Waves Across
the South

Waves Across
the South

A New History
of Revolution and Empire

SUJIT SIVASUNDARAM

**WILLIAM
COLLINS**

William Collins
An imprint of HarperCollins*Publishers*
1 London Bridge Street
London SE1 9GF

WilliamCollinsBooks.com

First published in Great Britain in 2020 by William Collins

1

ISBN (HARDBACK) 978-0-00-757554-1
ISBN (TRADE PAPERBACK) 978-0-00-757556-5

Typeset in Minion by Palimpsest Book Production Ltd, Falkirk, Stirlingshire
Printed and bound in Great Britain by CPI Group (UK) Ltd, Croydon

MIX
Paper from
responsible sources
FSC™ C007454

Contents

A Note on Transliteration and Images

This is a work of world history that spans a wide terrain of culture and I have done my best to highlight indigenous and non-European names, given the intent of the work to consider the age of revolutions from the oceanic South. When a colonial name is used for the first time, the equivalent vernacular or indigenous term is highlighted in square brackets. I aim to move between indigenous, colonial and post-colonial names as I move across historical periods. Diacritics, ʻokina and other marks have been used where possible.

The images used in this book form a central part of the argument; many of them are colonial images. Some of these depict colonial invasion. Other images are of Indigenous peoples who have been racialised and gendered. They have been included here to destabilise and expose the colonial vision that gave rise to them and to make space instead for Indigenous peoples and their perspectives in the history of the age of revolutions.

The beautiful cover for *Waves Across the South* was inspired by the maps used by Pacific islanders, to find their way across the vast expanse of the Pacific. These long voyages are discussed in the introduction. These maps consisted of various natural materials including coconut fronds and shells, denoting, for instance, the position of islands or currents. It is an appropriate cover for a book which considers world history from a 'sea of islands' in the global South. Each of these seas found its place within the rise and fall of the waves which indigenous navigators moved across.

List of Images

used as frontispiece in a book edited by John Martin, *An Account of the Natives of the Tonga Islands, in the South Pacific Ocean: With an Original Grammar and Vocabulary of their Language* (London: John Murray, 1816).

2.6   *Port au Prince* Memorial, Tonga and the beach where the massacre is alleged to have happened. Author's photographs.

2.7   'Tepoanah Bay of Islands New Zealand a Church Missionary Establishment' (watercolour, Augustus Earle, 1827), National Library of Australia, Canberra, NK 12/139.

2.8   'War speech' by Augustus Earle (published 1838); Earle wrote of a 'council for war', 'a rude parliament', National Library of Australia, Canberra, PIC vol. 532 U2650 NK 668.

2.9   'King George. N. Zealand Costume' by Augustus Earle (1828), National Library of Australia, Canberra, PIC Solander Box A37 T122 NK 12/84.

2.10 'The wounded chief Honghi [Hongi Hika] & his family' by Augustus Earle (London: Lithographed and Published by R. Martin, 1838), National Library of Australia, PIC vol. 532 U2643 NK 668.

2.11 'Waikato, Hongi Hika and Thomas Kendall' by James Barry, 1820, Alexander Turnbull Library, Wellington, G/618.

Chapter Three

3.1   A later image of a man with mixed ancestry with a racialised title, published in an account of the French voyage of Nicolas Baudin. 'Afrique Australe: Bastaard-Hottentot, ou Hottentot métis, revetu de ses habits de peau de mouton' [Bastard Hottentot or mixed blood Hottentot, wearing his sheepskin clothes], in *Voyage de Découvertes aux Terres Australes* [Voyage of Discovery to the Southern Lands], (Paris: Arthur Bertrand, 1824), 2nd edn, National Gallery of Victoria, Melbourne, 2010.96.56.

3.2   'A View of Table Mountain and Cape Town, at the Cape of Good Hope', 1787, National Maritime Museum, Greenwich, PAH2821.

3.3   'Bush Men Hottentots Armed for an Expedition', in Samuel Daniell, *A Collection of Plates Illustrative of African Scenery and Animals* (London, 1804), British Library, 458.h.14, part 1.2.

3.4–5 Bo-Kaap in Cape Town, formerly known as the Malay Quarter,

Timeline

British take Pondichéry from the French
Britain declares war on France; Louis XVI is guillotined
1794   Establishment of a Jacobin club in Mauritius
Abolition of slavery by revolutionary France
Sale of the vessels of d'Entrecasteaux's expedition in
Batavia
1795   *Trekboer* revolt in Swellendam, South Africa
British invasion of the Cape Colony
Unification of Persia under the Qajars
Michael Symes' first embassy to Ava
Setting up of Batavian Republic in the Netherlands
1796   British invasion of Dutch Ceylon (Sri Lanka)
Nationalisation of the Dutch East India Company
John Goldingham appointed astronomer to the Madras
government
René Baco de La Chapelle and Étienne Burnel are sent to
Mauritius by the French government to enforce the aboli-
tion of slavery but are forced to flee
French soldiers sail from France to invade Ireland
1798   Establishment of the first formal mosque at the Cape
Arrival of Tipu Sultan's embassy in Mauritius
Sultan bin Ahmad of Oman signs a cooperative treaty with
the British East India Company
Napoleon's invasion of Egypt, followed by Nelson's destruc-
tion of Napoleon's fleet at the Battle of the Nile
1799   Abu Talib ibn Muhammad Isfahani travels from Calcutta to
London, via the Cape
Death of Tipu Sultan and defeat of Mysore at the hands of
the British
Bungaree sails to Hervey Bay on a voyage with Matthew
Flinders
1800–3 Nicolas Baudin's voyage to the Pacific
1801–10 Matthew Flinders' voyage around Australia and capture in
Mauritius
1802   Michael Symes' second embassy to Ava
Planting of the British flag in Tasmania
Treaty of Amiens between France and Britain
1803   Establishment of a British colony in Tasmania
The Cape Colony is returned to the Dutch

Saudi invasion of Oman
Failed British invasion of Kandy
Britain declares war again on France as the peace of Amiens fails

1803–4   The Wahhabi-Saudi state invades Mecca and Medina

1804   Death of Sultan bin Ahmad of Oman, followed by a period of violent instability in the Gulf
First landing of convicts by the British in Tasmania
Castle Hill Uprising in Sydney
Haiti granted independence from France

1806–10 Arrival of the *Port-au-Prince* with William Mariner in Tonga; Finau Ulukalala II's raid on Tongatapu
Second British invasion of the Cape Colony

1807   Banning of the slave trade among British subjects by the British Parliament
John Warren observes a comet in the sky from the Madras Observatory and the comet is followed by his assistant Srinivasachari
Napoleon launches invasion of Portugal; Portuguese royal family flee to Brazil

1808   Slave rebellion in the Cape Colony led by Louis van Mauritius
French capture of Madrid leading to Peninsular War; British army under Wellesley [later Duke of Wellington] defeat French near Lisbon

1809   First British invasion of the Gulf, at Ras al-Khaimah

1810   Departure of William Mariner from Tonga
British invasion of Mauritius
Spanish *Cortes* establishes itself in Cadiz

1811   British invasion of Java

1812   Fall of Yogyakarta in Java to the British
Napoleon attacks Russia and enters Moscow

1812–18 Mehmed Ali's campaign against the Wahhabis
Prussia declares war on France

1814   First Christian missionary contact with Aotearoa/New Zealand
Congress of Vienna begins

1815   Defeat of Napoleon at Waterloo
British invasion of the kingdom of Kandy in present-day Sri Lanka
Mauritian Bonapartists plot to end British rule of the island

1816   A large fire tears through Port Louis, Mauritius
British return Java to the Dutch
Return of Pondichéry to the French

1817   Bungaree sails to north-western Australia with Philip Parker King
Negotiation of an anti-slave trade treaty between the Governor of Mauritius, William Farquhar, and Radama I of Madagascar's Merina empire

1819   Cholera epidemic in Mauritius

1819–20   Second British invasion of the Gulf at Ras al-Khaimah, after the failure of Hasan bin Rahma to negotiate a truce
British takeover of Singapore under Thomas Stamford Raffles

1820   Hongi Hika arrives in London
Signing of the General Treaty against piracy by Britain and the Arab city states
Arrival of the 1820 settlers in the Cape Colony

1821   Death of Napoleon on St Helena
Mutiny on board the *Bombay Merchant* between Bombay and the Gulf
The kingdom of Ava invades Assam

1822   Ratsitatanina's attempted slave revolt in Madagascar
Departure of John Goldingham's expedition to an island off Sumatra

1822–3   Withdrawal of British troops from Qeshm

1824   Singapore becomes a British possession outright after the signing of an agreement between the British and the Sultan of Johor
The British and the Dutch sign the Treaty of London, limiting the remit of the Dutch empire in Southeast Asia

1824–6   First Anglo-Burmese War between the British and the kingdom of Ava; ends with the treaty of Yandabo of 1826

1825   Establishment of the Van Diemen's Land Company
Peter Dillon sails from Valparaiso in Chile, in a voyage that eventually leads to the solution of the puzzle of the lost La Pérouse expedition

1826   Singapore and Malacca attached to the East India Company's presidency in Penang

1827   The Comité Colonial is convened in Mauritius
Dissolution of Cape Town's municipal Burgher Senate

1828 Use of martial law to police Aboriginal Tasmanians,
         followed by a 'Black Line' in 1830 to move them to confined
         ground
1830 Journey of Te Rauparaha to Sydney
         The July Revolution in France overthrows Charles X
1831 Baptism of Taufa'ahau, who takes the name George I to
         unify Tonga, initiating a monarchic line that lasts till today
         Press war at the Cape Colony over slavery, between the
         South African Commercial Advertiser and *De Zuid-Afrikaan*
         Abdication of Emperor Pedro I of Brazil
1832 Arrival of the abolitionist John Jeremie in Mauritius to
         serve as *procureur général*; his arrival brings resistance from
         Mauritian colonists
1833 Appointment of James Busby as Resident of New Zealand
         End of the British East India Company's monopoly over the
         tea trade
         Official abolition of slavery in the British empire
1834 First arrival of indentured labourers in Mauritius
         Robert Montgomery publishes *History of the British Colonies*
1835 Busby's declaration of a 'Magna Carta of New Zealand
         Independence' with Māori chiefs
         Abolition of slavery in Mauritius
1836 Renganghi moved into the 'protection' of George Augustus
         Robinson
         Queen Ranavalona of Madagascar renounces the official
         relationship between Britain and the Merina empire
1837 Chinese officials begin obstructing opium sales in Canton
1838 Arrival of Jehangir Naoroji and Hirjibhoy Meherwanji in
         London
         Establishment of the New Zealand Colonisation Company
1839 End of apprenticeships in Mauritius
         Arrival of William Wakefield in Aotearoa/New Zealand
1839–42 First Opium War between Britain and China
         First Anglo-Afghan War
1840 Signing of the Treaty of Waitangi in Aotearoa/New Zealand
         Grant of Municipal government to Cape Town
1842 French annexation of the Marquesas
         Signing of the Treaty of Nanking between Britain and
         the Qing

1843   French annexation of Tahiti
              Formalisation of the marriage between Puna and Tommy
              Chaseland
1845–6   First Anglo-Sikh War
1848   Abolition of slavery on the island of Bourbon/Réunion
              Outbreak of the 1848 revolutions in Europe
              Formation of a political Association in Mauritius
              Outbreak of rebellion in Sri Lanka
1848–9   A period of civil disobedience in Cape Town in response to
              the planned despatch of convicts to the Cape
              Second Anglo-Sikh War
1850   Beginning of municipal elections in Mauritius
              A new liberal newspaper, the *Commercial Gazette*, is estab-
              lished in Mauritius
1850s   Kīngitanga or Māori King Movement begins
1851   Official lighting of the Horsburgh Lighthouse in Singapore
              The first gold rush in Australia
1852   Death of Cora Gooseberry outside the Sydney Arms Hotel
              in Sydney
1853   Representative government granted to the Cape Colony

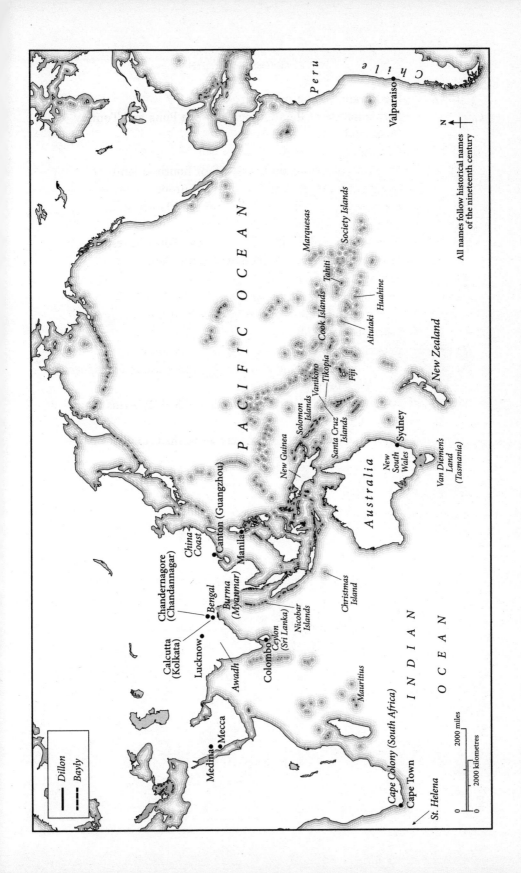

All names follow historical names of the nineteenth century

Dillon
Bayly

PACIFIC OCEAN

INDIAN OCEAN

Peru
Chile
Valparaiso

Marquesas
Society Islands
Tahiti
Huahine
Cook Islands
Aitutaki
Vanikoro
Tikopia
Fiji
Santa Cruz Islands
Solomon Islands
New Guinea
New Zealand

Australia
New South Wales
Sydney
Van Diemen's Land (Tasmania)

Canton (Guangzhou)
China Coast
Manila
Chandernagore (Chandannagar)
Bengal
Burma (Myanmar)
Calcutta (Kolkata)
Lucknow
Awadh
Colombo
Ceylon (Sri Lanka)
Nicobar Islands
Christmas Island

Mauritius

Mecca
Medina

Cape Colony (South Africa)
Cape Town
St. Helena

2000 miles
2000 kilometres
0
0

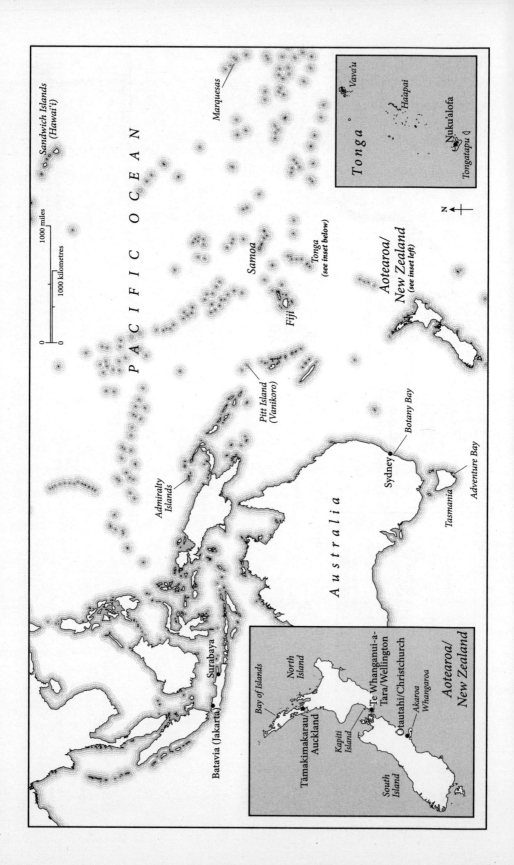

PACIFIC OCEAN

Sandwich Islands
(Hawai'i)

Marquesas

Samoa

Fiji

Tonga
(see inset below)

Aotearoa/
New Zealand
(see inset left)

Pitt Island
(Vanikoro)

Admiralty
Islands

Botany Bay

Sydney

Australia

Tasmania

Adventure Bay

Surabaya

Batavia (Jakarta)

1000 miles

1000 kilometres

N

Tonga

Vava'u

Ha'apai

Nuku'alofa

Tongatapu

Bay of Islands

North
Island

Tāmakimakarau/
Auckland

Kapiti
Island

Te Whanganui-a-
Tara/Wellington

Ōtautahi/Christchurch

Akaroa
Whangaroa

South
Island

Aotearoa/
New Zealand

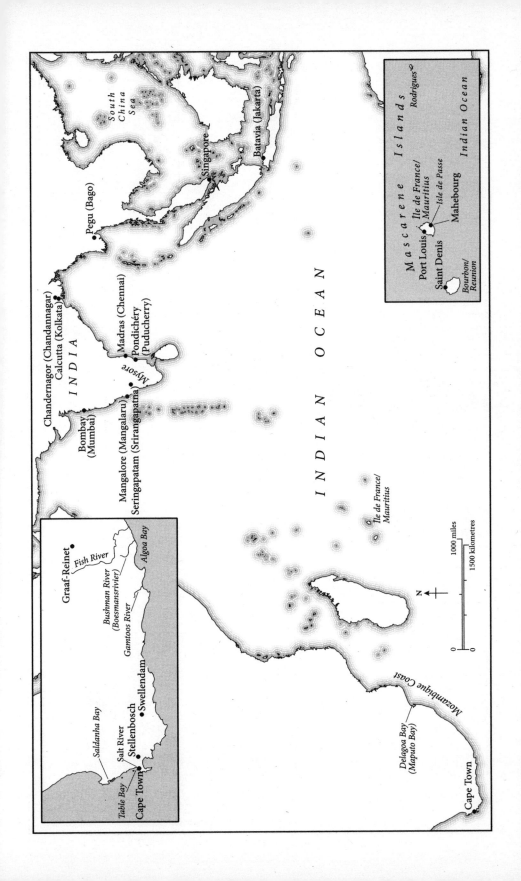

South China Sea

Batavia (Jakarta)

Singapore

Pegu (Bago)

Chandernagor (Chandannagar)
Calcutta (Kolkata)

INDIA

Madras (Chennai)
Pondichéry (Puducherry)

Mysore

Bombay (Mumbai)

Mangalore (Mangalaru)
Seringapatam (Srirangapatna)

INDIAN   OCEAN

Île de France/
Mauritius

Mascarene   Islands

Rodrigues

Île de France/
Mauritius

Port Louis

Isle de Passe

Mahebourg

Saint Denis

Bourbon/
Réunion

Indian Ocean

1000 miles

1500 kilometres

N

0

0

Mozambique Coast

Delagoa Bay
(Maputo Bay)

Cape Town

Graaf-Reinet

Fish River

Algoa Bay

Bushman River
(Boesmansrivier)

Gamtoos River

Swellendam

Stellenbosch

Saldanha Bay

Salt River

Table Bay

Cape Town

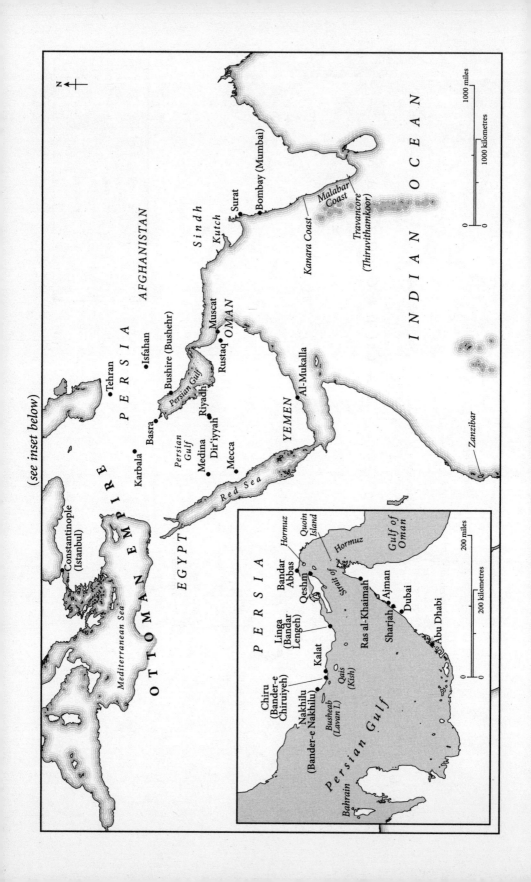

(see inset below)

Main map labels:

N

1000 miles
1000 kilometres

INDIAN OCEAN

Bombay (Mumbai)
Surat
Malabar Coast
Kanara Coast
Travancore (Thiruvithamkoor)

Sindh
Kutch

AFGHANISTAN

PERSIA

Tehran
Isfahan
Bushire (Bushehr)
Persian Gulf
Muscat
Rustaq OMAN
Riyadh
Al-Mukalla

Basra
Karbala
Persian Gulf
Medina Dir'iyyah
Mecca
YEMEN

Red Sea

Constantinople (Istanbul)
Mediterranean Sea

OTTOMAN EMPIRE

EGYPT

Zanzibar

Inset map labels:

PERSIA

Hormuz
Quoin Island
Hormuz
Bandar Abbas
Qeshm
Strait of Hormuz
Gulf of Oman

Linga (Bandar Lengeh)
Kalat
Chiru (Bander-e Chiruiyeh)
Nakhilu (Bander-e Nakhilu)
Qais (Kish)
Busheab (Lavan I.)

Ras al-Khaimah
Sharjah Ajman
Dubai
Abu Dhabi

Persian Gulf

Bahrain

200 miles
200 kilometres

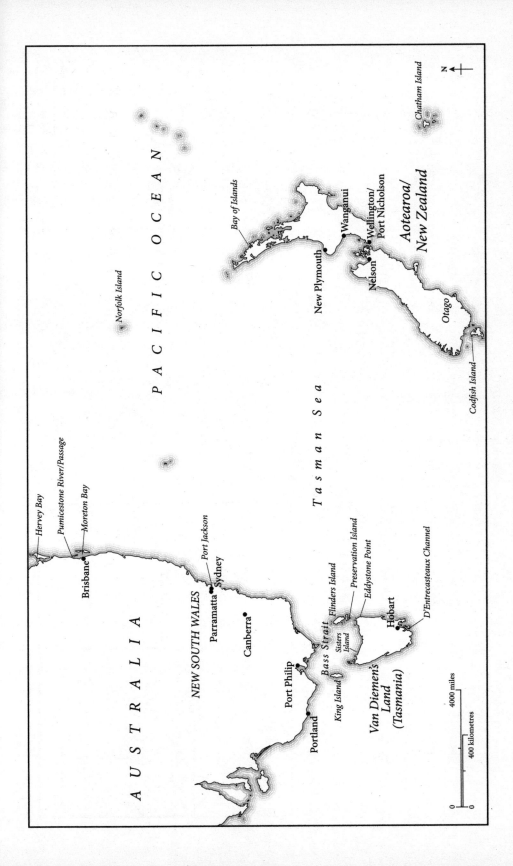

N

Chatham Island

Bay of Islands

Wanganui

Wellington/
Port Nicholson

Aotearoa/
New Zealand

PACIFIC OCEAN

New Plymouth

Nelson

Otago

Norfolk Island

Codfish Island

T a s m a n   S e a

Hervey Bay

Pumicestone River/Passage

Moreton Bay

Brisbane

Port Jackson

Sydney

Parramatta

AUSTRALIA

NEW SOUTH WALES

Canberra

Flinders Island

Preservation Island

Eddystone Point

D'Entrecasteaux Channel

Hobart

Sisters
Island

Bass Strait

King Island

Van Diemen's
Land
(Tasmania)

Port Philip

Portland

4000 miles

400 kilometres

0

0

(see inset below)

PACIFIC OCEAN

CHINA

Nanking (Nanjing)
Ningbo
Zhoushan
Fuzhou
Lintin Island (Nei Lingding Island)
Canton (Guangzhou)

Borneo

Java Sea

Java

Cilincing

Malay Peninsula
Queda (Kedah)
Selangor
Melacca (Melaka)
Singapore
Penang
Strait of Malacca
Sumatra
Palembang
Batavia (Jakarta)
Yogyakarta

Tenaserim (Thaninthary)
Junk Ceylon (Phuket)

Assam
Manipur
Chittagong

Calcutta (Kolkata)

Bay of Bengal

INDIA

Sri Lanka

INDIAN OCEAN

N

1000 miles
1000 kilometres

0
0

Amarapura
AVA
Irrawaddy
Arakan Yoma
ARAKAN
Pegu
Rangoon (Yangon)
Dalla (Dala)

Trincomalee
Sri Lanka
KANDY
Kataragama
Colombo
Ambalangoda
Galle

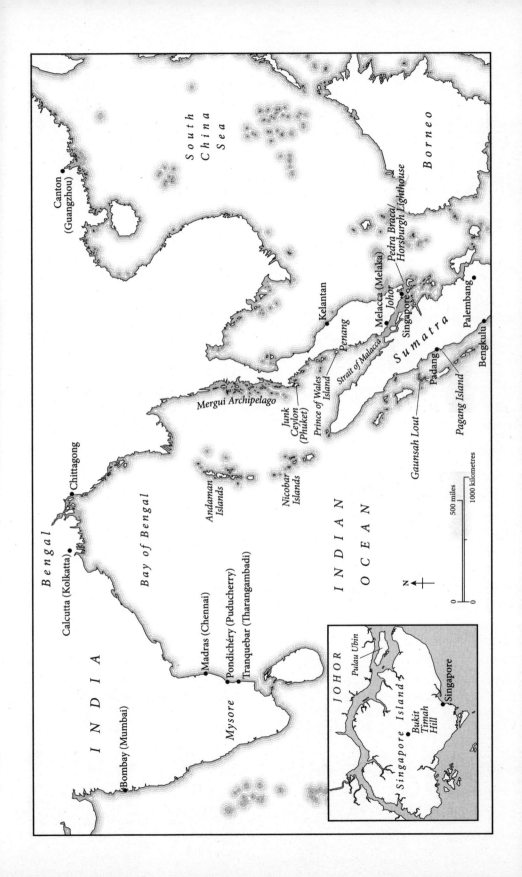

South China Sea

Canton (Guangzhou)

Borneo

Pedra Braca/ Horsburgh Lighthouse

Kelantan

Melacca (Melaka)

Johor

Penang

Singapore

Palembang

Strait of Malacca

Sumatra

Chittagong

Prince of Wales Island

Bengkulu

Mergui Archipelago

Junk Ceylon (Phuket)

Gaunsah Lout

Padang

Pagang Island

Calcutta (Kolkatta)

Bengal

Andaman Islands

Nicobar Islands

INDIAN OCEAN

Bay of Bengal

1000 metres

Madras (Chennai)

Pondichéry (Puducherry)

Tranquebar (Tharangambadi)

Mysore

500 miles

N

INDIA

Bombay (Mumbai)

JOHOR

Pulau Ubin

Singapore

Singapore Island

Bukit Timah Hill

Singapore

Introduction

There is a quarter of this planet which is often forgotten in the histories that are told in the West. This quarter is an oceanic one, pulsating with winds and waves, tides and coastlines, and islands and beaches. The Indian and Pacific Oceans – taken as a collection of smaller seas, gulfs and bays – constitute that forgotten quarter, brought together here for perhaps the first time in a sustained work of history. These watery spaces of the south, studded with small strips of land, facing gigantic landmasses, occupy centre stage in what follows. They are cast as the makers of world history and the modern condition.[1]

The decades straddling the late eighteenth and early nineteenth centuries, which historians call the 'age of revolutions', traditionally encompass an Atlantic triangle of grand events. This triangle of events includes the American Revolution, the French Revolution and revolts in the Caribbean, such as the Haitian Revolution, and then independence movements in Latin America in the early nineteenth century.[2] Many things changed dramatically in the midst of these revolutions and the wars that accompanied them. Among what was made anew are the organisation of politics, the conception of equality and rights; the mechanics of governance and empire; the status of labour and enslaved people; the workings of technology, industry and science; and characterisations of nation and self as well as public consciousness. By looking to the forgotten quarter of the Indian and Pacific Oceans, the intent is to turn the story of the dawn of our times inside out. It is to insist on the critical significance of the peoples and places in this oceanic tract in shaping the age of revolutions and so our present; and, accordingly, the need to meditate on this part of the world in considering the human future.

The age of revolutions is one of the most long-lasting labels of historical writing. It was used in the period and has carried on being used to describe the set of decades at the end of the eighteenth and the start of the nineteenth centuries. To look at this historical period again with a focus on the Indian and Pacific Oceans challenges the dominance of the West and Europe in the history we remember. This is especially important when what is at stake in descriptions of an age of revolutions is the lineage of our very rights and selfhood, and the memory of the contests and standoffs that gave rise to the world we inhabit. Approaching the past like this displaces the pernicious assumption that the soul of the world was crafted in the West and then travelled east; it rejects the notion that political subjectivity was forged in the Atlantic and that people elsewhere followed in the same tracks. The objectionable sentiment was phrased like this by one important early historian of the age of revolutions, R. R. Palmer: '[a]ll revolutions since 1800, in Europe, Latin America, Asia and Africa, have learned from the eighteenth-century Revolution of Western Civilisation.'[3] The history that follows refuses to cast Western and Atlantic Civilisation in the late eighteenth and early nineteenth centuries as the font of revolutionary sentiment. Nor was the West or the Atlantic the single origin of the modes of economic, technological, military and cultural expression that accompanied revolution.[4]

When the age of revolutions is reconceptualised from the oceanic south, an uncertain and violent tussle appears. Within the Indian and Pacific Oceans there was a contest between revolution and an imperial system which perverted the course of revolution and constituted a counter-revolution. Neither one of the forces of revolution and empire wiped the other out, but the balance shifted as the British empire in particular became the chief victor over these seas by the middle of the nineteenth century. While there were certainly other ideological, cultural and political impulses which drove the nineteenth-century British empire, one intent of this work is to track its origins as a counter-revolution.[5] The manner in which this empire suppressed the many possibilities of this time points to sinister imperial manoeuvring in the global South.

In these two oceans, the age of revolutions should be seen first and foremost as a surge of indigenous and non-European politics which met the invaders and colonists who washed ashore. In the late eighteenth and early nineteenth centuries, the inhabitants of the Indian and Pacific Oceans adopted and at times forcibly took from outsiders new objects, ideas, information and forms of organisation, all of which were used for their own purposes. One might think here of notions of monarchy, weapons, political association, science and medicine, and debate in the press. Oceanic peoples also recalibrated existent traditions and beliefs, modes of governance and war and relations with neighbours, in order to meet these new times. Here one might bring to mind Islamic or Buddhist reform or the changes in established long-distance relations for migration and trade. All this constituted the Indian and Pacific Oceans' age of revolutions. As a term of description, 'indigenous' has to be defined expansively in these seas. For oceanic peoples were often on the move and may be better described as diasporas than indigenous populations; they had complex cultural heritages. Settlers and indigenous peoples could also at times borrow from each other, making it difficult to draw a clear distinction between who and what was indigenous and who and what fell outside the category.

A sequence of voices across the sea embody an energetic indigenousness: Pacific Islander, Māori, Aboriginal Australian, Arab, Qasimi, Omani, Parsi, Javanese, Burmese, Chinese, Indian, Sinhalese, Tamil, Malay, Mauritian, Malagasy and Khoisan perspectives come into view below.[6] These and other peoples took passage as sailors, partners, fighters, labourers and travellers in these decades of unprecedented globalisation. Indeed, the most enjoyable part of researching this book was discovering links across the water through regions and territories that have not been cast together.

In addition to a surge of indigenous and non-European politics, the age of revolutions in these oceans saw a reconfiguration of political organisation. Empires, political units, kingdoms and chieftaincies were realigned or reorganised from Oman to Tonga and from Mauritius to Sri Lanka. Political tussles over water were poised such that relatively new forces could find their own way, acting as independent states or reacting to a colonial definition of what could count as a state. Venerable Eurasian empires, Ottoman, Mughal and Qing, were transformed at their maritime frontiers. New political formations, including monarchies inaugurated in the Pacific, could also cohere through the adoption of the maritime and military techniques of warring Europeans. Refugees of the Napoleonic wars could serve as advisers, for instance in Burma [Myanmar] to the kingdom of Ava as it fought Britain, or in Tasmania to a heavily militarised British colonial state. Oceanic peoples, including Asian sailors called *lascars* at the time, could establish a political pathway within the British empire's need for allies and collaborators without finding full meaning within empire. Those who took passage on European ships, or who worked on grand projects as labourers and technicians, could use this moment of opportunity to contemplate their selfhood and futures in radically new ways.

The British empire sought to neutralise or adopt the ideas, people, structures and modes of organisation which arose from the age of revolutions. It moved from sea to land and saw itself as an empire for liberty in sites as different as Singapore and Mauritius. In addition to seeing itself as spreading liberty, there were many ways in which the British empire acted in reactionary fashion in the age of revolutions. There was a lineage of wars over water across the first half of the nineteenth century, all of which employed the period's characteristic 'total war', including looting and wide-scale bloodshed.[7] In the Bay of Bengal, for instance, these wars drew military men and techniques from the revolutionary and Napoleonic wars linking them to the global warfare of this moment. Britain's invasive missions to the Gulf in 1809–10 and 1819–20 stood against a brand of Islamic reform which was compared with revolutionary sentiment elsewhere. The British fear of republicanism motivated invasions in Java and Mauritius in 1810–11. In all of these cases, British colonial and maritime war in these years was forged out of the age of revolutions in relation to tactics, ideology, motivation and forms of comparison.

Another way in which empire was made anew in the age of revolutions was through new classifications of peoples and kinds.[8] Scientific and natural historical classifications were linked with the surveillance regime of the expanding colonial state. The relation between science and colonialism can seem paradoxical; for new sciences were seen in the period as the harbingers of an age of reason. The way people engaged with water, from how they fished, to how they communed with sea creatures, to how they navigated the sea, or the artefacts they used or descriptions of their allegedly nomadic existences, easily led into colonial classifications of race and gender. The possibility of intensive comparison around neighbouring islands and settlements, which imperial writers cast as self-contained sites despite long histories of migration, meant that these oceanic basins became ideal for working through ideas of difference and for policies of segregation.

The consolidation of Britishness and whiteness in the new port cities from Port Louis to Sydney, which symbolised the forward march of this maritime Britannia, depended on sea-facing mariners, alleged pirates and private traders transforming themselves into respectable shore residents with families in situ and under Christian marriage. These colonists moved from itinerant sea-trades to settled interests in land and pasture. The moral duties of white maleness could overtake other ways of organising race and gender near the sea. Sporadic colonisation across the sea, for instance through escaped convicts, missionaries or private traders and slavers was made more 'systematic' for instance in New Zealand. The veto power of the slogan of 'free trade' was useful here. Maritime patriotism also became part and parcel of this transformation and its forward charge came partly from such enterprises as anti-slavery and anti-piracy and their legacy in more extensive land-based colonial enterprises. Such patriotism is often missed in existing retellings of this era which focus on large continental hinterlands and which point to 'agrarian patriotism', the glorification of land and agriculture, as an ideology which supercharged the British advance in the East.[9]

It is fitting, given the setting of this story in the Indian and Pacific Oceans, to describe this contest between revolution and empire as a clash of waves. To think with waves is to think with the push-and-pull dynamic of globalisation. It is to consider the surging advance of connection across the sea as well as turbulent disconnection and violence across waters.[10] It is to contemplate the formation of crests as well as the breaking of waves on the beach. All this was the case for revolution and empire, for both of these were susceptible to breakage and could never come to full success in these decades.

Thinking with waves is also apposite in reminding ourselves that the physical setting of this story matters. The physicality of rain, storms, squalls, cyclones, waterspouts, fevers and earthquakes had to be combatted to make global empire work, through regimes of study, tabulation, mapping, modelling, medicine and urban fortification and planning.[11] The irregular shape of the Earth itself had to be managed to allow ships on the sea to navigate their course and to lubricate free-trade empire, for instance between India and China or Australia. Surveying of the sea and the coastline was a first task that ran ahead of empire at a time when new scientific disciplines were being forged. Such surveying fed into the establishment of bases, transit points, ports and settlements across these oceans as definitions of sovereignty travelled from ship to shore and were transported into the interior.

The sea was not easily passed: ships featured here disappeared, caught fire, exploded, or were tossed into the air together with horses and fighting men, or ran aground in coral reefs. Ships were rebooted after being taken over by warring nations at a time of global war or pirated. In this sense too the ship was an unstable platform. The port city of these oceans was a place of meditation on shipwrecks, as the remains of vessels lined the shore. Water had to be safely navigated for purposes of colonial war, and the intersecting terrain of land, sea and rivers, close to the shore and leading inland, could be deadly for the British in terms of health and given the ill-suitedness of their techniques and logistics of conflict to such terrain. Conflict over water did not automatically privilege Europeans versus non-Europeans, though these two groups were erroneously separated as maritime versus land-based.

The significance of the physical setting to the history can be seen in some intriguing images. Take, for instance, 'Fishing Boats in the Monsoon, northern part of Bombay harbour' (1826), which is right in the middle of the period covered here. [Fig. 0.1] Produced in India, it was based on a sketch by Colonel John Johnson of the Bombay Engineers and shows two Indian craft battling the foaming waves.[12] It was not only fishermen such as those depicted here who used Indian craft. Take another image from another Indian port showing what it took to disembark, 'Surf boat landing European passengers at Madras' (c.1800) [Fig. 0.2]. Notably, there are just

Fig. 0.1 'Fishing Boats in the Monsoon, Northern part of
Bombay [Mumbai] Harbour' (1826)

Fig. 0.2 'Surf boats landing European passengers at Madras [Chennai]', c.1800

two Europeans in the foreground of this picture. Britons in red uniform feature in the ship behind. It is the Indians who battle the waves through their labour and this labour is co-opted to make an empire practicable. A good partner image for this one, which is in keeping with the uncharted connections across the Indian and Pacific Oceans in view in this book, is 'Landing Horses from Australia; Catamarans and Masoolah boat, Madras' (c.1834) [Fig. 0.3]. Though an incongruous European in hat and beard and jacket stands in the waters, it is the Indians who work with the animals in the boat who make it possible for poor horses to travel across vast distances of water. These images compare Indians with Europeans, but they also demonstrate an interest in Indian craft as well as European vessels. Notice Augustus Earle's 'Catamaran on Madras Roads' [Fig. 0.4].

It is the ingenuity of the seafarers of the Indian and Pacific Oceans, so strikingly illustrated in these images, which motivated me to write *Waves Across the South*. The book takes a chronological journey through these critical decades, from the dramatic voyages in the 1790s to the energetic debates in the press and in civil associations in the burgeoning port cities of the 1840s. As it does this, it tours the misplaced histories of the southern

Fig. 0.3 'Landing [Waler] horses from Australia; Catamarans and Masoolah boat', Madras, c.1834

Fig. 0.4 'Catamaran on Madras [Chennai] Roads', by Augustus Earle, 1829

seas in the age of revolutions and follows the rise of the British empire. Along the path from revolution to empire, our travels take into account the meeting of cultures, indigenous and colonial revolt, imperial annexation, conceptions of race and gender, conflict across the seas, global knowledge and the growth of public sentiment around programmes of liberal reform. Each of these seas had separate stories in the age of revolutions but the expansion of the British empire created dense connections between these distant realms.

Though spanning less than seventy years, these decades sit within a long and brilliant tapestry of history in the Pacific and Indian Oceans. European intrusion appears here as a late entry.

Long-distance voyages undertaken by so-called Austronesians saw the settlement of the vast realms of the Pacific Ocean, including more than 500 islands, from west to east from present-day Taiwan, and beginning from around 6,000 years ago.[13] Much before this, around 65,000 years ago or longer before human beings had migrated from the landmass called Sunda to Sahul, the latter of which linked today's New Guinea, Australia and Tasmania. Austronesians reached Aotearoa or New Zealand around 1300 CE and the distant foothold of Rapa Nui or Easter Island around 300–400 CE. They travelled in single outrigger or large double-hulled canoes, taking with them water, and fermented breadfruit, which could last for about three months. Sometimes they would take plants that could be grown on landing, and livestock, domesticated pigs, dogs and chickens. Settlers who roamed further into Oceania formed the 'Lapita' sphere of settlement; Lapita settlers valued obsidian or glass-like stone and took it to the region of the Pacific which was far distant from Asia. The styles of their pottery spread with them. There was a great deal of migration between these islands. As one archaeologist writes: 'Within the Lapita sphere you might have met the same man or woman one year in Tonga, and the next on New Britain or in Vanuatu. It would seem that about 3,000 years ago people from New Guinea Islands and out as far as Tonga and Samoa were more interconnected than at any time until the age of mass transportation began some two centuries ago.'[14]

There then arose a triangle of settlement across the vast Pacific, which had as its points Hawai'i, Rapa Nui and Aotearoa. This zone of settlement is huge; it is about the size of Europe and Asia put together. The 'Polynesian' and 'Micronesian' systems of navigation aided these successful voyages. The islanders relied on star positions at night and the sun during the day, the speed of wind and current, the swell of the sea caused by different kinds of winds, and the signs of birds and other natural elements. They waited for the right winds. They calculated their position by dead reckoning. But from about 1300, voyages became less frequent, and a series of islands in the triangle were abandoned. It was into an intricate world of shared language and politics that early modern European voyagers arrived: Spanish, Portuguese, English and French. And it was these voyages which once again reconnected indigenous peoples across the wide span of Oceania. Islanders recalled their historic migrations. The vibrant non-European politics of the seventy years covered in this book were shaped by these memories and the renewed connections with oceanic neighbours that European vessels brought.

The Indian Ocean too was long known from multiple cultural perspectives.[15] Coastal and regional trade was well established prior to the common era: by 2000 BCE there was contact between the civilisations of the Red Sea, the Gulf and the Indus Valley. South Asian merchants, Malay mariners and Buddhist monks, set a template for the Indian Ocean in the first centuries of the common era, as did the eventual emergence of empires like the Sasanians in Persia, the Guptas in India, and Funan in Southeast Asia.

South Asia has often been seen as a pivot of the Indian Ocean world, as it served as a stepping stone from east to west and the other way around. But connections across the ocean also involved the Middle East, East Asia and Africa. Islam should not be seen as the only factor which wove the ocean together from the seventh century; for the spread of Buddhist and Hindu doctrines to Southeast Asia occurred in the first five centuries of the common era. Trade and commerce were important to the making of the Indian Ocean world. Prior to the arrival of European empires, companies and private traders, there was a pattern of commerce across this sea which was under the control of sea-facing states, port cities and merchant diasporas. Trade was modulated by the seasons of the monsoon. Among the traded items were spices, precious stones and pearls, as well as rice and grain and indeed enslaved peoples.

Historians see the first European imperial enterprises as operating within this world, through partnerships with indigenous political elites, lenders and merchants. The Portuguese sought to reorganise trade through an insistence on the protection afforded by their licences and taxes. The Dutch, who were drawn to South Asia for cottons, indigo, saltpetre, silk, cinnamon and pepper, sought to follow in their tracks. Yet with the Dutch and the English came a new structure, the world-spanning joint-stock company. In India, this meant that Europeans established strategic settlements at ports. For the British the main bases became Madras, Bombay and Calcutta, around which their control of the Indian Ocean radiated. Even this quick sketch of the long histories of the Indian and Pacific Oceans points to the need to analyse the advent of the Europeans and the significant bridge between the eighteenth and nineteenth centuries which marked the powerful ascent of Europe in these oceans.

It is the starting premise of this book that revolution and counter-revolutionary empire did not obliterate these long-term histories. But the juxtaposition of new and old quickened with the extent of contact and globalisation making it difficult at times to differentiate what already existed from what had newly arrived. And with that quickening, the way that people thought of themselves, their territories and the globe itself was shifting. This was another characteristic feature of this age of revolutions and of the rise of empire.

The impact of the times as a phase of globalisation is evident in how indigenous peoples saw their seas, their histories and their place on the globe. Two treasures bear this out.

The First Fleet, the first detachment of convicts, arrived to found a colony at New South Wales in 1788, the year before the French Revolution.

In 1793, two kidnapped Māori were brought to Norfolk Island off the
coast of Australia, in order to teach convicts how to work the flax that
grew on many of the island's coastal cliffs. These two kidnapped men
are now commonly called Tuki and Huru. They came to Norfolk Island
on the *Shah Hormuzear*, which was crewed by *lascars*, and which had
arrived at Port Jackson [now in Sydney] from Calcutta.[16] On their way
to Norfolk Island they travelled in the company of 2,200 gallons of wine
and spirits, six Bengal ewes and two rams. They were the first Māori to
live in a European community, and the kidnapped Tuki, a priest's son,
and Huru, a young chief, became close to the commandant of the convict
settlement, Philip Gidley King. King was unable to discern much about
flax-working from the pair, given that it was women who worked the
flax in their communities. Yet he got Tuki to a draw a map.

One commentator noted the extent of Tuki's interests: 'Too-gee [Tuki]
was not only very inquisitive respecting England & c. (the situation of
which, as well as that of New Zealand, Norfolk Island and Port Jackson,
he well knew how to find by means of a coloured general chart).' If
Tuki's use of the coloured general chart indicated his adoption of
European cartography and his interest in locating his home in relation
to neighbouring territories, he was also 'very communicative respecting
his own country . . . Perceiving he was not thoroughly understood, he
delineated a sketch of New Zealand with chalk on the floor.'[17]

Tuki's map of his 'country' is extraordinary not only because it is
thought to be the oldest map drawn by a Māori. It shows 'Ea-hei-no-maue'
and 'Poo-name-moo' which should be read as He Ahi Nō Maui or Mauis's
fire, the North Island; and Te Wai Pounamu or Greenstone Water, the
South Island.[18] It combined a rich variety of elements: a double-dotted line
across the North Island shows the road taken by the spirits of the dead or
wairua and the place for leaping off into the underworld. On the map, this
road ends with the representation of a sacred pōhutukawa tree. Within this
map, and in the conversations that happened around its making, Tuki
attended to population, harbours, the concentration of fighting men and
the availability of water. All this demonstrates that there was an intermixing
of Māori topography with European cartographic interest, which was driven
for instance by the need to discover stopping places for their ships.[19] Tuki's
map sits within a larger set of Māori maps made for interpreters, surveyors,
explorers and whalers among others. On their return to New Zealand, Tuki
and Huru became important intermediaries between Māori and the British.[20]

If Tuki's map may stand here at the start of *Waves Across the South*

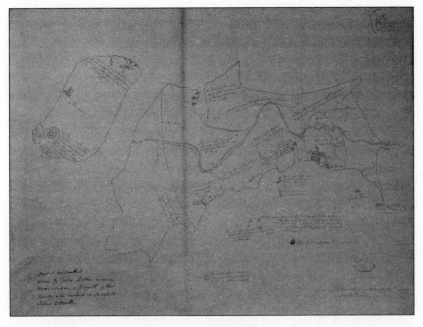

Fig. 0.5 'Tuki's map'

for the Pacific, from the Indian Ocean comes a second intriguing map, once more showing how people were responding to this age of dramatic change by attempting to find and place themselves in a world in flux. This is a Bugis map, inscribed with Muslim era date AH 1231 (1816), shortly after the end of the Napoleonic wars, and it is worth noting here that British Singapore was established in 1819. The home of the Bugis is Celebes in south Sulawesi in today's Indonesia and their wide circuit of sailing included northern Australia, where their vessels were known to Aboriginal Australians who traded with them. They converted to Islam from the seventeenth century.

The tattered and browned cowhide Bugis map, with coasts and islands in green and red ink, is one of a very rare set.[21] It has place names in Bugis script and records sea depths. It marks Dutch places of colonisation with flags, including Manila, which in fact was not Dutch but Spanish. It even shows a small section of the coast of Australia, and the Andaman and Nicobar islands. Once again, like Tuki's map, this chart can't be read purely as an indigenous artefact because it shows clear evidence of the impact of European traditions.

Fig. 0.6 Bugis nautical map, 1816

(One possible theory is that it was heavily influenced by a map of the region drawn by a French captain, Jean-Baptiste d'Après de Mannevillette.[22]) The map includes the sign of a compass, now an object which plays a critical role in Bugis navigation today. The compass was already in use by Bugis by the eighteenth century.[23]

Despite pointing to the adoption of European techniques, this map is consistent with established Bugis skills of navigation. Bugis navigators had to contend with the intersecting terrain of many islands and seas in Southeast Asia, a different challenge to that faced by Pacific islanders, including Māori, who navigated the open Pacific.[24] Noteworthy then is how the maritime fringe is presented in heavy and exaggerated detail, and islands and creeks are closely studied. This contrasts with the interiors of the land, where mountains alone are placed on the map, as they would have been seen from the sea.[25] These mountains probably helped with navigation.

The Bugis controlled Riau in the eighteenth century and made it a centre of trade between Europe, the Chinese and the Malay archipelago. Eventually, in 1784, the Riau Sultanate was taken over by the Dutch, like Makassar, another Bugis stronghold, which had fallen to the Dutch in 1667. This led to Bugis spreading across the region, roving the seas as traders, where they would be categorised as pirates by the British into the nineteenth century. They fought against the British in the fall of the Yogyakarta in Java in 1812.[26] However, the British relied on Bugis to connect up the early port of Singapore to regions further east as intermediaries, and the arrival of the Bugis fleet in Singapore, consisting of several thousand men, was a notable event in the port's calendar.[27]

As these two objects demonstrate, Europeans did not have a monopoly over mapping, a form of knowledge which is often cast as the centrepiece of European imperial expansion. These maritime maps demonstrate the creativity and confidence of indigenous perspectives in the age of revolutions. While these Māori and Bugis maps cannot be read for pure indigenous traditions, they provide evidence of exchange and tension with European knowledge, at a time of dramatic flux.[28] Fittingly then, in another Bugis map a European steamboat appears in the lower left corner; even one of the proudest tokens of progress in the era, the steamboat, could be placed within Bugis sensibility.[29] Across the waves of the south, it is these unexpected features of indigenous politics, knowledge and practice that this book hopes to establish. Despite the powers of mechanised steamboats, indigenous and non-European peoples could find their paths in these waves of the southern hemisphere.

1

Travels in the Oceanic South

'I will stick you on the Forecastle and set the Otaheiti men to shoot you.'[1] This was one of Peter Dillon's favourite expressions. He captained the 400-ton *St Patrick* as it sailed from Valparaiso in Chile, in October 1825, to Calcutta (now Kolkata), the bustling hub of the new British empire. Dillon had a penchant for storytelling. He was full of detail about the grand European voyages across the Pacific in the centuries that had just passed.[2] Dillon named one of his sons after Napoleon, whom he venerated: the son was nicknamed Nap. Seen from this perspective, perhaps his threat to use Tahitian men against his white crew was Napoleonic. The aim was to stem the possibility of mutiny.

Dillon was an erratic maritime adventurer and private trader with aspirations of greatness, an Irishman born in French Martinique in 1788. If he is to be believed, he had served in the Royal Navy at the Battle of Trafalgar in 1805.[3] He then sailed for the Pacific. He was known to foster close relationships with South Pacific islanders, an attachment which began when he was resident in Fiji in 1808–9, when he made 'considerable progress in learning their language'.[4] Pacific islanders called him 'Pita.'[5] From 1809, he set himself up in Sydney, using it as a base for his private trade across the Pacific. He moved to Calcutta in 1816 and traded between Bengal and the Pacific. By this time, he had married. Mary Dillon accompanied him on his voyages from Calcutta.

In these journeys, Dillon linked many of the sites of the *Waves Across the South* together. This is why his life is a good starting point for our travels. His voyage of 1825–6 falls squarely in the middle of the age of revolutions and Dillon's career is a telling gauge of changing times. For the British empire followed in the wake of people who may be placed next to Dillon, namely private traders, sailors, castaways, missionaries and so-called pirates. This new empire sought to reform their activities with more systematic colonisation, 'free trade' and liberal government.[6]

In keeping with this shift to formal empire, Dillon spent the later phase of his life in Europe. He now combined a new set of interests, presenting plans for the settlement of the Pacific to the governments of France and Belgium and publishing a proposal for the colonisation of New Zealand by the British. In the 1840s, he was an active member of a characteristic association of reform in mid-nineteenth-century Britain, the Aborigines Protection Society, which was tied up with the humanitarian heritage of anti-slavery. He also set out a plan for sending Catholic missionaries to the Pacific.[7] He died in Paris in 1847.

ASTOUNDING ITINERARIES FROM REVOLUTION TO EMPIRE

To return to Dillon's voyage of 1825–6, the link to the age of revolutions becomes clear through the history of Dillon's ship and its crew. According to its third mate, the St Patrick had been 'taken and retaken by different belligerents' involved in the independence struggles across Latin America in the early nineteenth century.[8] Under Dillon's command, it sailed under Chilean colours to Calcutta and on leaving Valparaiso, the Europeans on board were recorded in the port register as 'naturalised Chileans'.[9] The crew of the St Patrick thought it to be the second vessel to enter India under Chilean colours.[10] Dillon was entered in the register as 'Don Pedro Dillon'. The ship also had an 'enormous green flag with yellow Irish harp in it'. This meant that it could also fly Irish colours.

Around twenty British sailors who joined the crew had served in Chile's war of independence against Spain, under the command of Thomas Cochrane, a British naval officer who played a pivotal role in the rebel navies of Chile, Peru and Brazil in the 1820s.[11] These men and others combined with a crew who had laboured under Dillon's command in a previous voyage, in the Calder, from Sydney to Valparaiso. The Calder's crew had included 'eight Europeans and four Tahitians'.[12] Now, on the St Patrick, eleven Pacific islanders were said to be part of the crew.[13] In an act of mockery of the imperial establishment, Dillon named the Tahitians 'Governor Macquarie', after the governor of Sydney; 'Major Goulborn', after the colonial secretary of New South Wales, and so on.[14]

The Calder also had on board a Chinese cook and a Bengali steward.[15] Dillon's fondness for Pacific islanders did not extend to the Bengali. The captain kept a sheet headed 'Crimes' on which he listed the Bengali's wrongs, such as the breaking of crockery or the loss of spoons overboard.[16] Outbound from Valparaiso, a Marquesan on board the St Patrick died on the voyage, despite sailing for twelve months in the hope of returning to Tahiti, from where he could get back home.[17] When the St Patrick reached Calcutta, four of the eleven Pacific islanders who were part of the ship's crew died.[18]

Also on the St Patrick was the son of the governor at Valparaiso, Miguel Zenteno. A disturbing story told by George Bayly, the third mate, who kept a record of his time with Dillon, involves Dillon's wife Mary: 'His wife lived on board and he very frequently gave her a thrashing . . .'[19] Bayly himself later wrote of his release from Dillon's aggressive captaincy in reaching Calcutta: 'never was a captive bird more pleased to get its liberty than I was.'[20] There were other captives on board: horses and donkeys bound for Tahiti were also on the St Patrick.[21]

The crew of the St Patrick illustrates the unlikely comradeship which was typical of this period.[22] These ship-board relationships were unstable, unpredictable and violent and based on gender, status and race and this too was pretty characteristic of this time. Despite being so typical, the St Patrick's journey became important. Before docking in Calcutta, Dillon and Bayly solved one of the greatest mysteries of their age, the fate of the French navigator La Pérouse whose expedition had vanished in the Pacific. It was last sighted at the newly found colony of New South Wales in 1788.

When Dillon came to the island of Tikopia, the remains of an extinct volcano remotely located in the south-west Pacific, he looked for some old friends, whom he had left there when an officer on a different ship, the Hunter, in 1813. These friends had disembarked at Tikopia after a dramatic and now controversial episode. The Hunter had called in at Fiji to collect sandalwood and bêche de mer on a voyage between Calcutta and New South Wales.[23] Dillon resorted to force on that occasion in order to procure the goods. In a letter to the East India Company authorities of Bengal in 1826, Dillon noted that 'all the Europeans [on the Hunter] were killed except myself, a man named Martin Buchert, a native of Staten [Stettin?] in Prussia, who had been on the island, and one of the ship's Company, William Wilson.'[24] Elsewhere and sensationally, he noted that the Fijians were 'cannibal monsters' who wished to eat the bodies of those slain.[25] Dillon's account of cannibalism in Fiji was exaggerated in retrospective retellings and there is much to recommend a recent interpretation which casts it as a narrative of self-delusion; some self-delusion certainly characterised much of Dillon's life. [26] Cannibalism was too easily projected onto Pacific islanders in this era.

Now, fifteen years after the *Hunter*'s visit, when the *St Patrick* came to Tikopia in 1826, several canoes approached Dillon's ship and there appeared a man called Joe, a 'lascar', who kissed Dillon's hands and feet. He was the informant who helped solve the puzzle of the disappeared La Pérouse. The *Hunter* had dropped Joe off at Tikopia on Dillon's previous visit.[27] Buchert, the Prussian, had also decided to stay on in Tikopia on that previous occasion together with 'his wife, a Feejee [Fijian] woman.' Between the time when Dillon dropped Joe and Buchert at Tikopia and the visit of the *St Patrick*, only a couple of British whalers had touched at Tikopia and they had visited relatively recently.[28]

Trade conducted by the likes of Dillon opened up the Pacific to new connections in these years, and the sudden appearance of whalers makes sense in this context. Joe himself is representative. 'Lascar' was a racialised term for non-white seamen, which originated from Persian via Portuguese. Joe's South Asian heritage is clear from how Bayly told the story: 'He appeared to have almost forgotten his native language and spoke at random, Bengallee, English, the Fijee and Tucopean.'[29] Elsewhere he was described as 'married on the island and comfortably settled'.[30] Bayly noted that Joe's own 'countrymen', presumably South Asians on board the *St Patrick*, could not understand him. Buchert himself was an example of the unexpected figures one could encounter in the Pacific of the early nineteenth century. Bayly noted: 'His only garment now was a mat round his middle. He was tattooed all over his body and had several marks on his face.'[31]

The artefact which solved the mystery of the lost navigator was around Joe's neck. It was an old silver guard, which in Bayly's account he managed to buy for a bottle of rum. According to Dillon, Joe sold it for 'a few fishing hooks to some of my people'.[32] When it was examined, Dillon thought he could decipher the initials of La Pérouse.[33] The sword guard was taken back to Calcutta. In writing to the powers that be in India, Dillon reported that the sword guard had come from a neighbouring group of islands, 'a large group of islands under the general name of Mallicolo'. It was a two day canoe sail to the leeward of Tikopia and the islanders of Tikopia 'were frequently in the habit of making Voyages' to it. Joe had been there and reported that he had met two Europeans who spoke the language of the islanders, a tantalising account for anyone in search of a lost expedition. Dillon wrote:

'[Joe] also saw in the possession of the Natives, this Sword Guard, several chain plates belonging to a Ship, also a number of Iron bolts, five Axes, the handle of a Silver fork, a few Knives, Tea Cups, Glass beads and Bottles, one Silver spoon with a crest and a cypher and a Sword; all of French manufacture.'[34]

In Calcutta, the sword guard was inspected by the Royal Asiatic Society of Bengal; the society stood at the head of intellectual inquiries, scientific, geographical and 'oriental', undertaken in India. It was formed in 1784 by William Jones, an orientalist and judge. One of the society's meetings was attended by Dillon. The society responded to Peter Dillon's report by urging that all means be used to discover whether any of La Pérouse's crew were still alive so that they could be restored to their home country. This was consistent with the 'motives of humanity', a resonant phrase of the age of revolutions, which they alleged were shared by 'the whole Indian community'. The Royal Asiatic Society saw itself as presiding over such inquiries in 'this quarter of the Globe'. It also set forth its motivation, in confident imperial rhetoric, to 'extend our knowledge of the earth and its inhabitants, and to spread through yet barbarous lands the blessings of civilization'.[35]

It was not only this relic which created a stir in Calcutta when the *St Patrick* moored. Two Māori men who were sons of chiefs had taken passage with Dillon after the *St Patrick* stopped in New Zealand for timber, adding even further to the incredible itineraries which lace this story. The press coverage was larded with hype. The Calcutta newspaper the *Bengal Hurkaru* noted that the ship had on board Brian Boroimbe, a 'New Zealand Prince, who considers and by his *genealogical tree* can prove himself to be a lineal descendant from his namesake, the celebrated King of Ireland [Brian Boru], who died gallantly fighting for his country against the Danes at Clon'. Boroimbe's appearance was said to be 'prepossessing' and his 'demeanor in every respect indicative of the ancient and noble blood that flows through his veins'.[36] This description is in keeping with the way Europeans cast Pacific-islander elites as 'noble savages', indigenous peoples untouched by the corruption of civilisation. Māori were particularly in danger of being cast like this. Also among the arrivals was 'His Excellency Morgan McMurroch, aid-de-camp'. The so-styled Prince was feted in Calcutta, taken to breakfast, to dinner with the merchants in the settlement, and to a performance of Shakespeare's *Henry IV*. He was received by the Acting British governor general in the official country residence in Barrackpore, where the Pacific islanders with Dillon had to perform dances and chants. Boroimbe was given a captain's uniform, a sword, and a medal carrying the likeness of George IV, which he proceeded to wear around his neck.[37]

Even as the Indian and Pacific Oceans were being brought together by the likes of Dillon, on the same ships, indigenous peoples were making unprecedented long-distance travels. They were using these voyages for their own purposes. At Aitutaki, for instance, a 'great number' of Pacific islanders came aboard the St Patrick wanting to join the crew; 'they all had a great desire to see the world'.[38] This demonstrates the agency of the peoples of the Indian and Pacific Oceans within the age of revolutions and on expeditions like Dillon's voyage.

In 1826, Calcutta was gripped by its war in Burma with the kingdom of Ava. Anxieties connected to this war in Calcutta saw Morgan attacked as he landed from the St Patrick. According to a newspaper report, onlookers were 'struck with the form of the man, which combined Herculean strength with perfect ease, grace and symmetry'.[39] When he landed the chaukidars or gatekeepers drew their scimitars, thinking that Morgan was a Burmese general coming to Calcutta as a spy. Dizzying globalisation could generate mistaken identity. The gatekeepers thought it 'not improbable that his army would follow in the night, and storm Fort William'.

Some Europeans, or in another account, Peter Dillon's clerk, 'promptly interfered and [Morgan's] hand was arrested in the act of dealing a death-blow'.[40] Morgan was marched to the police, followed by what the newspaper recorded to be three thousand Indians. This story was surely embellished by the Bengal Hurkaru, in keeping with the newspaper's other comments on Morgan. It reported that Morgan had a 'very just idea of the initiatory principles of Political Economy' and that he was 'determined to perfect himself in the science before he leaves the Presidency [of Bengal]'. He had asked, it was alleged, for instruction in the making of railroads, steam coaches, wheels and the principles of phrenology, the science of the head. The India Gazette, meanwhile, poked fun at Boroimbe, noting the rumour around town of the cannibal propensities of New Zealanders, which once again highlights the currency of the idea of cannibalism. '[A]t least during the time that he has been on shore here, [he] has fed very much like a good Christian.'[41]

Dillon's travels with Māori indicate the reach of Pacific islanders, including Māori serving on board sealers and whalers, into the heart of the Indian Ocean.[42] The way in which indigenous peoples used these encounters is evident elsewhere too. Before the *St Patrick* had reached Calcutta or indeed Tikopia, it had called at Tahiti. Here, Dillon was surprised to find two other friends, Takai and Langi. Takai and Langi had met Dillon in Tongatapu on a previous voyage. They had served as intermediaries and Takai had even navigated the *Calder*, taking charge of the ship's passage. Dillon had last seen the pair in Sydney where they had attracted commentary in the press.[43] They had converted to Christianity, come to Tahiti with a British missionary and now hoped to return to their own islands to convert their peoples.[44]

The trade that Dillon undertook also fed into indigenous politics. When the *Calder* was lost in Valparaiso Dillon recouped some of the cost by selling a collection of Pacific weapons which were on board the ship.[45] In the opposite direction of exchange, Dillon brought muskets and gunpowder into the Pacific and especially to New Zealand. When the *St Patrick* reached New Zealand, Bayly wrote: 'for Muskets or Gunpowder we could procure anything that the Island produced'. The acquisitive Dillon busied himself in procuring spars which were valued for the making of masts. Yet, the trade in spars for muskets had the potential to misfire, and Bayly wrote of a conspiracy:

> All of our crew were employed in the Hold stowing away the spars as fast as they came off, except when a number of canoes more than ordinary came off; when all hands were immediately called to quarters, Captain D. having been lately informed by a native (who had been in on the whole plan) of a conspiracy which had been formed on the St. Patrick's former voyage, to take the Ship and murder all hands on board; and that the Chief whom Captain Dillon had behaved so kindly to in taking him to South America and procuring him a vast quantity of presents [perhaps muskets?] was at the head of it.[46]

In turn, the Māori who visited Calcutta were travelling in the shadow of an important leader and fighter, Hongi Hika. In 1820, Hongi had visited London from New Zealand. His story is a clear indicator of how these new voyages were opening up a terrain of new politics for indigenous peoples. Hongi was presented to the king and finally returned home with muskets, powder and shot. 'After [Hongi] returned to his native country,' Bayly noted, 'he gave out that he would never desist from killing and eating his countrymen till they made him King the same as King George in England.'[47] Accordingly, Boroimbe and Morgan too were to 'try their fortunes in obtaining Muskets and Gunpowder from the Merchants of Calcutta'.[48] Beyond New Zealand, at various other locations, Dillon got into conversations with indigenous elites and was enrolled, as in New Zealand, within local power structures and contests. Bayly noted how Dillon entertained 'Queen Pomarrè Vahine' and 'all the Royal Family' of Tahiti when the St Patrick called there to find Takai and Langi. 'They were received with a salute of musketry, and escorted down to the state-room. Here I was instructed to exhibit all our treasures.'[49]

The spread of the European musket across the far reaches of the Pacific in this period indicates how European wars and Pacific island contests were interrelated; the techniques and scale of war were shifting in the early nineteenth century. Those who went to war with Europeans as well as those fighting neighbouring regimes or political elites had to arm themselves as Europeans did. British imperial war was tied together with an extractive state and new ways of gathering information. In New Zealand, the rate of exchange adopted by the St Patrick was twenty spars for one musket or a proportionate quantity of gunpowder; on one occasion, however, 166 spars were purchased for 58 pounds of gunpowder and fifteen hatchets.[50] It is important not to romanticise the encounters between people like Dillon and the residents of Asia, Africa and Oceania because of the consequences that followed in their wake.

Note, for instance, the conversation between Boroimbe and Dillon at Budge Inn in Calcutta. Why, Boroimbe pondered, did the staff treat Dillon with such attention? When it was explained to him that this was because Britain had taken the country, Boroimbe observed: 'You will come and take my country too, I have no doubt, as you have taken this.'[51] Boroimbe was absolutely correct: these wandering maritime paths, which traversed the Indian and Pacific Oceans, were closely connected to colonisation. The Bengal Hurkaru, in reporting Boroimbe's visit to Barrackpore, imagined him returning home to New Zealand and providing a safe haven for British ships which would touch in any territory under his control. It added this line in support of Boroimbe's credentials as a friend of Britain: 'The dominions over which Boroimbe's father presides extend from Cape Palliser to the River Thames, and the largest, straightest and most durable spars in the world are easily procurable there . . .'[52] The reception accorded to Māori on Dillon's voyage pointed in turn to the prospect of an empire of trade riding the waves, an empire that would counter the age of revolution's many possibilities.

Elsewhere what would happen to Māori lands was part of the discussion. The *India Gazette* hoped that Boroimbe would be sent back not with weapons but with 'the instruments of agriculture and husbandry, and duly instructed in their use, and be provided with the means of raising in his own country, grains, vegetables, and fruits, that are not now indigenous to it'. Dillon, himself, in advocating the further colonisation of New Zealand in 1832 sketched the possibilities of a web of commerce. He envisaged that New Zealand would be a base for Pacific trades, including sandalwood, sperm oil and coconut oil, and mother-of-pearl, which was in demand on the China coast and in Manila. Timber could be traded from New Zealand to Chile and Peru. Empty convict ships arriving in New South Wales, he envisaged, could be filled with products like sandalwood, bêche de mer, shark fins and rope, which could be sent to India or Europe.[53]

It would be wrong to see the *Calder* and *St Patrick* as passing without company across the Pacific and Indian Oceans. The seas were becoming populated in new ways as Europeans were added in greater numbers and with greater reach. While the number of official British vessels in these seas was still small, nevertheless ships of all kinds came upon each other, private and official, British and non-British.[54] Valparaiso had a series of American and British vessels in harbour at the start of the voyage of the *St Patrick*, and during Bayly's time there a Spanish brig was brought to harbour by a crew that had mutinied, murdered their officers and wished to deliver the vessel to the patriots of Chile.[55] This episode was the talk of Valparaiso. At Tahiti, the *St Patrick* came across a British whaler, the *Fawn*, in addition to some American whalers and a merchant ship; at Huahine they encountered a 300-ton American whaler and in New Zealand they met the *Emily*, another whaler, the *Larne*, a British ship of war and the *Sir George Osborne*, on the way to pearl in the Marquesas.[56] In the East Indies, while between Papua New Guinea and Christmas Island, the *St Patrick* came across an American ship trading between Philadelphia and Canton.[57] After escaping the *St Patrick* as a freed bird, Bayly took up work on the *Hooghly* bound for London via Colombo and the Cape of Good Hope.[58]

Across these seas in the early nineteenth century ships kept track of each other and spoke with each other. Ships compared their passages between ports and determined which arrived earlier. Private traders watched the prospect of rival traders. They scrutinsed what the British colonial state was up to, in shipping convicts to Australia and making British bases in the Cape, Ceylon and Mauritius. They also watched and even participated as the British pushed against rival empires, political elites and private agents. On St Helena, Bayly wrote of how his vessel 'kept company' with another ship the *Harriet*; there was also an American vessel bound to Amsterdam with coffee from Batavia. On the way back home it came upon a French ship bound to Nantes.[59]

By the date of the *Hooghly*'s journey home, British fears of rivals were certainly abating. Yet in these busy seas, aggression and anxiety about the French still lay under the surface. There was a site which reassured the British of how they were overtaking the French in these oceans of the south. It was the tomb of Napoleon on St Helena. As soon as the *Hooghly* anchored at St Helena, the passengers went en masse to see the tomb. Napoleon had been exiled here after his defeat at Waterloo in 1815. He died on St Helena in 1821.[60] If Dillon named his child after Napoleon, a host of other Britons sought in this way to take up the legacy of the Napoleonic wars. The British empire adopted some of the features of the Napoleonic empire, a militarised logic of integrating territories combined with a rhetoric of free trade.[61]

Yet anxiety and aggression about the French could sit together with Anglo-French friendship. Indeed Dillon's return voyage from Calcutta to the Pacific, to the site of the disappearance of La Pérouse, attracted 'grateful acknowledgement' on the part of the French authorities at Chandernagore [Chandannagar], which was a French foothold in India returned by the British to the French in 1816. Dillon now took on board a representative of the French regime in India.[62] The *Hobart Town Gazette* of 7 April 1827 noted the docking of Dillon's vessel, which arrived with the official patronage of the East India Company:

Yesterday arrived for refreshment, the Honorable East India Company's ship Research, P. Dillon, Esq. commander (mounts 16 guns and carries 78 men), from Calcutta, 23d of January, on a voyage of discovery to the South Pacific, in search of the survivors of the French frigates La Boussole and L'Astrolabe, under the late Count de la Perouse. Passengers, His Royal Highness Brian Boru, a New Zealand prince, Morgan M'Murrah a New Zealand nobleman, secretary and aide de camp to the prince; Captain Speck of the Bengal Army, who remains here for the recovery of his health, and Monsieur Chaigneau of the French Consulate department.[63]

Despite the fact that this was an official voyage, it also had on board 100 muskets intended for 'the ships armament and [as] presents to native chiefs'.[64] The official instructions were set out in careful detail with the intent of restraining Dillon's entrepreneurial spirit. They also stated that firearms should be used against islanders only in 'cases of extreme danger'. Dillon was warned against too much interaction with the Pacific islanders on board and also on shore: 'The Board deem it proper to warn you against placing too much confidence in the Natives who accompany you from this Port.'[65] This new expedition also had within its aims the charting of this unknown stretch of the Pacific. Once again there was a link to the war in Burma: a medical 'dresser' who had also served in Burma was attached to it.[66] Dillon was instructed by his patrons to supply the naturalist on board the vessel at noon each day with the latitude and longitude of the ship. This proved a point of tension in a major disagreement between Dillon and this naturalist, Dr Robert Tytler, which led to a trial in Van Diemen's Land [Tasmania].[67]

As Dillon's story proceeded then – and as the grand voyages of the Pacific such as La Pérouse's gave way to the early nineteenth-century dispersal of settlers, traders, missionaries, governors and judges too – empire came into the space of revolution. To trace the trail of the *St Patrick* in 1825 and the voyages of Dillon and Bayly on either side of this journey is to find indigenous politics; dizzying and unexpectedly global itineraries spanning Latin America, the Pacific, Australia and New Zealand, India and Africa; the expansion of knowledge and reason and their relation to colonialism; the spread of British trade and rhetorical commitments to humanity and civilisation; and the spread of war, weapons and violent contests. This is all characteristic of the age of revolutions. Yet as we move across this tale, we move from revolution to empire, and the British empire emerges as a counter-revolutionary force that sought to adopt within itself the language and politics of what went before it. Indeed, this empire took charge of the very coordinates of this part of the Pacific. Even eccentric Dillon sought to insert himself within this new imperial structure.

Pacific islanders' assertiveness and their attempt to forge a new politics for themselves is evident in the detail of Dillon's life. Yet their voices and politics are difficult to extract because of the density of colonial rhetoric in these sources, including even in the names they were given. Telling here was how the people of Vanikoro (called Malicola in the commentary of the period) where La Pérouse disappeared, were racialised in press commentary. This offensive line comes from the *Colonial Times and Tasmanian Advertiser* of 1827: 'The Malicolans differ from almost all of the other islanders in the South Seas. They are as black as Negroes with wooly hair, and negro features.'[68]

The limitations of the sources and their ideological biases necessitate a different perspective to understand the history of this oceanic quarter in the age of revolutions.

PERSIAN WRITERS IN A WORLD OF WATER

South Asian writers and travellers who left accounts of voyaging across the south in this set of decades provide a good alternative lens, though they too were not without biases.[69] One such was Mirza Abu Talib Khan Isfahani, who was styled in a colonial idiom by British observers as being a 'Persian Prince', like the so-called Māori Prince who travelled with Dillon. Abu Talib noted: 'I never assumed the title'.[70] It was in 1799 and from Calcutta that Abu Talib departed for Britain. The ship he boarded was like the *St Patrick* in having an unusual registration and a diverse crew, including South Asian seamen. Abu Talib sought to distance himself from the band of sailors:

> On the 1st of Ramzan, A.H. 1213 (Feb. 8. 1799), we took leave of our friends, and embarked at Calcutta . . . We found the ship [a Danish vessel] in the greatest disorder composed of indolent and inexperienced Bengal Lascars; and the cabins small, dark, and stinking, especially that allotted to me, the very recollection of which makes me melancholy . . . The Captain was a proud self-sufficient fellow. His first officer, who was by birth American, resembled an ill-tempered growling mastiff . . .[71]

Abu Talib left Calcutta on the advice of an Scottish friend, in a bid to visit the West to dispel his despondency. As a young man, he had lived in Lucknow, in northern India. Lucknow was a magnet for scholars and he was educated by them. Earlier in the eighteenth century, his ancestors had come to India from Persia; his father had worked for the ruling elite of both Oudh [Awadh] and Bengal. The later eighteenth century created yet another phase of uncertainty for these scholar officials who relied so heavily on patronage. This uncertainty arose from repeated regime changes and from the ascent of British power.

Abu Talib's travel narrative in Persian, *Masir-i Talibi fi bilad-i afranji* or 'Talib's travels in the Land of the Franks', needs to be understood in this light. For his is an unsettled voice, that of an elite man trying to find his way in the midst of the age of revolutions, which was changing the world as he knew it. According to some authorities, these texts may have been encouraged by the British, though Abu Talib's view of Britain 'was not always flattering to the English, but congenial enough'.[72] After being dismissed from his work as revenue officer or *amildar* in Oudh, Abu Talib had taken up work under the British, serving as assistant to Colonel Alexander Hannay, who was in charge of revenue at Gorakhpur. He had also worked in Lucknow, once again for the British, tasked for instance with the suppression of a rebellion. He had been out of work for about a decade when he boarded the Danish ship in 1799 and all kinds of mishaps had overtaken him by this time: 'all my dependants and adherents, seeing my distress, left me; and even some of my children, and the domestics brought up in my father's family, abandoned me.'[73] His story did not end well. After returning from his travels in 1803, he died in 1806 without seeing a substantial change in his lot.

His writings reflect his literary skills as a poet; he was known for his recitation and writing of poetry. Note for instance his comparison of whales with elephants, from his sea journey to London:

Several fishes called *whales* approached so close to the ship, that we could view them distinctly. They were four times the size of the largest elephant, and had immense nostrils, whence they threw up the water to the height of fifteen yards.[74]

Abu Talib was close to the Cape of Good Hope when he observed these creatures. At this point in the voyage, the 'sight of land brought tears to [his] eyes.' Meanwhile in the next paragraph, he described how he felt being confined on board, in terms which were contrasted with those he used for the roaming whales:

In short, we passed our time like dead bodies shut up in dark and confined cells; and had it not been for the incessant noise and jarring elements, we might have supposed ourselves inhabitants of the nether world.[75]

While on his journey, Abu Talib paid a lot of attention to nature. This is unsurprising, for in the late eighteenth and early nineteenth centuries, people everywhere were changing their ideas of natural history. He tasted flying fish: 'I thought them good food, and fancied they had somewhat the flavour of a bird.'[76] At the Cape, he commented on the horses and their 'Arab blood', dogs and cats 'which run wild in the woods' and ostriches. He also wrote of coastlines and places, for instance noting that St Helena, where Napoleon was later to be buried, had cliffs which appeared 'black and burnt up'.[77] In the course of his voyage, Abu Talib was also very much aware of the stars. Close to the Nicobar Islands he was puzzled when he looked through a telescope and saw an island at sea, even though it was below the horizon.[78]

This interest in nature worked itself out in a commitment to classifying animals, landscapes and geography. All these were tabulated one against the other. On the classification of geography, he set out the following rules in keeping with how strips of the world's ocean were being defined on the globe in this period of expansive and regular globe-spanning navigation:

A *Channel* means a narrow part of the sea, confined between two lands, but open at both ends.

A *Bay* extends far into the land, is of circular form, and open only on one side.

A *Sea* (sometimes called a *Gulf*) is a large extent of the ocean, but nearly surrounded by land; as the Mediterranean Sea, the Gulf of Persia, the Red Sea etc.[79]

And even as places and other creatures were tabulated and located like this, people were too. Abu Talib was interested in skin colour, in origin and descent and in status and he was especially interested in women. In Cape Town, he wrote disapprovingly that 'all the European Dutch women' were 'very fat, gross, and insipid', but then added, 'but the girls are well-made, handsome, and sprightly; they are also good natured, but require costly presents.' He flirted with these younger women at Cape Town, wishing to give his handkerchief to the handsomest at a party. On his own account, in doing this he was attempting to adopt the practice of the 'rich Turks of Constantinople' who 'throw their handkerchief to the lady with whom they wish to pass the night'.[80] When in Britain, he wrote of a 'Miss Combe' to whom he took a particular fancy to and whom he once met at a masquerade. She was 'like the bright moon surrounded with brilliant stars'.[81]

Regardless of how these women interpreted his interest, Abu Talib's narrative is framed by the biases of status, rank, race and gender and their active defence. When describing Nicobar islanders, he wrote that they were 'very muscular' and resembled the 'Peguers [of Burma] and Chinese in features but [that these Nicobar islanders] are of a wheat colour, with scarcely any beard'. He showed no empathy, however, for South Asian seamen despite the fact that these sailors were 'much disgusted with the treatment they received on board'. While at these islands, these seamen deserted the ship and hid themselves in the woods.[82] *Lascar* revolt was a common feature of these years in the Indian Ocean during the age of revolutions.[83] But this revolt was pushed to the margins in Abu Talib's prose. On this particular occasion at the Nicobar islands, the deserting sailors were caught and brought back on board.

Despite his starting point as a non-European Abu Talib's writing, as with Dillon's, needs to be teased and taken apart in order to see the conflicts of the age. We see this with an intriguing argument that he penned about the 'liberty' of Asian women. It was written during his time in Britain and was first published in the *Asiatic Annual Register* in 1801 and then in other places.[84] He explained the origin of this essay:

> An English lady, addressing herself to me, observed, that the women of Asia have no liberty at all, but live like slaves, without honour and authority, in the houses of their husbands; and she censured the men for their unkindness, and the women, also, for submitting to be so undervalued.[85]

In response Abul Talib insisted on the greater liberties enjoyed by Asian women when compared with British women, but his reasoning fell back on patriarchal ideas and his position as an elite man. He reasoned that there were far fewer servants in houses in Britain due to the higher cost of labour. However, Asian women could have their own apartments and households and they could be released from their husband's company for several days and 'send [the husband's] victuals to him in the murda-nnah (or male apartments)'. In Abu Talib's view there were 'people of various nations' dwelling in the same cities in Asia, much more so than in Britain, and this necessitated segregated living arrangements between men and women; for to 'allow the women such a liberty [to live with their husband], where there is such a danger of corruption [from foreigners], would be an encroachment upon the liberty of the men'. Women in Asia were said to have more leisure, 'repose from the fatigue of motion' and the ability to preserve 'their honour, by not mixing with the vulgar'. On polygamy, Abu Talib wrote that it increased the freedom of the first wife. On those who didn't have the privilege of being the first wife, he wrote: 'those women who submit to marry with a married man are never of high or wealthy families'.

Abu Talib wrote in this way of liberty, a key concept of the age of revolutions. But like other writers of the time he twisted it in order to justify rather than tear down differences of gender, class and race. His argument about the women of Britain and Asia was an attempt to rela-tivise liberty and to make it subjective and culturally particular. Whereas his interlocutor, 'the English lady' perhaps, held that Asian women did not have the liberty to choose their husbands, Abu Talib replied:

On this head nothing need be said, for in Europe this liberty is merely nominal, as without the will of the father and mother, the daughter's choice is of no avail; and whatever choice they make for her, she must submit to; and in its effects, it serves only to encourage running away (as the male and female slaves in India do).

Abu Talib's travel narrative and his interactions in London and India were an attempt to insert himself within British class hierarchy even as he sought to defend the social structures and customary practices of South Asia.[86] It is important to note that he sold an enslaved person while in Cape Town whose 'manners and disposition', he wrote, 'had been so much corrupted on board ship'.[87] If his analysis of society, nature and the globe itself is in keeping with the times, this is also the case for his account of law and government. Here too were the characteristic contradictions of the time. He praised the use of trial by jury but had a generally negative view of British laws which often 'overruled equity', so that 'a well-meaning honest man was frequently made the dupe of an artful knave'. The law was a means, in this telling, of making money. He feared the insolence of Englishmen, exemplified in the assembly of 'mobs' in London, and was incensed at the increase in taxes and the price of provisions, seeing it as akin to that seen in France before the revolution.[88]

Abu Talib presented an account of the French Revolution: people 'disgusted with the tyranny of government, sent petitions and remonstrances to their King'. The king became a 'useless member' as is typical of a 'republican form of government':

> After this event, a complete revolution of affairs took place in France.
> The powerful were reduced to weakness, and the base raised to power.
> The common people elected representatives from the lowest classes; and
> appointed officers of their own choice, to defend their territories.[89]

If indigenous politics lay beneath the surface of Dillon and Bayly's accounts, Abu Talib's writing bears the evidence of European politics and Anglo-French tensions. Before the Danish vessel set off from Calcutta, it was delayed by more than twenty days when a French frigate was found cruising outside the port. The firing of cannons was heard. An English ship fell to the French. An Arab vessel flying French colours 'suspended under the English' was also spotted. The end of this contest was determined by an English ship from Madras which captured the French frigate.[90] Close to Mauritius, there was the fear that the ship would fall to the French. Abu Talib found that Cape Town had just been taken by the British, with sixteen vessels protecting the harbour from the French, and he wrote of five thousand soldiers garrisoned under General Dundas.[91]

The link to the age of revolutions lies in how Abu Talib narrated and interpreted these events of European politics and also in how he took on board and internalised the new knowledge and ideas of this time. The age of revolution's unprecedented globalisation is evident in the possibilities of travel which Abu Talib's journey exemplifies. But other clues to the fundamental changes of this era followed later. On his return journey, Abu Talib travelled overland from Britain to India. In the Middle East, Abu Talib described the Wahhabi movement, and noted that 'people could talk of nothing else'. At the hands of the Wahhabi, in his words, there had been 'sacrilegious plunder' of the cities of Mecca and Medina with the aim of eliminating idolatry. This Wahhabi reform of Islam was connected with the political changes across the Middle East, as we will soon see. It had within it a sense of revolution which was different to the European sense of revolution even as Europeans cast it as revolutionary. The concept of 'Wahhabism' as used today still carries with it a series of stereotypes about Islamic purism and fundamentalism. It is problematically traced back to the age of revolutions in an uninterrupted story of continuity. Abu Talib described the movement:

> Although the Vahabies possess great power, and have collected immense wealth, they still retain the greatest simplicity of manners, and moderation in their desires. They sit down on the ground without ceremony, content themselves with a few dates for their food, and a coarse large cloak serves them for clothing and bed for three years. Their horses are of the genuine Nejib breed, of well-known pedigrees; none of which will they permit to be taken out of the country.[92]

The idea of revolution also appeared in the writings of the class of Persianate chroniclers to which Abu Talib belonged. The word *inquilab* appeared frequently among Persian writers of this age, to mean 'revolution' or 'subversion'; it was used to describe the changes brought about by the invasion of the British too. According to one authority on these texts, this word 'literally meant turning'.[93] This means that these writings sit very squarely within the compass of the age of revolutions. In summary, the world around Abu Talib was turning in political terms; but there was also a churning in what it meant to live life. This was evident in his commentary on so many spheres, from nature to society and from gender to cultural difference.

This engagement with the turning of the times is also evident among those who may be seen as his compatriots. For instance there is the epic and valuable history of eighteenth-century India penned by Ghulam Husain Khan Tabataba'i, *Sair al-muta'akkhirin*. It stretched from the death of the Mughal emperor Aurangzeb in 1707 to the advance of the British in the early 1780s. Published in English translation in Calcutta, in the year prior to the French Revolution, it was written by a politician and landholder, whose aristocratic family hailed from Persia and who had served as a clerk to the East India Company.[94] Ghulam Husain presented an account of the American Revolution: settlers joined forces to resist the authority of the king of England, 'spreading full open the standard of rebellion and defiance'. In turn they called in the French, upon whom the English declared war.[95] Another writer, Mirza I'tisam al-Din, from a line of Muslim service gentry in Bengal, described the American revolution as the rise of the wealthy nobility of America against the English, and interpreted it as part of a broader conflict between the

English and the French.[96] Ghulam Husain meanwhile wrote that the
Spanish and the Dutch joined against the English. 'Time alone will point
out what may be the final intention of providence in this diversity of
concerns and interests; and time alone will discover what it has ultimately
predestined on those obstruse points.'[97]

Yet before closing his story with this resort to a long view of time
Ghulam Husain paused for another revealing reason. He gave his readers
a lesson in astronomy. This was in keeping with Abu Talib's interest in
the stars and seas. 'The circumstance and figure of land and water in
our globe are not as they were thought heretofore. They say that the
latter seems to encompass the former as a girdle.'[98] According to Ghulam
Husain, the New World was a hemisphere that had yet to be fully explored
and examined. He was aware of how medicinal drugs, fine woods and
gold and silver were to be found there. Would the feet of the inhabitants
of the two hemispheres meet 'sole to sole', if the earth were taken away
from them, he pondered. Even as their feet met like this, would their
heads still face the heavens? For this Persian chronicler, the changes of
the world sat together with changing knowledge of it; the rise of Britain
in India and its wars with France were tied together with events on a
further hemisphere. At the same time as these changes were unfolding,
Ghulam Husain was trying to find his own place in a world that was
shifting, and where new norms of patronage, government and rule were
emerging in India. For this reason, his voice, like Abu Talib's, was an
unsettled one that moved between old and new.

This uncertainty is clear yet again in the account of I'tisam al-Din's
journey to Britain. He too had moved between employment for Indian
and British masters. He had fought for the British in wars which led to
the 1765 grant to the British of the *diwani* of Bengal, the right to collect
taxes and decide civil cases. This was a key moment in the consolidation
of British expansion in India. He helped the British with the suppression
of unrest, just as Abu Talib would do. He left on a voyage to England
in 1767 as part of a diplomatic mission sent to the British king by the
Mughal emperor.

I'tisam al-Din's account of travel was titled *Shigarf-nama-i vilayet* or
'Wonder Book of England'. It was written in 1785 two decades after his
journey. It charted a history of exploration from the early attempts of the
Portuguese to reach India. Now, the British had taken the lead on the seas
above all the other 'hat-wearing nations of Europe'.[99] His account of travel
then proceeded with sections on the sea, the compass, ships and winds,

indicating a consistent and deep curiosity throughout. The sea was the conduit of European expansion but a mysterious medium: 'the blue of the sea is a reflection of the sky. A simple proof of this is that sea-water scooped up with the hand appears whitish, if not colourless.'[100] Contemplating the sea in turn brought with it the need to think of the earth itself, which was consistent with the prose of other Persian writers and in keeping with the nature of this age of revolutions and its concern with astronomy and other sciences. In poetic language, he wrote: 'The earth is a floating egg amidst the sea's immensity.' There followed the story that a European king had sought to find the depth of the sea by dropping a rope: 'millions of yards disappeared and yet the rope didn't touch the bottom.'[101]

He embraced western technologies of navigation, writing in detail for instance of the use of the compass, and describing ships which generally had 'five storeys': 'The topmost storey is aft and is occupied by the Captain and its officers.' During high winds a ship could be assailed by waves that could 'rise as high as palm trees'. In the midst of all this detail, I'tisam al-Din's refrain was to praise Allah. On the seabed 'complete knowledge of the secrets of the sea's depths belongs to Allah alone'.[102] In this way, there was a determined attachment to tradition and established ways despite his wide-ranging interest in the new. The twinning of these two, the old and the new, was beautifully expressed when he described European sailors climbing the masts during a storm as having the 'agility of Hanuman', the Hindu figure who appears in the epic *Ramayana,* and hanging from the masts 'like bats'. 'Their courage and industry', he noted, 'have made them the most powerful race on earth.'[103]

As for the voyage itself, his account of Mauritius, where the ship stopped, saw the appearance of Muslim *lascars.*[104] He was intrigued by how they had 'married into slavery', with wives who were enslaved to French masters. 'These slaves are brought as adolescents from Bengal, Malabar, the Deccan [all in India] and other regions and sold for fifty to sixty rupees each.' He benefited from the hospitality and advice of the *lascars,* who served as intermediaries in the market, enabling him to purchase 'mangoes, water-melons, cucumbers, musk-melons and several other varieties of fruits peculiar to the Bengali summer'. But he 'grieved inwardly' that these Asian seamen had forsaken 'their own land'. His description of Mauritius, an island that was taken by the British in 1810, partly in fear of republicanism and piracy, was attentive to people, settlement, history and nature.

I'tisam al-Din set Mauritius within a broader view of Indian Ocean territories. His passage to Mauritius had taken him near many interesting 'islands and coasts'. He incorrectly identified Batavia as Portuguese. Two months' journey from Bengal, he reported that there was 'an island, which is a part of the Chinese kingdom and is famous for its Chinaware'. There followed an account of Pegu in Burma. 'As we sailed down the Bay of Bengal,' he wrote, 'Malacca showed as a thin black line on the horizon . . . South-west of Madras, at a distance of one-hundred miles – or a day's sailing – from Pondicherry lies Ceylon, which Indians call Serendip.' The Maldives came next in this account, ruled by someone who was less than a *zamindar* or landlord of Bengal, and yet who had the affectation of sovereignty. And then an island where the inhabitants were said to be 'human' and yet they 'dress in the skins of wild beasts and eat half-raw meat'.

I'tisam al-Din's writing was as maritime as those of Pacific voyagers in its attention to ships, seas, islands, coasts and sailors; it also demonstrated some of the same predilections displayed by travellers like Dillon. He wrote of an island of cannibals:

The inhabitants of this island are human, yet their physiognomy is diabolical. They dress in the skins of the wild beasts and eat half-raw meat. They crave human flesh, and there being gold mines on the island, they will gladly barter gold for men. When they espy a vessel in the distance, they light a fire on a hill in order to lure the ship to their shores.[105]

It was not only the figure of the cannibal which united this travel account with colonial renditions of seaborne adventure. There were also mermaids in I'tisam al-Din's story: 'May Allah in his infinite mercy prevent anyone from seeing a mermaid, for it is a kind of genii.' And in keeping with Abu Talib's prose, there were of course flying fish and whales too. Whales were described by I'tisam al-Din in almost the same terms as were used by Abu Talib:

[A whale] is at least equal in bulk to two full-grown elephants; often it is larger. Its neck resembles an elephant's, and its nose too is rather like an elephant's trunk, only much smaller. Its nostrils are on the crown of its head.[106]

Though separated by so much including their own subject positions, there are many parallels in the content and concerns of this set of sources which arise from the Pacific and Indian Oceans. The travels of Dillon and Bayly as well as Abu Talib and I'tisam al-Din show us many if not most of the places that we will travel to in this book. Their stories encompass the breadth of the forgotten quarter and many of the scenes of what will follow. They also span the decades from the late 1760s to the late 1840s, a perfect introduction to the stories that are still to come. For these years constitute the age of revolutions as it turned to empire.

THE AGE OF REVOLUTIONS

Dillon and Bayly as well as Abu Talib and I'tisam al-Din reveal how difficult it is to find an indigenous perspective in the age of revolutions. The surge of indigenous politics, for instance of Tongans or Māori, arose in response to the infiltration of invaders and the new possibilities of this period. Some colonial biases and ideologies were taken up to forge this politics. The revolts, warfare and reformist movements of non-Europeans in the Indian and Pacific Oceans should occupy centre stage for once in this book; they were formed with one eye on global politics. Note the references to the American Revolution or French Revolution among Persian writers or how these travellers interpreted political changes in India with respect to a broader sense of the age of revolutions. Despite the problems in identifying a pure 'indigenous', the standard narrative of this era of change needs to be reordered, starting with the Indian and Pacific Oceans and their peoples, if this period is to be understood more fully. Otherwise oceanic peoples become simple recipients rather than active agents in crafting the modern world.

It is too easy to see how revolutionary currents flowed through the Atlantic and then moved outwards to spaces including the waterways of the south charted by the travellers we have considered. Accordingly, the declaration of American independence in 1776 served as a template for the global dispersal of assertions of the rights of states and the freedoms of individuals and communities.[107] The anti-monarchical offensive launched by the French revolutionaries in 1789 spread ideas of patriotism and liberty and called for self-government. There was a stirring of independence movements in Spanish America with the Peninsular War, which saw the French occupation of the Iberian Peninsula in 1808, the dissolution of the Bourbon monarchy and the establishment of the

Spanish Cortes from 1810 to 1814,. In Chile, the 1818 statement of independence held that 'the Continental Territory of Chile and its adjacent Islands, form in fact and right, a free, independent and sovereign State'.[108] Meanwhile, Haiti declared itself to be a 'black republic', drawing on the rhetoric of the French Revolution and rumours of slave emancipation in the late 1790s. These waves of revolt in turn were inescapably bound to the war between France and Britain, even as revolution and war have had intertwined lives to the present. The French supported the Americans, and the British government stood against not only French republicanism, but also Irish, Dutch and Belgian revolt. Britian went to war with France in 1792.

Yet if we are to leave this sequence of Atlantic events to one side, the age of revolutions needs to be defined less by grand moments and more by changing ideology, self-understanding, warfare, labour and political organisation. All these were being reinvented, but continuously so rather than at specific junctures or turning points. This reinvention occurred in small islands as much as it did in large states and nations in the global North. Each of these spheres of experience – political, economic, cultural, military and intellectual – was increasingly calibrated with respect to the rise of empire. The globalisation of the age was making people feel like the very world was shifting. The shift from plural revolutionary possibilities to the consolidation of empire saw imperialists who were naturalists, surveyors, astronomers and time-keepers seeking to control the shape of the globe and knowledge of it.[109] Writers in this space of water, like those just encountered, were reconsidering their sense of the globe and how bits of sea and land fitted together or how hemispheres were bound.[110] They were doing this while reconsidering themselves and others in relation to notions of race, gender and status which were unpredictable and yet powerful.

The flux of the age which gave rise to our times operated at many levels – the individual, the state, the region and even the globe itself – and if so this is in keeping with the multiple senses of the word revolution itself. Indeed, at the end of the eighteenth century, while 'revolution' was said to inaugurate a change for all humankind, it was nevertheless also seen as a return to the preordained status quo, a revolving back.[111] It was a naturalised process – commentators discussed it, like those who follow them to the present, in the language of currents, waves, winds and lava. There was also the sense of a perpetual revolt, rather than an identifiable event in a bounded window in time and with a definite goal in prospect. Revolution worked across deep time, linking past and future and intervening in the natural condition of humans everywhere. It is clear that indigenous peoples and certainly Persian writers in transit across the seas had a wide sense of revolution.

Given all this, empire was a counter-revolt not only in its attempt to adopt the ideology, knowledge, restlessness and mobility of the age of revolutions.[112] It was also so in substantially closing down the width of possibilities of the age of revolutions. The British empire was in this sense an invasive corrective, a force which countered its alternatives: republicanism and the dream worlds of so-called 'pirates', pilgrims and private traders, in other words the Dillons and Abu Talibs of this age. The outburst of republican feeling in Mauritius, with the formation of revolutionary committees and clubs; the diplomatic connections of Oman, ranging from Dutch Batavia to France via the so-called republican regime of Tipu Sultan of Mysore in South India; the traders involved in sealing and whaling on Tasmania, including Americans and Frenchmen, with links across the far south of the Indian and Pacific Oceans; the rise of millenarian religious fervour, for instance among the Wahhabis of Saudi Arabia, as they faced the Gulf; the spread of republican ideas and Napoleonic government in Batavia; the building of ships in Rangoon: these were some of the symptoms of the age of revolutions in the Indian and Pacific Oceans before the rise of the British empire. In each case another future was in view; waters were traversed for religion, politics and trade, bypassing empire, or feeding into other visions. The success of the British lay in altering the course of this turbulent world of change, association, debate and protest. The British empire co-opted the dreams of the global South and sent these dreams into reverse gear.

2

In the South Pacific:
Travellers, Monarchs and Empires

Four days had passed and there was yet no news of Comte de Trobriand. It was October 1793 and the French ships, *La Recherche* and *L'Espérance* lay impatiently moored twenty-five miles outside the Dutch foothold of Surabaya, now the second largest city of Indonesia.

The years of the French Revolution and the revolutionary wars saw a series of French exploratory voyages to the Pacific under dramatically different circumstances. To take three examples: first, there was an expedition under the command of Comte de La Pérouse (1785–8) and with the authority of an absolute monarch, Louis XVI; second came a voyage under de Bruni d'Entrecasteaux (1791–4), with the sanction of the National Assembly, and to search for the lost La Pérouse; and third, there was an expedition commanded by Nicolas Baudin (1800–3), under instruction from Napoleon. The *Recherche* and *Espérance* made up the second of this set of three voyages. The ships began their journey under the command of d'Entrecasteaux. But d'Entrecasteaux died about three months before the expedition reached Surabaya. Now the impact of the European age of revolution was about to overtake this voyage, for it too would soon be dissolved.

Waiting outside Surabaya, such was the crew's state of mind that any European might have become 'a compatriot'; 'any Frenchman would have been welcomed as a member of [their] families'.[1] With two-thirds of the crew ill, mostly with scurvy, they longed for refreshment and comforting assurances. Alexandre d'Hesmivy d'Auribeau, now the commanding officer, also very sick from an unknown ailment, and in all likelihood under the influence of laudanum, sent out another boat, this time flying a white flag as a sign of peace. Eventually a Javanese chief brought out the news of the age of revolutions: Louis XVI had been executed and France was at war with its European neighbours, including the Dutch. A republic had been declared. All the men on the voyage – and unbeknown to many, one disguised woman – were Dutch prisoners of war. The European family had been torn apart, and the diplomatic etiquette surrounding the provisioning of ships in the Pacific no longer held.

What could d'Auribeau do? One option was to make the six-week journey across the Indian Ocean to Île de France [Mauritius], and this would certainly be the most honourable option and that preferred by his crew. Yet d'Auribeau was a royalist and Île de France was known for republican sentiment. Add to this, his crew were in tatters and the prospect of another long sea voyage must have been unpalatable. After at first giving the order to sail to Île de France, d'Auribeau's quandary was solved in the nick of time. It was Comte de Trobriand, a naval officer on the expedition, bearing better news at last. The governing elite of Surabaya had contacted their superiors in Batavia, alarmed at the arrival of the French frigates at a time of war. Trobriand brought news of Batavia's ruling that the ships were to be received as normal. But the conditions stipulated by the Dutch became tighter with the passage of time: d'Auribeau's crew had to swear that they would not fight the Dutch and had to make themselves harmless by landing their armament. D'Auribeau also gathered all the crew's journals and papers.

Over the months of 1793–4 that the expedition waited in limbo in Surabaya, the new commander became more and more compliant to the Dutch. Perhaps it was his fear that if he returned to republican France he would be executed. His complicity was perceived as a sign of conservatism among some others of his crew who had more republican leanings, and this was especially the case among the large group of *savants*, or men of science, who were on the expedition, with the egalitarian aim of adding to human knowledge. While some of the crew of *L'Espérance* refused to give up their weapons, the pilot, from Brest, where republicanism flourished, threw his journal into the sea; others attempted to hide or make copies of their papers. This concern with keeping their papers arose partly from their interest in owning the discoveries which had been dutifully recorded in them. The Dutch were alarmed at the prospect of a ship-board revolution and took over the vessels. The expedition's termination came after an attempt was made by d'Auribeau to raise the royal flag.[2] It also came after the circulation of a rumour of secret orders from the National Assembly to some members of the crew.[3]

In December 1794, as the Frenchmen's debts had by this time mounted, *La Recherche* and *L'Espérance* were sold by auction in Batavia.[4] D'Auribeau himself died from dysentery before republican envoys from Île de France could take him captive as a traitor. In a token of the times to come, and where British explorations would overtake French missions in these seas, the papers of the d'Entrecasteaux/d'Auribeau expedition were seized in St Helena by the British. They were eventually kept in London under the protection of Élisabeth-Paul-Édouard de Rossel, who was the final commander of the expedition, after d'Auribeau's death. The British were particularly keen to detect any important material which they could use for their own imperial purposes.[5] Rossel was a royalist. He found London a good home in these tumultuous years until the Treaty of Amiens in 1802, after which he returned to France. Yet this was not the whole story. The republican Jacques-Julien Houtou de La Billardière, one of the surviving naturalists from the d'Entrecasteaux expedition, returned to Paris and ingeniously arranged with Joseph Banks, the British man of science, for the expedition's natural history cases to be transferred there.[6] The remains of the voyage were broken up in this way between the British and French, between royalist and republican commitments.

To track what happened to this voyage is to consider the impact of news from Europe on the other side of the planet; it is to turn the history of the age of revolutions inside out. This set of expeditions as a whole demonstrates how a new French nation and people were coming into being and what the values were for which they stood. Unlike the explorations of the land-hungry British, these Pacific voyages by the French were generally characterised by a lack of interest in territory; science took on a greater and greater significance, as each successive voyage had a larger number of individuals devoted to scientific discoveries. The philosophical residents of these ships increasingly conceived of themselves as citizens and contributors to humanity at large rather than as grandees out on a pleasure cruise of discovery. The transition from La Pérouse and d'Entrecasteaux to Baudin is itself revealing: for unlike the two aristocrats who went before him, Baudin was the first French captain without noble birth to sail through the Pacific.[7]

Beyond the decks of these ships, however, indigenous peoples were actively reworking their politics. In this era of unprecedented globalisation debates about authority and government had a parallel life in the Pacific. Indigenous elites, referred to as 'little Napoleons' by dismissive Europeans, used this moment to extend their domain of rule. They used alliances with Europeans as well as the material objects, weapons and ideas that came from their encounters with them.

So here's the argument to follow. Not only can the European age of revolutions be traced in these distant seas in the impact of the news from Europe, for instance at Surabaya, or even in the changing social composition and captaincy of crews. Once such a perspective is taken, it becomes possible to stand in the waves of the Pacific to see another more fundamental pattern of transformation in the waters of the South. Particularly striking is how these years saw the consolidation of Pacific monarchies.

Once Pacific royal lines were consolidated, as will be seen below, they could serve as the point of focus for colonial manoeuvring and diplomacy. Yet islanders could also use the notion of the monarch as a rallying symbol both for new politics and for resistance to invasion. Different conceptions of monarchy taken up by colonisers and indigenous peoples became a ground of controversy. The chapter ends with the controversial 1840 Treaty of Waitangi in Aotearoa/New Zealand and how Britain's maritime empire came into the Pacific and sought alliances with Māori *rangatira* (chiefs).[8] Alliances between colonists and indigenous elites set in place definitions of sovereignty which were colonial; these definitions encompassed land fit for 'improvement' and people in need of 'protection'. But Pacific islanders displayed their creativity in responding to intrusion of this kind.

FRENCH AND BRITISH VOYAGES
IN THE PACIFIC AGE OF REVOLUTIONS

To return to the d'Entrecasteaux expedition, it was an impatient national interest that prompted its failed attempt to search for La Pérouse. A petition drawn up early in 1791 from the Société d'Histoire Naturelle bemoaned how France had waited for two years for the return of its famous explorer:

> Perhaps he has run aground on some island in the South Seas from whence he holds out his arms toward his country, waiting in vain for his liberator . . . And the decent nation that expected to reap the benefits of his labors also owes him its concern and its assistance.[9]

La Pérouse hailed from a family of provincial nobles in Albi, far from the sea. He had seen action in the Seven Years War, against the British

off the American coast and in the Caribbean and also in India against
the Marathas. His instructions were driven by one of the recurrent themes
in Pacific exploration of the eighteenth century. This was the idea that
there were still large landmasses and strategic passages to be discovered
in the Pacific. British Captain James Cook, who died in 1769 in Hawai'i,
had done his best to put to rest the idea of a great undiscovered Southland.
Nevertheless, La Pérouse was still set the mammoth task of roaming the
Pacific in its widest extent, including the north as well as the south; Louis
XVI took a personal interest in the itinerary.[10] His agenda included the
search for a north-west passage across America, linking the Pacific Ocean
to the Atlantic. It included the survey of the coasts of Japan and Korea,
and the exploration of the relatively unknown western side of Australia
right up to Tasmania in case there lay there a continent rather than a
large island. Tahiti, which was idealised as a paradise among Europeans,
would have seemed a dominating landmark in La Pérouse's mind. He
was given detailed instructions to leave plants there which could be
propagated to add to the comforts of other voyagers who would pass
through this point of luxurious passage, known for its sexual liberty and
lavish hospitality.[11] These were tall orders in the programme of settling
European geographical knowledge of the Pacific. Before they could be
accomplished La Pérouse's expedition met with calamity.

La Pérouse's ships were as solid and heavy as those chosen by Cook;
and this was appropriate given that he was chosen to be France's response
to Cook. A French spy, taking the guise of a Spanish trader named Don
Inigo Alvarez, sought out information about Cook's expedition for La
Pérouse's mission. Alvarez found John Webber, Cook's artist, a particularly useful source of information. He sat for a portrait by Webber. The
expedition's connection to the politics of the time is also nicely illustrated
by one contemporary diarist who held that Napoleon Bonaparte expressed
an interest in joining the voyage, along with one of his compatriots at
the École Militaire.[12]

While the voyage was under way, the multiple eyes that watched it
clearly bore heavily on La Pérouse. He wrote home in 1787: 'The care we
have taken to preserve our crews' health has been so far crowned with
even more success than that enjoyed by that famous navigator [Cook]
. ... no one has died on board the *Boussole* and we do not have a single
man sick in either vessel.'[13] And commenting on his geographical exploits,
he wrote of 'a new strait leading out of the Sea of Tartary', of presenting
to geographers 'two islands as large as the British Isles' and of reaching

'in the same year' Mt St Elias after visiting Easter Island [Rapa Nui] and the Sandwich Islands [Hawai'i].[14] And on another occasion earlier in 1787: 'I am sure His Majesty will not fail to realise that his vessels will have been the first to undertake this navigation.'[15]

La Pérouse was anxious about whether his discoveries would be over-taken by the British successors of Cook, and wrote home of six vessels sent from India to the north-west coast of America. This was in keeping with the competitive spirit of this era, which related not only to politics but also to intellectual exploits. In commenting on this news, La Pérouse noted that British exploration showed 'evidence of the large means the English dispose of rather than of their judgement.'[16] Given the range of expectations heaped on it, the displeasure that arose when La Pérouse lost the whole of his crew – quite to the contrary of his boast about the lack of death to scurvy and other diseases – is indeed understandable. As the compiler of his journal, published from records sent home, wrote: 'our new Argonauts have all perished.'[17] And an English compiler who had sailed with Cook noted that La Pérouse had operated in a state of continual anxiety because of the enormity of the task combined with over-ambitious timetabling which created 'perpetual hurry'.[18]

D'Entrecasteaux, whose ships eventually ended up in Surabaya, came agonisingly close to success in his search for La Pérouse. Rumours had spread by this time that the navigator's end had come at British anti-republican hands.[19] La Pérouse himself had touched at Botany Bay, now in Sydney, just five days after the First Fleet had reached New South Wales in 1788 to found a convict colony there. There he had met the British captain John Hunter. Could contrasting modes of engaging with the Pacific world, tied to French philosophy and British colonisation, indicate antipathy to French voyagers on the part of the British and so explain the disappearance? From Botany Bay came La Pérouse's fateful last official letter, dated February 1788, promising to do 'exactly what my instructions require me to do . . . But in such a way as to enable me to go back north in good time to reach the Isle de France [Mauritius] in December.'[20]

A monument commemorating the place from where the last news of the navigator was received was later erected at Botany Bay. Fish and chip shops and couples having their wedding photographs taken at the weekend vied for attention with the monument when I saw it. La Pérouse had made a plan to end his voyage in Mauritius, his second home, where he had bought land, and from where his wife Éléonore Broudou originated. He had married her against his father's wishes.[21] The first news of La Pérouse reached d'Entrecasteaux in January 1792 while he was in Cape Town. In his journal he recorded a testimony received there via Mauritius of what had been seen by British captain John Hunter, in the Admiralty Islands, north of present-day New Guinea. Hunter later gave this account of his observations when at the Admiralty Islands:

> Five large canoes came off from the nearest island, in each of which were eleven men; six paddled, and five stood up in the center of the boat . . . they held up various articles, which they seemed desirous of exchanging; such as lines, shells, ornaments of different kinds, and bundles of darts or arrows . . . One of them made various motions for shaving, by holding up something in his hand, with which he frequently scraped his cheek and chin; this led me to conjecture, that some European ship had lately been amongst them, and I thought it not improbable, that it might have been Mons. de la Perouse, in his way to the northward of Botany Bay.[22]

D'Entrecasteaux believed that his compatriots in Mauritius, where he had served as governor general, had misunderstood or exaggerated the news. Surely Hunter would have persevered in a rescue if he sincerely believed that he had discovered shipwrecked Frenchmen or at least the signs of their influence? The 'sacred duties of mankind' would have overruled other considerations of weather or even national difference.[23] Regardless of his doubts, d'Entrecasteaux made up his mind; he would sail to the Admiralty Islands. When he finally got there, in July 1792, he decided that the reports of La Pérouse were uncorroborated. The islanders, he wrote, wore ornaments of white shells and dark red belts, and these could have been mistaken for sword-belts. He also noted that the colour of their skin was distinctly similar to the colour of the uniform of the French navy.[24] An engraving drawn up by the voyage's artist, Piron, shows an Admiralty islander, devoid of any context, except for a shell on his penis, a woven belt above his waist as well as on his arm, and woven wrist ornaments.[25] La Billardière, the naturalist, wrote that the most 'inflated part' of the shell was opened in order to lodge the penis, and that wearing the shell gave rise to 'very conspicuous tumour' of a white colour.[26] [Fig. 2.1].

In the forty years of uncertainty that followed the disappearance, the fate of La Pérouse led to much speculation across Europe, inspiring plays,

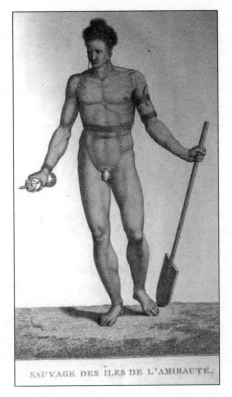

SAUVAGE DES ÎLES DE L'AMIRAUTÉ.

Fig. 2.1 'Sauvages des îles de l'Amirauté', Jacques-Louis Copia after Piron,
reproduced in La Billardière's *Atlas*, 1800

pantomimes and books, some with far-fetched romantic plot-lines.[27] The
solution eventually came from Peter Dillon and through his meeting
with Joe, the *lascar* in 1826. In a book published to cement his fame as
the problem solver and to add to his pocket, Dillon provided this account
of an interview with islanders on Vanikoro in late 1827:

Q. 'How were the ships lost?' – A. 'The island is surrounded by reefs at
a distance off shore. They got on the rocks at night, and one ship
grounded at Wannow, and immediately went to the bottom.'

Q. 'Were none of the people from the ship saved?' – A. 'Those that
escaped from the wreck were landed at Wannow, where they were killed
by the natives. Several also were devoured by the sharks, while swimming
from the ship.'

Q. 'How many people were killed at Wannow?' – A. 'Two at Wannow, two at Amma and two more near to Paiow. These were all the white men who were killed.'

Q. 'If there were only six white men killed on shore, how, or from whence, came the sixty sculls [sic.] that were in the spirit house at Wannow, as described by Ta Fow, the hump-backed Tucopian, and others?' – A. 'These were the heads of people killed by the sharks.'
. . .
Q. 'How was the ship lost near Paiow?' – A. 'She got on the reef at night, and afterwards drifted over it into a good place. She did not immediately break, for the people had time to remove things from her, with which they built a two-masted ship.'
. . .
Q. 'Had these people no friends among the natives.' – A. 'No. They were ship spirits; their noses were two hands long before their faces. Their chief used always to be looking at the sun and stars, and beckoning to them. There was one of them who stood as a watch at their fence, with a bar of iron in his hand, which he used to turn round his head. This man stood only upon one leg.'[28]

So what is the headline? La Pérouse's ships had come to their end in the midst of a hurricane. Though some of the crew remained, most of them sailed away in a small vessel they built never to be seen again. Evidently, before they left, their astronomical interests and their manners had bewildered the inhabitants of Vanikoro.

If the tragic ends of the expeditions of La Pérouse and d'Entrecasteaux are in keeping with the age of revolutions, the third French expedition, commanded by Nicolas Baudin and commissioned by Napoleon in 1800 at a different political moment, was relatively more successful. Baudin had sailed widely across the Indian and Pacific Oceans as a merchant captain. He focussed on precision rather than breadth and was instructed to concentrate on Australia. The need now was for voyages 'restricted to specific pre-determined, points, directed to the least-known coast-lines'.[29] However there were still squabbles on board which were typical of the broader character of this period. The commoner Baudin was seen as a social inferior by some of the scientists, and his first lieutenant even challenged him to a duel.[30] Social and ideological differences merged with scientific disputes: 'sketchers' and 'anatomists' on board, two classes of researchers, argued over the ownership of a dead porpoise; there was a similar fight about who got the right to dissect the first shark.[31]

Freycinet, who sailed with Baudin, published the first complete map of Australia in 1811. The credit for putting Australia in its place on a map belongs, however, to a Briton, Matthew Flinders. After securing British passports for the Baudin mission, the leading British man of science of this period, Joseph Banks, had the idea of a competing British mission. He arranged for Flinders to be sent off to chart south west Australia in a race with Baudin. Despite their common scientific interests, and the fact that Flinders had advised Baudin to stop in Port Jackson (the ria of what is now Sydney) when in need of refreshment, the impact of the revolutionary era dictated the outcomes for these two.

Before Baudin died from tuberculosis in Mauritius in September 1803, he wrote to the French Minister of Marine: 'I have enough strength left at the moment to assure you that the intentions of the Government have been fulfilled and that this voyage will be honourable to the French.'[32] Flinders pulled into Mauritius in December 1803, just after the death of Baudin, in urgent need of supplies and took confidence from his French passport, which asked all French agents to give him protection as the commander of a purely scientific expedition. Yet Governor Decaen, who reined in Mauritius' republicanism, took him captive for six and a half years, until the eve of the taking of Mauritius by the British in 1810. Flinders' books and papers were initially impounded and Flinders was accused of being an imposter. The navigator wrote that his daily routine consisted of learning Latin, writing up his ship's log, music and billiards; he was later transferred to a more relaxed residence on a plantation, where he worked at translations between English and French.[33] The British got wind of his captivity, via American traders who enjoyed a healthy commerce with Île de France in this period. Such traders allowed Flinders to keep up a regular correspondence home, while also sending scientific materials through them to London, including to Banks.[34] Flinders' health deteriorated while in captivity and though he returned to Britain, he did not live to see the publication of the account of his voyage.[35]

The French Revolution and its aftermath did not simply disrupt the passage of French and British voyages of exploration in the Pacific. The politics of the era certainly changed the nature and goals of voyaging. Gentlemanly culture still dominated British voyaging, but changing social orders were evident in the commoner Baudin's leadership of a French voyage, though aristocratic commanders did follow him. While scientific cords bound the missions of the French and the British together, the tensions of these years dictated that friendly assistance was no longer guaranteed, as is evident in the fate of the d'Entrecasteaux/d'Auribeau expedition. Even navigators – like Flinders – could become captives. As the British started to annex territory and build bases in the Pacific they used the tumult of the age to their benefit. The French had to find their own way to create an imperial presence, while coming to terms with their distinctive commitments to revolution and nation-building.[36]

Despite differences, these two national modes of engaging with the Pacific were interlinked too: not all Frenchmen were republicans after all, and neither were all Britons anti-French. Even Flinders wrote to his wife Ann: 'I am not without friends even amongst French men. On the contrary, I have several, and but one enemy [Governor Decaen].'[37] It was a story of a dance of European cousins. The French and British were trying to tame the Pacific, mindful of their related but different goals.

THE MAKING OF PACIFIC MONARCHS

The age of revolutions is evident not simply on the decks of vessels traversing these vast swathes of water, coming to terms with the news from Europe and working out the local outcomes of that news. To keep the story to that would still be to make the Pacific a distant planet orbiting Europe. In the exchanges between voyagers and islanders in the age of revolutions is a surge of indigenous politics and the rise of a counter-revolutionary British empire. At the heart of such exchanges was an eclectic range of ideas, techniques and materials and all of this made it possible for old systems of rule by chiefs to evolve into more centralised systems of monarchy right across the Pacific. Tonga is a good place to track this. It was here while in search of La Pérouse that d'Entrecasteaux had some of his most charged ethnographic encounters.

James Cook left a long shadow over those voyagers who followed in his wake in the two decades after his dramatic death at the hands of alleged cannibals in Hawai'i in 1779. D'Entrecasteaux referred to Cook's observations throughout the course of his journal, and sought to fill any gaps left by a man immortalised for his mapping of the

Pacific. Remarkably, European voyagers through the Pacific were already starting to leave their debris strewn across the islands as a mark of their passage through them. For the likes of d'Entrecasteaux, items of European trade, European clothing or even the remains of wrecked ships became symbols of those who had passed before: points of comfort as well as melancholic tokens of disaster. In Adventure Bay in Tasmania, d'Entrecasteaux saw signs of what he took to be 'temporary British establishments'; and suspected that there were remains of 'several wooden stands destined to hold instruments in place for astronomical or trigonometrical observations'. By deciphering inscriptions found on trees, he worked out that William Bligh, who had served with Cook and who would later govern New South Wales, and who is now remembered for the mutiny that overtook his own expedition on the *Bounty* in 1789, had left some plants in Adventure Bay. D'Entrecasteaux made a point of determining whether these trees had prospered, sending his gardener, who later turned into a rebel outside Surabaya, to inspect them. While some pomegranate trees, a quince tree and fig trees were found, they were not doing well: 'A five-and-a-half foot apple tree was found on the east coast of Adventure Bay which must have been planted several years before Captain Bligh's visit; it was struggling, and its chances were not very promising.'[38] Despite the tense intellectual competition between the French and British voyagers, the responses to the litter left by rivals across the landscape of the Pacific point to how these European cousins felt that they were following related paths across the sea.

In Tongatapu, the main island of what is now Tonga, there was the same French interest in whether British attempts at improvement had succeeded. While in Tongatapu from March to April 1793, d'Entrecasteaux reported that Cook's and Bligh's voyages were 'perfectly recollected' by Tongans, but that no account of La Pérouse was forthcoming even from 'the most intelligent' of them. [39] This was despite the fact that La Pérouse had made a brief stop in Tonga. Later investigators such as Peter Dillon and a French expedition under Dumont d'Urville were able to gather recollections in Tonga of the La Pérouse mission.[40] D'Entrecasteaux detected a large number of items of British manufacture but none of French manufacture. He quickly arranged for French medals to be given out, as if to rectify the imbalance and to test whether they brought La Pérouse to mind. When a feast was held in d'Entrecasteaux's honour by a chief called Tupou, the navigator took a billy goat and a pregnant nanny goat along as a gift, as well as a pair of male and female rabbits. But d'Entrecasteaux regretted Tupou's indifference in receiving them and turned the conversation to the cattle that Cook had left in Tonga. The sheepishness of the Tongans' response indicated that something was amiss.[41] Was it that they worried that he would ask for the cattle as gifts? This was a minor particular for d'Entrecasteaux to devote such energy to while exploring the other side of the world. But towards the end of the mission's time in Tonga, the royalist d'Auribeau (who later took over from d'Entrecasteaux) wished to solve the puzzle. He visited a chief, Fuanunuiava, whose father had received the cattle from Cook, only to discover 'a kind of mausoleum, which [Fuanunuiava] offered to dig open, so that the bones of these animals could be recognized'.[42]

This nicely illustrates the keen competition between French and British voyagers over natural husbandry. Such competition was tied to a shared commitment between these rival explorers to the idea that agricultural improvement was central to the making of settled and progressive societies in the Pacific. As empire moved from sea to land, maritime missions like this set the terms for commercial exchange of crops and plants and also for further schemes of land-based control. It was not coincidental that European voyagers themselves required replenishment when they called at islands.

D'Entrecasteaux was troubled by the nature of authority on the island of Tongatapu. He wrote: 'I believe, like Cook, that this government has a lot in common with the old feudal regime, where the inconveniences increase in proportion to the weaknesses of the principal chief.'[43] Tonga was seen to be in anarchy; what was needed was proper governance tied to the agricultural uplift of the land. For d'Entrecasteaux anarchy was evident in the prevalence of theft, which arose from the insecurity of property. The chiefs owned all the property and could demand from their inferiors anything that they wished. The chiefs' privilege lay also in how they had the right to multiple wives. D'Entrecasteaux noted the appearance of these women in heavily patronising terms:

Most of the women of the class in which the chiefs belong have very good looks: their aspect is interesting; they are expressive, without being flirtatious. They usually have beautiful hands, and their fingers could easily be used as models.[44]

Yet d'Entrecasteaux was plagued by the riddle of identifying the monarch of Tongatapu. Between Cook's visit and his own, he would have expected that the throne would have passed to Fuanunuiava, the son of the man denoted as sovereign by Cook.[45] Perhaps it was because of Fuanunuiava's youth, he pondered, that this had not occurred. D'Entrecasteaux also puzzled over the fact that Queen Tiné, whom he now took to be the head of state, could not confer the throne on her death to her immediate relations. For d'Entrecasteaux the complicated rules of succession were part of the problem. There was too much confusion in 'distinguishing men who exercise power and to whom respect is given'.[46] D'Entrecasteaux was a man who wished for authority, but for the kind of authority held up by rules and constitutions and hemmed in by a market in trade and land and also by familiar gender norms. D'Entrecasteaux's naturalist de La Billardière, later one of the leaders of the republican faction, wrote meanwhile of 'King Tuoobou' or Tupou of Tonga.[47] Tupou was in fact the Tu'i Kanokupolu, one of three paramount titles in Tonga; the highest ranking however held another title, Tu'i Tonga. Fuanunuiava was named as Tu'i Tonga in 1795. La Billardière also observed how Queen Tiné was conscious of her privileges as the paramount authority on Tonga. Lower ranking chiefs including Tupou were obliged to pay their respects by taking her right foot to their heads.[48]

D'Entrecasteaux's portrait of Tonga reveals more of himself than the Tonga of this period. Despite how the terms of King and Queen pepper so many European reports of the Pacific, in this era, until the arrival of Europeans, there were no European-style kings and queens. In Tongatapu, the status of chiefs was determined on the basis of descent from a chosen ancestor, where age and gender were important as in Europe; but in Tonga sisterhood was ranked as a higher privilege than brotherhood in determining succession.[49] The differences between chiefs and others did not lie in the labour they undertook, if any, and so the language of class that d'Entrecasteaux used to observe Tonga was misplaced. Objects were not sold and did not retain a value on the basis of the work that had been put into making them. Rather value was determined primarily by the rank and status of the creator of the object: it was no wonder that Tongans wished to possess European objects. Yet those whom the Tongans called *papalangi*, or men from the sky, introduced into these islands a new language of politics, class and organisation. It was through a European insistence on the value of labour, the market and industry, together with a supplanted language of kingship, that political change was ushered in. Such change was consistent with the broader political transformations across the world in this age. In this region, these changes counted as a firming up of monarchy whereas elsewhere it could see monarchies torn down. Items like d'Entrecasteaux's medals – and European weapons in particular – fed into the intense wars and political instability in early-nineteenth-century Tonga. Chiefs quarrelled over the arrival of European ships, trying to attract them to their harbours. [Fig. 2.2] And those who resided at ports inevitably did better than those based elsewhere. As

Fig. 2.2 'European ships as depicted on a Tongan clapping stick'

Europeans sought for kings and queens, islanders reinvented their politics.

Sexual favours also became part of this market and a means of establishing strategic friendship with Europeans. La Billardière's account of the d'Entrecasteaux expedition includes an image titled 'Dance of the Friendly Islands in the Presence of the Queen Tiné', showing bare-breasted women draped from their waists down in what is probably bark cloth. D'Entrecasteaux entertained Tiné with the music of a violin and cittern and she returned the favour, instructing Tongan women to sing of the great deeds of warriors. Some of the younger women wear girdles around their waists, probably *sisi fale*, worn by high-born women in dances in honour of the Tu'i Tonga.[50] [Fig. 2.3] Yet Tiné desired to firm up her relationship with the commander. She invited him to reside in her house: 'the Admiral had no opportunity of appreciating justly the motive for these obliging offers, for he did not accept her invitation.'[51] This report of Tiné's invitation to d'Entrecasteaux was in keeping with how 'Queen Oberea' was alleged to have greeted Cook's voyage and had sex with Joseph Banks, the gentlemanly naturalist, who later went on to

Fig. 2.3 A fragment of *sisi fale*, 'Coconut fibre waist garment, in all likelihood collected during the voyage of d'Entrecasteaux'

organise papers for Baudin.[52] When the reports of Cook's journey went
to press, this supposed queen of Tahiti became an emblem of the exotic
in Europe. As she slept with Banks, she was seen to have given her
kingdom to her lover. Despite the differences between Europe and
Polynesia, between monarchic and chiefly systems of rule, sex crystallised
powerful unions.

In an age of revolutions that saw active debate about the nature of
politics and about monarchies and republics, it is striking to see how
indigenous peoples created centralised Pacific kingdoms. Pacific islanders
participated in and crafted the age of revolutions too, a point which
historians have struggled to see. These new monarchies made identifiable
representatives of island societies, who could serve as the point of focus
for collaboration with British and other foreign agents as well as resistance against invading imperialists. In Tonga, at the same time as the
arrival of a range of European settlers in the 1790s, including traders,
evangelical missionaries as well as those who had escaped from the
convict settlement in Australia, there came a long civil war between rival
chiefs. The investiture of the paramount chief, Tu'i Tonga, was laid aside
and there was a conflict between the lineages of the Tu'i Tonga and Tu'i
Kanokupolu.[53] Chiefs fought over tribute and connections to missionaries
and other Europeans. The wars between chiefs were attended by the
spread of European diseases and weapons, and the fleeing of many chiefs
to neighbouring Fiji or Samoa. One chief fled with his wife to British
Sydney.[54] In the midst of these radical changes, there was a loss of
cohesion and the chiefly system of rule was in crisis.

If Pacific notions of monarchy drew from contact with Europeans in
political and material terms, religion also played a vital role in the new
order of politics that then arose in a place like Tonga. The work of
Protestant missionaries is notable here. A new age dawned in Tonga with
the conversion of the uninstalled paramount chief Taufa'ahau to
Protestantism through the work of Wesleyan missionaries who arrived
in 1822. This man changed the political make-up of Tonga and transformed it from a competitive set of chiefdoms to a united monarchic
polity. Taufa'ahau took the name George I at his baptism in 1831 and
used the support of British missionaries to unify Tonga. The change in
religion signified a drastic change in political organisation: for where
chiefs had received their sanction from lineages tied to gods, the spread
of Christianity now brought a different relationship between political
and sacred authority. Now the missionaries were the purveyors of the

Fig. 2.4 George I of Tonga (1880s) in his eighties

Word, and George I was the keeper of the law. Taufa'ahau's opponents feared that soon the missionaries themselves would become chiefs. Many of George I's followers adopted Christianity, though there continued to be a great deal of wavering and movement in and out of Christian faith and church attendance. George I boasted: 'I am the only Chief on the Island . . . When I turn they will all turn.'[55] He was right: George I's monarchic line has survived till today, priding itself on never being formally colonised. [Fig. 2.4]. Tonga is a microcosm of changes which were afoot across the wide expanse of the Pacific.

In Tahiti, where Banks had apparently slept with his lover, the queen, Cook used the vocabulary of royalty in ordering his observations. In contrast with d'Entrecasteaux's comments on Tonga, Cook noted that Tahiti's was a benevolent monarchy. All had free access to King Tu in Tahiti: 'I have observed that the chiefs of these islands are more beloved by the bulk of the people, than feared. May we not conclude from hence that the government is mild and equitable?'[56] By the time that Bligh arrived the Tahitians knew the line themselves: the Pomare family had established a kingly lineage. Pomare II invited Bligh to a ceremony allegedly involving human sacrifice, where the victims were the violators of some *tabu* (taboo). The ceremony ended with a prayer for the British monarch. When Bligh celebrated the birthday of the British monarch, George III, with fireworks, free alcohol and a twenty-one-gun salute, the alliance of monarchs was complete. European weapons were central to the consolidation of this monarchic line.[57] Further to the east in Hawai'i, a dynasty was founded by Kamehameha, who was also visited by Cook and other European navigators. By the 1820s, the monarchy of Hawai'i could be idealised as perfect for a post-revolutionary world. As the Russian commander Otto von Kotzebue explained in arriving in Hawai'i, Kamehameha had got the right balance between tradition and change. He was already preparing for succession.

The intertwined changes in politics between Europe and the Pacific in the age of revolutions run across commitments to monarchy, agriculture, land, gender and sex. These changes seem unexpected because the Pacific is so far away from Europe. How did they become possible in practical terms? The entanglement of Europe and the Pacific might be described through the image of raiding. Islanders raided Europe for everything that came on their ships, from political ideas to animals and plants, and used them for their own purposes in the light of the old.

RAIDING EUROPE

In 1806, more than a decade after d'Entrecasteaux's time in Tonga, an Englishman called William Mariner was taken captive in the Tongan islands, at the age of fifteen, to the north of where d'Entrecasteaux made his observations. Mariner arrived on the *Port au Prince*, a private English ship, which was formerly French, and which was now deployed to raid French or Spanish vessels. The sailors on board were allowed to keep the booty. The ship was 'nearly 500 tons, 96 men, and mounting 24 long nine and twelve pounders, besides 8 twelve-pound carronades on the quarter-deck'.[58] It was because of vessels like this that the French feared that

La Pérouse had met a death at the hands of English anti-republicans. Spanish bases in the Americas were particular targets of the *Port au Prince* but so were the whales that roamed the Pacific and which were valued for their oil.

In Tonga, the *Port au Prince* was taken over by about 300 islanders who went aboard the ship and attacked the surprised crew. This was in spite of the warnings that there was a conspiracy to take over the vessel; these warnings were issued by some Hawai'ians (who understood Tongan) and who were part of the *Port au Prince*'s crew. The Tongans eventually grounded the ship. Gunpowder, carronades, guns and stripped iron were taken ashore, and after the ship had been summarily looted for everything that was deemed valuable it was burnt. About half of the crew were massacred by the Tongans in what followed. According to Mariner, the attack was led by a Hawai'ian, who probably arrived in Tonga on an American ship.[59] Mariner wrote evocatively of the noises that were let off by the guns on board:

> In the evening they set fire to her, in order to get more easily afterwards at the iron work. All the great guns were loaded, and as they began to be heated by the general conflagration they went off, one after another, producing a terrible panic among all the natives.[60]

The survivors, their skills and their possessions were recycled in the wars that gripped Tonga around the decline of chiefly lines and before the consolidation of George I's monarchic state. The story goes that the future George I was himself involved in the raid of the *Port au Prince*, when he was about nine, and that he nearly drowned in the whale oil in the hold of the vessel.[61] Mariner was a key asset. He was so liked by the chief Finau 'Ulukalala II – who raided the ship – that he was adopted by one of his wives. Another of the survivors of the *Port au Prince* was serving as 'prime minister' to a chief on Vava'u as late as 1830.[62]

From his base in the Ha'apai islands 'Ulukalala wished to attack the political centre of these islands in Tongatapu from where he had been driven away. In seizing the *Port au Prince* he was arming himself for his wars with the powers that be in Tongatapu. Mariner and fifteen other Britons participated in the raid that followed on Tongatapu, undertaken with the use of a fleet of canoes and the carronades looted from the *Port au Prince*.[63]

In the end one of the most important forts at Nuku'alofa, now the capital of Tonga, fell into the hands of 'Ulukalala's forces. Mariner described the fort as made of walls of wicker-work supported by posts, making nine-foot high fences; it had stood for eleven years but was now ravaged. It was a truly awful rout: 'The conquerors, club in hand, entered the place in several quarters and slew all they met, men, women and children.'[64] These inhabitants were awe-struck by the new weapons used by their assailants. They described balls as if they were alive, entering houses, going around their dwellings looking for someone to kill, rather than exploding straight away. While the battle was in progress, 'Ulukalala sat himself in an English chair taken off the *Port au Prince* and surveyed the scene from the reef.[65] After this attack, his further attempt to take the fort in Vava'u harbour was not as successful.

Despite using European articles of war, 'Ulukalala preferred Tongan military customs and did not take the advice that Mariner gave him on how to consolidate his power. When at peace, he took up the opportunity for conversation with Mariner to learn about the outside world, and one topic that was particularly interesting was that of politics. He wished to be the king of England. This again highlights how islanders were taking up new notions of monarchy:

> Oh, that the gods would make me king of England! There is not an island in the whole world, however small, but that I would then subject to my power: the King of England does not deserve the dominion he enjoys; possessed of so many great ships, why does he suffer such petty islands as those of Tonga continually to insult his people with acts of treachery? Where [sic.] I he, would I send tamely to *ask* for yams and pigs? No, I would come with the *front of battle*; and with *the thunder of Bolotane* [the noise of the guns of Britain].[66]

A central component in the spread of the global market into Tonga was also tied up with these conversations. For Mariner explained the role of money to his patron. He explained that the silver discs that had been taken off the *Port au Prince* by the Tongans and which had been thrown and bounced across the surface of the sea, and called flat stones or *pa'anga*, were in fact money. *Pa'anga* is now the currency of Tonga; it was introduced as such in 1967.[67]

When 'Ulukalala died, Mariner was also highly favoured by 'Ulukalala's son, Moengangongo.[68] Mariner finally escaped in 1810. Though wishing to escape before this point, he had not been at the right place at the right time to intercept a vessel. When he left, it was a painful parting because he had integrated himself into Tongan ways.

In 1832, Mafihape, Mariner's adoptive mother in Tonga, sent him an intriguing letter.[69] In her letter, written or probably transcribed for her by someone very familiar with Tonga, she notes that 'everyone has become a Christian'. She asks Mariner to send a ship:

> If you have genuine affection [for me] it would be wonderful if you could send your younger brother, if you have one – or your son, if you have one, so I can see him, and also so that you be shown, in the Lord, to be manly – if you are so determined not to come yourself and see me. He can come and live here instead.[70]

Mafihape herself had by this time converted to Christianity but wanted Mariner to know that she was 'very poorly off'. Despite the spread of a new religion, and its associated trappings of paper and writing, as also new conceptions of behaviour, Mafihape still hoped to utilise the customs of chieftaincy, where chiefs adopted powerful sons, to circumvent her allegedly lowly situation. Her plan was to arrange for a rerun of William Mariner's time in Tonga, by asking for the arrival in Tonga of Mariner's younger brother or son, and perhaps even hinting that Mariner himself should return. Her letter points back to patterns of chiefly rule, which pre-dated contact, while also bearing the markers, in the use of 'in the Lord' in the extract, of newly Christianised Tonga.

In the course of investigating the disappearance of La Pérouse in the mid 1820s, Peter Dillon records meeting this woman and showing her the portrait of Mariner. Dillon writes that she exclaimed 'it is Tokey', the name that 'Ulukalala gave to Mariner, in remembrance of a favourite child of his who had died. She 'wept bitterly' at the sight of the image. In Tonga today the story is told that she may have been Mariner's concubine rather than his adoptive mother.[71]

Sadly, Mariner could not read Mafihape's letter having forgotten most of his Tongan. He complained that the 'orthography' of his mother's letter was in too unfamiliar a form, indicating the impact of the English missionaries, perhaps.[72] After returning to England, he gave up his life of adventure and became a stockbroker in London, married and fathered eleven children and, rather unfittingly, drowned in Surrey Canal at the age of fifty-three.[73] In the Pacific meanwhile there is a line which carries the name Mariner, from Mariner's son George, who settled in Samoa

Fig. 2.5 'Mr. Mariner in the Costume of the
Tonga Islands' (1816)

with a Tongan wife. As for Mariner's own end in the canal, a speculative
Tongan theory is that he committed suicide, being unable in the end to
come to terms with his life in England.[74]

William Mariner's account of travels was written up for him by a
doctor, John Martin, citing the excuse that Mariner had become so
accustomed to Tongan ways that he had been out of the habit of writing
and reading in English. The image facing the title page is a full-length
view of Mariner, which was shown by Dillon to his Tongan mother,
dressed in Tongan clothes and bare-bodied above the waist like the
women who danced for d'Entrecasteaux. [Fig. 2.5.] Mariner had straddled worlds. A product of the European age of revolutions, and its
commitment to global war at any price, he had been taken captive to
fight in a series of other wars, which were Tongan tussles in aid of
monarchy. These wars too, arose within the changing political currents

Fig. 2.6 The beach where the ship is said to have been raided (above) and the
Port au Prince Memorial (below), Tonga

of this period. The age of revolution had bred a surge of indigenous monarchism in the Pacific.

The dispersal of European weapons was critical to the story around the *Port au Prince*; so it is appropriate that three of the cannon from the *Port au Prince* are today placed in front of the former site of the British High Commission in Tonga. Other cannon are dispersed elsewhere including on Ha'ano where, according to one story told by the inhabitants of this island in the Ha'apai group, the ship was finally taken.[75] In 2012, the discovery of a sunken ship thought to be the *Port au Prince* gave rise to a treasure hunt in the waters off Tonga.[76] Today, in Ha'apai, which I visited in 2017, stories still circulate about the site of the *Port au Prince* wreck, together with accounts of how the Japanese mafia as well as New Zealand criminals had found gold from the wreck and taken it out without the knowledge of the Tongan government. A monument has been erected close to the beach where the *Port au Prince* was raided. It is overtaken by the lush vegetation of Ha'apai. [Fig. 2.6]

The beach itself is simply a thin strip of sand, bearing no evidence of its history. However, perhaps fittingly, given the history of exchanges on Tonga, including of animals brought by voyagers, there was a dead pig floating in the water when I walked its sands. The carcass was accompanied by plastic bottles, broken coral and fallen coconut trunks rotting in the water. The signs of modern consumption – part of the history that followed the whale oil on the *Port au Prince* – were evident on the beach.

When published, Mariner's account was one source of inspiration for the poet Byron's idyllic description of South Pacific island culture. 'The Island' was written in 1823. In Byron's telling of the politics of Tonga, republicanism is rife on the island of Toobonai, the fictional island where the poem is set. It is the 'equal land without a lord'.[77] Here nature is bountiful and the islanders are relatively uncorrupted by sin. Labour is unnecessary because of what nature provides:

> Where all partake the earth without dispute,
> And bread itself is gather'd as a fruit;
> Where none contest the fields, the woods, the streams: –
> The goldless age, where gold disturbs no dreams,
> Inhabits or inhabited the shore,
> Till Europe taught them better than before:
> Bestow'd her customs, and amended theirs,
> But left her vices also to their heirs.[78]

This is a telling fact of the contradictory effects of the age of revolution on either side of the world: European literary representations, full of romanticism, could be utterly disconnected from the reality of the Pacific. If Tongans raided Europe to remake their politics, Europeans in turn often missed the import of what was happening in the Pacific in the age of revolutions.

The need to challenge European depictions of this sequence of events is clear in the writings of recent Tongan historians. They react against a view of the burning of the *Port au Prince* as indicative of the 'treachery' of Tongans: instead they hold that the crew of this vessel behaved 'like pirates and robbers' in the first place.[79] In other words, these were two systems of raiding, European and Tongan, which faced each other around the *Port au Prince*. The two-way exchange included materials, ideas and culture, too.

AOTEAROA AND THE IMPERIAL MONARCHS

This indigenous language of political consolidation and monarchy usefully fed into the advance of the British empire. In looking further south, to Aotearoa/New Zealand, the forward march of the British is in full show. The story from New Zealand that follows corresponds with some of the features of the transformation in Tonga with the consolidation of monarchy.

First, customary forms of warfare, chieftaincy and decision-making evolved in contact with British traders and missionaries. Second, warfare spread in range and intensity as exchanges with Europeans deepened and as weapons and affiliations proved politically useful as signs of *mana* (status) to Māori *rangatira* (chiefs). Third, and in contrast with Tonga, the British state came in claiming to protect Māori through the introduction of law and bureaucracy. There were plans for flags and discussions of constitutional arrangements, set piece indicators of the age of revolutions and the dawn of our times. Fourth, Māori asserted their standing as political agents able to resist the British, sometimes picking up on the tactics of the revolutionary era, for instance through the identification of a Māori monarch. If the articulation of monarchy occurred across the Pacific, this in turn allowed bigger monarchs or the British empire to rise up as a counter-revolutionary force. The 1840

Treaty of Waitangi saw the status of the political elites of New Zealand tied up with that of the British monarch.

In general terms across the Pacific, the number of settled Europeans was dramatically increasing as the nineteenth century began. In Hawai'i, while there had been ten European residents in 1790, there were nearly a hundred by 1806.[80] In Tonga a visiting captain wrote in 1830 that there were many Englishmen in the islands, who had been treated with great kindness, and who had married, settled and accommodated themselves to Tongan manners and customs.[81] By the late 1830s there were as many as two thousand Europeans settled in New Zealand, including missionaries, and 'beachrangers', meaning people who were cast out of sealing and whaling missions for various crimes, and escaped convicts. The greatest concentration of these settlers resided in the Bay of Islands district in the North Island.[82] Occasional and exoticised encounters gave way to more sustained contact, and formal imperial takeover was just around the corner.

After the British established a base for themselves in Australia in 1788 and in Tasmania by 1803 the game of imperial takeover had begun. This game saw New Zealand following a different course to Tonga. One vital difference between the two was the closeness between Australia and New Zealand, which made New Zealand a resource frontier for Australia. The significant turning point for imperial advance was the British signing of the Treaty of Waitangi with Māori chiefs in 1840, which the colonists interpreted as a deed of cessation. The French responded by annexing the Marquesas in 1842 and Tahiti in 1843. Though a tit-for-tat battle for islands marked Anglo-French relations in the Pacific through the course of the mid to late nineteenth century, the convict colony that the British had established in Australia in the eighteenth century meant that the Pacific came increasingly under the purview of the British.

One source for the early history of New Zealand is the travelling writer and painter Augustus Earle, who visited in 1827–8. Despite the increasing presence of Europeans, Earle's watercolours of the Bay of Islands show romanticised scenes of nature and Māori going about their business while paying no attention to arriving European ships. These visual illustrations do not exaggerate the impact of styles of European settlement on Māori habitation and deserve scrutiny for revealing indigenous social and political features which sometimes go missing in the textual sources kept by Europeans.[83] One large watercolour shows Te Puna in the Bay of Islands. Māori canoes and a large tree in the foreground play a bigger

Fig. 2.7 'Tepoanah Bay of Islands New Zealand a Church Missionary
Establishment' (watercolour, Augustus Earle, 1827)

Fig. 2.8 'War speech' by Augustus Earle (published 1838)

role than the missionary settlement behind the beach: no Europeans are
in sight. [Fig. 2.7][84] A *pa* or Māori defence fortification appears at a
height on the hill above the bay. In keeping with such a reading of this
image, it is important to insist that prior forms of organisation, navigation and politics in New Zealand set the terms for early encounters with
Europeans. For instance, existent systems of patronage allowed missionary
work to proceed under the powerful auspices of Māori chiefs.[85]

In one offensive myth, these islands are a nation founded by Captain
Cook. It is true that the *Endeavour* voyage gave rise to remarkably
accurate charts of the coast of New Zealand in 1769–70.[86] Yet this is an
offensive narrative because ideas of people were long extant in Aotearoa/
New Zealand. *Iwi* denoted people of common descent, a fundamental
identity, tied up with the arrival of Māori from a place denoted as
Hawaiki. In political terms Māori also organised for warfare in *hapu*,
groups subordinate to chiefs, fighting as units.[87] Plans for war were
made and discussed in various kinds of ceremonial meetings, which
early missionaries called 'councils of war' and which Earle called 'a
rude parliament'.[88] [Fig. 2.8][89] *Whakapapa* are Māori genealogies.
Teachers and experts in Māori genealogy possessed genealogical staffs
that were notched with references to their ancestors, providing a means
for keeping up a sense of their past.

European observers were quick to interpret and exaggerate traditional
styles of Māori war – caused by the resolution of wrongs that resulted
from the killing of high-ranked individuals, or from offence to the sacred
or untouchable status of elites. Europeans saw these conflicts as signs of
the 'savagery' of Māori. The resulting view of the 'heathen' Māori was
central to the early colonisation of New Zealand. As time passed there
was also the trope of the enfeebled Māori, which justified liberal protec-
tionist empire.[90] Religious encounter and rapacious trade oiled these
tropes.

The taking of the Gospel to New Zealand was pushed through by Rev.
Samuel Marsden, an Anglican cleric and a Yorkeshireman who engaged
in extensive agricultural pursuits in Paramatta, now a suburb of Sydney.
Under Marsden's auspices, the first evangelical contact with New Zealand
was made in 1814, in a vessel captained by Peter Dillon who appears
again in our story.[91] Marsden was troubled by the brutality of European–
Māori interaction and stated his agenda as a making of peace.[92] He took
a liking to Māori who came to Sydney and saw their land as a 'great
emporium of the South Seas'.[93]

In 1809 the *Boyd*, a vessel on its way to London with sixty Europeans, was returning a Māori chief Te Aara to New Zealand when it was raided at Whangaroa in the Bay of Islands district. Its passengers were killed by Māori, including women and children. Another vessel under the command of the Sydney trader Alexander Berry, who was procuring spars for the Cape Colony, was only able to rescue a woman, two children and a boy from among the *Boyd*'s passengers.[94] Marsden presented his own view of the violent episode around the *Boyd* in the *Sydney Gazette*, using the account of a Tahitian called 'Jem' who deserted a European ship.[95] Berry's and Marsden's views of the civilisational capacity of the Māori differed; authoritarian settler politics were aligned against reformist Christianity in these two alternative renditions.[96]

One contemporary explanation of the cause of the attack is that the master of the *Boyd* had been especially harsh to the returning Māori chief, Te Aara, in the course of the voyage. In conversation, Earle noted that one of his interlocutors, 'King George' [Te Uri-Ti], mimicked the ill-treatment of the returning chief on board the ship, 'his cleaning shoes and knives; his being flogged when he refused to do this degrading work'.[97] Another explanation is that Te Aara was dismayed by the death of his relatives in New Zealand, brought about by the spread of European diseases.[98] Cultural misunderstanding ran ahead of the *Boyd*'s problems. This included a pocket watch accidentally dropped into the waters by a visiting captain, which Māori believed cursed the coast with disease. A group of two hundred whalers decided to exact revenge, massacring the settlement of Marsden's friend Te Pahi, who had spent time in Sydney, meting out their revenge on the wrong group of islanders.[99] Such dramatic altercations changed Māori–British politics.

Yet the idea of the violence of Māori culture and its interaction with ruthless and unthinking Europeans, in a cycle of revenge and counter-revenge, is a rhetorical relic of the period. To the contrary, Māori were mobile peoples who undertook war in order to restore their integrity and status.[100] If there was no possibility of war against offenders, war could be undertaken against distant non-kin to this end of restoration. The arrival of Europeans expanded these customary forms of politics in new directions, making wars more intense and wider in their radius. As in Tonga, the appropriation of European weapons was significant. Newer styles of war, sometimes termed 'muskets wars', unified and concentrated power.[101] They generated unprecedented fatalities and a decline in population. But they transformed what already existed by way of conflict rather than giving rise to a simplistic fatal impact with no room for indigenous response.

The physical power of muskets was not the sole determining factor of these wars. Some historians have cast the new culture of the potato as equally significant as muskets to the unfolding of these wars – in providing food to enable long-range war parties. [102] In the words of the first British Resident of New Zealand in 1837: 'there seems to be good reason to doubt whether their wars were less sanguinary before Fire Arms were introduced.'[103] Established military tactics involving close combat, evolved in order to accommodate these new long-distance weapons. [104] The symbolism of these muskets was critical too. Particular chiefs, who acquired weapons, were cast as great leaders and warriors; they could be seen as operating within pre-existent modes of righting wrongs. Gradually, over the decades that followed, and beyond the signing of the Treaty of Waitangi, the concept of the Māori monarch appeared as a result of this entanglement between old and new, the Pacific and Europe. As an example of the attribution of monarchy, Earle drew 'King George' or 'Shulitea' (Te Uri-Ti), who served as his friend and protector in New Zealand.[105] [Fig. 2.9]

Fig. 2.9 'King George. N. Zealand Costume' by Augustus Earle (1828)

Fig. 2.10 'The wounded chief Honghi [Hongi Hika]
& his family' by Augustus Earle, 1827

The so-called 'Māori Napoleon', Hongi Hika (1772?–1828), was an early initiate to the power of European muskets. Hongi used muskets in the wars between Nga Puhi and Ngati Whatua in the Bay of Island district of North Island.[106] The loss of the Nga Puhi in a battle of 1807 or 1808, which killed two of his brothers and many chiefly kin, was a formative moment in his life. Travelling to Sydney, on a missionary ship, he supported the first missionary settlement in New Zealand. This missionary settlement was later criticised for being under his personal monopoly.[107] Hongi's relationship with the missionaries lasted until his death.

As a Māori account holds, Hongi operated within established ways of avenging the wrongs against kin:

> The primary reason Hongi set himself up as a war leader killing people was the wrongs of former times, that is the farewell requests (concerning them) of those who died earlier, which Hongi carried out to honour the words of his ancestors who died.[108]

Yet Hongi innovated and changed these traditions. Following the Europeans' advice he grew wheat and corn, and potatoes, that he could use to buy muskets and gunpowder from arriving vessels, and he put the captives he took in war to work on these plantations.[109] As a result of these wars, and the interplay of new and old, Hongi's people came increasingly to refer to themselves using a larger collective name, 'Nga Puhi'.[110]

Hongi created quite a stir when he arrived in London in 1820 accompanied by the evangelical Thomas Kendall and an aide, Waikato [Fig. 2.11]. Global travel supercharged Māori customary practice. Tellingly he was presented to the British monarch, George IV. He allegedly observed: 'There is only one king in England, there shall be only one king in New Zealand.'[111] He also spent some time at the University of Cambridge, was entertained by the Vice Chancellor and helped create a Māori dictionary.[112] In the oral tradition of his descendants, he is said to have taken a great interest in maps of the Napoleonic wars deposited in Cambridge.[113] A representation of Hongi's face had arrived in England prior to his person. Marsden had asked him to carve a likeness of himself; a copy of the carving was later published in the *Missionary Register* of 1816.[114] One MP wrote of Hongi's appearance in the House of Lords and compared his face to a carved specimen:

Fig. 2.11 'Waikato, Hongi Hika and Thomas Kendall' by James Barry, 1820

I went round, and got near enough to touch his Majesty; when I found his royal face to be one of the very finest specimens of *carving* I have ever beheld. The Chamberlain's face [Waikato] was fair; the sunflowers on it were highly respectable; but the King's nose, which surpassed the average size, was one blaze of stars and planets.[115]

When he returned to New Zealand, the fact that he came with gifts and patronage and a personal bond with the British Crown allowed him to immediately mount a series of campaigns to consolidate his power. He traded many of his presents in Sydney on the way back to New Zealand, preferring muskets, powder and shot. (He had hundreds of muskets in his possession when he returned to New Zealand.) He retained a suit of armour which was presented to him.[116]

Hongi's story is reminiscent of that from Tonga: local wars were part and parcel of the global contests of the age of revolutions. For the spread of armament, political consolidation and notions of community arose at the intersection of Māori traditions and British imperialism in a mutually reinforcing dynamic. Such a dynamic was evident with respect to the interpretation of Hongi's face: it was a product of Māori carving as much as European notions of race. Hongi Hika's wars in the 1820s covered a wide area, allowing hundreds of people to leave the Bay of Islands, and, according to one historian, 'set almost the whole of the North Island on the move, caused numerous wars and expeditions in both the North and South Islands, and eventually brought about a major redistribution of population'.[117]

In extensive and often negative European commentary appeared another iconic fighter of the musket wars.[118] Te Rauparaha (?–1849), the Ngati Toa leader, was involved from the late eighteenth century in a series of war parties to right the wrongs done to his people. He extended his expeditions south, in order to find a home for his people. His iconic status is illustrated in how his dance of war and welcome, 'ka mate', is now used widely by the All Blacks rugby union team, a signifier in its original sense of the triumph of life over death that has now become a cultural symbol of the Māori to millions of rugby fans. He reached down to Kapiti Island, close to today's Wellington at the southern end of North Island, and established a base there.

It was partly as a result of European assistance that Te Rauparaha's migratory wars spread into the South Island though he came from the North Island. His son, Tamihana, a Christian convert and one of the

first Māori to enter a missionary school, wrote of the events which
unfolded when John Stewart of the *Elizabeth* arrived at Kapiti island in
1830. Te Rauparaha asked the captain whether he would transport him
and a war party to Akaroa, close to today's Christchurch on the South
Island, to right the wrongs caused by some murders. Te Rauparaha took
seventy fighting men with him aboard the *Elizabeth*, and Stewart participated in a scheme whereby the offending chief Tamaiharanui was lured
aboard. Stewart called out to Tamaiharanui's people: 'Go and bring him
to get some gunpowder.' In Tamihana's words:

> When his canoe reached the ship, Tamaiharanui, his wife and daughter
> came aboard and went below to the captain's quarters. When
> Tamaiharanui had sat down Te Rauparaha tied his hands and took him
> and his family to another cabin. Nothing was said. Then Rauparaha
> came up on deck with his warriors to capture the 30 men who had
> accompanied Tamaiharanui; not one escaped. When it was dark the 70
> warriors got in the canoes and went ashore. They entered the villages
> at dawn, the slaughter began.[119]

With time, the extent of Te Rauparaha's contact with whalers expanded
greatly and Europeans readily transported his canoe aboard their ships.[120]
Widening his reach by foreign assistance, Te Rauparaha followed the
path earlier trodden by Hongi and other Māori, arriving in Sydney and
meeting Marsden in 1830. He also came into dispute with the New
Zealand Company, formed to create settlements for British migrants. Te
Rauparaha attacked land surveyors, ending with the killing of the
Company's Captain Arthur Wakefield (1799–1843).[121] These disputes over
land point to the connection between this period of war and trade which
pitted Māori against outsiders and what was to come in terms of colonial
settlement, when Te Rauparaha signed a copy of the Treaty of Waitangi.[122]

So far, two steps in the sequence of change in New Zealand are clear.
First, the encounter with the British transforms existent customs connected
to righting the wrongs of the past. Second, the spread of weapons and
the entrenchment of violence make their impact on these existent customs.
Warriors and monarchic figures emerged who used the British to expand
their ambitions. Te Rauparaha employed the transport provided by the
invaders in this way. And at the same time British bureaucracy and law
arrived in New Zealand. It presented itself as keen on protecting Māori,
even from the effects that Europeans were having on their land.

In 1814, the year of his arrival in New Zealand, as part of the first contingent of missionaries, Thomas Kendall was appointed Justice of the Peace.[123] The British created a position of Resident to New Zealand, taken up by the Tory James Busby in 1833, who was seen by the Māori as the British 'king's man', just as men-of-war were called the 'king's ships' and their sailors the 'king's warriors'.[124] The British empire could in this way project the language and symbolism of monarchy for its own imperially benevolent purposes. Busby's letter of appointment from the governor in Sydney made specific reference to how the *Elizabeth* had contributed to the wars of New Zealand. He came to New Zealand in the direct context of that violent episode in 1830.[125] Busby arranged for a Māori flag, previously used by the missionaries, to be flown by vessels built in New Zealand as they entered Sydney, as 'the Flag of an Independent State'. A declaration of Māori independence was also signed by fifty-two chiefs by the end of the 1830s in the name of 'The United Tribes of New Zealand'.[126] It was first signed by Māori chiefs in 1835.

The 1835 declaration was conceived by Busby as a 'Magna Carta of New Zealand Independence', though it was clearly a first step on the way to formal British control.[127] Busby saw a confederation of chiefs as the constitutional body of the Māori people and wrote soon after his arrival that he wished to build a Parliament House for the Māori chiefs.[128] His view was that they were the 'aristocrats' of their society, under the absolute power of the primary chief, who functioned like a king.[129] He hoped to school these chiefs in keeping the peace and in moral principles of government. In return they were to be awarded a salary and a medal marking their distinction.[130] The Resident, the post that Busby filled, would legislate and present the congress of chiefs with the laws needing approval. This British representative would seek the advice and information of missionaries and other settlers. A militia, composed of settlers who could act in an emergency or a trained 'native force', were also part of Busby's vision. In conceiving of his post in these terms, Busby took up the role played by Marsden's religious mission. He bitterly complained at times that the missionaries of New Zealand did not defer to him.[131] He also diverged from his orders from Sydney. The governor in New South Wales criticised the 1835 declaration for vesting exclusive legislative power in the confederation of chiefs.[132]

Despite the liberal humanitarian discourse, the 1835 declaration arranged by Busby was partly a strategic response to the manoeuvring of a French aristocrat, Baron Charles Philip Hippolytus de Thierry, from a family who had fled the French Revolution, who threatened to found a colony in New Zealand, free from taxation. The baron planned for marriage and collaboration between Māori and Europeans. Before the 1835 proclamation, in the early 1830s, a direct petition had been drawn up by the Māori chiefs and addressed to the British king, William IV and it specifically referred to French plans:

> We have heard that the tribe Marian [a reference to Marion du Fresne, the French explorer who was killed by the Māori in 1772] is at hand coming to take away our land, therefore we pray thee to become our friend and the guardian of these islands, lest the teasing of other tribes should come near to us, and lest strangers should come and take away our land. And if any of thy people should be troublesome or vicious towards us (for some persons are living here who have run away from ships), we pray thee to be angry with them that they may be obedient, lest the anger of the people of this land fall on them.[133]

In the mid 1830s Thierry sailed through the Pacific, after offering a colony to both the Netherlands and France, and he wrote from Tahiti to the British Resident of New Zealand, styling himself 'Sovereign Chief of New Zealand and King of the Island of Nukahiva [in the Marquesas, which he had claimed in the course of his voyage]'. It was in response to this eccentric French bid, and the growing worry about both French and American interests in New Zealand, exemplified by French Catholic missionaries and by American whaling, that Busby presided over the proclamation of the sovereignty of the united tribes.[134]

Busby also noted how two Belgian brothers were buying land in New Zealand and how a 'Polish Count' was writing of his travels in the country.[135] French Catholics in New Zealand, meanwhile, were said to be joining forces with the Irish; and a Catholic bishop was alleged to be plotting the arrival of a vessel of 'Soldiers and Missionaries and traders' for the formation of a French settlement.[136] The way in which humanitarianism cloaked strategic imperial calculations is especially evident in Busby's bid to educate 'half-caste children' lest they fall into the grip of Roman Catholics in Aotearoa/New Zealand and be educated in 'sentiments and principles adverse to British interests'.[137] In one instance of the prevalent paranoia, which in this case was linked to revolt in the Americas and was racist, Busby wrote to his brother of 'American negroes from the whalers' who he had found teaching voodoo to Māori in the bush:

Here were some twenty or thirty Natives of New Zealand seated round the side, and in the middle was a sort of brushwood altar with some articles on it, and busy about it three or four Negroes, who were, by signs, apparently instructing a New Zealand *tohunga* in some mystic rite. With the New Zealanders were four or five white men from near Hokianga who were known to me as being undesirable characters, and these men were already under the influence of an intoxicant.[138]

With such a dizzying range of global interests at play, which are consistent with the age of revolutions, the scene was now set for the controversial Treaty of Waitangi of 1840. Like the treaty arranged by Busby in 1835, the Treaty of Waitangi was framed with a dual purpose: while establishing the legal independence of New Zealand, it also sought to bring the islands under British protection. The balance between these two aspects of the treaty is what has caused protest ever since it was signed, resonating until this day in rival land claims. The most debated words of the treaty are: 'to the Chiefs, the Tribes, and all the people of New Zealand, the entire supremacy of their lands, of their settlements, and of all their personal property'.[139] At the heart of the paradox lies the relationship between ideas of kinship and kingship.

Māori imagined that they were binding themselves to a familial relationship with the British, and choosing them over the French, the 'tribe of Marion'. Māori kinship with the British was seen to come from shared ancestry and religion. This relatedness allowed them also to become kings. In 1839 they had the idea of a meeting 'for the election of a king'.[140] In commenting on Māori bids for kingship, however, Busby wrote: 'I believe we are all agreed that a King from amongst themselves is quite out of the question.'[141] To his brother he noted that a Māori chief had alluded to how Busby himself may be their king: 'I told him that the *"ritenga"* [custom] of this land was not to have a King, that the authority must be in the confederation of chiefs.'[142]

The 1835 declaration called upon the British king to be 'the parent of their infant state'.[143] This language arose directly from the Māori chiefs.[144] The reason Busby did not support a Māori king or even himself as king, was because for the British, who were now annexing territory, ultimate sovereignty did not reside with Māori chiefs. Rather it lay far away with Queen Victoria, now the British monarch, and was delegated by her to her representatives in New Zealand and Sydney. Chieftaincy could continue but only under subordination to Victoria. Notions of independence were a façade that propped up a counter-revolutionary empire, an empire which reactively adopted the language of politics and independence of this period.

In the decades that followed, it was no wonder then that Māori involved themselves in a series of skirmishes with the British. They too could be monarchs. The 'King Movement' or Kīngitanga appointed the first Māori king in the late 1850s and opposed the take-up of ancestral land by the British empire. It successfully mounted armed resistance against the British. It declared the boundaries of the Kīngitanga, or kingdom in 1858. The movement expected to govern alongside the settler state. Intriguingly, Kīngitanga could creatively adopt the narrative of the age of revolutions: for instance, the Haitian Revolution became a point of reference to the Kīngitanga movement. Haiti was interpreted from a Māori cosmology: Haitians had built a *pa* on a hill (fortification), from where they had flown their *kara* (flag), calling the French to attack them. 'Now that island possesses law and its independence [*rangatiratanga*] is established; its flags have been raised; also, the councils [*runanga*] of that place are working for the good of the country. The chiefs [*rangatira*] have united their word; the law has effect; its many harbours are rich.'[145]

A change in the order of politics had come to pass in slow motion and through the evolution of established concepts such as *iwi*, *hapu* and intra-tribal identity, as well as war and Māori attempts to respond to British and global ideas and events. When the British state intruded it did so by cleverly adopting the instruments of the age of revolutions to counter their revolutionary power, from declarations of indigenous independence to flags. And Māori too adopted the mantle of monarch and the legacy of the age of revolutions, including on one occasion events in Haiti, to respond to the British. Yet the fact that similar types of political consolidation were occurring elsewhere in the Pacific makes this more than a Māori story. It is a feature of these years in the Pacific. Arms and ideas, Christianity and the British state, Anglo-French rivalries and shared aims forged these changes. But these changes were not created simply by outside forces; rather change drew in Māori and Pacific political vocabularies. The British were able to use the result of these encounters for imperial gain.

3

In the Southwest Indian Ocean:
Worlds of Revolt and the Rise of Britain

Even in our own times, rebels, insurrectionists and fleeing dictators have sought refuge in underground caverns. By blocking out the world with the darkness of the earth it has been possible to sustain grand dreams of upheaval.

It was 1788: the year of the First Fleet's arrival in Australia to establish a penal colony and just prior to the French Revolution. It was also the day before the expected fulfilment of a prophecy of the end of the world. This prophecy was issued by a rebel, Jan Paerl, at the frontier of the Dutch colonial presence in South Africa. Constant van Nult Onkruijdt, the *landdrost* of Swellendam had the pleasure of discovering Paerl's subterranean dwelling.[1] As *landdrost*, Onkruijdt was the chief representative of the Dutch government of Cape Town in the frontier base at Swellendam, about one hundred and twenty miles to the east. When in force, Jan Paerl's millenarian movement had a following of about two hundred people who were charmed by his charismatic oratory and who saw him as the God of the Khoikhoi or *Onsen Liewen Heer* (Our dear Lord).[2] He was preparing his followers for a new world where divine intervention would allow Khoikhoi to claim back their possessions, land and livestock.[3]

In Paerl's dwelling, Onkruijdt immediately ran through the rebel's personal belongings and discovered a knife, which he took into his possession.[4] This was perhaps the knife that Paerl had used when addressing his followers for the first time. He had stabbed himself with it twice to show that a knife could not injure him. For Onkruijdt, the discovery of the dwelling was a moment to savour; his policy of aggressive intervention had paid dividends.

At the frontier, Onkruijdt had established a tradition of doing what he thought best while ignoring the theoretical advice given by the powers that be in Cape Town. More than a week earlier he had written to Cape Town that the Khoikhoi, the indigenous peoples who performed hard labour on the farms of Swellendam, were attempting through a 'conspiracy' to regain 'control of their entire land and to bring it under their control and rule as in the time of their forefathers'.[5] In responding to this news, Onkruijdt took the side of the migrant farmers or *trekboers* of Swellendam. After cross-examining several captured rebels, he hatched a plan. While the rebel Khoikhoi were congregating on high ground he ordered his men to attack and loot the Khoikhoi settlements in River Valley and Rivier-Sonder-End. Given Khoikhoi impoverishment, their retreat to high ground in this way signified their sacrifice of any connection with European capital and culture. It was a radical statement of resistance.

After discovering Paerl's dwelling, Onkruijdt pursued an extensive investigation and even resorted to bribery. He was still unsuccessful in his search for the rebel. He had a description to the effect that Paerl was tall and of mixed origin. Paerl was labelled a *bastaard* in the midst of the search. He was born to a Khoikhoi woman in Swellendam, after she had a sexual relationship with a man of at least some European ancestry. Though no precise details of this liaison exist, informal and often violent sexual intercourse across the colour line was common in South Africa in the late eighteenth century.[6] Paerl was arrested in 1790: Onkruijdt had resigned his post more than a year before this date.

Despite its idiosyncrasies, Paerl's was a movement of its time. By the late eighteenth century, the Cape colony and its surroundings were entering a point of crisis in demographic terms, in terms of ownership of land as also in settlers' relations with indigenous and enslaved peoples. As this crisis unfolded the language and practice of revolt took off not only among the Khoikhoi but among other groups too. This includes *trekboers*, other indigenous peoples and enslaved persons from elsewhere in the Indian Ocean world. In the period that linked the eighteenth and nineteenth centuries, the dreams of remaking the world of the Cape were remarkably multitudinous: its location as a bridge to a continent inhabited by a wide spectrum of protesting peoples and communities, allowed interwoven revolts to appear here. Modes of revolt drew their power through waves of contact: from people on the move and the news of political change that they brought with them, and from millenarianism and the cultural symbols of far-away places, and even supplies from other Indian Ocean territories. Though linked

Fig. 3.1 A later image of a man with mixed
ancestry with a racialised title, published in an
account of the French voyage of Nicolas
Baudin, covered in the previous chapter,
published 1824

to land-based agriculture there was a maritime pathway to many of
these revolts too.

In the midst of these myriad uprisings was another transformation,
the militarised arrival of the British, who took over this Dutch foothold,
first from 1795 to 1803, in fear of French advance, and finally from 1806
onwards, in fear of Napoleon. The British also made a charge through
the French Indian Ocean world. The arrival of the British was a reactive
response to these many kinds of revolt. The island of Mauritius, then
Île de France, is important too. Mauritius' republicanism served as a
model for onlookers in French India. This south-western Indian Ocean
island's republicanism was hemmed in first by a Napoleonic governor

and then by the British, who took it over in 1810 wishing to put an end to its reputation not only for republicanism but also for piracy. Once again this was the British imperial counter-revolution in action.

Across these sites of the watery South, a surge of indigenous resistance and uprisings of various kinds set the context for the rise of the British empire. This surge was connected in turn with a tumult of Dutch and French descendants seeking for more self-rule. Though indigenous politics are in view, it is also the case that the truly indigenous is difficult to extract given the range of migrants, labourers and settlers who figure here. Indigenous protest was tied up with the resistance of enslaved peoples and *trekboers*. This resistance in turn was forged through connections which have been largely forgotten until now. Connections which linked the Cape and Mauritius across the waves of the South stretched towards Batavia as well as India and even to the Gulf.

FACING OUT OF INDIGENOUS LANDS

Paerl's millenarian movement is indicative of the forces that were building and within which revolutionary thinking could flourish in so many different ways. A Dutchman called Johannes Nicolaas Swart took possession of fertile land occupied by a Khoikhoi community. The community's leader Cobus Valentijn protested that this was illegal, taking it up with both Onkruijdt's predecessor and Onkruijdt. But Valentijn's complaints did not receive a proper reply. It was after observing how the law failed to work to protect him that Paerl underwent an 'inner conversion' to become god.[7]

Forty-three years before Paerl mounted this resistance, Swellendam was taken under the wing of the VOC or the Dutch East India Company, through which this part of Southern Africa was governed. A sub-*drotstdy* or area of jurisdiction was established. About ten years before this resistance movement the settlement comprised merely four houses, one of which was used by the *landdrost*. This indicates not a lack of population but more how *trekboers* were spread thinly across the vast countryside around the settlement.[8] Each farmer had open to him the right to farm six thousand acres. Population pressures and the lack of prospects in Cape Town had forced them to take up residence here. In the later eighteenth century these *trekboers* began to feel that land was increasingly scarce.

Rivers served as boundary markers to their haphazard expansion: first Swellendam and its neighbour Stellenbosch, to the north, were demarcated as extending up to the Gamtoos River to the west. Then in response to complaints, the frontier was pushed back to the Fish River and Bushman River further to the west. Yet still the farmers complained: in 1775 they wrote to the Dutch governor: 'unless this colony expands farther east – and northward, the inhabitants will not be able to obtain for themselves or their children any more farms and therefore will not only remain in their present poverty-stricken state but must fear that it shall become worse.'[9]

As the grumbling grew louder, there arose a gap of understanding between the Dutch of Cape Town and these frontier men which led to stereotyping of these *trekboers*. Cape Town elites feared that *trekboers* and their kin were turning into heathen and lawless barbarians, and they insisted on portraying the farmers as lazy. One Scottish botanist and traveller wrote of how he visited a 'Dutch boor [boer]' who was 'possessed of numerous herd of cattle; but had no corn, and scarcely a house to live in, though the place was favourable for both'. He carried on: '[t]he generality of those people are of so indolent a disposition, that they seldom trouble themselves either to build houses or to cultivate the ground'.[10] This impression was of course inaccurate. For working the land was a hard existence which necessitated a culture of self-sufficiency among these poor whites who had left Cape Town. They sent on meat and butter to Cape Town, but transport was difficult and costly. The Swedish natural historian Anders Sparrman urged the establishment of better navigation between the ports of the Cape Colony, writing that 'many thousands of days work are unnecessarily lost and thrown away every year on the roads leading to the Cape'.[11]

Tellingly, just as the lack of understanding between the city and the frontier was building, giving rise to a political rift, the economies of the frontier and Cape Town were increasingly entangled. Indeed, *trekboers* had not been isolated in economic terms even before this point in time. Frontiersmen were indebted to the city and the city depended on the frontier for meat. Bursts of economic growth – tied for instance to times of global war when more ships called at Cape Town – were followed by times of economic depression. As the 1770s closed depression gripped the frontier and the falling of the price of slaughtered stock served as the context for revolt.

In addition to this economic element, the crisis at the frontier on the eve of the French Revolution was also connected to relations with

Fig. 3.2 'A View of Table Mountain and Cape Town,
at the Cape of Good Hope', 1787

indigenous peoples. Paerl's life and story constituted a piece of a bigger
jigsaw which encompassed the changing fortunes of the Khoikhoi and
other indigenous and mixed peoples in these years. In 1713, a smallpox
epidemic had dramatically reduced the Khoikhoi's numbers 'so that
they lay everywhere along the roads as if massacred by the Dutch,
who they said had bewitched them'.[12] In the middle of the eighteenth
century, Khoikhoi had perhaps appreciated European weapons, tobacco,
brandy and livestock farming. Indeed, there were important similarities
between the Khoikhoi and *trekboer* cultures: both groups were subsistence
agriculturists and pastoralists in the earlier eighteenth century. These
similarities inevitably led to a system of dependence. But by the late 1770s
the picture was rather different and there was a growing sentiment of
resistance and detachment, as is evident from the millenarianism
surrounding Paerl. By 1797 a pass system limited the free movements of
Khoikhoi in Swellendam.[13]

Otto Friedrich Mentzel, a German immigrant to Cape Town, provides
a disturbing and highly racialised account of Khoisan, whom he called
'Hottentots' and 'Bushmen'. Their lack of a permanent abode served as
the pretext for European expansion. Of the San he wrote:

They live scattered in all the mountains to the East and North of the Cape, have no fixed abode or kraals, but wander about from one place to another, sometimes in groups, hide in ravines and among the rocks, and live in the greatest idleness and laziness as long as they have any means of subsistence; they never attempt an attack until they find nothing more to eat, when exhausted from hunger they are compelled to look for booty. By nature they are apparently not savage nor cruel, but the persecution of the Europeans who shoot them like dogs, and the bitter hunger when they have nothing to eat, make them audacious and desperate, so that they risk their lives and become bloodthirsty.[14]

What Mentzel described as an active process of expansion, which in turn generated a response on the part of a feeble and nomadic people, was in fact a project of dispossession and resistance, and violence was solidified in the years before and after the Paerl incident. The nature of this expansion is illustrated in the taking of war captives: Graaff-Reinet had around one thousand war captives in 1795, taken in the

Fig. 3.3 'Bush Men Hottentots Armed for an Expedition', in Samuel Daniell, *A Collection of Plates Illustrative of African Scenery and Animals* (1804)

midst of *boer* raids directed at indigenous settlements. As a leading historian of the Afrikaners writes: 'in the final decades of the century, some Graaff-Reinet farms were the scenes of acts of great cruelty'.[15]

In addition to increasing tensions with the Khoikhoi, in the late eighteenth century there began a hundred-year war between European descendants and another indigenous people, the Xhosa, who had settled to the east of the Cape Colony. The Xhosa had come to a stronger sense of themselves as ethnically separate from Khoikhoi, while also exchanging a great deal with the Khoikhoi. The word 'Xhosa' comes from Khoikhoi and means 'angry men'.[16] In the late eighteenth century the Xhosa were forming more politically centralised structures and establishing settlements for the first time in the area to the east of *trekboer* farms. As these two rival streams of settlement – one *boer* and the other Xhosa – came into contact with each other conflict ensued. The Xhosa found that Europeans stole their cattle and took them and their children captive. The struggle between these Europeans and Xhosa took the form of raids and counter-raids. As war with the Xhosa unfolded, it stoked wide-scale rebellion among the Khoikhoi in turn, who escaped from and then also raided *trekboer* farms. Conflict with one group of indigenous peoples bred conflict with another.

A particularly sustained period of unrest came between 1799 and 1803, eleven years after the Paerl affair and after Britain's first taking of the Cape between 1795 and 1803, where in some farms rebels killed all the Europeans. In this period 470 farms were scorched and it is estimated that rebels took into their possession 584 horses, 3,137 oxen, 22,230 cattle and 19,766 sheep and goats.[17] Rebellion for indigenous peoples therefore amounted to taking possession of items that were highly valued in the agricultural economy which they were challenging. In addition to conflict with the Xhosa to the east, the *trekboers* also had to come to terms with a third group, the San people to the north, whom colonists called 'Bushmen', and who assembled in large numbers to mount raids on farms. Despite the racialised ways in which settlers differentiated them, the San were not necessarily separable from the Khoikhoi. They too were experiencing the pressure of European expansion and responding with violence in turn.[18]

The revolt of the indigenous peoples of Southern Africa – Khoikhoi, Xhosa and San – was moulded by the form of European pastoral expansion at the ground level. Population pressures and the instability of agrarian and subsistence economies were vital factors, and accordingly revolts were also characterised by plunder. But if *boers* sought to stamp out revolt they also sought to take the revolutionary ideas of this moment as a weapon in their own arsenal.

TREKBOER PATRIOT REVOLT

Despite the age of revolutions being defined here from the South as a surge of indigenous politics, *trekboers* also participated in the age of revolutions. They did so as people who saw their identity as tied up with a southern land. Their revolt was fundamentally local at the same time as it was attuned to global news.

From the 1780s, a tradition of patriotic opposition to the policies of the Dutch East India Company took off in Cape Town and then later at the frontier. If Cape governors had sought to see the Khoikohi as a nation, the *boers* at this time started to assert their own nationality. *Trekboers* used the term Afrikaaner to describe their community, distinguishing themselves in this way from the Dutch officer class. The disquiet among *boers* began in Cape Town, among those who saw the Dutch East India Company as an institution representing the *ancien régime*. Boer patriotism drew inspiration from changes in the Netherlands, where a Batavian Republic came to exist in the aftermath of the French Revolution. Yet this South African patriotism was not determined by events in Europe.

To start with events in the far-away northern hemisphere, a Patriot Revolt that lasted from 1785 to 1787 saw the takeover of a number of towns in the Netherlands, drawing inspiration from the American Revolution. At its heart the movement sought to revive the Dutch nation's past and its federal administration, while deprecating the perceived decline of the Orangist monarchy. These Dutch patriots in the Netherlands, like their southern compatriots, were no friends of the Dutch East India Company. They spoke for natural rights and primitive democracy, while also cherishing populist Christian piety. At first they were roundly set upon by their opponents, with the help of a Prussian army, only to regroup in the aftermath of the French Revolution. In 1795, when a French army invaded the Netherlands, it set up the Batavian Republic, which stood until 1805, governed by Dutch patriots. The Prince of Orange fled to England.[19] The VOC (Dutch East India Company) was nationalised in 1796. It was exactly then that deep within the Cape Colony there

was a surge of patriotic feeling. Against a view of cause and effect tying
metropole and colony, patriotism took off in the Cape prior to the
consolidation of the Batavian Republic in 1795 and even prior to the
Patriot Revolt of the 1780s.

For it was in 1779 that a petition was launched by the *boers* in Cape
Town, demanding for their number the same rights as the officials of
the Dutch East India Company. They desired free trade and denounced
the Company's monopolistic practices. They accused the Company of
corruption. They complained of their 'narrowly circumscribed way of
life' and the prospect of 'complete poverty'. They put this burden down
to the 'oppression under whose burden the entire citizenry [*Burgerstaat*]
must groan'; the oppression in view was caused by Company officials.[20]
According to one *boer* description of the governorship of Plettenberg,
which lasted until 1785: 'no transaction with government could be carried
out without bribery, in which many of the officials farmed and traded
openly and the colonists generally became discontented.'[21] Indicating
how this pattern of politics was a local one, these patriots held that *boers*
should have the right to punish their own enslaved peoples. At the heart
of their pleas was a racial vocabulary of distinction between themselves
and their others, meaning that their revolt was set not only against
traditional authority, but also against indigenous and slave revolt.
According to another of their petitions of 1784, which had been drafted
in Holland, they warned of the 'approach of a complete bastardi[s]ation
of morals'; their community's threat to the colonial state would become
as 'dangerous . . . as the Bushman-Hottentots [Khoisan] now are'.[22] All
this denotes the dangers of reading this protest simply as the diffusion
of political currents from the Netherlands.

This culture of *boer* patriotism also took off in the very place where
Paerl had been active. In 1795, in Swellendam, *trekboer* revolt set in. Sixty
trekboers under the command of a man styled as *Nationale Commandant*
and calling themselves 'nationales' stormed the settlement.[23] The
landdrost at this time, Anthonij Faure, was deposed and in his place a
'national' *landdrost* was appointed. Among the demands of these rebels
of Swellendam was the withdrawal of paper currency and the institution
of free trade. They criticised the conduct of Faure in the war with the
Xhosa, alleging that he had taken the side of the indigenous peoples, a
constant refrain among these southern-hemisphere patriots.

In the neighbouring district of Graaf-Reinet patriotism became more
sustained in the 1790s. Once again the *landdrost*, Honoratus Maynier,

was evicted by rebels wearing the tricolour cockade, who imagined themselves to be directly under the control of the States General of the Netherlands, the legislative body of the Dutch state.²⁴ Various 'Representatives of the People' forced themselves onto the district council. These rebels took particular issue with how Maynier had opened his court to the Khoikhoi. One of their leader, Adriaan van Jaarsveld, wrote of their agenda, using the word *volk*, meaning the people or nation:

> The volk demanded the defeat of the Xhosa. The reason why they did not want to say it unequivocally was that they feared the consequences of arbitrary conduct and desired that the attack take place on higher authority. The volk would long ago have come to blows with the Xhosa again but they feared that they were too weak and would need help.²⁵

The rebelliousness of Graaff-Reinet carried through into the British rule of the Cape Colony and drew in the maritime connections of the Dutch. In 1797, Andrew Barnard, the secretary to Lord Macartney, the governor at the Cape, wrote to Robert Brooke, the military officer of the East India Company, about how the rebels of Graaff-Reinet had sought to arm themselves. He described the 'volcanic disposition' of the rebels, which remained 'smothered for a while in order to burst forth with redoubled violence'. Barnard wrote of how a British vessel called the *Hope*, a South Sea whaler, had reached Delagoa Bay, where it was in need of water and sent a brig in to get some. A few days later, the *Hope* noticed another vessel which they took to be a French privateer and immediately pretended to be American by hoisting American colours. However, the *Hope* learnt that the vessel was in fact Dutch, and:

> that they were laden at Batavia with Six Hundred Barrels of Gunpowder and Eight Pieces of Artillery, from 12 pounders and four gun (?) Field Carriage, which shot in perfection, they had besides Bale Goods and Coffee on board, the whole of which was intended to be landed in Algoa Bay, which is at the Mouth of what is called the Swarte Kops River and within a day or a half's journey of the Drosdy, or village of Graaf Reynet . . . The whole of this was intended for them on the receipt of which they meant to declare themselves independent of the Cape and establish a Government of their own after the French System.²⁶

A three-week stand-off between the whaler and the Dutch brig *Haasje* followed, before the assistance of some men from a Portuguese vessel arriving on the scene allowed the British to take the upper hand. The Dutch headed up a river. Most of the Dutch ship's crew were taken as prisoners. Yet 'the natives', Barnard wrote, 'contrived during the contest . . . to steal all the Bale Goods and Coffee . . .' Earl Macartney, the governor, wrote to London that the expedition was 'ignorantly and injudiciously planned'.[27] The *Haasje*'s captain Jacob de Freyn had 'despatched a negro' with a letter to Graaff-Reinet; from Delagoa Bay he had hoped to get to Algoa Bay, where the governor of Batavia had instructed him to land his supplies.[28] According to the statement of the third mate of the *Haasje*: 'At the time she left Batavia no person knew her destination except her Captain and the governor of that place.' The crew had believed the vessel to be bound for Ternate.[29]

Another alleged attempt to provide support to the rebels was reported by Barnard in 1799, when the *Prenouse*, a French vessel flying Danish colours, was fired upon and chased for 200 miles, after detection in Algoa Bay.[30] By this time the British were building a fort at Algoa Bay, 'a second Gibraltar'.[31] The conflict with the *Prenouse* gave rise to the false rumour that the French had landed troops to support the Dutch patriots. By March 1800, when the vessel was captured and blown up, a 'finishing stroke to the French marine in these seas' was reported, despite the continuing action of French privateers working out of Mauritius.[32] Mauritius was still under French rule at this point. If the *trekboer* patriot revolt was forged locally and in relation to news from Europe too, it also drew in contact across the South, pulling in supplies from Batavia.

The episode around the *Prenouse* coincided with the Graaff-Reinet *trekboers*' attempt to found a free nation in 1799. They perceived that the British regime was weak. They adopted the slogan of Liberty, Equality and Fraternity, what Barnard dismissively called 'cursed French principles'.[33] Van Jaarsveld, the Graaff-Reinet *trekboer* leader, had been imprisoned for forgery and was being taken by armed convoy to Cape Town when he was released by his comrades. The rebels then gathered in considerable number and insisted on having 'an English Landrost' as they were 'no longer Dutch subjects'. In response, the British stamped out revolutionary feeling by sending in forces, who disarmed rebels and announced martial law. Barnard wrote to Macartney on the subject of the rebelling *trekboers* in this area: 'They will then be sent out of the Colony for as long as they remain in it that District will never be quiet.'

Yet the frontier broke out in full-scale revolt as its organisation was unravelled by the presence of such a large British force: Khoikhoi now took the opportunity to raid *trekboer* farms and combine forces with the Xhosa. This is the revolt that was encountered above and which was tied with the first British occupation of the Cape Colony. The vulnerability of the *trekboers* arose from the British denying them gunpowder.[34] They fled in fear when a rumour spread among them that they were to be captured and killed and that their women were to be given to 'blacks': accordingly, 'this year their wives still had white children on their laps, but next year they would have black'.[35] The English statesman and South African traveller, John Barrow, reported the tragic violence between *boers* and 'Hottentots' in the context of British military operations and reported this among a catalogue of what can only be called war crimes:

> We had scarcely parted from these people when, stopping at a house to feed our horses, we by accident observed a young Hottentot woman with a child in her arms lying stretched on the ground in a most deplorable condition. She had been cut from head to foot with one of those infernal whips, made from the hide of a rhinoceros or sea-cow, known by the name of sambocs, in such a barbarous and unmerciful manner, that there was scarcely a spot on her whole body free from stripes, nor had the sides of the little infant, in clinging to its mother, escaped the strokes of the brutal monster.[36]

In this manner, *boer* revolution set some of the context for British intervention, which in turn allowed a revolt of the indigenous peoples of Southern Africa to deepen at the close of the eighteenth century. For Barnard, force was critical to distinguish Britain from their Dutch predecessors. The *boers*, he noted, 'thought themselves out of the reach of Government & that they could play the same game they had done in the Dutch time when the government was too weak to oppose them'.[37] Revolt and imperialism became interrelated. Tragically, in the end, only with the firming up of imperialism, through a greater military response and a consolidation of the administrative apparatus of British colonialism, could its opponents be driven underground.

The language of the American and French revolutions, and the example of the Batavian Republic, was used in this way by *trekboers* in support

of a conservative culture of settlement. This culture of settlement generated a local age of revolutions. It included the *boers*' commitment to the
harsh discipline of slaves and aggressive conflict with indigenous peoples.
Such practices set a context for the expansion of the counter-revolutionary
British empire.

ENSLAVED PEOPLES IN REVOLT

If the revolutionary landscape of the Cape Colony was fractured along
multiple lines, there is still one other group who mounted their own
kind of revolt in Southern Africa in this period. These are the enslaved
people who arrived at the Cape from various parts of the Indian Ocean.
Neither indigenous nor settler, they played a vital part in supercharging
the Cape Colony's age of revolutions.

The multiple backgrounds of enslaved people and their dispersal across
the colony prevented the kind of camaraderie which was important as
a condition for rebellion. Violent resistance could take personalised
forms, including the poisoning of masters, using expertise gained from
Khoikhoi; or setting fire to slave owners' property.[38] Suicide was also a
desperate and tragic means of resistance and one which was economically
costly for the owners of enslaved people. In order to strike fear in the
minds of other slaves, two years before the Paerl episode gripped
Swellendam, the body of a drowned female enslaved person was taken
out of the river and laid out to be observed until it decomposed.[39]
Runaway slaves joined forces with the indigenous peoples at the frontier.
The emergence of mixed communities, categorised in racial terms as
bastaard hottentots, made the recognition of an escaped enslaved person
a difficult undertaking for the state.[40]

Among enslaved people, the revolutionary rhetoric of these decades
drawn from overseas was fundamentally reworked to suit local agendas.
The year 1808 saw a significant slave rebellion in Cape Town. [41] It began
when two Irishmen told the thirty-year-old Louis, the keeper of a wine
shop, who was an enslaved person owned by the 'separated wife of Willem
Kirsten', that in Ireland, England, Scotland and America 'there were no
Slaves, but all free people, that all people ought to be free'.[42]

These two Irishmen were in their early twenties and had travelled
across the Atlantic and Indian Oceans at a time when ideas connected

to the abolition of slavery were circulating, once again showing the importance of the wider context to the events of Southern Africa. One of them had worked for the East India Company as a soldier in India and arrived at the Cape as an invalid.[43] Following the leadership of Louis, who had been in contact with the Irishmen, a group of enslaved people proceeded to take control of thirty-four farms in Zwartland, Koeberg and Tygerberg, districts where grapes and grain were grown. After the revolt's suppression, about three hundred prisoners were taken. Sixteen of them were sentenced to death, 244 were returned to their masters with a serious warning. The Irishmen were apprehended while attempting to escape by sea from Saldanha Bay.[44]

The 1808 slave revolt was in some ways the opposite of the Paerl movement. For here, instead of renouncing the culture of Europe, the rebels sought to imitate it. They took up European clothes, whereas Paerl had given these up. They also rode horses, a right reserved for whites, and sought to hunt down farmers on the run, as farmers hunted down enslaved people. Take for instance the testimony of Jacomina Hendrina Laubscher, the wife of Petrus Gerhardus Louw, a farmer in Zwartland, who told the Court of Justice that when her husband was away, a wagon drawn by eight horses had arrived at the farm, with two white men, who claimed to be English officers and 'a black person was with them, who they said was a Captain of the Spanish Navy', which was presumably Louis.[45] The take-up of settler culture was evident in how these rebels had seven enslaved people with them:

> That the said three persons supped at Table with her that evening, in the cloaths above described, sitting the pretended Spanish Captain between the two Englishmen opposite her, the appearer, and her children & were served by one of the Slaves they had brought with them . . .
>
> The next morning, the party went off with ten of this household's slaves, leaving behind them 'a few dressed feathers, painted with different colours, together with some cartridge, with powder in two pillow cases . . .'

When questioned, Louis let on that he had had a prior conversation with one of this farm's slaves, Jephtha. Jephtha had been in Cape Town with grain from the farm. In preparation, Louis had asked Jephtha to speak to other slaves in the interior about the plot; he hoped to assemble enslaved people at Salt River, to arm them, and to come to Cape Town in the night, to take charge of a battery, and to demand freedom from the governor.[46] 'And in case of a refusal to make themselves masters of the Magazines to storm and force the Prison, release the Prisoners and fight for the liberty of the Slaves.'[47]

While all this indicates how revolt was forged in a local context, it nevertheless drew from the wider Indian Ocean. Louis himself had the name van Mauritius, to indicate his birth on Mauritius. He claimed to have arrived in Cape Town aged three.[48] Others listed as involved in the plot by the Court of Justice included an enslaved person specifically noted as 'Adonis' who came from Ceylon, and appears to have been an enslaved person used for fishing, and another 'Cupido' from Java, 'Geduld' from Mozambique and 'Damon' from the Malabar coast of India.[49] The questioning of the rebels paid particular attention to their clothing, and the specific role of the feathers, jacket, epaulets and sword acquired for Louis. Louis appears to have consciously modelled his apparel on that of the rebels of the Haitian Revolution.[50] According to one of the Irishmen, Michael Hooper, the function of the feathers was as follows:

> Louis told me that he was to be Governor over the Blacks at the Cape, and James [the other Irishman] said that these feathers were for Louis and James put a few of them on the Hat of Louis before he went to sleep [at the house of Louw] – but when we went away, James took the new Hat of Louis, on which the feathers were with him and afterwards took the feathers off.[51]

The rebels also spoke of flying a red flag, like that flown by mutinous sailors.[52] Yet the context for this slave resistance at the Cape is not simply that of Caribbean revolt, and this is especially apparent in the spread of Islam among enslaved people in the Cape in this period, which once again makes the case for the importance of seeing the revolts of Southern Africa from the perspective of the global South.

By 1807–8 the British were deeply concerned by 'the most general spreading of Mohametan principles amongst the slaves' compared with the relative lack of baptisms to Christianity amongst them.[53] Islam had already been a significant element of slave resistance at the Cape in the 1760s especially among those who called themselves 'Bugis'.[54] Louis was questioned explicitly on his religious beliefs: he answered that he was a Christian but that he had not been baptised. He was asked to give an account of Christian doctrine and this line of interrogation indicates British fears of Islam:

My mistress always held forth and impressed on my mind the Christian
Religion. She warned me against the Mahometan Religion . . . I believe
in God and Christ, and that I shall be punished hereafter if I have
committed evil and rewarded if I do well, that my Soul shall not perish,
but be responsible for everything: this my Mistress taught me.[55]

The arrival of Muslims at the Cape in 1658 occurred shortly after its
first establishment as a base for Dutch trade.[56] Though they drew on
Sufi traditions, these adherents created novel constellations of communities and rituals. They had to come to terms with the dominant context
of slavery within their ranks while trying to find leaders among the
home-grown faithful. In the early nineteenth century, the community's
leader and the critical agent in establishing the Awwal Mosque was Frans
van Bengalen. The Awwal Mosque was the first formal mosque in South
Africa, its founding normally dated to 1798. Van Bengalen was an
enslaved person who bought his freedom and then became a slave owner.
Among the rituals that became markers of the Cape Muslims in the
nineteenth century were elaborate birth ceremonies intended to ward
off evil, the recitation of the Qur'an in religious school as a rite of
passage and dignified burial rituals. Burial sites such as that of Shaykh
Yusuf from Southeast Asia, who had been brought to the Cape as a
political prisoner and who died in 1699, also served a ritual role in the
early nineteenth century. Just as ideas from Europe were localised and
mutated so also was Islamic discourse and practice from across the
Indian Ocean.

Looking back at the multiple worlds of the Cape Colony, for enslaved
and indigenous peoples as well as *trekboers*, the last two decades of the
eighteenth century and the start of the nineteenth century marked a shift
in the strategies of resistance. Revolt had occurred before in numerous
ways. Yet new elements which can be traced either directly or indirectly
to the age of revolutions, such as patriotic ideology, news of revolt elsewhere, economic fluctuations and population pressures, mounted to
create a cycle of revolt. Revolt crossed between communities as different
indigenous groups' resistance fed into each other, or as mixed communities led revolt. The wider maritime world of the South framed the
intensity of the age of revolutions in Cape Town and its frontier, even
if local circumstances dictated its particular form.

The local circumstances of the Cape Colony were particularly wide,
encompassing so many different types of settlers and labourers, and this

Fig. 3.4–5 Bo-Kaap in Cape Town, formerly known as the
Malay Quarter, and where Awwal Mosque, shown below, was built in 1798

meant that the types of revolt evident here were incredibly heterogeneous. Even as revolution was localised, the values and meanings of
revolt could be turned on their head and take dramatically divergent
forms, particular revolts could still uphold enslavement. Those indigenous and other people who saw their residence and identity to be tied
up with this southern land set the agenda of this age of revolutions.
Revolt was also sandwiched by counter-revolutionary empire; imperialism sought to take it under its wing and to suppress it. If this was a
small place at the end of the earth, nevertheless there were worlds in
worlds in the Cape Colony.

MAURITIUS AND THE NEWS

If Cape Town was the centre of Dutch colonialism in the South Indian
Ocean, Mauritius was the headquarters of the French empire. It was
modelled to some extent on the way the Dutch controlled its neighbouring settlement to the west. Though Mauritius had first been colonised
by the Dutch, it was abandoned by the Dutch East India Company, only
to be taken by the French East Indies Company, or the Compagnie des
Indes, from 1715. In the later eighteenth century, when the company went
bankrupt, control of the island passed to the French crown. By royal
edict in 1785 it became the administrative centre of French operations
in the Indian Ocean. Though uninhabited when the Dutch arrived, the
island was from its early stages of colonisation a diverse society. Residents
included Europeans of many nations, as well as enslaved people and
mixed communities, and today it seeks to project itself as a 'rainbow'
nation, which is evident even in its flag.

The news of the French Revolution arrived in Île de France in late
January 1790, on board a ship from Bordeaux, under Lieutenant Gabriel
de Coriolis. The captain and all his crew were sporting the tri-coloured
revolutionary cockade. Charles Grant was born into a Scottish family
who had emigrated to France; his father, Louis-Charles Grant, had
become a colonist and governor in Mauritius. He wrote that 'the flames
of revolutionary conflagration instantly burst forth in all parts of the
colony, and the cockade was very generally adopted'.[57] The effect of the
news was electric: within four days three hundred people were wearing
the cockade, including some women, and those who didn't wear it were
heckled. Advertisements were posted on the streets, asking 'citizens' to

form themselves into assemblies, imitating the assemblies that had emerged in France.

The governor, Comte de Conway, however, could not stomach revolution: he summoned the ship's commander, de Coriolis, and criticised him for causing such tumult. He ordered that the men who posted the advertisements should be taken into custody and also called upon rural whites who were more conservative to turn up in force in Port Louis. But the 'citizens' would have none of it: they freed the pamphleteer of revolution and insisted that de Conway also sport the national cockade. The first meeting of the newly constituted Colonial Assembly took place in April 1790, with sixty-one members, under the presidency of Ange d'Houdetot.

There was a tradition of protest which pre-dated this moment, for instance under the liberal governorship of Bruni d'Entrecasteaux, the French Pacific voyager who spent time in Tonga and died before the termination of his voyage in Surabaya (as retold in the last chapter). In 1789, under d'Entrecasteaux's governorship, an assembly of whites who had the right to vote convened on the island.[58] With the arrival of the latest news in 1790, this commitment to franchise turned radical. In further developments, republicans soon succeeded in curbing Governor de Conway's power, insisting on having a role in determining the representatives of Île de France to be sent to Paris to sit in the National Assembly. In July they marched on and took control of Government House.

The radicalising impact of news was also evident in February 1793 when the island learned of the abolition of the French monarchy. The Colonial Assembly decreed that all symbols and titles be stripped of royal connotations and references: the royal courts became the Tribunal of First Instance and the Council of the Judiciary became the Tribunal of Appeal. Public documents were sealed with the figure of liberty associated with the words 'French Republic'. The President of the Assembly, Julien Barbé, addressed the governor, Malartic, with these words:

Citizen Governor, you were the representative of a king that the love of the people had conserved given his veritable grandeur but which the sovereignty of the people has reversed because he did not know how to be the King of the French people . . . The monarchy has been abolished forever in France; but the power which it was the deposit of is maintained. The executive power subsists in all its force. You remain the representative of this power in the colony that could not exist in more sure hands. You will prove this by the attentiveness with which you will surrender to the wish of the Assembly to swear an oath of loyalty to the French Republic. Swear that you will be loyal to the French Republic and that you will maintain it with all your power.[59]

The republican commotion was fundamentally maritime. Henri de Macnémara, the Irish commander of the French navy in the Indian Ocean, arrived in May 1790 after serving as an envoy of Louis XVI to the court of Tipu Sultan of Mysore.[60] He was particularly disturbed by the 'criminal seductions' evident among crews at port.[61] He described the sailors as being far too swayed by the 'desire for an independence which they well know can never be in a monarchical state' and that they were 'easily led astray by the vain hope of a chimerical sense of equality'.[62] He also sought to take an account of the defection of the island's soldiers back to the French Minister of Marine. It was rumoured that he was plotting to arrest the two representatives appointed by the Colonial Assembly in Mauritius who were to take seats in the National Assembly, Charles Alexandre Honoré Collin and Antoine Codère, while they were on their way to Paris. When the soldiers got wind of his views they marched down to the harbour and stormed his ship, took Macnémara into custody, and placed him before the newly constituted self-governing assembly:

> The fermentation of the soldiers had risen to such a pitch, that it was not possible to appease it; so that the members of this constituted assembly found it necessary . . . to send him to prison for his own security . . .

Various different accounts of what happened to Macnémara have survived and have been embellished for their readers. The later-nineteenth-century commentator Albert Pitot has Macnémara appearing several times before the island's Assembly, on one occasion forced to announce his patriotism and on another made to wear the uniform of the National Guard.[63] According to Pitot, the change of uniform was taken as a change of heart and the swarming crowd shouted, 'Long live Macnémara!' According to the commentary of Grant, while being conveyed to prison by soldiers, Macnémara made a desperate bid to escape. Passing the door of a watchmaker whom he knew, Macnémara decided to rush into the shop. As a man of authority in the French empire, Macnémara held a high opinion of his physical powers and believed that he could with the simple use of his pistol intimidate the crowd who dared to follow him. But the episode only angered the soldiers further and there was a general stampede. Macnémara was murdered and beheaded.

A later commentator added that his severed head was paraded through the town and thrown into a sewer.[64] Another wrote of how his 'mutilated body' was dragged to Pont Bourgeois and first abandoned and then interred by a marine.[65] Violence often took theatrical and ritualised forms in this small society: beheadings of maroons or escaped enslaved people are examples of this.[66] Grant saw that this violence was directed at those of his class and wrote that it made him 'shudder with indignation'.[67] He migrated to Britain. Macnémara's death, if the rumour is believed, prevented him from chasing after the two representatives from Mauritius on the way to Paris on the *Amphitrite*. These representatives were lost at sea off the coast of Brittany.[68] Before arriving in Mauritius, Macnémara had travelled from Paris to Mysore in South India, under instruction from Louis XVI, in order to accompany home the ambassadors sent by Tipu Sultan, the ruling prince of Mysore, to the French court. Now, the letters that Macnémara was carrying by return from Tipu Sultan to Paris did not reach their destination.[69]

While *trekboers* of Swellendam and Graaff-Reinet were taking over the governmental apparatus at the Cape colony's frontier, these colonists of Mauritius also sought to use the opportunity of the age of revolutions for themselves.

Racial dynamics were a major part of the story. The bigotry of this Assembly is evident in how it excluded free people of colour from membership. Free people of colour were a rapidly growing number on Île de France in this period, including freed slaves and new migrants from overseas. Their exclusion from the Assembly arose despite the demand of people of colour in 1790 to 'exercise a right which they [believed] to be founded in nature and the law'.[70] The request to set up a Special Assembly for free people of colour was also denied in 1794.[71] The 1791 Constitution of the Colonial Assembly allowed the 1,800 whites to dominate all the aspects of the state and to appoint an electoral body of 36 members, which in turn appointed 300 public men who controlled the legal, executive and legislative arms of the government.[72]

The prejudices of the colonists were also evident when news arrived four years later that slavery had been abolished by the French. The colonial republicans opted not to do the same. When Paris sent two representatives, René-Gaston Baco de la Chapelle, a lawyer, and Étienne Burnel, a former Mauritius-based journalist, to enforce the abolition of slavery in 1796, they had to flee in fear for their lives. This was after 'some young Creoles' entered the government house where they were staying and announced that these two deserved to die. Grant notes: 'one of the agents narrowly escaped being killed by the discharge of a pistol'.[73] Meanwhile, the two representatives of Île de France in Paris argued that the abolition of slavery would lead to 'the misfortune of free men and slaves and will spark a civil war that will not end without the complete destruction of one or the other, or even both parties'.[74] They continued by claiming that a petition from free people of colour asking for abolition was the work of the British who were trying to divorce French colonies from the Republic.

In further evidence of the local texture of what unfolded, the Colonial Assembly was contested within Mauritius, when a Jacobin club was set up in 1794, trying to initiate a reign of terror on the island. This arose from the union of two societies, 'The Friends of the Constitution', with the more radical 'The Reunion of Sans-culottes'.[75] The club's most daring endeavour was to charter a sloop from Mauritius and to convey about a hundred men to the neighbouring island of Bourbon, which had over time been a rival centre of European colonialism to Mauritius. The aim was to arrest Bourbon's governing authorities. The accusation was that they had corresponded with the British. The club's agents brought back to Mauritius several prisoners, including the governor of Bourbon, the Civil Commissary, the former minister of foreign affairs of Louis XVI and the former Commandant of the Marine.[76]

When these officials of Bourbon reached Mauritius the president of the Jacobin club announced: 'the people accuse you, and the people will judge you.' Grant notes: 'They were then conducted to the dungeon, where they were fettered, and they remained there about six months.' A guillotine was also constructed by these Port Louis Jacobins. Bearing out Mauritius' role as a centre to be imitated, a Jacobin club was also set up in Bourbon. The 'Popular society of Sans-culottes' of Bourbon introduced themselves to their compatriots in Mauritius as:

> brothers and friends hoping to maintain a fraternal correspondence of which the end is and will be to thwart the plots of enemies of the French Republic, to correct abuses; restore peace, unity, and public tranquillity.[77]

This connection between Mauritius and Bourbon in turn points to the revolutionary links across the Southwest Indian Ocean. Neighbouring colonies could have an impact on each other.

Returning to Mauritius itself and bearing out internal divisions, a row erupted about the relative judicial purviews of the Colonial Assembly and the Jacobin club, the *Chaumière*. Eventually the more powerful and well-supported Assembly managed to have thirty Jacobins arrested and the guillotine and the *Chaumière* disbanded. Counter-revolutionaries were released from captivity in 1795.[78] It was the arrival of news of the abolition of slavery that turned the tables in the Assembly's favour blunting the revolution. The spectre of the Haitian revolt was very much in mind. On an island in which 55,000 of the 70,000-strong population were enslaved it was natural to ask: would the slaves of Île de France also rise in revolt?[79] Such a question and the fears it generated subdued revolutionary feeling.

In the midst of these events, a smallpox epidemic gripped the island starting from 1792. This dampened revolutionary feeling, as did a famine on the island.[80] Yet, other uprisings followed, requiring the National Guard to violently oppose French soldiers on the island, forcing them to depart. There was also a showdown in 1799 between creditors and debtors, when laws concerned with settlements of debt in France were to be applied on the island.[81] In the end, revolution and dissent were abruptly ended with the arrival of Napoleon Bonaparte's governor General Decaen in 1803, and the disbanding of all the island's republican institutions and ideas.

Until this moment, however, Mauritius successfully served as a centre of revolt in the Indian Ocean. Revolutionary ends – though circumscribed by race, class and many sorts of self-interest – took off in pronounced fashion on the island and were followed in a radical spirit of local independence, even more accentuated than in Southern Africa. It was as if the inhabitants of this island saw themselves as a world unto themselves.

As one later abolitionist commentator, John Jeremie, put it: 'Mauritius from its isolated position, has always cherished false ideas of importance and independence; and its inhabitants succeeded . . . in setting at defiance the whole power of France.'[82] The small island asserted its right to make its own decisions. Indeed, in 1795 in the midst of the discord over slavery, Mauritius was effectively an independent nation. In adopting revolution and in working it out conservatively, it had to distance itself from France.

In April of that year, Paris decreed that it did not recognise the Colonial Assembly of Île de France and that it would be reformed by French agents who would be sent there. French ships arriving in Mauritius were initially classed as enemy vessels, with the use of an elaborate system of signalling to sound the alarm when a ship approached.[83] The island's independence from France was also evident in how it refused to house any of the seventy extremists involved in the Terror who were deported to the Indian Ocean, and who eventually landed in the Seychelles.[84]

This strain of revolutionary independence prospered partly because of the economic conditions of Mauritius. Revolution provided an opportunity for privateering, slaving and raiding. Profits coming from maritime plunder were critical in supporting the expanding sugar plantations, which would become a staple of the landscape by the 1820s and which still cover the island. The consolidation of a sugar interest came directly as a result of the revolutionary tumult elsewhere, particularly in Haiti, which disturbed supply from established sugar-producing areas.[85] It is estimated that 500 ships were captured, plundered or destroyed by action arising from Mauritius, 'representing a value in excess of 5 million pounds sterling'.[86] The slave trade also continued in this period, just when abolition was gathering force. In these circumstances, the full force of revolution could be blunted by elites, who combined it with plunder and profiteering. Indeed, as one recent historian writes, the Colonial Assembly was composed of residents, rich merchants, lawyers and military officers; these were the classes who benefited most from this period.[87]

As clinching evidence for how Mauritius could stand as a beacon over more than ten years, immediately after the French Revolution, a striking series of delegations arrived in Île de France. A delegation of republicans from Graaff Reinet came to Mauritius in this period to ask for help with the British. Others came from other parts of the Indian Ocean world: from Tipu Sultan of Mysore who was at war with the British and who sought French assistance; and also a delegation from Pegu in Burma, which too was fearing the advances of the British.[88] If news from Europe had a radicalising impact, not only was it localised in the social, political and economic milieu of Mauritius; in turn news of what was being effected in Mauritius drew other peoples and movements to this island.

ACROSS THE FRENCH INDIAN OCEAN WORLD

In following one of these missions that arrived in Mauritius – that from Tipu Sultan of Mysore in southern India – it is possible to see how events in Mauritius converged and diverged from those on the further shores of the Indian Ocean. The fact that Tipu Sultan of Mysore wished to collaborate with Mauritian republicans bears out the interconnections between this settler uprising in Mauritius and a culture of resistance which was South Asian.

Fig. 3.6 Tipu Sultan of Mysore, 1792 by an unknown
Indian artist

Tipu's embassy arrived in Mauritius in 1798. It would not have arrived without the work of a French privateer, François Ripaud de Montaudevert. Ripaud had lived on Mauritius and married a woman who was the daughter of Bourbon settlers. Tipu Sultan had already been to war with the British three times and his kingdom had been curtailed by about half by these conflicts. It was no wonder that his hopes were raised rather spectacularly by Ripaud's arrival in 1797 in Mangalore on the coast of India, after he 'nearly foundered at Sea'.[89] When he was arrested, Ripaud disingenuously announced that he came as a representative of the governors of Île de France and Bourbon. Ripaud offered 10,000 men to fight for Tipu from these islands. Without taking account of the scepticism of his ministers about Ripaud, Tipu appointed Muhammad Ibrahim and Hussain Ali Khan, to form an embassy to Mauritius.

Tipu's trust of Ripaud was matched by great suspicion of the British. He asked his ambassadors to dress as merchants and false passports were arranged. He insisted that the mission should be conducted in complete secrecy.[90] Tipu adopted an active policy of sending embassies far and wide in this period, attempting to connect his kingdom to others on the world stage, as an equal player. He aimed to consolidate a kingly ideal which was typical of South India in this period, where tributary relations could incorporate friends and inferiors as members of his court. These embassies also had the agenda of trade. He hoped to found 'factories' as bases for commerce.[91] Embassies were sent to or touched at among other places: Paris, Constantinople, Muscat, Kabul, Bushire, Basra, Baghdad, Tehran, Shiraz, Bandar Abbas, Cairo, Mecca, Medina, Bourbon, Pegu and Cape Town. An earlier embassy to Paris in 1787 had also stopped for a prolonged period for repairs at Île de France.[92]

The 1798 embassy to Mauritius left under Ripaud's direct oversight and authority. This was not a liberal cosmopolitan voyage but an authoritarian one.[93] The ambassadors allegedly complained to Tipu:

> Refuge of the World, health! He [Ripaud] assigned for our accommodation the part of the vessel appropriated to the Lascars, without any place for us to sleep or sit down.

Ripaud did not provide these emissaries with any more water than was usually given to Indian mariners. The scarcity of water meant that they could not cook their own food, a signifier of cultural violation. The complaint about water has within it two different orders of cultural and racial hierarchy. While the ambassadors see themselves to be superior to petty labourers, Ripaud sees the South Asian emissaries to be beneath his status. This nugget points to the social limits that both parties had set to the revolutionary potential of the age.

Eventually, Ripaud assigned the ambassadors a special 'doney' or small boat in which to sleep and eat, which presumably kept pace with the main ship. Ripaud did not recognise another basic right. The ambassadors sought to establish their own channels of communication across the ocean. On the ship were cases of tissue or silk into which special letters addressed to important nobles or persons of rank were inserted. Tipu's letters to the governing authorities of Mauritius were placed here. Ripaud took these despatches and sought to tear them open. It was only when the ambassadors reminded Ripaud about the dignity of France that he relented and restored these letters to them.

The provisions provided for this embassy were carefully recorded and lists are still extant in the archives in Mauritius. The provisions included: kid or goat, poultry, clarified butter, beans, aubergine, bananas, pineapple, calabash, pepper, saffron, salt and chilli pepper, mangoes, peaches, cabbage, onions, garlic, flowers, bread, wine for the interpreter and packages of betel.[94]

When it arrived in Mauritius, the offer made by Tipu's embassy was bold. Tipu would eliminate every single British soldier in India, and in return he would supply any Frenchman who would fight for him with provisions, with the notable exception of wine, which he could not provide as a Muslim prince. He also promised horses, camels and bullocks and porters and palanquins for the wounded.[95] There were discussions about the possibility of setting up 'a factory' on the island to 'buy and sell', so that the produce and products of Mysore could be sold in Mauritius in exchange for a supply of military articles. The embassy also asked to be accompanied on their journey home by people skilled in navigation and ship-building.[96] As negotiations got under way, the crafty Ripaud slipped away. Yet Tipu's political ambitions had been realised. For he saw his fate and that of Mauritius to be intertwined. Accordingly, the ambassadors instructed Île de France:

> Turn your thoughts only to the protection of your island, for our king will keep the English so employed and embarrassed, that they will be unable to turn their attention towards you. Further Zemaun Shah, king of the Afghauns and the greater part of the Indian powers, are united with our king for this purpose, and will not cease until they shall have driven the English out of India.[97]

General Malartic of Mauritius was in the embarrassing situation of feeling rather weak in the midst of such an advance. He had no forces to offer, given that the number of soldiers in Mauritius had been depleted. Soldiers had also been sent from Mauritius to help the Dutch regime of Batavia. All he could do was to publish a proclamation:

> We invite citizens who may be disposed to enter as volunteers to enrol themselves in their respective municipalities and to serve under the banners of Tippu. This prince also desires to be assisted by free citizens of colour. We therefore invite all such who are willing to serve under his flag to enrol themselves.[98]

A vessel was also despatched to Bourbon to seek recruits there. Around eighty men responded to this advertisement and distinctions were drawn among them according to whether they were 'white or 'coloured'.[99] Tipu received them well but was rather surprised at their meagre number. The passage of these troops followed a prior history of troops from Mauritius arriving in India. Significant numbers of predominantly creole or mixed troops from Mauritius were used by the French to fight the British in India between 1781 and 1783; French forces meanwhile had also supplemented the troops who fought the British under Tipu's father Haidar.[100]

Tipu's connections to Île de France were monitored by the British at the Cape and St Helena.[101] Malartic's proclamation arrived at Cape Town and was reprinted in British Calcutta later that same year, which defeated Tipu in his desire to disguise his plot.[102] It was a public testament to the embassy. This news provided further grist to the British attempt to oust Tipu, who saw the arrival of French forces as 'an act of war'.[103] British troops were soon afterwards assembled in Madras to go to war with Tipu. Some fruitless correspondence did not change the political stand-off. As early as 1799 Tipu was killed by invading British forces.[104]

The alleged evidence of Tipu's revolutionary sentiments was successfully employed as symbolic capital by the British. They demonised Tipu as an oriental despot; this was a counter-revolutionary ploy to undermine a confident indigenous ruler. For this reason, one has to tread very carefully in interpreting the sources connected to Tipu's alleged republican sympathies. Prior to the 1798 embassy to Mauritius, a club was supposedly inaugurated in Seringapatam [Srirangapatna], Tipu's capital, under the presidency of Ripaud, who styled himself as a 'Lieutenant in the navy of the French Republic'. According to the controversial papers of this club, Tipu took the contradictory title of 'Citizen Prince'.[105] Historians rightly dispute the labelling of this club as 'Jacobin', pointing out that this was a British wartime characterisation of this society. Its papers may have been fabricated.[106]

Such an interpretation is persuasive but should be seen in the context of the wider Indian Ocean. The club operated within the force field of Mauritius' relations to India and Mauritius' own republican assemblies. Indeed, the club's papers sit together with a whole range of other documents connected to exchanges between Mauritius and India. The club bears out the local flavour of the political possibilities of the age of revolutions and also the potential of exchanges across the Indian Ocean. It is necessary to separate these events in French India, Mauritius and the Cape from Europe. They need to be assessed on their own terms. indigenous agency needs to be prioritised over categories of universal assessment and comparison like 'Jacobin'.

Certainly, the club only met a few times, and after Mass on Sundays, making it a fleeting and ritual institution.[107] Tipu's own role within it is uncertain: the society seems more like Ripaud's publicity stunt. Ripaud called members to 'swear hatred to all Kings, except Tippoo Sultaun, the Victorious, the Ally of the French Republic'.[108] When the national flag was unfurled Tipu was said to be present and a parade progressed through the city, to be greeted by cannon fire. Could this ceremony have been interpreted as a *durbar*, a ritual festival to view the king and to order his subjects? Tipu allegedly announced:

> By this public acknowledgement of your national standard, I give you a proof of my affection for it. I declare myself its Ally and promise you that it shall be as firmly supported throughout my dominions as ever in those of the Republic, my Sister. Go and conclude your festival![109]

In addressing the club which consisted at first of fifty-nine members, Ripaud educated them on the rights of man and constitutional ideas. The club's members also put in place a set of laws based on those promulgated in France in the Reign of Terror. These governed the conduct of citizens who were members of this association.[110] These early definitions of citizenship in South Asia were intimately related to violence. Every citizen swore by oath to defend the French nation and to 'die at arms at [their posts], in the defence of the sacred right of a citizen to live free or perish!'.[111] All those who gave themselves up to the enemy, the British, or who even displayed some weakness in the fight, were to be put to death. The preponderance of soldiers in the club indicates how republican ideas could be useful for disciplinary authority in Seringapatam. For his part Tipu had embarked on a campaign of reforming his army, making it the most powerful in India. Republican laws may have been a useful tool in binding fighting forces to this activist ruler.[112] The way the club was classed in exaggerated terms as 'Jacobin', by the war-mongering British, then parallels the military utility and symbolism of this association in Tipu's Mysore.

The punishment envisaged by the laws laid out by Ripaud was primarily concerned with the violation of brotherhood and the proper relations between so-called superiors and inferiors. Though no mention of slavery appeared in the club's papers, the undue use of violence against enslaved people was cautiously restrained: '[e]very superior who shall threaten to strike his inferior, even though he should not execute his threat, shall be cashiered, and deprived of the rights of a citizen for one year.'[113]

Tipu conceived of his state as *Sarakar-i-Khudadi*, or God-given government. He allegedly proposed a family relationship of alliance with Île de France and Bourbon which is consistent with the way South Indian kings sought to incorporate people into their realms: 'you and your Nation' and 'myself and my people may become one Family; that the same oath may bind us for life and for death'.[114] This is in keeping with how Tipu assigned a high degree of sovereignty to himself. He declared that he was *padshah*, which was the title used by the Mughal emperor.[115]

Unlike in Mauritius where there had been an attempt to make the colony an exact replica of France and even an independent state, such a programme could not work in South Asia, given the existent political and princely culture of the subcontinent. Yet there were five French colonial outposts elsewhere in India, which sought to emulate Mauritius rather more wholesale. The pattern becomes even more complex when these sites are brought into the picture.

In Chandernagore and Pondichéry, on the opposite coast to Mysore, paler copies of the sequence of events in Mauritius unfolded. In Chandernagore the governor's house was stormed, in what one historian calls a re-enactment of the storming of the Bastille, soon after the arrival of news of the French Revolution. Its public divided into royalists and rebels. As in Île de France, these revolutionaries were able to depose the conservative French governor, replacing him with a republican assembly.[116] In Pondichéry to the south, events were more sombre. Revolution took shape as a local assembly was brought together with a permanent committee and with representatives selected to be sent to Paris.[117] The permanent committee sought to curb the powers of the French governor. For six governors had taken office in the period from 1785 to 1790. These governors had undertaken a series of unpopular reforms with a view to making the administration more financially efficient, and this served as a context for the committee's work.[118] The committee also took issue with the colony's relegation to an inferior status under Mauritius.

In objecting to its inferior status, Pondichéry, divided between its white and non-white quarters, which respectively constituted the coast and the interior, sought to take the lead in the French settlements in India. It now saw itself as the centre of the French empire in the East. In 1791, it formed a Colonial Assembly for French India, and sought to fill the twenty-one seats with representatives brought from other French territories. Given that fifteen of these twenty-one seats were to be reserved for its own representatives and only three for Chandernagore, it was no wonder then that Chandernagore did not recognise Pondichéry's lead. Chandernagore sought instead to constitute itself as a separate state with a direct relationship with France.[119]

Questions of who belongs and who does not, and who could be a revolutionary citizen and who could not, once again took on an urgency and particularity in these two French settlements, just as in Mauritius. In Pondichéry, local Tamils looked for membership of the assembly. The self-styled 'President of the Nation', who headed the assembly, denied them this right, patronisingly assuring them that the assembly would call on them for help when needed. This closing of the doors was especially potent and illiberal given that many Tamils had arrived in Pondichéry in the context of the wars fought between Tipu and the British and after experiencing looting.[120]

Yet if this was a clear-cut issue for the authorities a more vexed one was the question of the *topas* community of this settlement, who were equivalent to the free people of colour who had campaigned without luck for entry into the assembly in Mauritius. The *topas* represented the earlier colonial presence of Portugal in the subcontinent. They had Portuguese names, and some had French descent. French men often married *topas* women, given the small numbers of white women in Pondichéry. After being admitted at first into the assembly, the *topas* community was thrown out six months later. In protest they wrote:

> The *topas* believe that the National Assembly [in Paris] . . . has already promulgated a decree giving the rights of active citizenship to any free colored man born and having his home in the French colonies of América. Nevertheless it is certain that this principle has not been decided definitely in regard to the *gens de couleur* of the islands [a reference to Mauritius and the Caribbean] . . .[121]

In looking across the oceans like this, the *topas* then made their plea for rights as citizens, through an act of comparison. By 1792 they were allowed back in. This back and forth shows how tortured was the working out of rights in the age of revolutions in the Indian Ocean. Its participants were being defined in different ways in different localities, even as these widely dispersed communities had a sense of each other's plights.

The French Indian Ocean world was as varied in texture as Dutch Southern Africa. Even if Mauritius drew delegations to itself, South Asian states could never become politically equivalent to this island. Nor could republicanism or Jacobinism travel unaltered. Instead, in Mysore, these revolutionary times and connections were used to support a particular kind of authoritarian, incorporative and militaristic politics in the princely reign of Tipu Sultan. Meanwhile the settlements of French India, despite copying Mauritius, sought too to own the revolutionary moment and to become centres themselves. If patterns of contact and exchange linked Mauritius to South Asia, nevertheless in each locale the copy-and-paste dynamic hid local social and ideological differences. Decisions of who belonged within republican assembles could shift with time. This then is a forgotten geography of protest, assistance and revolution.

THE COMING OF THE BRITISH

Yet both these overlapping and distinct worlds of land- and sea-based revolt tied to Dutch and French imperialism in turn were to receive a rude shock as the nineteenth century began and its first ten years took their toll. Within this space of time, the British intruded into these territories, affected by revolt and republicanism. Worlds that were over-lapping and yet particular and localised gave way rather slowly.

What follows now spans the sites that we have travelled across, looking back to the first arrival of British forces at the Cape in 1795, and forwards to the fall of Île de France in 1810. The arrival of British colonialism was of course a maritime event, and the fall of Dutch and French bases in the Indian Ocean to the British drew from support and supplies on further shores and fears of rival imperial expansions across the Indian Ocean. Meanwhile, the arrival of the British saw a change not simply of politics and governance, but also of ideology, trade and culture, an installation of a monarch, an emphasis on free trade and the policing of possible Jacobin troublemakers. All this was counter-revolutionary.

When William V, the Prince of Orange, was exiled to Britain, after the victory of the Dutch patriots with French assistance, he issued a letter from his residence at Kew in London. He called the governor of the Cape of Good Hope to receive into 'Table and False Bays and other Harbours and Places where Ships can remain with Safety' the forces of 'His said Brit. Majesty' and to consider them to be friendly forces in alliances with Holland who came to the Cape of Good Hope in order to prevent the colony from invasion by France.[122] The British had long sought for the Cape and had been unsuccessful in an earlier bid, when an expedition sent to take it in 1781 was thwarted by a French fleet under Pierre André de Suffren. De Suffren had been sent to reinforce France's bases across the Indian Ocean and to defend Dutch territories which were in danger of falling to the English.[123] After the Cape, de Suffren called at Île de France and fought naval battles against the British in Indian waters. Now in 1795, a further British fleet was sent out without further delay to take the Cape. The eagerness of the British to establish a toehold is apparent in how a party comprising a battalion of five hundred men under Commodore John Blankett and Major General James Craig went before the six warships under the command of Admiral Keith Elphinstone.[124] This eagerness arose from a fear that the French would take the Cape from their bases in Île de France and Bourbon.[125]

When in receipt of the Prince of Orange's letter from Kew, the acting governor of the Cape, Commissioner A. J. Sluysken was left in a quan-dary. How should he interpret this extraordinary advice? Was he to trust the British fleet? Was there a Franco-Dutch counter-fleet on its way to the Cape as in 1781? His own troops were a ragtag lot, comprising many different European nationalities, and he would need to call in the many groups who were mounting resistance to the *ancien régime* in the Cape Colony, including the Khoikhoi and the *trekboers*. The correspondence between the British forces moored outside Cape Town was characterised by a monarchic flourish. The commanders of the British forces envisioned republicanism as giving way in the end to monarchism, even in the Netherlands, once the Batavian Republic fell away:

> His Britannick Majesty considers the Republick of Holland under its ancient & legal constitution, as His Friends & Allies; and although it has pleased Providence in its wisdom to permit the Country to fall under the dominion of a foreign power, yet His Majesty is so far from considering the re-establishment of that constitution as impossible, that he looks forward with confidence to the blessing of that same Providence on the justice of His arms for the success of His efforts to bring about so desirable an event, and in the mean time it is His Majesty's wish to preserve for the Republick His friend & ally under its ancient Constitution as much of the Possessions belonging to it as can be saved from the ambitious grasp of the common Enemy.[126]

It was almost as if Britain would imagine a world without revolution and treat the Cape in accord with the status quo prior to the revolutionary events of Europe. Ancient constitutions and polities would be imagined as staying in place, bound by Providence and friendship. Elphinstone and Craig, the authors of this letter, compared the future French and British regimes which could conceivably come into being. One would be characterised by the 'too captivating idea of universal freedom and the rights of man among your Slaves', giving rise to a 'total want of money . . . the failure of your markets and the entire annihilation of the little commerce' and the other would generate 'protection, peace and an extended commerce', 'the continuance of your Laws, Customs & Usages' and much 'domestick happiness'.[127]

Sluysken however did not give in to this rhetorical fare. His mind was made up when he received a newspaper smuggled off an American ship, reporting that the States General, the governing body of the Netherlands, had ruled that allegiance to the House of Orange was no longer necessary.[128] The British request that the colony be ceded was denied. Despite this opposition, British troops marched into the town with some ease.

Dutch officials and *boers* alike were called to swear allegiance to King George. A monarch was symbolically installed where so many rebellious, liberal and republican strains had flourished in the years prior to this. Very quickly, the prospect of a free trade between India and the Cape opened up as a point of discussion between merchants based in Cape Town and Bombay and Madras. A thousand barrels of gunpowder were transferred from India to South Africa in 1797 on the ships *Britannia* and *Isabelle*; five hundred further barrels were struck by lightning and blew up en route.[129]

The 1795 taking of Cape Town came from a complicated imperial game across the Indian Ocean. From 1780, the perceived decline of the Dutch East India Company combined with the start of the Fourth Anglo-Dutch War, which was sparked in part by the American Revolution and disagreements over how Holland conducted trade with Britain's rivals. In this context British aggression directed towards the Cape went up a gear. The British also sought in these years to found a penal colony in Southern Africa, before the founding of New South Wales as a convict settlement. A virulent cultural criticism of the style of the Dutch empire had also developed among British observers and politicians. This criticism shared with *boer* patriots an idea of the Dutch East India Company as corrupt and monopolistic.[130]

In planning the 1795 expedition, the British had in mind the stereotype of the 'most tyrannical and oppressive' Dutch company, which in turn had generated hungry people, who could only live off plunder and who were characterised by a disposition to revolt. 'I apprehend', Henry Baring wrote to Dundas, 'they are very much tinged with Jacobin principles.'[131] Meanwhile, the defeat of the British in North America and also the rise of the patriot party in the Netherlands made it possible for the French to dream of a consolidation of their empire in the East as their influence over the Netherlands was on the rise. In 1792, the French ambassador to the Hague described the tug of war for the Netherlands: 'in freeing Holland from the fetters of Great Britain, the commercial preponderance of the latter will speedily decline. France will regain in the East Indies everything that her rival will lose.'[132] Events in Europe and North America had combined in this way to open up a new set of geo-strategic possibilities for the British and French in the Indian Ocean.

These years also saw the culture of the Cape Colony swing between poles. After the French victory over the British fleet that sought to take

Cape Town in 1781, the settlement had become increasingly French.[133] The French language took off in the Cape of this period. Increasing trading alliances also built up between the Cape and Île de France and Bourbon. Yet in the period of the British occupation of the Cape, which followed from 1795 until 1803, the culture of Cape Town became a more policed one. Private letters seized by the British from Dutch vessels in this period of war demonstrate the emotional strain that their presence had on the Cape. These letters never made it to their addressees and lay deposited in the Admiralty archives. In these letters, the British were largely seen as occupiers rather than as liberators. The women of the Cape were chided for running away with the English, and English coffee houses were frowned upon. One correspondent from the Cape wrote: 'our terrible circumstances will already be known over there, what will the outcome be? To me everything is like an awful dream, and that's that!'[134]

In the Cape Town archives meanwhile lie volumes of reports on 'strangers' arriving at the Cape. These reports, written first in Dutch and then English, bear out a concern with the spread of Jacobinism into the colony, especially from people arriving at the Cape from Batavia. An oath of allegiance to the British monarch became a condition of migration. Regulations calling migrants to come with licences and 'passports' caused difficulties to arrivals who were fleeing political change in Europe, for example Dutch refugees fleeing disorder at home.[135] Resident 'native' burghers or European-descent settled citizens in the Cape District above the age of sixteen were called to register themselves with the town's Burgher Senate, which held municipal powers.[136]

The tension surrounding the taking of the Cape by the British was particularly evident in the letters of Andrew Barnard. In 1799, after the news of the defeat of the French fleet by Nelson in Egypt had arrived in the Cape, and George Macartney had departed from his position as governor at the Cape for ill health, he noted: 'Almost every night there is an alarm of fire . . . the day before yesterday a small faggot was found made of dry thatch all dipped in Pitch and tied up with oakum, the day before a long reed was found with some of the combustible materials at the end of it . . .'[137] The insurgent world of the Cape had as yet not been overtaken by the British, which would only come with the co-option of institutions such as the Burgher Senate. The takeover would also be interrupted by a short interlude where power was returned to the Dutch between 1803 and 1806, to be ruled in these years by Batavian patriots.

They sought to introduce a series of liberal reforms connected to schooling, as well as the founding of improving societies and Bible study as a yardstick for morality.[138]

Moving across the Indian Ocean, the shock of British advance was also felt in French India, and that shock was especially pronounced given the revolutionary feelings that preceded the advent of the new invaders. The French Revolution had generated a greater interest about India in France.[139] Yet on the eve of its taking by the British the residents of Pondichéry felt that they were in a 'state of weakness and abandon' given the 'very thin' military provisions of the settlement and the news which arrived on 3 June 1793, from Madras via Suez of the declaration of war between France and Britain.[140] There was a dream of assistance from Mauritius, as some residents believed that ships were anchored there waiting to come to Pondichéry's aid as soon as resources arrived from Paris. Yet in fact Île de France was more concerned about its own plight, asking whether there was any plan in India to attack the French base in the Southwest Indian Ocean. The Colonial Assembly in Pondichéry worked together with the governor, in forming a war council which met at Government House, and assembled a company of civilian soldiers, including a troop of *topas*.

Republican ceremonies were critical in forging the self-confidence of these beleaguered men. On 25 and 26 June 1793, 'constitutional flags' were delivered to the soldiers, followed by speeches. By August, a conflict between the British and Pondichéry had begun. This was a war not only of firepower but also for the hearts and minds of French settlers as the British sent in propaganda, described, in the narrative of a member of the war council, as 'bombs in small sizes'. Before taking Pondichéry the British despatched into the settlement an advertisement showing Louis XVI with the caption, 'I die innocent.' They also despatched a supplement of the *Madras Gazette* with news of Europe and how there would be a need to reinstate the monarchy.

Once it fell, revolution was soon transformed into its opposite: many of Pondichéry's self-proclaimed citizens went into mourning for Louis XVI. Others who could not become royalists left for Île de France.[141] In the words of an anonymous contemporary observer involved in the changing of the guard: the residents of Pondichéry 'removed their masks'; some soldiers asked for a church service as a memorial for Louis XVI and to celebrate the feast of St Louis. The service ended with cries of 'Long Live the King!', 'Long Live the English!'[142] Though Pondichéry was returned in 1816 to the French, and though it remained under French control until 1954, it never became more than a vestige of a bygone era. The French had to agree to British sovereignty in India in order to be granted Pondichéry back again in 1816.

If the mid 1790s saw one wave of advance, then another came in 1810–1, when Île de France and Bourbon fell to the British alongside Dutch Java, which was also an integral part of this Indian Ocean world of revolutionary conflict. The invasion of Java will come into view elsewhere in our travels. But to return to Île de France, the raiding of British vessels undertaken out of this island, that 'nest of pirates', had to be stopped, and the British were increasingly aware of the weak defences of these French isles.[143] Yet the challenge lay in how to take such isolated settlements in the Southwest Indian Ocean effectively. The island of Rodriguez was the solution: from 1808, the British used this base, about three hundred miles to the east of Mauritius, in order to launch a blockade against the French and to spy on French activity. Bourbon was the first to fall without much fuss into the widening net.

The taking of Île de France wasn't as easy. In the lead up to the first failed attack in August 1810, the British anxiously gathered information. A royalist pro-English French informer reported that Governor Decaen had been strategically reducing his troops, sending some to Java, in order to orchestrate an 'honourable capitulation'. Decaen was said to have sent the bulk of his own fortune to Europe. The informer also alleged that the services of French troops were being sold on to privateers in the immediate run-up to the British attack. The informer set out details on the coast and singled out the Isle de la Passe, off the south-east coast of Mauritius, as a good first point of attack.[144] Communications were also seized from a French vessel, including correspondence from Mauritius to Java.[145] An officer wrote to the future governor of British Mauritius, Farquhar:

> Let us now turn our eyes to the Isle of France, whilst we are laying idle here [in Bourbon], cooling the ardour inspired by successful achievement – looking calmly towards the glorious prize for which we must contend. Is not Decaen exerting all the energy – genius & abilities of a soldier to put it further from our grasp? . . . The occupation of Isle de la Passe which you directed with such promptitude on my suggestion, will materially affect him: it will effectually secure the Grand Port and interrupt his communication on that side of Mauritius.[146]

Despite this bluster, on this first occasion, the British were defeated on this very coastline in the south-east, in a major embarrassment to the navy, because of their lack of knowledge of the extensive coral reefs and sandbanks. Farquhar had been consulting charts and maps in the run-up to this battle: all to no avail.[147] In the panicky report of a captain of one ship involved in the battle, writing from Isle de la Passe: 'sad to say Sirius [the writer's ship] grounded on a small bank not known'. Of the grounded *Sirius*, which was later set on fire, the writer reported:

> I must now inform you that the very moment we took the ground every possible exertion was made to get the ship off by carrying out stream and kedge anchors but both anchors came home together. I then got a whole Brown cable and Anchor hauled out . . . we could not move her one inch from the nature of the Ground and the very heavy Squalls at that time.[148]

And of another ship *Nereide* which had been summarily fired at by the enemy and grounded: 'sorry I am to say that the Captain every officer and Man on board were killed or wounded.'

This French victory of August 1810 is still remembered and actively commemorated along this coast. In Mahébourg, overlooking Grand Port Bay, a simple late-nineteenth-century monument recalls the loss of both French and British lives in naval battle. It faces the crystal blue water and is surrounded of an evening by young couples in love gazing at the sea. At the town's museum the British defeat takes pride of place. When I visited in 2018, there was even a relatively large segment of a wrecked British ship on display, and also bolts, nails and other ship fittings recently rescued from a wrecked British vessel involved in the war. On the other side of the room was a celebration of French 'corsair' activity, including a handsome portrait of the 'king of corsairs' who was dreaded by the British, Robert Surcouf (1773–1827). All this indicates Mauritius' continuing Francophile culture to the present. Yet, despite this first defeat for the British, a few months later, in December 1810 – with military and naval help from the two sides of the Indian Ocean, from the Cape as well as India amounting to in excess of 10,000 men – they strangled these islands.

A series of panoramic images emphasise the orderly landing of the British troops in Mauritius.[149] [Figs. 3.7 and 3.8] One taken from the deck of one of the transport vessels shows radiating lines of small boats bound for the shore with disembarking troops.[150] On board the transport ship, vigorous discussions are in progress, presumably about supplying the troops. Another in the set of images presents an aerial view of Port Louis, with the British fleet in the harbour. It is a scene of picturesque quietude; no crowds or troops are in sight. Instead red flags fly in the wind on board the ships as well as on the defences of the town.[151] In responding to this assault, Île de France had desperately sought to muster enough men and had to turn even to British prisoners of war.[152] One officer involved in this successful attack hoped that the French would now be remembered by 'the memory of their defeats'. 'The name of the common enemy is now erased from the map of these countries; we have struck a death-blow to [France's] colonial system, and in the same act, supplied a vacant link in the great chain which binds the eastern to the western empire.'[153] A large hoard of arms and ammunition were seized in Mauritius by the British, including over 8,000 muskets of French and English manufacture.[154]

Just as in Pondichéry, the political culture of Île de France changed, or perhaps it is more fitting to say that royalism returned after a period of suppression as an acceptable political ideology.[155] The new British governor Robert Townsend Farquhar fraternised easily with the noble

Fig. 3.7 'Isle of France, No.1: View from the Deck of the
Upton Castle Transport, of the British Army Landing', 1813

Fig. 3.8 'Isle of France, No.5: The Town, Harbour, and Country, Eastward of Port Louis', 1813

families of Mauritius straight after his arrival, organising balls and other social events. Freemasonry also linked the governor to his elite; indeed freemasonry also had an important life in the early British Cape as a bond between the British colonial elite and their Dutch predecessors. Exiled royalists from France found Mauritius a congenial home in the years after 1810. Farquhar's popularity with the island's elite stemmed from his embrace of free trade, which was to the taste of the merchant families, and his controversial acceptance of slavery, despite British abolitionism. A proclamation of December 1810 emphasised a commercial vision of amity, and included this clause:

> The English have come to establish a firm and perpetual friendship with the inhabitants of Isle de France, who will be able to sell their produce in excellent conditions and will enjoy all the advantages of Commerce as all the other subjects of His Britannic Majesty.[156]

THE PATH FROM REVOLUTION TO
COUNTER-REVOLUTIONARY EMPIRE

There were myriad different kinds of revolt in this era, even in one place or locality. The Cape Colony saw revolts of the enslaved, *boers* and indigenous people and each of these was enmeshed with the other. Local dynamics were evident in how Mauritius responded to the news and sought to assert its independence and place as a model and centre for the rest of the Indian Ocean. The wide range of revolts also denotes the different economic, religious, and social bases for protest. Whereas the Cape Colony spilled over into the interior of Africa, and in turn drew to itself many different indigenous peoples as well as the enslaved, Mauritius was a tightly bound launch pad from which revolutionary principles spread across the Indian Ocean. There were many different peoples on Mauritius but nobody who claimed to be indigenous. In French India and the French isles, there were intense debates about relations with each other and the mother country, now in revolt. The situation in Dutch Southern Africa was affected by the less certain revolutionary results in the Netherlands and the ambiguous status of the Dutch East India Company.

Despite all these differences, right across the Dutch and French worlds of the Indian Ocean, there were attempts to remodel politics and redefine belonging, assembly and citizenship in a time of militarism and punishment for treachery or conservatism. The differences could be forgotten in the forming of unusual alliances, for instance between Tipu Sultan of Mysore and the republicans of Mauritius. Kingdoms or communities of indigenous peoples and settlers could be defined as nations or states able to exert their own diplomatic power in the age of revolutions. At the same time, local circumstances dictated access to the rights of citizenship for mixed communities, freed slaves or Asians and Africans. There was a marked conservative pull that excluded indigenous peoples and people of colour from this age of revolutions, despite the charismatic story of someone like Jan Paerl.

As the 1789 French Revolution passed into memory, Napoleon entered Egypt in 1798 and the Napoleonic Wars took off from 1803. Now revolution was increasingly turned into its opposite. A counter-revolutionary imperialism arrived in the Indian Ocean, propelled by fear of the French and stereotyping of the Dutch, or the creation of Tipu Sultan of Mysore as an oriental despot. It sought to install monarchy, free trade and bureaucratic monitoring of radicals. The local assemblies and clubs that sought to reshape revolt were interrupted and dismantled by the rise of a singular power, the British, in what had been a textured imperial landscape including the French and the Dutch.

Both the spread of revolutionary politics and the arrival of British imperialism took place over water: drawing in supplies, news, strategy and manpower, and cultural and ideological baggage from other places. What this meant in practice is that dreams of worlds to be changed rested on connections across this great sea: from Batavia to Graaf Reinet, or from Pondichéry to Île de France or from British India and the Cape to Rodriguez. The sea was certainly a conduit of the revolutionary and imperial age as was the ship. Yet what came across the sea took force as it was planted in particular places that faced the water. In this spirit, Europe was certainly not the only point of reference. The Atlantic entered this story too, through reference to Haiti, for instance, on the part of slave rebels; yet it too was not the only or the prime space which rebels and revolutionaries had in mind. There were patterns of connection and divergence across the waters of the South.

4

In the Persian Gulf:
Tangled Empires, States and Mariners

The Persian Gulf is one of the world's most closeted stretches of sea. It opens to the Indian Ocean through the narrow Strait of Hormuz and also the Gulf of Oman. The Gulf should occupy a central place in the story of the transformations of the revolutionary age as also the narrative of the steady but uneven rise of Britain.[1] It has largely been forgotten in this wider literature.

The emergence of new political formations at the outer frontiers of the long-standing Ottoman empire and fallen Safavid empire in Eurasia, and the competitive pattern of engagement with this region between the British and French is vital to the Persian Gulf's age of revolutions. Ideas and concepts such as state, independence, rational religion, piracy and free trade were used here, in keeping with the time, and generated calls for violent imperial action. Fundamentally, however, the Gulf's age of revolutions is about the initiative of people of a diversity of cultural heritages who found their path in the midst of a world that was changing rapidly. The British adopted and turned to their own advantage the flux of this period, mounting a counter-revolutionary imperial manoeuvre. This counter-revolution worked through paperwork as much as invasive warfare.

The story begins with a dramatic incident of saving the mail in the Persian Gulf in 1804. Bushire [Bushehr], now in south-west Iran and on the Gulf coast, was critical to one of the routes for transferring mail to and from India. The route linking Basra to Constantinople [Istanbul] saw the London-bound mail deposited at Bushire by sea from India.[2] This colonial obsession with guarding the mail against all comers, perfectly demonstrates the dizzying agents and political forces which contended for control of passage across these waters before the British military expeditions to the Gulf in 1809 and 1819–20.

THE DRAMATIC BRITISH QUEST TO SAVE THE MAIL

François-Thomas Le Même (1764–1805) was born in St Malo. He was taken prisoner by the English in 1778–9 during the American Revolution, when he was a volunteer on a French merchant ship. He was later employed by the French navy until 1783. It was he who first jeopardised the transit of the mail through Bushire in October 1804.[3]

Le Même had based himself in Mauritius, after arriving there in 1791, and he used it as launch pad for his privateering from 1793. In 1804, he took captive a quick succession of British vessels in the Persian Gulf, including the *Fly* where a Mr Flower was a passenger. The *Fly* was taken off a small island called Qais, ten miles off today's Iran. He also captured the *Nancy*, commanded by a Captain Youl, taken at Muscat; and the *Shrewsbury*, commanded by R. W. Loane, taken in the Bushire roads. Incredibly, he returned to Mauritius with a fleet of eight captured English vessels, in keeping with how Mauritius was a base for privateering and piracy.

However, the British were able to score what appeared a moral victory. When the *Fly* ran aground before being taken by Le Même, the ship's captain instructed his men that the English India Company's packet of correspondence, together with its treasure, should be thrown into the sea before the French got their hands on them. This was the starting salvo in a battle which typified the period, a grand contest to reclaim the British mail lost to the enemy.

Surely a packet of letters in the water was almost as bad as a packet lost to the French? Not so. If Le Même represents the French aim of intervening in the comings and goings of the Persian Gulf, Flower, Youl and Loane tell another story. These three seafaring men joined forces to rescue the mail. Mr Flower had taken accurate bearings off the island of Qais when the lost packet was put to sea. So the three men purchased an Arab vessel at Bushire, a large *dhow*, called a *baghla* (literally 'mule' in Arabic). A *baghla* was among the largest Arab ocean-going vessels and displayed some traces of European design. After 'creeping for the packet' for three days, Loane wrote that they were 'fortunate' to procure it.[4] This successful search for the packet of letters followed Loane's prior safe despatch of the treasure on board the *Shrewsbury* to Bushire. Here then was a man who had come to prize his abilities to defend imperial and naval Britain from the French.[5]

In yet another turn, on 1 November 1804, just after the rescue of the lost packet from the *Fly*, the *baghla* was met by 'two large Dows' (common sailing vessels in the Indian Ocean, sometimes regarded as 'Arab'), which altered their course and bore down on it.[6] These *dhows* were said to be part of the Qasimi fleet, arising from Qawasim, a set of maritime political units or shaikhdoms which were on the Arabian coast. Today's rulers of the emirate states of Ras al-Khaimah and Sharjah are of Qasimi descent.[7] According to Loane, his crew 'set every stitch of canvas' to escape and then 'hoisted an English ensign' to indicate submission. Yet sixty Qasimi raiders leapt aboard. Loane complained of their assailants' incivility. In contrast with Le Même, who had displayed 'handsome behaviour' in dropping Loane off at Bushire, these 'barbarians', he noted, in racialised language, were 'ignorant of the laws of nations, and insensible to those of humanity' in enacting such unnecessary violence. As will become clear, this reveals more of Loane's ignorance about Qasimi codes of conduct and political organisation than the ignorance of his assailants. According to *the Mariner's Chronicle*, these attackers began 'cutting and stabbing all whom they met, [and] forced the whole crew overboard'. In his telling, Loane and the rest of crew were stripped naked and thrown into the hold.

Eventually the Qasimi raiders decided to sell their captives as slaves at Ajman, now the capital of the emirate state of the same name. In anticipation of the sale, these captives were housed in a mud hut and left to fend for themselves, only being supplied with dates and brackish water. Pearls were the chief item of trade in Ajman and the shore around it was covered in shells. Some women supplied the captives with fish, vegetables and rice; and the men had to scavenge, finding shellfish to sustain themselves. James Silk Buckingham, the liberal critic and campaigner for reform of the East India Company and traveller in this region, wrote that '[t]he Joassamee [Qasimi] ladies were so minute in their enquiries, indeed that they were not satisfied without determining in what respect an uncircumcised infidel differed from a true believer.'[8]

Given the extent of curiosity raised by their presence, the band of sixteen started to charge for a view of their persons. Loane saw the irony here, as people of colour from around the world were being displayed in London in this period for the entertainment of the British. He took the view that a similar eagerness for novelty surely existed everywhere. The comparison with London's shows certainly humiliated him, but he remembered the adage that necessity has no law.[9] Strategising as best he could, he also pretended to be a medical man, in order to get access to Shaikh Abdullah of Ajman, where he helped the Shaikh with a sight impairment: 'I persuaded the Sheikh to suffer me to cut an issue in his arm, thinking it would lead off all the gross humours which then affected his eyes.' Three weeks later, this Shaikh announced that visiting merchants would buy the captives: soon the cook was bought for thirty dollars and the South Asian carpenter, described by Loane as a 'Hindu', disappeared.

The intervention of a Wahhabi chief on his way to 'join the army of his confederates', who was acquainted with Samuel Manstey, the British Resident at Basra, changed the fate of the captives. He asked for the captives' release, making note in particular of the power of the British to chastise any who dared insult their flag, and speaking of his 'high opinion and friendship for the English nation'. As will become clear, this statement of friendship was a contradiction, given the events to unfold in the Persian Gulf in the years that followed, when Wahhabi action and militancy alarmed the British. In response, Abdullah took the captives with him while going on a 'cruize, to recommence his depredations', and released them on Qais island, advising them that they would be able to get a boat to Bushire from there.

Much of the next ten days was spent hiding on Qais, watching a torrent of violence around them. A Qasimi fleet attacked Qais. Qais' inhabitants fled to the mainland, leaving its main settlement to be set on fire by the invaders. Meanwhile, the men with Loane struggled with thirst and hunger and eventually satisfied their needs when they came across some goats grazing near abandoned houses. Loane wrote of how he 'occupied' the teat of the first that was captured and that it yielded 'the most pleasing beverage I ever tasted in the course of my existence'.[10] The men eventually became the sole residents of the island and dressed their 'lower extremities' in goat skin. After building a raft from timber which had been burnt in the sacking of Qais, and getting a lift from a boat which called at Qais, the group made their way to Kalat, on the Persian mainland.

The next challenge was to make a long journey overland to the west: they eventually reached Bushire in January 1805. Before reaching Bushire, a fever and ague struck and some of the crew died on the very last stages of the journey, and even in Bushire, including Flower and Youl.[11] On the way, one *lascar* named Christian Seacunny ('seacunny' indicated a steersman and this man was evidently a Christian), died while passing through a valley between Kalat and Chiru.

The party had been 'crawling from rock to rock, whilst continual cries and howlings of the jackals and other animals' were heard.[12] These were the years which saw the uncertain rise of Britain. In a fitting gesture for the time, in response to the jackals in the valley, the group began to sing 'Rule Britannia'. It was a tune which Loane supposed was 'never heard before in these deserted and inhospitable regions'. From Chiru, a search party returned to the valley after the group's arrival there, to find 'a corpse, nearly half devoured by the jackals'. It was the body of Seacunny. The thought of a Muslim 'degrading' himself by touching a dead Christian, it was said, prevented the party bringing his body back to Chiru.

Yet despite the loss of life and the intervention of the French and the Qawasim, the packet was kept safe and eventually reached Bombay. In return for a sextant, Loane successfully persuaded Shaikh Abdullah to return the correspondence to him before their release from captivity. On Qais, two days were devoted to drying the letters on the beach, where they were turned over during the day but collected at night to be kept safe from a heavy dew.[13] When Qasimi raiding began on Qais, Loane and his companions hid the packet in a 'deep hole in the earth'. [14] On one occasion Loane came to blows with Muhammed Agi of Nakhilu, a subordinate of Shaikh Rahma, the ruler of Nakhilu. According to Loane's narrative, Muhammed Agi took the packet into his possession by duping some of the party:

> Exasperated at this unparalleled piece of insolence, and not being able to bear the idea of losing (at last) the object, for the preservation of which, we at first had thrown ourselves in misfortune's way, and had afterwards suffered so much to retain, I [Loane] felt every feeling and passion aroused into action, and careless of my existence, in the first emotions of my rage, rushed upon the deceitful scoundrel, and seized him by the collar, thoughtless at that moment of what might be the consequences of such rashness.[15]

After this altercation, Muhammed Agi returned it to the party. Buckingham approved of how 'these unfortunate sufferers' guarded the mail 'with an almost religious zeal'. He criticised the government for its illiberal response to the packet's receipt in Bombay, writing that they were only rewarded by a letter of thanks.[16] But perhaps a letter was a fitting gift for those so concerned with the preservation of correspondence. Though Buckingham did not note it, the government paid 4,000 rupees to the family of the deceased Flower and 2,500 rupees to Loane and also the same figure to the deceased Youl's representatives. It also compensated the families of the dead *lascars*.[17]

It is certainly the case that these sources embellish the events that unfolded. Yet the dramatic quest of 1804 to save the mail points to the dogged and aggressive determination that individual Britons deployed against the French and the Qasimi and other rival forces, as they mounted their slow triumph over the waters of the Persian Gulf. In the Gulf, the British had to find a pathway through a concatenation of politics and religious traditions. They sometimes succumbed to violent fisticuffs as did Loane and his companions, and they faced sickness too, in this unfamiliar geography of water and land. In this tussle, the British saw themselves as set apart by their devotion to civility, rationality and writing. Letters and packets were accordingly prized. Yet if stories like that of the saved packet point to the slow triumph of the British, it is important to add that it was not only the British who sought to conquer through writing, law and a code of conduct.

CODES OF REVOLUTION:
THE BRITISH AND THE WAHHABI THREAT

Local political elites navigated their course through this age of revolutions with as much skill as the British. Such a claim is in keeping with the broader argument about indigenous and non-European peoples' creativity in the Indian Ocean's age of revolutions.

This is borne out in Loane's description of the island of Busheab [now Lavan island, off the coast of today's Iran], which was under Shaikh Rahma, the superior of the man with whom Loane had come to blows. Rahma had amassed his wealth directly from the plunder of the *Hector*, which was on the way to Basra, in 1803, with a cargo of immense value, including 850 bales of Company cloth. Rahma refused to return the cargo to the British, despite the arrival of three vessels of the Bombay Marine in Nakhilu on the Persian coast. Only in 1806, when the Shaikh's son was taken hostage, was he more accommodating.[18] Rahma's military standing came also from British armaments. In this region, it was common to use armaments taken from Indian vessels for fortification.[19] In 1803, when the *Alert* was plundered, after it came ashore in the middle of a storm, Rahma used the ship's guns to erect a small battery, 'with a breastwork thrown up before it, as if determined to repel any attempt that might be made to compel him to restoration of his ill acquired wealth'.[20] Rahma held to different laws to those of the British, despite the fact that they labelled him a pirate: 'the right of every country to the property which might be shipwrecked on its coasts'.[21] Perhaps it was in fear of British attacks that Rahma dealt with Loane and his companions favourably. He arranged in the end for their arrival in Bushire at the end of their long journey.

Just as much as armaments and property passed between sides, showing a shared history, the story of the packet should not indicate an easy differentiation of the British from their unlearned piratical opponents, who may popularly be characterised as uninterested in texts.[22] If the British were devoted to text, code and law, they were not alone in this. The intensification of maritime plunder in this period came as Wahhabi ideology took hold among the Qawasim, from 1800, and especially from 1808.

The Wahhabi movement emerged out of an alliance between a scion of a family of *qadis* or Muslim judges, Shaikh Muhammad bin Abd al-Wahhab, of Hanbali clerical lineage, and the rulers of Dir'iyyah, close to Riyadh in 1744–5. These rulers were of the Al Sa'ud family, now the royal house of today's Saudi Arabia. As a set of teachings the Wahabbi movement stressed the Unity of Allah, and criticised the sin of polytheism, the association of Allah with any other. Abd al-Wahhab preached *tawhid*, the importance of professing the oneness of God. Combining rigid dictates about prayer and fasting, the Wahhabi movement also sought to eliminate any kind of infidelity to a monotheistic doctrine, by tearing apart shrines of Muslim saints, outlawing minor pilgrimages and standing against the invocation of the names of angels, prophets or even the Prophet Muhammad. All this was labelled as *shirk* or polytheist. The Wahhabi movement pursued a course of *jihad* in Arabia in the late eighteenth and early nineteenth centuries, so allowing the alliance to be politically useful to the Al Sa'ud family, in creating a stronger state, the first Saudi state, which superseded tribal allegiances as well as alleged superstitions.

From 1795, the Wahhabi-Saudi state undertook raids against Ottoman

Iraq, sacking Karbala, the holy Shi'ite shrine. It made raids into Syria, Yemen and the Hijaz, taking over Mecca and Medina in 1803–4, the indisputable centres of the Islamic world. The arrival of Wahhabi ideology at Ras al-Khaimah, which headed the Qawasim states, is evident in the desecration of the tomb of a Sufi teacher of the ruler of Ras al-Khaimah. The ruler was Shaikh Rashid, who had to flee to Linga, on the opposite coast, in present-day Iran, being unable to come to terms with how his teacher's tomb was taken down stone by stone.[23] In the end, the response to the Wahhabis came from Egypt, when Muhammad Ali launched a sustained attack on the new Wahhabi-Saudi state, retaking Mecca and Medina. Abdullah bin Sa'ud, the Saudi ruler, was sent to Constantinople and executed.[24]

In the words of the historian C. A. Bayly: 'the Wahhabi revolt against intrusive Ottoman rule and the decline of proper religious observance in the cities of Saudi Arabia should be regarded as a variety of world revolution.'[25] And more recently, in the words of another historian: 'The Wahhābīs' exclusivist and absolutist outlook, ambition to impose one identity [which was Sunni] on those they ruled, prioritisation of religion over commerce, and destruction of free ports challenged the outward-looking hybrid communities of the Gulf.'[26]

The glorification of Wahhabi revolt, and the interpretation of it as revolutionary, emerged partly from the period's colonial writings. Indeed, in the early nineteenth century and in the context of the Napoleonic era, the Wahhabis could be cast as akin to the people of the Swiss cantons or the Dutch United Provinces set 'against crusading Catholic potentates'. In this rendition they could be glossed positively for how they stood up to Ottoman tyranny.[27] If this was a period when 'revolution' was an unstable term of reference, especially in the British perception of the concept, the Wahhabis were revolutionary. In addition, European commentators sought to make sense of the Wahhabis through analogy to the Christian past. These were the inspired 'Protestant' Muslims. To make the point, one of the earliest accounts of the Wahhabi movement among English observers comes from Harford Jones, the Resident of the East India Company in Baghdad in this period. Jones wrote of the Wahhabis as '[a] sect of *Puritan* Arabs', who if not stopped might 'be the occasion of considerable *revolutions* in this part of the Globe'.[28] He defined the tenets of the Wahhabis to include a 'literal' embrace of the Qu'ran:

That a Mohammedan, who deviates, in religious duties, in the smallest degree from the literal forms, injunctions and precepts of the Koran is as much a Cafer or Unbeliever or Christian as a Jew; and that, therefore, to make war against him is the positive duty of every Wahambee, or as they call themselves, all true Mussulmans.[29]

Yet beyond these European descriptions, within the Wahhabi movement itself was a commitment to revolution, quite outside any equivalent sense of it in the Christian past. In such a view, plundering the British or the Indians, or indeed Omanis, the last of whom were mostly of an Ibadi tradition marked out by *shura* (a distinctive emphasis on consultation), was sanctioned by law and by text. The legality of violence was determined by whether it was directed within or outside the community of adherents. For the purpose and definition of the Islamic community was to follow the strict law, and to expand the community by *jihad*. What was 'acceptable' maritime violence was subjective, for Arabic did not have a single equivalent word for 'pirate'; yet it is wrong to see such violence as sporadic and without a code of conduct.[30] Water-borne plundering was akin to raiding enacted against neighbouring tribes, and some part of the proceeds fed back into state-making enterprises.

In the encounter between the British and their opponents in the Gulf, it is tempting to assume that the British were set apart. To assume this would be to take at face value the heroism of Loane, which drips off the account he left of his adventures with the mail. Yet text, law and code of conduct, together with the contemporary usage of 'revolution' itself, cut across Europeans and non-Europeans, colonisers and indigenous peoples. Wahhabism could be compared – by British observers – with the Puritan past of the British or indeed with the Reformation. The Wahhabi movement itself was revolutionary in its own terms and this is in keeping with the surge of indigenous agency in the age of revolutions in the global South. For this was not a revolutionary sensibility that diffused out of Europe. The opposing sides were all trying to enact change in politics in similar fashion. Britain was just one political force among many.

It was the scale of British intrusions which would follow, the militarism, uncontrolled violence, treaty-making and wars that would not cease, which altered the political scene, creating a counter-revolutionary imperialism. The British empire overtook its opponents by employing

Fig. 4.1 'The Troops Landing at Rus ul Kyma [Ras al-Khymah] in
I. Clark, W. William Haines and R. Temple, 'Sixteen Views
of Places in the Persian Gulph' (1811)

the same techniques that they did. This empire cast its opponents as fundamentally distinct in civilisational and racial terms. Intervention on a grand scale followed the lone actions of people like Loane.

INVASIVE EXPEDITIONS TO THE GULF:
WAR THAT WILL NOT CEASE

From Bombay, in 1809–10 and 1819–20, the British launched two invasive operations against Ras al-Khaimah [or Ras al-Khyma], which sat at the apex of the Qasimi confederacy, in the present-day United Arab Emirates.[31] These military expeditions, which should be placed in the history of British invasions of the Gulf, were driven by fear of Qasimi piracy and the Wahhabi movement. Such fears coincided with the rise of British India's trade with the Gulf after 1790 and the expansion of the threat which the British labelled as piracy.

Concerns about French activity in the Gulf and Persia fed into the first operation. The second was post-Napoleonic. These were gunboat missions that aimed to secure sea lanes; such an aim was in keeping with Portuguese engagement with the Gulf which preceded that of the British. The Portuguese had established themselves at Hormuz and at other bases from the sixteenth century, well before the Dutch, English or French sought to intrude into the Gulf with a view to controlling strategic commercial passages.

Critical to the British expeditions of 1809–10 and 1819–20 was their desire to stand by their ally, Oman. A Wahhabi chronicler described the result of the 1809–10 expedition in metaphorical language: Ras al-Khaimah had been set alight by the great crystal which was wielded by Britain to focus the sun's rays on it.[32] Bearing out the significance of Britain's friendship with Oman, Sa'id bin Sultan of Muscat wrote to the governor of Bombay in 1809: 'I take God to witness that all my own resources are at your disposal and I trust in heaven that prosperity and success will ever attend the British Govt. that it may vanquish and subdue all its enemies.'[33]

Visual images of the 1809–10 expedition pay attention to how the British burnt the settlement, including merchandise, naval resources and buildings.[34] 'Sixteen Views of Places in the Persian Gulph' gives a visual narrative of the military expedition. It begins with the departure from Apollo Gate, Bombay, and includes an image of Ras al-Khaimah on the

Fig. 4.2 'The Storming of a Large Storehouse near Rus ul Kyma
[Ras al-Khymah]' in I. Clark et al., 'Sixteen Views'

Fig. 4.3 'Rus ul Kyma [Ras al-Khymah] from the S.W. and the
Situation of the Troops' in I. Clark et al. 'Sixteen Views'

horizon beyond choppy waters. A closer image shows troops preparing to land [Fig. 4.1], using smaller vessels to get to the beach. Then two prints follow of Ras al-Khaimah burning [Figs. 4.2 and 4.3]. While a British officer lies wounded in a sacrificial pose in the middle of one of the images, another shows local settlers desperately attempting to save their possessions. The visual rhetoric contrasts the manly devotion of the British military with the self-serving interests of the people of Ras al-Khaimah, who are barely clothed.

The official record reported a complete destruction of Ras al-Khaimah. Fifty vessels allegedly used for piracy, including thirty large *dhows*, were said to have been destroyed. Some captured property was passed on to Muscat.[35] Vessels were also destroyed elsewhere on the Arabian and Persian coasts. In the expedition's instructions, burning vessels with fire was specifically advised. It was the appropriate response to the alleged plunder of goods.[36]

Like all such interventions and despite the visual propaganda, the political results of this expedition were incomplete. In one account, the hold of the Wahhabis was accentuated as the political structures of Qawasim crumbled.[37] The ruler of Muscat noted that, unless another expedition was sent out, he might be overwhelmed by the Qawasim backed by the Wahhabis. In response the British opted to arm him with 'several articles of Guns, muskets and ammunition'.[38] Muscat's request for troops was eventually complied with about ten years later, when a further British expedition was sent off to Ras al-Khaimah in 1819–20.

Though diplomacy between the British and the Qawasim was pursued in the intervening years, including a short-lived truce of 1814, the loss of authority at Ras al-Khaimah meant in turn that its elites could not control the acts of maritime violence which occurred in the Gulf. One particularly embarrassing occasion in 1814 involved the capture of an official *baghla* belonging to the East India Company; this *baghla* was engaged in diplomacy with Ras al-Khaimah.[39] In 1819, Hasan bin Rahma of Ras al-Khaimah sought to prevent a British expedition by proposing a new truce. This time he sought to embrace the British legal culture of the sea. He spoke of the need for 'signals and boundaries' and the proper use of flags, which issue had angered Loane, when his vessel was boarded by the Qawasim.[40] But it was too late: the second expedition destroyed twice as many boats and fortifications too. As the wife of one of the leading lights of this expedition noted of the demolition of Ras

al-Khaimah: 'The atmosphere seemed absolutely on fire – there was no
air to breathe, and I was burning with fever. I recollect the appearance
of the horizon all in flames.'[41]

In British reports, the rise of the Wahhabi movement fed into the
reasons why the second expedition of 1819 was launched. After the 1819
expedition, the British signed a series of truces with the rulers of what
they saw as the city states of the Gulf, enabling this coastline to become,
in popular British parlance, the Trucial Coast. These truces were an
attempt to diffuse into the Persian Gulf the liberal imperial definition
of good conduct at sea, critical to the expansion of British trade. The
penetration of these agreements into this region should not be over-
emphasised.[42] According to the terms of the General Treaty of 1820, there
would be a cessation of piracy and plunder, such conduct which was
defined as 'an enemy of all mankind'. The illegality of piracy arose in
opposition to the legality of warfare:

> An acknowledged war is that which is proclaimed, avowed, and ordered
> by Government against Government; and the killing of men and taking
> of goods without proclamation, avowal, and the order of a Government
> is plunder and piracy.[43]

In this view, vessels needed to have national identities and alliances,
and so the language of nations and citizenship which was part and parcel
of this age of revolutions was here applied to the nature of shipping.
Arab vessels became tied by the treaty to carrying by land and sea 'a red
flag, with or without letters in it'. This flag's peculiar characteristics were
spelt out: the red colouring was to be set 'in a border of white, the
breadth of the white in the border being equal to the breadth of the red
. . . the whole forming the flag known in the British Navy by the title of
white pierced red.' Elsewhere Keir explained his logic. Given that a red
flag was taken to indicate pirates, the intention was to combine it with
a border of white to signal peace.[44] A regime of paper and bureaucracy
now overtook the Gulf.[45]

Under the terms of the General Treaty, each Arab vessel also had to
carry a registration paper, with 'the signature of the Chief', specifying
the name of the vessel, the length and breadth and capacity. Diplomacy
tied the vessels to their chiefs and in turn generated the chief's identity
as someone who proclaimed their subjugation to the British. This subju-

gation was symbolised through the chiefs' sending of an envoy to the British Residency in the Persian Gulf. The issue that so troubled Loane – that his *baghla* had been attacked even as its crew put down their arms – was specifically picked up by the Treaty:

> The putting of men to death after they have given up their arms is an act of piracy, and not of acknowledged war; and if any tribe shall put to death persons, either Muhammadans or others, after they have given up their arms, such tribe shall be held to have broken the peace; and the Friendly Arabs shall act against them in conjunction with the British, and God, willing, the war against them shall not cease until the surrender of those who performed the act and of those who ordered it.

The 'war that . . . shall not cease' may be reminiscent of the language of the Wahhabi movement, but in this rendition it is transposed into a statement of British legal culture. The treaty ends with two further identifying marks of British imperialism: the abolition of slavery and the pronouncement of the benefits of free trade, as friendly Arabs would be welcome at all British ports. This treaty was signed at Ras al-Khaimah on 8 January 1820 by Hasan bin Rahma of Ras al-Khaimah, the Shaikhs of Dubai, Abu Dhabi, Sharjah, Bahrain, the chief of Ajman, where Loane was first taken, and others. It is said that the ruler of Muscat, who had an established trade in enslaved people procured via East Africa, was not too enthusiastic about the accord's commitment to anti-slavery. Muscat's base in Zanzibar was critical as a source of enslaved people for the French isles of Mauritius and Bourbon, a story that we will return to later.[46] Yet this was now no barrier to the British maritime empire.

The signing of the treaty confidently marked out states and their representatives on the coast of Arabia. This might be contrasted with the situation a decade earlier when the British struggled to determine which entity to recognise as a state on the coast of the Gulf.[47] Meanwhile, the British surveying of the Gulf coast, its islands and its sea lanes proceeded apace too.[48]

In the new expansive regime of written code and instructions, colonial law turned against those who allegedly did not recognise paper, namely pirates or fanatics. Wahhabis and Omanis had their own legal and cultural norms for acceptable practice over water. The British writing machine responded defensively to raiding. It then began to triumph over its alternatives, even reorganising political units in the process. Treaty-making and bureaucracy, and then cartography, came immediately after war and fire. These various strategies were related, as shown even in how commitments to warfare appeared in the midst of a treaty.

The British military expeditions, full of destruction as well as bureaucratic ordering, allowed the colonists to expand their counter-revolutionary control into this corner of the globe. Similarity in techniques between invaders and insiders gave way dramatically with the military expeditions from 1809 onwards. By the middle of the nineteenth century the superior authority of the British was clear in bureaucratic terms. Meanwhile, Arab political units facing the sea had to live with what they had signed in 1820, as also the implicit conception of states. The General Treaty of 1820 fed into the Perpetual Mandate Truce of 1853.[49]

EURASIAN EMPIRES AND MARITIME POLITICS

There is a side note to the expedition of 1819 which is relevant in tracing the deeper links between the age of revolutions, the rise of Britain, and these events in the Persian Gulf.[50] For behind these maritime political units facing the Gulf were large venerable Eurasian empires. If political organisation and ideology was in flux in the Persian Gulf, this mirrored significant changes in these land-based imperial realms and the interaction of these empires in turn with outside European forces. All of this flux coincided with a moment of unprecedented globalisation.

So here's the side note. In instructions to William Grant Keir, who took a leading role in the 1819 expedition, the Government of Bombay was especially careful to ask the military expedition to avoid interfering in the affairs of the Persian and Ottoman empires. Keir was directed to destroy 'piratical vessels and craft of every description' and to exact 'exemplary punishment'. Yet the intention was for Ras al-Khaimah to be given back to the Ottoman empire, which in turn had been victorious against the Wahhabis. In this manner, the British expedition was cast as completing the work begun by the Ottoman empire in attacking the Wahhabis. Indeed, Keir was instructed not to undertake any military actions against territories which may have recently 'submitted to the authority of Ibrahim Pacha', the son of Muhammad Ali Pasha of Egypt. Keir was also told to move cautiously with Persia, so as not to infringe the sovereignty of 'His Persian Majesty, the ally of our august Sovereign'.

To Persian officers, the commitment of the British Government to free trade was to be proclaimed in order to underline the utility of the expedition to Persian interests.

The maritime violence in the Persian Gulf, undertaken in all directions, might be placed in the context of the tenuous hold of the Ottoman empire over this part of the Gulf. It was also connected to the fall of the Safavid empire which gave rise to Afshar, Zand and, finally, Qajar Persia in the late eighteenth century. These empires and, states at their margins, including Egypt, could not keep up with the imperial and military toolkit of France or Britain. Oman's resurgent port city in Muscat is a good place to trace this history. It was a political unit which attempted to pursue a sea-facing policy, in order to benefit from the new style of trade and global maritime politics orchestrated by the Europeans. Thinking about the transition from grand Eurasian empires to smaller political units such as Muscat is fundamental in characterising the age of revolutions across Eurasia. These political entities were utilised by non-Europeans to forge their own paths.

An Omani commercial and political centre in Muscat was consolidated following the inauguration of the Al Bu Said dynasty, which rules Oman still today.[51] The dynasty's first ruler was Ahmad bin Sa'id (r.1749–1783), whose father was a coffee trader, marking the importance of commerce to the founding of this line. Ahmad bin Sa'id was elected Imam in 1749 and based in Rustaq, which is not on the coast but about seventy-five miles away from Muscat. Meanwhile, the increasing significance of coastal Muscat drew on a prior tradition of Ya'ariba rule in the seventeenth and early eighteenth centuries, which sought to link the interior and the coast in the aftermath of the expulsion of the Portuguese. Omanis in turn also had a longstanding maritime culture which went back to the period of the Sasanian Empire in Persia, prior to the rise of Islam and into the early history of Islam. This tradition set the context for the maritime impulse of the late eighteenth century.[52] Indeed, by the time of the age of revolutions, the rulers of Oman had many ships at their disposal.[53]

The aim now was to make Muscat the Gulf's new gatekeeper and port of choice. Ahmad bin Sa'id's grandson Hamad bin Said (r.1786–1792) and his successors at Muscat oversaw this agenda. Muscat became the indisputable prize of Oman.[54] Like his grandfather, Hamad was particularly interested in maritime trade. Under Hamad's hold of Muscat, commercial links were further developed with the Sindh and Afghanistan.

His successor and uncle, Sultan bin Ahmad (r.1793–1804) consolidated sea-facing trade and politics by establishing agreements with ports such as Batavia, Shiraz and Abyssinia, and enjoying friendly relations with a wide field of others.[55]

Sultan bin Ahmad formalised a cooperative relationship between the British East India Company and Muscat, which supported the military expeditions to Ras al-Khaimah. A treaty or *qawlnama* was signed with the 'High and Potent English Company' in 1798 and a Resident was stationed at Muscat.[56] This was driven by the British in part because of their fears of the French desire to establish a factory in the region. Sultan bin Ahmad agreed to 'an increase of the friendship' with 'the State' of Bombay; 'and from this day forth the friend of that Sircar [Bombay] is the friend of this . . . and in like manner, the enemy of that Sircar is the enemy of this . . .' This language of stately friendship – also seen for instance in the accord between Mauritius and Tipu encountered before – was defined in relation to war:

> whilst warfare shall continue between the English Company and them [the French and Dutch], never shall, from respect to the Company's friendship, be given to them throughout all my territories a place to fix or seat themselves in, nor shall they get even ground to stand upon within this State.[57]

Sultan bin Ahmad also stepped back from his trading relations with French Mauritius and agreed that the English were free to establish a factory at Bandar Abbas. At the heart of this relationship was the British bid to make a base for maritime free trade in the Persian Gulf, and the eager eye it cast over Bahrain.[58] The language of friendship licensed this aim while isolating competitors and rolling out an imperial definition of states.

With this alliance, Muscat's dream of making itself an entrepôt of maritime trade came to life for a brief period. In the words of one historian: 'Oman's great need in the nineteenth century *was* for strong leadership and military strength. Instead the country received ineffectual government from a dynasty of merchant princes whose talents and resources were almost wholly connected with the sea.'[59] Yet it is ill-placed simply to tell the story as one of internal governmental weakness. For the turn to the sea reflected changing global circumstances, the rise of France and Britain, as well as the plight of large land-based empires, and it showed a rather vibrant attempt on the part of Muscat's leaders to place themselves within such developments. It was not ineffectual. It is better expressed as 'a move to take a position with the "globalising" world-system by extending and enhancing its participation in existing Indian Ocean networks'.[60]

Regional dynamics played a part. The consolidation of the Saudi state and the rise of the Wahhabi movement had a negative impact on Oman as the doorkeeper to the Gulf. These fed into opposition from Bahrain and Qawasim directed to Muscat.[61] When Sultan bin Ahmad invaded Bahrain for the first time in 1799 he angered Persia; on another of his attempts on Bahrain the Wahhabis intervened and expelled Muscat. Oman itself was invaded by the Wahhabi forces by land and sea in 1803, necessitating its payment of a tribute to Dir'iyyah.[62] On a mission to get the Ottomans to assist him against the Saudis, Sultan bin Ahmad met his death in 1804. In the years after his death and with the dominance of Sa'id bin Sultan (r.1804–1856) at Muscat, the region entered an even more volatile period, full of raids and counter-raids and a tangled network of alliances between Qawasim, Bahrain, Muscat, the Saudis, Persia, the British and French. The 1809–10 expedition to Ras al-Khaimah occurred in this context. Despite a persistent desire to proclaim its independence and sovereignty, Oman now found itself in collaboration with Britain in military terms too.

If the 1819 British expedition was undertaken without a full knowledge of the internal politics of the region, it is notable that in the long run the British military interventions changed the economic landscape of the Gulf. Raiding was no longer profitable and the region's politics was reconfigured as a result; the global trumped the regional. The British brought about peace by treaty and this meant that traders no longer needed to look for security to Oman. This was a further step that followed from treaty-making: the consolidation of colonial commerce. More than two decades earlier, in 1786, it is estimated that Muscat's customs duties equalled its internal tax revenues.[63] However, in the new context of quietude across water, Oman had to look elsewhere in order to bolster its coffers.

The Omani state increasingly based itself in East Africa after 1820. This followed a longstanding set of connections between Omani migrants, religious groups and traders and the Swahili coast. Yet this redirection also came from the rise of British free-trade ideology as it met Oman's continued desire to engage in maritime politics and trade.

By the middle of the nineteenth century as Oman came under even more British influence, Oman proper and Zanzibar were divided into separate political arms in the midst of a succession dispute which followed the death of Sa'id bin Sultan.[64]

It was no wonder then that early-nineteenth-century British visitors to Muscat commonly praised its peaceable and civil inhabitants, and delighted in its fish, pomegranates and mangoes, though there were some concerns about the unhealthiness of the climate.[65] This was the cultural life of British free trade which changed the foundations of Muscat and the politics of the Gulf. It was this free trade which the British emphasised repeatedly to Oman as the benefit of their relationship.

The flexible course adopted by Oman to navigate these new times, on either side of the two invasive expeditions, should be contextualised within the events inland on either side of the Gulf in the Ottoman and Persian worlds. It was the reconstitution of these historic empires which allowed this particularly vibrant politics and commerce to come to life at Muscat.

The Safavid empire – which had at its core the longest-lasting dynasty of Iran – came to an end in 1722 when Afghan invaders met an Iranian army at Gulnabad, outside Isfahan, only to score a decisive victory.[66] The empire had reached its high point around 1600. Isfahan was ravaged by the siege that followed which saw the scarcity of food and the spread of disease dramatically reduce its population. From the seventeenth century, the Safavid realms experienced a series of intertwined problems. Critical here was the spread of silver from Latin America through European fleets into Asia. One historian explains the result: 'Iran fits neither the classic European core or Asian periphery role – it bought Asian products (as the Europeans did) and sold its own silk (as the Asians did), but the European companies profited twice on these transactions.'[67] Occupying a middle ground between Asia and silver-rich Europe, the Safavid rulers found their currency depleted, and they also found themselves to be gripped by inflation trouble. The result in social and political terms was an attempt to centralise and economise the military in particular, at the cost of a series of tribal rebellions that engulfed the empire, the most virulent of these in the end being the Afghan threat. The period was also marked by the increasingly independent control exercised by the 'ulama or Muslim legal scholars, who exerted pressure on rulers. Religious minorities, including Zoroastrians, left Iran in the midst of religious persecution.

After the fall of the Safavids and into the later eighteenth century, Persia fell into disarray, allowing military adventurers to rise to prominence in place of the centralised control which came before them. The most well-known ruler, who founded the Afsharid dynasty in Isfahan, was Nadir Shah. He was vigorously militaristic and attempted to impose Sunni Islam. He aimed to find a course of accommodation between sects, instead of the realm's traditional commitment to Shi'ism. He ransacked Delhi in 1739. For a period, central and western Persia was ruled by the Zands of Shiraz after the 1750s. From the 1760s to the 1780s the Zands followed a maritime policy, taking over Bahrain and Basra at times and flexing their muscles in war with Oman. The death of Karim Khan Zand in 1779 saw Zand rule disintegrate in a rapid turnover of seven successors and it was the year of the French Revolution when Lotf-Ali Khan came to the throne.[68] His rule saw Shiraz fall to the Qajars who went about unifying Persia under one rule in 1795. The Qajars chose Tehran as their capital.

These events set the deeper conditions for the emergence of maritime Muscat as a political unit whose strident confidence in its sovereignty allowed it to play the age of revolutions. The emergence of the Al Bu Sa'id line came directly after a period of Persian domination over Oman, which began with the arrival of a Persian army of 5,000 men in 1737. Yet later in the century, with Persian strength reduced, the situation could reverse. Muscat was opposed by Karim Khan who sought to make Bander Abbas and Bushire the lead staging posts of the Gulf, in order to collect revenue and customs there. Tellingly, Muscat won out as the key entrepôt: Persian writers bemoaned how Muscat took Iranian vessels captive and allowed them to be plundered by heretics.[69] Meanwhile Muscat wrote to British Bombay asking it not to allow Karim Khan to purchase ships from the East India Company:

> The people belonging to Carem Caun [Karim Khan] having settled at the Island of Carrack, Bunderich & Bushire did plunder & take several English Ships, bound to Bussora and also molest many poor people, they had an intention after inlisting [sic] a number of troops to meddle with me too, which obliged me at last to send my troops & Vessels against the said Island, who fought there the whole afternoon with Arrows, Swords, Shots &c Arms & got a compleat Victory over the said Carem Caun's forces, taking one of his Vessels and about 6000 Men, Horse & foot Prisoners, but they were since released thru Compassion, they still intend to raise

disturbance against me. I therefore write your Honor this as a Friend
hoping you will write the Governor of Bombay, not to permit any of the
Azeems (or Persians) either to purchase or build any Ship or Ships in
your Dominions because Carem Caun is an Enemy & watches the opportunity for if he gets fighting Vessels he will stop our & other Merchants
in their way to Bussora. Your Honour will also be pleased to write Hyder
Ally Caun not to give him the said Carem Caun any Ships doing which
will turn to our mutual advantages. Your Honour will please me with an
account of your Welfare, & command my Services this Way, & I will not
fail to execute any of your Commands. God grant you prosperity for
ever.[70]

While Muscat had a brief period of supremacy in the late eighteenth
century, especially after the death of Karim Khan, the uncertainty next
door meant that Persia was ultimately unsuccessful over the sea. Instead
of finding its own way within the age of revolutions, Persia became a
pawn in the diplomatic tussle between the Russians, the English and the
French. The English and the French both competed to modernise Persia's
army as the Qajars went to war with Russia over territory in the very
early nineteenth century.[71]

The rise of Muscat and by proxy the turn to the sea by small political
units facing the Gulf was also determined by the fortunes of the other
large and historic agrarian and landed empire which lay to Oman's west.

The Ottoman empire, like the Safavid and Mughal realms, was a
Eurasian superpower which relied on an agricultural surplus of peasants
at the base level. It connected that surplus to the emperor, via a network
of intermediaries, who could take up military, revenue or administrative
roles. The Ottoman empire, like its neighbours to the east, also relied
on the horizontal loyalties developed by its intermediary officers in
particular provinces, for war, tribute or cultural cohesion. The crisis
resulted, in one important explanation, from 'tribal breakout' which
arose as the centre declined, and as millenarianism spread.[72] The decen-
tralisation of the imperial economy also gave rise to processes of
urbanisation, which allowed the emergence of a new set of social classes
at the fringes who challenged the authority of the imperial high court.
Rather than seeing these empires as having suffered inevitable decline,
historians now emphasise the flexible and resilient control exercised over
peripheral regions and political units.

If Oman was one such polity, Egypt was another. It was drawn directly into the Napoleonic wars with Napoleon's invasion from 1798 to 1801, which was aimed as an assault on the British empire. The rise of Saudi-Wahhabism in the early nineteenth century in Arabia may be explained in light of the diminishing powers of Egypt with Napoleon's arrival there, and also the changing character of the Ottoman empire. Egypt's response to the Wahhabi movement came with Muhammad Ali's campaign against the Wahhabis from 1812 to 1818. Egyptian troops continued to be stationed in Arabia, and a further expedition from Egypt arrived in 1837 when the Saudis refused to pay tribute to these troops. According to a Briton in Tehran, by 1819, the Imam of Muscat was expressing a 'dread of having so enterprising a neighbour as Mahomed Ali Pacha, whose late success against the Wahabees [Wahhabis] have gained him a great name in this part of Asia.'[73]

This tangle between Ottoman Egypt, the Wahhabis and Oman, which in turn drew in Persia as an ally of Oman, can be seen as surprising. The interior of Arabia was seen as a commercial and economic backwater, without a surplus even with respect to its dates and livestock. It had aroused only sporadic Ottoman interest. The key reason for keeping hold of Arabia lay in the holy sites of Mecca and Medina (Makkah and al-Madinha), but these were not in the arid interior of the peninsula. Given that the Ottoman empire was in a period of change, why did it absorb this outer fringe so determinedly in the Egyptian expeditions against the Wahhabis?

One explanation might emphasise that the Ottomans were responding to raids on Mecca and Medina. In addition to being driven by Wahhabi theology, the lack of surplus in the Najd, in the interior of the Arabian peninsula, drove Saudi raids into the richer provinces of Iraq or Syria, and even the Hijaz, which in turn had benefited from the pilgrimage traffic to Mecca and Medina. The stripping of shrines and the taking of pilgrim caravans was at one and the same time an economic end and a theological principle, tied to a monotheistic faith. The Ottoman empire then responded to this potent combination of economically driven ideology. Yet the full context for Muhammad Ali's expedition to the centre of Arabia to dampen millenarian Islam does not lie simply in a clash of cultures between the Saudis and Egypt. It doesn't lie in a pattern of Wahhabi raiding of the interior cast against Ottoman opposition which was realised by Egyptian invasion. Nor does it lie simply in what one historian terms the Ottoman's 'fear' of the Wahhabis, 'the most basic of human instincts'.[74] Rather the changing circumstances of maritime commerce and the politics of the age of revolutions, as also the threat of Britain, are important to keep in view.

At the other end of Arabia, the Wahhabis and their Qawasim collaborators benefited from the changing circumstances of maritime trade in the Persian Gulf. The late eighteenth century saw a resurgence of sea-based trades, connected to pearls, dates, wool, and opium in the Persian Gulf. The rise of these trades required labour, which also came via the ocean, primarily as enslaved people from East Africa. These slaves arrived as a result of Omani merchants' contacts and the developing political alliance between Oman and Zanzibar.[75] The sea-facing placement of these burgeoning centres of the Gulf is noteworthy. Earlier factors that determined settlement in Arabia, such as access to water and the potential for agriculture, were no longer constraints.[76] Slavery itself was reconstituted as a result. It shifted from being primarily domestic and agricultural to being connected, for example, with pearling, with loading and unloading at port and with work aboard *dhows* or other ocean-going craft. Ras al-Khaimah was a major slaving entrepôt, and there were other such sites: Basra, Bushire, Bandar Abbas and also Dubai. From this coastal region a large number of enslaved people were taken further into Iranian and Ottoman lands. In the port of Muscat there arose an eclectic group of peoples who supported this maritime trade: Hindus, Armenians and Jews were involved in lending money or providing insurance and did not need to adhere to Islamic law.[77] The connections to the wider Indian Ocean were also apparent in the fact that Bombay slowly became the leading entrepôt for pearls from the Persian Gulf as the century progressed.

The resurgence of small political units that faced the sea – and particularly Oman – can be explained in this way by the deeper history of the Ottoman and Persian lands and the increasing role played by maritime trade in these decades. This was in itself a revolution in political practice. It was engendered by the appearance of stronger local elites and religious zealots, who sought to ride the waves. Yet the critical fact is that these agents interacted opportunistically and with some success with the larger forces of the age of revolutions, namely the opposition between Britain and France and their allies in the Napoleonic wars. Muscat's diplomacy is particularly revealing of this interplay between the global and the regional, which did not see the Persian Gulf's particularity disappear.

Oman actively turned away from the French to develop its agreement with the British, having observed that France made but did not keep its promises, for instance the promise to appoint a Resident. It also observed that Britain was taking an increasingly critical role in India. Even Tipu Sultan of Mysore had a factory in Muscat.

In fact, after signing the agreement with the East India Company, Muscat did not annul its relations with the French, to the chagrin of the British.[78] Such manoeuvring arose from the changing political landscape at the crossroads of the Ottoman and Persian worlds, which produced in Oman a new confidence which could then be wielded in global diplomacy. Note this description of Sa'id bin Sultan, in an instruction to the expedition of 1809: 'a prince of great activity and judicious management [maintaining] not only his own dominions in good order, but [overawing] the licentious spirit of his maritime rivals'.[79] Meanwhile, beyond Oman, the structure of maritime plunder which the British critiqued as 'Wahhabi piracy' was itself not a reflection of the decline of trade, as contemporary British observers explained it, but an indicator of the resurgence of trade.[80] It arose together with tribal migrations to the Gulf Coast at a time of drought.[81] In this sense it was also an opportunistic response to both local and global pressures and their consequences for trade too.

The correspondence of Henry Willock, Resident at the Qajar Persian court in Tehran, and formerly of the Madras Army, is intriguing.[82] Willock was asked to secure the Shah's agreement in advance of the 1819 expedition, to Ras al-Khaimah, and even to ask for land forces to supplement the British naval forces, but such cooperation was not forthcoming. In the first instance, Persia sought to give Britain a lesson on how states should relate. Willock reported that the 'ministers' at the court:

> stated that if the Natives of the Persian Coast had offended, H.P.M [His Persian Majesty] would undertake the punishment of His own subjects; and if the Property of British subjects had been plundered, the regular and proper method of obtaining redress was to have stated such grievances to the Persian Government; no such intimation had ever been made; it was therefore adviseable that the British Force should act only against the Jewasamees [Qasimi] . . .[83]

In response, Willock held to the position that the inhabitants of the Persian coast involved in plunder of the seas were in fact 'independent' of Persia and that it was Britain's desire to 'establish the Persian Authority in these Ports' and to quell Qasimi influence.[84] This is related to how the British operated with an ethnic sensibility in distinguishing the Persians and Arabs on this coast.[85]

In the aftermath of the expedition, a new contest over sovereignty opened up. At issue were islands in the Gulf and the question of who had sovereignty over them as Britain sought a base. Britain eventually landed troops at Qeshm Island, a long island very close to the Persian mainland. Britain declared this action legal, by turning to Oman, which it said had jurisdiction over some of these islands. Yet Persia declined to recognise this right and Oman's relationship with Britain was also put under a strain.[86]

Despite defining states, law and sovereignty in this watery geography, both Persia and Britain were not taking on board the real spirit of the age of revolutions. Rather Persia and Britain's play with concepts such as 'independence' hid empires at work. Their aims were counter-revolutionary. Wilcock noted what lay behind Persia's hesitation: 'as practical Politicians, they recall to mind the nature of our first establishment in India, from the small extent of our original possession, to the final attainment of an immense Empire . . .'[87] Having reflected on this transformation, 'the vanity of the Persians makes them regard their Country as the most favoured spot of the Universe and the object of envy and desire to all neighbouring States.'[88] When the language of states and rights of access did not work and when Britain landed troops in Qeshm, Persia adopted a notion of natural territory. Surely, it asked, 'everyone who has been in the Persian Gulph or coasted on the Arabian & Persian shores, or who has examined charts & geographical works where the territories of Empires are defined', must know that the long island belonged with the coast of Persia?[89] British forces at Qeshm were withdrawn in 1822–3, following some heated diplomacy and even the threat of war between Britain and Persia.[90]

The British were certainly flexing their muscles. But right into the 1820s, the Persian Gulf's revolutionary age could still encompass the agency of older empires and newer political units. Many political forces intervened in this moment with opportunism, to expand the terms of trade, politics and state-making.

The Persian Gulf was a stretch of sea hemmed in by land. It constituted a fault-line. Evolving sea-facing political units, venerable empires and outside imperial forces wrestled to take control of the ascendant techniques of statecraft, even as the British increasingly defined the terms. Concentric circles of politics – local, regional and global or Omani/Egyptian/Wahhabi, Persian/Ottoman, and French/British – were creating tensions when set against each other. Within each circle, agency and limitation were in evidence, before this organisation of tiered politics was increasingly overtaken by the power of British free trade and British imperialist diplomacy. The level of the small political unit – and indeed its peoples – needs to be kept in view in tracing the surge from below on the part of indigenous and non-European peoples in the age of revolutions. Burgeoning maritime trade drew political forces into this watery geography. The flexible course adopted by people is also apparent in their need for ships which now comes into view.

PARSIS IN THE AGE OF REVOLUTIONS

It is time to take a radically different perspective on the Gulf, to look from Bombay to this stretch of sea. For there was another political force that impinged on this region: British India. The Gulf was not simply a closed sea, it was a body of water approached from multiple axes and directions in the age of revolutions. It is these multiple engagements that generated the changeable possibilities of this period. The Gulf's place on the emerging mental globe needs to be approached in the round.

On 10 February 1819, a new ship was floated on the middle dock of Bombay harbour. Named the *Shah Alum*, it did not receive the customary ritual of naming where wine was poured over a new vessel.[91] The *Asiatic Journal* reported that there was simply a 'conspicuous effusion of rosewater and ottar', and that the ship was saluted by all the Arab ships in the harbour on the following morning. The ship was bound for the Gulf, to Muscat and for the navy of Sa'id bin Sultan.

The *Shah Alum* had been constructed by Parsi shipbuilders who had by this time become renowned for their skill in making sturdy teak ships which could hold their own in a test of seaworthiness against European vessels. The *Asiatic Journal* noted the expectation that the *Shah Alum* would receive a benediction from a Muslim holy man. But it was named by a European, with the advice of the agent of Muscat who was resident at Bombay. The year the *Shah Alum* took to water was also the year of the second British expedition of 1819 against Ras al-Khaimah, which marked yet another step in the consolidation of Britain's relationship with Oman.

The late eighteenth and early nineteenth centuries saw a great deal of debate about the merits of oak versus teak as the wood of choice for shipbuilding.[92] The debate was informed by the French revolutionary and Napoleonic wars, which saw a shortage of ships and the arrival of Indian-built ships in London, carrying rice and wheat in 1795.[93] This was a set-piece discussion of the age of revolutions. In one of the key pamphlets, the subject of casualties in conflict was used to argue for teak over oak. According to the testimony of General Abercrombie who landed British troops in Mauritius in 1810, 'the effect of Shot upon Teak is far less dangerous than upon Oak'. In arguing for teak, Abercrombie cast the safety of sailors as a winning argument against the economic plight of shipbuilders in England and their concerns about losing their livelihood to Indian dockyards.[94]

Fig. 4.4 'Jamsetjee Bomanjee Wadia [Jamshedji Bamanji Wadia] (c.1754–1821)', by J. Dorman, oil on canvas, c.1830

This debate and its associated tensions was handled by partitioning the Indian Ocean. Beyond the Cape of Good Hope to the west, the trade was restricted to British-built ships. Meanwhile, there was a defined role for so-called 'country ships', or Indian-built ships. They could be used by British private merchants in a trade which ran from India to the East Indies and the Malay peninsula, to China and to the Persian Gulf, but not to Europe.[95] At times these ships could also be hired by the East India Company to carry the mail and to take troops; indeed the *Fly*, from which the mail was lost, had been built in Bombay in 1793.[96]

In such a story, the Parsi shipbuilders and their wider community of merchant families, ship owners, moneylenders, brokers and printers are seen as one of the most successful 'comprador classes' of British imperialism.[97] Their easy adaptation to British culture is evident for instance in the series of portraits drawn of the 'Master Builders' of the Bombay Dockyard to celebrate their dedicated and accomplished service to the British.[98]

The first master builder of Bombay was Lavji Nasarvanji who moved from Surat in 1735 and gave rise to the Wadia family of Bombay. A portrait of his grandson, the third master builder, Jamshedji Bamanji [also referred to as Bomanji] (c.1754–1824), displays how Parsis accommodated themselves to British norms. Jamshedji Bamanji held his title jointly with his cousin, Framji Manakji, who was also portrayed for British eyes.[99] Jamshedji Bamanji's portrait is a richly textured image. It shows the effervescent beauty of Jamshedji's white robe, which in turn is wrapped within a pashmina shawl embroidered in gold, red and green. [Fig.4.4] The painting incorporates markers of technical skill, including a divider and two rules, one of which is tucked into Jamshedji's robe. The second rule sits on the table and may have been the one given to him by the East India Company in 1804, inscribed in praise of his 'continued Fidelity and long tried Services'.[100] The workmanship of his clothes matches his own expertise in building ships, which is also on show.

Through the window is the *Minden* (1810), 'the first and only British ship of the line built out of the limits of the Mother Country', in keeping with the plan in Jamshedji Bamanji's hands.[101] Unlike the *Shah Alum*, it took to water after the ceremony of 'breaking the bottle' and in the presence of 'some thousands of spectators'.[102] Consistent with the tradition of European portraiture and exploration, this painting includes a chair, a curtain and a window out of which one sees the outside world.

Fig. 4.5 'Nourojee Jamsetjee [Naoroji Jamshedji] (1756–1821)',
by an unidentified artist, likely J. Dorman, c.1830

Accordingly, Jamshedji's son was portrayed before a wide landscape of
a mountain, coconut palms and a sailing ship in clear water. [Fig. 4.5]

Jamshedji Bamanji's portrait does not emphasise effortless genius or
manly heroism, such as that deemed to characterise British explorers.
Rather it speaks of hard work. Jamshedji Bamanji himself appears rather
weary, with one eye almost totally closed and frowning. His cousin Framji
Manakji poses with his spectacles in hand.[103] The character and excellence
of the work carried out by Jamshedji Bamanji was a constant refrain
when the *Minden* was launched, as was the quality of the teak that was
used. Note the words of the Commissioner of the Admiralty:

. . . at the period of forwardness I first viewed the ship, her principal timbers were all open to inspection; with such timbers I could not but be highly delighted, as certainly very many of them I have not seen equalled in the building of any ship in England; the mode of securing the beams by dovetailing them into strong clamping planks, (a method not used in the King's Yard) gave me such satisfaction, as much strength is thereby given to the ships. As the work was carried on toward completion, I continued daily watching the progress and must declare was at all times pleased with the solidity of the work, as well as the manner of its being put out of hand . . .[104]

At times the master builders felt particularly aggrieved that their considerable and skilful labours were not sufficiently rewarded by the British. When Framji died, Jamshedji and Rustamji Manakji wrote of how they could have become much wealthier if they had taken up free-trade commerce rather than shipbuilding. They also noted how Europeans who built ships in Calcutta with inferior timber could go home with 'a certain provision for themselves and families'.The same could not be said for Framji's family of eighteen, nor of Jamshedji's family.[105]

Parsis first arrived in Gujarat from Persia, perhaps in the eighth century, after the Arab conquest of Iran, to escape persecution for their Zoroastrian faith.[106] From the seventeenth century they turned to ship-building at the port of Surat, while taking up an increasingly urban style of life. They moved in increasing numbers to Bombay, reacting perhaps to recurrent famines, so that there were ten thousand Parsis in the city in 1811. Most of these arrived as farmers and artisans, but then turned to trade and industry. Their increasing wealth came partly out of profits in cotton and opium and moneylending and brokerage. In time they took a pioneering place in Indian politics. In Britain the first three Asians to become members of the British parliament were all Parsis.[107] The argument is made that they were sub-imperialists. To follow this perspective, they adapted to the British empire with greater occupational mobility, when compared say with Hindus or Muslims. Within the British empire, they were unimpeded by a sense of a loss of status in political or administrative terms, unlike some established Indian elites. Instead they embraced English-language learning and maritime culture.

Yet this established interpretation only goes so far. The *Shah Alum* and also the *Tajbaux* (1802), *Caroline* (1814) and *Nausery* (1822), which too were built for Oman rather than for Britain, throw open and critique this story. The Parsis were building vessels for Muscat too, not just for the British. This fits alongside the migratory history of this community as well as the long-standing reliance on the part of Arab sea-facing political elites for timber and ships from India. There is a theory that Omanis had ships built in India in the seventeenth century, when Omanis serviced Portuguese shipping which connected the Gulf and India.[108] According to one estimate eight ships were built for Muscat in Bombay between 1802 and 1835.[109] It is likely that other vessels operated by Arabs and Persians were also built along the coast of India. Earlier in the eighteenth century, Nadir Shah of Persia had ships built and repaired in India.[110] In the aftermath of the 1809–10 expedition to Ras al-Khaimah, the British Indian government enforced a ban on the import of timber to the Gulf, in order to put a stop to what they saw as the menace of Wahhabi piracy. Yet it was possible for the Qawasim to continue to get their hands on timber, for instance from Travancore, on the furthest south-west Indian coast.[111] There was a similar discussion yet again in 1820, after the second expedition.[112]

The British could not control the making of ships on the coast of India, just as they could not monopolise access to valued hardwoods, which could be used to build ships.[113] In fact they were anxious to get a good estimate of the forests on the south-west Indian coast in Malabar and Kanara, which could be used for shipbuilding.[114] The arrival of an Indian-built vessel made a great impact in Muscat. The Caroline for instance came to Sa'id bin Sultan's navy just when he was assailed by the Wahhabis. In order to bolster morale, it is said that he boarded the vessel 'attended by a thousand men, armed with lances, and among whom were a crowd of his own slaves'. The ship was immediately engaged in firing on the enemy.[115] However, according to Francis Warden of the Bombay government, the Caroline was almost taken over by the Qawasim of Ras al-Khaimah.[116]

Until the 1820s, after which the Bombay shipyard declined, finally giving way to steamships built of British iron, an earlier history of connection between the Persian Gulf and Bombay continued to operate under the nose of the British.[117] This connection was in keeping the age of revolutions, in the value placed on well-built ships at a time of war and when war impacted on commerce. Parsis may have benefited from the British empire, but they should not for this reason be excluded from the class of people who were agents of the age of revolutions.[118]

Their early politics in Bombay further supports this characterisation, for Parsis began to conceive of themselves as a nation and took an active interest in their own history in Persia in response to the British Christian missionary critiques of Zorastrianism.[119] The extent of Parsi migration to Bombay strengthened their community identity and supported a desire not to assimilate into Hindu culture. They also attempted to reorganise the mechanisms used to govern their community. A Parsi *panchayat* (an assembly of community governance, theoretically of five chosen leaders) was founded in Bombay to regulate the community in the early eighteenth century. By 1818 this assembly was run by eighteen members who were elected in a public meeting.[120]

Self-governance through assembly is a classic signifier of the age of revolutions. Among the families who took a leading role in this *panchayat* were the Wadia family. The assembly took into its purview matters connected to marriage and adoption, property and charity. A series of tensions between the newly monied and long-standing Parsi merchant elites and between new Western customs and traditional rules took the political force out of the *panchayat*. By the later 1830s it was already in decline, accused of corruption, bigamy and idolatry by a new generation of Parsis.

Parsis began travelling to London from the early eighteenth century to proclaim their rights and to observe and criticise the English. Among Parsi travellers to London were two shipbuilders of the Wadia family, who were grandsons of Jamshedji Bamanji. Jehangir Naoroji and Hirjibhoy Meherwanji were sent to acquire new skills in shipbuilding at a time when the Bombay dockyard was in decline, arriving in 1838. They visited the dockyards, but also the British Museum, the zoological gardens and other sights of London and wrote of the progress made 'by that giant Steam' and how it was 'becoming more extensively applied to marine purposes'.[121]

Under the patronage of Charles Forbes, these two shipwrights also visited the House of Commons. Forbes had lived in Bombay and headed Forbes & Co., before returning to England to take up politics, being elected as an independent to parliament and opposing the East India Company's monopoly.[122] The shipwrights' observations about how Britain decided between 'Reform or Revolution', in adopting the 1832 Reform Bill which expanded franchise, drew on a later visit to the parliament, where they witnessed a debate in progress. They sat in the 'foremost' seats in the gallery, dressed in what they called 'our costume', supposedly watched by every member of parliament, for eight and a half hours through the night, until 2.30 in the morning.

Naoroji and Meherwanji's journal issues the judgement that 'the British constitution is acknowledged to be the best in the known world, and a perfect model to be imitated by others for the legislation of their countries'. Yet they twinned this sentiment with a condemnation of the 'bribery' which characterised elections, and how the Reform Bill had increased such 'bribery' by allowing poor votes to be bought. These comments can be read in the light of the problems which beset the Bombay Parsi *panchayat*. Debates about reform in Britain in the late 1830s were happening side by side with the questioning of rights in Bombay.

In summary, the Parsis' story of shipbuilding is consistent with the circles of political activity in previous sections of this chapter: for the Parsis kept up links with the Gulf and the British empire and reworked local politics. The story in other words is simultaneously local and global. Parsi agency is in keeping with the surge of indigenous activity which characterised the age of revolutions. Like the Qawasim or the Omanis, these were people and communities on the move with unexpected connections. The traditional sense of 'indigenous' might be widened to include complicated mobile paths and heritages such as these.

Yet Bombay's links to the west via ships did not simply rest with socially ascendant shipbuilders. It also included labourers, traders and enslaved people aboard the vessels which plied this sea route. On these ships the age of revolutions from the Persian Gulf to West India had fewer elite constituents who reworked the culture of constitutions, some-times formenting more violent forms of revolt.

REVOLT BETWEEN ARABIA AND INDIA

The British Indian Ocean world was partitioned by type of ship between British-built ships and Indian-built ships engaged in the 'country trade', but matters were not this simple. For in the age of revolutions, the Persian Gulf and Bombay and other western Indian ports were becoming increas-ingly connected by Arab vessels.[123]

In the early nineteenth century there were years where the number and tonnage of Arab vessels arriving and departing from Surat exceeded that of British ships.[124] The counting of Arab ships is a difficult enterprise, because some Arab ships sailed under British flags, while others were probably unrecorded. The increase in Arab maritime activity arose directly from the Napoleonic wars. Arab vessels were seen as neutral and were not attacked by either the British or the French. Such was the advantage that some European ships, especially French and Dutch, took up Arab colours adding a further complication to the counting of Arab ships. While *baghlas* and their smaller equivalents, *battils*, were used for Arab trade between the west coast of India and the Gulf, European-style ships were also increasingly prevalent in this trade. Some European-style ships were bought by Arab merchants from the French, who in turn had taken them captive from the British.

A whole range of commodities went back and forth in this trade, including the export of chinaware and grain from India and the import of aloes, copper, beads, horses and pearls from Arabia. Enslaved people could also travel in both directions. It was only with sustained opposition from British merchants, who accused Arab merchants of spying and disguising French trade, that measures were tightened in the mid 1830s, so that Arab vessels were classed as comparable to any other foreign craft. In this perspective, the relationship between Muscat's rulers and Bombay's shipbuilders fits into a wider context of regional connections. These connections between Arabia and western India were becoming more intense in these decades and the British were seeking to spread their bureaucratic net over them.

In piecing together the relatively small number of travel journals in English for the early-nineteenth-century Persian Gulf, Arabia and Persia, it is possible to reconstruct something of the experience of the labourers and enslaved people aboard the Arab vessels as much as on the country ships under British flags. James Silk Buckingham, who also wrote on the quest to save the mail of 1804, noted the nature of the language spoken on the vessels which travelled between Muscat and Bombay: 'on board their own large ships, even the names of the masts, sails, and ropes, as well as the orders of command in evolutions, are, as in India, a mixture of Arabic, Persian, Hindee, Dutch, Portuguese, and English . . .'[125] Yet the breadth of these languages flattened out, he noted, to make 'Hindoostanee' the language which was understood most widely by the diverse crews of these vessels. There were also some remnants of the Portuguese language evident among them, apparent in the words for flag, compass and squadron.[126]

The range of languages was matched by the backgrounds of the crew. Lieutenant William Heude of the Madras army, who travelled from India to the Persian Gulf and overland to England in 1817, was on an 'Arab ship' with British colours named the *Fuzil Kareem* for the first leg of the journey and provided a map of the ship by ethnicity:

> with a crew of 50 Lascars, and 90 passengers on board; of these, 30 were Persians, stout, able, and turbulent; the rest were Arabs, Turks, Jews, and Gentiles, of every quality and degree, of every trade and occupation that can be named. Merchants, and pilgrims to the holy tomb at Kurbulla [Karbala]; horse-dealers, soldiers, gentlemen, and slaves; they had reached Bombay from every part . . .[127]

Heude also showed the suspicions of the period: was one of the Turks on board in fact a disguised Frenchman, 'under the protection of a beard and turban'? He wrote of the superstitions of the men on board too. When they were delayed at Devil's Gap, sixty miles away from Muscat, without winds, the 'finger of the Prophet' was allegedly the cause. When an Arab and a Jew were washed overboard, one of the Turks blamed them as evil men. Indeed, the loss of passengers in the course of journeys between Bombay and the Gulf appears to have occurred regularly in these years. The loss of life was aggravated by the fact that conditions on board were crowded, with many people huddled together, with their cargoes and produce.[128] Stereotypically, Heude wrote that the two men were forgotten within a day.

As they approached Muscat, twenty-five craft were sailing out to Bombay, under convoy with the *Caroline*, built by the Parsis. Heude also gave a titillating description of the slave-bazaar at Muscat:

> Twenty or thirty young Africans, brought across the desert, and chiefly from the coast of Zanguebar [Zanzibar], were ranged in rows on either side of the bazar, and according to their sex . . . [Their owners] in walking between the ranks, seemed extremely particular in handling and feeling the bodies and skins of their intended purchases; extending their inspections to such minute particulars as quite astonished me; who was by no means a connoisseur, in any animal more rational than a camel or a horse.[129]

At a time which emphasised the powers of reason, humans were seen as distinct from other animals, but enslaved peoples contradictorily and disturbingly were compared by Heude with the camel and horse. This denotes the cultural anxieties and racist views that plagued the British about slavery even in the second decade of the nineteenth century, after the slave trade had been abolished. Meanwhile, there was a persistently gendered quality to the observation; for Arabs were presented as being particularly careful in the selection of 'young females'.[130]

Much of Heude's description was presented rather nonchalantly. Indeed the *Edinburgh Review* lambasted the author for being full of 'idle and ill-told stories about drunken Turks', rather than having as his aim 'the gratification of that rational curiosity respecting the countries he passes through'.[131] Such a reception aligns with Heude's account of an insurrection that overtook the *Furzil Kareem*, the ship he was on board, on its journey out of Muscat. The Persians tried to strangle a *lascar*, after a quarrel, and when the mate interfered they rose against him. The commotion overtook the vessel in the early morning; the 'mutineers' were driven 'towards the poop' and 'happily without bloodshed'.[132]

The linguistic and social hybridity of these vessels did not, then, entail smoothly functioning relations between rival communities. This episode occurred just prior to the vessel meeting a 'pirate dow' [*dhow*] [b]ound by no law, by no respect controlled, their wanton barbarous cruelty has set them beyond the pale of civilised intercourse, of mutual trust and sacred confidence.'[133] The insurrectionary events on this 'Arab ship' occurred in the same space and time as other revolutionary events connected with the Wahhabi movement in the Persian Gulf. Indeed, observers, travellers and sailors of all kinds brought together and compared shipboard insurrection with maritime plunder undertaken by alleged pirates. Both rebellion and piracy were said to be threats to the law and to involve unnecessarily 'barbarous mutilation'. [134]

Another very colourful traveller was Vincenzo Maurizi who was in Oman in 1809–10 and 1814–15. On the title page of his book, he announced that he was 'Physician in many parts of the East . . . Commander of the Forces of the Sultan of Muscat, against the Geovasseom and Wahabees Pirates [Qawasim and Wahhabi pirates]'. Yet he was accused by Muscat's Sa'id bin Sultan, upon the advice of a British officer, of being a Napoleonic agent, which may indeed have been the case. He had left his home in Italy after falling into trouble with his family for pro-French feelings.[135] On one occasion, when Maurizi was fleeing from Muscat, without the permission of Sa'id bin Sultan, who wished to keep him in his employment, he took to a small vessel made of teak, 'composed of one tree, brought from the coast of Malabar [Southwestern India]'.[136] His journey was full of hazards. The crew consisted of two pilots, Arab and South Asian, and 'many Jedegals' who were in the service of Indian merchants. Maurizi's own servant from a village between Barka and Muscat was also on board.

The dangers of the journey lay partly in how fragile this vessel was in the high waves, for instance when it was assailed by 'a tremendous waterspout': 'My Moslem [Muslim] companions immediately began to cry out Allaá, Allaá, while the Jedegals exclaimed as vehemently Burda, Burda.'[137] Maurizi tried to shed some of the vessel's weight, by pushing a bag of dates overboard, and then he did the same with bags filled with scales of fish, which were destined for India and China, 'to be used in the composition of that beautiful lacquered ware called Japan'. Maurizi came to safety at long last, back ironically in Muscat, and yet the voyage made him wonder at the perils of small vessels, which were 'patched like the shoe of an Italian peasant', and which were 'constructed for no other purpose than to waft its crew to the other world'.

Maurizi's experience neatly captures the environmental conditions of the trading world connecting the Gulf and Arabia to the west. The entrance of the Gulf at Quoin Island was a waypoint where prayers could be offered to deities. In 1817, for instance, a British country ship set afloat a little ship here as a sacrifice, 'rigged and in sailing in order, bearing a sample of all merchandise carried for sale in the vessel which sends her forth'.[138] In the harsh circumstances of voyaging between Bombay and the Gulf, with vessels of all kinds making an increasing number of journeys and asking a lot of their crews, a fertile ground for revolt was laid.

Because of the detailed records kept by the East India Company, including testimonies from captains, servants, slaves and sailors in revolt, it is possible to trace the occurrence of revolt among *lascars* on the country ships after the 1780s.[139] *Lascars* were part of a gang, under the command of a headman or *serang*, who was a recruiter, who negotiated a contract with a European sea captain for the labour of his gang. Though mostly Indian, the same gang could include men with diverse origins from across the Indian Ocean. The partitioning of the trade of the Indian Ocean by type of ship was related in turn to the impact of the Navigation Laws, according to which British ships arriving and departing from

London had to have predominantly British crews; this despite the heavy reliance on Indian *lascars*.[140] In practice this meant that *lascars* often took up work on vessels on the way to London, for vessels like this needed sailors for the homeward journey from India to Britain. But such *lascars* found themselves stranded without work on getting to London, at times having to become passengers on the return journey.

There was also an increasing feeling of rivalry, resentment and conflict on the part of *lascars* directed towards British officers and crew members on ships, connected to differences in pay and their exploitative use, given the legislative constraints of the Navigation Laws. The *lascar* issue became a point of debate for liberal reformers of the British empire and was picked up by humanitarian activists.[141] However, attempts at reform generated further bureaucracy rather than an improvement of conditions for *lascars*. The so called 'Lascar Act' after the end the Napoleonic wars further precluded the legal use of Indian seamen on British vessels.[142] These wider conditions framed the types of insurrections which occurred among *lascars* in the circuit of country trade between Bombay and the Gulf.

Lascar revolt aboard country vessels involved complex alliances and grievances. The *serang* or his deputy could serve as a rebel leader or as a point of protest; there were even times when isolated Europeans joined the rebel cause. The character of revolt could range from work stoppage to violent upheaval which could amount to taking control of the ship. Country ships were ill-defended against such revolt. By the middle of the nineteenth century, accounts of *lascars* who allegedly burnt ships in Calcutta, Bombay and Madras were picked up by sensationalist journalists across the British empire as examples of 'wilful incendiarism': fourteen ships were burnt in 1851.[143]

The progress of revolt could be marked by imitation, such as that displayed by the enslaved people in revolt in Cape Town. Rebel captains could seek to imitate their deposed captains or to occupy their cabins. This was the case when the *Alert* was taken over by its *serang* in 1804, in the middle of a voyage from Calcutta to Bombay. This *serang* took it to Al-Mukalla in present-day Yemen, under Arab colours. News circulated that the rebels had murdered all the Europeans, and the British government of Bombay sent a cruiser to recover the ship. In published reports, the crew were cast in racist terms as 'woolly headed men, originally slaves procured from the east coast of Africa by the Arabs, and by these meta-morphosed into mussulmans [Muslims]'.[144] The Bombay government were keen to take charge of this 'most horrible and successful conspiracy' and that 'as many of the pirates may be secured' on the return journey of the *Alert* back to India.[145]

In another instance, revolt occurred between Bombay and the Gulf on board the *Bombay Merchant* in 1821. Here a relatively simple request when the *Bombay Merchant* arrived at Al-Mukalla, that the *serang* and the crew be allowed to go on ashore, turned into a full-scale revolt when Captain Hyland declined the request, announcing that 'only one [man] at a time could be allowed to leave the vessel'.[146] Eventually: '[t]he Serang and some of the crew laid hands on the Captain, who extricated himself with some difficulty from them.' The crew managed to leave the boat and go ashore, and the captain had to give up the ship and return to India on another vessel. The *serang* commanded the *Bombay Merchant* successfully back to Bombay, where he managed to deliver the cargo 'to the satisfaction of the owners'. In fact the *serang* reached Bombay some months before his captain. Captain Henry William Hyland's description of these events which overtook the *Bombay Merchant* is telling. In a petition to the Bombay government he wrote of the 'mutinous conduct' of the crew and described it as 'insurrection and piracy', which could be avoided by 'lawful prosecution to that condign punishment they are so deservedly entitled to'.[147]

There was then an ideological slippage between the categories of protest in the Indian Ocean. Pirates could be compared with rebel *lascars*, racial and religious attitudes to Wahhabis could come to set the terms for understanding the 'superstitions' embraced by the passengers on board 'country ships' who were on Islamic pilgrimage and such suspicion could also feed into fears that *lascars* were increasingly converting to Islam. This blurring of contexts was also evident in the histories of the vessels upon which these events unfolded. For instance, the *Bombay Merchant* was previously used in the taking of Mauritius by the British in 1810. It transported the French garrison of the island to Europe under the terms of a truce, which marked the British take-over.[148] Ships passed between and were repurposed by the British, the French and the traders and rulers of the Persian Gulf. If there were so many types of politics, religion, law and statecraft around the Persian Gulf, the social experience of traversing these seas was also heterodox as also the ownership and use of ships.

TANGLED POLITICS OF REVOLUTION
AND COUNTER-REVOLUTION

The tangle of political possibilities which formed the age of revolutions in the Persian Gulf is quite astounding. In the words of Francis Warden, the Secretary of the Government of Bombay, writing in 1819: 'complicated interests' and many 'Powers' had 'contended for superiority' in the Persian Gulf, in the midst of 'various revolutions'. Together with these interests, 'the unsettled state' of Persia and the Ottoman world had given rise to Wahhabi power.[149]

The expansion of maritime politics, plunder and commerce in this period came about partly as a result of the reconstitution of land empires and the consolidation of political units which engaged the sea, like Muscat. Yet the political circles in the Persian Gulf also encompassed rival Europeans, and particularly the British and the French as they tussled for control over channels of correspondence, trade and strategic access to Asia and the Middle East. The picture includes British India and how the Gulf depended on the line of passage to Bombay and how Bombay sought to exercise control over it, sending off military expeditions to Ras al-Khaimah for instance.

The true complexity of this age cannot be understood simply by listing the tiers of political units like this. Rather, communities of migrants, technicians, sailors, enslaved people, soldiers and diplomats made the Persian Gulf come alive, and found their own paths. The history of the age of revolutions in the Gulf should not simply be told as the story of Wahhabi revolt. Indeed, the 'Persian Gulf' doesn't stand simply for the geographical region marked by this name on a modern map; rather it was a space on the mental globe of the age of revolutions. When the Gulf is approached from multiple directions, it is possible to locate this conception of it in opposition to today's debate on whether to name this gulf alternatively, 'Persian', 'Arab' or even 'Ottoman' or 'Islamic' and the associated programme of excluding African or Asian connections with it.[150] In contrast, the history of the Gulf told here has been determinedly plural by way of cultural heritage. This is in keeping with the larger enterprise of charting a series of indigenous and broadly non-European practices that constitute the age of revolutions in these forgotten regions of the world.

The British, with their legal norms and paper, started to insert their own notions of rights and citizenship into the Gulf, aimed at determining states, politics, trade and even labour. Indeed their dominance over France could be seen by the late 1830s in the fact that French ships were being refitted in British Bombay.[151] Before this occurred, it was possible for a short period for Muscat to assert its confidence in its own sovereignty, while playing the age of revolutions. And prior to the age of steam, the need for sailing ships at this time could bolster the prospects of Parsis. The political context of the Napoleonic wars benefited Arab shipping vessels, before new legal norms came in during the 1830s.

In these ways, the Persian Gulf and those who engaged with it could be characterised by types of agency which arose from below, but they were aware of the wider pressures and possibilities. It was in undertaking their own politics across this web of forces that elites, trading communities or technicians found their way. Those who were imprisoned in one vector of relations, for instance, on board ships under the constraints of the Navigation Acts – such as the *lascars* – did not meet much success. Those who were able to creatively remould the culture of historical empires, by adopting reformist religion or those who used existing connections in shipbuilding between South Asia and the Middle East while moving between patrons, did best in the age of revolutions.

It is tragic to see how this plural landscape of revolution became tied up with a counter-revolutionary imperialism. Laws, state-making and assertions of sovereignty were shared on all sides, but the scale of British intervention outstripped their opponents. As time passed, it was Bombay that defined the Persian Gulf. This shift in turn indicated the ascendance of the British Raj in India by the middle of the nineteenth century. Yet British travellers and officials also found their categories in contest and blurred by the stretch of water linking the Persian Gulf to India. Right under their noses, trade, pilgrimage, slavery and ship building could still carry on apace. Though legal norms sought to define piracy, theft, slavery and diplomatic friendship, in practice there was a categorical confusion. Forms of protest in the age of revolutions did not only straddle different geographies, political times and communities. The British imagination itself linked different contexts of slavery and rebellion for instance; this was despite the empire's pretensions to exact discursive definition.

The temptation is to use big politics to explain the tussles of the age of revolutions and the transformations of political organisation and commerce. But as the Parsis' rise or the rebellion of the *lascars* demonstrate, these shifts had personal consequences for the plight of individuals or even how they were portrayed. What follows – on the Tasman Sea – links the high politics of imperial stand-off in this age to changing orders of gender and race. It begins with individual people caught in the middle of a world that was changing. If this chapter has told a story of the agency of communities in the midst of a multiplicity of political configurations, such as the Parsis or Muscat between local, regional and global, the next places Aboriginal Australians' agency at centre stage. Aboriginal agency was a statement at a time when counter-revolutionary imperialism was surging forwards through liberal and bureaucratic experiments of state-making.

5
In the Tasman Sea:
The Intimate Markers of a
Counter-Revolution

Fig. 5.1 'Cora Gooseberry, Freeman Bungaree,
Queen of Sydney & Botany', brass breastplate

It is tempting to think that the closest that one can get to the deceased is in the company of their possessions. For Cora Gooseberry such a notion is false and true in turn. Cora was an Eora woman. Eora is a term for over thirty clans of Aboriginal people who resided in the coastal Sydney region.[1] She was the widow of Bungaree, who is often said to be the first person to be called an Australian in print.

R251B, a crescent-shaped brass breastplate said to have been worn by

Cora, doesn't weigh much as I examine it at the Mitchell Library in Sydney. The four walls of the library's reading room are covered from the floor almost to the ceiling in Tasmanian-blackwood bookcases.[2] [Fig. 5.1]. The engraving on the breastplate's front may be mocking how Aboriginal Australians engaged settlers. But I wonder whether the engraving provides some evidence of a sense of status adopted by Cora. It records in capital letters: 'Cora Gooseberry, Freeman Bungaree [her husband's name], Queen of Sydney & Botany.'

Then there is R252, another object attributed to Cora, described as a 'rum mug', in bronze with a handle. It was a colonial idea that the Aboriginal Australians in Sydney of these years were addicted to drink.[3] R252 was collected in the nineteenth century by David Scott Mitchell, the book collector, whose name now graces this library. Without citing any evidence, Mitchell told his assistant that the mug was larger at the top than at the bottom because: 'it had been enlarged by a marlinespike for her so that it would hold more rum.' It lived on a mantelpiece 'behind his chair'.[4] Yet might this roughly formed mug show how Cora carried on finding her path within the port of what is now Sydney? Rum was itself a currency in colonial New South Wales. If so, the colonial trope of alcohol addiction needs to be forcibly rejected.

According to a Sydney newspaper of the 1840s, Cora was the 'sister as far as regality goes of Queen Pomare' of Tahiti. This is in keeping with the use of a royal signifier – Queen – in the breastplate too. Pomare IV of Tahiti intentionally deployed an image of herself as a queen, woman and mother in the Anglo-French tussle over her fabled home.[5] Yet there is a difference between Pomare IV and Cora. For Sydney was a city founded by a mass influx of white settlers, where Aboriginal Australians were wiped off the land. Indigenous peoples didn't consolidate royal lines in Australia akin to those in Tahiti, Tonga or elsewhere in the Pacific. If so, is the attribution of queenship to Cora simply an indicator of colonial rhetoric once again like the use of the stereotype of alcohol addiction?

One way of tracing an Aboriginal Australian perspective from Cora's breastplate, to get to a truer sense of her, is through a focus on water and gender. Both Cora's remaining breastplates are engraved with fish and this may not be an accident. One of her names means 'goat fish'.[6] It is now known that coastal Eora Aboriginal women played an important role in fishing with hook and line from their *nowie* or canoes, prior to the arrival of European nets and boats.[7] These women are pictured in early drawings on their canoes. Early diarists in Sydney comment on Aboriginal Australian women's wonderful skills with boats and their ingenious hooks and lines. Aboriginal women fished with children in tow, while men usually fished with spears from the shore.[8]

For instance, a set of watercolours attributed to George Charles Jenner, the nephew of Edward Jenner, the pioneer of smallpox vaccination, and thought to be from the early nineteenth century, show Aboriginal Australians in portrait. An Aboriginal Australian man waits, looking down into the water with his spear, as if in expectation of a fish. In another image, an Aboriginal man passes a fish on to someone outside the image. A woman sits in a canoe with her child and a line.[9] [Fig.5.2] Eora Aboriginal women's involvement in fishing along the coast of the Sydney region also highlights the mobile and maritime character of their lives. These were women who navigated the rivers and coastal seas around New South Wales, not as nomads and wanderers.

The woman who has dominated accounts of early Sydney is Barangaroo, the wife of the Aboriginal Australian man Bennelong.

Fig. 5.2 'Natives of New South Wales' (undated, thought to be pre-1806), attributed to George Charles Jenner and William Waterhouse

Governor Arthur Phillip, Sydney's first governor, took Bennelong with him to London. Bennelong returned to Sydney in 1795. Barangaroo's rebelliousness and dislike of how her husband took on British ways has attracted recent commentary. In one analysis, she took up a 'determined nakedness', preferring it to a petticoat, even at the governor's table.[10] As a fisher, it has been suggested that she could not keep up with the hauls brought in by British fishermen, and begrudged the dependence on colonial men which this entailed.[11] Her determined agency fits a narrative of the age of revolutions as indigenous presence and resistance.

Women's involvement in fishing led at times to British men portraying them as sexually unattractive. George Worgan, a surgeon on the First Fleet, noted that Aboriginal women smelt of 'stinking fish-oil'. He wrote that they coated their bodies with the oil and this oil mixed with the soot which collected on their skins, because of the fires they kept on their canoes while on the water. Bearing out the sexual culture of settlement, he carried on: '. . .[F]rom all these personal graces & embellishments, every inclination for an affair of gallantry, as well as every idea of fond endearing intercourse . . . is banished.'[12]

In Cora's story, in place of the Aboriginal woman as fisher there arose the Aboriginal man as aide in navigation. For her husband Bungaree totally overshadowed Cora in the British vision. He had several wives. He circumnavigated Australia with the explorer Matthew Flinders, in the voyage that established the contours of the great island in 1801–3. The image that defines Bungaree's reputation among the eighteen or more that remain of him is the oil painting produced by Augustus Earle.[13] [Fig. 5.3] It shows Bungaree in a chiefly pose. He is greeting the viewer and dressed as a general. He stands before Sydney harbour with three British warships and a vessel which may belong to the French expedition of Jules Dumont d'Urville. He wears a scarlet jacket.

Bungaree was gifted military and naval gear that was no longer needed by the colonists. Lachlan Macquarie, the reforming governor of Sydney, gave him an outfit on the day before he left for London in 1822. In Macquarie's words: 'I gave him an old suit of General's Uniforms to dress him out as a chief.' The coat was presented in the midst of a 'plentiful feast, with grog' and Macquarie asked his successor as governor to provide Bungaree with a 'Fishing Boat with a Nett'. The conferral of the uniform coincided with the resettlement of Bungaree and his 'tribe' in a farm on George's Head. This gift-giving and settlement was a

Fig. 5.3 'Portrait of Bungaree, a native of New South
Wales, with Fort Macquarie, Sydney Harbour in
background' by Augustus Earle, c.1826

reformist project consistent with Macquarie's autocratic attempt to reorganise the colony.[14]

The oil painting by Earle of Bungaree is in keeping with the recurrent
colonial description of this man as the entry point to Sydney. Russian,
French and British travellers routinely commented about how Bungaree
greeted ships in his 'bark canoe' and saw them to port, bidding them
'welcome to his country' and 'endeavouring at the same time to take
likewise what [they] are probably less willing to part withal – namely, a
portion of your cash'.[15] When viewed in a wider context the painting is
reminiscent of how indigenous peoples such as Louis van Mauritius of
Cape Town or Toussaint Louverture of Haiti took up the theatre of
military clothing to play with and overturn colonial culture.[16] Earle

himself drew an image of a female soldier of Brazil, Dona Maria de Jesus, involved in Brazil's struggle of independence from Portugal, making a perfect link to Latin America's age of revolutions.[17] Another man who greeted visitors to Sydney in this period beside Bungaree was 'Billy Blue', a Jamaican boatman; this is another Atlantic connection.[18]

The belittling of chiefly authority was obvious by the time a later version of this image appeared. [Fig. 5.4] An image from a collection titled *Views in New South Wales and Van Diemen's Land* (1830), shows Bungaree next to a woman:

> The accompanying likeness represents him in the act of taking off his hat and bowing to the strangers landing, with one of his wives in company smoking her pipe.[19]

Fig. 5.4 'Bungaree, a native of New South Wales'
in Augustus Earle, *Views in New South Wales and
Van Diemen's Land: Australian Scrapbook* (1830)

The ships have now been replaced with bottles that glisten in a very dark blue. The houses in the background indicate the expansion of Sydney, and yet Bungaree and the woman with him, perhaps one of his wives, are detached from that project. The cut-and-paste style of representation which characterised British views of Aboriginal Australians had separated the genders. This new representation brought Bungaree to the foreground and there is also a stronger view of racial difference in this image.

In Earle's image a breastplate hangs around Bungaree's neck, which reads, 'Bungaree, Chief of the Broken Bay Tribe 1815'. Governor Macquarie initiated the tradition of presenting breastplates to Aboriginal Australians, drawing perhaps from his experience in America. Bungaree may have been the first recipient.[20] After Bungaree's death his assertions of headship were retold in a racialised mockery of his alleged kingship. When he died a broadside parodied the title which had appeared on the breastplate: 'Aboriginal Majesty King BONGARIE, Supreme Chief of the Sydney tribe.'[21] Another described him as the 'revered antipodal Majesty'.[22] In 1857, in an age of anthropometric measurement, his skull was reportedly received at the Australian Museum, though no trace of it remains. In 1852, Cora was found dead of natural causes at the Sydney Arms Hotel on Castlereagh Street, having reached the age of 75.[23] *Bell's Life in Sydney* in publishing her obituary noted that she 'was the last descendant of the Sydney tribe of Aborigines; and her kingdom now is consequently not worth a gooseberry'.[24]

In the cases of both Cora and Bungaree and as evident in the story of Cora's breastplate as well as Earle's image of Bungaree, the British adopted characteristic vocabulary for the time, connected to monarchy and chieftaincy. They did this to reorganise Aboriginal Australians in line with reformist imperial programmes of gift-giving and schooling. Patronising and changeable characterisations overtook indigenous practice, for instance Aboriginal women's fishing. All this counted as a new order of race and gender. The sequence of steps in which this order was constructed is apparent in how Earle's image was reproduced in cut and paste or how the obituaries of these two people of colour found it humorous to represent them as monarchs. There is undoubted violence in this conception of race and gender. Yet it is still possible to break this order apart to find indigenous perspectives and presence.

Fig. 5.5 'The annual meeting of the native tribes of Parramatta' by Augustus Earle, watercolour thought to depict 1826 meeting

COUNTER-REVOLUTIONARY ORDERS
OF RACE AND GENDER

Curiously, the colonial emptying of chieftaincy and monarchy in New South Wales occurred alongside rare descriptions of Aboriginal Australians as republican in their social organisation. This once again highlights the specific link to the ideas of the times.

Earle's images are among the most revealing of early Sydney. The artist painted a watercolour of a Native Conference, said to be that of 1826.[25] [Fig. 5.5] The *Sydney Gazette* noted that there were 210 'natives' and 100 'inhabitants'. The silencing of revolt and unrest was a theme of these meetings. Aboriginal Australians were said to be as happy as 'so many princes – indeed we question whether Bonaparte in his most brilliant career, was ever so exempt from outwards care or mental disquietude'. The journalist noted that there were 'subjects, constables, chiefs, wives, daughters, mistresses, and even kings, all mingled higgledy-piggledy, and as familiar with the other as if they were all down-right Republicans'.[26]

The link to republicanism appears elsewhere too. Watkin Tench, the now-beloved commentator on early Sydney, wrote that 'theirs is strictly a system of *equality*'.[27] The writer in the *Sydney Gazette* also observed that missionaries would get to the bottom of their 'political intrigues', and the benefits of trial by jury, taxation and representation would enable the British to 'hail and embrace these hundreds and thousands and millions of fellow-creatures, not only as fellow subjects — but as fellow-Christians.' There was then a great deal of variety in this political language: Aboriginal Australians were alternatively humoured as monarchs, chiefs and republicans. All these authorised liberal and humanitarian intervention as much as settlement.

Settled family relations with ordered gender norms were critical to the project of civilisation which Macquarie and his aides had in mind. This means that there were intimate dimensions to the transformation afoot as colonial vocabulary dominated indigenous peoples. In writing to London on the 'Character and General Habits of the Natives of this Country', Macquarie wrote of how Aboriginal Australian lives were wasted in wandering through woods, in small tribes of between twenty and fifty, acquiring subsistence from possums, kangaroos, grub worms, and 'such Animals and Fish as the country and Coasts Afford'.[28] He enclosed a letter from William Shelley, who presided briefly over the Native School connected to the Native Conference.

Shelley laid out the links between schooling and race and gender. The problem with raising indigenous peoples to Englishness was that 'they were generally despised, especially by *English females.*' In advocating classes for boys and girls in separate apartments, in a school under his care, Shelley wrote:

> No European Woman would marry a *Native*, unless some abandoned profligate. The same may be said of Native Women received for a time among Europeans. A Solitary individual, either Woman or Man, educated from infancy, even well, among Europeans, would in general, when they grew up, be rejected by the other Sex of Europeans, and must go into the Bush for a Companion.[29]

The implication of Shelley's argument is that 'native' men needed to marry 'native' women in as much as Europeans would marry Europeans. His school would serve the purpose of training such a corps.

With colonial norms imposed in this way, masculinity was Bungaree's passport. It allowed him to become visible to Europeans and to come to the foreground of British representations of Aboriginal Australians. He first sailed with Flinders in 1799 on a survey voyage to Hervey Bay, north of present-day Brisbane, in a sloop named *Norfolk*, made out of the pine wood of Norfolk Island. In addition to later circumnavigating Australia with Flinders, he also sailed with Philip Parker King, son of the former lieutenant governor of Norfolk Island, to north-western Australia in 1817. It is significant to note his entry into the large corpus of texts connected with Flinders' work: 'Bong-ree, a native of the northside of Broken Bay, who had been noted for his good disposition and open and *manly* conduct [italics mine].'[30] Elsewhere in the account of David Collins, later governor of Van Diemen's Land or Tasmania, Bungaree was termed 'undaunted', and 'gallant and unsuspecting'.

In meeting indigenous peoples at Moreton Bay, while on the *Norfolk*, Bungaree wished to serve as emissary for Flinders. He opted to go ashore naked and unarmed, just as Aboriginal Australians appeared on shore. If the adoption of European clothes, as has been recently argued, confounded the gauging of gender by Aboriginal Australians in Sydney, Bungaree's decision to go with no clothes may be seen as a statement of

his Aboriginal masculinity.[31] When with Flinders, Bungaree sought to
fish as an Aboriginal male would around the coast of Sydney, by using
his spear, without using the hooks and lines with which women would
fish. On one occasion in a side-by-side show, three large fish were fired
at by Flinders and speared at by Bungaree. But neither brought the catch
up. On another occasion, Bungaree gave a spear and throwing stick to
local people and showed them how to use them at Pumicestone River.[32]
Bungaree also presented himself as a naked emissary and also a spear
thrower in the course of his circumnavigation of Australia and later while
accompanying King.[33]

Flinders was especially curious about how the people near the head
of Pumicestone River fished and noted that their method was completely
new to Bungaree, indicating perhaps Bungaree's interest in their fishing
too:

> Whichever of the party sees a fish, by some dextrous manoeuvre, gets
> at the back of it, and spreads out his scoop net: others prevent its escaping
> on either side, and in one or other of their nets the fish is almost
> infallibly caught. With these nets they saw them run sometimes up to
> their middle in water; and, to judge from the event, they seemed to be
> successful, as they generally soon made a fire near the beach, and sat
> down by it; no doubt, to regale with their fish, which was thus no sooner
> out of the water than it was on the fire.

From these observations about fishing Flinders built up a theory of
cultural and racial difference. European notions of difference were overlaid on Aboriginal ones. Where nets rather than spears were used, Flinders
argued that people would form associations with each other. Because
nets provided a more certain means of procuring fish their users would
settle more regularly. Spears on the other hand explained the violence
of Sydney: 'An inhabitant of Port Jackson is seldom seen, even in the
populous town of Sydney without his spear, his throwing-stick and his
club . . . It is even the instrument with which he corrects his wife in the
last extreme . . .'[34]

In 1804 the *Sydney Gazette* reported how Bungaree created a spectacle
in Sydney in throwing 'a bent, edged waddy resembling slightly a Turkish
scymetar'. This was a reference back to the Ottoman world. For this
writer, Bungaree's was a display of malignant 'native warfare'. Conflict
had erupted despite the fact that Bungaree was a 'native distinguished

Fig. 5.6 W. H. Fernyhough, *A Series of Twelve Profile Portraits of Aborigines of New South Wales, Drawn from Life* (Sydney: J. G. Austin, 1836). This lithograph is of Cora. There are hand coloured originals in the National Library of Australia

by his remarkable courtesy'.[35] Bungaree's value could only be tolerated then if he conformed to the British class-driven type of masculinity which was often equated with gentlemanly warfare in the age of revolutions; Aboriginal senses of gender had to be subservient to this greater colonial identity and its polite civility.

The apogee of the new colonial conception of race and gender is evident from the mid 1830s when a series of black-and-white lithographs of Aboriginal Australians, ready for hand colouring, became popular in Sydney. They were produced by William Henry Fernyhough, who took up employment in a Sydney printing firm, a short time after his arrival in the city. They were probably based on drawings and sketches done by Charles Rodius, a German artist.[36] There is a distance between viewer and sitter in these lithographs. The starkly darkened Cora Gooseberry facing to the left, without any features, would not have called for a conversation.[37]

Yet the rise of this order of race and gender, linked in turn to the whitening of Sydney as a colonial space with the dominance of white people in demographic terms, still relied on information provided by Aboriginal Australian women. Cora was seen on the streets of Sydney together with her family camping close to hotels and in the Domain, the open space in central Sydney, which was walled by Macquarie as a pleasure garden. The group of Aboriginal Australians with whom she camped provided demonstrations of boomerang throwing.[38] Cora was more than a token of the indigenous. Her biography fits into an important argument about colonial Sydney until about the 1830s: 'It is time to shake off the idea that Sydney was a "white city", that Aboriginal people simply faded out of the picture and off the "stage of history". It is simply untrue.'[39] Aboriginal Australians found a place for themselves in the city.

Accordingly, a rare mid-nineteenth-century account sees Cora providing information about Aboriginal rock carvings to the artist George Angas on North Head. At first she objected to the request that she show Angas these carvings, saying that such places were 'forbidden ground, and that she must not visit them'. Yet Angas continued: she 'became more communicative as she filled her pipe with some of the negrohead tobacco . . .'[40] In doing this she conformed to the role of the Aboriginal woman as a cultural go-between in early Sydney, a role which was racially stereotyped in turn.[41]

Outside the Mitchell Library stands a statue of Matthew Flinders, and it looks, in what would have seemed to British colonisers as proud and youthful manliness, at the street named after Governor Macquarie. It was dedicated in 1925 in return for the deposition of Flinders' papers in the library. Importantly, Bungaree does not figure here nor of course Cora or Matora, another of Bungaree's wives. Yet Flinders has recently been given another companion. It is Flinders' favoured cat Trim. Trim the cat is an Australian celebrity. Even the library's café is named after him. Unveiled here in 1996, the plump Trim stands on his four legs behind Flinders and looks up to the right from beneath one of the outer faces of the library's stained-glass windows. One of two plaques devoted to him reads:

Trim. Matthew Flinders' intrepid cat who circumnavigated Australia with his master 1801–3 and thereafter shared his exile on the island of Mauritius where he met his untimely death.

It is partly as a result of a tribute penned by Flinders, while in captivity in Mauritius under Governor Decaen, that his cat has been raised to this pedestal. Flinders' tribute bears the marks of someone with too much time on his hands, and is ironic and overly affected in turn. Trim appears as an astronomer and practical seaman and is said to be a cat of Indian origin. Flinders proposes that Trim is related to a cat who entered Noah's Ark. Trim is also said to have formed a special relationship with Bungaree: 'If he had occasion to drink, he mewed to Bungaree and leaped up to the water cask; if to eat, he called him down below and went strait to his kid, where there was generally a remnant of black swan.'[42]

The rise of Flinders as hero, together with his cat, corresponds to the displacement of indigenous peoples like Bungaree and Cora from historical memory. Colonial norms of gender and race were used to reorganise Aboriginal Australian senses of self. In the stories of Cora and Bungaree is also evidence for how marine encounters could lead into projects of settlement colonisation, including the attempted settlement of Bungaree on a farm at the shore from which he could greet incoming ships. Bungaree as a navigator's assistant was more visible than the Aboriginal women who fished. Politicised but empty concepts such as chief and monarch were applied to Aboriginal Australians to allow counter-revolutionary empire to attempt to manage these people. Yet this counter-revolution was not a complete one: there were still spaces, including at the heart of the city as seen in Cora Gooseberry's later life – and as we will see, in the Tasman Sea – where indigenous presence was still apparent.

THE TAKING OF TASMANIA IN THE AGE OF REVOLUTIONS

The stories of these individuals are in keeping with that of the British advance in the late eighteenth and early nineteenth centuries. To move from mainland Australia across the Bass Strait, the colonial rivalry of the age is perfectly clear in the origins of the settlement that was initially called Van Diemen's Land and later Tasmania.[43]

In the first years of the nineteenth century, concern was brewing in Sydney about the infractions caused by French and American interests in this region to the south of New South Wales. When a sealing expedition from Île de France was wrecked on the Sister Islands between mainland Australia and Tasmania, Governor King in Sydney wrote to London, almost in relief, that the disaster would put a stop to any more 'adventurers from that quarter', perhaps pointing to Mauritius' reputation among the British as a bastion of republicanism and piracy.[44] It was not just the French who were a concern. In 1804, King published a proclamation about how Americans were acting in 'violation of the Law of Nations' by building vessels in the Bass Strait, between Tasmania and Australia, connected to their sealing operations.[45] Indeed, the wrecked sealing expedition also included American crewmen.[46] The governor underlined the significance of this poaching to the settlers of Sydney: there were 123 men, 'exclusive of ship-builders and many other artificers and labourers' whose livelihood was at risk from these outsiders.[47]

While in harbour in Sydney, the sealing expedition from Mauritius overlapped with the French exploratory expedition of Nicolas Baudin. The Baudin expedition had left Sydney just a few hours earlier when a rumour spread in the settlement that the French voyagers had instructions to set up a base in Tasmania in the d'Entrecasteaux Channel. King alleged that an English officer, Lieutenant-Colonel Paterson, had been in a discussion about the site of the intended settlement. The governor proudly reported that he did not lose an instant, despatching a 'colonial vessel' with as many 'scientific people' as he could gather.

A set of instructions and counter-instructions were speedily devised to foil the French. The ship's midshipman was officially instructed to examine the channel, hoist the British flag there and to leave a guard.[48] As one leading historian of Tasmania writes: 'had Britain not been at war with France, it is unlikely that it would have occupied Van Diemen's Land at this time.'[49] The 1802 raising of the flag, which in fact occurred on King Island in the Bass Strait, was followed by the 1803 landing of a band of soldiers on the Derwent River and the 1804 landing of convicts in modern Hobart, marking the formal annexation of Tasmania.

Anxious to note the successful result of his outmanoeuvring of the French, King reported to Joseph Banks, the botanist who had accompanied Cook:

The mid. [midshipman] was received by Mons'r Baudin with much kindness. In the later's answer to me he felt himself rather hurt at the idea 'that had such an intention on his part existed that he should conceal it,' &c. However he put it on the most amicable footing, altho' the mid. planted His Majesty's colours close to their tents, and kept them flying during the time French ships stayed there.[50]

Private antagonism and public wariness lay side by side in this inter-change. For a domestic bond had formed between Baudin and King's family in Sydney. 'How valuable your friendship has been and will ever be to me,' wrote Baudin in leaving King.[51]

There was yet another layer to the Anglo-French rivalries of the Napoleonic Wars. François Péron, who was with Baudin, was an impet-uous strategist, a radical patriot and naturalist, on the tradition set by those men of science who rebelled against their captain on the d'Entre-casteaux voyage. He was the zoologist on the expedition.[52] Inspired by the insult of King's gesture, and until his death in 1810, Péron compiled a memoir to the French government on why it was necessary to annex New South Wales, accusing the English of an 'invasion'.[53] He asked: 'and so is this the only flag [the British one] that can be raised over the Southern Continent and over those countless archipelagos of the Great Ocean?'

In the wake of the flag incident on King Island, Péron commanded his reader, addressed by the imperial title of 'Monseigneur' that there was 'not a moment to lose'. 'We must strike a blow at this international bogeyman at all costs, otherwise world trade will be in England's hands.'[54] Consistent with British visions generated out of Sydney, Péron stretched his eyes to the east and the west and imagined how the holders of New South Wales would command of the southern fishery, would determine the fate of Western America as also of the Maluku Islands. He was insistent: 'New Holland [Australia] must therefore be taken from the English . . . without delay.'[55]

There is no evidence that Péron's calls were directly heeded, except that a version of his views of New South Wales, when they came to light in the published version of the Baudin voyage, came to frame the terms of a debate on penal colonies in France. Additionally, in 1813, a French plan to capture New South Wales circulated once again in Australia, and this has been traced back to Péron.[56] If the flag incident fed into the settlement of Tasmania, there was another way in which he had an impact. Péron's actions also contributed to Matthew Flinders' impris-onment. Flinders was taken captive partly as a result of Péron writing to Decaen, the Napoleonic governor of Île de France, saying that the navigator was on the lookout for a military base.[57]

Péron's memoir read the local politics of Sydney in the light of the global age of revolutions. Revolt was a local enterprise in Sydney where the Irish played a role and they called international events to their aid. Péron wrote of the Irish in Sydney:

How often did we not see all of these unfortunate deportees, their eyes bathed in tears, heap curses on England, implore Bonaparte and call down upon their oppressors the moment of vengeance? How many attempts did they not make to escape on board our vessels, which they persisted in seeing as manned by their liberators and friends! Oh! How often did we ourselves not weep at being compelled to hand over these unfortunate souls or even to cast them out on neighbouring shores.[58]

The French patriot included an account of the Castle Hill Uprising in 1804 which was led by the Irish, and included some English too. He noted how the Irish had experienced significant fatalities and deportations in the aftermath of the rebellion as well as increased surveillance. He imagined that such ill feeling would lead the Irish to join the French cause with 'unswerving devotion' in the event of an attack.[59] He suggested that some of the Irish in Sydney were involved in General Humbert's army in Ireland. This was the army which had mounted resistance against the British on the basis of revolutionary principles in 1798.[60] In Péron's view, in the days after the French takeover of New South Wales, the training of Irish regiments would be critical in ensuring that the French colony in Sydney would not fall back into the hands of the English.[61]

The Irish in turn had their own global imagination. This is seen in their efforts to escape New South Wales and find their way overland to China in this period.[62] Reporting on one such Irish group, Tench wrote about how they believed that to the north of New South Wales lay a river which separated it from 'the back part of China'. When the river was crossed 'they would find themselves among a copper-coloured people, who would receive and treat them kindly'.[63]

Like all the other observers and travellers passing through Sydney in these years, Péron and his compatriots on the Baudin expedition saw it as a maritime hub. The commander of the *Naturaliste*, the second vessel in the expedition, described the ships which connected the port to Tahiti and traded in meat. He noticed that there were others which undertook sealing that traversed the waters to India and China. There was a company of traders who owned ships in New Zealand which travelled back to England, and ships bringing convicts which came via Brazil. The colony had 'two corvettes to defend it'.[64] For the French, the value of Sydney lay in its command of these comings and goings at the southern extremity of the world. This assessment was shared by the British.

Anglo-French exchanges and competitiveness are not simple. Friends in Sydney could become competitors to plant a flag in Tasmania. Yet this complex relationship fed the advance of the British. The age of revolutions inflected the story not only with respect to elite stand-offs, maritime rivalries and trade. The cultural, intellectual and environmental dynamics in the commentary on Tasmania were in keeping with the period's modes of operation. Militarised data-gathering and natural 'improvement' went together.

ISLAND TASMANIA

Today's Hobart, Tasmania's capital, can seem like the edge of the earth. When I visited it the gigantic bright orange Aurora Australis ice-breaker was moored in its deep waters, fitted out for work in the Antarctic. Along Salamanca Wharf, before a line of 1830s Georgian warehouses, now converted to trendy shops and restaurants, was a reminder of what first made the early colony of Tasmania: a large black whaler's trypot, used to boil stripped whale blubber so as to produce oil. Close by was the monument in honour of Abel Tasman, replete with ships and stars, a curious combination of humour and elaborate symbolism, in honour of the first European to sight Tasmania. The trypot reminds the viewer that sealers and whalers working out of Tasmania were critical to the early economy of colonial Australia before they were overtaken by the wool trade in the 1830s. While whaling was dominated by capital-intensive companies operating out of the south of Tasmania, sealing was carried out from the north of the island.[65]

Seals and whales appeared in Péron's writings. The southern seal fishery is estimated to have taken seven million seals in fifty years in this period, an extreme case of natural exploitation. Péron described a 'remarkable trade – one of the most audacious, without a doubt, and one of the most lucrative that man has yet opened up'.[66] He bemoaned that the circumnavigation of the world, once seen as a voyage of grandeur and importance, had now become a commonplace among these traders and sailors.[67] Meanwhile, Flinders also wrote about seals in his journal as he was finding his course through the Bass Strait. The random distribution of the seals was 'beyond [Flinders's] comprehension'. 'They

Fig. 5.7 Elephant seals at King Island off Tasmania. Victor Pillement, 'Nouvelle-Hollande, Île King, l'elephant-marin ou phoque à trimpe, vue de la Baie des Elephants' 1824

will leave one Island unoccupied close to several others where they cover the shores; nay one point upon the same Island will be so left and totally without any apparent reason . . .' He conjectured that the answer lay in 'streams and eddies and perhaps many other causes', which were 'imperceptable'.[68]

Péron's observations of the seals take an ethnographic character. They bear the marks of close encounter and arose from a period when he was stranded on King Island in the Bass Strait for twelve days in 1802. [69] Indeed the French naturalist's theory of the distribution of seals was more complex than that penned by Flinders.[70] In the official account of the voyage, Péron sketched the southern geography of the seal, 'particularly in deserted islands', from the Bass Strait to the Falkland Islands and Juan Fernandez Island.[71] In making sense of the anomalous fact that elephant seals appeared in some such islands and not others, Péron proposed that their presence depended on 'small ponds of fresh water in which sea elephants like to wallow'.[72]

The temperature was also said to be a factor in these distribution patterns, as the elephant seal was said not to like extremes of heat and cold. Péron noted that the pregnant seals were guarded by their males, who 'drive them back' to the task of tending to their pups 'by biting them'.[73] 'The period of lactation lasts seven or eight weeks, during which no member of the family eats or goes down to the sea.' Once three years had passed, the pups grow into males aware of their sexual needs and willing to 'hurl themselves at each other; they fight relentlessly.'[74] The easy comparison that came to Péron, which he attributed to sailors, was between the victorious seal and the 'master of a Turkish harem', allowing the 'jealous and despotic seal' to be nicknamed 'The Basha'.[75]

This attention to seals shows an empiricist, romanticised, anthropomorphic, and even gendered and racialised, observation of nature. Such commentary is consistent with an ideology of natural 'improvement', typical of the time, according to which colonists sought to theorise, uplift and make more perfect and useful the bounty of nature.[76] The taking of Tasmania in the revolutionary era was sandwiched by the natural historical observations of seals both by the British and the French; on both counts natural history was not too far from annexation. The control and ordering of the sealing trade was important not only because these voyages stepped across emerging political boundaries, like the wrecked sealing ship from Mauritius which contributed to the argument for the British taking of Tasmania. Rather, natural exploitation was commercially lucrative and there was a contest to benefit from it.

In keeping with a commitment to the utility of nature, new settlers wrote of the lush and hospitable landscape of island Tasmania. For Collins, the later governor of the island, Van Diemen's Land did not sicken the heart with those 'excessive tracts [in mainland Australia] which at once disarm industry, and leave the warmest imagination without one beguiling project'. For Flinders, voyaging through the Bass Strait, on one occasion, Tasmania provided the best water he had ever tasted.[77] By way of contrast, New South Wales was found to be unexpectedly sterile, as evident in the tussle over fish that ensued between Aboriginal Australians and colonists.[78] It was bound on one side by the Blue Mountains, which were not crossed by Europeans until 1813.[79]

The notion of Tasmania being naturally bountiful fits with how islands in the late eighteenth and early nineteenth centuries were taken to epitomise natural luxury. Flinders and Péron's ethnographic and scientific description of seals also falls in line with the commentary of the time on Aboriginal Australians. Indeed, colonial descriptions of seals and humans show symmetric features. The depopulation of seals happened side by side with the horrific depopulation of Tasmania's Aboriginal peoples.

SEALERS, INDIGENOUS WOMEN AND COLONIAL HUMANITARIANS

Sealers were cast as 'seawolves' in the period, a term which places them next to the age of revolution's pirates, such as those labelled as such in the Persian Gulf. [80]

From 1810, populations of sealers lived with indigenous women in the Bass Strait. The community was polyglot, including English, Irish, American, Portuguese, *lascar*, New Zealander, Tahitian and Australian Aboriginal members. [81] By the second decade of the nineteenth century reports of these communities were circulating in Sydney, allowing Rev. John McGarvie to write of them as 'runaways' who had come ashore in the strait, become acquainted with 'old Munro', who with his 'black wife' led them into 'all the secrets of the mysterious traffic & routes in these dangerous straits'. James Munro, one of the earliest resident sealers, was described as the 'owner & king' of Preservation Island.[82] The mention of 'runaways' indicates that some sealers were escaped convicts.

The events which occurred in these sealing communities may be seen as an outworking of the revolutionary moment. Before turning to that history it is important to stress at first that the trade is one aspect of the extraordinary violence which unfolded in Tasmania as Aboriginal Tasmanian resistance spiked from the late 1820s. One of the driving factors of the brutal Tasmanian wars, which saw the hunting down of Aboriginal Tasmanians and retaliatory violence towards settlers, was the arrival of people who had served in the Napoleonic wars, and other refugees, to settle Van Diemen's Land, including the offspring of colonial officials and the aristocracy of Britain. As the colonial population increased by six times from 1817 to 1824, the island was changed from 'a creole society based on small-scale agriculture, whaling and sealing, to a largely pastoral economy based on the production of fine wool'.[83]

The policy taken to contain the violence between the settlers and the Aboriginal Tasmanians was a counter-revolution, an intentional and careful manoeuvre to outwit indigenous agency. It was also driven by contradictory commitments to militarism and humanitarianism, a characteristic blend for the period. There are several clear signs of the imperial counter-revolution in Tasmania. For one, there is the establishment of military posts, a field police and the scouring of the land by armed parties, making this one of the most policed territories at this time.[84] There is also the use of martial law over more than three years from 1828, justified as bringing about reconciliation through terror but used to kill Aboriginal Tasmanians. Then there is the 'Black Line' in 1830, devised perhaps from strategies against the French and using expertise of warfare in India and in the Peninsular War and the model of imperial hunts. It comprised a human chain of troops, convicts and settlers, which sought to drive the Aboriginal Tasmanians into a confined ground. And finally the counter-revolution didn't only amount to military tactics to capture Aboriginal Tasmanians. The counter-revolution was also an ideological move. It saw the application of commitments to civilisation, honed after the abolition of slavery and as a result of evangelical religion, to the transportation and confinement of Aboriginal Tasmanians in the Bass Strait, leading to their deaths.

The language of the times – including that arising from humanitarianism – was used to describe and intervene in the sealing and whaling communities in the Bass Strait. Take the important writings of the evangelical humanitarian and later 'protector' of Aboriginal peoples, George Augustus Robinson.[85] For Robinson, the sealers were 'wretched men': for 'to abolish the Slave Trade the Govt. at home has expended millions – and that it should exist in this her colony is certainly improper and Disgraceful. These men put the Govt. at defiance.'[86]

Already by this point, there were calls for the management of these sealing communities. These calls were in keeping with the reform of imperial government in a liberal imperial age. One 1826 report addressed to Governor Arthur of Van Diemen's Land by a naval officer described the Strait as 'one continual scene of Violence, Plunder, and the commission of every species of Crime'. It called for tighter checks on the passengers of sealing vessels in order to stem the arrival of escaping prisoners from Sydney to the Straits who would then become sealers. It also called for a restriction of the sealing season to five or six weeks in order to prevent seal pups being killed too young, and the making of a 'Government settlement' on one of the islands, with civil and military force.[87] This call for a military settlement presaged the eventual formation of Robinson's reserve for Aboriginal Tasmanians.[88] An act regulating the shipping of Van Diemen's Land, including measures to prevent the stowaway of escaped convicts in vessels, was passed in 1833 in the midst of the Tasmanian War.[89] In the end the sealing communities were overtaken by the rise of steam-shipping and agricultural commerce across the Bass Strait.[90]

For Robinson himself, the exercise of liberal reform was exemplified in the rescue of indigenous women who lived with sealers. As a 'humanitarian', he wrote that they had been 'taken from their country' and that the kidnaps had involved white men tying the women's hands and forcibly conducting them to their boats, transporting them to the islands of the Bass Strait. When a 'plurality' were 'possessed', a 'favourite [was] selected, who is exonerated from labour and to whom the others are compelled to submit'.[91] One sealer – Thomas Tucker – allegedly shot male Aboriginal Tasmanians while being 'most active' in the pursuit of indigenous women. The 'unmerited cruelty' was evident in the scars on the women. Robinson presented a catalogue of these women's names and stories and he made certain to indicate who had been rescued and placed in his establishment. Among the lists is a woman who was taken by a 'man of colour', another who still had a 'husband among the Blacks' and others who were passed, bartered and sold between the sealers. There are accounts of women beaten with sticks, for instance one woman who reportedly told Robinson how a sealer had wounded her on the head when she lost one of his dogs. In one horrific story, Robinson describes Worethmaleyerpodyer:

> About 20 years of age fine . . . Woman native of the District of Pipers river was forcibly taken from her country by a Sealer name James Everitt [who came to the Strait after the wreck of a whaler in 1820], by whom she was afterward murdered on Woody Island by maliciously shooting her through her Body with a Musket Ball because she did not clean the Mutton Birds to please him . . .[92]

Worethmaleyerpodyer's grave was pointed out to him.[93]

Yet despite the commitment to the extension of liberty and freedom evident in Robinson's work which was tied to its lineage in the abolition of slavery, he attributed minimal agency to these women. Robinson's writings are probably the most controversial in the early history of Tasmania and they became a focal point in the History Wars which gripped Australia around the status of indigenous histories.

For some he is the agent of 'genocide'. According to these commentators, with the blessing of Governor George Arthur, Robinson rounded up the majority of the Aboriginal Tasmanians and transferred them in the mid 1830s to Flinders Island in the Bass Strait, after a series of missions of conciliation, which had the aim of civilising them. Adrift on this remote outpost, disease took a rapid toll on the Aboriginal Tasmanians. For other historians, Robinson is a self-seeking mercenary. For others still Robinson exaggerated the violence against Aboriginal peoples, concealing the wrongs done by Aboriginal peoples against settlers, and simply reporting settler killings of Aboriginal peoples in Tasmania. If in the words of one recent commentator, Robinson was 'constantly in contention with his fellows, forever asserting himself', the same is true of his place among historians.[94] Later in his career his restlessness took him across the Bass Strait. He became chief protector of Aboriginal peoples at Port Philip on the Australian mainland in 1839.

Robinson reported on women who escaped the sealers and rejoined their communities. This means that his writings cannot be taken, even in their own terms, as indicators of a complete lack of female agency. For instance, a woman whom Robinson named Tarerenorer was said to have committed 'dire outrages on the Settled Districts' after escaping from the sealers, and to have then returned to the sealing community. It was then that she was placed in Robinson's custody.[95] Yet the minimal agency that Robinson attributed to Aboriginal Tasmanians becomes clear when one reflects on how these women were the prime providers for their families, responsible for gathering food from both coast and sea, and known for their swimming, diving and sea-voyaging.[96] In contrast, James Kelly of Hobart provides a fuller account of their role along these lines and prevents them being seen only as abducted females.

Kelly's crew gave six women a club each and watched the unfolding events. The women crept up close to the seals and lay down with their clubs alongside them, 'some of the seals arose their heads up to look at their new visitors and smell them'. The women then imitated the seals, following the same motions, lifting elbows and hands and scratching themselves as the seals did. It was only an hour later that they suddenly rose and struck the seals on the nose, thus killing them. 'In an instant they all jumped up as if by Magic and killed one more each . . . they commenced loud laughing and dancing as if they had gained a great Victory over the seals.' They then swam with the dead seals, which presumably required great strength, and brought them to the watching men. On the following day, the women took the lead in killing seals. They also proceeded to roast seal flippers and shoulders.

Kelly's vivid portrayal of the women workers could not have been penned without George Briggs as his aide. Briggs was recognised by these communities, having resided in the strait as a sealer, and having 'two wives and five children' in the straits. Kelly wrote that Briggs had 'acquired the Native Language'.[97] Kelly reported that the women cried when they were about to leave, and they asked Briggs to wait for a dance, the marker of the end of an agreement or exchange.[98] Three hundred people, including men and children, proceeded to dance at Eddystone Point. The women began 'forming a circle and dancing round the heap of dead seals . . . putting themselves into the most singular attitudes.' 'The men then commenced a sort of sham fight with spears and waddies then – dancing round the heap of dead seals and striking their spears into them as if they were killing them . . .'[99]

In the debate over Robinson among historians, it is a pity that very few readers have gone back to his original diaries, choosing instead to use a

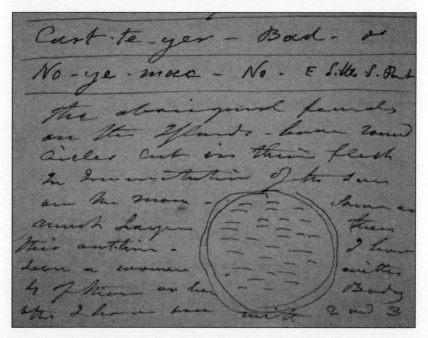

Fig. 5.8 Papers of George Augustus Robinson, vol. 8, part 2,
Van Diemen's Land, 30 September–30 October 1830

sanitised and republished compilation of his diaries as the key bone of
contention. The originals, in the Mitchell Library, are a rich set of objects.
Of various sizes and textures, some of these are in duplicate hand copy,
some in ink and others in pencil. They convey the hurried work of his
field explorations and contain a range of jottings which are as interesting
as the main journals. Within these scribbles are indicators of how Robinson
engaged with the Aboriginal women of Tasmania. He observed them
intensively. For instance, the back pages of a tattered cream-coloured
journal for 1830 written in pencil and ink in turn was used by Robinson
to jot down the names of the Aboriginal Tasmanians. Also included were
some bits of biographical information, the names of 'nations' inhabiting
various islands, rough vistas of scenes, such as 'Rugged mountains near
Cape Portland', the names for places and then suddenly a line across the
page followed by a circular drawing in ink accompanied by this note:

> The aboriginal females on the Islands have round circles cut in their
> flesh in imitation of the sun and the moon. Some are much larger than
> this outline. I have seen a woman with 4 of them on her Body, others
> I have seen with 2 or 3.[100]

Interspersed in this assortment of information are collections of words,
arising from the women, including, in pencil, 'Try-yer-lee', which is 'East,
white man' and 'Parlee', which is 'Black man East'. *Tyereelore* was the
name that the women used to refer to those who lived with white men
in the Eastern Straits.[101] There is also attention to differences in age: the
words for young woman and old woman and young man and old man
are noted. This mode of operation was an ethnographic one, the precursor
of later anthropology, where the fieldworkers immersed themselves in
the language and customs of the people and observed them as specimens,
surveying their features and in this case their skin. As imperialism arose
in the midst of the militarised struggle in Tasmania, it was accompanied
by an order of information-hunting, evident in the natural history of
seals as much as the ethnography of Aboriginal Tasmanians. Yet this
information gathering could not have proceeded without the assistance
of indigenous peoples.

Mutual reliance is seen in the pencil sketches of a dance of the *tyereelore* which appear in another journal. The scene is set at the sealers'
camp opposite Robbins Island. This island was hastily sketched in ink
in the journal.[102] The women – and there are only women here – are

without their kangaroo skins and naked except for their caps, which are usually brightly coloured.[103] In the accompanying notes Robinson writes that the women gave him necklaces made of shells, in return for which he gave them beads, pincushions and buttons.[104] In his words, probably copied in the hand of a clerk: 'the night was remarkably fine, and the sealer women and myself made up a fire and danced and sang until it was time to depart, they appeared to engage each other's company much.'[105]

According to a scholar with descent from *tyereelore* and who grew up on Flinders Island, the Aboriginal Tasmanians began to perform new dances in the 1820s. At times women imitated seals, followed by children and men.[106] In another of Robinson's sketches the women appear alongside the sealers, dressed now in kangaroo-skin dresses, and despite the crude production, it is possible to make out one of the sealers' faces coloured darkly in pencil. This may be the 'native of New Zealand named John Witieye', from the Bay of Islands district, who was apparently known to Rev. Samuel Marsden, the evangelical promoter of Christian missions, encountered in a previous chapter. This man was a Māori named Matarra. He travelled to England and, in the Bass Strait, he married an Aboriginal woman.[107]

These *tyereelore* were Robinson's helpers and mediators, and assisted him in making contact with inland Aboriginal communities as also with other women whom Robinson hoped to take into 'protection'. It was from the sealers and their information in turn from these Aboriginal Tasmanians that Robinson learnt that the body of an Aboriginal female speared by an Aboriginal male was lying on Robbins Island.[108]

To stress mutual entanglement, in the passage of information like this, before the undoubted power of empire and its classificatory project is to make it possible to appreciate one continuing legacy. Some descendants of these mixed communities live into the present and claim the heritage of the Aboriginal Tasmanians as their own. This runs contrary to nineteenth-century accounts of the extermination of Aboriginal Tasmanians.[109] To follow scholars of Aboriginal descent, this continuing heritage should not be denied despite the dramatic reduction of the population of Aboriginal peoples in the north-west of Tasmania, especially at the hands of armed parties during the Tasmanian Wars.[110]

The history of Tasmania is a story of tremendous violence and colonialism. Yet indigenous perspectives and traditions as well as the reliance of colonists on indigenous peoples are not absent from the story. The British imperial counter-revolution had to take account of what existed before in mounting a militarised humanitarian intervention which violently and intentionally overtook Aboriginal presence. Robinson's need of Aboriginal women as go-betweens sits alongside his ethnographic and intrusive styles of representation which gave these women so little agency.

INDIGENOUS PEOPLES ON THE
MOVE ACROSS WATER

There is another context for understanding Robinson's meetings with sealers. Indigenous peoples not only from Tasmania but from Australia and Aotearoa/New Zealand too travelled the oceans. The waters of these southern seas showed both indigenous and colonial activity.

George Briggs, the sealer who resided in the strait, was accompanied by indigenous women on voyages to Sydney and perhaps to New Zealand. Among James Munro's wives were indigenous peoples of the Australian mainland and one of Munro's wives was from New Zealand.[111] In the Bass Strait was at least one Indian woman, who was a Hindu who lived with a sealer. The extent of this water-borne migration means that the Tasmanian story of sealing should be contextualised alongside the sealing and whaling communities in New Zealand and off the coast of mainland Australia. The connective tissue of British commerce linked these places up and so provided a new terrain for the travels of indigenous women and men too.

The result of these connections was evident in the cultural life of sealers and whalers. Creole dialects emerged, Europeans were 'nativised' and Aboriginal people were 'Europeanised'. Knowledge about fishing and hunting passed between the Europeans and indigenous peoples.[112] Aboriginal ideas of gender played a role here as Aboriginal women instructed white men on how to survive in harsh conditions.[113] The women who hunted seals extended their traditional roles in order to find their path in the quickly evolving complex of European trade.

As with Cora and Bungaree, colonial understandings of race, gender and marriage were overlaid on Aboriginal notions of self. The changing status of the Aboriginal woman (Māori, Aboriginal Australian and Tasmanian), as the British empire and its commerce and culture took hold, appears in two histories of partnership. These biographies have been pieced together by other historians.[114]

The first is the story of William Pelham Dutton. He was born in Sydney, grew up in Hobart, and has a claim to being the pioneer of Portland, in the Australian state of Victoria. He established a partnership with Renganghi, also called Sarah, an Aboriginal Tasmanian woman.[115] From his base in Portland, Dutton traded seal skins with London and China and moved from sealing to whaling. Renganghi sailed with Dutton when he captained the *Henry*. Dutton allegedly rescued her from a sealing community on Kangaroo Island, off the coast of Australia. The couple lived in a hut in Portland and had a daughter. When Dutton was away whaling, Renganghi managed the whaling station they owned and worked alongside the whalers. In the end, when Dutton was away on a whaling mission, Renganghi was removed into the 'protection' of Robinson in 1836, and to Flinders Island.

Dutton and Renganghi moved in a maritime world which bridged Tasmania, New Zealand and Australia. A logbook from the *Africaine* commanded by Dutton in 1840–1 is revealing. In this source, it is difficult to locate where the *Africaine* is as its itinerary moves between mainland Australia and Tasmania and New Zealand. Rather than taking the land as a point of reference, the log is marked by the catch. This dry account of wind and sea is interrupted by drawings of fish tails to indicate success with whaling, a practice adopted by other whaling voyage logbooks at this time. The number of tails amounts to the number of whales taken.[116]

Recovering Renganghi's life has necessitated an archival feat. The reconstruction relies on shreds of evidence, such as this account of her, by Edward Henty, who is held responsible for her deportation to Flinders Island:

5 January 1835, Monday
. . . Sailed the Schooner Thistle for Launceston. Passenger H. Camfield, & 1 Black Woman belonging to Wm Dutton to be landed at Kings Island.[117]

The second story is of Tommy Chaseland, who in contrast with Dutton is well remembered on the South Island of New Zealand, given that a district of Otago and a promontory are named after him. He was the son of an Aboriginal Australian woman and an English convict. He had been involved in crewing between Tasmania and Sydney, and the wider Pacific, including the Marquesas and Tahiti, and also Calcutta and Mauritius, before he settled in New Zealand in 1824.[118] He came to have the Māori name Tame Titirene, possibly after *titi*, the mutton bird.[119]

His integration into the Māori world was not without violence. He was involved in retaliatory revenge on Māori for what sealers took to be crimes committed against them.[120] He became the headman of the sealing boats in Foveaux Strait, off South Island, belonging to Robert Campbell, a Calcutta merchant who had moved to Sydney.[121] His relationship with a Māori woman, Puna, first comes into the archive when he navigated an open sealing boat from Chatham Island, after being wrecked there. According to an oral history collected in the early twentieth century, Puna helped Chaseland by sitting in the bow of his boat 'karakia-ing' or praying till the storm abated.[122] After he settled at Codfish Island, which was set aside for sealers by Māori chiefs, he once again found himself in total debt to Puna. When shipwrecked, Puna is said to have dragged Tommy ashore. By 1844, Puna had taken on 'household duties of cooking and bed-making', and in another recollection she was described as 'one of the few Māori women . . . capable of being a helpmate to a civilised man'.[123] By this time Chaseland had become renowned as a whaler, perhaps the best in New Zealand. He is said to have become quite a 'dandy', enjoying the white shirts which were ironed for him by Puna.[124] In historian Lynette Russell's words: 'although he never *becomes* white, he is described in terms that imply he was not seen as merely coloured.'[125]

In contrast with the story of the Renganghi–Dutton relationship, the Puna–Chaseland partnership made the transition to an age of liberal imperialism: it was blessed and formalised by Rev. James Watkin in 1843. Puna was also baptised.[126] She died six years later. Tommy then married a young woman, the daughter of a Māori woman and a Portuguese sailor.[127] Before her death, however, Puna was able to determine her fate; this possibility was open to her in part because of her birth as part of a powerful Māori chiefly family of the Ngai Tahu.[128] Yet that hereditary privilege was placed first within the complex of sealing and whaling and then within the cultural expectations of British settlement.

These two stories are not exceptional. The fact that they can be retold depends on the men in question being unusual and working at the head of the sealing and whaling communities which they represent. This means that they left more historical traces. Despite their differences, they show that sealing and whaling allowed women and men to develop strategic partnerships in several sites of the triangle between Tasmania, New South Wales and New Zealand. All this points to the role that British commerce, religion and empire played as the context for the continued presence of indigenous peoples.

There were differences according to locale. Southern New Zealand, Chaseland's base, followed the changing pattern of sealing slightly earlier in Tasmania. Indeed, the development of sealing in New Zealand came in the wake of people moving out of the Bass Strait.[129] In turn, by the 1830s, in southern New Zealand, with the movement of people from sealing to whaling, whaling stations became sites of inter-cultural relationships, where whalers engaged in marriage with indigenous women to get access to land.[130] Meanwhile, in Tasmania, a narrative of 'the extermination of the native' took hold, despite the continuing evidence of mixed-heritage communities. In turn, the southern New Zealand story should be set in contrast to that from the Bay of Islands, encountered in an earlier chapter, and where the Treaty of Waitangi was signed and the seat of government was established.[131]

SYSTEMATIC COLONISATION

The rise of British settlement, as it moved from the sea to the taking of land and the creation of pasture, was the next step in the sequence of events.

One critical aspect of this transition was the link between sealing, whaling and land-based settlement. First, those involved in sealing and whaling became more sophisticated in their commerce, linking their trades across the Tasman Sea with London, Calcutta, Canton, Cape Town and the Pacific islands. They broke free of the control over trade exercised by an officer class in Sydney.[132] Second, they began to set their own terms, where earlier they were hemmed in both by the control of the East India Company in India, which enjoyed the exclusive privilege of trade from the Cape of Good Hope to Cape Horn, and the lack of a local currency. Third, they shifted from sea to land as the oceans were plundered without moderation. The turn to terra firma came as war, economic blockade and depression in Europe changed the context of maritime trade.[133] Fisheries gave way to other trades.

Supporting this shift was an ideology of 'systematic colonisation'. This ideology stood opposed to the supposed illiteracy, racial mixing, slavery and plunder of a previous age. 'Systematic colonisation' was a philosophy which aimed at correcting the pragmatic dispersal of settlers; it saw the setting up of joint-stock companies for colonisation across the Tasman Sea. The Van Diemen's Land Company, formed by an Act of the British parliament, was set up in 1825 with the aim of applying its capital in Tasmania for the supply of wool to British factories. It was granted a block of 25,000 acres on the north-west coast of Tasmania, bordered by the sea on one side. By 1830 it had acquired a series of plots of land.

In its early years, the company was the envy of other colonists in Tasmania who saw it as 'nothing more or less than a monopoly'.[134] Despite seeing agriculture as its prime end, the company wanted to take sealing and whaling under its patronage. Its first annual report noted the intention of making loans to whalers and sealers and to keep houses, wharves and other buildings.[135] The company's indentured servants escaped and made complaints about their treatment. Humanitarians like Robinson documented the violence that erupted between Aboriginal Tasmanians and company agents.[136] It was not successful at raising sheep for wool, but diversified, and the Van Diemen's Land company exists to this day as Tasman Agriculture Ltd.

Across the sea in New Zealand, the link between sealers and whalers and company-endorsed taking of land is seen in the impact of the ideas of Edward Gibbon Wakefield, the chief thinker behind 'systematic colonisation'. Wakefield proposed the sale of land rather than the allocation of free grants, believing that this would allow the colonial economy to expand by promoting labour and restricting the rapid transformation of settlers into landowners. Wakefield took a specific interest in New Zealand, which fed into the establishment of the New Zealand Colonization Company in 1838. His brother William Wakefield arrived in New Zealand in 1839; also among the arrivals was Edward Gibbon Wakefield's son, Edward Jerningham Wakefield. When the Treaty of Waitangi was being negotiated, William Wakefield was bargaining for land from Māori and noting how speculators from Sydney and Hobart were haphazardly taking up land in New Zealand.[137] At its height the Company owned a million acres and four towns: Wellington, New Plymouth, Wanganui and Nelson.[138]

Maritime workers keep appearing in William's and Edward's journals.[139] William wrote that whalers were anxious for an English settlement. He described whaling stations in the midst of his tour, including one

headed by Taiaroa of Otago, 'the most Europeanised chief of New
Zealand', with numerous whale boats. Despite presenting his negotiations with chiefs as his own work, a Mr Barrett intrudes into his writing.
Dicky Barrett was a whaler who knew the geography of New Zealand.
Wakefield credited him with having great influence on the Ngai Tahu
tribe, having married the daughter of a chief, Wakaiwa Rawinia.[140] In
William's negotiations at Port Nicholson for the purchase of land, Barrett
was a critical aide allowing William to intervene in the ceremonial debate
which unfolded among the chiefs about whether to sell the land.[141]
Wakefield's journal slipped between 'through Barrett' and 'I' in recording
the result:

> At [the debate's] conclusion I formally asked the Chiefs, through
> Mr. Barrett, whether they had made up their minds and they asked me
> 'Have you seen the place? and how do you like it.' I replied that I had
> seen all I wanted and that it was good . . .[142]

Even as the Company's work turned after the purchase of this land
to surveying, town planning and wharf building, Wakefield wrote in 1840
that he had appointed Barrett, 'agent for the natives', in which office he
would be 'the medium between the settlers and their dark neighbours'.
A salary of £100 per annum was attached to the job.[143] It should be no
surprise that Wakefield also made Barrett harbour master.[144] The incor-
poration of a whaler into the core of the company highlights the intent
of this systematic colonisation to appropriate and transform existent
contacts and settlement in New Zealand.[145] Barrett eventually set up a
hotel, Barrett's Hotel, which became a civic hub in Wellington. Tellingly,
denoting the shift from sea to land, he also took up cattle farming.[146]

The resonances of the age of revolutions were still evident in this
history. This is well illustrated in the career of the Copenhagen-born
Jorgen Jorgenson, who accompanied Flinders and was involved in sealing
and whaling. He proceeded to become an employee of the Van Diemen's
Land Company, traversing and exploring the interior as he had done
the seas before.[147] In the interim, while in Europe, he became embroiled
in the Napoleonic wars, and was taken a prisoner of war in England after
he attacked English ships in the wake of the occupation of Copenhagen
by an English expeditionary force. He took the title 'His Excellency, the
Protector of Iceland, Commander in Chief by Land and Sea', after
attempting a revolution in Iceland, in order to set it free of Denmark.[148]

In his last incarnation in Tasmania, to which colony he was sent as a convict, the privateering, trading and adventure for which he was renowned at sea was directed towards bushrangers, sheep thieves and to the policing of Aboriginal Tasmanians.[149]

In Sydney, new modes of free trade fed into the colonial regularisation of settlement. Another key life story, that of the Scot Robert Campbell of Campbell & Co. is an excellent example of the phases of this transformation. After arriving from India Campbell quickly became interested in sealing expeditions to pay for merchandise brought into Sydney. His was not the only Calcutta firm testing Sydney waters in these years.[150] Campbell built a private wharf, constructed whale boats from teak imported from Calcutta, and stocked the colony and Tasmania too with horses and cattle from India. He enjoyed wide popularity in the early nineteenth century for lowering the prices of foreign articles in Sydney, and was celebrated for his assault on monopolies.[151] He eventually defied the East India Company's monopoly, by attempting to trade directly with London. In 1805 he sailed to London with his family and a cargo of 260 tonnes of seal oil and 14,000 skins.[152]

As the decades passed Campbell shifted from trade to politics. Taking up an appointment as a magistrate and naval officer, he became embroiled in a rebellion against Governor William Bligh, already famous for the mutiny on the *Bounty*. In 1825 he became a member of the Legislative Council. He petitioned for the end of the transportation of convicts, arguing that free immigration should be encouraged. He opposed the liberal principle of trial by jury, and when it was passed wrote that if it had not been carried: 'my children would not have been exposed to the degradation of being brought in association, day after day, in the Jury Box, with the refuse of the Gaols and Hulks of the Mother Country'.[153] His political work came together with an increasing investment in choice land, well fitted for pasture, including a tract in what is now Canberra. According to his calculation of 1831, he owned 2,000 sheep and 600 cattle.[154]

To move to another biography that demonstrates the changes that engulfed maritime traders, the name of James Kelly, encountered earlier as the watcher of Aboriginal sealers, still resonates in Hobart. Kelly's Steps, a historic outdoor stairway, is a stop on the tourist trail. Kelly was born in New South Wales as a 'currency lad', a term for the first generation of free children born to convicts. He became involved in sealing in the Bass Strait, working as an apprentice for the Sydney firm of Kable and Underwood 'to learn the art or mistery of a mariner'.[155] He went on to be renowned for his circumnavigation of Van Diemen's Land in 1821. From Hobart he also sealed towards southern New Zealand, where he came into a violent encounter with Māori, when he sought to mete out revenge. He was appointed harbour master in Hobart in 1821 and moved into whaling. He developed his whaling stations together with farmland which provided supplies to whalers.

The contracts of agreement for his whaling voyages – which form a large part of his papers – are tokens of the indeterminacy of this trade. Kelly's crews had to sign up for a voyage on which they promised to navigate and travel from 'place to place as they may be directed'. They were paid in ratio to the marketable products, such as oil and whale bone resulting from the voyage.[156] In 1842 Kelly was declared bankrupt.[157] This last fact bears out that individuals like Kelly did not meet with unqualified success. Indeed, lesser-known individuals went from one financial crisis to another.

The uncertain rise of the merchant and landed class was felt not only on the streets of the burgeoning settlements across the Tasman Sea and Bass Strait. These were intimate changes which had domestic consequences. Where Aboriginal or indigenous women as well as men had liaisons with traders, sealers and whalers, in these new circumstances of settlement, a policy of 'whitening' was unleashed.[158] William Wakefield, in his journal from New Zealand, wrote that the taking of a 'native female' in a 'quasi marriage' was a natural result of 'irregular colonisation'. It would now give way.[159] The extent of immigration into Australia and New Zealand, with the extension of agriculture, the opening up of rural frontiers and finally the discovery of gold, allowed white settlers to create households far beyond the urban centres. With this arose a legal sanction for the dispossession of indigenous peoples, with the proclamation of their land as rightfully owned by the Crown.[160] These were two related effects of systematic empire.

In the Campbell household, Mrs Sophia Campbell, the sister of the commissary, who was Campbell's close associate, mothered seven children. It was no wonder then that Robert could write that he had 'a numerous Family to maintain and educate'.[161] Campbell's house was by the wharf and its openness to 'depredation' was quite evident. Robert wrote on one occasion: 'my family were alarmed last Night by a Man (a Prisoner in the Dock-Yard) being detected in one of the upper rooms'.[162] In Hobart, Kelly built a grand house for his family, arranged music lessons for his daughters and sent his sons for schooling to London. He had a pew in

St David's Church.[163] As an archaeologist of the Kelly whale-stations writes, Kelly was part of the 'generation between' and 'caught between the older mentality of rank and the new, modern divisions of class'.[164] The rising status of his family arrived together with tragedy. His bankruptcy coincided with the death of his wife after the birth of their tenth child and the death of his eldest son in a whaling accident.[165]

As these two vignettes reveal, the makings of the colonial family were precarious, and especially so when respectability had to be built on the foundations of dangerous and speculative trades.

The anglicised landed and settled family had arrived, and so had empire come out of the waters to land, through a philosophical commitment to systematisation. Systematic colonisation saw a reversal of revolutionary principles; it was a counter-revolution with intimate consequences for family arrangements, based around new norms of race and gender. It transformed the culture of contact, reliance and violence between traders and indigenous women across water.

CONCLUSION

The picture of the Tasman World sketched here is unusual. Though a maritime swing is evident in histories of Australia and New Zealand, it remains the case that these two states are rarely bridged in the same historical telling for this period.[166] The separation of Australia and New Zealand arises partly from the view that British relations with Māori, including the Treaty of Waitangi in 1840, contrast with their general lack of treaty-making with the Aboriginal Australians. At the heart of this contrast are differences in attributed sovereignty and assignations of race and gender.[167] In addition, the contrast is shaped by the fact that Aotearoa/ New Zealand was not a convict settlement like New South Wales or Tasmania. The separation of these national stories is a symptom of how politically useful it has been to separate out the pathways taken by indigenous peoples. Yet in moving from New South Wales (and the stories of Cora and Bungaree) to Tasmania (and the horrific account of the Aboriginal Tasmanians and particularly the women sealers), on to Aotearoa/New Zealand (and the emergence of the settled family), the narrative has taken seriously the range of maritime links which were evident in the period.[168] Ideas, people and forms of representation moved across these sites making these places show parallels.

Across these sites, radical differences around the future of indigenous peoples for instance, emerged through this period, even as places were connected and disconnected in a rhythm which accompanied the move towards systematic colonisation. Throughout this story of relatedness and difference, indigenous people were able to make their presence felt and to move themselves. This set the framework for colonial mobility over these waters. Classifications of race and gender were overlaid upon indigenous agency and engagement with water. Colonial imposition and indigenous activity were tied together – the former did not proceed without having to come to terms with the latter in the period.

The counter-revolution of the British empire, as it established outposts here in the southern seas, includes the elite rivalries of exploratory voyages, for instance in the quest to plant a flag in Tasmania which riled Perón. It encompasses programmes of natural historical 'improvement' at the water's edge, including empiricist and romanticised descriptions of sea creatures. The counter-revolution is evident in the militarism, humanitarianism and reform that intervened here, and also in how these programmes utilised and ridiculed notions of chief, monarch and republican. The British deployed the idea of the civilised and settled family, allowing new conceptions of gender and marriage to be painted over Aboriginal understandings of self. The counter-revolution includes surveying and schooling, as much as patterns of free trade and anti-monopolism, of the kind supported by Campbell, which allowed the expansion of cities such as Sydney, Hobart or Wellington. This wide sensibility of how empire came to take shape in a moment of contestation between British and French travellers, and of war, allows Aboriginal peoples and their histories to be told alongside Europeans, when Aboriginal lands were taken to create the modern world.

It is easy to consider the histories of Australia and New Zealand as tied to land and pastoralism, and yet throughout this story water and land were bridged. Aboriginal women's and men's engagement with water were reconfigured around European gender norms about exploration, for instance in navigator Flinders' engagement with Bungaree. Indigenous women on the north coast of Tasmania taught vital skills of seal-hunting to sealing men and sealers; whalers influenced the programme of systematic colonisation on land in New Zealand. A language of maritime patriotism, evident for instance in anti-slavery and anti-piracy, ricocheted across this world and influenced the rise of the bureaucratic state, and the management of trades.

The biographies of settlers in turn point to the phases of transformation, from maritime trade to pastoralism, sometimes as was the case with Jorgenson, dramatically punctuated by the events of the European age of revolutions. Among those whose biographies were told, whalers and sealers settled down, changing from the sea to land, and from trade to politics, from mobility to Christian marriage. To write a history across the water is then to reconsider the origins of the British empire in this part of the world. At the same time, it is to connect up the separate entities of the continent of Australia and the islands of New Zealand and Tasmania. These places were born together as colonies – and yet their paths diverged.

Given the brutality of the Tasmanian war, and also the brutality of settlement colonisation, it isn't enough to leave the age of revolutions as an abstract and structural process of modernisation or a scheme of politics or political ideas. We need to consider how it gave rise to counter-revolutionary British imperialism. At the same time, it needs to be peopled. It needs to be considered for the transformations it gave rise to in conceptions of gender. And conceptions of race too. And thinking of the seals and whales, it needs to be populated with other creatures. For the consequences of this rapid expansion were environmental as well. This theme will be picked up next from a small sea in the Indian Ocean, the Bay of Bengal. And warfare will be a significant feature of the events that unfold.

6

At India's Maritime Frontier:
Waterborne Lineages of War

In the mid 1820s, the waters of the Bay of Bengal created a new danger for the kingdom of Ava in upper Burma.[1] Invaluable and unusual letters written by a Buddhist monk called Kyi-gan shin gyi, or 'The Elderly Novice of the village of Kyeegan [Kyi-gan] Lake' are indicators of what was afoot.[2]

This monk's real name was Maung Nu. He did not rise above the status of a novice monk. Instead, he led an itinerant life and moved in the circles of trade and the law. When his fame as a scholar spread, he was invited by King Bo-daw-hpaya to take up residence at his capital in Amarapura, now within reach of Mandalay in northern Burma/ Myanmar. Kyi-gan shin gyi's epistles were written on palm leaf. They are *Myit-taza* or letters of loving kindness, cast in a language which was meant to seem familiar to the Burmese villager. They were probably written on behalf of people who could not write to their relatives. They point to the plight of people caught up in the changes brought about by the centralisation of the Burmese kingdom of Ava and greater European trade. These changes led to migration from the north to the coasts to participate in this trade.

'The Elderly Novice' wrote for a young man, 'Lotus Leaf', who had travelled down the Irrawaddy to Rangoon: 'I should have written before I sailed. But in such trifling matters, the only important thing is love and affection.'[3] For 'Lotus Leaf', Rangoon was a city to which people came from across the Bay of Bengal: 'all sorts of sailors, strangers and aliens in habit and custom, and belonging to many races all of which I cannot name'. Among the people listed were Armenians, Roman Catholics, Portuguese, Africans, Arabs, all kinds of Indians including 'Hindu Sardhus [holy men], Muslim crewmen and Bombay merchants'.

They are hairy people with moustaches, side-whiskers, beards and shaggy legs. Energetic and alert, they hustle and bustle from place to place, round and round and up and down, in and out and to and fro, winding and curving, to all nooks and corners, east and north and west and south.

Particularly interesting is how this giddiness was contrasted with the steadiness of the people up the Irrawaddy in the north: 'I hope that my dear people at home remain constant and true to me, like that silver lizard, undisturbed by the scandalous and untrue accounts of what I did and what I do . . .' The silver lizard referred to the mariner's compass, which in the words of the letter, 'remains quietly constant always pointing to the north'.

According to one explanation which circulated at the time, in these years before the First Anglo-Burmese War (1824–6), Burma was a regime conceited with the certainty of victory against the British.[4] Such a characterisation of indigenous rulers and kings as 'oriental despots' was common across Asia. The European idea came to influence other conflicts which we will turn to shortly, including in Java, Sri Lanka and China. But Maung Nu's letters demonstrate instead a sensitive perception of danger, which is mapped on the land. The regions in the south along the coast and also the frontiers with British India are seen to be rife with turbulence. This was not then a kingdom uninformed of the wider world.

In another epistle written by this monk, for an anxious father addressing his son, new and troubling songs are said to be sung in the heart of the kingdom. The stars are lined up against King Bo-daw-hpaya:

Both the astrologers and the general public are agreed that times are bad, the planets are unfavourable and dangers are ahead for both the King and kingdom . . . Unfortunately for you, my son, you are in the path of his mighty army of destruction, as your business takes you to the great towns on the seaboard, for example, Dallah, Syriam, Martaban, Sittang, Thaton, Moulmein, Pegu, Hmawbi. These maritime regions of our country shall be the scene of our King's greatest victory, but they will also be the scene of disaster and destruction wrought by his might.[5]

Kingdoms like Ava and Kandy, the latter being the interior highland kingdom of what is now Sri Lanka, and the island's last remaining independent foothold, are often presented as landlocked. Asian regimes of the period are traditionally seen to have not had the skills to engage the technological and military capacities of maritime Europeans. This applies especially to their response to the advance of the British who invaded these territories during and after the Napoleonic wars and across the seas. Yet contrary to such an interpretation, there was a stand-off on the Irrawaddy River in the midst of the First Anglo-Burmese War. In Sri Lanka, the British, coming from the coast again, first lost rather spectacularly to the interior kingdom of Kandy in 1803, before defeating Kandy in 1815.

During the late eighteenth and early nineteenth centuries a critical technical gap opened up between European armies and navies and non-European forces. Yet this did not give rise to automatic success to colonisers. In Asian environments, logistics, terrain and transport continued to be difficult. One might add that this was particularly so in sea-facing places, where the terrain could change rapidly, ranging across coastal territories, highlands, rivers and swamps. Asian regimes responded actively, finding their path in the midst of European advance. Meanwhile, in these theatres, the fact that Europeans could not be certain of victory meant that they turned to extensive looting.

BOATS AT WAR

The First Anglo-Burmese conflict is a neglected war in histories of the early British empire. This neglect is unwarranted. For it cost the British 5 million pounds and 15,000 lives and lasted two years.[6]

War began as the kingdom of Ava pushed to the west, led by Ba-gyi-daw, the grandson of Bo-daw-hpaya, seeking greater control of territories outside his purview in Manipur, Arakan, and Assam. The British based in Calcutta began to worry. Reports circulated of Burma's wish to take Calcutta.[7] Ava invaded Manipur in 1758 and 1764 and finally subdued it just prior to the First Anglo-Burmese War.[8] Arakan was annexed in 1785 and 20,000 men marched on Assam under the command of Maha Bandula I in 1821. They took apart the Ahom court in Assam. Streams of refugees from this region, fears of further expansion by Ava and frontier conflict over the Arakan border led to British India's declaration of war in 1824.

The First Anglo-Burmese War is correctly interpreted as arising from a contest over land boundaries, and its tortured course was determined partly by the monsoon and the terrain, for instance in the mountains of the Arakan Yoma in western Burma/Myanmar today. Yet it was won by the British because of their action by sea, with the arrival of a naval fleet in Rangoon, which stopped first in the Bay of Bengal in the Andaman Islands.

The sea advance surprised the Burmese forces, under Bandula, who were conducting a well-planned two-pronged raid, originating from Assam and Arakan. They were attempting to open up the way to Chittagong and on to Calcutta over land.[9] This overland campaign might have met with some surprise results in Ava's favour, given the bare British defences in Chittagong. Yet the arrival of the British ships at Rangoon necessitated an about turn for Bandula's forces who had to meet the British there.

After the arrival of the British fleet, both sides played out their politics on the Irrawaddy River. An important phase of war saw boats in combat. The Burmese were aware of British advances elsewhere and had clear ideas of their sovereignty. Ava defined its sovereignty against the ideal kingdom, Zambudipa (or Jambudipa), the island of the Buddhist cosmos.[10] Ava was at this time consolidating itself against internal rivals by creating a pan-Burmese ethnic sensibility and this fed increased warfare. The ethnicised title Myan-ma was used for Burma for the first time in the late eighteenth century. As the historian Victor Lieberman notes: 'imperial and pan-Burman loyalties increasingly superseded local identities.'[11] The use of boats, the kingdom's response to Anglo-French rivalry, its adoption of European objects of display and its attention to maritime trade, point to a reflective and reactive politics, which is in keeping with global developments and regional changes. Theirs was not a naïve militarism.

On arrival in Rangoon the British were greeted by its dockyards. Employing famous Burmese teak, a key export trade in Rangoon, these yards functioned under half a dozen foreign shipbuilders. Most of the ships were built for Armenians or Muslim traders. The arriving Rangoon expedition met two large vessels of 300 tons, built for the ruler of Muscat, whose reach extended even here.[12] As an example of the Armenian connection, one shipbuilder was the merchant Manook Sarkies. He acted as an interpreter for the British.[13] Sarkies' family firm traded in indigo, betel-nut and stick-lac.[14]

The British interest in maritime Burma is evident in the intense scrutiny that troops paid to Burmese war boats. One published account noted the use of 'magnificent teak, for the construction of boats, first roughly shaped, and then expanded by means of fire'. The author, Captain Thomas Abercromby Trant, ranked these war boats above British vessels. This was on the basis of their rapidity, which arose from their lightness and their small surface above the water, combined with the 'uniform pulling of the oar falling in cadence with the songs of the boatmen'. Trant gave his readers the musical notation for Burmese war boat songs over three pages.[15] War boats were said to carry about fifty or sixty rowers and to 'sail in fleets' and to mount 'impetuous' attack.[16] In a splendid image, Captain Frederick Marryat, who became the chief naval officer in Rangoon, presented a captured long gilt war boat, eighty-four feet in length, snaking up the Irrawaddy, with its rowers arranged in precise order.[17] [Fig. 6.1]. In one version of the image the gilt on the boat matches the gilt pagodas on the shore.[18]

The glorification of the war boat went together with the classification of two inferior kinds of Burmese boats: flat bottoms, which belonged to traders, and the 'mere canoe'.[19] Before the war, the traffic in large boats

Fig. 6.1 'One of the Birman Gilt War Boats Captured by Capt.
Chads, R.N. in his successful expedition against Tanthabeen Stockade', 1826

up the Irrawaddy included a trade in rice to the north, and guns for the court passed on this route too.[20] The advantage of Burmese riverine and coastal craft was their shallow draft combined with the power of oarsmen, which performed very well in the intricate creeks and rivers of Burma. In these waterways European sea-going vessels ran aground or could not cope with river currents or the twists and turns of the river.[21]

The published visual sequence of the war went from the gathering of the British fleet at the Andaman Islands, in the Bay of Bengal; the fleet's arrival at Rangoon; the taking of Rangoon, with its brilliant pagodas, of which images were drawn in order to point to the gilt; and the onward passage of British vessels up the Irrawaddy.[22] British boats, with the assistance of land forces, were shown facing off Burmese war boats.[23] The visual repertoire of the war was maritime and allowed a maritime conflict to be redrawn in inland Asia.

At the end of the war, British interest in the seaboard was especially evident in how the colonists took Manipur, Arakan and Tennasserim, by the 1826 Treaty of Yandabo, dramatically reducing Burma's access to the Bay of Bengal. After the war, in the Burmese court chronicle, *Kon-baung-zet Maha Ya-zawin-daw-gyi*, the king is advised by the princes and ministers that the towns and villages along the river from Rangoon are the 'gateways through which war may find its way'.[24]

In the midst of the war, the British need to take Burmese navigation seriously was combined with their alarm at the eruption of another type of conflict on the river. 'Earth oil', as petroleum was called by some of the British commentators in Burma, was an ill-understood resource, supposedly present wherever the Burmese could transport it by water. It was used to light lamps and smear timber to protect it from insects.[25] During the war, the Burmese constructed rafts and placed jars of petroleum on them, launching them ablaze to encircle British vessels, as 'moving volcanoes'.[26] In Captain Marryat's private log is evidence of how the British responded to fire with fire:

> 1824
> June 30   Fire rafts came down
> July 1ST   Mr. Fredk Brown. Mid[shipman]: died
>   Fire rafts sent down
> 3RD   Burnt Dalla [town].[27]

Fire had a rich symbolic politics within Burma. Wood-built towns were in constant danger of burning; the king had to appoint fire officers to keep them safe. Amarapura, the capital, had burnt down in 1810. Royal usurpers were also known to use fire.[28] For the British fire was part and parcel of scorched-earth techniques. With fire too, as with the marine character of the conflict, there was symmetry and entanglement.

War by boats led in time and after the conflict to diplomacy by boats. John Crawfurd, who had accompanied the British expedition which took Java from the Dutch in 1811, entered Burma at the conclusion of the war in 1826, as civil commissioner in Rangoon. Crawfurd headed an embassy to Ava, to negotiate a commercial treaty. He was made to witness a water festival which included an exhibition of boats. On his arrival by boat at the festival, he noted the monarch and queen in a large barge:

> This vessel, the form of which represented two huge fishes, was extremely splendid: every part of it was richly gilt, and a spire of at least thirty feet high, resembling in miniature that of the palace, rose in the middle.

Crawfurd wrote of gilt war boats and gilt state boats where the gilt covered all the oars and paddles. As a statement of royal power, the king paraded under his white umbrella and the state vessels had thrones for the king and his queen. The monarch and his wife sat under a green canopy at the bow of the large barge, 'the only part ever occupied by persons of rank'.[29] In this way, the sacred kingdom, centred on the king's person with his subjects in circles around him, was arranged on water. Crawfurd and the British were being enrolled, unwittingly, in this symbolic politics. The spectacle of the court on water, accompanied by war boats, was also depicted in the illustrated *parabaik*, or folding manuscripts, and the temple art of the period, indicating a wider visual life. [Fig. 6.2][30]

In the court chronicle, now translated into English, the import of all this is clear: the king still saw himself as lord, or literally the sole and supreme monarch, of the whole of Burma.[31] At the conclusion of the war, the chronicle does not speak of defeat at the hands of the British, but rather of how the British had over-extended themselves, necessitating a negotiation of peace. The king would make a gracious payment of the expenses of the British, in keeping with Buddhist sensibility. The king would be 'overcoming by giving'.[32] In turn, this is what the British referred to as an indemnity.[33] Elsewhere the king is recorded as proclaiming on the waxing of Tagu, 1187, which corresponds to 11 March 1826: 'I have observed all rules of kingly conduct.'[34] All these elements were intended as statements

Fig. 6.2. *Parabaik* image, showing royal festival on water

of political power. Burma was not silent or unversed in how to do politics with strangers. Though a gap in techniques of war may have been opening, in practical terms the British and Burmese were still a matched pair.

Despite this symmetry, rather than demonstrating understanding or a depth of curiosity, Crawfurd's narrative descended into a stereotypical view of the Orient. The end of the boat festival, for instance, was a profusion of 'barbaric gold', 'the most splendid and imposing which I had ever seen, and not unworthy of Eastern romance'.[35] This orientalist vision continued in the portrayal of Burmese artefacts which arrived in England from the war. Rev. John Skinner was one observer of a collection, brought back by Marryat, and displayed at the Asiatic Society in Bond Street, London. He wrote that the model of the Burmese war boat was comparable to a Norman vessel, 'as represented in the Bayeaux tapestry'. Skinner's diary included watercolours of the Marryat collection. In one image, the war boat was depicted without the customary rowers, alongside an isolated paddle, a rudder, a pole, a Burmese bell and Buddha images.[36]

There was another way in which techniques of war and the symbolism of politics orbited around a boat in the First Anglo-Burmese War. This time it concerned a British vessel. The ship which created the most talk around the First Anglo-Burmese War was the steam vessel *Diana*. It reveals the lack of easy success which the British experienced through the use of new technologies of war.[37] It was Marryat's idea to use it in combat, and it was the first time a steam vessel was deployed by the British in war. In one illustration of the war, in the background, the town of Dalla, 'a considerable place' is up in flames, fired upon by British forces. [Fig. 6.3] Yet there is no detail of the destroyed town. Instead, there is an array of British vessels. The *Diana* sits on the left, accompanied by a Malay prow, the gun-brig *Larne*, under Marryat's command, a captured Burmese war boat and a transport vessel. The assembly of ships in calm water indicates how British war relied, especially in this terrain, on gathering a range of vessels, including those used by Asians in the Bay of Bengal or on the Irrawaddy.[38]

Despite this reliance and mixture of modes of navigation, the advantage that the *Diana* provided is undoubted, for instance for launching rockets. According to British reportage these amazed the Burmese for their rapid succession, fatal aim and 'ominous hissing'.[39] In the words of one Englishman, who came aboard the *Diana*, after being kept captive by the king for the two years of the war, the steamship was a 'work of Enchantment',

Fig. 6.3 'The Conflagration at Dalla', from Joseph Moore,
Rangoon Views and Combined Operations in the Birman Empire, (1825-6)

for the terror it induced among the local people.[40] They approached it like
some 'infernal beast called into existence by superior art in sorcery'.[41] This
enchantment was well appreciated by the British. The steam boat kept
pace with Burmese war boats, and allowed for their capture.[42]

Later, Crawfurd travelled on the *Diana* in the course of his embassy,
writing repeatedly of how anxious the Burmese were to see the steam
vessel.[43] The king allegedly proclaimed a wish to own a steam vessel and
took note of the coal, asking whether the mineral was found within Burma.[44]
If the Burmese choreographed a spectacle of boats to communicate the
ideal of the Buddhist king, the British hoped that steam power itself was
a symbol of their rising imperial prowess with machines. The symbolic
power of the steam vessel was also set against Burmese traditions. British
observers recorded a prophecy in circulation among the Burmese that the
kingdom would not be overtaken until a vessel ascended the Irrawaddy,
at the time of the monsoon, without the assistance of rowers or sails.[45]

Contradictorily, Crawfurd noted that it took his embassy on the *Diana*
thirty days to reach Ava from Rangoon. This compared with a Burmese
war boat, travelling both night and day, taking four days 'in the freshes'

and ten days 'in the season of the rains'.[46] The steam vessel struggled on the return journey, given the drop in the level of the river, and it required the assistance of three hundred Burmese at one point to drag it off a sandbank.[47] The triumph of British technology was still not a full one and the dramatic impact of steam should not be assumed. By 1844, the Burmese had bought their first steamship. They used *mi* or 'fire' to refer to the steam, making a steam ship a fire machine in Burmese.[48]

In all these ways, both the British and the Burmese engaged with water, for diplomacy and symbolism as well as for warfare. If this high-lights the entanglement and symmetry between the British and the Burmese, the global context of the Napoleonic Wars generated a degree of looting in the course of this war. This looting is a key indicator of how the balance of the scales was altered.

POST-NAPOLEONIC LOOTING

The Shwedagon Pagoda remains a mesmerising icon for the newly arrived visitor to Yangon, the city that was colonial Rangoon. [Fig. 6.4] It is believed to enshrine relics of the Gautama Buddha and three of his predecessors. After ascending one of its staircases, past a myriad of vendors, one reaches the upper terrace. At twilight this fills with devo-tees and tourists, who pass clockwise, as I did, around the pagoda and its many associated halls, shrines and temples. Given the other-worldly atmosphere which soaks the site, it is difficult today to imagine that this pagoda was the epicentre of one phase of the First Anglo-Burmese War. After Rangoon was taken the British made the Shwedagon Pagoda the headquarters of their operation.[49]

The choice of this base was surely strategic given the pagoda's height. But the use of the pagoda was also a statement of cultural arrogance. Where Buddhist priests 'sung the praises of their deity', one commentator wrote, 'a British soldier was now seen cleaning his musket, or smoking a cigar'. '[A] chakoh [military cap] sacrilegiously adorned the head of the god Buddha, whilst his arms supported red jackets, knapsacks, and other accompaniments of a soldier's equipment.'[50] A bell found within the complex was prized for its gold and silver and its inscriptions in Pali and Burmese. It was hauled onto a raft to be sent to Calcutta, only to sink in the river, to be dredged up in January 1826 and restored to the Shwedagon.[51]

Elsewhere the pillage of cultural artefacts was even more successful. In the midst of the war, it became the norm to 'rifle' through temples and sacred sites, with a view to claiming the relics within.[52] Looting fed hungry troops. On one occasion, it was reported that there were four thousand Burmese bullocks within the ranks of the army. Men hid ducks and other fowl stolen from houses.[53] The manner in which British forces scoured the landscape for small cells or chambers enclosing silver- or gold-covered images was compared to a form of 'sapping and mining'; indeed, it was driven by the perceived value of the metals.[54]

This generated a market in Burmese artefacts; objects were advertised in Calcutta and fell into private hands in London.[55] Marryat had a collection of at least 173 items, including the model war-boat sketched by Skinner. He proposed that he become a trustee of the British Museum,

Fig. 6.4 Shwedagon Pagoda, Author's photograph

in view of the loot he brought back from Burma. He also presented a
'Colossal Gilt figure of the Burmah deity Guadma', a Buddha statue, to
the British Museum. According to one important early orientalist scholar
of Buddhism, this artefact came from the Shwedagon Pagoda.[56] This was
a hollow lacquered figure, which was first displayed in the museum on
the main staircase next to the giraffes when the museum was at its
original site, Montagu House.[57]

The maritime stand-off, the pillage and the prolonged conflict which
make up the First Anglo-Burmese War all help sustain the argument
that this conflict is a child of the Napoleonic wars. It needs to be placed
within the age of revolutions. Sticking with objects, the lineage is evident
in the history of another extraordinary object, 'one entire blaze of gold,
silver, and precious stones', which was pillaged to arrive on the streets
of London.[58] This object speaks of a history of exchange and imitation.
It was taken from the seaport of Tavoy in Burma. It was built in keeping
with the pattern of a previous gift given by the British to the Burmese.
It was then sold in Calcutta and reached the popular Egyptian Hall in
Piccadilly, London, from where it was resold to a private individual after
attracting much attention in the press.[59] The object in question was the
magnificent Burmese Imperial State Carriage or Rath.

Unlike the carriage which had been given by the British to the Burmese,
which had a low seat for the king, this imperial carriage allowed the
monarch to sit at a height and perform the symbolic politics of kingship.
It had a moveable seat.[60] The hype that built around the display was
inspired by the memory of another carriage taken in war, which had
brought the crowds in: the carriage of Napoleon, displayed in the Egyptian
Hall in 1816. *The Times* introduced the display of the carriage as a direct
successor to the display of Napoleon's carriage, predicting that it would
'be equally attractive with the carriage of Buonaparte'. It continued: 'It
bears we are told an exact similitude to the chief pagoda at Shoemandro
[Shwedagon], and consists of seven stories, progressively diminishing in
the most skilful proportions.'[61]

For the journalist, and by extrapolation the resurgent British, both
the king of Ava and Napoleon were seen as vanquished and over-
confident foes:

> The King of Ava, during the late war with France, expressed his
> wonder that our Government did not apply to him for assistance
> against Buonaparte. He could find, he said 40,000 men, who could

sweep the whole French nation from the face of the earth. After such a presumptuous piece of arrogance our readers will not be surprised at hearing that he had the candour to warn our Indian Government, that after he has driven us from India, he will *march* an army to subjugate England.[62]

FRENCH AND BRITISH ENGAGEMENTS
AROUND THE FIRST ANGLO-BURMESE WAR

The reason why the Napoleonic wars could provide the point of comparison and the frame for the First Anglo-Burmese War is evident from a consideration of a longer period.

French and English connections from India played a role in lower Burma in the eighteenth century, and these outside connections were embroiled in the mid-eighteenth-century war between Pegu in the south and Ava in the north.[63] The rebels of the south were incensed by Avan taxation and immigration to the south.[64] Both the French and the English set up footholds in Lower Burma to refit ships.[65] Before the fall of Pondichéry, the French could consider the possibility of moving their headquarters in the Indian Ocean to Burma. Admiral de Suffren, encountered before, was the chief protagonist of this scheme.[66]

Two successive British embassies were led by Michael Symes, in 1795 and 1802, who later fought in the Peninsular War in Spain and died at sea. They had as one of their aims the intention of persuading the Burmese monarch to sever his links to France.[67] Burmese links to France were animated via Burma's contact with Île de France, a fascinating episode of long-distance diplomacy and trade, which has been overlooked by historians of the Indian Ocean. On Symes' first embassy, negotiations were adversely affected when:

> . . . advice came of the arrival of a small vessel at Rangoon from the Isle de France, under Birman [Burmese] colours, which brought an unfavourable account of the situation of affairs in Europe; exaggerating the disappointment of the Allies on the Continent to a total defeat; and adding, that the Dutch and Spaniards having joined the republicans, the utter ruin of the English was not far distant.[68]

On the second embassy, Symes had to wait at court while a French delegation from Île de France, with 'letters and presents from the governor of Mauritius,' made its way up the river.[69] When the French arrived in Amarapura, Symes sneered at their composition: an American supercargo of a French ship, sent from Île de France, a liberated prisoner from Calcutta and two sons of a French man and a Burmese woman.[70] The contact between Burma and Mauritius tailed off in the years before the fall of Mauritius to British control. But before this, Ava had asked the French island for ammunition and muskets. Meanwhile, French privateers arrived at the Burmese court. These aspects of the relationship align with those which characterised Tipu Sultan's Mysore in its relationship to Mauritius.[71] They are in keeping with the non-European assertiveness which is a definitive feature of the age of revolutions in the Indian Ocean.

In 1802, Symes reported that a ship from Mauritius had arrived in Burma with a cargo of firearms.[72] An account of French assistance with ammunitions also appears in the royal records of Burma.[73] When Mauritius was blockaded in 1809 Britain sent a mission to Ava, to allay any fears that Britain was also set against Ava.[74] In addition to diplomacy and ammunition, trade also played a role in this link between Burma and Mauritius and could have included oil and teak.[75] In the wider Indian Ocean arena this indicates how Burma took up a reactive position in the politics of Anglo-French rivalries.

Given this earlier history, the concerns at the frontier noted before which fed into the First Anglo-Burmese War confirmed to the British the need to exert their control over Burma's borders, lest the way be opened once again, in a post-Napoleonic age, for French interests to prosper in the state neighbouring India.[76] Exaggerated worry about French relations with Burma carried on well into the nineteenth century. After the Second Anglo-Burmese War of 1852–3, there was a report of French subjects in Amarapura, who had been kept against their will. According to a letter in the archives in Yangon, one individual had arrived at the kingdom of Ava expecting to take up a commercial pursuit, but was 'required to assist in the manufacture of arms, gunpowder & so on, but he state[d] [that] he declined'. In this letter to British India, it was alleged that this man's wife was on occasion 'heavily beaten in a shameful manner'.[77] Anecdotes of this kind allowed the British to construe their work as that of the true liberators. They indicate the persistence of British India's fears at its frontier.[78]

Additionally, the lives of the men involved in the First Anglo-Burmese War deserve filling out in order to show the links between this war and the age of revolutions. Take Marryat, whose diary on the war was cited earlier. Here was a lifesaver: a man who got a medal from the Royal Humane Society for his plans for a lifeboat. He made rather a habit of jumping into the sea to save those in danger and an archived scrap book contains several pasted certificates which attest to Marryat's valiant masculinity as a lifesaver.[79] He also fought the French and was involved in the Anglo-American war of 1812–14. He later became a novelist. It was perhaps his experience of war which led to his drawing up a code of signals, to align the navy and the merchant marine.[80] His personal undated manuscript signal book is a carefully prepared artefact. Beautifully coloured flags set in clear grids denote messages, directions and signals, and there is a register of shipping, indicating how to read the nationality of ships.[81]

Yet the clinching fact for why Marryat was formed by the Napoleonic wars lies in his obsession with one event, the death of Napoleon on St Helena, which he witnessed.[82] Marryat drew several sketches of Napoleon lying dead and it is uncertain which of these is the original sketched in

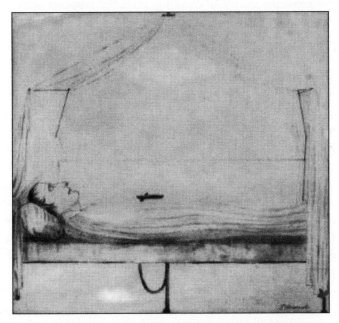

Fig. 6.5 'Sketch of Napoleon Bonaparte after his death
at St Helena', by Captain Frederick Marryat, 1821

the death chamber. One of them carries a handwritten subtitle in English: 'Napoleon Bonaparte, as he appeared on Sunday Morning on the 6th of May, 14 hours after his decease – laying upon the bed that he died in.' [Fig. 6.5]. The images are dignified in their black-and-white simplicity. The dead man lies totally at peace, shrouded in a long garment, and the deathly peace is accentuated by the figure of a crucifix lying on his body.[83]

For Marryat, and by proxy for others – including General Sir Archibald Campbell, who led the forces involved in the First Anglo-Burmese War, and whose curriculum vitae reads as a history of the Napoleonic wars – the Burmese war allowed a new lease of life for careers forged in the Napoleonic wars. One account of the war on the Irrawaddy notes how the troops were composed of young officers, who had not seen action since the end of the Napoleonic conflict, 'with the sincerest pleasure . . . [of] this chance of seeing service'.[84] In other words, at a time of peace, soldiers in need of work took up service in an unnecessary war. After all, the real threat posed by Burma to India was minimal. References to Napoleon's campaign therefore appear in the middle of the sources quite by chance.[85] From another perspective, foreigners within the court of Ava, who provided advice to the king, included refugees of the revolutionary and Napoleonic wars. One figure who takes a prominent role is a Spaniard, Sr Lanciego, who had married into the court, and who was a privateer, wrecked 'by the changes and chances of the French revolution'.[86] He was the king's collector at the port of Rangoon.[87]

If wars led on to other wars in the global history of this period, in fact there is another lineage to the First Anglo-Burmese War besides that which places it in a post-Napoleonic world. This alternative lineage is a regional one.[88] The First Anglo-Burmese War marks an end point to a story of the Bay of Bengal at war in the early nineteenth century. From that perspective, there is an arc from the British invasions of Java (1811) in today's Indonesia, and Kandy (1815) in today's Sri Lanka, to the Anglo-Burmese War. All these were colonial conflicts orchestrated from or which benefited from assistance from India. They were about stabilising the maritime frontier of British India at a time when the subcontinent was falling more securely under British control.

The regional pathway of war over water which stretched across Sri Lanka, Java and Burma encompassed local changes in the organisation of politics as well as religious orders. It included the movement of religious teachers or fighters and saw news of colonial advance reaching

Asian elites. Also evident among Asian regimes was an oceanic imagination. These dynamics constitute indigenous connections across the Bay of Bengal. Yet colonial scholarship, war and naval deployment, followed these indigenous pathways and transformed their content. This colonial manoeuvre once again suggests the counter-revolutionary dynamic of empire as it folded the possibilities of the age within its structures.

FROM BURMA TO SRI LANKA

When Burma is placed together with Kandy, the last independent kingdom of Sri Lanka, what is clear in both cases is that both experienced rejuvenated Buddhist monarchies.[89] Each kingdom had devoted attention to cultural refashioning in the eighteenth century. In each case this reformation fed into and in some ways set the context for British colonialism and colonial territorial advance.

Lankan monks appear more regularly in some sections of the royal orders of the kingdom of Ava than do concerns with French and British intrusion. In 1806, the king of Ava gave careful orders for the planting of saplings of the Bo tree [*ficus religiosa*] brought by monks from Sri Lanka. The tree was specially regarded because Buddha was said to have attained enlightenment under its boughs. In the royal orders, there followed a list of questions to be put to the monks from the island: Why had they come to Burma? How long was their journey? Which calendar was in use in Sri Lanka?[90] Later on permission was granted to these monks to go to Rangoon to collect other holy men who had arrived from Sri Lanka and a teacher called 'Ambagaha'.[91] Orders were given by the king to ask people to offer food and flowers to the Lankan Buddhist relics as they were transported to Ava.[92]

The next year, the royal orders decreed that monks from Sri Lanka should meet Burmese monks, and that Buddhist manuscripts and medical works brought by the Lankan monks on palm leaf should be translated into Burmese.[93] In return, monks going back to Sri Lanka in 1810 were given religious texts from the Royal Library. After being transported down the seaboard, these monks returned to the island with travel arranged by the court.[94] A group of monks from Sri Lanka were also able to meet and converse with other holy men visiting the kingdom of Ava from what was called 'Middle India', and they were able to see Buddhist objects brought from Benares, the holy city of India.[95] All these are revealing vignettes. They show not the isolation of the highland kingdoms of Ava and Kandy, a dominating trope in British descriptions, but rather their interconnection, and their reach into mainland India, just before the advent of greater British control.

In Sri Lanka, connections with Burma gave rise to a new fraternity among monks in the early nineteenth century and this took as its name 'Amarapura', the capital city of Ava.[96] While the dates connected to the fraternity's origin in the royal records of Burma do not match exactly those in Sri Lankan palm-leaf sources, nevertheless it is clear that in the early nineteenth century a series of delegations of monks from Sri Lanka travelled to Burma. This was partly with a view to rejuvenating Buddhist sensibility on the island.[97] Connections from Sri Lanka to Burma and Siam were longstanding, and among the aims were the preservation of the rite of higher ordination and the passage of religious texts.[98] In the mid eighteenth century, in line with these links across the Bay of Bengal, the Buddhist clergy in the kingdom of Kandy were comprehensively reorganised. Kings who celebrated Buddhist learning and preaching, scholar monks who turned to old languages, and student monks who were trained in a new system of education illustrate these changes. Kings orchestrated spectacular displays, such as the procession of Buddha's tooth in the kingdom's capital, which still occurs annually – and they patronised new temple art. The resurgence of kingship at the core of the island of Sri Lanka had a parallel life to events in Burma where also kings patronised programmes of palm-leaf writing and where there were attempts to purify religion.[99]

If the similarity between Kandy and Ava might be understood in light of the connections between these two kingdoms when the British went to war with Kandy in 1803, to a remarkable failure, and then once again in 1815, when they took the kingdom, there appeared other common features. These were similarities in imperial practice. For British colonial war and the orientalism that accompanied it followed similar tracks to indigenous links across the Bay of Bengal

Britain's first war with Kandy was a brutal affair. Having taken the coastal territories from the Dutch in 1796, the British sought to take the inland kingdom and assert their sovereignty over the whole island. It was driven by the practical and economic expedience of such island-wide rule. The colonisers took the capital city of Kandy and found it to be deserted. They were then surrounded by the king's forces. With the monsoon and disease taking its toll, and Indian and Malay soldiers deserting to the other side, the colonisers opted to evacuate but were intercepted by the Kandyans.[100] Only three Britons survived the slaughter. It is likely that the number of deaths among the Indian, Malay and Sinhalese men involved in this war was even higher than that among the Britons. As with the First Anglo-Burmese War, this was a poorly planned war, where terrain and bad weather, together with the guerrilla tactics of the opposition, created a disaster for the colonisers.

The *Ingrisi Hatana* is a palm-leaf poem written in honour of the Kandyan king's victory against the British in 1803. It is likely to have been written in sections over a period from around 1805 onwards. It is perhaps a transcription of an oral ballad performed before the king. It is a gory celebration of victory, replete with details of the smashing of British bodies, but this violence is not unlike that enacted by the British in their 'total wars' against colonial opponents in the period. The violence is consistently linked with the assertion of the superiority of the king and the ethnic identity of the kingdom. As in Burma there is the assertion of the unity of the Buddhist kingdom, here as 'Tri Sinhala', three historic principalities united under one kingdom. Across the Bay of Bengal, then, war with the British was a pretext for the assertion of political, spiritual and ethnic unity.

Ingrisi Hatana provides a fascinating picture of the advance of the British forces. All these are on the move with the British: 'cannons, pistols, guns . . . strong and sharp spears, axes, discs, swords, bows and arrows, javelins', 'strong horses and an innumerable number of carts drawn by bulls', 'tents for camping, beds and chairs, copper vessels, paper, books, cauldrons of vinegar, bullets, ammunition, drums, boxes of preserves . . .', 'chicken, sheep, snipes, ducks, cattle, goats', 'rice, coconuts, salt', 'a large amount of money in rupees and in gold coins needed to pay the salaries' and, of course, 'a large army consisting of violent elephants, horses and foot soldiers'.[101]

On the departure of the forces from the British Colombo on the coast, the poet notes:

> With the booming sounds of gunfire and the sound of five-fold musical instruments, bearing parasols, flags etc., the English soldiers set out from Colombo riding palanquins and horses.[102]

On the taking of the deserted city by the British, there is the following commentary:

The idiotic British, having seen [Sinhalese forces] thus retreating, entered the city like a herd of cattle that rush into a deserted field from which the farmers had taken away all the grain. The way they took up residence in the city, having crossed the river, shows that they are doomed to be food for crows, dogs and foxes.

The portrayal of British techniques of war as without wisdom, and British conduct as greedy and plundering, is contrasted with the tasteful procession of the king and his troops:

Many different elephants that roar violently like the roll of thunder in the battlefield, who look like clouds moving on the earth, and who touch the ground with seven parts of their bodies.

Lines of horses on either side of the road looking like waves in the milky ocean. Look! They have prevented the sun from shining on the earth with the clouds of dust they stir when they run.

Thus the sound of the wheels of horse-drawn carriages filled the air while some soldiers took shields with swords, arrows and bows and spears wearing glittering armour as the four-fold forces got ready in this manner.[103]

Celebrated are the king's careful choice of his men, his adornments, 'made of nine-fold gems' and fine clothes, and the selection of music together with the accompaniment of female dancers. It was no wonder then that the king could proclaim: 'Let as many enemy forces like these come! I will beat and defeat and will become famous in this world hoisting my sceptre of victory. You rest assured without a worry.' Yet, as with Burma, this is not a kingly statement of oriental and despotic ignorance. And this is important, for the colonial typecasting of the last king as a tyrant was critical in justifying British expansion as the conduit of liberty.[104] Rather the Kandyan victory speaks of the lack of superior knowledge on the part of the British, cartographic, military and technological. Also evident is how the Kandyans were able to exploit this gap in information to their advantage. They made use of the jungles and hills in their guerrilla warfare against an army which favoured controlled fighting formations, ill-suited to the Kandyan landscape.

As with Burma, the kingdom at the core of Sri Lanka adopted a variety of practices from Europe in the years and even centuries before the war and this contributed to their victory. Kandy had been at war with the Portuguese and the Dutch before the British. In the midst of these wars, deserters crossed over to the Kandyan side. In 1803, an artilleryman, Benson, crossed from the British side to the Kandyan, where he was put in charge of gunpowder. This is reminiscent of how Ava learned about weapons from European refugees of the Napoleonic wars.[105] More than Europeans, however, was the significant crossover of Malay troops from European armies to Kandy, numbering in the hundreds. Eighty Africans or 'Kaffirs' were also among the troops of Kandy that surrounded the British in 1803. In addition, Kandyans took some firearms and artillery from Europe or made their own versions of these.[106]

The difference between the two sides may at first glance indicate the difference between the maritime British empire and the highland kingdom of Kandy, literally ringed by the hills. This would cast sea versus land. Again, as with the war in Burma, this is too simple. The taking of Ceylon, as Sri Lanka was called by the British, occurred in the context of the Napoleonic wars. As with the Cape Colony, the Prince of Orange's flight to London gave rise to an instruction to the Dutch in Ceylon to welcome the British. Instead of allowing the maritime provinces to fall to the French, the British then took up, and in this case did not return, a Dutch territory. The British desire for Ceylon was a maritime one. An island so close to their increasing Indian territory, with a large natural harbour in Trincomalee on the eastern coast, was too good to give up to the enemy.[107] If maritime concerns dictated in part Britain's imperial policy in Sri Lanka, Kandy was not without an oceanic imagination. For Kandy saw itself as owning the whole island. The kings of Kandy had prided their right of access to the ports on the coast, a key part of the diplomatic game which characterised Dutch–Kandyan relations.[108] Once again like in Burma there was symmetry between colonisers and colonised.

It is not odd then to notice the motif of water in the *Ingrisi Hatana*. It is in keeping with the glorification of the king's project of building a lake at the centre of his capital, which was seen to be akin to the milky ocean churned by the gods.[109] In the *Igrisi Hatana*, the hostile soldiers of Britain are 'like waves who march bearing arms in hand and roaring aloud' who are then stopped at the 'beach' of the majesty's feet. The king himself has 'churned the ocean of enemies with the churning-stick that is his sword'. The music that accompanies the king is like 'the roar of

the ocean at the end of the world'.[110] This is not purely a metaphor, for
land and water, the natural and the masculine, the religious and the
ethnic, were tied together here in the proclamation of what it meant to
be a king, who was politically triumphant in the late eighteenth and
early nineteenth centuries. [Fig. 6.6] The British interpreted the symbolism
as ornamental, as in Crawfurd's response to the Burmese water festival,
not realising that these symbols created a link between the ruler and the
people. British misunderstandings of these symbols, and the colonial bid
to instead proclaim the liberty and rationality of Britain meant that they
were enrolled as a subservient force, as in Burma.

Unlike in 1803, the war that led to the fall of Kandy in 1815 was relatively quiet in the capital itself and the Kandyan elite signed a convention
with the British. A very different palm-leaf ballad attributed the British
victory to the help given them by Ahelapola, a minister who fled to the
British:

Fig. 6.6 'The late King of Kandy from a drawing by a Native', from John Davy,
*An Account of the Interior of Ceylon with Its Inhabitants with
Travels in that Island* (1821)

Like the waters of the great ocean at the end of the world. The great army bearing flags, parasols and weapons with the sound of the music. Like Rama the hero entering the city of Ravana [the characters of the Indian epic *Ramayana*]. He [Ahelapola] entered the city of Senkada [the capital of Kandy] by the power of the Buddha.[111]

Elsewhere, outside the capital, the British troops plundered Kandyan provinces, just as they later looted Burma. Villages were ransacked by troops in search of supplies and assistance after the inhabitants fled at their arrival. Buddhist temples witnessed an assault as in Burma. In Kataragama, a centre of pilgrimage in south-east Sri Lanka, the 'wealth of the Temple' was taken by a British detachment and many of the houses were 'unroofed for firewood'.[112] In the three years that followed, as an anti-British rebellion engulfed the Kandyan provinces in 1817–18, this violence became more entrenched, with the British using scorched-earth techniques and starving and terrorising people with a view to ending the rebellion. In the words of a palm-leaf poem, the English, 'spreading in ten directions armed with bows, swords and guns', set houses on fire and went looting, 'killing uncountable numbers'.[113]

In the midst of war and rebellion is the shadow of the Kandyan kingdom with ties across the Bay of Bengal. For just as war with the British took a similar form in Burma and Sri Lanka, so too did the Kandyans' attempt to resist in line with outside connections. Take one specific incident which reveals the surge of connections in the age of revolutions in rich detail. In 1816, before the start of the wide-scale rebellion against the British in Kandyan territories, the colonists received information of a 'conspiracy' to overthrow the British government. The information arose from Eknaligoda Nilame, an office-holder in Kandy, who was loyal to the British and who had played a decisive role in the capture of the last king of Kandy.[114]

Eknaligoda Nilame was visited by a young monk about thirty years of age. After the rest of the household retired for the night, the young monk laid out the plan to attack the British. He told Eknaligoda Nilame that: 'The [British] Governor was to send for all the Headmen [chiefs] to attend from Kandy [in Colombo and] intended to take that opportunity of putting them on Board Ship, and sending them away *beyond the sea*.' The issue, as the monk explained it, was that the coast and inland provinces had been united under one regime, namely British rule, with no space of escape.

The monk's briefing and invitation to Eknaligoda to join the cause continued. The idea for a 'conspiracy' had been hatched in a series of conversations between Chalia Mudliyars, the headmen working under the British regime in the maritime provinces and in control of cinnamon workers. Other Mudliyars said they couldn't join in the first instance but would send on 'Thieves and rogues (black guard fellows who certainly do abound).' They would also send a Malay Muhandiram, another titled officer who was a trained fighter, and other Malay Captains and Corporals. Also involved in the plan was Madugalle, a minister of the late Kandyan kingdom who would organise the support of the chiefs of the fallen kingdom. 'Kaffir' or African-descent troops would be invited to join the cause.[115] The Malays would rescue prisoners, purported to be the last king's son-in-law and brother, who were 'Malabars'. This was a term which later became 'Tamil', and referred to the island's minority, at the centre of the protracted civil war which gripped Sri Lanka until recently.[116]

In view then was the assembly of a composite community of rebels, whose own stories reflect the history of indigenous oceanic linkage between Kandy and its Asian neighbours. The tooth relic, the signifier of Kandyan kingship, would also be secreted away; a message was said to have been sent to the temple at Kataragama. The plot included instruction on the route through which the rebels needed to march into Kandyan territory. The idea was to use the pretext of a Muslim feast in order to undertake this resistance.[117] There was said to be 'an abundance of arms all over the Country', from the reign of the last king, which could be utilised. It was thought that only a small proportion of the king's arms had fallen into British hands.

The rebels' imagination of Burma played a role in the plot of 1816. There was the idea of getting a 'King from Ava', to serve as the focus of revolt, and Ihagama, the main priest who pursued this conspiracy, appears to have tried to travel to Burma.[118] The British governor reported his intelligence of the conspiracy together with the account of how a party of seven priests had departed to Ava, with a long-term resident on the island who originated from Ava.[119] Prior to this, the governor noted how a delegation from Ava had made their way to Kandy without permission and without being much noticed. He suspected devious motives. These 'missions to Ava', he wrote, were undertaken with the 'pretence of sending for Religious Books to that great seat of Boodhoo [Buddhist] learning and under that cloak they can carry on any negotiations they please'.

The plan laid out by the young monk was overtaken by the British; the Buddhist monks at its centre were arrested. When they later escaped, two were recaptured and Ihagama went into hiding.[120] Control over the waters increasingly passed to the British naval war machine. Yet before this occurred Asians used water-borne connections for their own purposes.

Eknaligoda Nilame's intelligence referred to a Malay headman, Asana, who had agreed to organise support for the rebel cause. Ihagama's conversations with Asana were at the heart of this plot. Asana had fled Kandy and helped the British invade the kingdom in 1815. In that expedition he had served with Captain Lewis de Bussche, who had a high regard for Malay fighters. In a book published in 1817, the captain wrote that the Malays were 'a hardy, bold and brave race of men' and attested to their bravery in the British taking of Java in 1811.[121] Prior to fleeing the kingdom, and taking the side of the British, Asana had been one of the last king's fighters. In 1816, however, this Malay fighter offered his support to the anti-British rebels.

The British governor decided to banish Asana from the island and 'to send him to Batavia [in Java], the Native place of his Family', citing his readiness to take up any cause of 'dangerous enterprize'. [122] He was placed on a ship at Galle, in southern Sri Lanka. Yet Asana managed to escape at Ambalangoda further up the coast. He was recaptured and placed under military guard at Galle awaiting the next means of deportation to the East Indies, together with his two grown sons and other family. This was not effected, for in the ensuing rebellion of 1817–18 there was a further attempt to communicate with him.[123]

There were a series of striking parallels in the wars undertaken by the British in Burma and Sri Lanka in the early nineteenth century. Monarchic centralisation, religious reform, colonial military knowledge-gathering and British inability to cope with guerrilla warfare in an unknown tropical terrain appear in both cases. Ways of articulating royal power, tied to ethnicity and marine culture, were misunderstood or ornamentalised by the British. Yet pillaging proceeded on a vast scale, so that materials and informants or fighters such as Asana were increasingly adopted by force by the British. Witness for instance the radically different courses of the wars of 1803 and 1815 in Kandy. If the First Burmese War occurred in a post-Napoleonic world, the Sri Lankan case was coincident in time with the Napoleonic wars; the British bid to take Ceylon arose partly out of the rivalry between Britain and France. Yet it is important to stick with Asana, lest we lose another part of the lineage of wars in this region.

AND TO JAVA

This Malay fighter connects the story of Burma and Sri Lanka to yet another context further south and east, on the other side of the Bay of Bengal and beyond it. Java was where he came from and Java is a critical component of this part of the world in the age of revolutions. Java was composed of a Dutch colony ringed around south-central Javanese princely states. It was the Dutch who had brought Malays from Java to fight in Sri Lanka and there were at least one thousand Malays in Sri Lanka when the Dutch surrendered to the British.[124]

Java was violently taken by the British in 1811. In some sources it is named not as Dutch but as 'French'. This is because it was seen as an outpost of republican ideas, governed by Herman Willem Daendels who had fought alongside French republican forces in their invasion of the Netherlands in 1794–5, before the Batavian Republic was set up. By the time of Java's invasion in 1811 it was under the command of Jan Willem Janssens.[125] After the fall of Mauritius to the British, it was thought very likely that the French would try to reinforce Dutch Java. Stamford Raffles, the later pioneer of Singapore, wrote that the French flag had been substituted for the Dutch flag throughout Java.[126]

Following the fall of Java and Île de France, Lord Minto, the governor-general of India wrote, 'the British nation has neither an enemy nor a rival left from the Cape of Good Hope to Cape Horn.'[127] In this view, the achievement of the 1811 Java invasion was to tie together the British footholds in Australia and India with a chain of islands, 'with intervals of no great importance'. As Raffles noted, they 'extend nearly from the Bay of Bengal to our settlements on the continent of New Holland [Australia]'.[128] If in Sri Lanka we witnessed the Asian oceanic imagination, this was the colonial equivalent.

However, after a five-year stint, the British returned Java to the Dutch in 1816, to the emergence of uprisings and rebellion in the 1820s. These agitations cohered around the messianic figure of Dipanagara, a 'just king'. He tapped into economic and social anxiety, and the longing for an old order, and he organised these around millenarian Islam. Though backward-looking, this revolt has been read as indicative of the emergence of Indonesian nationalism, though such an interpretation leaps ahead too quickly.[129] Regardless, Java became a global centre for Dutch colonialism in the nineteenth century. This bears out the claim of historian Jos Gommans that the Dutch empire was tied to a pattern, becoming 'more intensive in more restricted territorial colonies', rather than assimilating peoples and places spread everywhere.[130]

The British invasion links Java to events elsewhere in the Indian Ocean. In India and among the ruling elite, the 'complete expulsion' of the enemy from the 'Indian seas' required the conquest of 'the French islands', to be followed by the 'subversion of the Enemy's establishments in the Eastern islands'. A force no greater than that which took Mauritius was thought to be sufficient for the task. The two attacks on Mauritius and Java were seen to be part of the 'same plan . . . recommended by the same principles of policy'. [131] Major William Thorn, who had by this time fought many wars in India and had also been involved in the taking of Mauritius in 1810, produced an account of the British arrival in Java from notes taken 'on the spot'. He later fought at Waterloo.[132]

Thorn began his story with the journey of the British fleet from Madras.[133] Included at the front of the volume was a precise plotting of the track of the ships, across the Bay of Bengal, the rendezvous at Penang on the Malay Peninsula, a voyage through the Strait of Malacca and on to the Java Sea. The force from Madras combined with a second division which met them at Penang from Calcutta. All this points to the regional colonial dynamic of warfare operating at the British Indian maritime frontier.

The string of islands spreading between mainland Asia and the Pacific were seen by the British as add-ons to India and essentially maritime spaces. In the words of John Crawfurd, in his book on 'the Indian Archipelago': '[f]rom the nature of the countries they inhabit, the islanders are necessarily a maritime people.'[134] He wrote of their use of boats as equivalent to how the camel, the horse and the ox served the 'wandering Arab' and added that 'the sea is to [these islanders] what the *steppes* and the *deserts* are to the latter'.[135] Again, like with Burma, there was a classification of the boats in this sea of islands: Malay 'prahu' or *proa* were said to be more than a match for British vessels.[136] In planning the Java expedition of 1811, Stamford Raffles classed this maritime activity, very much in keeping with colonial frontier fears, as 'Malay piracy':

The Malay governments have this in common with the feudal states of
Europe, that the chiefs are only rich in hands and in the rough produce
of their grounds. A Prahu or war boat can be easily constructed wherever there are hands and timber and to man her costs no trouble to the
chief of the clan or any of his family. To go a roving is the next step
which implies no dishonour in the present state of Malay morals and
having surprized some unsuspicious merchant the pirate proceeds coolly
to dispose of the goods which he has thus seized wherever he can find
a market.[137]

Further into the long treatise he wrote to Lord Minto prior to the
expedition, he explained that this 'piracy' arose from ancient custom:
the 'old Malay romances' and 'fragments of their traditional history'
constantly refer to piratical cruisers. He also blamed the spread of
Islam for the plague of pirates.[138] Elsewhere Raffles presented a maritime code held by Malay peoples which he translated from the Malay
language.[139]

At the first moment of the expedition to Java, the weather played a
bad trick. It was hit by a 'tremendous hurricane' which affected vessels
on the Madras roads, driving them on shore and causing some to be
lost. News of the wreck of a supply ship reached as far as recently taken
Mauritius where a request arrived for 'good Europe salt provisions' for
the consumption of the troops heading to Java.[140]

Across the Bay of Bengal, in the course of the voyage, particular
attention was paid to the health of the horses and the men, given the
sweltering heat and confinement on board. It was perhaps because of
these conditions that the troops were given a plentiful supply of beef
while in Penang. Thorn described Penang as seen from the deck of a
ship, including the appearance of the harbour and the height of mountains rising above it. His book cast Java together with the isles of
Madura, Timor, Maluku, Banda and Amboyna, as a string of maritime
settlements. Thorn wrote of how ships of all sizes were constructed at
Penang. Since the British established control of Penang in 1786, it had
become a centre of commerce, attracting 'the trade of Junk Ceylon
(Phuket), Queda, Selanger and other Malay ports', including pepper,
beetle nuts, rattan and some gold.[141]

From Penang, the expedition journeyed on to Melaka, where another
maritime calamity hit. This time the problem was not the weather but
the danger of transporting gunpowder on ships. A store ship from

Bengal with gunpowder on board caught fire and exploded. It was a relief that the ship did not explode close to the rest of the fleet. At Melaka, an event which was characteristic of the maritime culture of patriotism and colonialism was celebrated, the fourth of June birthday of the monarch. 'Royal salutes from the men of war expedition, and from the batteries on shore, announced the happy day . . .'[142] A calculation of the weather determined the expedition's onward course to Java. The expedition had to arrive before the rainy season. Troops had to be kept healthy, a task which became more difficult after the rain began.[143] The decision was made to travel across to Borneo and then down its coast to Java.[144]

Raffles had arranged for the surveying of this passage prior to the expedition, and indeed he took the credit for pushing the government of India to pursue the invasion of Java in the first place.[145] The survey he had arranged established the 'facility of working along the coast of Borneo by the sea and land breezes [and] likewise of making Borneo through the Straits of Sincapura [Singapore]'.[146] Near Borneo, the shallowness of the sea struck together with a stiff squall, creating a dangerous spectacle:

A more frightful sight can scarcely be conceived; – large vessels with a hundred horses, and double that number of men on board, were tossed up into the air at one instant, and precipitated the next to the bottom of the ocean, with such violence that their keels actually struck the ground, and the earth thereby torn up with great force, gave the sea all around a thick muddy appearance.[147]

After meeting on the extreme south-west coast of Borneo at Point Sambar, a discussion began of how to attack the Dutch forces gathering in Batavia in Java. A 'vigorous opposition was to be expected at landing; and, some risk, and much loss must of course attend a disembarkation in the face of an army of twenty thousand men'. Twenty thousand men was the British estimate of the Dutch forces. Lieutenant Colonel Colin Mackenzie, who had made his name in India as a surveyor and orientalist, was despatched to survey the coast with a view to determining the best landing place. A resolution was made to land at Cilincing, ten miles from Batavia.[148]

The fleet of one hundred ships, including gunboats, carrying 11,000 troops, anchored on Sunday 4 August 1811.[149] Thorn immediately compared the landing to what had unfolded in Mauritius, noting that they were landing safely at a difficult place. 'This idea of security', he wrote in reference to this landing place, 'enabled us to effect our debarkation without loss, in the same manner as happened at Isle of France.'[150] The link with Mauritius is also evident in how armament and reinforcement which arrived in Mauritius after the conquest of 1810 were redirected to Java.[151]

On land, the travails of the army as it moved on Batavia, followed the commentary on the voyage over sea, with attention to the lie of the land, the course of rivers and the coast. Thorn described it as 'intersected country' for the prevalence of so many 'swamps, salt-pits and canals'.[152] Colonel Gillespie wrote of the 'fatigue' experienced by the troops in the 'almost impassable country'.[153] This terrain was also documented in a sketch of the 'Plan of the Route of the British Army' showing its passage since the point of landing.[154] Crawfurd described the archipelago as 'thickly strewn', noting large alluvial tracts, considerable rivers and innumerable straits and passages in the sea.[155] The forces took Batavia without opposition, finding the settlement deserted. On the streets were strewn plundered stocks of coffee and sugar: 'the peacable inhabitants had undergone a period of extreme terror'.[156]

Soon the British colours were hoisted.[157] Open conflict then erupted between British forces marching from Batavia and Dutch forces based in Weltevreden close to Batavia. The strategy of the Dutch was to use nature as an element in the campaign. Janssens had sought to tempt the British with Batavia, hoping that 'the unhealthiness of the town and the noxious climate of the seashore' would have an effect on the health of the troops. In this plot, the British would be taken ill while Dutch troops were well provisioned in Weltervreden. But the 'salubrious' cantonment in Weltevreden fell to the British. [158]

After a sustained battle at Fort Cornelis, only a small party headed by Janssens escaped.[159] A maritime chase unfolded as other ports fell to the British.[160] Janssens was pursued and an offer of terms held out, which was full of the British rhetoric of liberty.

> . . . if, Sir, you continue deaf to the cries of a distressed people, – if
> blood must be unnecessarily shed, – if the Natives must be let loose to
> plunder and massacre the European inhabitants of Java, we shall hold
> you, Sir, and those who continue to support you, as answerable for the
> consequences.[161]

Janssens eventually made a stand near Salatiga, where he gave up unconditionally. At the conclusion of the first phase of the invasion, Thorn took specific note of how the British did not resort to plunder at the fall of Batavia. 'Scarcely a single instance,' he alleged, had occurred.[162] When action was directed towards those he called 'Native Powers' in the interior a dramatically different course unfolded.[163]

One aspect of the stand against indigenous regimes was an expedition to Palembang, 'the Emporium of the inland Commerce of the Island of Sumatra'. This expedition was said to be driven by British outrage at the alleged murder of the residents of the Dutch factory there.[164] A riverine contest took place, a foretaste of what would occur in the First Anglo-Burmese War. The contest included the use against the British of fire rafts, an 'Arab ship' and piles of wood in the river.[165] For Crawfurd, however, the naval tactics of the islanders were no match for British strategy. All they could muster over water was 'predatory warfare . . . the only one suited to the genius of the Indian islanders'.[166] In other words, these were said to be 'pirates' working outside the law. Indeed the alleged spread of 'piracy' in the eastern isles, and the need to suppress it, served as another early factor feeding the expedition to Java.[167]

Colonial plunder and predation on a grand scale is surely the only way to explain how the prior practices of the Franco-Dutch regime were extended by the British. It offers a radically different interpretation to Thorn who wrote about the clean hands of the British. Looting is in full display in the tragic events that unfolded as the British turned on the sultanate of Yogyakarta.[168] As the leading historian of this episode writes: it was the exchange of 'one form of colonial tyranny for another'.[169] In the shameless words of the treaty the British concluded with the Sultan of Mataram after the fall of Yogyakarta, the conquest was said to arise, from the need for 'the preservation of the Country from the oppression of a cruel and relentless Tyrant . . .'[170] Here once again was the trope of the 'oriental despot' which was seen at work in Burma and Sri Lanka to justify invasion in the guise of liberation.

The invasion of the Yogya *kraton* [the structure of a fortified royal capital] in June 1812 arose during growing cultural and diplomatic tensions. The looting carried on for four days and booty was carried out on the backs of porters and on ox-drawn carts; jewels, fine clothing and weapons were available for sale in the market outside the fort.[171]

A Javanese chronicle on tree bark was written by Bendara Pangeran Arya Panular, a member of the ruling elite, which became part of a collection of manuscripts brought to England by John Crawfurd. It has been recently been expertly rendered into English summary, and details how complete confusion and chaos unfolded inside the *kraton*. The sale of looted items persisted for a month, and quick profits were made by burghers and Indo-Europeans.[172] Women were seized and demands made for diamonds.[173] Court manuscripts were plundered and opened by Crawfurd. The Indian soldiers, who are described here as actively involved in the looting, are said to be like lions at the kill. Senior British officers are like blood-red giants who have just eaten human beings.[174]

War and scholarship were tied together. Colin Mackenzie was chief engineer to British forces in Java. Mackenzie became the president of a committee charged with the study of the island for British interests. This committee's work ranged widely from land tenure and taxation to religion, culture and history, allowing Mackenzie to poke around 'almost every part' of Java, including surveying the River Solo.[175]

Given the counter-revolutionary and anti-Franco-Dutch politics of the expedition to Java, it is particularly interesting to note that Mackenzie sought to complete rather than overturn the work undertaken by the Dutch regime. He made a 'complete register of the whole Charts, Plans & Maps', undertaken by the Dutch. He noted that a lot of information about coasts, harbours, rivers, mountains and natural history had already been amassed and called for 'a complete Geographical & Cartographical Survey of the whole Island, to complete what was so well begun . . .' He located his intellectual work in the light of the age of revolutions:

> It would appear that the American War & Revolution, so productive of changes in all the established relations of the Europeans Nations, had in its consequences given the final blow to the Commerce and Prosperity of the Dutch East India Company; & their ruin was only protracted by a time by various efforts at reform, change & improved system at the very same time nearly that the same subject, an Exclusive Monopoly attracted the attention of our own National Councils . . .

In other words, the reforming impulse of the Dutch needed now to be followed by the British, through a commitment to the 'Cultivation of the Science of Political Economy'. The age of monopolies would give way to free trade.[176] Yet it is ironic that this period of reforms – linking the policies of the Dutch and the British – was later overtaken by more draconian state control over lands by the Dutch, and an intensification of the regime of taxation after the Dutch return to Java. The line of inheritance from the Dutch to the British and back to the Dutch again was uneven; there was no simple continuity.[177]

Mackenzie placed Java within the realm of the British empire in India, seeing it as a further maritime periphery. It was for him 'the reverse of India', in its medical topography. It was unhealthy on the sea coast, while it was salubrious 'in the Upper Country & Woods'. These environmental conditions were caused by 'the flat marshes found at the junction of the Rivers, with the Sea'. The marshes allowed deposits of rich soil to be carried down to a shallow sea, where there was 'formentation & putrefaction', and the emission of a vapour.[178] Mackenzie's instincts as a surveyor were evident as he approached a series of problems, including this medical commentary. The same skills were evident in his military strategising and observation as in his survey of the Yogya *kraton* before its fall.[179] It also extended to the study of cultural remains, where he described antiquities with the precision and terminology of a surveyor.[180]

The invasion of Java was affected by the natural terrain, as the expedition moved from sea to land and from India to Batavia. The sea had to be contended with in planning the expedition and also in understanding the peoples of this region. Java's invasion fitted alongside events elsewhere in the Indian Ocean: it occurred alongside the taking of Mauritius. Meanwhile, the global context of anti-French and anti-republican sentiment supported this advance, and the negative characterisations of tyranny and monopoly set against free trade and the securing of liberty, which the British alone were seen to provide. Beneath these colonial connections of war and ideology, the Asian and indigenous connections in this story are pretty evident too. They include religious and trading exchanges which Europeans cast as piratical.

THE OPIUM WARS AS END POINT

As a closing vista of this survey of bloody wars on the boundaries between land and sea in the period of the Napoleonic wars and afterwards, it is apposite to consider the Opium War in the South China Sea (1839–1842), more than a decade after the First Anglo-Burmese War.[181]

The Opium War was as bloody as the prior events of Java, Sri Lanka and Burma. According to Britons who had fought in the Peninsular War, the Battle of Ningbo in 1842 was unmatched for the concentration of mangled dead bodies in a small area: 'the howitzer only discontinued its fire from the impossibility of directing its shot upon a living foe, clear of the writhing and shrieking hecatomb which it had already piled up.'[182] This battle saw the forces of the Qing empire attempting to take back a fort which had fallen under British control in 1841. Thousands of Qing soldiers were defeated by a few hundred British men. This fact bears out how the new technology of field guns – howitzers – which had transformed land battles in Europe was having an impact on the Chinese coast.

A technological gap was finally opening to yield success for the British in their wars with Asians, where entanglement and symmetry played such a key role in those conflicts narrated above. This technological gap included firearms, cannon and powder, the theory of ballistics and the organisation of drill. It stretched from land to sea. For it included carron-ades aboard ships which had the capacity to destroy multiple Chinese ships called *junks*. And critically, the use of a steamship in war had now been mastered. The steamer – *Nemesis* – was a key tool of the British war effort. In the 1841 Battle of Chuanbi, in the words of the Chinese who watched the work of the *Nemesis*: 'He-yaw! How can! My never see devil-ship so fashion before; but go all same man walkee.'[183]

The causes of war in East Asia were tied to the increasingly global reach of British shipping, 'gentlemanly capitalism' and a commitment to free trade, part of the makeup of an industrialising world power, now more confident as the period of Anglo-French rivalry abated. Concern about France still lingered: one immediate context for the Opium War was France's closure of Buenos Aires to British trade in 1838.[184] The long origin of the Opium War lay in British consumption of tea, which meant that the balance of trade between Britain and China was very much to the latter's favour in the late eighteenth century and disastrous for the English East India Company.

How might the Company offset the drain of silver in payment for tea on the Chinese coast? Opium was the perfect answer. It was already an elite commodity in China. Grown in India, shipped to China through private 'country' traders both British and Indian, and sold to Chinese consumers, opium offset the British loss of bullion. The flow of silver reversed direction in 1808, so that there was no drain on the Chinese coast. When the East India Company's monopoly over the trade in tea was annulled in 1833, this trade expanded further with the involvement of private merchants, and in turn expanded the opium trade into China too. But the Qing government stamped down on this exchange, wishing to take more control while also seeking to correct what was seen as the corrupting habit of opium-smoking.

All that was needed was a spark that would set off a war, and tensions erupted over a series of events. There was the arrival of Lord Napier, who had fought at Trafalgar, in Canton in 1834, wishing to press for a relaxation of trade restrictions imposed by the Qing empire. Napier did not conduct himself according to diplomatic etiquette, unlike for instance how Crawfurd had followed or been hemmed in by the royal etiquette of Burma. Napier took the view that a force from India would settle the differences with China, but in the end he died of a fever in Macao. By the end of the decade tensions were also stoked by opium merchants in Canton.

Matters came to a crisis from 1837 when Chinese officials obstructed an illicit trade in opium emerging from the floating warehouses of foreigners. This obstruction was so successful that opium was massed unsold in chests on Lintin Island. The Qing Emperor appointed a special commissioner, Lin Zexu. The commissioner asked for the handover of this opium to the Chinese and confiscated 20,000 chests without compensation. Unlike with the wars in Sri Lanka, Java and Burma, London politicians played a critical role in deciding the course of events which followed. This again signifies the altered possibilities of governance and imperialism in the mid nineteenth century, where communications travelled faster. The honour of the British flag had to be restored and Lord Palmerston sent out a naval force to make its presence felt on the Chinese coast through a blockade.[185]

This was still diplomacy on water but not in the midst of Burmese war boats arrayed on the Irrawaddy. Rather this was aggressive gunboat diplomacy that yielded results. The victory of the British in China resulted in the signing of the treaty of Nanking (1842), which opened five treaty ports to foreign merchants and saw the British takeover of Hong Kong.

Yet the rise of the British may also be appreciated from a view of boats and water and the tropes surrounding vessels. The period saw a racial dismissal of the Chinese *junk* and its fighting power. In the words of a correspondent, writing in 1836 to the Canton-based Protestant periodical, *China Repository*, the junks of the Chinese imperial navy represented a 'monstrous burlesque'. A demeaning comparison came to this correspondent's pen stretching across from the Pacific to South Asia. When the Chinese navy was faced with the 'the most savage states that we [the British] know of', the correspondent noted, 'a couple of New Zealand war canoes' could outdo it. But the ships of China could be outdone when placed against a 'single unarmed merchantman, manned by Lascars.'[186]

This dismissive representation of Chinese ships was typical of the Protestant press and missions which vociferously cast China in negative terms in these years. Yet it is important to note that vessels which were so dismissed by this correspondent were not an essential part of the defence of the Qing empire. For instance, only twenty-nine war junks participated in the first clash of the Opium War off Canton.[187] As one authority explains: 'in Ch'ing [Qing] times, the water force was strictly an antipiratical force'.[188] This meant that the British were able to wreak havoc for the vessels were not meant for war. As in Burma, fire rafts were also used here in warfare against the British. But instead of being shocked by engulfing flames on the water, in 1842, the British seized thirty-seven such fire rafts near Ningpo.[189]

The Qing sought to emulate and learn how to build ships, but this happened slowly. There were early attempts at building 'wheel-boats' or human-powered paddle vessels which were adapted junks with cog wheels. Lin Zexu also bought a Western merchantman, the *Cambridge*. Yet the Chinese were not well versed in how to use these vessels, allowing the British to easily take them in the Opium War. The *Cambridge* was blown up, 'to strike terror into the Chinese, far and wide'.[190] In addition to shipbuilding, this practice of copying stretched to weapons: in 1842 in Zhoushan the British found a cannon foundry that was manufacturing carronades.[191]

Underlying these experiments were attempts at translation of Western works and spying on Western technologies; there was also the aim of reforming Qing education to include naval study. Wei Yuan's *Illustrated Treatise in the Maritime Countries*, first published in 1842, advocated the testing of naval knowledge in official examinations.[192] Ding Gongchen

(1800–1875) described the action of steam power and built a model of a steam engine. Meanwhile Lin Zexu's successor described the power driving a steamship: 'it is rumoured that there are men or oxen driving the gears. But this is a speculation.'[193] The charisma of the steam engine, witnessed elsewhere on the Irrawaddy, evidently lived on, yet it fed into attempts to describe and build replicas.

Later in the nineteenth century, the Chinese stepped up their attempt to build ships, including iron-hulled vessels, while purchasing warships from Europe. The Jiangnan Arsenal became a key centre for the manufacture of arms in East Asia. It engaged in the translation of scientific and technical texts, the promotion of a new category of 'engineers' and the making of machines. As one historian notes: 'By mid-1867 the arsenal was producing fifteen muskets and a hundred twelve-pound shrapnel daily. Twelve-pound howitzers were produced at a rate of eighteen per month and used as munitions in the northern Nian wars of the 1860s.'[194]

In addition to the Jiangnan Arsenal, there was also a naval yard at Fuzhou, which stretched over a large campus. It employed 3,000 workers at its peak, and included forty-five buildings on a 118-acre site. Foreign advisers – both British and French – were key to the work of these sites. Yet by the end of the century, the shipping technology of Japan outmatched that of China. In 1884, the Chinese had fifty European-style ships, half of which were made in China. As a result of a lack of centralisation and lack of preparation for warfare, the navy lost out once again to the French in 1884–5 in a war over northern Vietnam. This then set the stage for loss against the Japanese in 1894–5.

This later history bears out the dangers of adopting a narrow perspective from the beginnings of the Opium War, to see an easy technological gap which allowed the domination of Western science, technology and the war-machine over China. For Chinese responses were creative and sustained. In the end once again, like wars elsewhere in this chapter, the regional dynamic, this time between China and Japan, was key to the future of this part of the world as it faced the twentieth century. Japan was cast as the modern nation which had successfully adopted from the West.

CONCLUSION

The mid-nineteenth-century rise of the military machine of the British empire in Asia is usually appreciated from its land frontier in the north-west of India. Here, costly wars were fought, pushed by the emerging 'Great Game', as Britons worried about Russian invasion of India. These wars are no longer seen to be driven by high-level strategy, but more by men on the spot who manufactured crises which called for intervention. The lack of secure communication – until the laying of telegraph lines – allowed such belligerent men to take the initiative. Buffer states such as the Punjab, Sindh and Afghanistan felt the force of British might. Wars against the Sikhs of Punjab were fought in 1845–6 and in 1848–9, when it was finally conquered. Sindh was taken in 1843. Wars against Afghanistan proved difficult: the creation of a puppet ruler did not work and wars were fought in 1839–42 and 1878–80. This set of conflicts demonstrates the volatility of frontier politics.

Yet it is possible to turn this story inside out by shifting from the land frontier of British India to its maritime frontier. At the water's edge too, wars were costly and deadly and the tropical climates, and the intersecting terrain of rivers, canals, flatlands and highlands, proved unfamiliar to the British. British boats, logistics and diplomacy did not perform well here. Meanwhile, resistance to British advances could also generate strength from fighters across the sea, from religious ideas which had spread across water, or from modes of political imagination which were also shared or which at times took water as a theme of inspiration. Oceanic conflict took new form as boats faced each other in inland Burma on the Irrawaddy. All this indigenous marine activity is part and parcel of the age of revolutions.

The wars put together here as a lineage, Asian and colonial, regional and global, have never been brought together before this. This is because the land model of colonialism, which surely became more important in the later nineteenth and early twentieth centuries, with the rise of 'geostrategy', has been retrospectively applied to understand this earlier period of warfare. This way of approaching war from the water at the dawn of our times is in keeping with the scepticism now levied against a famous thesis, of a 'military revolution' in early modern Europe. According to this thesis, the military's expansion in numerical terms, its increasing cost and its new forms of organisation, led to a militarisation of society and the rise of modern states which monopolised power. The bureaucracy arose out of military planning. Yet the sea and navies, and the wider world, often disappear from such predominantly land- and Europe-focussed explanations.

In this watery world, colonial men and machines were first entangled with other modes of gathering information and going to war, stretching across Burmese, Javanese or Qing craft for instance. This wasn't an easy transformation in the military and technical capacity of Britain – note, the slow progress of the *Diana* on the Irrawaddy, the first steamship used in war. The way colonialism overtook the indigenous and Asian connections, running across religion, politics and trade and forms of imagination, is in keeping with its counter-revolutionary character.

Tussles between the British and the French in the age of revolutions were being worked out in the midst of these wars. Refugees from Europe could serve as advisers, for instance in Ava. Those with careers forged in the Napoleonic wars could engage in acts of looting and surveillance which were consistent with the 'total war' of Europe at the start of the nineteenth century. For the British, this moment allowed scientific data-gathering, the use of costly armies, new technology and aristocratic militarism disguised with a language of liberation and free trade, to go inland from the water's edge.

The impact of the fear of France and the impulse of a counter-revolution, was explicit as Britain sought to take Dutch bases in Java and Ceylon. They did so in case they should fall to the French, and in the case of Java, because it was said to be a stronghold of republicanism in the Indian Ocean. British aggression against other Europeans supercharged competition with indigenous regimes. The looting of Yogyakarta, for instance, came in the aftermath of the British taking Dutch bases in Java. British policy meanwhile – in Java or Sri Lanka – could follow upon that developed by the Dutch.

If there were such overlapping connections over water, Asian as well as colonial, regional as well as global, Britons often found themselves enrolled by indigenous peoples in alternative ways of engaging with water and land. These alternative modes were diplomatic as well as military and pertained to cultural and cosmological understandings too. Yet the success of the British lay in tracking and then overtaking what already existed. The British followed the route of Buddhist connections or Javanese fighters or sought to eradicate what it classed as 'piracy'. The surge of indigenous peoples was followed by a counter-revolution of empire.

The rise of war for free trade is apparent at the end of this story in China. The triumph of British aims in this context may be compared with the difficulties faced by Crawfurd in Burma in the 1820s who was also after a trading agreement. Asians no longer had easy access to the keys to military success: British gunboats, capital or insurance. What this meant in practice is that the international rise of British commerce, together with the industrial-technical capabilities which the British now deployed, allowed Britons to rule peoples on the coast of Asia. Local modes of making ships, doing commerce across the sea, or exchanging information, as for instance on palm-leaf, were affected by the advance of colonialism. As the terms of warfare turned, this indicated also the turn of the terms of the knowledge economy, a gap in technical expertise and a command over commerce. These last three themes – knowledge, technique and commerce are at the heart of what follows.

7

In the Bay of Bengal:
Modelling Empire, Globe and Self

Astronomer John Goldingham was planning an expedition to the equator from Madras. 'In selecting a station on the Equator', he wrote in 1822, 'care should be taken that it be as far as possible out of the sphere of the attraction of Mountains, and close to the sea.'[1] The Equator is now a taken-for-granted marker in our understanding that the Earth is a perfect sphere or globe. Yet that belief does not often reckon with the fact that the planet should instead be described as an oblate spheroid.

The variation of the distance to the centre of the Earth is especially apparent near to where the Equator now lies. The planet bulges close to the Equator, and the consequent variation to the distance to the centre of the Earth is accompanied by a slight fluctuation in gravitational acceleration. Spreading a net of numbers, calculations of longitude, tidal determinations and coastal marking points, was an effort launched in this context to standardise the misshapen form of the planet. It was part of a programme of making the Earth more like a spherical globe.

As this data-collecting proceeded, it bridged disciplines and displaced informants and mediators in privileging the interests of global imperialism. And as colonial settlements and cities were consolidated, regions and territories were fitted into grids within which they found their place, for instance on maps or in tabulations of local times. The infrastructural projects that came in the wake of this knowledge at waterside, like lighthouses or dockyards, smoothed the passage of colonists, traders, travellers and technicians of various kinds. Indigenous peoples had to come to terms with how this rule of knowledge transformed their seas and lands in an age of free-trade empire, when steamships called at port. Yet the detachment and classification which was so characteristic of this project, where nature and the Earth were seen to be tableaux worth plotting and exploiting, was not met without response from individuals.

The Madras Observatory, over which Goldingham presided, was first established privately in 1786, and officially under a resolution from the Court of Directors of the East India Company in 1792. When founded in 1786 it was thought to be the first astronomical observatory instituted by 'any European in the East'.[2] Its prime function was nautical: the determination of longitude and the correction of shipboard chronometers, timepieces that helped with the determination of coordinates. Goldingham himself wrote:

> A public observatory . . . is an establishment for observing the heavenly bodies to ascertain exact position and motions with a view to the improvement of the tables and geography of navigation.[3]

Yet other activities and disciplines overlapped with the nautical agenda of this institute. The observatory shared staff with an institute set up to train surveyors, the Revenue Survey School in Madras.[4] The survey of the South Indian coast was an important function of this set of experts. The reference point for longitude calculations was provided by Madras Observatory. Meteorology also played a role at the observatory, which is unsurprising given the difficulties faced by East India Company vessels in navigating the Bay of Bengal's monsoon (more on this anon). Meanwhile, Goldingham observed the changes in the tide, and these observations were put together with data from other parts of the world and across South Asia, including from Henry Burney, the first British Resident in Ava, which shows that the observatory's tentacles stretched to Burma.[5]

The extent of disciplinary cross-fertilisation evident at the observatory matched the geographical reach of the observatory's work. Both of these were in keeping with how the sciences practised here stretched over different spaces, for instance, sea, land, the atmosphere and the sky. The observatory was not simply a place from which to watch the heavens. The different sorts of extensions – disciplinary, geographical and topographical – were consistent with the expansive character of empire itself.

A MULTI-DISCIPLINARY OBSERVATORY FACING THE SEA

Goldingham had already made lunar observations and observations of Jupiter's moons at Bombay, and chronometer readings between Bombay and Madras before becoming astronomer to the Madras government between 1796 and 1830.[6] His published scientific work bears out his interest in multiple observations: he weighed up the value of observing the moons of Jupiter and their eclipses to determine the position of a point. He deemed this to be far preferable a route to using 'eclipses of the sun, of the moon, or of occultations', which 'happen but seldom'.[7] He determined the longitude of Madras as also Madras Time, which he correlated to Greenwich Time.

He worked out the velocity of sound at Madras, noting the results of observations of the sounding of a gun on the ramparts of Fort St George in Madras and also on St Thomas' Mount. The observatory was placed between these two sites: 'each observer begun to count the beats in the interval of the flash and report.' These beats were correlated with the thermometer, the barometer and hygrometer and the state of the wind and weather at the time. Goldingham concluded with satisfaction: 'The mean velocity of sound deduced from these experiments appears to be 1142 feet in a second which closely corresponds with the estimate of Newton and Halley.'[8] Elsewhere he also roamed into antiquarianism and architecture.[9] The generality of observation is what is noteworthy – the tabulation of all this data was interrelated. The more data there was, the more systematisation resulted and the more extraction from the physical space of the Earth and its peoples. The folding of data and space regularised nature as an understandable and universalised tableau.[10]

This regime of calculation thrived at the seafront because sea-facing locales could provide especially good platforms from which to observe the sky. Accordingly, John Warren, who between 1805 and 1810 acted instead of Goldingham at the observatory, wrote that he spent much time digesting observations which could not be undertaken in Europe. On one occasion in 1809 he wrote with pleasure of how he observed stars 'of a higher Southern Delineation which from circumstance of their not being visible in Europe, are in many instances very inaccurately laid down in the Catalogues in the hands of most Navigators'.[11]

Warren, along with others, was successful in detecting comets at Madras. A 'Great Comet' of 1807 detected by Warren was probably easier to spot from a location like Madras, despite the interruptions of bad weather. Warren wrote that it had been seen in Bengal, Penang and at sea before he spotted it on 2 October. Nevertheless he was probably one of the first to observe this comet.[12] A sea-facing observatory allowed different kinds of questions and results to be related. For instance, in publishing readings of the barometer, Goldingham pondered whether the action of the moon on the sea, in creating the tides, had a counterpart in its action on the air. In his words, were there 'tides of the atmosphere'? Using his calculations, he answered negatively.

The Madras Observatory's central nautical aim, given its location at the heart of the Indian Ocean, was as a calibration point for ships across this vast ocean. Warren wrote, for instance, of bringing order to an 'extensive mass of observations for the Longitudes taken for nearly 22 years in Madras'.[13] East India Company ships were floating observatories of a kind, 'part of the hardware of longitude determination'. In these ships' logbooks a column was introduced in 1791 for the determination of longitude. It was only by about the 1840s that chronometer readings became the most secure means of determining longitude. Before this period, ships continued to use chronometers next to lunar calculations and dead reckoning to determine longitude. If ships on the sea functioned as observatories of the heavens, and as sites from which to measure longitude, this in turn relied on the secure position of Madras Observatory as a point of reference for them, fixed in time and space.[14]

This partly explains why 'solidity', 'steadiness' and 'stability' were some of the words used to describe how the Madras Observatory would be built. The observatory's construction plans paid close attention to material: for instance, granite supports would be set in place for instruments, like the stone used in 'Indian temples'. These stone supports would prevent any alteration caused by vibration. The observatory's walls would be made of 'Brick and Chunam' deemed to be the best materials for the making of a 'solid mass', and the floor was to be made with teak from Burma. The construction was deemed to be strong enough to withstand the monsoon.[15] A granite tablet was placed on the western door of the observatory with an inscription.

This inscription was also engraved in three Indian languages on the cone at the centre of the observatory. These languages were Persian, Telugu and Tamil. On this cone was a gallery from which instruments could be directed to the sky. [Fig. 7.1] The words of the inscription celebrated 'British liberality in Asia' and the arrival of the astronomical sciences which would be a blessing to the 'future generations of this extensive [British] Empire'.

Fig. 7.1 Length of Pendulum Experiment at Madras, from J. Goldingham, *Madras Observatory Papers* (1827)

THE EXPEDITION FROM MADRAS
TO AN ISLAND OFF SUMATRA

In planning his expedition of 1822, Goldingham brought to his mind's eye 'a small healthy Island' off Sumatra, 'at a moderate distance from the Mainland'.

This expedition was to be launched from Madras Observatory. It was not like the voyages encountered in an earlier chapter where British and French explorers competed and cooperated over the plotting of islands on maps in the oceans of the south. Goldingham shared with the Dutch the results of the voyage that he proposed and saw through with the speedy and full patronage of the East India Company authorities on the Indian subcontinent.[16] By this time, geographical pursuits were important but secondary to commercial or political concerns, unlike in an earlier period of grand voyaging.

Goldingham was searching for a particular sort of island for a specific task of calculation and calibration, which was less about the island and its inhabitants than about its place on the globe and the rise of new style of empiricism:

> The primary object of the Expedition is to make the requisite Experiments and observations for ascertaining the Length of the Pendulum at the Equator, to combine with examinations which have been made at Madras, and in other parts of the Earth.[17]

The pendulum-length experiment – now standard fare for physics students – is in simple terms a calculation of the impact of gravity on the time a pendulum's bob takes to swing, and this time slightly varies from place to place on the Earth's surface. Close to the equator, from repeated observations up to fractions of seconds Goldingham proposed a calculation to determine the acceleration due to gravity and to confirm the exact shape of the Earth. From a previous round of Madras experiments Warren had given the verdict: the Earth was a 'heterogeneous spheroid'.[18] The systematic determination of the acceleration due to gravity was a global pastime in this period driven partly by the studies of the physicist Henry Kater in Britain, who sent Goldingham in Madras an invariable pendulum in 1820. Kater's new designs for experimental pendulums allowed a greater degree of accuracy over the very difficult calculation of minute differences in acceleration due to gravity, allowing in turn a greater degree of empirical precision over the determination of the shape of the Earth.[19]

Kater himself had served in the survey of India from 1794 to 1806, inventing 'a very ingenious method for ascertaining the amount of moisture in the atmosphere', using a seed known to Tamils.[20] About forty different calculations of the length of the pendulum had been conducted across the world by 1826, including at Mauritius, Guam, the Cape and Sydney. The reconciliation of the results of these various experiments proved a huge headache: 'At the Isle of France and at

Guam and Mowi, the errors appear enormous.'[21] The coordination of the results benefited from the support of the Board of Longitude but depended on informal patterns of sociability that straddled the globe.[22] Illustrative of this sociability was the patronage of Stamford Raffles, at this point governor of Bengkulu, in response to the direct approach of Goldingham. Raffles agreed to receive the expedition at Bengkulu and to send it on to Sumatra with further advice and assistance, together with a guard.

Off Sumatra, eight hundred experiments were conducted by those whom Goldingham called 'observers', namely two surveyors trained in the East India Company's Surveying School. Peter Lawrence and John Robinson were trained for hours on end under his watch at the Madras Observatory before their departure. According to one of his superiors who was a Madras surveyor, Lawrence had once been in trouble for 'constant intoxication'. This superior asked for confirmation from the governing authorities of the East India Company that Lawrence had indeed returned to 'habitual sobriety', consistent with a disciplined observer in releasing him for service with Goldingham.[23] In being disciplined like this, Lawrence and Robinson had to perform the role of regulated human instruments of observation, creating a composite in a system of data-gathering, encompassing alongside humans the many scientific devices which accompanied them.

Lawrence and Robinson carried instruments which included an astronomical clock, a pendulum, thermometers, pocket chronometers, a sextant and 'one with a stand'; 'Artificial Horizons with Glass covers – Quicksilver for the same', a large telescope, a portable transit instrument, a theodolite, and a circumferentor, which is a compass used for survey.[24] In addition to ascertaining the pendulum's swing, Goldingham gave his aides a further list of observations that needed to be conducted:

> During the time of making the Experiments, the rate of the Clock must be correctly ascertained, both by the Stars and the Sun – and all the Observations carefully registered. A small Pillar may be built for the Transit Instrument, sufficiently to the right in the Observatory, not to obstruct the view of the Pendulum through the Telescope, but so as to take advantage of the opening in the top of the Observatory, for taking the Transits. Meridian Altitudes of the Sun, if not too high for the Artificial Horizon, and of the Stars on each side of the Zenith should be observed; the more numerous the Observations are the

better – as a result to the nearest second is required. The Longitudes must be found by the Chronometers, and Eclipses of the Satellites of Jupiter.[25]

Despite all this precise training and instruction, the expedition encountered severe obstacles. This shouldn't be a surprise: for here were observers seeking to study the Earth's shape at the boundaries of two of the planet's tectonic plates. An earthquake provided an alarming shock to the travellers while they were at Bengkulu; a severe squall overtook them after they had left and forced them to take refuge in the hold of the vessel, where with the hatches down they faced a danger of suffocation. So then they had to return to Bengkulu, where they were gripped by fever. Fever was later said to have affected every single member of the party by the end of the expedition.[26]

A further series of tremors struck the expedition as they travelled through islands and settlements off Sumatra in search of the perfect site for the pendulum-length experiment. On one occasion at Pulo Panjong [Pagang Island]: 'a shock of an Earthquake was felt, which is stated to have given the earth, an undulatory motion for some minutes – another (but slighter) shock was felt shortly afterwards . . .'[27] After many observations – for instance at 'Sugar Loaf Peak', close to Tapanuli Bay, where longitude, bearings and angles were determined, the expedition finally decided on a site for pendulum-length experiments, and began the erection of an observatory. The chosen site was the island of Gaunsah Lout [probably Gangsa Laut], just above the equator on the western coast of Sumatra and off-present day Pulau Pini.[28]

Gangsa Laut was described in the expedition papers as an island '365 feet long by 200 feet broad'.[29] One illustration shows the party of investigators: four Europeans in hats gesticulating and making plans before a line of white tents, before which in turn are a set of Asian assistants who are clothed in blue. [Fig. 7.2] To the left is an indigenous vessel, a reminder that however isolated and however perfect for equatorial experimentation, this was an island in an inhabited terrain of sea. The idea of a self-contained experiment set apart from any interference was impossible.

The British observers were themselves assisted by *lascars*, who presumably are the figures in blue in the illustration. The official papers noted the fear of attack by '*The Padres*, a sect of Musselman Fanatics'. This was a reference to the early-nineteenth-century Padri movement, which

Fig. 7.2 'View of the Island of Gaunsah Lout [Gangsa Laut] with the Observatory and Encampments', from John Goldingham, *Report of the Length of the Pendulum at the Equator . . . Made on an Expedition . . . from the Observatory at Madras* (Madras, 1824)

was an accelerated programme of religious renewal in West Sumatra, an attempt to cleanse Islam of *adat* or local customary law and practices. In one historical interpretation the Padri movement was set off through the activity of returning hajjis with knowledge of Wahhabi reform, connected to the events encountered before in the Persian Gulf. It also drew on longstanding scholarly networks between Southeast Asia and the Middle East.[30]

The Padri movement was concentrated in the highlands but Padang on the West Sumatran coast, close to the island chosen for experiments, had come under the influence of Padri ideology. It had also seen the arrival of anti-Padri refugees. When some Sumatran territories were retaken by the Dutch from the British in 1821, the Dutch sided with anti-Padri elements, especially traditional nobles. Islamic renewal was set against colonialism. The conflict between the Dutch and Islamic reformers was perhaps why Raffles provided the party with a guard. Though the Padri movement may easily be seen as part of the age of revolutions for its concern with the purification of religion and the reorganisation of politics so as to create more centralised rule, it made no mark on the expedition. This despite the fact that the sciences of 'logic' and 'ideal realities' were part of the programme of scholarly renewal at its heart.[31]

Rather, the problem faced by Goldingham's expedition was the theft of instruments. 'Savage inhabitants' were blamed: they came on the pretence of fishing, entered the tent and took 'the Transit Instrument, Azimuth Compass, Circumferentor, and a small box belonging to Captain Crisp.'[32] The explanation provided was that these indigenous peoples thought the brass was gold. From dark until daylight Goldingham's men patrolled the 'experiment island' to keep visitors away. A second image of Gangsa Laut appeared as an oblong egg-shaped island, with layers of coast and vegetation, leading to a central observation point [Fig. 7.3] An idea of a scientific fortress was in this manner superimposed over a terrain where Muslim reform operated and where indigenous peoples displayed the desire to take – instruments, for instance – from Europe.

Among the results of this attempt to confirm the exact shape of the Earth, was the precise plotting of islands such as Gangsa Laut on the map of the globe. There was another result. The expedition results fed a view from nowhere in the sense of allowing the creation of a scientifically detached view of the Earth; around forty sites across the world provided data points which were integrated by 1826.[33] Intermediaries were important in the experiments undertaken by Goldingham and his

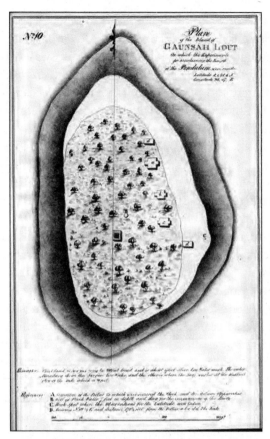

Fig. 7.3 'Plan of the Island of Gaunsah Lout on
which the Experiments for ascertaining the
Length of the Pendulum were made',
from Goldingham, *Report of the Length
of the Pendulum*

coterie. Yet the progress of these experiments demonstrates the increasing
disappearance of the markers of indigenous work as the Earth emerged
as a tabulated object.

PEOPLE IN A BRITISH MACHINE OF SCIENCE

At Madras Observatory, where Goldingham was personally involved in
pendulum-length experiments which he conducted in advance of the

expedition to Sumatra, he used *brahmin* assistants: Tiruvenkatacharya counted the clock and Srinivasacharya took down the time. *Acharya* at the end of their names is a title marking their status as a teacher. Given the care with which Goldingham trained Lawrence and Robinson, the importance of these tasks should not be lost – even a fraction's error would jeopardise the resulting calculations and yet here were Indians entrusted with this role of observation.[34]

John Warren also employed assistants like this. In 1809 he had used Srinivasacharya in pendulum-length experiments in Madras.[35] In reporting on the 1807 comet he noted how he was taken ill in early December, making it impossible to make further observations, but 'the Bramin Assistant Senivassachairy [Srinivasacharya] continued to notice it'. Srinivasacharya took measurements of its position in relation to the stars: 'The last sight he had of it was on the 13th after which the light of the Moon prevented his perceiving it any longer.'[36]

Yet this long-lasting story of personal relations between local elites, indigenous informants and Europeans, including, elsewhere in the oceans of the South, Pacific islanders who provided information to voyagers, took on a new hue in the midst of these enterprises. This detached, aerial, multi-dimensional and exalted scale of global modelling, dependent on a vast array of instruments and sites, while combining longitude and latitude, seas, lands, airs and sky, made it less necessary to rely on local information. Or even if there was a reliance, the stamp of the intermediaries who helped form the models disappeared from the results which arose. In the case of Goldingham's experiments in Madras and Sumatra, the results comprised long lists of statistics and figures, without visible indication of labour or personality.[37]

This manoeuvre might be placed within the broader set of claims marshalled so far for a British imperial counter-revolution. The British turned their war machine, as also their commitments to international commerce, interventionist humanitarianism, law, racial and gendered civility, cultural study and collecting, to their own interests and displaced subjects, informants and workers. They did so while also owning a vocabulary of liberation, protection and freedom from tyranny and monopolism. Their attempt at ownership extended to the peoples whose pathways of oceanic travel, protest and agency were moulded by this era of the age of revolutions. There was entanglement and borrowing – across the axis of colonised and coloniser, and also across European rivals. Yet, violence, exemplified in looting witnessed alongside the 'total war' of the era for instance, tilted this balance, as in Burma. So also did the dense set of colonial itineraries across the water, for war as well as scholarship. The information that was collected as a result of the British empire's aggressive mobility was critical in allowing the British to ride supreme over the waves of the South. It is that information that the activities of the Madras Observatory highlights. In the age of revolutions, indigenous peoples were active participants in knowledge-making. The sciences of reason were vastly expanding in scope. But the British co-opted informants and didn't credit their agency and assistance in creating a global view.

For instance, in 1825 Warren completed a tome on Indian timekeeping, titled *Kala Sankalita*. It was published by the Madras Fort St George College Press and the subtitle gives a good idea of its contents: *A Collection of Memoirs on the Various Modes According to Which The Nations of the Southern Parts of India Divide Time: To which Are Added Three General Tables, Wherein May Be Found By Mere Inspection The Beginning, Character, and Roots of The Tamul, Tellinga, and Mahommedan Civil Years, Concurring Viz. the Two Former with the Europeans Years of the XVIIth, XVIIIth, and XIXth Centuries, and the Latter with Those From A.D. 622 (A.H. 1) to 1900.* This then involved the communication in print of knowledge that had previously resided in palm-leaf texts: 'to disclose to Europeans the contents and structure of those humble annual Kalendars [Calendars] which, written on palmyra leaves, have, during nearly two centuries, been sold under their eyes without even suspecting the skill and labour which their computation required'.[38] The agenda was to make much easier the task of converting between different calendars in South Asia, and specifically between the European calendar and its South Asian equivalents.

The book resulted not only from the patronage of the East India Company and especially the College of Fort St George, but also through the patronage of British governments across the Indian Ocean. Warren thanked the governments of Ceylon, Prince of Wales Island and Mauritius.[39] The Company noted that Warren's work of correlating Indian and European calendars would be of great use to 'officers of Government'.[40] Merchants and 'all classes of people in the Company's territories' were envisaged as being among its users. As the title indicates, it was hoped that the planning of civil and religious ceremonies would benefit from the data it brought together. Warren also thanked an assistant – one of the 'best informed natives of Madras' – who had helped him for three years.[41] In completing the work Warren's calculations were checked and verified by the 'Hindu Astronomer and other natives' at the College of Fort St George.[42]

Yet signs of this astronomer *pandit* are absent in the copious descriptions and tables which comprise the work. There was only this line in the preface about thanks due 'to R. Audy Shashya Brahmini, the Native Astronomer attached to the College, for his professional assistance during nearly two years that he communicated with him on the subject of these Memoirs'.[43] The creation of privileged and expert knowledge in place of localised and personalised information is evident in the public diary of the Madras Presidency of the East India Company, which comments on the *Kala Sankalita*:

> none of our Members, were sufficiently versed in Hindoo Astronomy to estimate with earnestness and report with confidence on the merit and value of Colonel Warren's Work . . .

It called in the judgement of Mr George Hyne of the Medical Service, who had in fact worked alongside Warren on the publication, and noted his verdict:

> The Kala Sankalita of Colonel Warren is a work which must have required much laborious research and a very considerable knowledge of Hindoo Astronomy. It reports itself to be key to the Hindoo Solar and Lunar Kalendars. It contains an abundance of materials for constructing a Kalendar of the positions of the Sun and Moon, and exhibits numerous examples and illustrations of the mode in which the construction may be accomplished, and a variety of useful tables for the purpose of abbreviating labour and facilitating the apprehension of the object of investigation.[44]

If labour could thus be 'abbreviated', it relied on the abbreviation and substitution of the work of indigenous intermediaries. Yet there was another way in which the Madras Observatory abbreviated the work of its employees. Within this institution other European nationals were made to serve the British state.

Of note in tracing the rise of the British in the aftermath of the age of revolutions is that Goldingham was not English but in fact Danish: he was one of a class of Danish naturalists and technicians who worked across India in this period. His original name is said to be Johannes Guldenheim.[45] Denmark had minor colonial outposts in South Asia, which were useful bases for Protestant missionaries, until they accessed English East India Company territories. One was on the south-east Indian coast – Tranquebar, now called Tharangambadi, where the Danish established a fort, Dansborg. It was only ceded to the British in 1845, though it was occupied during the Napoleonic Wars between 1808 and 1814.

The man who stood in for Goldingham when he took a long leave was himself not British and had anglicised his name. He had left Paris after the French Revolution in 1791, and one line of his family had settled in Ireland. John Warren's real name was Jean-Baptiste François Joseph de Warren (1769–1830). He fought against Tipu Sultan of Mysore, and went on to survey Mysore. One of Warren's concerns, in keeping with his obsessive calculation of information, was an interest in milestones on highways. At his own expense he placed 262 milestones on some roads in southern India. After the restoration of the French monarchy, he returned to France in 1815 and was reinstated in the French army, but made his way back to India and to Pondichéry.[46]

In co-opting individuals like this, the British colonial data-collecting matrix bore the marks of the earlier age of the revolutions. Fighters and people from conflicting empires took up their places within the edifice of the British information machine and its commitment to empiricism. The determination of navigational problems and other associated sciences included an important cross-continental enterprise which was directed across the globe.[47] The colonial British took increasing hold of this continental network as is evident in the anglicisation of the names of these two key astronomers in Madras.

If this denotes how times were changing in the Indian Ocean, the same may be said for the legacy of revolutionary ferment. Madras was a far more confident metropolis by the second decade of the nineteenth century after the Napoleonic Wars.[48] The city itself was stamped by the age of revolutions, as it expanded and breathed in the light of the military victories against Tipu Sultan of Mysore, who had constituted the greatest threat to colonial Madras. Mysore, as we have seen, was finally defeated in 1799. In the aftermath there occurred an urban programme of imposing colonial civility, stretching from the installation of public lamps and pavements to the greater separation of an anglicised British fort from a multifunctional and socially heterogeneous 'Black Town'. As colonial residents in Madras felt an embattled isolation in being far from Europe, this gave rise in turn to a 'a Southern patriotism', connected to the adoption of distinctive local practices, set apart not only from London but also from Calcutta in the north. The growing urban confidence of Madras was evident also on the beach, as a formal trading quarter was established here.

The reorganisation of the settlement had repercussions along racial and gendered lines. The difference between coloniser and colonised – like the lineaments of the city – were more carefully laid out in the nineteenth century. The changing place of intermediaries at the Madras Observatory needs to be understood from this wider social and political perspective. Also critical here was how Madras served as a hub from which empire expanded across the seas.

WEATHER WATCHERS AND IMPERIAL MODELLING

The monsoon was a maritime challenge over which control had to be exercised as the British empire spilt over from India to Southeast Asia. The results were evident as the colonial settlements of Southeast Asia took their shape, under the patronage of figures such as Raffles. They took form as a string of ports and water-facing settlements, along the western coast, including Penang, Melaka and Singapore. Colonial bases were determined by the routes of ships, buffeted by winds, in need of a safe haven, especially those charting a course between India and China for trade. Weather and empire were interlocked.

With scientific work on the monsoon too, as with Goldingham's and Warren's experiments, there was an effort to create global models that would facilitate empire and explain and tame the winds. In the late eighteenth and early nineteenth centuries, the voyagers of navigators in the East Indies, in the employ of the East India Company, rather than the armchair philosophers in Europe, were key voices in the discussion and theorisation of the monsoon. Madras was a launch pad for this group.

James Capper, an officer of the East India Company, was a keen weather watcher and illustrates the pattern. Based in Madras for successive periods, where both of his daughters were baptised, Capper had fought in the Madras Army. While in Madras, Capper kept records of the weather. His *Observations on the Winds and the Monsoons* (1801), written after retreating to Cathays in Wales to restore his health, included a sample of his observations on the weather at Madras for the whole of

1776, together with the mean monthly thermometer and barometer read-ings. A weather diary can seem a dry digest of empirical detail. Take this entry in Capper's Madras diary:

> June. – On the 1st and 2d, regular land and sea-breezes; the 3d, violent long-shore wind. On the 4th, morning fair, noon cloudy, in the evening rain. – N.B. More than two hundred pieces of cannon fired in salutes; query whether it occasioned the rain? – On the 5th, land-wind all day, and likewise on the subsequent days to the 24th; on that day a sea-breeze at ten A.M. and in the evening cloudy and rain. On the 29th, the land and sea wind changed alternately four different times. On the 30th, it rained in the evening. To the 15th, the mean of the thermometer 86 degrees; to the latter end of the month 94.[49]

Yet the rise of this empiricism is deceptive – for what it did, for Capper and other weather watchers, was to provide tools of control over a whole series of data. The data allowed the possibility of creating a regularised pattern of explanation that encompassed winds, seas, rains and heat, while also taking in the relation between human action and the weather.[50] Note this comment in Capper's tract on waterspouts which drew on his expe-rience of observing them, including in the straits of Malacca: '[i]t is found that in some instances they have been destroyed by firing a gun at them.'[51]

He concluded that waterspouts appear where the atmosphere 'near the earth' is in a 'high rarified state and of course during the most violent heat'.[52] The ascent or descent of 'electrical fluid' was said to cause cold air to force itself through the 'rarified medium' to produce hurricanes, a whirlwind, a squall or a waterspout.[53] The interrelation of data, together with the attention to relations between people and the weather, and a multidimensional view is perhaps best illustrated in Capper's eccentric advice on 'late hours'. He gave advice on how best to sleep given how life in the modern metropolis had turned 'day into night'. The suggestions were addressed to readers in Great Britain. He constructed an elaborate set of rules on how beds should be made up and what kind of mattress should be used, all in order to regularise the circulation of heat in the body. He advised that a thermometer should be kept in the bed chamber and that stagnant air should not be repeatedly breathed nor 'sweet-scented flowers' in bedrooms.[54]

This general methodology – running across a commitment to the interrelation of humans and environments, the task of collecting data of

all kinds and in all contexts, as also to a theory of the universal occurrence and comparability of weather phenomena like waterspouts – is all
in evidence in Capper's account of the monsoon. Capper began by
classifying winds ranging from the 'perennial' to the 'general'. He
provided a global survey of the circulation of winds and a comparison
of the rainfall of India with the Americas, and commentary on rivers
and mountains, temperatures and the sun and moon.[55] Such a survey
linked winds and seas:

> The currents in the Indian Ocean . . . the Gulf of Sind and the Bay of
> Bengal, almost invariably take the same course as the winds. During the
> S.W. monsoon they constantly run from the S.W. to the N.E. to the
> S.W. The cause of this connection between the wind and water seems
> almost to speak for itself.[56]

He also explained the surf on the Coromandel coast, the coastline of
Madras:

> The immense body of water which is brought from the southward into
> the Gulf of Sind and the Gulf of Bengal, during the S.W. monsoon, very
> probably arises from the quantity of ice and snow, which has been
> dissolved in the southern polar regions during the summer solstice of
> that hemisphere . . . [t]o these causes very probably may be ascribed
> likewise what is usually called the surf or surge, which breaks with great
> violence during the S.W. monsoon.[57]

The interrelation of data did not simply generate explanations of
phenomena on and above the water, such as the surf and waterspouts and
their relation to the monsoon. Capper also moved into an account of the
heat of the Earth as generative of winds. 'Electric fire' which exists in both
the 'body of the Earth and in the atmosphere', when disturbed, as when
a common fire is kindled, was thought by Capper to produce winds.[58]

Plotting data like this allowed a rationalisation of the world's geography. For the empiricism drove a commitment to classification which
was in keeping with the making of global models. Accordingly, Capper
advised that the Bay of Bengal, to which Madras opened out, should
probably be labelled a Gulf rather than a Bay, leaving the category of
bays only for small gulfs, where gulfs in turn were 'inferior' portions of
great seas.[59] The Bay of Bengal's ferocity was explained by how it shut

things up: the northern Indian Ocean did not allow for the escape of the winds, generating the pattern of the monsoon.

Similarly, to follow Thomas Forrest who had extensive experience in navigating the seas around India as a country trader, and had been involved in gathering intelligence about French naval activity in the Indian Ocean in his *A Treatise on the Monsoons in East-India* (1783): 'I mean the whole contained between the Cape of Good Hope to the north-east; then east as far as the China seas; and then south, by New Holland, has no exit northward . . .'⁶⁰ Forrest immediately followed up this observation with an analogy, asking the reader to imagine an Atlantic with Europe stretching all the way across to North America. In such circumstances, he argued, the Atlantic would also have a monsoon. A great deal of Forrest's treatise was devoted to delineating the correct tracks to be kept in navigating the Bay of Bengal in specific periods of the monsoon. Forrest insisted that theoretical writings on the monsoons and the practice of navigating the seas should go together.

The illusion of modelling – its potential to recreate the relationship between humans and nature, by making the whole Earth an object – is especially evident in how Forrest finished one of his works, *Voyage from Calcutta to the Mergui Archipelago, Lying on the East Side of the Bay of Bengal* (1792). This book was designed to raise interest in the Mergui islands, off Burma, which Forrest saw as a good stepping stone for voyagers, as the islands lay in a regular order, forming a connected barrier against the south-west monsoon. They were a good point of access to a series of good harbours on the eastern side of the bay.⁶¹

The dense description of sites and precise instructions about sailing which Forrest provided ended with an off-hand suggestion about yet another model: 'Why does nobody turn a level verdant plain of a few acres into a map of the world?' Forrest suggested that such a map could be laid out in the gardens of 'men of fortune'. The idea came to him when he had been detained by the south-west monsoon and constructed a large map from two thick planks. He provided detailed measurements for such a garden: 'the continents and islands may be made in turf, the sea in gravel'; and at particular places 'gravel posts may be fixed up, indicating particular circumstances of monsoons, trade-winds and currents'.

The intention was to expose nature to widest view, to expand the powers of the mind, and so to come to a deeper engagement in turn with particular places. For Forrest such a project would highlight how a passage from the Downs in coastal England to India 'is nothing'

compared with the hardships and fatigue of narrow seas.[62] Models multi-
plied in this period of time. Forrest's final proposal was interesting for
blurring the distinction between models and nature; he aimed to natur-
alise the map of the world in a garden. In this early moment, British
trade and empire reorganised existent traders and assistants – ranging
from Bugis, Chinese, Malays and Dutch – within new centres of control
such as the colonial bases on the eastern side of the Bay of Bengal. In
keeping with this, Forrest incorporated Jawi Malay navigational information in his charts.[63] The global model once again depended on and
effaced indigenous information.

It was the global modelling of this knowledge which slowly made
possible a more instrumentalist imperial form of control which radiated
outwards from British India. Britons used their science to create long-
lasting footholds down the eastern side of the Bay of Bengal. These
contrasted with the mutating pattern of Asian maritime states which
existed prior to this time. In other words, the emerging model of knowledge and data was not only global but generative of empire and
settlement. The way it bypassed indigenous intermediaries was of a piece
with the way it established territorial control.

In 1786 Penang came under East India Company rule, because of
the activities of country traders like Forrest. Francis Light, one of
Forrest's associates, and soon superintendent of Penang, wrote to India
of how Penang was 'a convenient Magazine for Eastern Trade' and of
the need for some 'useful and convenient Port for the protection of
Merchants who trade to China . . . in time of War in either Monsoon.'[64]
Another trader, James Scott, gave an even more systematic argument
for Penang:

1ST Because it is easy and safe access and recess, in all seasons.

2ND because it may be established with the consent of the Natives, because
of the northern Ports of the Streights of which it is the centre, is unconnected with the Dutch.

3RD. Because we want such a Port having no place of Retreat in case of
Accidents but Malacca . . . were the Dutch well diposed to do so, which
they are not, yet this is the thoroughfare of our Europe, Madras, Bengal,
Bombay & China Ships . . .'[65]

The consolidation of Penang followed a thorough assessment of its potential and – taking up the work of Forrest prior to this – the suitability of other islands in the Bay, including the Andamans, the Nicobars and Junk Ceylon, what is now Phuket.[66] Its superiority lay in its supply of good timber for shipbuilding, and as a good site for the repair of ships. The role of agents like Forrest in making this come to pass needs to be emphasised: Forrest spent a great deal of time arguing for British bases on the east side of the Bay of Bengal, though in the end he lost his reputation in the eyes of the Company's directors, and didn't see his proposals for the Mergui islands taken forward.[67]

By 1805 Penang had become the fourth presidency, or unit of govern-ance, of the East India Company territories directly under the Court of Directors, alongside Calcutta, Bombay and Madras. The year 1826 saw Singapore and Malacca attached to Penang, after a period of a few years when Malacca was returned to the Dutch, thus making a set of three harbours on the way to China on the east side of the Bay.[68]

Noteworthy is the fact that a treaty signed between the British and the Sultan of Johor and his Temenggong or minister, marking the 'cessa-tion of the Sovereignty and property of the island of Singapore', extended to the 'Seas, Straits and Islets (the latter probably not less than 50 in number) within ten geographical miles of [Singapore's] coasts'.[69] This 1824 agreement marked the moment when Singapore ceased to be governed in alliance and became an outright British possession.[70] The imperial march was about the construction of seaborne passages between India, the Bay of Bengal and the South China Sea: it was the sea which was in view before the land. It was from the definition of ownership over the sea that territorial control was made possible.

This seaborne British advance on the eastern side of the Bay of Bengal came about because of the ambiguities surrounding the limits of the Dutch empire in Southeast Asia, only resolved on paper with the signing of the Treaty of London in 1824. Though this treaty was meant to settle boundaries, even as late as 1840 the Dutch could accuse British surveyors of being up to no good, dressing up their strategic ventures as enterprises of science and mapping.[71] Knowledge-making and empire were inseparable.

The maps which arose from these surveyors contained various visions of empire. James Horsburgh's chart of the *Bay of Bengal* (1825) centres the ocean as an object and sketches lines of passage across it, indicating the best passages for ships from Europe, Madras and Calcutta, during

alternative monsoon seasons, towards the Malacca strait.[72] Geostrategy
was not too far away. An instance of this is George Romaine's *A Sketch
of the Bay of Bengal* (1802). In this map, drawn to suggest ways of
protecting the empire from French privateers, the naval commander lays
out the possible track of three cruisers that would guard strategic
passages.[73] A similar strategic vision generated discussion about the limits
of the Bay of Bengal, in a tense stand-off between two naval men in 1805,
about how to divide up the Company fleet between Penang and Bombay.
The sticking point was whether Ceylon and Madras should be placed
under Penang or under Bombay.[74]

Tellingly for the links between marine surveying and empire, Raffles'
taking of Singapore in 1819 occurred side by side with its marine surveying
by Captain Daniel Ross. Ross drew up a *Plan of Singapore Harbour*
(1819).[75] Most of this map, which uses 'Singapore' for one of the first
times, is taken up by the expanse of water in the proposed harbour.[76]
The map is annotated 'deep water' at one spot and with 'Malay village'
at another. Along the line of the coast in the top left of the chart, there
is a creek and mangroves. Some profile views of the harbour were undertaken alongside it, with clear ideas of elevation, and showing vessels on
water, a flag flying, and a 'watering place', all classic elements of this
phase of maritime empire.[77] Attention to the coast is also seen in the
very large *Plan of the Island of Singapore* (1822), probably the result of a
survey of Captain James Franklin which contains a very detailed assessment of the coastal belt with no attention to the interior, which is blank,
except for Bukit Timah hill.[78]

Control of the sea face made it more possible to consolidate protected
land settlements. The assertion of maritime 'sovereignty' by the British
was connected, if one is to follow John Crawfurd, the Resident of
Singapore, writing in 1824 with the 'military protection of the Settlements',
'towards [their] internal security, and towards [their] safety from the
piratical hordes that surround [them]'.[79] By the middle of the nineteenth
century, as revolution and war gave way to the certainty of Britain's
ascendency, this chain of stepping stones down the bay took up another
imperial cartographic representation. They were not points of shelter
and safety, but radials and magnets of free trade, emporiums in the sea,
halfway between India and China.

UNSETTLED SELVES IN STEAMBORNE BRITISH SINGAPORE

The danger of this new mode of global knowledge and modelling lay in how it scientifically positioned places – islands such as the 'experiment island' off Sumatra as well as Singapore – on a tabulated model of the Earth. In turn, global knowledge worked across sea and land, and from sea to land, allowing stations like the Madras Observatory to serve as platforms for data collection, and this allowed ships to ply the Bay of Bengal with an accurate sense of their position on the globe and with knowledge of how to cope with the wind and find harbour. The rugged-ness of the globe, close to the equator, was controlled and smoothened. If this was then one aspect of the transformation of knowledge, the rise of a newly empiricist regime of data collection was deeply connected, as just sketched, with the evolution of the empire itself. Here too there was a spiralling history of land bases which linked sea routes. Conceptions of sovereignty and control moved from sea to land alongside surveying. Because of the flattening of personal relations and the reconsideration of locality, these changes were perceived both as totally novel and dangerous by human observers.

It is easy to think that the models were effective and transformative, but the rise of the global view fractured self-understanding as local intellectuals sought to comprehend the new in the light of the old. This knowledge had an impact on the body, and indeed the relation between the body and weather was already of interest to East India Company navigators. This history of the unsettled self in the midst of big global data and empire is especially evident by the second quarter of the nine-teenth century as a port such as Singapore was consolidated and settled.

Take Mr Siami, who hailed from Thailand and was probably present at the negotiations undertaken by Stamford Raffles which gave rise to Singapore in 1819. Here he describes a decree given by the British:

> It hit us like a raging storm accompanied by thunder and lightning, that blows ships and prows adrift in all directions, most with broken rudders and splintered oars, stays and halliards sliced through, rigging snapped and left dangling, with only the fore-mast and main-mast remaining. Ah! Alas, it is truly pitiable. We, ships at anchor that have dragged their moorings, can now find no safe haven. We feel utterly desolate.[80]

Siami took up an appointment with the Master Attendant's office in Singapore. In 1823 his name appeared in the list of officers, as a 'Chinese & Siamese Writer & Interpreter'.[81] Yet the decision of the Directors of the East India Company to move the Master Attendant to Penang, meant that he lost his job, and this was why he felt so bitter – as a ship adrift without shelter. Indeed the way he used a ship as a metaphor for his selfhood is especially striking and suggestive of how maritime empire was generating fundamental change for a man like him.

Siami might be compared with another of Raffles' Malay scribes, Abdullah bin Abdul Kadir (1797–1854), who worked as a language teacher alongside missionaries and other foreigners in Singapore, and who remembered that Raffles was 'just like a father' to him. Writing like this helped him to claim a personal relationship with the great man, who proposed the 1811 invasion of Java.[82] Abdullah travelled constantly between Singapore and Melaka, to visit his family, and died in Mecca in 1854, while undertaking the *hajj*.[83]

Hikayat Abdullah or 'The Story of Abdullah' was completed in manuscript in 1843 in Singapore. Abdullah writes of when accounts of steam shipping first arrived, the next advance on the elements of nature in the Bay of Bengal. He was reluctant to believe such accounts without 'visual proof'. When a picture of a steamship arrived, he finally came to 'absolute assurance'. But his friends ridiculed him for 'magnifying the prowess of the English and [telling them] the most impossible things'.[84] Abdullah visited a steamship in 1841, the *Sesostris* which was involved in the Opium Wars in China.[85]

Abdullah then took up the invitation of the American missionary Alfred North to write a Malay text on the steamship.[86] He used what he knew already to come to terms with the new, writing for instance that the fire on the steamship does not arise from wood, like that used by Malays for fire: 'The coal looks like a rock or a stone, shiny, hard, and as if it were removed from the ground or from the mountains.' The ship itself seemed to have a speed like that pulled by six to seven hundred horses on land. He noted that its cannonballs were as big as his head. In perhaps the ultimate indicator of placing new machines in the light of existing ways of thought, he described the *Sesostris* as 'a gift bestowed by Allah upon man for his thought and enterprise'.[87]

As a translator, involved in missionary publications of useful knowledge, Abdullah worked on 'the nature of the physical world, the atmosphere, the invention of steamships and steam-engines, the making of gas, water-supply systems in America, the uses of steam, the whaling industry, and all sorts of other things about science and western civilisation . . .' This sentence from his *Hikayat* ended with his aim in undertaking all of this: not to kowtow to Britons, but rather so that Malays could also 'make new things'.[88] As Abdullah presented it, his engagement with Western knowledge, from the rise of empirical data to steamships, followed a path: from unbelief to assurance through evidence, and from assurance to writing through physical demonstration. In the midst of this he was undertaking another journey. He was aiming to change Malay views of machines and to generate what he saw as inventiveness.

Yet, even as Abdullah engaged with steamships and wrote and translated material on science and technology for the press, he also kept alive an older tradition of contemplating the sea. The entanglement of old and new is evident in his record of a voyage undertaken in two British cutters, among the fastest vessels in Singapore. He was taking a letter from George Bonham, the British governor of the Straits Settlements, to the ruler of Kelantan on the eastern coast of the peninsula.[89] It was printed in both Jawi (Arabic Malay) and romanised script, with the two scripts on opposite pages and with the title *Kisah Pelayaran Abdullah ke Kelantan* or 'Account of Abdullah's Voyage to Kelantan'. Abdullah was pleased to learn that it had also been translated into French.[90] As Abdullah sailed, he recalled the goodness of God in 'saving me from so many dangers – the shooting, the bullets, the pirates, and the fighting in Kelantan'. This led him to sing a *pantun*, a Malay four-lined poem, which often focuses on love.[91] His *pantun* places the European journey and European ships in the context of this long-standing genre, while also, like Siami, moving between life and the sea and voyaging:

> Good step! Anchors set loose!
> The oars have fanned out, the cannons fired.
> If it is a bullet, bullets lodge deep.
> If it is love, it is not momentary.[92]

In another seaborne narrative, the record of his voyage on the *hajj*, Abdullah once again provides a dramatic account of tempestuous seas, and a comparison of his ship with 'a coconut husk' thrashed in the water.[93]

Abdullah wrote that knowledge 'is the most wonderful of the things created by Allah': 'it does not encumber or weigh heavily upon those who carry it, or require room for its accommodation. It requires neither food nor drink to sustain it, yet it is ready to satisfy our needs at any time.'[94] His theory of knowledge was expressed in a bodily idiom, while he was insistent about the immaterial nature of knowledge.

His concern with what knowledge does to the body was clearly evident in his retelling of surgery undertaken to treat a hydrocele. He had used many Malay, Chinese and Indian medicines but there had been no cure. When examined by a visiting British doctor, who told him that he needed to be cut and drained of fluid, he was terrified. This terror was like that experienced by Muslims who feared vaccination, in this period of time, as an incision in the body.[95] Mulling it over all night, Abdullah discussed it with his friends, who told him: 'Don't you do it. With these white men it is an even chance: if you die you die and if you live you live.'[96]

Yet in contrast with the divided respect accorded to Western innovation by his compatriots, as a game of probability, rather than the generator of a certain outcome, Abdullah placed himself under the knife. He then took two bottles of the drained liquid and sent them back to his parents in Malacca [Melaka]. He wrote that in Malacca people were saying of him: 'His mind accepts the ways of the white man. If it had been any of us we would rather have died of the disease than summon up the courage to do what he did.'[97] If his compatriots saw his mind being changed by his assent to Western medicine, and if Abdullah himself was concerned about incision, it is vital to note the man's refrain in the midst of the record of the operation: praise to Allah for his grace.[98]

The story is replete with questions about how knowledge and the body interact and change each other. It is this train of questions that was opened by the ascent of Western global science and technology. This was a line of contemplation that did not have a simple resolution, even from the perspective of a man who appeared to be loyal to the British empire.

Among scholars, Abdullah's status in the early history of Singapore is controversial. Much better known and read than Siami, he is now valorised as one of the earliest Malay writers of the modern age: 'probably the first Peninsular Malay to confront the moral dilemma presented by Western contact'.[99] But to call him Malay is to attach an uncertain label to him. At this time ethnic understandings were being purified and rigidified under the impact of colonial terms, even as Malay indicated something looser and open to contact across the waters of the Indian Ocean.[100] In the account of one of Abdullah's students in language, J. T. Thomson, the government surveyor of Singapore, Abdullah's father was the son of a Tamil from Nagore in South India and his grandfather was the son of an Arab of Yemen. Thomson described Abdullah's physiognomy as of 'a Tamilian of South Hindoston'.[101] In today's Singaporean lexicon, Abdullah is a Peranakan, an individual of mixed ancestry rather than a Malay.

The difficulty of pinning Abdullah down is also evident with his *Hikayat Abdullah*. On one side it is seen as a radical rupture in Malay literature, because of its autobiographical form, including his use of 'I' and its appearance in print.[102] On the other side, however, the *Hikayat* is an evolution in the form of the longstanding Malay court chronicle, with its combination of advice and admonition and its attention to the genealogy and moral quality of rulers. According to this second reading, it was because of Abdullah's attempt to resuscitate rather than change Malay literature, that he wrote the *Hikayat* in Jawi, or Arabic Malay, at a time when Malay was being romanised by Christian evangelists and translators. Modernist or revivalist? Keeper of tradition, or mimic-man of the West? These established dichotomies are rather caricatured ways of coming to terms with this important voice, and also with Siami. For these were both men living in a time of great change and contending with the innovations of new knowledge.

The *Hikayat Abdullah*'s interest lies precisely in the way Abdullah moves between alternatives, from Christians to Islam, from traditional healing to Western medicine and from Malay engagement with the sea to the British steamship and camera. This movement is itself indicative of the changes afoot in the midst of the counter-revolution of British rule. The unsettled times in which Abdullah lived and the stresses they created for him, match the jumps back and forth, in the placement, form and intent of the *Hikayat*. The human subject in Singapore – for Abdullah and Siami – was on a seaborne voyage, and the ship itself as a motif signified a life in transit here. At the same time, and in what appeared as physically very real, the newness of ships and other mechanical technology resituated the body in new worlds of mobility, trade and empire. For Abdullah and Siami the response was to attempt to ride these waves, metaphorically, intellectually, and materially, to address the needs and problems of the colonised. Life was in flux. But so was the body. And so also what the body needed to contend with in a new age of global knowledge.

INSTRUMENTALISM AND SUBJECTIVITY AT A LIGHTHOUSE

Turning from Abdullah and Siami's views on water and empire to British subjects and their selfhood, it is interesting to return to the surveyors, working out of bases like Madras, who sought to tame the winds and waves. Though Britons active in the late eighteenth and early nineteenth centuries, such as Forrest and Capper, sought to create successful global models, the impact of such knowledge on their sense of self remained destabilising into the middle of the nineteenth century. Additionally, grand programmes of infrastructural improvement – such as a grand lighthouse project designed to allow the transit of ships – demonstrate not simple success but also moments of resistance, and the reliance of these British men on indigenous and colonised labour.

Writing of the programme of surveying undertaken by the British, Abdullah described a deep friendship which he formed with an East India Company surveyor. He named his friend Smith and noted their discussions on the history of Singapore and Malacca and eclipses and stars.[103] Smith was sounding the depths and surveying islands and channels in the waters around the settlement. At their parting, Abdullah records the exchange of a watch for a *kris* [a type of dagger].[104] This was perhaps the template for his relationship with J. T. Thomson, who published an English translation of the *Hikayat*. Thomson arrived in Singapore in 1841 at the age of 21 and was appointed government surveyor, in which position he played a critical role in laying out the settlements' buildings, bridges and roads. He is celebrated for building Horsburgh Lighthouse on the eastern side of the Singapore Strait and also for undertaking a survey of the eastern side of the Malay Peninsula in 1849.[105] A chapter of Thomson's memoir of the Malay lands is devoted to Abdullah, and notes how Abdullah retained a determined commitment to Islam despite his long acquaintance with Christian missionaries.[106]

Thomson's Horsburgh Lighthouse was named in memory of James Horsburgh, who became the East India Company's hydrographer in 1810. Horsburgh was an authority on sailing information. He published and updated such information in his *East India Directory*, on the basis of the close inspection of the accounts of voyages and the charts drawn up by marine surveyors in Company territories.[107] The lighthouse named after him towered over the sea and tumultuous waves in monsoon

Fig. 7.4 Horsburgh Lighthouse today

season, and was intended as a physical marker of British triumph over
the sea route to China. It was strategically placed at the halfway point
on the route and as an aid to mariners who wished to enter Singapore
on the way from China. [Fig. 7.4] The proposal for the lighthouse
appeared in the midst of a series of shipwrecks and was pushed by
merchants who raised a subscription in memory of Horsburgh.[108]
Thomson noted that it was the 'only lighthouse in India occupying a
position on a small solitary rock far out to sea'.[109] Much more recently,
Pedra Braca, the rocks which house this lighthouse, became a point of
dispute between the Malaysian and Singaporean governments who both
claimed it, until the International Court of Justice awarded it to
Singapore.

The progress of this grand project was beset by all kinds of environmental challenges. Infrastructural interventions that came in the
midst of the advance of global knowledge in this period were difficult
to fully realise. The papers connected to the lighthouse charge that its
location proved costly as the rocks were much 'exposed to the influence

of the waves during the South East Monsoon' requiring its structure to be 'entirely faced with granite set in cement'.[110] Despite the winds, mosquitoes proved a particular problem. They caused the Temenggong of Johor, who visited the project, to quickly leave with his followers.[111] After it was built, the surf which struck the western rocks was sufficiently strong to strike a man down at twenty-two to twenty-five feet above the level of the sea, while at times making it impossible to stand at the entrance to the lighthouse.[112] The protests of the labourers, including convicts, who were deployed for the task, and who were said to speak eleven languages, slowed things down. Then there was the difficulty of access to the rocks from ships, and the waves which washed away some of the temporary settlement during the construction.[113] In Thomson's words: the works were 'a source of fear and uncertainty at all times'.[114]

Thomson's success depended on how well he was able to regulate and control the bodies of labourers. Eighty Chinese stonecutters from Singapore, speakers of the Hakka dialect, were employed on Pulau Ubin to the north-east of Singapore island.[115] Pulau Ubin is now visited by tourists, on 'bumboats', who journey there, as I did too, in search of nature after an overdose on hyper-urban Singapore. Escapism was not the lot of the Chinese workers who cut the granite for the lighthouse, splitting huge monolith stones into smaller pieces. In a two-plate sketch, Thomson drew up the passage of the work in a fantasy of step-by-step control. In these images, the stones are blocked out, marked up with a string soaked in China ink or charcoal mixed with water, and then straightened and smoothed by a chisel.[116] [Fig. 7.5] If the stone needed to be broken further, small holes were made and filled with wedges until the granite divided.[117]

Thomson's attention to procedure is matched by his attention to the posture of the labourer. Making a good stone required mastery not only of technique, but for the labourer and stone to 'accommodate' themselves one to the other. Thomson wrote of such accommodation:

> . . . in doing this [the labourer] places himself in many postures; sitting on his heels or squatting, is the favourite position, and the one which comes most easy to him, but at times he sits on the floor, at others he works with the left hand under the thigh, sometimes he crouches so as almost to be doubled up.[118]

Fig 7.5 J.T. Thomson, Chinese Stonecutters, 1851, from Thomson's
sketchbook, 1851

The problem – according to Thomson – was that these labourers were not up to European standards of correctness. He complained that their work did not bear out the test of the plummet, level or straight edge.[119] Theorising further (or fantasising further), and creating racial ideas, Thomson wrote that the labour of a Chinese man working 'under the heat of the equator' does not equal half that undertaken by a European in a temperate climate. In his view, this resulted not from the lack of physical powers but from the effect of climate.[120] In other writings, he argued for the critical importance of climate in determining racial difference, and after settling in New Zealand and becoming the country's first surveyor general, his Malay experience fed into a theory of the migration of Māori from 'Barata' or South India. He also wrote positively about the ability of Chinese migrants to adapt to New Zealand.[121]

If building the lighthouse was a project that tested European surveying and the Asian body at the extremes of nature, it was also an opportunity for Thomson to undertake ethnographic observation and calculation. Ethnographic observation proceeded, in this manner, in the enforced conditions of a construction site. It was the next step in the control of indigenous peoples. Such intense study and manipulation marked a step change from the way in which a *pandit* observed a comet without supervision in Madras Observatory

In the construction of the lighthouse, the resistance of the labourers to the oppressive work which they had to complete was visible and material. One of Thomson's images illustrates 'a riot' on Pedra Braca, drawn much later in New Zealand. The Chinese labourers are shown trying to capture a supply ship, as a result of their unhappiness at their difficulties working on the rocks.[122] Compared with the precise depiction of the labourers at work, their bodies merge here into each other. The relation of weather and bodily unmooring is also evident in how this resistance of the Chinese is followed in Thomson's narrative with an account of a mutiny on board the *Nancy*. This was a ship involved in the lighthouse project. The crew, said to be Malays and 'Indo-Portuguese', were alarmed at the severity of the weather and the onset of squalls, and went on strike.[123]

Thomson's work in Southeast Asia took a great toll on his own frame, necessitating his removal from the tropics, perhaps as a result of malaria contracted on the rocks. He complained of 'sickness' throughout his report on the works on the lighthouse and declared that 'the rock seemed inimical to me'.[124] Meanwhile, picking up Malay traditions of meditating on the sea, at an early moment in the project, the Malay *lascars* put themselves to bed by singing a *pantun*, somewhat in fear of the elements to which they had exposed themselves.[125] On all sides then, this work necessitated reflection on selfhood on the rocks.

Thomson ended his report on the building of the lighthouse with meteorological commentary on waterspouts, reminiscent of Capper's writings. He saw more than twenty of these in the period of the light-house's construction. He notes how the first waterspout he saw 'played', allowing its tube to be shortened and lengthened, while the vapour around it moved as a spiral. He drew an image of the waterspout – again demonstrating its mobility and changeability. According to Thomson, waterspouts resulted from the effect of electrified clouds. In his analysis, the mobility of weather phenomena such as squalls in these waters was connected with the monsoon.[126]

Despite these subjective, bodily, contemplative, puzzled and resistant responses to global knowledge, this was also the period of an advancing rule of nature allowing colonisers to rise to ascendance. The Horsburgh Lighthouse was officially lit in 1851. Navigators immediately commented on the 'great utility and brilliancy of the [revolving] Light'.[127] It opened the way for discussions about the building of other lighthouses in the region. Meanwhile, surveying was taken up and followed by the wider population of the Straits. This is evident in disputes over land bound-aries in this period.[128]

Maps continue to be lauded today as artefacts worthy of attention in Singapore.[129] A highly instrumental understanding of land and sea has carried through as vividly demonstrated in the advance of the land into the sea with grand programmes of reclamation from the late twentieth century into the present. This late-modern instrumentalism descended from the transformations wrought by British colonialism as it engaged with existent systems of culture, trade and politics in Southeast Asia.

FREE TRADE CITIES: HYDROGRAPHY GOING INLAND

Looking down the decades further into the nineteenth century and considering the relation between the British empire, knowledge and modelling, Singapore overtook Malacca and Penang as the definitive emporium of the three and attracted to itself Chinese, Indians and Malays who created a cosmopolitan colonial city.[130] In the mid 1830s, in excess

Fig. 7.6 'Singapore town from the Government Hill looking East' by
John Turnbull Thomson

of five hundred square-rigged vessels and more than one and a half
thousand 'native craft' called at the port of Singapore in one year, setting
the context for urban expansion.[131] This expansion made itself felt in
maps of Singapore.

The techniques of hydrographic surveying turned inland, as surveyors
laid out streets in neat grids.[132] Maps also contained more detailed navigational information to assist regular commercial shipping. For instance,
J. T. Thomson's maps of the straits of Singapore, included information
about the pattern of tides and currents on both sides of the strait, and
soundings related to the depth of the water. Also included were measurements from the magnetic observatory established in Singapore, to allow
navigators to calibrate their compasses accounting for magnetic deviation.[133]
This information sat side by side with attention to settlement. Thomson
wrote that his 1845 topographical survey of Singapore was undertaken 'in
the manner of Nautical surveys'.[134] Forwarding a map of rivers, he wrote
that he had used Malay names at their mouths and Chinese ones at their
heads, because this indicated the pattern of settlement. Attention to rivers

drew in a concern to discover whether these were navigable by gunboats. If Madras Observatory had served as a platform from which seaborne navigation could proceed, now the nautical and maritime became the template for the surveying of settlement and land.

Related to Thomson's maps was his description of Chinese settlers' gambier and pepper plantations in the interior of the island. He alleged that these settlers led 'a laborious and industrious life' without much exposure to the sun, a 'pleasanter' existence than some others in the straits. And yet, he wrote, they were already moving on to Johor, finding their plantations in Singapore 'exhausted'. With an ethnographic and racial eye, he observed that these labourers were of a 'muscular and healthy appearance', in '9 parts out of 10 unmarried' and addicted to opium. In their defence, given their isolated settlement, Thomson carried on that their smoking of opium did not have a more general effect.[135] As is evident, early Britons in Singapore were generally quite ignorant of the conditions of thousands of Chinese planters who arrived on the island before their own arrival in Singapore in 1819.[136]

The way the seafront set the terms for understandings and mappings of British settlement is best demonstrated in one of Thomson's letters of 1851 about plans for 'drainage and Scourage on Scientific principles'. He noted that the use of surveying to plan sanitation was very recent even in the 'Mother Country' and that he was unaware if it had been tried in India:

Connected with the surveys [to aid sewerage], it would be very desirable to have careful observations on the rise and fall of tide – and on the ideal currents that run in the creeks into which the drainage would be carried – these observations would be useful in denoting the level practicable at which the Sewerage of the Town could be delivered – to this end also the influx and reflux of water with the creeks should be estimated in quantity so that data might be afforded for the improvement of their channels. They would also allow of the estimate as to what effect such improvements would have on the sewerage and drainage of the Town ... Hourly observations on the pluviometer would also be useful in ascertaining the greatest fall of rain within short periods so that the capacity of the Sewers in draining a given surface may be calculated – and the expence of making unnecessarily large sewers avoided.[137]

In this view, mapping the position of Singapore in the straits broad-
ened out – allowing the undulations of water and land to have a bearing
on a pressing concern of modern British colonialism: the question of
hygiene. The realities of modern urban life were worked out in practical
terms here around water and land.

The dissonance within this scheme, however, was that the Straits
Settlements, with their scattered geography in a sea of islands, were
difficult to administer and govern. India saw them as a burden, especially
after the East India Company lost its monopoly in the China trade in
1833.[138] With light governance and heavy immigration, they became
changeable centres of culture, migration and capital. Penang and Malacca
were seen by Singapore as appendages or backwaters. The problems that
beset the idea of these settlements as bastions of urban free trade with
a fringe of plantations beyond, are best illustrated by the figure of the
pirate.

Well into the nineteenth century in Singapore, pirate problems didn't
go away, despite the first flush of optimism that steam power would
keep pirates at bay.[139] Fears about strategic vulnerability also did not
recede, showing how earlier cartographic imaginations of the Bay of
Bengal were still alive and well in the vision of Singapore as a port of
free trade.[140] The Horsburgh Lighthouse was seen as vulnerable – open
to marauding pirates and needing the defence of a mounted gun.[141]

CONCLUSION

Unemployed Siami was well aware of the workings and contradictions
of imperial free trade in Singapore. He wrote a poem, 'Trading, Selling
and Buying', in the 1820s, which was lithographed and recited aloud in
the settlement. Before going into the details of a dispute between a Bugis
shipmaster and Chinese and Indian merchants, presented as a ruling
against the mariner, Siami noted:

> Now the merchants are governing the land
> A sign that the world has come to an end'.[142]

Abullah's writings can also be read for their critique of new styles of
consumption. Of note is 'Malay Poem on New Year's Day', which was
published in Jawi in a Singapore periodical in 1848. This is not a simple

account of merriment. Abdullah pointedly notes the commercialism of the New Year celebrations. Writing of sack races:

> Now there was another curious thing,
> People were going into sacks in pairs,
> For the sake of money, they were willing to put up with
>   anything,
> So they hopped slowly on, each and every one of them . . .
> It ain't easy trying to get the *Orang Putih*'s [white man's] money.
> You're done in until your body is weary and worn,
> While your sweat perspires like beads of grain.
> Thus people rose and fell upon each other.[143]

Abdullah described the spectacle of what he saw as many races of people engaged in racing each other on the Singapore seafront for the enjoyment of their colonial masters. In recognition of the effort, the 'English tossed their coins'. Fittingly, given the location of the celebration, Abdullah wrote:

> The uproar thundered like a storm,
> Young, old, small, large went all a'grabbing,
> Falling and rising on the grass,
> Some had their clothes torn, some
> Had their hair rent askew.

At the end of his poem, Abdullah commented that food and drink of 'various kinds' was on offer. This was the 'the day where money was asking to be spent'. For this Muslim, free-trade consumption had tainted the joys of sport and entertainment. It had generated an excess and brought about a race, allowing people to become uncivil.

As many recent writers have contended, the older world of Malay connections, born of the sea, definitely carried through into the nineteenth century, and so did South Asian oceanic connections with Southeast Asia.[144] But at another level, empire generated a break and made a world come tumbling down. The start of the nineteenth century saw the rise of a global model, which was generative of imperialism. Such modelling stretched across land and sea, the local and the regional as well as the human frame; all these were placed within huge piles of numbers and data.

This kind of observation – like at Madras Observatory – ranged across a series of interrelated disciplines, from the study of the stars to underwater currents and tides, from the body and medicine to engineering and sanitation. Global knowledge-making spilt over from sites like Madras to Singapore. It gave rise to big projects such as the building of lighthouses. Despite being concerned with safety and positionality on the seas – global modelling made ships sink. In its course, with the penetration of new knowledge and machines, the Bay of Bengal was reforged in a world of imperial free trade even as it was replotted in cartographic terms on the world map. Nature, the seas and the body were instrumentalised, just as 'experiment island' off Sumatra had been. Indigenous assistance was overtaken; though in other spaces, indigenous traditions of navigation carried on.

Such an argument is akin to the discussion of how Aboriginal peoples made a stand in the Tasman Sea in the midst of the rolling out of counter-revolutionary discourses of race and gender and humanitarian intervention. It is consistent with how Parsi shipbuilders found their path within and beyond empire and across the seas, stretching even to Oman as imperialism sought to overtake various kinds of revolt. Here, this claim has proceeded further with exploration of subjective responses to empire. Bodies and selves were uprooted in new globe-sprawling schemes. Accordingly local intellectuals had to come to terms with the seas and their place in them anew. They had to find themselves on the maps designed for use by the new steam vessels that made Singapore, or indeed Madras, a stopping point of uneven global commerce.

If the Napoleonic wars unleashed an aggressive British imperialism, connected to worries of republicanism, unruly maritime frontiers, despotism and oriental luxury, the surety of the British advance came also from empirical progress. It came from the disciplined collection of data and facts which supported territorial expansion and commerce, while giving Britons the resources to think big and global. In the midst of this, the physical markers of the age of revolutions – note the fate of the anglicised Goldingham and Warren – were themselves adopted within the British information machine. Even more critically, indigenous peoples who were participants in the age's quest for knowledge were overtaken or effaced. Knowledge spread outwards in the shadow of war – for instance against Mysore. It slipped from sail to steam.

Such knowledge became central not simply to the planning of settlement but also to life in port cities. And it is in such public spaces that responses to global British imperialism began again as we will see in the final chapter of this book. It is apposite that Abdullah's poem was dated to the New Year of 1848, for this was once again an important year in global revolutionary history and one which reverberated in particular ways across the newspapers of the Indian Ocean.

8

Across the Indian Ocean: Comparative Glances in the South

If there is a need to prove the moral righteousness of the British empire many often turn to the abolition of slavery. But there is little under-standing among those who retell this story that the end of enslavement was slow, protracted and resisted on multiple fronts. There is even less understanding of how abolitionism was part of a programme of reform, directed to the wider world, that kept running into the middle of the nineteenth century, set against rival arguments on one side or the other. In other words, the abolition of slavery was not a definitive event.

Our travels move into the end years of this book, the 1830s and 1840s, and especially the pressure point of 1848, which provides a final lens through which to view the relationship between the age of revolutions and empire. The 1830s and 1840s witnessed an intensifying imperial counter-revolt, with the increasingly successful outcomes that colonists saw in war, for instance on the China coast. These years were also char-acterised by the advance of technology and information. There were attempts to reform colonial government and a surge forward in what was called 'free trade'. In cultural and social terms, the classification of peoples, regions and territories, and even the tabulation of the globe's sphericity, gave rise to a colonial perspective on the world as a model, which had the potential to bypass the actions of assistants, rebels, religious revivalists and mutineers.

If resistant and puzzled colonial subjects, like Siami or Abdullah, were overtaken but not effaced, in the middle of this march of knowledge, they regrouped again as public spheres came to life in port cities. Debates around abolition set the template for campaigns about self-government. The virulence of these discussions was shaped by recently established private newspapers. Debating 'emancipation', its politics and its means of expression in print and urban clubs, set in train a series of comparisons across the global South. These comparisons were self-assessments and claims of progress towards self-rule. They occurred at a time when steamships were advancing and accelerating contact but where better contact between distant places was more prospected than realised.

If the abolition of slavery is approached in this context it becomes a characteristic episode in this broader era of tussles between divergent ideologies, politics and forms of social organisation. In 1848–9, coincident with a new moment of revolution across Europe, there was debate and agitation across the Southwest Indian Ocean, the region in focus here. This constituted a parallel sequence of events to what had happened in this region after the French Revolution, including assembly, petition and the setting up of alternatives to colonial governmental control. However, this was not simply a rerun; the nature of the events was affected by the character of growing port cities such as Cape Town, Port Louis and Colombo. The stand-off was also altered by new possibilities of expression, and also the different dreams of the future, more than half a century after the French Revolution. Indigenous and colonised peoples' voices were also constrained by the conservatism and racism of some of the debates seen in the press about the nature of 'emancipation'.

ABOLITIONISM: NO MORAL TURNING POINT

For Mauritius the relevant dates for the abolition of slavery may be stated like this. The slave trade had already been abolished when Mauritius was taken by the British in 1810. Slavery itself was abolished in Mauritius in 1835. Apprenticeship, a scheme through which former slaves had to work for their masters for six years, apparently to be trained for freedom, was annulled in 1839. Despite the neatness of such a recital of dates, in the five years after its taking by the British, a commission sent to investigate the island's government in the 1820s found that 20,000 enslaved persons had illicitly landed on Mauritius. There are higher estimates.[1] Mauritius' longstanding British governor, who first took office in 1810, harboured pro-slavery sentiments: Robert Farquhar urged London to give Mauritius an exemption from the 1807 annulling of the conduct of the slave trade among British subjects.

In further evidence, by the 1830s, slavery itself morphed into other modes of coerced labour. Most significantly, South Asian labourers arrived in Mauritius, under indenture contracts. They arrived for the first time in 1834 to join an existing community of Indian labourers. These labourers accounted for as much as 35 per cent of the population by 1846.[2] There was also an aborted attempt in the late 1820s to introduce Chinese indentured workers here from Singapore.[3] The question of whether indenture was a new kind of slavery was debated by humanitarians at the time. The debate carries on among historians to the present.[4]

The differences then between freedom and unfreedom, slavery and non-slavery, became increasingly muddied and confused by the British rule of Mauritius. Indeed, freedom could in some ways run ahead of abolition: enslaved persons exerted considerable agency in seeking for manumission, buying their freedom, prior to the formal end of slavery. On Mauritius, rates of manumission were comparatively high.[5] As one recent historian writes: 'They did not wait for their owners and the British colonial authorities to free them, but they were able to earn enough money through their wages, mostly as skilled and semi-skilled slaves and apprentices, to secure their freedom.'[6] Meanwhile, the British compensated for the loss of enslaved people by payment to owners. Just over two million pounds were granted to Mauritians out of a total of twenty million to British colonies.[7] Some of this compensation was fed back into the sugar plantations, again dissolving the moral triumph of abolition and casting the shadow of slavery over the post-abolition plantations of Mauritius.

In addition, the dramatic expansion of sugar plantations in Mauritius, which in approximate terms doubled between 1825 and 1830, generated a greater need for labourers on the island into the middle of the century. The sugar boom in Mauritius was stimulated by the annulling of a preferential tariff that encouraged Caribbean sugar to enter Britain. Given the labour-intensive regime that now characterised big sugar plantations, labourers were depersonalised objects of work, under different regimes of management to the personal and yet cruel relations of power which characterised slave–master relations in Mauritius before sugar.[8]

This dramatic expansion of sugar tied Mauritius to the ups and downs of the market while making the island reliant for supplies on Madagascar, the Cape and India.[9] Apprentices and freed slaves transformed themselves into a lowly peasantry, mostly giving up work on plantations and demonstrating a determination to become smallholders of land.[10] After the island was taken by the British, marronage, or running away, became more extensive among enslaved people. Rules governing marronage were used as a template to deal with runaway South Asian labourers.[11] For all these reasons too the dates of 1835 and 1839, and the procedures to abolish and reform labour, reveal very little. Flows of capital, labourers' own agency and the symmetric plights of ex-slaves and new labourers, in addition to the gradual and incomplete nature of imperial policies, cut across these supposed moral turning points, the dates marking the alleged end of slavery.

RERUNS IN MAURITIUS?

Mauritius was encountered in a previous chapter as news of the French Revolution reached it in 1790, after which republican assemblies were constituted. In that period the island asserted a centrifugal force over the currents of revolution across the Indian Ocean, until the arrival of a Napoleonic governor who reaffirmed slavery in 1803 and of the British takeover in 1810.

The British were incensed in the run-up to annexation that Mauritius had served as a platform for anti-British attacks, for instance by privateers, who fed capital from raids on British vessels into the plantation system of the island. In 1815, island-based Bonapartists, including whites and people of colour, plotted to get rid of British rule, picking up grievances about slavery once again. The removal of the British, in the words of one contemporary man of colour, would be followed by the 'murder of every royalist or man of respectability' and then by revolution in neighbouring Bourbon. The rebels, he envisaged, would organise 'a Bonapartean' government or some other which was equally 'infamous'.[12]

By 1827 leading Franco-Mauritian planters created the Comité Colonial, as a parallel structure of government, led by the lawyer, Adrien d'Épinay. This Comité Colonial, which resembled the revolutionary assemblies of the turn of the century, was another reason why the end of slavery in Mauritius was not definitive. The committee presided over a conservative revolution – linking governing Englishmen, such as the governor Charles Colville, to planters, lawyers, merchants and volunteer corps versed in French law. These men resisted the reform of the laws governing labour and the emancipation of enslaved people.

This revolt of the elite slaveholders on Mauritius was perhaps a 'bloodless coup' and 'a storm in a teacup', to use the description of it by one historian.[13] However, writing in 1832, the chief justice of Mauritius,

Edward Blackburn, who supported the cause while alleging that he had stayed aloof from both sides, claimed that aggrieved colonists saw 'a question of life and death' and 'blindly determined to sacrifice everything at once . . .'[14] To turn to this moment in detail now is to trace the continuing stand-off between, on the one hand, assertions of independence of a conservative kind; and on the other hand, the reforming counter-revolutionary impulses of the British empire.

In the early 1830s, Governor Colville's laxity allowed slave-owning elites under the leadership of the Comité Colonial to arm themselves, conduct drills and hold public meetings. They wore the uniform of the French National Guard and were led by an officer, who had served under Napoleon, and divided the island into military districts.[15] They refused to pay taxes and boycotted cases initiated by the Protector of Slaves, who investigated complaints of illegal treatment towards enslaved peoples.[16] News of the July Revolution which saw the overthrow of Charles X in 1830 gave them momentum, and news from Brazil in 1831 about the abdication of the Emperor Pedro I, and also news from the Caribbean, was reported in the local press in the period that followed. What occurred was not the collapse but the neutralisation of the British government of Mauritius, 'watched by a garrison of 1,600 British troops confined to barracks by [Governor] Colville's express orders'.[17] One exaggerated estimate put the number of volunteers who stood against the government as high as 6,000.[18]

In order to impose the latest legal order about slavery, London sent John Jeremie to Mauritius in 1832, to serve as *procureur général*, the chief legal officer in the French system, the public prosecutor of all cases. The problem was that Jeremie was an ardent British abolitionist and news of his support for immediate emancipation spread in Mauritius. As he described it to some of the inhabitants of Mauritius: 'had he professed himself an absolutist or an Atheist, he might perhaps have obtained their pardon, but he was said to be what they called "a negro's friend" . . .'[19] Jeremie's arrival in Mauritius focussed the mind of the elite anti-reformist rebels who threatened to 'revolutionise' the island unless Jeremie was sent home.[20]

The way Jeremie was greeted on arriving in Mauritius by ship, the *Ganges*, echoed the events which unfolded around the arrival of France's representatives, Baco and Burnel, sent to free slaves in 1796, who had to flee for their lives.[21] In the words of the rebels' French-language newspaper *Le Cernéen*, Jeremie's arrival was:

the final signal for the explosion of public sentiment. All business was suspended; all shops were closed immediately. The militia, armed itself, augmented by all the citizens.[22]

Jeremie faced assassination threats and was assaulted on the threshold of the courthouse, where he was due to take up office. Inside the court, according to his account, 'the Public who had assembled there in great numbers, hooted, shouted & conducted themselves so discreditably, that I directed the Chief Commissary of Police to clear the court.' When leaving without being able to take up his office, he wrote that his 'hat was knocked off'.[23] In print he asserted that he was 'collared and struck'.[24] Le Cernéen took a different view. It accused Jeremie of attempting to assassinate a citizen, whereas Jeremie alleged that he had acted in self-defence. The general closure which greeted his arrival lasted forty-five days.[25] Jeremie wrote that this was the 'exact counterpart' of the events in Mauritius during the French Revolution. He described what he saw as 'Anarchy the most complete'.[26] When Governor Colville summoned the legislative council to determine what should happen the verdict was that Jeremie should be sent back to London.

Observers at the time drew attention to the presence of a few 'revolutionary Frenchmen of the worst principles and the lowest character' who carried on despite the law and who led the proceedings against Jeremie.[27] In the words of another commentator: 'With liberty and equality ever on their lips, these adventurers opposed every act, which had the liberty of others for its object.'[28] After being despatched home, Jeremie did an about-turn and arrived in Mauritius for a second time in 1833, backed by military force. In the end, he was forced to resign after falling into disfavour with the new governor of Mauritius, William Nicolay, over accusations that he made against the legal officers of Mauritius.

One context with which to explain this virulent stand-off in 1832 is the rhetoric of British abolitionism and its perception in Mauritius. Abolitionist propaganda cast Mauritius as an especially inhumane case in cruelty towards slaves, where for instance punishment of enslaved people was said to involve strict flogging, the tearing out of teeth or the cutting of noses.[29] Even if the coverage of Mauritius in Britain never overshadowed that from the Caribbean, the nature of the abolitionist critique and the degree of elite resistance to abolition in Mauritius, created a matched pair. To counter abolitionist attack in print, the recently freed press in Mauritius poured its scorn against the flurry of legislative reforms from London and spread rumours of slave rebellion.

The rebel organ, *Le Cernéen*, described how colonists had 'sounded with the full force of their weak lungs, the great voice of the press'.[30] Mr Laing, the collector of revenue, who didn't support the rebels and whose house had been pelted for this opposition, held that the press 'by preventing any other voice than their own, even that of Govt, from being heard', had contributed substantially to transforming the rebel cause into a 'popular movement'.[31] The press in other words became a conduit of rebellion and antagonism against the government, at the very moment when a 'public mind', to use another of the phrases Laing used, was emerging in Mauritius.

Another way to explain the revolt is to point to the class of elite Franco-Mauritians who hemmed in their governors. They were intimately related by marriage; their judicial and civil establishment was reputed to be the most expensive in the British empire.[32] They were aggrieved by the rejection of their request for a local assembly which would give them greater powers over the island's affairs. They were dissatisfied with the legislative council of advisers to the governor, which was granted in its stead. Their antagonism towards the reform of slavery fell alongside this other grievance.

In addition there was a glut of sugar in London around 1830, which depressed the market. According to Laing, this 'Colonial party' resisted the implications of the transfer of power from France to Britain: 'every attempt to render the Colonial Institutions relative to Property, Education, Language, Religion or the Administration of Justice more consistent with the English system than they were originally . . . [was resisted] with extreme jealousy.'[33] Their quest, he continued, was to re-establish the assemblies existent on the island during the French Revolution to give themselves more control over civil and judicial matters. Concerns with self-government therefore sat together with pro-slavery sentiments. One can see why the colonial secretary in London gave this extraordinary interpretation of events:

> It is impossible to avoid the acknowledgement that, on the subject of Slavery and the Slave trade, the People of Mauritius have been too strong for the People of Great Britain. Neither Acts of Parliament, nor Orders in Council, nor local Ordinances, have been of force to secure the

obedience of the handful of white Inhabitants of that small Island, or even to induce them to mask their disobedience under the ordinary forms of decorous and respectful Courtesy.[34]

In these ways, the tussle over the reform of slavery was not simply a tussle over ideologies connected to labour, or indeed modes of capital; it was also seen and discussed at the time as a contest for the independence and sovereignty of Mauritius in the light of a more interventionist regime of imperial governance. Jeremie certainly interpreted it in this way, which is unsurprising given that he wished to protect the position of humanitarian abolitionists. He wrote that: 'it was not a question of Negro freedom but of Empire! The blow was aimed not at British philanthropy, but at England's supremacy.'[35] The colonists were said to have held a 'long cherished dream of independence'.[36] But *Le Cernéen* took a not too dissimilar position, though arguing for the colonists' respect for empire in their bid to pursue their privileges within it. The newspaper cited Edmund Burke's line: 'The body and mass of the people never ought to be treated as criminal.' It continued:

> In vain do they try to persuade us, that a desire of domineering over their fellow-subjects is love to their country; and that the amiable and conciliatory virtues of lenity, moderations, and tenderness to the privileges of those who depend upon the Empire, are disrespect to the Monarch, and treason to the State.[37]

REVOLT STRENGTHENED BY THE WAVES OF THE SOUTH

Within the documents connected to the so-called 'Jeremie affair', however, is evidence that leads in another direction. This pro-slavery revolt in Mauritius wasn't only, or seen only, as pitting France against Britain or at least the combined heritages of the French empire and the plantocracy and bureaucracy against the reforming impulses of Britain.

There were interconnections across the waters of the South, forged by indigenous peoples as well as by colonists, rebels as well as conservatives. Beneath the layers of accusation and rhetoric is evidence of an Indian Ocean of resistance and militancy which supported and supplied these rebels. The waters of the Southwest Indian Ocean – including its islands – were still beyond the control of Britain and so even as Britain sought to assert its humanitarian, political and commercial stranglehold over the island of Mauritius, it had to contend with the region as a whole.

Jeremie's accusatory letters describe legal proceedings in the 'Grand Port Trial' against the rebel Colonel Brodelet, formerly of the French army, and four others, providing names, dates and witnesses of people involved in the uprising. Also relevant is a pamphlet published to clear Jeremie's name.[38] Jeremie argued that from early April 1832 the Comité Colonial 'publickly governed the country', managing the militias, and plotting to neutralise and stand against the governor's military force. When addressing inhabitants of Mauritius, he already noted that these were 'unconstitutional bodies, organised and affiliated usurping the functions & powers of Government'. In Grand Port district, for instance, there were 350 men ready to 'act as guerrillas in the wood', and in other areas too similar preparations had been made in advance of Jeremie's arrival.[39] Armament had been distributed and pikes were made to arm more free people and some 'portion of the Slave Population' who consented to join the rebels.[40] The call was to strike for independence so as to 'make their own Laws themselves and pay no more Taxes'.[41] The reward for those killed or wounded in such action was to be the donation of five acres of land and an enslaved person to their families.[42]

Jeremie reported evidence that new muskets had been brought into Mauritius to arm the rebels. This was contrary to the rebels' view that the muskets used by them were 'old slaves plantation muskets withdrawn from the Watchmen [guards]'.[43] Jeremie described the depots where these arms were sold. He also gave accounts of vessels including those which were searched:

> from the month of March 1832 to the month of January 1833 arms were introduced into the Colony clandestinely by different vessels from Bourbon and elsewhere. The 'Aure' was seized in June 1832 – The 'Saucy Jack' in January 1833 – the 'Angelique' the 'Constance' and 'Tiger' vessels trading between this island, Bourbon and Madagascar are proved to have been thus engaged.[44]

At least one vessel involved in this clandestine trade flew American colours; there were French vessels involved too.[45] These rebels attempted to secure muskets from a visiting whaling ship.[46] Brodelet was a key agent in this trade. He disguised arms in cases filled with wallpaper and arranged the distribution of arms among the militias.

More circumstantial was the evidence of a ball given in Grand Port. A conversation between Messrs Brodelet, Valentine Keating and a Monsieur Chenaux, in control of a battalion at Bourbon, which was under the French, was overheard in the courtyard by a man of colour, Jean Louis Jeannot. Jeannot was formerly of the police, but now aged and 'in humble life'.[47] The three ball-goers were moving between the ballroom and the supper room. *La Balance*, a newspaper read by people of colour, gave an account of the testimony of Jeannot. The ball-goers discussed manpower for the strike for independence:

> M. Chenaux said to these gentlemen, 'Hold yourself ready; in a fortnight it will be done. I will arrive here with five hundred men of Bourbon [under the French].[48]

Jeremie noted that communication between Mauritius and Bourbon had been 'incessant' until the British takeover. In response to Chenaux's proposal, Keating is alleged to have replied that all the Indian convicts were for their cause. Madagascar was discussed too as a source of support. And a black corps of fighters was thought possible.

Though this conversation surely amounted to no more than scheming – for no men arrived – it points to the political imagination and strategising of the anti-abolitionist rebels of Mauritius. Their quest was pushed along by neighbouring kin in the region. Meanwhile, in further evidence of the cosmopolitan networks within as well as against the revolt, Jeannot's information was first conveyed to the government by a man of colour from the Seychelles.[49]

The reference to Indians meanwhile shows how the rebels reached out to those who had travelled across the Indian Ocean to Mauritius. Nadir Khan, an Indian convict, accused Keating of attempting to 'corrupt' the group of prisoners from India, by distributing muskets, swords and presents among them and inviting them to join the volunteer militias.[50]

Indian *lascars* were on the scene too. *La Balance* provided the account of seven *lascars* who appeared before the court. A Muslim priest said a short prayer and asked them to swear on the Koran to tell the truth and nothing but the truth. Ibrahim, a *lascar* from Bombay, then proceeded to give an account of his work on the *Constance*, under Captain Régnaud. In 1832, long crates were transported from Bourbon to Mauritius, 'heavy as if there was iron in them'. The sailors were not advised of what they contained. There followed another Indian sailor, 'Sounalla', who worked on the *Tiger*, who gave evidence of voyages connecting Mauritius and Foulpointe [now Mahavelona] in Madagascar, where muskets were exchanged for oxen, at an exchange ratio of three to two. The muskets were usually in the hold of the ship, wrapped in coarse cloth.[51] And on one occasion 400 muskets were taken to Madagascar, but only 120 were sold. The remainder, it was alleged by this *lascar*, were brought back to Mauritius as an illicit trade.

Another *lascar*, named as Miajan in the sources, provided further evidence from on board the *Tiger*, noting the transport of weapons from Mauritius to Madagascar being returned to Mauritius. In one instance these weapons were put into a boat near the isle of Coin de Mire [now also called Gunner's Quoin] on the north coast of Mauritius. The boat was said to have a Frenchman and Englishman on board; according to Jeremie, 'there were two Whites and four Negroes'. The Englishman on this boat was an overseer of Indian sepoy convicts. Miajan's father was a convict in his charge. In court, and in order to support his testimony Miajan was asked to identify the overseer, who was seated among the onlookers. '[I]n a court crowded to suffocation', Jeremie wrote, 'Miajan at the expiration of about five minutes, fixed his eye on Carver [the overseer] and pointed him out,' and this despite his being seated relatively far away from him.

The waterborne connections that then underwrote the rebel cause meant that the British attempt to comprehensively reform one island in a great ocean could only produce limited results. To reform slavery necessitated the control of trade, but in a maritime zone such as this it was a difficult undertaking. In the words of the early describers of Mauritius's lost dodo, who were making a case for the organic unity of the region, this set of islands was: 'a meagre fragment of an archipelago ... connected with Madagascar'.[52] This fragmented and oceanic geography was challenging when an empire such as the British empire sought to reform, standardise and centralise the mechanisms of power.

BETWEEN MAURITIUS, BOURBON AND MADAGASCAR

Relations between Mauritius, Madagascar and Bourbon generated pressures in defining the limits of British sovereignty. The British had to consider the status of French interests close by and the way to approach trade and the abolition of slavery in a complicated political geography.

The passage of labour, cattle and rice between Madagascar and Mauritius was longstanding. Farquhar, the first governor of British Mauritius, had sought despite London's lack of interest to create an informal sphere of influence over Madagascar. This interest began at the very moment of the 1810 British conquest in a prospective plan to search for French settlements on the Madagascar coast.[53] In support of this ambition, Farquhar held that before Mauritius' taking by the British, Madagascar was an 'immediate dependence' of the French government based at Mauritius.[54] Accordingly, the British taking of Mauritius legitimised control of Madagascar too. In summarising the history of Madagascar, Farquhar sketched what the French empire in the West Indian Ocean looked like. He attached a map of the zone which he sought to take from France:

> Before the conquest [of Île de France] the boundaries of the Government General of the French possessions in this hemisphere were marked on the North by the Equatorial Line. On the South by the circle of latitude of the Cape, on the East by the Meridian of Point de Galle in Ceylon [Sri Lanka], on the west by a Line proceeding from the 47th degree of East Longitude down the centre of the Mozambique Channel till it cuts the latitude of the Cape.[55]

By extending his reach to Madagascar, Farquhar also sought to divert attention away from the slave trade in Mauritius. He argued that the trade needed instead to be suppressed at the point of supply in Madagascar.[56] He cultivated personal relationships with the elites of the Merina empire, assisting the chief Radama to fight against his rivals and to establish himself as 'king'. In 1817, in an agreement with Radama, Farquhar sought to stop the trade in enslaved persons from Madagascar to Mauritius in return for British military and commercial cooperation. Farquhar also signed an agreement with the ruler of Muscat in order to stem the slave trade out of Zanzibar.[57] Farquhar's personal ambitions

overrode a consistent commitment to anti-slavery and he benefited from
the array of possible maritime relations, which allowed him to play
politics across the Indian Ocean.

Radama, for his part, initially proclaimed that his ports were free to
the British and that he encouraged the residence of Britons in Madagascar
for 'the better civilization of [his] people and the introduction of various
arts and sciences'.[58] This friendship with the British resulted, for instance,
in the furtherance of Radama's interest in the cultivation of the mulberry
tree and the culture of the silkworm in Madagascar. This project relied
on the assistance, in the first instance, of two Indian convicts from
Mauritius, 'No. 172 Goluck Harree and No. 610 Turce Sirdar'. The friendship saw the arrival of Malagasy youth for training in seamanship and
other skills in Britain.[59] Relations with Britain assisted the expansion of
Radama's kingdom in central Madagascar. British correspondence with
Radama demonstrates, in a story that would intensify with his successor,
the greater consolidation of a sovereign state as it established the terms
of it exchanges with Britain. Radama allegedly took pride in the British
flag and objected to the recognition of any other chief's flag by the British.
He also devised his own flag.[60]

One result of this cross-island exchange was the arrival in Mauritius
of Ratsitatanina, a prisoner of Radama, who had escaped captivity in
Mauritius and tried to set off a slave revolt in 1822. He was beheaded by
Farquhar. In the next decade, the official relationship between Britain
and Madagascar was renounced by Radama's successor, Queen
Ranavalona, in 1836, in a bid for self-sufficiency.[61] At this point, the
queen's officers reminded Mauritius of Madagascar's own right to set
its rules and agreements with outside forces. The letters of the queen's
chief secretary, addressed to Mauritius, are striking for their tone:

I inform you plainly that with respect to the people that you want [as
labourers to work on Mauritius's plantations], that you will not get a
single Malagasy to go across the sea if money was not be the means
of taking them away – even if you was to give 10,000 or 100,000 for
a single person . . . I inform you plainly, that with respect to our
friendship, the English was not to rule Madagascar and the Malagasy
was not to rule the English, for each possess the land which God gave
them, and each do as they like in their own country . . . for each has
its own laws . . .[62]

Britain chided Madagascar, however, that it could not be independent in a world of imperial superpowers and that it ought to renew a treaty of friendship: 'for if Madagascar was even invaded by any Foreign power, the Queen could expect no assistance whatever from the English, as there is no Treaty now existing between the two Nations'.[63] In this period, trade between the Merina empire and British Mauritius – in cattle, wax, gum and wood – was now subject to monopolies.[64] But there continued to be unsuccessful bids on the part of the planters in Mauritius to secure cheaper labour from Madagascar for their expanding sugar concern. For these labourers could take the place of Indian indentured workers. Slavery out of Madagascar – directed up the East African coast and across the Indian Ocean and even at times across the Atlantic – continued in various guises until the French takeover of the island and their abolition of slavery in Madagascar, much later in the nineteenth century in 1896.

Two historians describe the geographical factors that allowed the continuation of slaving in this region, despite British abolition from London: 'the proximity of Mauritius and Bourbon to the major sources of supply [for example, Madagascar] and the presence of numerous small islands in the region greatly facilitated the task of the colonists.'[65] If Madagascar was one point of reference for the anti-abolitionist rebels of the early 1830s in Mauritius, the neighbouring island of Bourbon or Réunion was another.

In 1815, Britain returned Bourbon to the French, though they had taken it together with Mauritius five years earlier. This generated a complicated prospect for British abolition laws. They were to apply in 'their full force and rigour' to Mauritius and even in the island's 'most remote and minute' dependencies, including the Seychelles and the island of Rodrigues, but any 'parts as relate to the Island of Bourbon' were annulled.[66]

At just over 120 miles away from each other, the voyage from Mauritius to Bourbon in these years took around twenty-four hours, but five or six days the other way.[67] Slavery was only abolished in Bourbon in 1848 and it is estimated that something like 45,000 slaves reached the island illegally between 1817 and 1848, though numbers dropped after about 1830 to just a smattering.[68] Enslaved people sent to Bourbon from across the Indian Ocean were: 'exposed without pity on the shore of the sea, they waited only for death to end their cruel suffering'.[69] Coffee was smuggled from Bourbon to Mauritius in the 1840s.[70] There were also waves of indentured labourers who arrived here from India and China.[71]

There were 3,440 Indians on the island at the end of 1848. The presence of this French colony next door inevitably affected the politics and trade of Mauritius.

Farquhar for instance announced that Bourbon had to be kept in view in his diplomacy with Madagascar. He wrote of the 'weighty responsibility' in his hands if he:

> [acquiesced] even for a moment in any measure by which, the inhabitants of Bourbon, who are authorised to carry on the slave trade, would be admitted to establish any commercial relations in places, which had been previously open to that traffic, and over which [he] had every reason to consider that the authority of the Government confided to [his] care extended.[72]

In the Bonapartist plot of 1815, once again the relation of the two islands became critical to the passage of political intelligence and schemes to overthrow government, not only in Mauritius but also in Bourbon.[73]

All this means that despite the efforts of British abolitionist law and treaties, attempts to stem the slave trade had limited effect in the network of islands in the Southwest Indian Ocean. The ties of capital, the expansion of plantations, the arrival of new labourers both as indentured workers and as illegal slaves, and the different chronologies of abolition, for instance between Mauritius and Bourbon, all took away from the singular significance of abolition as an event or moral and controllable victory. Additionally, the battle over the slave trade led to initiatives to define sovereignty and the terms of politics between territories under and outside the British empire, including Mauritius, Bourbon and Madagascar. This was accentuated with the passing of territories from France to Britain and sometimes the other way too. Discussions of labour also galvanised the emerging public sphere – through newspaper wars, for instance, by the colonists of Mauritius who stood against Jeremie.

Even as the newspaper, such a token of modernity, spread in the midst of this battle over slavery, programmes of reform and counter-reform were also tied to the expansion of sea-facing port cities across the Indian and Pacific Oceans. Maritime cities expanded because of the arrival of new labourers. They were home to journalists and the emerging public spheres of the South. In turn, the debates that surrounded labour were linked to changing conceptualisations of race, civility and gender, and the governance and organisation of these ports. Various classes of inhabitants had to settle their relations with each other, with the arrival of new migrants after emancipation, and this generated a need for new mechanisms of government. From discussions of how the city was physically laid out to how it was constructed and governed, the imprint of the earlier tussles between the likes of d'Épinay and Jeremie around reform and anglicisation made their presence felt.

TWO NEIGHBOURING PORT CITIES
AND THE MODERN WORLD

The modern city in this region was impacted by debates over slavery as they expanded into concern about new migrants, urban living, governance and civil association and representation. Two cities in this region are representative.

'The scenery may be described as intermediate in character between that of the Galapagos and of Tahiti.' So wrote Charles Darwin on arriving in Port Louis in Mauritius in 1836.[74] Many travellers and traders called here as Darwin did. This is evident in announcements of the arrivals of ships in the island's press in the 1830s.[75] Maritime passages stretched from the Pacific islands and Australia to the island, and from Indonesia, India and the coast of Africa, Arabia, and on to Latin America, the United States and Europe. Ships were packed in rows in the harbour and many noted that the bustle of life at the harbour was astonishing.[76] In 1823, approval was given to make a dockyard for the repair of ships.[77]

The trades conducted via Port Louis, according to an 'official resident' in 1842, included rice, wheat and gram from India; horses, mules, wheat, oats, barley, flour, beef, dried fish and poultry from the Cape; fish and flour from America; wine from France; and cattle and grain from Madagascar. This writer particularly noted the role played by vessels from Sydney and Van Diemen's Land [Tasmania] in the sugar trade out of Port Louis.[78] All this marks the fact that this was a different moment in the history of Port Louis to the 1810 annexation when it was taken in a military manoeuvre by the British. Now, the prosperity and busyness of Port Louis was tied to the cycles of the sugar market and free trade.

Those jumping on and off ships often noted the majesty of Port

Fig. 8.1 'Vue de la ville du Port Napoleon prise de la Montagne du Pouce', from J.G. Milbert, *Illustrations de Voyage pittoresque à l'Île de France*, 1812

Louis' appearance on the horizon at a distance, such as at daybreak when the low-lying features of the island were covered in mist and revealed only the craggy summits of mountains above. As the day wore on, the 'exhalations [were] diffused by the power of the sun, the pleasing vision disappear[ed]'.[79] Port Louis stood within an 'amphitheatre' of mountains; and the range of mountains was centred on one which was shaped like a human thumb, accordingly named the 'Pouce', which Darwin climbed. The port stood on a stretch of ground in the figure of a square. The square was bounded by the sea at its face and had a plain named 'Champ de Mars' at its rear. The east and west 'like two wings' enclosed various suburbs.[80] The artist M. J. Milbert, who was part of the Baudin expedition, produced an image showing the many mountainous vistas of the island. There was also an image of Port Napoleon [Port Louis] as seen from a distance.[81] [Fig. 8.1]

The population of Port Louis was calculated at 27,645 in 1835, which compares with 24,839 in 1817.[82] It then grew rapidly with a quickening inward migration of Indian indentured workers. It had reached 41,031 by 1840 and roughly doubled from the time of Darwin's visit to the midpoint of the nineteenth century.[83] A greater expansion might have been expected when Darwin wrote if not for the ravages of a series of epidemics, of smallpox and cholera. In 1819, with the appearance of cholera, the colonial establishment targeted precautionary measures towards the enslaved population and people of colour, urging that they should use warm clothing rather than exposing themselves to the weather.[84] In addition to disease a great fire tore through Port Louis in 1816. It was caused by a young enslaved woman, who brought a light too close to the curtains near her bed. The French traveller Auguste Billiard described these curtains as a mosquito net. The woman did not call for help. The fire spread rapidly on a strong wind:

> The hoses of the only three fire engines were in such a state that they burst at every moment. The buckets brought would not hold water, and the washing and bathing tubs of the neighbouring houses were the only utensils left.[85]

Governor Farquhar reported: 'one Black burnt to death, two soldiers missing and forty persons dangerously scorched or wounded.'[86] Wooden houses stacked close to each other were easily combustible. The lack of an easy supply of water was another factor in the spread of the fire, as was 'the quantity of Rum, sugar, wines, cotton, wheat, Rice, maïs [maize], cordage, tar, pitch and other inflammable materials' which filled the stores caught in the fire.[87]

A large part of the business area of Port Louis was devastated as was the principal street of Port Louis and property, which was estimated to the value of 1.2 million pounds.[88] As Billiard noted, it was the area of the city where the first French settlements had been formed which was lost: 'fire destroyed in an instant the labours and fortunes of a century.'[89] Papers in the Port Louis archives reveal that in the aftermath of the fire, streets in the burnt part of the city were widened and various half-destroyed structures were torn down and indemnities paid.[90] By 1823, a fire brigade was formed but no regular firemen were attached to it: 'in case of fire, requisitions on the large Slave Establishments are the present, and only means of procuring men to work the engines.'[91] The police force was also reorganised.[92]

In addition to disease and fire, given its location in the middle of the Indian Ocean, Port Louis was subjected to extreme weather events. Two cyclones arrived in 1818 and 1819 and another in 1824. The year 1818 saw an especially severe one, bringing nearly all the ships in the harbour to the shore with great damage.[93] Roofs made of slate, copper and tin were blown off the tops of houses, while those made of 'bricks joined by a resinous cement' withstood the trial.[94]

If population figures changed slowly, and then rapidly in the second quarter of the nineteenth century, there are other ways of charting the rise of the modern city as it overcame the furies of nature. One change – connected to the fire – concerns how buildings were made to withstand the elements. Builders in Port Louis moved from wood to stone.[95] The streets of Port Louis were 'macadamised', or paved with compacted stone. By 1828, there was a proposal to surround the bazaar in stone walls, for security and also for the collection of duties.[96] Canals were further developed to deal with the difficulty of accessing water which the fire had highlighted. Street lighting spread.[97]

The newly laid streets also had their names changed in 1818, no longer commemorating either French governors or 'the wars of the Revolutions', just as the city's name Port Napoleon had become Port Louis.[98] Farquhar also established a Commune Council in 1817 to manage town administration after the fire; this was a forerunner of the later town council.[99] Among the matters it took under its charge in 1818–20 were the price of bread and wheat, the disposal of rubbish, the burial of the dead and the health of the settlement.[100] The early 1820s saw discussion of how to fund the upkeep of the streets, including water and lighting and the town's theatre.[101]

Against an argument for transformation, Darwin found that Port Louis was still rather French, writing that 'Calais or Boulogne was much more Anglified'. French was the language which was 'universally spoken' in the 1830s and the food was of the 'French style'.[102] Writing in the period of the anti-abolitionist uprising, one commentator noted that the English resident families associated little with the French, 'excepting at the annual ball given at Government-house, given in honor of his Majesty's birth-day.'[103] This was in keeping with how royalism and freemasonry bound the French and the British elite together at the time of the 1810 British takeover.[104]

The commission which came from London in 1826–8 aiming to reform the island and abolish slavery had anglicisation in mind. They were worried about the consumption of French alcohol, given that burgundy with water was the 'common beverage' at dinner, and sought to open the market to Cape wine.[105] Though anglicisation could never be fully successful the desire to apply it was most apparent in changing language policies. Royal College, first established in 1799, saw the introduction of an English education system and in 1847, French was replaced by English as the language of the courts while a closer relationship grew between the state and the Anglican church.[106] Yet French is still far more widely spoken than English in today's Mauritius.

Connected to this, Protestants were worried about the spread of 'Popery', and even saw it in the Islamic celebration of 'Yamsey' in the month of Muharram, undertaken by indentured workers, which drew in Asians of various religions. The Quaker missionary, James Backhouse, who before visiting Mauritius had sought to bring Christianity to Australian penal settlements, including Tasmania, gave a description of 'Yamsey' or the *ghoon* procession, which saw pagodas carried down the streets, in commemoration of the death of the grandson of the Prophet Muhammad. Backhouse wrote of how the 'Lascars and Hill Coolies from India' were carrying structures 'with balloon-like tops', made from 'coloured and gilt paper, upon bamboo frames'. 'Representations of the sun and moon, and some stars' were visible on these structures. The 'gayest' was broken over the water. He noted in disapproval of how Roman Catholic Christians also participated in 'Yamsey', by taking vows when ill to make a contribution to the priest at this festival. 'Such does the wreck of Popery mix itself with heathenism.'[107] Another perceived threat came from the arrival of Chinese settlers who ran many of the shops of Port Louis. According to one set of petitioners to the governor in 1843, 'one half of the minor shops for the sale of *comestibles* besides many of the larger ones, are kept by men of *Chinese* birth of extraction.' These petitioners objected that this was unfair and that there was no open competition given the collectivised interests and underselling practised by the Chinese.[108]

Despite the removal of traces of the French Revolution from the names of the streets of Port Louis, the Anglo-French faultline, or the Protestant–Catholic one, endured. The question of whether Port Louis was English or French became less relevant when placed next to other questions of identity. As in Madras, distinctions of ethnicity and class started to play a greater role in the mid century and this is another way to trace the emergence of the new city. Visitors of the period routinely noted the diversity of the city. Billiard, the French writer, wrote of Port Louis in characteristic racial prose for the time, that one could 'go through all the shades of colour, from pale pink to coppery red and up to the darker black'.[109] The bazaar was said to display 'at a glance the productions and physiognomies of the four parts of the world'.[110] Backhouse himself wrote that the island was 'one of the inns of the Southern hemisphere', a 'motley multitude, of all nations, kindreds, tongues, and people'.[111] Certainly Port Louis drew to itself people from across the waters of the south.

Whereas creolisation was a longstanding feature of social life in a settlement like Port Louis, racial and class demarcations became more apparent. Tabulations of population were pretty stark in their simplicity in the early British years. Take this one, which accompanied a list of views published in 1831:

> 2387 whites
> 7511 free blacks
> 15717 slaves
>
> ———
>
> 25615
>
> ———

The categorisation of white versus black could not keep up with the arrival of waves of labourers and settlers after slave emancipation.[112] Already by the 1830s and 1840s, the range of communities were laid out on the streets of Port Louis in separate quarters. In the early 1830s Port Louis was said to have a 'principal town' inhabited mainly by the French elite, who were traders, while two other suburbs were respectively occupied by 'Malabars' or Indians, and by free blacks in turn.[113] The arrival of new workers meanwhile stretched the city out to the south-west and north-west, 'like the horns of a crescent'.[114] The diversification of Port Louis after slavery had a physical effect on the city; the expansion of the suburbs coincided with the multiplication of ethnic categories as well as with discussions about the relative status of different kinds of workers.

The size of the city, its increasing diversity, and the problems of modern life, from fire prevention to sanitation, required reformed forms of government. And the urban bureaucratic order was another emblem of the mid-century character of the city. When Adrien d'Épinay was dispatched to London as a representative of the Mauritian slaveholders, he asked for a municipal committee; the idea was taken up again by a journalist of colour, Rémy Ollier.[115] Young Ollier was obsessed with the legal proceedings against the rebels of Grand Port, even visiting them in prison and attending the trial, which highlights the connection between his bid for a municipal council and the early 1830s moment around Jeremie.

Ollier had been exposed to the political works of Lamennais, Montesquieu, Diderot, Rousseau, Voltaire, Adam Smith, Horace Say and Ricardo at the literary club in Port Louis, La Société d'Émulation Intellectuelle. In 1843 he set up a newspaper, *La Sentinelle*, written in French. This replaced the now defunct *La Balance* which had catered for a readership of colour. Unlike the men who stood against Jeremie, Ollier wished not for the withdrawal of the English, but the reform of English institutions, in order to give more rights to people of colour. This again highlights how the Anglo-French tussle was now replaced with another politics of representation. Individuals like Ollier sought to take up the badge of Englishness for the advancement of rights. He wrote for instance:

We are English today, we are not a conquered people, we are English people . . . We belong to England. Why do we not possess the institutions of England? If she wishes to make us love our nationality, to endow our island with that which makes for the glory of our mother-country; this, we shall not be able to know or appreciate if we are strangers to all that which makes it cherish its children and respect its people.[116]

His writings led to municipal elections in 1850 and the appointment of twelve councillors.[117] The municipal corporation had 820 voters when first established, who enrolled or had the requisite property worth £300 to make them eligible as voters. Among them were listed traders, advocates, physicians, and a 'harness maker' and 'Pharmacopolist'.[118] The setting up of the municipal council coincided with a widening of the civic and mercantile life of the city, including agricultural and commercial chambers, which also flowed out of Ollier's efforts. The first mayor was the businessman Louis Léchelle and the council's seal bore the word 'Union', while its councillors were asked to wear 'a little silver medal tied by a silver chain to [their] button holes, and bearing on one of its faces the words "Municipal Councillor".'[119]

The first praised successes of the municipality included the addition of new street lamps, the repair of a canal, the extension of the town bazaar and arrangements for new street paving. Stones for paving the streets were cut by prisoners.[120] The prevention of fire was one the very first concerns directed to the municipality, which was put in charge of fire engines.[121] In keeping with the attention to ornament, in case of fire, councillors were asked to wear 'a scarf half white and half red, in order to have themselves known among the crowd'. [122] Another concern was epidemic disease.[123] Le Cernéen taunted the municipality even in song and criticised its delay in publishing decisions and resolutions. They saw the municipality as aligned with a rival English language paper, the Commercial Gazette, committed to liberalism.[124] Certainly, the matters with which it dealt were at times mere trifles: like the case of a Mr Rendle, whose carts knocked against a suspension bridge due to bad driving.[125]

After Darwin had visited Port Louis he journeyed to Cape Town. Here once again, like with Port Louis, he saw a city which was more European than English.[126] Yet he sought to distinguish Port Louis and Cape Town in relation to the degrees of Englishness each of them displayed, writing of the latter:

> It is laid out with the rectangular precision of a Spanish city: the streets are in good order, and Macadamized, and some of them have rows of trees on each side; the houses are all whitewashed, and look clean. In several trifling particulars the town had a foreign air, but it is daily becoming more English. There is scarcely a resident, excepting amongst the lowest order, who does not speak English. In this facility of becoming Anglefied [sic.], there appears to exist a wide difference between this colony and that of Mauritius.

Fig. 8.2 Thomas Bowler (1812-1869)
'Cape Town and Table Mountain from Table Bay'

Though Cape Town is now much better known than Port Louis, with a population today of over three and a half million compared with Port Louis' population of about 150,000, at the time of Darwin's voyage the two cities were comparable by population. Darwin noted Cape Town's ethnic heterogeneity and how Table Mountain served as a backdrop to the city, the upper sections of which 'forms an absolute wall, often reaching into the region of the clouds'. This view was made iconic through art: for instance in the work of Thomas Bowler who over and over again produced watercolours of the view of the coastline of Cape Town, and who had arrived in the city two years before Darwin.

The arrival and departure of ships crossing the southern oceans, as also their shipwreck on its shores, was of abiding interest in Cape Town like in Port Louis in these years. Disease – for instance smallpox and measles epidemics in 1839–40 – punctuated life and generated great hardship for the poor.[127] Commentary on the Asians of Cape Town – like Backhouse's writing on the *ghoon* festival celebrated by the new indentured workers of Port Louis – romanticised this community or demonstrated fear of them. Asians were labelled as 'Cape Malays' despite their multiple origins and their distinctively localised religious festivals and customs.

Darwin's view that Cape Town was comparatively more anglicised than Port Louis was placed next to a comment on class: there was a poor white working class in Cape Town who spoke English. However, the predominant group at the lower end of society were 'coloured' residents, ex-slave apprentices, Khoisan and others.[128] There was also a heavy British-military presence; the navy based in the city had within its orbit the island of Mauritius and Madagascar too. New British settlers – refugees of the Napoleonic wars – moved here. A large contingent of settlers arrived in the Cape Colony in 1820 as a result of a state-aided scheme. These circumstances were different to those of Port Louis. Meanwhile, there had been a concerted attempt to anglicise the public face of Cape Town before the Jeremie affair in Mauritius. Interestingly, given the role of the lawyers of Port Louis, part of the anglicisation programme in Cape Town was directed towards the use of English in the courts and the civil service. English became the main language of administration by the 1830s.[129] There was also by this time a class of 'Anglomen', a term used for Cape Dutch inhabitants who actively embraced English ways, sometimes through intermarriage.[130]

As the authorities on the urban history of Cape Town note, reminding us of the rise in the use of stone in Port Louis: 'Large glass window frames replaced small shuttered windows, plastered ceilings succeeded open beams, and thatch roofs gave way to tile.'[131] Architectural styles also moved from rococo and baroque to a new enthusiasm for classicism.[132] This story of the increased use of glass, plaster and tile and new styles should keep in view what it was like on the other side of the fence. Houses were increasingly overcrowded after emancipation and people of colour had the worst accommodation in Cape Town with several people at times in one bed.[133] This fact shows the limitations of the English gaze and the anglicisation agenda. The British elite also preferred privacy in the design of their houses with halls and corridors which gave access to rooms. This was an attempt to distance themselves from the organisation of Dutch households.[134] Meanwhile, just like in Port Louis, slave emancipation created new pressures on the colonial layout of the city. There was a great deal of building in the city from the late 1830s.[135]

English schools marked the expansion of mid-nineteenth-century British Cape Town. Scottish Calvinists were trained to take up ministry within the Dutch Reformed Church, another curiously contradictory example of anglicisation.[136] The rise of British middle-class values was deeply gendered, necessitating the making of a settled family, where the male forged a public role and the woman was at home, her lack of work a signifier of middle-class status. Such households were contrasted with slave-holding Dutch predecessors in the Cape Colony which were cast as immoral.[137] In addition to gender, race also placed limits on the social mobility of ex-slaves, and emancipation created new kinds of racial tensions between residents of the city.

Racial ideology was supercharged by the expansion of the press. These followed the era of emancipation: 'humanitarian disillusion, more widespread stereotyping and the rise of racist science in the 1840s and 1850s'.[138] The consolidation of an interest in land at the frontier, among Cape Town dwellers, with the expansion of the wool industry from the 1830s, for instance through mortgages on farms and estates, once again hardened racial commitments to the dispossession of indigenous peoples. Race and science had been connected practices before this period – but they now came to live in the midst of these cities.[139]

These intriguing similarities and differences in how a French and Dutch colonial citadel mutated into an English commercial city of the nineteenth century stretch across to the history of institutions too. A sequence of foundings – the first unofficial newspaper and private bank, new cultural institutions and commercial associations, literary and scientific societies and libraries – constitutes a shared history for Port Louis and Cape Town. The 1820s saw the rise of middle-class liberalism in Cape Town, led by John Fairbairn's newspaper, the *South African Commercial Advertiser*, and the consolidation of a localised community of merchants. This class relied on an ethos of Protestant hard work, self-help and free trade; their language of status and rank was open to newcomers but not to poor members. It has been argued that they represented an English nationalism, to which Afrikaner and African nationalism later responded.[140]

The hold of this liberalism in Cape Town and its ties to the press and merchants mean that it is difficult to find a comparable event to the Jeremie affair of Mauritius in the early 1830s. Worth noting is how Fairbairn and his wife, Eliza, were physically attacked on the street in 1836, by a Dutch farmer, A. P. Cloete, who objected to emancipation. There was a current of anti-abolitionism and anti-Englishness in 1830s Cape Town, but it certainly wasn't as powerful as that in Mauritius.

The Dutch newspaper *De Zuid-Afrikaan* was one of its vehicles; a paper with a mostly rural reach, it was set up in opposition to Fairbairn's organ, though they were united in the quest for political representation. There was a press war between the two in 1831 around slavery.[141] In the words of one historian, 'the launching of *De Zuid-Afrikaan* amounted to an organised challenge to the humanitarian-mercantile solidarity in favour of liberal reform among the Cape Town bourgeoisie which had marked the 1820s.'[142] Another difference of course is that Cape Town serviced an agricultural economy and was an entrepôt, reacting to trouble in the colony's hinterland, while Port Louis was an island-based port city dependent on sugar plantations. This meant that these cities faced somewhat different pressures with respect to the global economy, the war on the frontier, or to internal and external migration.

Regardless of these different political, geographical, social and economic tenors, these cities displayed a similar pattern of events in the lead-up to representative government. If in Port Louis there was a chain from revolutionary assemblies to the Comité Colonial and on to a municipality, in Cape Town a Dutch legacy lived on within the expansion of urban Englishness. Municipal government was granted to Cape Town in 1840. As with Port Louis, this municipality descended from other assemblies. There had been a Burgher Senate, which had charge of building and fire regulations and the 'moral health' of the city, which was dissolved in 1827.[143] The Cape Town municipality was seen as a victory for liberalism, though it was greeted with lukewarm public interest in elections.[144] The duties of the new municipality in Cape Town ranged from the provision of fire engines to the regulation of weights and measures. Elections as wardmaster or commissioner on the council were open to all ethnicities but not to all classes, or to women.

Despite the aim of anglicisation pursued by the British, in its first decade or more, Cape Dutch burgers were the majority among the commissioners of the Cape Town municipality. These commissioners were not an old elite but a newly rising commercial class who used the structures of this assembly to advance their local propertied interests.[145] Curiously then, anglicisation allowed here in Cape Town for Dutch descendants, the creation of a newly formed collective and its insertion into the structures of British government. Indeed, the Cape Dutch had to campaign for their rights as British subjects to forge their political future.[146]

As an institution, the municipality operated in parallel to and in some tension with the Commercial Exchange, which was dominated by an old mercantile elite of 'gentlemen', who had more contacts overseas. The municipality's investment in the keeping of the streets of Cape Town reflects the concerns in the pages of John Fairbairn's *South African Commercial Advertiser*.[147] The upwardly mobile colonial class, who were tied to the municipality, also sought to initiate a rival forum to the Commercial Exchange, in establishing a Cape of Good Hope Chamber of Commerce.

In these ways, the politics of class, race and gender which are evident in cities like Cape Town or Port Louis were consolidated in the era after emancipation and within institutions of very many kinds. These institutions expanded in these decades and included and excluded particular groups and had complex relations with each other. The desire to civilise slave-holding societies was part and parcel of the programme of anglicisation which lay behind some of these institutions. Sovereignty had been central to the tussle over the abolition laws around Jeremie in Mauritius. Similarly, the demand for representative government saw sovereignty come to the fore once again, and the clamour was first met by the grant of municipal powers for Port Louis and Cape Town. This became a necessary step on the part of the colonial authorities because of how both reform of labour and free trade had been embraced by those who lived in these cities.

Moving into the years bridging the 1840s and 50s, the dangers of a colony falling back in its progress towards self-government, was critical in shaping the events which unfolded in Cape Town and Port Louis. Additionally, the interlinking of these maritime territories was very much evident in the sideways glances that framed their politics, as city elites and middle classes assessed their plight in relation to Europe and to other colonial territories in the global South. The idea of the city, in travelogues or as depicted by artists, as also the public debates of the city in its press, represented the place afar and made it a point of comparison and critique in programmes of reform which were maritime and global.[148] This style of South–South comparison was in keeping with the archipelagic geography of the region which was evident in the midst of the Jeremie affair.

In the era of emancipation, Cape colonists had looked to the Caribbean to assert the comparitive mildness of their own slavery and for the displacement of anxiety connected to ownership of slaves.[149] Mauritius

– as noted above – had fared badly in the comparative stakes, being branded by abolitionists as a particularly severe case study in cruelty to labourers. Now in the late 1840s, comparisons in print made the case for the alleged progress achieved in the age of reform and the rewards due in turn, both in Cape Town and Port Louis.[150] More and more the language of British subjecthood was squeezing out the most virulent strains of disloyalty in Port Louis.

1848–9

'Be it known that the revolutionary genius of the age has reached even unto the Cape: and that we are now in a state of war with the government.'[151] So wrote F. S. Watermeyer, then in his early twenties, in his editorial in the *Cape of Good Hope Observer* in 1849.

The debate over slavery did not give rise to an urban commotion in Cape Town of the scale of the Jeremie affair in Mauritius in the 1830s. The context for Watermeyer's editorial was a protest which paralysed the government and allowed an alternative structure of rule to come into being. The events in Cape Town in 1848–9 did not involve weapons and were not bound to a particular class of slave holders or bureaucrats. They are described by historians as a form of 'civil disobedience' and an 'agitation' which was 'more or less universal, and visceral'.[152] In Fairbairn's newspaper they were seen not as armed rebellion but as a *'rebellion of the heart'*, premised on a 'difference of opinion'.[153] When the commotion became more factious, the newspaper sought to prevent the occurrence of riots.[154] In keeping with this sentiment, Watermeyer's editorial was titled, 'A QUIET REVOLUTION'.[155]

The disarray originated when the Cape was declared a penal colony. The order arose in response to the Cape's governor, Harry Smith, writing misguidedly to London to welcome the suggestion that convicts should be introduced, and calling Earl Grey, Colonial Secretary, to move ahead in making measures for conferring the 'boon' of convicts into the Cape, 'with as little delay as possible'.[156] London took this enthusiasm at face value and arranged for 288 Irish ticket-of-leave convicts – convicts who had served their sentences and were now free to work with some supervision – to be sent to the Cape on the *Neptune*. For Fairbairn's newspaper in April 1849 the colony was 'to be converted into a *large prison*, for every description of felons, each district being a separate ward!'[157] It was an 'invasion of "Exiles".'[158] In May 1849 there were two public meetings in Cape Town to express opposition to the measure, and which saw the gathering of five or six thousand people on each occasion. As the *Cape Town Mail* described it:

> THE Nineteenth Day of May, One Thousand eight hundred and forty-nine, will long be memorable in the annals of this Colony, as the day on which the Inhabitants of the City of Cape Town arose as one man to protest against one of the most flagitious and tyrannical acts ever attempted by Power in its maddest moods . . . By the decorum which they observed on this occasion the People of this Colony gave evidence of their progress in education and civilization, and of their fitness and ability to take in hand, and give a decision upon, the most important questions.[159]

A meeting was also held on the significant date of the American Revolution, 4 July, and it extended the boycott to all who aided the government's policies.[160]

The vital issue at stake though unconnected to slavery was how to secure labour for the colony; free or 'healthy' emigration was now threatened by what was planned.[161] Indeed the programme of emancipation, so tied up with debates about slavery, was now taken up by colonists who argued for their own freedoms and emancipation. They had been born 'with titles for freedom written on their hearts', but as the *South African Commercial Advertiser* bemoaned, because of metropolitan tyranny over their affairs, they were to 'receive the slave's collar'.[162] For the *Cape Town Mail* also, the imposition of convicts on the colony was a return to an age of slavery:

> The older Colonists having being deprived of the slaves which they formerly held as lawful property, – there being here, as in every new country, an opportunity of employing labour with advantage, – and considerable exertions having been made to increase the numbers of the operative classes by immigration, – it seems to have been thought that compulsory labour of any kind would be eagerly received, and that so deadened were our feelings to all sense of humanity, that the moral and social evils of convictism would be accounted as nothing, in comparison with the profits which might be wrung from the labour of the miserable and degraded beings to be sent amongst us.[163]

Of great concern was also how to square the colony's now advancing anglicised and morally middle-class compass with an interventionist measure which went so far against both as also against local opinion. Given this, it is curious that the crisis came to be partly because of metropolitan politicians' desire to placate the middle classes of Britain.[164]

Harry Smith, the governor, received a stream of petitions of protest. An Anti-Convict Association sent almost daily orders. A slew of institutions, bodies and individuals had to give way: justices of the peace resigned; unofficial members of road boards, prison boards, school committees, the harbour commission and even the unofficial members of the Legislative Council stepped down from office. Watermayer's editorial noted: 'At present is the Government already crippled.'[165] And in an issue which followed shortly afterwards: 'The Legislative Council is dead.'[166] This then was akin to the Jeremie affair of Mauritius, almost two decades earlier.

For five months, from the ship's arrival in September 1849, the convicts on the *Neptune* were unable to land. They lived docked in Simon's Bay outside Cape Town. Those who supplied the ship had their businesses boycotted.[167] Unsuccessful escape bids were mounted.[168] It was like a 'Pest Ship', a vessel seen as conveying deadly diseases.[169] Eventually, the ship sailed on to Van Diemen's Land. Fairbairn now wrote: 'the people of the Cape of Good Hope have shown to the world what it is that constitutes a state.'[170]

The municipality of Cape Town played an important role in the anti-convict protests, giving the Town Hall for the Anti-Convict Committee's meetings. One onlooker gave the municipality the title, 'Anti-Government'. The role played by the municipality makes sense when viewed from the perspective of the large number of voluntary associations which were sprinkled across the colony by this date. At the end of 1848, a local almanac filled thirty or forty pages with their names. For the *South African Commercial Advertiser*, these libraries, agricultural societies, banks and other such associations were 'local administrations', which prepared the people for 'Government' and gave evidence of the strength of 'the democratic element'.[171] The municipal commissioners gave this notice to the governor: 'the people have determined that the convicts must not, cannot and shall not be landed or kept in any ports of this Colony.'[172] In the aftermath of the agitation and its victory, the municipality pushed for a new constitution. Representative government was indeed granted in 1853. To qualify for the franchise one needed to have property valued at £25 or to be paid either a salary of £50 or £25 with board and lodging provided.[173]

That one of the anti-convict public meetings was held on 4 July was in keeping with how journalists and observers made references to the French and American Revolutions and to the events which had convulsed Europe in 1848. The *South African Commercial Advertiser* noted that Benjamin Franklin had also objected to the imposition of convicts on America, asking whether the Americans might send rattlesnakes to England in return. And so 'the hearts of the loyal people were irrecoverably alienated, and the British Empire was cut in two'.[174] In his editorial Watermeyer referred to the French Revolution of 1848 and to the liberal politics engulfing Italy which necessitated the departure of the Pope from Rome. He described the state of war with the government as:

> not a whit less earnest than that which in France transformed Louis Philippe into the Comte de Neuilly, or elsewhere compelled the blessed Pope Pius to date his Bulls from Gaeta instead of his venerable seat in the Eternal City.

He noted that there was among the colonists a demand for 'a free and liberal constitution'. Once aroused, the passion for this had replaced their listless confidence in the colonial state. 'And then, laying the axe at the root of the mischief,' he continued, 'they insist that the Representative Legislature which has been so long promised them shall be withheld no longer.' If the news and language of events far away fed into the agitation, the connection should not be assumed to be too direct, for months passed between what occurred in Europe and the convict agitation in the Cape.[175] It has recently been argued that news travelling between Europe and the Cape in the early press sometimes lost its sheen by the time it arrived – it was not seen to be up to date or entirely accurate because of the time lag.[176]

One might add that this was an especially acute problem in these years of transition to steam. Expectations of the global circuitry of news and markets was rising but these expectations were hard to fulfill. Rather than playing a determining cause, the European year of revolution of 1848 may instead be seen as a piece of convenience, a story to be deployed at will and over which local interests could triumph in the global South. It could quite literally be cut and pasted in newspapers which then played a critical role in the anti-convict agitation. Such reportage allowed forms

of comparison about rights and governments to arise between Europe
and the Cape. This is a more meaningful way of analysing these events
than to say that the tumult of Europe in 1848 directly or indirectly caused
the anti-convict agitation.

The flow of news and the style of comparison that operated around
the agitation had a colony-to-colony or South–South dimension to it
too, which again necessitates a turn away from a view of Europe as
dominating the story of protest at the end of the 1840s. In pushing for
representative government, Fairbairn's organ reproduced the Canadian
Constitution of 1840 (the so-called Act of Union which brought together
Upper and Lower Canada into one legislative entity), and the *Cape Town
Mail* discussed it too.[177] The *South African Commercial Advertiser* asserted
that the Cape Colony was happier than New South Wales, Jamaica or
Mauritius, where financial ruin came more easily due to speculation or
problems with labour. The Cape's happiness – in its view – gave grounds
to oppose the plan to send convicts to the colony.[178]

In keeping with this classificatory project, this newspaper exclaimed
in moralist terms against the grouping of the Cape with Van Diemen's
Land and Norfolk Island, 'the Sodom and Gomorrah of the British
Empire' or a 'moral dung heap'.[179] At other moments, however, the Cape
press wished to join arms with colonists in Australia, fearing that that
'insular continent' of Australia would become an 'earthly pandemonium',
a 'nuisance and terror to all nations' if transportation continued.[180]
Meanwhile, across the southern ocean, the Sydney press reported on the
events in Cape Town. Anti-convict agitations also occurred in Australia
in 1849. In the Sydney press the need not to be outdone by the patriots
of the Cape was voiced.[181]

Closer to the Cape than Australia was Mauritius, which too could be
made into an 'other' with respect to race, gender and moral values in the
Cape press of these years. In 1848, in *Sam Sly's African Journal*, artist George
Duff took Cape Town and Port Louis to be moral counterpoints and used
a language of race and class to distinguish the two. People of colour in
both cities were compared and 'the poorest Hottentot [Khoikhoi] in Cape
Town' was said to look better than 'the drunken Malabar [Indian] women'.
French colonists in Port Louis were said to look ungentlemanly, 'a d—
sight too much of the monkey about them'.[182] In the same year, Fairbairn's
South African Commercial Advertiser also kept an eye on Mauritius,
predicting that news from France of revolution would jeopardise the
relationship of the 'classes that call themselves French and English', making

one talk of 'Independence, or re-union with the French Republic' while the other would want to move 'closer than ever to the pillars of the British Monarchy'. This choice facing Mauritius was seen to be different to the prospects facing the Cape: the colonies' Dutch and British settlers were said to share 'the character of being slow to heat and slow to cool', explaining the nature of the united and determinedly sustained non-violent protest that greeted the convict question. At the Cape, they were all seen to be 'embarked in the same boat' to 'sink or swim together'.[183]

In the run-up to the convict agitation, the newspaper wrote of how Mauritius also feared the arrival of convicts to the island. It quoted the *Mauritius Times* as proof of the danger of introducing convicts into a colony 'in a transition state of political and social existence'.[184] In the months to come, it turned indignant at the news that military convicts, or soldiers who had been punished for crimes, would be sent to the Cape from Mauritius to work on the roads, and that other convicts were scheduled for arrival in the Cape from elsewhere in the British empire, though these plans later evaporated.[185]

In Port Louis itself, the news from Europe could be deployed for local purposes, even if no convicts were on the way. In October 1848, an association was formed which had as its published purpose the creation of a channel of communication to the governor. It was an economically dire time for sugar planters. The formation of the association also came directly in the context of a so-called 'July Manifesto', written by the editors of *La Sentinelle*, *Le Mauricien* and *Le Cernéen* and in favour of the French rather than the British.[186]

Le Cernéen took the view that the Mauritian press could not 'remain a stranger' given the events of Europe which echoed 'all over the Globe', and to do so would be to fail 'in its own dignity'.[187] It noted rather extraordinarily and bravely:

> We should be concealing the truth, and be advancing a notorious falsehood, did we presume to maintain that Mauritius is not, by its origin, its language, its laws, habits and affections, impelled towards France.
>
> The Government is well aware, that, if Freedom reigned in the world, if the inhabitants of Mauritius were allowed to select a protecting power, their option would be for the Nation which founded this colony, the Nation from which they have been severed by force, provided however they received from Her their liberties, without which they would refuse her flag.[188]

However, *Le Cernéen* reprinted a speech from the 5 October meeting of the association, in which its organisers insisted on their loyalty to the English and that an interrogation of England's commercial policy was consistent with this duty of loyalty.[189] The Anglophile and pro-government *Mauritius Times* noted that though no political ambition was acknowledged in its formation, there was nothing to stop the association from stepping outside the remit envisaged at its founding.[190]

On 12 October between eleven and twelve o'clock at Hôtel d'Europe in Port Louis, the association attempted to hold a meeting to receive the votes of the inhabitants of the island. All who took up the right to vote had to pay two dollars to the association. Though there was a debate about dropping the 'two dollar qualification' to allow ex-apprentices to participate, such an amendment was not passed. The limitations that were set to democracy and the continuing exclusion of labouring classes are in clear view.[191] The association set out its aims thus:

> They are: 1st Those of agriculture and sugar cultivation in particular. 2nd to obtain from Her Majesty's Ministers the institution of an Elective Administrative Council. 3rd A diminution of our enormous taxation, and a corollary measure, reform in the Colonial Administration.[192]

The Deputy Commissary of Police broke up the meeting at Hôtel d'Europe. The governor of Mauritius – William Gomm – declared the plan for the association unlawful and rebellious. Though he was clearly worried about the events around its formation, describing it as a 'revolutionary movement' to the Colonial Office, he insisted that it did not have a popular following among the population at large. It had only aroused 'ordinary curiosity' among onlookers. This appears to be accurate, meaning that the association's agitation should not be seen as comparable to the events that would follow in Cape Town around convict arrivals.[193] Gomm noted, however, that he warned some unofficial members of the Legislative Council of the dangers of participating. He feared the possibility of another Jeremie moment or an episode like the convict agitation, with the formation of an alternative structure of rule.[194]

When disrupted by the police, the association's organisers decried the 'public act of dishonour and insult'.[195] *Le Mauricien* insisted:

Who were the rebels and violaters of the law? . . . Were they a few republicans who wished to set at defiance the British Government? . . . No; they were honest, independent, loyal and intelligent Colonists.[196]

The association denied that it hoped to form an alternative structure of rule.[197] Eventually it trimmed its plan to suit the law by appointing a central committee of fifteen rather than a body of sixty-four elected representatives. This change resulted from the advice of Prosper d'Épinay, the brother of Adrien d'Épinay who was at the centre of the 1831 protests. He advised that the law, inherited from the French, only allowed fifteen people to meet without the government's express permission, to consider 'religious or political subjects'.[198] In November that year, the *ghoon* procession came under strict regulations and surveillance by the police; the festival was only to be open to those who were, in an extraordinary description, 'entirely mahomedan [Muslim]' and no fire-arms or 'clubs or sticks' were to be allowed.[199] The central committee of fifteen now drafted petitions to Governor Gomm and the queen. The first was more strident than the second, including one capitalised request: 'AN IMMEDIATE REDUCTION OF TAXATION'.[200] The link with the debates over slavery was clear from the first point in the petition to the queen:

That your petitioners have since the year 1833, when Slavery was abol-ished in Your Majesty's dominions struggled by every possible means to produce with free labor, Sugar, the staple and almost only produce of Mauritius, so as at once to remunerate themselves, and to furnish cheap sugar to the British consumers.[201]

The queen's petitioners carried on highlighting the costs of labour and machinery, heavy taxation and the burden of an expensive system of local government. They had been plunged into ruin, they asserted, by the sugar bill of 1846, 'whereby Foreign slave grown sugar was admitted for consumption in Great Britain at so small a discriminating duty, as to bring it into immediate competition with the produce of this Island'. And point 15 came to the issue of representative government:

That your petitioners, being deprived of any participation in the Government of the Colony either by means of an elective representative assembly, or any sort of municipal institutions, are unable to control the public expenditure, so as to reduce it in conformity with the resources of the colony, and to what is strictly required for an effective government, on a rigid economical footing.

They also pointed out the problematic effect of the queen of Madagascar's politics on their trade. The petitioners had been deprived of their supplies of cattle and a source of labour:

The price of meat having risen in consequence four fold, whilst Draft oxen on which the Planters are dependent for the cheap working of their Estates, are not to be procured to replace the large numbers destroyed by murrain.

They asked for a restitution of free trade with Madagascar and the formation of an 'elective assembly' and a municipal corporation by royal charter for Port Louis. No taxes should be imposed, they insisted, without the consent of the elective assembly. All this was consistent with the global moment of 1848. The two petitions were presented to Gomm in a flourish of ceremony as the central committee processed through the streets of Port Louis, followed by about three hundred people.[202]

In the end the central committee of fifteen had to disband when a paper war erupted between the island's newspapers. The spark occurred on 4 July 1849, the very day when anti-convict protests were happening on the streets of Cape Town. When men of colour were not allowed entry to a ball, a telling sign of the racial limits of this protest, five members of colour of the committee sent in their resignation.[203] The *Mauritius Times* declared that ethnic divisions were tearing apart the identity of the French population, necessitating a turn towards Englishness. The newspaper's view is reminiscent of some of the assertions of loyalty and British subjecthood around the Cape's convict agitations:

The feeling of the mass is unequivocally English, they desire to see the English language established in the Island; but the press being until a few years ago exclusively in the hands of the French or *old colonial party* [of the Jeremie days], the English and the coloured race had no means of advocating their views.[204]

THE CHARACTER OF GLOBALISATION
IN THE MID NINETEENTH CENTURY

If the press of these years represented factions at war and differences of opinion, these tussles were outworkings of the imperial birth of the modern world. The genre of the newspaper was still an unsettled one; the nature of the press should not be seen as totally different to other modes of writing in this era. Communication between cities like Port Louis and Cape Town and the wider world was starting to be transformed through the spread of steamshipping. Yet globalisation's impact was still uneven. Different sites were able to follow related but separate chronologies of change. News from Europe had an impact, but so also did travelling pieces of information and politics across the oceans of the South. All of this makes it necessary to mount a much more multi-sited account of 1848, especially if we are to understand the internal make-up of the Southwest Indian Ocean.

In Port Louis, in these years, there was an avid correspondent with a painfully close relationship with his mother in Britain. The letters written by James Egbert Simmons (1810–1857) epitomise the emerging character of the mid nineteenth century for colonists: they felt far from Europe and yet news from far and near in turn could be turned to local purpose as it arrived in irregular sequence. He told his mother everything and one of his letters, from a batch of about one hundred letters written between 1847 and 1855, was written together with Caroline Casaubour, whom he fell in love with and who wrote in French. He worried that his mother would not forgive her for the 'double defect' of being 'neither English or Protestant'.[205] This liaison was very much in keeping with the gender politics of anglicisation as French-speaking 'creole' women became partners to British men in Mauritius. In demonstrating how much times had changed since the Jeremie affair, Caroline Casaubour was the niece of Prosper d'Épinay. Her family had been at the centre of the 1831 protests against the British and also the advice given to combat the pro-French 1848 political association. This means that it had stood both against and with the British government in a short sequence of years.

Simmons arrived in Port Louis together with his regiment, and died in India 'in action', when shot in the mouth. He had been posted to Calcutta during the Indian Rebellion. Simmons' letters are obsessively concerned with the passage of the mail and the circuit of communication between Port Louis and the rest of the world. He constantly provided advice on the best way to reach him, comparing transit times for the mail through different routes. On 21 August 1848, writing to his 'dearest Mother', he noted:

> I am sadly behind hand in receiving letters, my last being dated 23 March (your no.13), we have overland news to the 24th June, but none by ship later than the 14 May, the English ships making just now most account-ably long passages . . . I hope very shortly there will be a regular line of packets to Ceylon, when we shall get our Letters regularly in less than two months, until they are established it is no use your sending Letters overland, if you do send them via Columbo [sic.][206]

These letters were written at regular intervals, sometimes rushed to make the call for the mail before a vessel departed. 'Ebby' (the nickname he used in his letters) and his mother numbered their correspondence (as is clear in the extract). He waited for numbers to arrive in sequence and complained when they were out of order, and this generated anxiety when he hadn't heard from his mother before his wedding. All this means that these letters may be usefully compared and placed next to the early newspapers of Cape Town and Mauritius. Though letters are of course more personalized forms of writing, both letters and news-papers in these years and from this region were experimenting with marking time in regular periods and operated with a sense of their point origin as placed in a globalising world.

Indeed, periodicals accompanied letters: Simmons sent his mother Mauritian newspapers. He also promised lithographs of Mauritius and sent seeds too and for a Christmas present in 1849 sent his mother 'a little book of Chinese drawings on nice paper'.[207] Plans were also made for the transport of wedding cake. Among the things which passed with the letters in the other direction were a 'Bible and Testaments'. They were for the new couple and for Caroline's mother. A 'quarter Cheese and quarter wedding cake' also travelled on this route; the latter from the wedding of a family member in Britain.[208] Though the letters span only a few years the acceleration of steam is also evident in them. By 1852 Simmons worried whether his mother was unwell because no correspondence had arrived. He hoped that it was because she had missed the date of the departure of the Cape Colony steamer: 'in these days of regular communication it is rather alarming not to receive a letter from so regular a correspondent as you dear Mother have always been.'[209]

If political news faded in immediacy and power in encountering delay in the 1830s and 1840s, before the transition to an era of steam, this made it possible for such news to be deployed for local purposes. This is evident in Simmons commentary on the events of 1848 in Mauritius and how they had generated rumours:

> As for the politics of this little place, I believe the Creoles to be much disaffected and inclined to follow the French example, but they cannot help themselves. They have been amusing themselves by spreading all sorts of alarming reports here relative to the disaffection of the Troops . . .

He provided his mother with an account of the 'very ridiculous' association formed in Port Louis in 1848, led by 'some ruined English merchants' of the sugar plantations. In denying any dignity or political force to the assembly, he distanced it from Europe. This was also why he apologised for the dullness of his commentary on local news, seeing Mauritius as 'completely out of the world' in relation to events in Europe.[210] Though the island could be placed alongside European news it was not equivalent to it. The political association of 1848 was for him:

> a sort of representative assembly under the Title of the Mauritius Association, 64 members were to have been returned, and the qualification for a vote was to be a subscription of 2 dollars . . .

If belittled and humoured in his account, he still used the word revolution to describe this body: 'This has been the nearest approach to a revolution we have had, not withstanding the revolutionary cravings of a portion of the press.' Immediately following this line, Simmons moved not into European politics but to the political context which was more immediate to Mauritius: 'We yesterday had newspapers from the Cape, that is to say a rumor of a fight between Sir H. Smith [governor] and [Andries] Pretorius [the Afrikaner leader] . . .'[211] Simmons was insistent that the news from Europe was awful but that it was unlikely to affect Mauritius unless a war broke out between England and France, which looked increasingly improbable.

Instead, the challenge for Mauritius was to integrate a cohesive

society while being so far from Europe and also surrounded by other
colonies such as French Bourbon and the Cape. He wrote of his plan
of visiting Bourbon with Caroline, noting that she had plenty of relatives there:

> there is a mountain there some 10,000 feet high, with some celebrated
> springs near the Top of it, the waters they say would be very good for
> her and the Climate perhaps still better. She has plenty of relations there
> and very nice people, upon whom, one might quarter oneself . . .[212]

The French in Mauritius could be incorporated into this programme
of anglicisation; Simmons' own personal life attested to this. They were,
in his words, 'poor fellows', 'they are all most thoroughly Anti-
Republican.'[213] Anglicisation was a tool then for further transforming
anti-republicans.

In keeping with this style of comparative glances across the oceans of
the South, in 1850, a new daily paper called the *Commercial Gazette* was
established in Mauritius. It took upon itself not only to hold government
to account but also to keep an eye on Port Louis' municipal council set
up after the agitations of 1848. The *Commercial Gazette* sought to extend
liberal principles and repeatedly advocated a steam line between
Mauritius and the Cape in 1850.[214] It was comparable to Fairbairn's
newspaper in Cape Town. In an early issue, the way comparison between
places drove politics was in plain view when it asked:

> A Municipal Institution for the town was thought sufficient for us, whilst
> our neighbor the Cape is to have a complete representative system. What
> is the difference with regard to the two colonies? Mauritius is a conquered
> colony – so is the Cape. Part of the population of Mauritius has a
> different European origin – it is the same at the Cape. The only reason
> we can find for the preference the Cape has enjoyed is that since 1841
> the inhabitants have petitioned for a representative government . . .[215]

A couple of months later, it raised the question again and noted one
of the objections: 'the existence of *hostile races*' in Mauritius. The
Commercial Gazette insisted in response that class hostility had ceased
in Port Louis and that education had banished prejudice and attachment
to rank.[216] Despite the rhetoric of comparison and the shared history in

the grant of municipal government between Cape Town and Port Louis, it is important to note that Mauritius was given representation by election much later in the nineteenth century; the first elections were held in 1886.[217]

The newspaper did not only look to the Cape to make its argument for representative government. It pointed to the political status enjoyed by Bourbon in being represented in the National Assembly in France. A resident of Bourbon, P. de Greslan, whose letter it reproduced, was said to have undertaken a noble struggle in the Assembly, being rewarded if not with press freedom for Bourbon then at least with assistance to repair damages arising from two hurricanes, and with plans to procure labourers for the island. The newspaper concluded: 'Bourbon by having two representatives in the Assembly, who pass all their time in making known the wants of the Colony, in defending her interests, in preventing legislation in ignorance of the locality, has a great advantage over us . . .'[218] Mauritius was seen to suffer the decisions of people who did not know where it was on a map or who had not seen it.[219]

Meanwhile, the *Cape Town Mail* used material from the Mauritian newspapers to alert its readers to the events of Bourbon, where, riven by various political factions, a general assembly had lately formed independent of the government.[220] In Mauritius itself, the formation of a general assembly in Bourbon was in the news just before the island's 1848 association was formed. These developments in Bourbon were one context for the signing of the petitions to the queen and Governor Gomm.[221]

In sum, the press did not simply report the news. People in places like Mauritius did not only adopt and follow the ideologies of Europe. Print and letters ordered the colonies of the Cape, Mauritius and Bourbon in relation to each other. Newspapers allowed a debate about emancipation, rights and government to occur between these sites which in turn drew in comparisons which were more global.

FAR DISTANT GLANCES ACROSS THE SOUTH

This style of comparisons is in keeping with this moment of protest and civil disobedience in the British empire around 1848, stimulated as it was by the extension of free trade, the need to transport prisoners from

Britain and to economise and extend taxes overseas while easing the tax burden at home.[222]

From the debate about slavery in the 1830s there is a line of descent to the debate about self-government in the 1840s and 50s; both were seen as being concerned with 'emancipation'. If enslaved labourers had been emancipated, now the middle classes, the emergent public and commercially minded elites, sought to use the idea of emancipation to talk about their rights to petition and assembly. These classes of people adopted the language of the time for their own purposes and did so while excluding those who didn't belong with them. A call for constitutional reform was evident across these locales as in Europe. In both Cape Town and Port Louis municipal government was used as a foundation from which to argue for representative government, with different outcomes.

Reform and its overtaking by conservatism created a pattern, just as revolution and imperial counter-revolt had done. Indeed, the twists and turns of this story were mapped directly onto the events after the French Revolution. The challenge now for those who were socially mobile or part of the elite was to present evidence of Englishness and loyalty to the British in order to secure rights and advancement.

Alongside the reporting on the news of tumult from Europe, just as the political association of Mauritius was being formed, there appeared in the columns of the Mauritian press a sustained study of a revolt from the other side of the Indian Ocean. In 1848, a rebellion broke out in British Ceylon [Sri Lanka]. Government buildings were attacked in the interior heartland of the old kingdom and urban commotion took place in the port city of Colombo. A meeting in Colombo, to sign a petition to the governor against a new regime of taxes, degenerated into a violent clash.

The rebellion was crushed ruthlessly by Governor Torrington but there were many striking similarities between the conditions of Sri Lanka and those of Mauritius where no violence occurred in 1848. Taxation was once more at issue and in Ceylon the series of new taxes which had been introduced ran from stamp duties to licence fees for carts. Concerns about labour conditions fed into this revolt: a road ordinance made it obligatory for men to work on the roads for six days per year. This was akin to a regime of compulsory labour or *rajakariya* abolished by the reforming commission, sent by the metropolitan British government, which arrived in Sri Lanka after visiting the Cape and Mauritius and which recommended measures to reform slavery. In other words, in 1848, it was thought that slavery was being reintroduced whereas it was formally, if not practically, abolished in the previous decade. In the words of a letter in Ceylon's *Observer*: 'I think the Singhalese people [of Sri Lanka] will show they are not a race of slaves.'[223]

Together with news from Europe, the possibility of creating village-level municipalities and an 'elective franchise' for the Legislative Council were being discussed in the press of Sri Lanka in the run-up to this agitation. Petitions and memorials were signed on all sides. And newspapers were at the heart of the rebellion: Dr Charles Elliot, an Irish physician and editor of the *Observer* was accused of fathering the revolt. For the *Times* of Ceylon, Elliot was the 'arch traitor', 'the man who ha[d] sown the seeds from which this monster rebellion began'. The letter above, which objected to the new slavery of the Sinhalese people of the island, was published in the *Observer* on 3 July 1848 under the pseudonym, 'An Englishman'. It was translated into Sinhala and distributed in pamphlet form. The similarities between Sri Lanka and Mauritius appeared intriguing when viewed from Port Louis. The two islands were seen in 1848 to have similar economies and societies, facing parallel challenges.[224] For *Le Cernéen* for instance: 'the Ceylonese are no happier than we are; rural property is overburdened with debts and sells at a low price when it is sold [to coffee planters].'[225] *Le Mauricien* gave updates on the developments in Ceylon as they arose, including this account of Elliot:

> At Colombo a large body of natives of Cotta (from 5 to 7000) have assembled, the troops of the garrison were under arms and stationed to guard the gates of town. The Police in one part of the town had interfered, and six or eight of the poor people got broken heads. Dr. Elliot (the principal Editor of the *Observer*) took a very active part, and used all his influence to calm the people, at the same time calling on the Governor who was present to order the troops and police to retire, as he said the people only met to sign a petition and then separate . . .[226]

Yet the similarity between Ceylon and Mauritius was not only due to the global economy or discussions of rights. The similarity was used by the newspapers of Mauritius in order to map their own politics as a debate ensued about the implications of the events in Sri Lanka. This constituted a further set of comparative glances across the waters of the South. The *Mauritius Times* poked fun at how *Le Cernéen* and *Le*

Mauricien wished to make the Sri Lankan papers, the *Observer* and the *Examiner* 'grand favorites' while presenting the Ceylon *Times,* a pro-government paper, to be like the *Mauritius Times.* Yet in biting commentary, the *Mauritius Times* noted in response: 'Unfortunately Doctor Elliot [editor of *The Observer*] is not disposed to fraternize with his admirers in Mauritius.' Elliot's view, it reported, was that it was not the paper he edited but the Ceylon *Times* which was the parallel paper in Sri Lanka to the *Le Cernéen* and *Le Mauricien.*

In other words, in the midst of the transference of the news between Mauritius and Sri Lanka alliances between sites and politics were attempted across the global South. Newspapers cut and pasted reports, aligned themselves with each other, and debated the implications of 1848 across territories which were seen as neighbours. Yet, despite the attempt to fit the liberal politics of an Irish newspaper editor in Sri Lanka next to the conservative politics of an old elite in Mauritius, the presumption of common cause between these journalists and also the political events they were feeding, namely the 1848 Ceylon Rebellion and the formation of a political association in Mauritius, was certainly inexact as a form of comparative politics. Dr Elliott was quoted by the *Mauritius Times* as he criticised the racial supremacy advocated by the planter elites of Mauritius who were allied to *Le Cernéen* and *Le Mauricien.* Elliot didn't believe in the 'liberal professions of faith of the Dutch and the French creoles'. The *Mauritius Times* alleged that the Mauritian elite wanted freedom in order to 'exterminate' the blacks or to 'reduce them in slavery'.[227]

In the Cape Colony, however, the reporting on the Sri Lankan rebellion was muted, despite the strength of liberalism and shared Dutch colonial heritage in both South Africa and Sri Lanka. Cape writers saw race as a differentiating factor as they looked upon the events of Sri Lanka. For the *South African Commercial Advertiser*:

From the India papers it appears that a most wicked insurrection or rebellion in Ceylon, has been quickly put down and smartly punished by the governor, Lord Torrington. Some party writers [Dr. Elliot] are accused of having excited the Cingalese to this miserable movement by acrimonious attacks on the British Government. The proceedings of the loyal inhabitants on this occasion, are highly honorable to them, and the Reports of Speeches, &c. given below, will be read with peculiar interest here at the present time.[228]

Elsewhere, the rebels of Ceylon were distant others: 'wild and vicious' insurgents.[229] Their excessive violence was evident in how they had 'tortured an unfortunate planter who fell into their hands'. This specific commentary followed directly after the unremarked-upon fact, which appeared in the report, that many rebels had been killed in Matale, in the interior of the island at the hands of the British government.[230] The *Cape Town Mail* wished also to rehabilitate the reputation of Dr. Elliot as a liberal, noting that there had been an attempt to fix the blame on him. The 'insinuations against him are couched in language so utterly indefensible, and worthy only of a Country Chronicle of the days of William Pitt when describing a reform meeting of those times . . .' It also used some extracts from non-Cape papers to make the point that the governor of Ceylon, Torrington, had overstepped his mark in the way he handled the rebellion. Just as the events of the Ceylon rebellion were interpreted to suit Mauritius, here in the Cape they were inflected by the concerns of Englishness, loyalism, liberalism and anti-authoritarian government. These were commitments which were circulating in the Cape Town of these years.

CONCLUSION

The Sri Lankan rebellion of 1848 is so often lost out of the European narrative of the springtime of nations as a wave of political change engulfed the European continent in 1848. It is a good event from which to mount a retrospect on the argument in this chapter about the 1830s and 1840s across Indian Ocean sites which were becoming more anglicised and modernised in the 1830s and 1840s. Abolition was not a programme which ceased in the 1830s. It fed into calls for self-government and the language of 'emancipation' was applied to colonies wholesale. The fact that abolition had been embraced was now used to argue against the interventionism of the colonial state, for instance in the introduction of convicts or the economic impact of its policies on plantations on the coast of the Indian Ocean.

If in the 1830s, abolitionism faced difficulties in the Southwest Indian Ocean, the emergence of new public spheres and the prospect of steam-shipping in the 1840s gave rise again to a politics of comparison, where neighbouring locales across the South were used to push forward local concerns. Far-away Europe was certainly in view, but so also and perhaps more so were neighbouring colonies with similar histories, societies and economies. Yet the news – like that of the Sri Lankan rebellion or the politics of French Bourbon, when it arrived in the Cape and Mauritius – was inflected by local factors. News dulled as it travelled, losing its immediacy, and events around the Southwest Indian Ocean should not be read simply as caused by the European revolts of 1848.

An emerging urban and institutional politics of race, gender and Englishness is also evident in this story. To assert rights and potential for self-rule it was increasingly necessary to adopt the notion of British subjecthood and this was undoubtedly exclusionary. Extraordinary moments – such as when in 1848 Mauritian journalists longed in print for French rule – were the exceptions. The Mauritian journalist of colour Ollier could proclaim a manifesto of Englishness, as could those who campaigned against convicts at the Cape. This Englishness was becoming increasingly connected with liberal middle-class values and to racialised and gendered notions of morality, and was set against the slave-holding cultures of France and the Netherlands which Britain wanted to replace. Even as it sought to replace what came before, this Englishness allowed the assimilation of Dutch and French heritages in both Cape Town and Port Louis, as seen in the relationship between Simmons and his French 'creole' wife. This woman came from one of the families who stood against Jeremie in the early 1830s in Mauritius. Ascendant Englishness didn't erase Dutch and French heritages; it incorporated these and bypassed them as a new politics of class, race and status emerged in the burgeoning port cities of Port Louis and Cape Town.

This story is about the coming to be of many things which we identify with the modern urban world – the private newspaper and civic culture. Yet the tragic fact is that these elements coincided with the consolidation of the British empire amidst its rivals. The legacy of the revolutionary years was still here, as people appropriated the memory and symbolism of revolution, in the year 1848, and in its public meetings and associations. But the memory of the revolutions was literally wiped off the streets of Port Louis, and Englishness as a cultural and social practice was a tool of anti-republicanism. This in the end was the tragedy of the mid nineteenth century. A counter-revolt of modernity tied up with the British empire suppressed so much of the potential of the age of revolutions.

Yet the British counter-revolt was not a fully successful event nor did it progress in a linear fashion. Indian Ocean peoples still creatively manipulated the spaces and gaps of empire for their own purposes. The march towards representative rule followed a parallel pattern across different sites. Legislative councils were reformed and municipalities created before the franchise was introduced in a limited fashion as in the Cape. Yet this sequence took on a different pace in different localities. Though a municipality was created in Port Louis it came ten years after the grant to Cape Town. And though Port Louis sought to point to its neighbour in seeking representative government, this policy did not work as representative government Mauritius was much delayed. Though the setting up of an alternative government is one way of interpreting the Jeremie affair, there was no equivalent in Cape Town, until the anti-convict agitations perhaps of the late 1840s. Beyond the parallel but separate paths, these perceived differences were the openings which created political pressure across the Indian Ocean and fed into protest. Not only did a straightforward story of one place impacting another become impossible because news took a while to travel, the fact that different places followed different paths was problematic for those who lost out. In the Cape, Sri Lanka could be a racialised other, while in Mauritius there was an attempt to map local politics through the rebellion of Sri Lanka. The geographical and temporal patterns, the waves across the South, were complex, but in their midst modernity came to be in the midst of the British empire.

Conclusion

In the middle of the nineteenth century, there was a boom in history writing on the British empire.[1] The age of revolutions and the Anglo-French and Anglo-Dutch tussles in the wider world faded into memory; Chartism failed and the 1848 revolutions on the continent met with a lack of widespread success. At this juncture, where this book ends, it was easy to assume that the British empire would last long.

A nostalgic look back into Britain's supposedly revolution-less, pragmatic and ordered past supported the view that the British empire would have a long life. The empire's longevity was sketched as a forward march of unending progress, reform and liberty. The uncertainties, the twists and turns, the revolutionary and counter-revolutionary stand-offs of the decades just passed were mostly forgotten. If they found a place within these histories they were epsiodes in the inevitable rise of the British. The distinctive and plural histories of small seas in the Indian and Pacific Oceans were obliterated by narrators who focussed on colonial units in a network of relations with a centre, London. These books mostly surveyed as if the authors were sitting in the sky and looking down on the earth below; they did not work from the ground or sea upwards.

The mid-century boom in writing on the British empire encompassed many overlapping but different genres, in various measures, globe-sprawling, empirical, statistical, fictional, biographic, cartographic, orientalist, encyclopedic and moralising. Within this avalanche of print were some of the first published English-language histories of what became the nations of this part of the world. These were authored by colonial travellers or officials and residents based in the Indian and Pacific Oceans. They included an eclectic set of information: ranging from personal anecdote to natural historical observation. At times, they proposed schemes for the 'improvement' of the colony in question.

Waves Across the South has told the story that ran before and behind this tide of print. It has challenged the forgetting that these mid-century works allowed. This makes it possible to see the rise of empire in an age of revolutions in the Indian and Pacific Oceans. At the heart of this story is a clever and unexpected manoeuvre: a surge of indigenous agency which was followed by an empire which folded and overtook the aims and agency of such indigenous peoples within its expanding structures. It was revolution followed by counter-revolution. If such is the case, the same manoeuvre was evident in the writing of history itself.

Colonial historians of the mid nineteenth century could rely on indigenous oral and genealogical accounts or cosmologies tied to lines of monarchs and chiefs. Yet indigenous accounts of the past became supplementary information in English-language printed histories. They were cast into separate disciplines outside history such as ethnology, oriental studies or philology. The writing of colonial and Eurocentric history was linked at times to the collection and study of indigenous remains, including human remains. These mid-century histories naturalised a gendered and racial order. The reams of paper involved in this writing were consistent with the rapid expansion of information and scientific knowledge in the age of revolutions.

One characteristic figure of the mid-century avalanche of print about the British empire is the Ulster Protestant, Robert Montgomery Martin (1801?–1868). To his name may be credited an astonishing 267 printed works. He travelled across some of the sites covered in *Waves Across the South*. Having worked as a doctor in Ceylon and at the Cape, he joined a survey expedition as a naturalist and surgeon from 1820 to 1824, and made his way up the coast of Africa and reached Mombasa, and then returned to the Cape via Mauritius.[2] He then proceeded to New South Wales in 1826. He went on to work as an editor and surgeon in Calcutta, coming into contact with Indian liberal reformers, such as Dwarkanath Tagore and Rammohan Roy. He sailed to Britain and turned to his career, writing on the British empire. It was punctuated by a short and disastrous stint in the mid–1840s as treasurer of the newly-taken Hong Kong.

The years 1834–5 saw the publication of Martin's *History of the British Colonies* and 1839 saw *Statistics of the Colonies of the British Empire*. He had access to 'blue books' in an office on Downing Street. 'Blue books' were compilations of statistics and information sent from individual colonies. These books were a visible sign of the close linkage between London and far distant outposts in the 1830s and 1840s.[3] Martin also had access to the commercial returns of the East India Company. His books were positively reviewed, despite their hasty and somewhat erroneous content. They sold well and were reissued.[4] *Statistics of the Colonies of the British Empire* was said to include '*three million* figures'. The lines of data were seen to speak for themselves.[5]

The first large foldout table in *Statistics* had telling headings. It lists possessions, against 'Date of Acquisition', and with an indication of whether these possessions were 'Ceded, Conquered, or Colonized'. There immediately followed a geographical classification: were these possessions 'Insular, Peninsular or Continental'? Next was 'Latitude' and 'Longitude' and there followed length and breadth in miles and 'Extent of Sea Coasts in Miles'. Population was determined as 'White' or 'Coloured', religious difference appeared next and then military strength, finance, money and 'Maritime Commerce' and 'Shipping (Tons)'. There were also columns for 'Vessels Built in the Colony from 1814 to 1837' and information about the 'Chief City or Town', including its location and whether it was coastal.

Through this table, so much of the history charted in *Waves Across the South* was reduced to data and to a single sheet of paper. The interest in the sea was still evident in the attention to maritime trade. And yet 'Continental' concerns were also entering the imperial mind. Martin's *History of the British Colonies* was dedicated to the king as the empire's '*first* Colonial History', arising from an active life across 'our transmarine possessions'. He used a form of description which persists to this day in popular memory of the British empire: 'In fine, SIRE, on this wondrous Empire the solar orb never sets.' Elsewhere his verdict on the global spread of the British empire and its eternal destiny went even further:

> On our Empire the sable curtain of night is never complete, for while the bright light luminary of the heavens is temporarily illuminating the skies of Albion, it is but to shed light and life on another section of our wondrous social frame; may this astronomical phenomenon be typically that of our national history, – may the sun of Britain's glory never set in eternity until the great globe itself shall have passed away. . ..[6]

In the first volume, on possessions in Asia, he included a plan for steam-packet communication between England and India, via the Cape. In another phrase that would last, this project was intended for 'the annihilation of space' and for 'connecting and consolidating our maritime empire.'[7] Indeed, this is what Simmons in Mauritius would have wished for in communicating with his mother. This triumphant prose cast the British empire as a singular entity moving forward almost as an astronomical body.

Martin nailed his colours to the quest for the unification of the empire under a federal mode of government, consistent for instance with the quest of the Cape Town protesters who were recently encountered. Martin's aim was to promote the exploitation and improvement of all the British territories under a system of free trade, the spread of British education, Christianity and liberal goals. His wasn't an original set of ideas, which is one reason why he is largely forgotten by historians. It was the enthusiasm and style with which he illustrated and articulated this agenda which is striking.

Martin's works also included, in a ten-volume series, histories of some of the regions covered in this book. These formed a popular accompaniment to his *History*:

History of Austral-Asia: comprising New South Wales, Van Diemen's Island, Swan River, South Australia, &c. (1836).

History of the British possessions in the Indian & Atlantic Oceans: comprising Ceylon, Penang, Malacca, Sincapore, the Falkland Islands, St. Helena, Ascension, Sierra Leone, the Gambia, Cape Coast Castle, &c., &c. (1837).

History of southern Africa: comprising the Cape of Good Hope, Mauritius, Seychelles, &c. (1836).

These books created a flat imperial and global world of historical narrative and with it the possibility to survey as a monarch in the sky, to recommend reforms and benefits, and to have the information at hand to form a view of a distant place. As one historian explains, it was now possible to believe that there was a British empire.[8] One might add that it was possible, for instance, to believe that there was a colony called Mauritius. Martin's overviews made India seem central to this empire. His personal travels and the corresponding emphasis which followed also brought the Indian and Pacific Oceans into the heart of a global vision of empire. To bear out such a claim, Martin was one of the first to publish a map of the world coloured pink to indicate Britain's territories. His map was drawn by

James Wyld, and appeared in Martin's *Statistics of the Colonies of the British Empire*. It was centred on the Indian and Pacific Oceans. North America appeared in the distant top right.

Martin did not only allow his readers to imagine the British empire. His history writing squeezed indigenous peoples out of the narrative and relied on the racist collection of human remains. This was a humanitarian who was active in the Aborigines Protection Society, founded in 1837 partly through the inheritance of British anti-slavery. His was an interest in indigenous peoples which was motivated by wanting the satisfaction of doing all that was possible for such people. Striking in this respect is Martin's *History of Austral-Asia: Comprising New South Wales, Van Diemen's Land, Swan River, South Australia &c.* which drew on his experience as a surgeon in New South Wales. Readers waded through accounts of the 'Discovery of New Holland' [Australia], a line of great white explorers, the establishment of the penal colony of New South Wales and a whole page of sequential and somewhat melodic 'firsts' indicating the progress and 'prosperity' of the colonial project, including:

> 1789, one year after the establishment of the colony, *first* harvest reaped (at Paramatta); 1790, *first* settler (a convict) took possession of the land allotted him; 1791, *first* brick building finished; 1793, *first* purchase of colonial grain (1,200 bushels) by government; 1794, *first* church built; 1796, *first* play performed; 1800, *first* copper coin circulated; 1803, *first* newspaper printed; 1804, Fort William built; 1805, *first* vessel built; 1810, *first* census, free school, toll-gates, police, naming of the streets, establishment of Sidney market, races and race-ball; 1811, *first* pounds; 1813, *first* fair; 1815, *first* steam engine [and so on, and so on..][9]

There followed an account of the various towns, counties, mountains, rivers, minerals and discussion of geology and natural history. And it was only then that there was a chapter on 'POPULATION', on the 'white' and 'coloured' peoples and their 'numbers and condition'. Martin noted how he had obtained a male and and a female body of Aboriginal Australians for 'osteological measurements'.[10]

One of these was the body of '*Black Tommy*, who was hanged for murder at Sydney, in 1827'. Martin attended the trial and believed that this Aboriginal Australian was innocent. There was only unconvincing circumstantial evidence. The man had run away from a crime scene where a shepherd had been killed, at the sight of the arrival of mounted police. He had also previously been at the dead shepherd's hut 'with a party of natives, bartering with Europeans'. This was enough to condemn the Aboriginal Australian to execution. Martin humanised the accused, whom he described as smiling innocently in the dock. But he had no qualms in applying for the body: 'I applied to the sheriff, and obtained his body, dissected it, and prepared a skeleton therefrom, which I took with me to India.' The female Aboriginal Australian whose body Martin obtained was an indigenous woman like Cora; she had been 'long known about Sydney'. Martin showed no restraint in disturbing her grave: 'I brought the old woman home in my cabriolet, and her skeleton is also in India.'[11]

In Martin's description of Aboriginal Australians' anatomy, weapons and alleged cannibalism, racism is in full evidence. Gender also played a key role. Martin's observations on the female Aboriginal Australian included the story of how her skull, which he had placed in the Asiatic Society of Calcutta, had been struck by sticks. He interpreted this as arising from Aboriginal Australian customs of sex.[12] The difference between the 'civilised' and their opposites was also linked to how 'polygamy' was said to be common among these indigenous peoples: 'women are treated in the most inhuman manner, wives being procured from adjacent tribes by stealing . . .'[13]

Martin believed that if Rousseau, the exponent of the idea of the noble savage who is untouched by civilisation, had visited the indigenous people of New South Wales, he would not have hesitated as to 'whether savage or social life is to be preferred'.[14] This was a short interlude in Martin's history of 'Austral-Asia' which described Aboriginal Australians amid reams of detail on settlement and exploitable natural resources; it worked on the premise that these indigenous peoples were dying out and needed rescue:

> Notwithstanding these unfavourable signs, I think we ought to persevere in our endeavours to save the wild and untutored savages from perishing; self-interest, humanity, christianity call on us so to do; we have occupied their hunting and fishing ground; the kangaroo and the emu have disappeared before the plough and the reaping hook.[15]

Martin's account of New South Wales ended with a prediction that it would become a vital colonial outpost, at one of the 'most essential extremities' in an empire.[16] As indigenous peoples gave up their land, they were studied and collected by the likes of historian Martin. They were also simulatenously pushed out of the very structure and organisation of historical works written by men like Martin.

The next section of Martin's *History of Austral-Asia* moved to Van Diemen's Land. Once again, Aboriginal Tasmanians only entered this history after his descriptions of supposed discovery, the physical geography of the island and its various outposts and police districts, its geology, soil and climate, its vegetation and animals, and birds and fishes. Even then, Aboriginal Tasmanians were given little more than two short pages:

> The total number of the aborigines probably does not exceed 300; and in a few years (owing partly to the small number of males in proportion to females), these also will have entirely passed away.[17]

The rest of the chapter in which this commentary appeared was devoted to convicts and the free population. In Martin's *History of the British Colonies*, the account of Van Diemen's Land included this in its introduction: 'It cannot be expected that this colony would present many features of interest to the historian . . .'[18] Martin's boundless optimism about settlement, and his advocacy of empire, subsumed his interest in Aboriginal Australians and Tasmanians. He confidently omitted them from the pages of his statistical and globe-sprawling history.

The structure of his work on the history of 'Austral-Asia' is similar to that of other books in this series. His account of Mauritius also went through its discovery and colonisation, the republican tumult, and its taking by the British. Its 'physical aspect' was next, followed by its geology and climate. Of particular interest here is an interlude on the phases of the moon and their impact on the weather, taking as its departure point the report of an inspector of hospitals on the 'violent commotions in the atmosphere' in Mauritius.[19] Martin's account of the population of Mauritius noted its French-descent population, as well as the 'creoles', and he took time to include an account of the 'beauty' of French women. He then proceeded to describe 'slaves' of 'two races': from Mozambique and the east coast of Africa and from Madagascar. He presented these enslaved people as being in desperate circumstances. They were seizing boats and mounting escapes from Mauritius and elsewhere towards Madagascar or Africa. He gave a personal testimony of the situation of the enslaved and wrote of how his vessel had 'picked up a frail canoe' with 'five runaway slaves, one dying in the bottom of the canoe, and the other four nearly exhausted.' They had fled from the Seychelles.[20]

On the next page came his other interest, namely the anatomy, demography and death of indigenous peoples. There appeared a bloody account of the execution of an enslaved Malagasy person in Mauritius for arson. Martin provided the story of how this enslaved person walked with his coffin for a mile. Before dying, he prayed a Christian prayer. In Martin's account this Malagasy slave had committed the act of arson out of desperation. Martin held that this enslaved person now wished to be beheaded.[21]

Martin's observations and globe-sprawling statistical compilations and narratives show that the first makings of the history of the British empire were violent. This was an effort to scientifically chart the past and predict the future of an empire. Leaving Martin's moment for our own, despite the recent rise of new ways in which to write the history of Britain and its place in the world, there are still too many books on the British empire that universalise its story or which see the British empire as a singular entity.[22] Such galloping historical writing descends partly from the mid-nineteenth-century boom which came at the end of the age of revolutions.

Waves Across the South is intentionally not a history of the British empire told from the nerve centre of London, nor a comprehensive globe-sprawling account of it.[23] It has not been a discussion of the history of the British empire's strategised ascent, or of 'rise and fall', the usual arc in which an empire's path is surveyed. Rather it is a history of empire in the physical setting of the oceans as a surging and never complete form, not a historical event as much as a responsive and reactive process that was never fully completed. In placing empire within an age revolutions, the aim has been to show that the rise of the British empire in the Indian and Pacific Oceans was not a forgeone conclusion, despite all the retrospective flourish of writers like Martin.

We must contend with the violent evacuation of indigenous peoples from modern historical writing. *Waves Across the South* has tracked a surge of indigenous agency. This pattern of agency includes politics, forms of organisation, religion, warfare, protest, knowledge and material objects. In all these spheres and others, indigenous peoples took from invaders in as much as they resituated their own traditions, beliefs and commitments. Throughout this book the indigenous has been cast inclusively, especially as this was a period of accelerated globalisation where many people were on the move and where labourers, migrants, rebels and imperial aides led peripatetic lives. The ocean itself has been in central view. Over the fluid medium of the sea indigenous and colonised experience was mobile and changeable.

In repopulating a key label of historical periodisation, the age of revolutions, from the oceanic South and from the perspective of its islanders and coast-dwellers, the aim has been to make space for a radically different view of the origin of our times. In this view, empire was not the force that spread concepts of rights, democracy or forms of political organisation; nor indeed were these concepts born exclusively in continental heartlands or in the Atlantic world. Rather in sites which have often been marginalised and cast to the fringes of historical memory, there was sustained creativity in the late eighteenth and early nineteenth centuries.

The British neutralised this age of revolutions, an age of indigenous assertion, and co-opted concepts of liberty, free trade, reason, progress, printed expression and even projections of selfhood. The imperial counter-revolt followed the agency and rebellion of subjects.[24] The power, violence and clever manoeuvre of the British, as they combated opposition and bypassed the agency of colonised people, has been a key concern. The British placed the seas and lands of the South on a newly plotted globe, while deploying notions of race, gender and classification. War, commerce and government have been narrated here, but from the waters and also in relation to culture. They have been approached from the perspective of the colonised and rival European colonisers and in relation to connections, divergences and glances across the South.

This historical telling doesn't separate off the story of the British empire from that of its rivals. Nor does it partition it from the perspectives of its subjects or the terrain in which empire expanded. Rather the histories of other peoples, environments and objects intrude into this story as they resist, interrupt and reframe empire. In all these ways, this argument breaks the history of the British empire, which Martin cast as an entity, into a series of stories set in the waves of the South, while never underestimating empire's invasive force.[25] Within this set of decades, entanglement slowly and uncertainly gave way to detachment, segregation, depopulation, settlement and colonial technological advance. Yet again it is important to add that this wasn't total or fully complete.

Even in the middle of the nineteenth century, there was still space left open for indigenous peoples to make passages across the sea. Indeed, the imperial counter-revolt in turn saw a response from colonised peoples as cities and public spheres close to the sea expanded and as prospected political goals shifted, for instance, in the aftermath of the abolition of slavery. Just as history writing on the empire was booming, the public spheres of the colonies were coming to vibrant life.

Martin's books show that the type of information that constituted a history was remarkably diverse. This was in keeping with how English-language historical writing came from many locales as exchanges between Britain and its colonies increased in the nineteenth century.

Colonial writing, including history, was aimed at multiple audiences, from children to prospective settlers, and from those in Britain to those in the colonies. In Britain, knowledge of the wider world was growing, as a broad range of travel texts, metropolitan exhibitions and the expansion of missionary work brought far distant territories to life and into the home. Yet the width and depth of this interest in empire in the metropole is rightly a matter of vigorous debate.[26] Regardless, the relations of centre and periphery were being reorganised by publications such as the 'blue books'. There was new emphasis on efficiency and facts as set against what was identified as personal networks, luxury, corruption and jobbery in the decades just passed.[27]

Mid-nineteenth-century imperial historical writing also overlapped with another genre as Britain's heft became manifest: fiction which took colonialism as its inspiration. By the end of the nineteenth century there was a significant collection of imperial fictional works, including some for young readers. Yet the early ingredients of this genre were already there in Martin's time. The Indian and Pacific Oceans and some of the sites that have been traversed in our travels were critical. As these islands and coasts were converted into numbers, tables and facts by authors like Martin, they were also perfect subjects for stories, romance and propaganda. These were related techniques of imagining indigenous peoples.

Take, for instance, Frederick Marryat (1792–1848), who has already appeared in this book in the midst of the First Anglo-Burmese War and through his portrait of the dead Napoleon. Marryat wrote a sequence of novels which romanticised and sanctified the naval career. He cast good naval men as knights errant. In keeping with the reforming impulse of the second and third decades of the nineteenth century, such men were seen as better representatives of the British nation than the corrupt aristocracy or those in parliament. Naval chivalry was set against the allegedly debased morality of colonial subjects. Such chivalry was super-charged by the conflict between Britain and France. This popular fiction sat at the border of the factual. Marryat modelled one of his characters on himself.[28]

For young readers, Marryat published *Masterman Ready; or the Wreck of the Pacific* (1841–2). Put together in order to correct what Marryat saw as the errors of Jan Wyss' *The Swiss Family Robinson* (1812), it tells the tale of the shipwrecked family of an Australian farmer, Mr Seagrave. Seagrave's family was stranded on an island, together with their working-class sailor, Ready, and a female ex-slave Juno. Lessons in natural history pepper the story. The use of fiction to make facts digestible to readers is conspicuous. Story telling is folded together with the history of British imperial expansion and an unfailing attachment to racialised and gendered views. At one point the same phrasing that Martin used appears in a conversation between the eldest child of the stranded family, William, and his father, Mr Seagrave, about the history of empires and nations:

> '. . . the sun is said, and very truly, never to set upon the English posses-sions; for, as the world turns round to it, the sun shines either upon one portion or another of the globe which is a colony to our country.'[29]

At another point, William asks: 'What sort of people are the islanders in these seas?' Mr Seagrave answers:

> 'They are various. The New Zealanders are the most advanced in civi-lization, but still they are said to be cannibals. The natives of Van Diemen's Land and Australia are some portions of them of a very degraded class – indeed, little better than beasts of the field: I believe them to be the lowest in the scale of all of the human race.'[30]

Indigenous peoples are here compared and placed on a scale of civilisa-tions and in relation to the very category of the human. The conversation takes another turn when Ready tells of his encounter with Andaman Islanders. In his words: 'I saw them once; and, at first, thought they were animals, and not human beings.'[31] Later Ready explains how he viewed Andaman Islanders through his telescope, and how he conversed with a soldier at Calcutta who had 'caught two of them'. He discusses whether or not Andaman Islanders had arms and whether Andaman Islanders were even 'lower in the scale' than the 'New Hollanders.' William's next question was: 'Where did the people come from who inhabit these islands, papa?' There followed a series of other questions which are totally consistent with the kinds of knowledge which were central to the counter-revolution of the British empire: 'What is a typhoon, Ready?'; 'But what are monsoons, Ready?'; 'And what are the trade winds . . .?'; and 'Is it the sun which produces these winds?'[32]

Islanders only appear at the margins of this story. They are 'savages', who communicate in yells rather than words. The first two islanders to appear in the story are indigenous women who arrive in Marryat's story exhausted and without food and water, needing the help of the stranded British family. Those who follow in their wake are depicted as 'swarming like bees'.[33] Marryat visualised a horde of attackers, intent simply on plunder, who finally dispersed with the arrival of a European ship which rescues the family from the island where they are shipwrecked. Sailor Ready dies a sacrificial death as a virtuous man who knew his place and duty. The ex-slave Juno is cast as God-fearing and grieving for the loss of her parents but she is ever-courageous in her duties to the Seagrave children who are in her charge. She is thankful for her freedom. This characterisation fits with the model ex-slave whom Britons sought to imagine.

Marryat's fiction may be placed usefully next to the intellectually more serious novels of Harriet Martineau, who also wrote of the global spread of the British empire. Martineau's writing too was located in some of the very sites of the Indian and Pacific Oceans which we have travelled through. Tasmania, Sri Lanka and South Africa had a novel each in her series of stories, *Illustration of Political Economy* (1832–4). This series brought her public acclaim. However, it is important to add that she did not travel in these places. Her use of fiction indicates how her audience didn't expect women to write directly on politics or philosophy, though of course she did. For the Unitarian Martineau, the rise of the British empire is a historical turning point which is a rational stage of development which will last long. Her writing too sees an accumulation of data and facts. She relied on 'blue books' and on people with experience of the colonies.[34]

Martineau's works demonstrate a conscious attempt to work through the thinking of Adam Smith, Thomas Malthus, or David Ricardo. The ambition of the writing was evident at times where Martineau gave non-Europeans more agency than Marryat did. She showed an inclination to engage alternative ways of life, especially where she considered indigenous peoples to be more 'civilised'. As has recently been noted: 'the enslaved of Martineau's imagination are more fully imagined than those of much abolitionist literature.'[35] The writing still displays an unbounded confidence in progress and in the ability of Britons to better the conditions of all, free and unfree, and those populations deemed to be dying out as well as those which were demographically stable. Like Marryat, Martineau used forced conversations between characters in the middle of her tales to get across the points she wished to communicate. Unlike Marryat, the sailor was less in view and the settler more so.

The way these fictional works incorporated history is evident for instance in *Cinnamon and Pearls*, set in Sri Lanka, and part of *Illustrations of Political Economy*. It is a lesson in the negative impact of monopolies, presented through the island's pearl fishery and its cinnamon plantations. The novel relied on information provided by a returning judge, Alexander Johnston, and other colonial returnees from Sri Lanka. The monopolies that Martineau exposed were being abolished in Sri Lanka even as her work was being published. The narrator notes:

> If the government would give away its pearl banks to those who now fish those banks for the scantiest wages which will support life, government would soon gain more in a year from the pearls of Ceylon than it has hitherto gained by any five fisheries.[36]

This was not simply recent historic facts converted into stories, it was also a mythic history of colonial expansion in Sri Lanka. The trade's optimistic future predicted by the narrator is misplaced: the pearl fishery brought minimal returns by the 1830s. Meanwhile, a long-term history of colonisation was superimposed over the story of the pearl fishers, cinnamon peelers and planters of Sri Lanka. In centuries to come, in Martineau's vision, 'civilized' and 'uncivilized' helped each other, as parent and child:

> Let this connexion be modified by circumstances as time rolls on, the child growing up into a state fit for self-government, and the mother country granting the liberty of self-government as the fitness increases.[37]

This kind of philosophical musing was interspersed throughout *Cinnamon and Pearls*, in the story of a pearl diver, Marana and his partner, Rayo, and their dependence on their superiors. The peoples of Sri Lanka were cast as being in need of help. For the island was full of 'struggles of poverty by day, or of death by night'.[38] Though Sri Lankans were not erased from the story, nevertheless they were seen as dependants, children who needed British liberty and reason.

Elsewhere in this series of tales, the colonised could take far more marginal roles. For instance, *Life in the Wilds*, set in South Africa, sees a band of self-improving settlers face and overcome a series of trials. These trials arise from the attack of San people, or for Martineau, 'Bushmen', who destroy their settlement. Rather than playing an active role in the story, indigenous peoples serve simply as a threat to the main characters. Meanwhile, the forward-looking advance of history and the British empire relies on nature being improved. Machines are deployed and human ingenuity is realised without attention to hierarchies of class or property, but also with no engagement with the inhabitants of the land. In the pages of *Life in the Wilds*, the marginalisation of indigenous peoples and the shared bond of the settlers and their unstoppable forward march are all of a piece.

Martin, Marryat and Martineau do not of course comprise the full range of writing on the British empire in the middle of the nineteenth century. What is clear from them, however, is how history writing itself followed the manoeuvre of an age of revolutions. Indigenous agency was overtaken but not totally eradicated. Indigenous peoples were taken out of the narative and this writing described and predicted their depopulation and at times was related to the collection of remains. Different narrative techniques for silencing indigenous peoples worked in concert. On one hand, indigenous peoples could be made into stereotypical fictional characters who revealed more of British imagination and ideology than indigenous worlds. On the other hand, they were squeezed out of the recitation of facts and figures which charted the forward march of settlement and colonisation.

Attending to the mid-century boom in writing is important because the period from 1780 to 1850 is often held to be less definitive of the British empire than the 'new imperialism' which followed by the end of the nineteenth century.[39] Accordingly, in the age of 'new imperialism' from around 1860 and into the early twentieth century, there was the rapid annexation of vast territories; hardened and more scientific conceptualisations of race and gender; imperial culture which some historians assert was heavily popularised or made public in grand rites and festivals; and demographic change and migration which are cast at times as unprecedented. Yet by returning to the late eighteenth and early nineteenth centuries, it is possible to see that the foundations and techniques of modern globalisation and imperialism, and imperial history writing too, were set in an earlier uncertain age in the age of revolutions and directly afterwards.

Yet there are other ways to hear indigenous perspectives in the midst of all the rhetoric, fiction and fact-gathering in the mid century.

Turning again to Sri Lanka, it saw many colonial printed works by the middle decades of the nineteenth century, which flowed from the pens of travellers, administrators and clergymen. One of most influential texts was a two-volumed account written by James Emerson Tennent, *Ceylon: An Account of the Island, Physical, Historical and Topographical* (1859). Tennent (1804–1869) was secretary to the government of Ceylon between 1845 and 1850, prior to which he had been Member of Parliament for Belfast. Each of the volumes of Tennent's *Ceylon* ran to more than six hundred pages. These volumes bear out the eclectic types of information which were brought together in mammoth works like this authored out of experience in colonial territories.

The first volume included sections on 'Physical Geography', 'Zoology', 'The Singhalese Chronicles', 'Science and the Social Arts' and 'Medieval History', while the second volume covered 'Modern History', which led into the so-called 'British period', followed by an overview of the various regions of the island, including detailed asides on 'elephants' and 'ruined cities'. In his text, Tennent represented his intellectual compatriots as discoverers of indigenous chronicles. In bringing indigenous texts out of obscurity, they were saving these texts from hyperbole and exaggeration while creating a factually accurate history of the island. Consistent with this characterisation, Tennent himself presented his readers with a table which sought to rationalise the reigns of the 'native sovereigns of Ceylon', by date and by kingdom.

This kind of factual analysis could be placed alongside the first colonial publications of the *Mahavamsa*. The *Mahavamsa* ranges over twenty-five centuries and was put together in the sixth century, with additions in the thirteenth and eighteenth centuries.[40] It charts a line of kings through time and ends with the fall in 1815 of the last independent kingdom of the island, the kingdom of Kandy. It was a compilation of palm leaves which was transformed into paper and print by British orientalists. It is still the key historical text of today's Sinhala Buddhist nationalism in Sri Lanka. Traditionally palm-leaf texts were created by Buddhist monks on the island. The leaves of the talipot or palmyra tree were rolled and boiled and oiled so as to prepare them for use in the writing of a manuscript. The leaf was cut into long thin strips, and once the writing was complete, the leaves were punched with a hot iron rod and strung together by a cord.

The first publication claiming to be the *Mahavamsa* in the English language came out in print in 1833 under the name of Edward Upham, a retired bookseller and mayor of Exeter who had not travelled to Sri Lanka. Alexander Johnston, the judge who supplied Martineau with information, was one of Upham's sources too. Buddhist monks provided relevant materials to Johnston when he was in office in Sri Lanka. In an indicator of colonial confusion, the Upham translation was undertaken from a commentary on the text rather than the text itself. Another version soon followed, published by George Turnour (1779–1843), a civil servant in Ceylon who had learnt the Pali language. Turnour's text appeared in 1836 in English and Pali rendered into Latin script. This was hailed as the first publication in the Pali language and consisted of the first twenty chapters of the *Mahavamsa* and an extended introduction. More chapters followed the next year. An indigenous chronicle moved, in this way, from palm leaf to paper. Yet this shift did not see the death of palm-leaf historical memory.

For mid-century colonial publications on Sri Lankan could not cope with the flexibility and linguistic complexity of these indigenous chronicles: Upham's confusion about text and commentary is one indicator of this. Meanwhile, in early to mid-century Sri Lanka, colonial administrators were forced to acquaint themselves with the character of palm-leaf texts, especially given the ceremonial function of such manuscripts in governance. In new narrations in palm leaf, British governors appeared at times like the kings of the past, as their deeds were assessed according to whether they were meritorious or not. In the eyes of the colonised, how the British printed texts could be seen as akin to how kings patronised palm-leaf scholarship. The passage from palm leaf to print did not see the eradication of indigenous perspectives and responses. There was still a creative ability on the part of the colonised to respond to the aggression and violence of colonialism. [41]

And to move across the seas to the other ocean of *Waves Across the South*, the Pacific's colonial and orientalist historical writing is not dissimilar. Take the New Zealand governor George Grey's *Polynesian Mythology and Ancient Traditional History of the New Zealand Race as Furnished by their Priests and Chiefs* (1855).[42] Grey (1812–1898) was a serial colonial governor: he first served in South Australia (1841–5), then in New Zealand (1845–53 and 1861–8) and also in South Africa (1854–6). One formative early moment in Western Australia, which plagued him for the rest of his life, saw an Aboriginal Australian wound him. Grey shot and killed the Aboriginal Australian in turn.

The first section of *Polynesian Mythology* was titled 'The Children of Heaven and Earth', and subtitled in Māori, 'Ko Nga Tama A Rangi – Tradition Relating to the Origin of the Human Race'. It began:

> Men had but one pair of primate ancestors; they sprang from the vast heaven that exists above us, and from the earth which lies beneath us. According to the traditions of our race, Rangi and Papa, or Heaven and Earth, were the sources from which, in the beginning all things originated.[43]

Once again this was a long-term history which started with indigenous cosmology. When Grey arrived in New Zealand in 1845, he accumulated notes on poems and legends at every opportunity. He participated in Māori gatherings. A fire in Government House destroyed a lot of his collection.

Yet again he 'collected a large mass of materials', which he put together in 'a scattered state'; 'different portions of the same poem or legend were often collected from different natives, in very distant parts of the country.' The way in which Grey's research was done, where several versions of poems were collected at different times and compared, is evident in the finished published text of his history. Though Grey attempted to impose colonial order and European historical norms, his book is a 'cut and paste' compilation of indigenous historical knowledge. Genealogies of the Māori past lived on within this text. For Māori like other Pacific islanders had stories of arrival across the sea and descent over generations. In Aotearoa/New Zealand these are *whakapapa*. They are part of the shared culture of genealogical history across the Pacific islands. For all the power in the hands of the makers of imperial history in the mid century, the perspective of indigenous peoples did not disappear.

These islands are different; local traditions of rule, cosmology, religion and commerce and engagement with the water, lasted the rise of the

British. At the same time, a long-term vision of the British empire centred on the mother country arose. This long-term vision was mythic in naturalising the rise of Britain as a global power. It erased other histories and even collected the narrations and remains of indigenous people in order to craft its vision of itself.

There are vast realms of histories of the Indian and Pacific Oceans beyond and outside the encounter between revolution, empire and counterrevolt. These include alternative dynamics of trade, religion, migration and cultural understanding. These non-British, indigenous, Asian, Pacific and African encounters across the ocean didn't need to engage intensively with the expansion of the British empire. This means that *Waves Acrosss the South* should not be read as a comprehensive history of the Indian and Pacific Oceans even in these decades. Yet the dance of revolution, empire and counter-revolt, around the British empire and its rivals, is critical to understanding the histories of these oceans. It is also critical in coming to terms with the missed and foreclosed opportunities in this plural period of the late eighteenth and early nineteenth centuries.

To forget this story is to repress the tragedy of the birth of the modern world and its relation to imperialism in these seas. Such forgetting effaces the full violence of empire and the way empire reformulated forms of cultural exchange, consumption, exploitation and connection. The extent of this British empire, as it stretched across the global South in these years and responded to so many different traditions which it placed anew on the globe, is astounding. Its ability to move across so many environments and over such a vast geography marks it out as related but quite distinct from what came before. This means that the British empire cannot be seen simply as a continuation of a long-term and global practice of imperial power and hegemony.

In the mid nineteenth century, the impact of print was very evident, but even within this print are the legacies of indigenous perspectives and voices. The mesh of genres that made imperial history is striking: from fiction to hyper-empiricism, from local information to global overview, and one might add other genres, such as the religious and commercial, here too. These pairs were not opposites, but rather mutually reinforcing forms of recording the past and justifying the present.

In response, *Waves Across the South* isn't a history that is told as if looking down on the aqueous Earth from above. If in decades past, debates about how to tell the history of empire have centred on the relative weight of economics, politics and culture, this argument brings an environmental lens. It insists on the material and physical terrain as significant.[44] Empire and settlement moved from sea to land, in relation to the pathways of traders, or forms of scientific study and urban planning or in relation to warfare. Because of this alternative focus, a host of people who have largely been misplaced in broader accounts of the origin of the modern world are brought instead to centre stage.

It is because of the long-term legacies and present realities of indigenous agency, politics and protest, that a book such as *Waves Across the South* is possible and necessary. Islanders and ocean-goers from the Indian and Pacific Oceans are still often caricatured. This has been an attempt to make space for them and to challenge caricatured histories. A surge of indigenous assertion was part and parcel of the age of revolutions. It was followed by a counter-revolution of imperial expansion which sought to overtake and silence voices. Yet indigenous peoples continued speaking across the waters.

Afterword

THE SUN SWALLOWED BY THE WAVES

So much for words, their publication and their use to analyse the past. What about the waves? In this book, I have sought not to take the privileged view of the historian looking from on high, but to write from the small seas in the Indian and Pacific oceans.

As I write these words, I am in Port Louis in Mauritius and have just returned from swimming in the sea and watching the sun set after a day in the archives. Unlike Martin or Marryat, I didn't find myself imagining the setting sun moving to another part of the world, to illuminate another quarter and to keep day and night in predictable and never-ending imperial rhythm. The sun setting on the waters outside Port Louis, on this day at the end of the Mauritian winter in 2018, looks to me like the yolk of a fried egg. It is wondrously orange. The sun bloats and descends into the water and is swallowed in chunks by the waves out at sea. Mauritians tell me that the summers are getting hotter and hotter.

For a Sri Lankan used to big waves, swimming in the lagoon (the reef-calmed waters that stretch around a large part of Mauritius) is a surprisingly waveless experience. Today, in Port Louis' Blue Penny Museum an exhibition on mid-nineteenth-century images of multi-coloured fish is under way. These brilliantly coloured fish seemed more alive to me than this still sea, even if their American artist, Nicholas Pike, froze his fish with their mouths open.[1] In the reef, I can't see any fish. Port Louis residents say that the land is bleaching the sea and that fertiliser has entered the groundwater after centuries of heavy cultivation. Dead coral lies strewn on the beach. A young and clever Mauritian oceanographer explained to me that the public beaches, like the one I am now on, are too heavily used for coral or fish. The small number of public beaches is itself an indicator of the march of big tourist resorts on Mauritius' coastline.

Along the public beach where I've just swum, and right around
Mauritius, are dozens of characteristic pirogues, historic wooden boats
prized as a national treasure and used by local fishermen. One I've just
seen is named in big capitals: PIRATE. It makes me smile, a nice echo of
Mauritius' history which I've charted. The landscape of Mauritius shows
the afterlife of colonisation. Incredibly, about a quarter of Mauritius is still
covered in fields of sugar. The Port Louis tourist trail includes the statue
of Rémy Ollier in Jardins de la Compagnie, the garden at the centre of
the city. Along the street named after Ollier I buy my Indian sweets and
walk into Chinatown. I gaze enchanted at Jummah Mosque built at the
point in Port Louis' history where the last chapter ended.

The history of *Waves Across the South* has led into our present, and
the signs of that past are still around us. It isn't the case that globalisation and imperialism have flattened islands and ocean-facing places, or
the seas, into a universal equivalence. This is despite the dramatic political, environmental, social and cultural change enacted in sites like those
covered in this book. Mauritius' polyglot and energetic people are indicators of this. They include South Asians who speak creole at home and
are fluent in French and South Asian languages. These South Asians first
arrived in the island mostly as indentured workers and go on pilgrimage
to Grand Bassin, where gigantic Hindu statues rise out of the Mauritian
mountains. Even when indigenous people have faced tragic and fatal
circumstances, including slavery, enforced labour, warfare and decima-
tion, they have responded with ingenuity and ridden the waves. Outside
Port Louis's municipal theatre, first built in 1822, I pause next to a plaque
titled 'Universal Declaration of Human Rights': *No one has the right to
treat you as a slave nor should you make anyone a slave.* But the island's
Truth and Justice Commission's recommendations, which include the
bid for a Slave Museum to memorialise this history of the island were
halted for a long period. Meanwhile, as I write, historic buildings are
being brazenly pulled down for a metro line.

To think of the dawn of the modern age as a contest of agents and
ideologies – human and non-human, indigenous and colonial, revolutionary and counter-revolutionary – makes sense to an islander like me.
To think like this contends with the violence of modern imperialism
without letting it fill all the picture. It makes sense of the opportunities
and foreclosures, the twists and turns of power. While writing this book
I've worked across the Indian and Pacific oceans, from Tonga to Aoteaora/
New Zealand and from Burma/Myanmar to India and Singapore, from

Australia to Tasmania, from the United Arab Emirates to Sri Lanka, Mauritius and South Africa. It has been an immense privilege and also a reminder that history looks so different when read from the ground, from the streets, the beaches, local bookshops, archives and libraries, and in the context of so many conversations with brilliant historians in each of these sites. The chapters of this book have also been written on site and the writing has flowed much better when I'm here – as in Mauritius – rather than in my office at the University of Cambridge. Some of the stories in *Waves Across the South* have come as much from sniffing the ground and smelling the sea. They have also arisen from turning countless pages in archives such as that in Port Louis, set in an industrial estate, where drills and hammers or trucks unloading crates interrupt the experience of contending with the remains of the past.

But as I sit in the sand as the sun sets in Port Louis, allowing the drilling and banging to leave my head, with my feet in the ebbing sea, I start to worry again about the way the sea is changing. On another evening, I see the bright lights from the long line of ships on the dark horizon waiting to enter Port Louis harbour. One of the points of this book is that waves do not stop; revolution, empire and counter-revolt were part of a sequence of politics. Indigenous peoples continued to ride the waves despite the unprecedented onslaught of modern empire which sought to evacuate, bury and silence. But might it be that the constellation of waves, the connection and disconnection, the globalisation and imperialism, has now reached more and more interventionist and speedy concatenations in the twenty-first century?

Scientists theorise that wave heights are changing with global warming. If the sea's creatures are dying just like the land's creatures, and if human actions are having a now unstoppable impact, what will this mean for the people of the Indian and Pacific oceans? Will our distinctive seas become more alike? I think back to the flatness of Tongatapu or how Beach Road in Singapore now lies far inland. Will the tsunamis become greater than the waves across the South that I've been following? Will the pirogues, the catamarans, the dhows, and the double-rigger canoes, now need to contend with winds, waves and currents that they have never encountered before? Will the fear of being sunk in the tides of the modern, which was already evident in the period of this book and in this very language, become even greater in the years ahead? Will the scale of the infrastructural projects in the sea or of reclaiming land from the sea radically accelerate all this?

As a historian, all I can say is that there is no better time than now to reflect on the histories of oceans and ocean-goers in the origins of our world. Indeed, we may be at a point in human history where the story of ocean-facing peoples has a particular role to play. Now or never we should think on how modernity has impacted on small societies and sea-facing places while the clock ticks for what can still be done to turn around the environmental impact of globalisation and imperialism. We might draw inspiration from how such societies faced the turn of the eighteenth and nineteenth centuries and used the age of revolutions despite the dramatic imperialism that they lived amidst.

Given that 70 per cent of the Earth is covered in water, we are all islanders. We will all soon be islanders if the seas rise. To reflect on what happened at the birth of our age at the bridge of sea and land is then to think in mirror-image about the challenges that face all of us now. It is also to engage with history in a humane way, reflecting the density and diversity of the human past. It is more humane because it is isn't a view of the universally common story of the world's past. Nor is it a globe-spanning equation such as those written by the first historians of the places and times charted above. And it doesn't cast humans as being separate from their environments.

This book is a history of particular places in the context of the world and seas around them. We need to guard this diversity of indigenous perspectives going forward, a diversity which is consistent with how waves and land have interacted, a diversity which is consistent with our Earth and with how people have responded to structural and material changes in the places they live. A commitment to such a history is consistent with the urgent need to protect the ecological niches of the World Ocean and all that might be at peril in the twenty-first century. Only then will it be possible to appreciate the sun going down on the waves, outside empire, globalisation and their effects.

Acknowledgements

I am immensely grateful to have had the privilege and opportunity to work through what it means to write history across such a range of sites in the global South. As I finish what has been a project which has lasted many years, the many interlocutors, friends, colleagues and advisers who have helped me to get my thinking straight and also provided essential encouragement come to mind. If one speaks to a Tongan philosopher about the past; if one engages with the memory of enslavement and indenture in conversations with Mauritian scholars in the island; if one writes about the monsoon in the midst of torrential storms in Singapore and in the midst of the country's triumphal celebrations of the fiftieth anniversary of independence; and, if one goes on a long walk on the Tasmanian shore to think about why histories of convicts and indigenous peoples are so hard to reconcile, it is unlikely that one will ever be the same historian. Writing this book has been a learning experience for me and I hope it will be the same for readers of *Waves Across the South*.

In practical terms, the book would never have come to be without the funding provided by the Leverhulme Trust. The Trust honoured me with a Philip Leverhulme Prize in 2012. This prize gave me the ambition to build on a commitment to tiny, and often forgotten, sites as revealing places from which to consider the transformative moments of world history. It also made me widen out a methodology that is attentive to the local, the particular and the indigenous as they meet the imperial. The prize made me consider how to tell the history of the late eighteenth and early nineteenth centuries from the perspective of the Indian and Pacific Oceans, and for a public audience.

The National Maritime Museum awarded me a Sackler Caird Fellowship, which once again gave me precious time away from teaching to use the museum's collections and also to travel overseas for archival work. The Faculty of History at the University of Cambridge supported me by approving research leave. The Cambridge Humanities Research Scheme was generous in allowing me funding to complete this book. Further afield, I benefitted greatly from being based at the University of Sydney's Centre for the Foundations of Science and also at the National University of Singapore's Asia Research Institute. The research was also aided by a visiting professorship which I held in Paris at the invitation of Ines Županov, who was a host par excellence at the EHESS. I thank Ines for her very memorable Parisian hospitality.

The book would not have come to be without my colleagues in Cambridge who discussed it with me over lunches and dinners. I thank all the members of the World History Subject Group. Early drafts of some parts of this book were powerfully directed by discussions over drinks next to the Cam with the late Christopher Bayly. I was writing on Java in Cambridge's University Library when I heard the very sad news of his demise. More recently the book has benefitted from conversations with Alison Bashford and Saul Dubow; and it has also benefitted from the work of Megan Vaughan. Additionally, I am grateful to Andrew Arsan for taking time to read and comment on the chapter on the Persian Gulf; John Slight also made helpful comments on this chapter. Over the years, other members of the World History Subject Group contributed in other ways and I should particularly note: Bronwen Everill, Tim Harper, Shruti Kapila, Gabriela Ramos, Gareth Austin, Samita Sen, Ruth Watson, Rachel Leow, Hank Gonzalez, Christina Skott, Jeppe Mulich, Joya Chatterji, David Maxwell, Helen Pfeifer, Arthur Asseraf, Simon Layton and Leigh Denault.

At my college, Gonville and Caius, I am so very fortunate to have excellent history colleagues who have created a vibrant community of students, researchers and teachers. Peter Mandler was a fantastic reader of this manuscript and I deeply appreciated the time he spent with an earlier version of the book. Lunches with Melissa Calaresu have been enriching and intellectually engaging in so many ways. Vic Gatrell was there for me at a critical moment and told me what I needed to hear. Annabel Brett and Richard Staley asked me good questions. At one moment the research benefitted from a collection of oceanic projects in a day entitled, 'Caius At Sea', including the work of Naor Ben-Yehoyada, Cyprian Broodbank and David Abulafia. Successive generations of history research fellows at the college have provided suggestions.

But even more than my colleagues, I must admit that the book has been shaped by the work of my students, who have been with me through this journey from the start to the finish. The Cambridge undergraduate students who have taken my final-year paper on the Indian and Pacific Oceans have been outstanding and I have enjoyed their essays and class discussions. There has been no greater joy in my academic life over the last ten years than to see the work of my doctoral students come to fruition. I thank all of my doctoral students for their close friendship, their intellectual energy and for keeping me on track. I owe an especial debt to James Wilson, who helped me for a period of weeks as a research assistant after the completion of his PhD; I have especially valued his digital skills. I also thank Jake Richards who did a short period of work for this project before he started his PhD. James de Montille was adviser on all things connected to Mauritius. He sparked my interest in Mauritius through his undergraduate thesis and MPhil thesis. Alix Chartrand did a few hours of work on a batch of sources. Additionally, I thank Scott Connors, Tamara Fernando, Lachlan Fleetwood, Taushif Kara, Jagjeet Lally, Steph Mawson, Tom Simpson, Hatice Yıldız and other members of the graduate reading group that meets in my room at Caius. In the last two years, I have taken up the role of Director of the Centre of South Asian Studies and my life has been immeasurably brightened by the community on the third floor of the Alison Richard Building and the three pillars of the Centre: Barbara Roe, Rachel Rowe and Kevin Greenbank. Their devotion to scholars and students and to fairness is remarkable.

The hospitality and intellectual generosity of scholars in many places across the Indian and Pacific oceans has been critical to what has resulted. In Australia, Bronwen Douglas has been a wonderful friend and has read the latest draft amidst bushfires and has provided incredibly detailed notes. She kept me well entertained in Canberra while I was working in the National Library of Australia. In Sydney, Kristen McKenzie, Warwick Anderson, Mike McDonnell, Kate Fullagar, Robert Aldrich and Hans Pols were engaging fellow travellers. In Aotearoa/ New Zealand, Tony Ballantyne was a wonderful host and I enjoyed conversations with John Stenhouse, Michael Stevens, Angela Wanhalla and Lachy Paterson. Francis Steele's recent work has helped this project. In Auckland, Tony Smith broke up the rhythm of archival work by taking me to dinner. In Brisbane, I was delighted to give a lecture from research afoot for the book at the David Nichol Smith Seminar; Peter Denney and Lisa O'Connell were brilliant hosts and interlocutors. One place that mattered greatly for the writing was Tonga. I had some especially memorable conversations with 'Okusitino Mahina [Hufanga], among many other Tongans at various sites I visited while I was writing and researching.

In South Africa, Isobel Hofmeyr took time out of her busy schedule to spend a day with me and Dilip Menon and Keith Breckenridge hosted me at their homes and at WISER. Vivian Bickford-Smith kept me much amused in Cape Town while I was doing archival work; Nigel Worden has been an absolutely generous reader of the manuscript in recent weeks. In Mauritius, once again I felt very lucky to have a conversation with Vijaya Teelock and to be driven around the island with historical commentary by Marie-Hélène Oliver. In Singapore, while I was based at the Asia Research Institute, I enjoyed intellectual exchanges with Prasenjit Duara, Arun Bala, Gregory Clancey and scholars who were passing through. In India I punctuated archival work with conferences including a memorable meeting in Delhi which I had the pleasure of co-hosting with the always inspiring Simon Schaffer. Rohan Deb-Roy, Charu Singh and Devyani Gupta were hosts of this meeting too. Another very memorable occasion on which I presented an early account of this project was at the conference in honour of Chris Bayly convened by Shruti Kapila and Faisal Devji in Varanasi. Around that event, I benefitted from conversations with Ruth Harris, Susan Bayly, Robert Travers, Richard Drayton and Seema Alavi among others. Ruth's husband Iain Pears was incredibly generous in reading an earlier draft of the introduction of this book. Sadiah Qureshi, a long-term friend and historian, also did the same and provided astute commentary.

Before I travelled to Burma/Myanmar, Mike Charney was incredibly generous in providing detailed advice on research and contacts in the country. I especially appreciated the advice and introductions of Yangon University's former librarian, Professor U Thaw Kaung, and in Mandalay, it was a pleasure to meet various intellectuals. In the Gulf, I thank Lauren Minsky for wonderful hospitality. In Europe, I am so pleased to enjoy common cause with Martin Dusinberre, an excellent scholar of Japan. Roland Wenzelhuemer has been generous with his invitations and kept me abreast of the latest developments in the writing of global history in Germany. Joan-Pau Rubiés, a long-term friend and scholar, hosted me at Universitat Pompeu Fabra in Barcelona to share aspects of this book. Ricardo Roque did the same at Instituto de Ciências Sociais in Lisbon. Isabel Corrêa da Silva and Annarita Gori have continued to engage with the project after my visit to Lisbon. Marek Tamm at Tallinn University in Estonia invited me to give a keynote on aspects of this book at a conference on global cultural history; he was a most engaging host. I also benefitted from a couple of visits to the EUI in Florence and from meetings of the European network of global historians (ENUIGH).

Work in progress for this book was presented in many universities in the UK, from the University of Exeter to St Andrews University. I especially appreciated the opportunity to use material from this book as the basis of the University of Edinburgh's annual Fennell Lecture and thank Emma Hunter in particular for being a long-standing interlocutor. It was an absolute honour to give the Royal Historical Society's Prothero Lecture during Margot Finn's presidency of the Society. Margot has also read and commented on a chapter.

This book appears in the year of my former doctoral supervisor's retirement. The example of scholarship and writing that Jim Secord has set for me is hard to match as is his deep humanity and creativity. It would be totally amiss not to mention the community of Sri Lankan historians who have journeyed with me through my research career. The friendship of Nira Wickramasinghe, Alicia Schrikker, Zoltán Biedermann, Mark Frost, John Rogers, Farzana Haniffa, Sandagomi Coperahewa and others mattered for this project. I have also much appreciated engagements on some materials in this book with Sunil Amrith, Clare Anderson, David Armitage, Lauren Benton, Chris Clark, Lizzie Collingham, Douglas Hamilton, Maurizio Isabella, Renaud Morieux, John McAleer, Anne Secord and Jonathan Saha. In the USA, I particularly appreciated speaking on my work in Los Angeles at the invitation of Ravi Gunewardena and LACMA at a special moment for the study of island Sri Lanka.

Andrew Gordon has been the perfect literary agent: attentive and committed to the things that matter most. Arabella Pike championed this book from the moment she heard me speak on it. At William Collins, a whole team of people have worked carefully and energetically on various aspects of the book. I particularly appreciated the way they have listened to my views and fully engaged with them. Jo Thompson, Katy Archer, Eve Hutchings, Anthony Hippisley and Luke Brown have done the book a huge service. Elsewhere, librarians and archivists have fetched materials, answered queries and dealt with me patiently in collections from Hobart to Port Louis and from Singapore to Paris. I hope that they are pleased at the appearance of the treasures that they curate in the pages of *Waves Across the South*.

This book is dedicated to my parents Ramola and Siva for being with me at every turn. They have listened to tales of the strange world of academia without ever being bored. Rather, they have provided steadfast love and assurance to me. The wider family of Samarasinhes and Rendles have provided welcome rest. Toby Tarun, Anjali Alice and Maya Mae have travelled the world for this book and it is wonderful to see them emerge as responsible human beings. Caroline has been a constant anchor who has kept me on the right path with her love and care and ensured that I do not get lost in the late eighteenth and early nineteenth centuries. I would not have been able to write this book, nor to be so bold, without her.

Sujit Sivasundaram
Gonville and Caius College, Cambridge
1 March 2020

References

INTRODUCTION

1 For introductions to the histories of the Indian and Pacific oceans, see Edward Alpers, *The Indian Ocean in World History* (Oxford: Oxford University Press, 2014) and Nicholas Thomas, *Islanders: The Pacific in the Age of Empire* (New Haven and London: Yale University Press, 2010). For recent historical writing which has focussed on oceans, see David Armitage, Alison Bashford and Sujit Sivasundaram, eds, *Oceanic Histories* (Cambridge: Cambridge University Press, 2018). For an excellent account of a small sea as constituting the centre of world history, see Sunil Amrith, *Crossing the Bay of Bengal: The Furies of Nature and the Fortunes of Migrants* (Harvard: Harvard University Press, 2015).

2 For a classic but now dated work on this era, see E. J. Hobsbawm, *The Age of Revolution, 1789-1848* (New York: Mentor Books, 1962); for the need to widen the compass and geography of this period, see David Armitage and Sanjay Subrahmanyam, eds, *The Age of Revolutions in Global Context, c.1760-1840* (Basingstoke, 2010) and also Alan Forrest and Matthias Middell, eds, *The Routledge Companion to the French Revolution in World History* (London and New York: Routledge, 2016).

3 R. R. Palmer, 'The Age of the Democratic Revolution', in L. P. Curtis, ed., *The Historian's Workshop: Original Essays by Sixteen Historians* (New York: Knopf, 1970), 170.

4 For critical commentary on the shape of the field of the Atlantic age of revolutions, see Sarah Knott, 'Narrating the Age of Revolution', in *The William and Mary Quarterly* vol. 73 (2016), 3–36. For an important work that has influenced this book: Peter Linebaugh and Marcus Rediker, *The Many-Headed Hydra: Sailors, Slaves, Commoners, and the Hidden History of the Revolutionary Atlantic* (London, New York: Verson, 2000). For some work on the Atlantic age of revolutions, see Nathan Perl-Rosenthal, *Citizen Sailors: Becoming American in the Age of Revolution* (Cambridge, Mass.: The Belknap Press of Harvard University Press, 2015); Gabrielle Paquette, *Imperial Portugal in the Age of Atlantic Revolutions: The Luso-Brazilian*

World, c. 1770–1850 (Cambridge: Cambridge University Press, 2013) and Paul E. Lovejoy, *Jihad in West Africa During the Age of Revolutions* (Athens, Ohio: Ohio University Press, 2016); and on Europe, see Janet Polasky, *Revolutionaries without Borders: The Call to Liberty in the Atlantic World* (New Haven: Yale University Press, 2015).

5 The late eighteenth and early nineteenth centuries are often misplaced in galloping histories of the British empire. The last critical work of scholarship to interrogate this period as a whole is C. A. Bayly, *Imperial Meridian: The British Empire and the World, 1780-1830* (Harlow: Longman, 1989). For an account linking the Atlantic and India in the mid to late eighteenth century, see P. J. Marshall, *The Making and Unmaking of Empires: Britain, India, and America, c.1750-1783* (Oxford: Oxford University Press, 2005).

6 For a recent attempt to place indigenous peoples at the forefront of the age of revolutions, see Kate Fullagar and Michael A. McDonnell, eds, *Facing Empire: Indigenous Experiences in a Revolutionary Age* (Baltimore: Johns Hopkins University Press, 2018). For recent histories of exchange across the Indian Ocean, see, for instance, Tim Harper and Sunil Amrith, eds, *Sites of Asian Interaction: Ideas, Networks and Mobility* (Cambridge: Cambridge University Press, 2014); Engseng Ho, *The Graves of Tarim: Genealogy and Mobility Across the Indian Ocean* (Berkeley: University of California Press, 2006).

7 For this era as a period of unprecedented naval war, see Jeremy Black, 'Naval Power in the Revolutionary Era', in Roger Chickering and Stig Forster, eds, *War in an Age of Revolution, 1175-1815* (Cambridge: Cambridge University Press, 2010), 219–42.

8 For some work on race and gender in oceanic contexts, see Bronwen Douglas, *Science, Voyages and Encounters in Oceania, 1511-1850* (Basingstoke: Palgrave Macmillan, 2014); Barbara Watson Andaya, 'Oceans Unbounded: Transversing Asia across "area studies"', *Journal of Asian Studies* 65, no. 4 (November 2006), 669–90; and Margaret S. Creighton and Lisa Norling, eds, *Iron Men, Wooden Women: Gender and Seafaring in the Atlantic World, 1700-1920* (Baltimore: Johns Hopkins University Press, 1996).

9 This is the argument for instance of Bayly, *Imperial Meridian*.

10 For more on this, see Sujit Sivasundaram, 'Towards a Critical History of Connection: The Port of Colombo, the Geographical "Circuit" and the Visual Politics of New Imperialism, ca. 1880-1914' in *Comparative Studies in Society and History* 59, no. 2 (April 2017): 346–84.

11 For global science, see Sujit Sivasundaram, 'Sciences and the Global: On Methods, Questions, and Theory', *Isis* 101, no. 1 (March 2010): 146–58.

12 Robert Melville Grindlay, *Scenery, Costumes, and Architecture, chiefly on the Western Side of India* (London: Smith, Elder & Co., 1828).

13 For some entry points into the histories of long-distance Pacific navigation,

see D. Lewis, *We, the Navigators: The Ancient Art of Landfinding in the Pacific* (Canberra: ANU Press, 1972) and Damon Salesa, 'The Pacific in Indigenous Time', in David Armitage and Alison Bashford, eds, *Pacific Histories: Ocean, Land, People* (Basingstoke: Palgrave Macmillan, 2014), 31–52.

14 Matthew Spriggs, 'Oceanic Connections in Deep Time', *PacifiCurrents: EJournal of Australian Association for the Advancement of Pacific Studies*, vol. 1 (2009), 7–27; citation, 14.

15 For further information and bibliography for this account of the long history of the Indian Ocean, see, Sujit Sivasundaram, 'The Indian Ocean', in Armitage et al., eds, *Oceanic Histories*.

16 For an account of Tuki and Huru's time on Norfolk Island, see Anne Salmond, 'Kidnapped: Tuki and Huri's Involuntary Visit to Norfolk Island in 1793', in Robin Fisher and Hugh Johnson, eds, *From Maps to Metaphors: The Pacific World of George Vancouver* (Vancouver: UBC Press, 1993), 191–226; see also R. R. D. Milligan, *The Map Drawn by the Chief Tuki-Tahua in 1793* (Typescript, Mangonui, 1964).

17 Cited in Salmond, 'Kidnapped', 215.

18 See Alison Jones and Kuni Jenkins, eds, *He Kōrero: Words Between Us, First Māori-Pākehā Conversations on Paper* (Wellington: Huaia, 2011), 29.

19 See Philip Lionel Barton, 'Māori Cartography and the European Encounter', in David Woodward and G. Malcolm Lewis, eds, *Cartography in the Traditional African, American, Arctic, Australian and Pacific Societies*, in *History of Cartography*, 3 vols (Chicago: Chicago University Press, 1998), vol. 2, book 3, 493–533.

20 Tony Ballantyne, *Entanglements of Empire: Missionaries, Māori, and the Question of the Body* (Durham, NC: Duke University Press, 2014), 43–4.

21 For some further information on Bugis maps, see Frederic Durand and Richard Curtis, *Maps of Malaya and Borneo* (Singapore: Editions Didier Millet, 2013), 59 and Joseph E. Schwartzberg, 'Southeast Asian Nautical Maps', in J. B. Harley and David Woodward, eds, *The History of Cartography: Cartography in the Traditional East and Southeast Asian Societies*, 3 vols (Chicago: University of Chicago Press, 1994), vol. 2, book 2, 828–838.

22 M. Storms et al., eds, *Mapping Asia: Cartographic Encounters Between East and West: Regional Symposium of the ICA Commission on the History of Cartography* (Cham, 2017), 50–1.

23 Gene Ammarell, *Bugis Navigation* (New Haven, Conn.: Yale University, Southeast Asian Studies, 1999), 117. What follows also draws on Gene Ammarell, 'Astronomy in the Indo-Malay Archipelago', in Helanie Selin, ed., *Encyclopedia of the History of Science, Technology, and Medicine in Non-Western Cultures* (Springer: New York, 2008), 2nd edn, 324–333.

24 Ammarell, *Bugis Navigation*, 2.

25 Ibid., 149.

26 See Peter Carey, *The Power of Prophecy: Prince Dipanagara and the End of an Old Order in Java, 1785-1855* (Leiden: KITLV Press, 2007), 333. For more on the Bugis and their history, see Christian Pelras, *The Bugis* (Oxford: Blackwell, 1996) and James Francis Warren, *The Sulu Zone, 1768-1898: The Dynamics of External Trade, Slavery, and Ethnicity in the Transformation of a Southeast Asian Maritime State* (Singapore: NUS Press, 2007), 2nd edn.

27 See Mark Frost and Yu-Mei Balasingamchow, *Singapore: A Biography* (Singapore: National Museum of Singapore, 2009), 87–8.

28 For a striking example of such intellectual exchange, see L. Eckstein and Anja Schwarz, 'The Making of Tupria's Map. A Story of the Extent and Mastery of Polynesian Navigation, Computing Systems of Wayfinding on James Cook's *Endeavour*, and the Invention of an Ingenious Cartographic System' in Journal of Pacific History 54, no. 4, 629-61.

29 Schwartzberg, 'Southeast Asian Nautical Maps', 834.

1 TRAVELS IN THE OCEANIC SOUTH

1 George Bayly, 'Journal on the *St. Patrick*, 8 October 1825 to 31 August 1831', reproduced in Pamela Statham and Rica Erickson, eds, *A Life on the Ocean Wave: The Journals of Captain George Bayly* (Melbourne: The Miegunyah Press, 1998), 79.

2 The biographical details of Dillon's life that follow, if not otherwise noted, arise from: J. W. Davidson, *Peter Dillon of Vanikoro: Chevalier of the South Seas*, ed. O. H. K. Spate (Melbourne: Oxford University Press, 1975), 13 and J. W. Davidson, 'Peter Dillon: The voyages of the *Calder* and *St. Patrick*', in J. W. Davidson and Deryck Scarr, eds, *Pacific Islands Portraits* (Canberra: Australian National University, 1970), 9–30. Davidson notes how Dillon used the narratives of past explorers as pilot books, see 'Peter Dillon', 11; for the name of his son, see 12.

3 Davidson, *Peter Dillon*, 13.

4 Ibid., 16–17.

5 Davidson, 'Peter Dillon', 11.

6 For the private traders of the Indian Ocean, see Anne Bulley, *The Bombay Country Ships, 1790-1833* (Richmond: Curzon Press, 2000). For whalers of the southern ocean, see Lynette Russell, *Roving Mariners: Australian Aboriginal Whalers and Sealers in the Southern Oceans, 1780-1870* (Albany, New York: State University of New York Press, 2012).

7 Davidson, 'Peter Dillon', 29–30.

8 George Bayly, *Sea life Sixty Years Ago: A Record of Adventures which Led to the Discovery of the Relics of the Long-Missing Expedition Commanded by the Comte de la Perouse* (London: K. Paul, Trench & co., 1885), 91.

9 Davidson, *Peter Dillon*, 98–9 for this and other citations in this para.
10 Bayly, *Sea life*, 73.
11 Ibid., 110 notes that these sailors numbered sixteen.
12 Bayly, *Sea life*, 82.
13 Ibid., 108.
14 Davidson, *Peter Dillon*, 95.
15 Ibid., 95.
16 Ibid., 96.
17 Bayly, 'Journal on the *St. Patrick*', 48.
18 Peter Dillon, *Narrative and Successful Result of a Voyage in the South Seas: Performed by the Order of the Government of British India, to Ascertain the Actual Fate of La Pérouse's expedition*, 2 vols (London: Hurst, Chance & co. 1829), vol. 1, 102.
19 Davidson, 'Peter Dillon', 25.
20 Bayly, 'Journal on the *St. Patrick*', 79.
21 Bayly, *Sea life*, 51.
22 This mixture is in keeping with what has been called the 'many-headed hydra' of the Atlantic, see Peter Linebaugh and Marcus Rediker, *The Many-Headed Hydra: Sailors, Slaves, Commoners, and the Hidden History of the Revolutionary Atlantic* (Boston: Beacon Press, 2000).
23 Letter dated 19 September 1826 from Peter Dillon to Chief Secretary Lushington, IOR/F/4/ 961, British Library (hereafter BL).
24 Letter dated 19 September 1826.
25 Peter Dillon, *Narrative*, vol. 1, 21.
26 For this claim see, Gananath Obeyesekere, *Cannibal Talk: The Man-Eating Myth and Human Sacrifice in the South Seas* (Berkeley, Calif.: University of California Press, 2005), 192–222.
27 Bayly, 'Journal on the *St. Patrick*', 65.
28 Letter dated 19 September 1826.
29 Bayly, 'Journal of the *St. Patrick*', 65. See also, Peter Dillon, *Narrative*, vol. 1, 32.
30 *Bengal Hurkaru*, 26 September 1826.
31 Bayly, 'Journal on the *St. Patrick*', 65.
32 Letter dated 19 September 1826.
33 Bayly, 'Journal on the *St. Patrick*', 66. See also, Dillon, *Narrative*, vol. 1, 39–40.
34 Letter dated 19 September 1826.
35 Letter dated 4 November 1826, from the Secretary of the Asiatic Society, IOR/F/4/ 961, BL.
36 *Bengal Hurkaru*, 5 September 1826.
37 *India Gazette*, 14 September 1826, for how Brian wore the medal of George IV around his neck.

38 Bayly, *Sea life*, 122.

39 *Bengal Hurkaru*, 11 September 1826, for all information in this paragraph.

40 For the other account, see the *India Gazette*, 14 September 1826.

41 *India Gazette*, 4 September 1826.

42 For the resettlement of New South Wales convicts in Calcutta, see Clare Anderson, 'Multiple Border Crossings: Convicts and Other Persons Escaped from Botany Bay and Residing in Calcutta', *Journal of Australian Colonial History* 3, no. 2 (October 2001), 1–22; Brian and Morgan's journey is in keeping with the spike in the global dispersal of Māori in the first three decades of the nineteenth century. See Vincent O'Malley, *Haerenga: Early Māori Journeys Across the Globe* (Wellington: Bridget Williams Books, 2015).

43 Davidson, 'Peter Dillon', 20.

44 Ibid., 24.

45 Ibid., 23.

46 Bayly, 'Journal on the *St. Patrick*', 59.

47 Ibid., 56.

48 Ibid., 62.

49 Bayly, *Sea Life*, 120–1.

50 Ibid., 126 and 143.

51 *India Gazette*, 14 September 1826.

52 *Bengal Hurkaru*, 12 September 1826.

53 Peter Dillon, *Extract of a Letter from the Chevalier Dillon, to an Influential Character Here on the Advantages to be Derived from the Establishment of Well Conducted Commercial Settlements in New Zealand* (London: Nichols & Sons, 1832).

54 H.V. Bowen, 'Britain in the Indian Ocean region and beyond: Contours, Connections, and the Creation of a Global Maritime Empire', in H. V. Bowen, Elizabeth Mancke and John G. Reid, eds, *Britain's Oceanic Empire: Atlantic and Indian Ocean Worlds, c.1550-1850* (Cambridge: Cambridge University Press, 2012), 45–65, at 52.

55 Bayly, 'Journal on the *Calder*', 42, 46.

56 Ibid., 51, 54, 56, 62.

57 Ibid., 73.

58 Bayly, 'Journal on the *Hooghly*', 3 November 1826 to 5 April 1827', in Statham and Erickson, eds, *A Life on the Ocean Wave*, 81–3

59 Bayly, 'Journal on the *Hooghly*', 83–5.

60 Ibid., 83.

61 C. A. Bayly, 'The first age of global imperialism c.1760-1830', *Journal of Imperial and Commonwealth History* 26 (1998), 28–47, see 37.

62 Letter dated 23 November 1826 from E. Molony, Acting Secretary of Government to the Secretary to the Right Honble Governor in Council, IOR/F/4/961, BL and letter dated 30 November 1826 from Governor General in Council to Captain Cordier, Chief of the French Establishments in Bengal, IOR/F/4/961, BL.

63 *Hobart Town Gazette,* 7 April 1827.

64 Letter dated 7 December 1826 from G. Chester of the Marine Board to the President in Council, IOR/F/4/961, BL.

65 From the Marine Board to Capitan Dillon Commanding the Honble Ship Research, December 1826, IOR/F/961, BL.

66 Letter dated 29 November 1826 from G. Chester, Marine Board to the Vice President in Council; and Letter dated 30 November 1826 from Acting Secreatry Molony to Dr. Tytler M.D., IOR/F/4/961, BL.

67 For more details on this see the voluminous materials on this trial in IOR/F/4/961, BL.

68 *Colonial Times and Tasmanian Advertiser,* 13 April 1827. For more on engagements with Vanikorans, see B. Douglas, *Science, Voyages and Encounters,* chapter 5.

69 For a long-term genealogy of this travel writing, see Muzaffar Alam and Sanjay Subrahmanyam, *Indo-Persian Travels in the Age of Discoveries, 1400-1800* (Cambridge: Cambridge University Press, 2007). For a recent exploration of the legacy of this genre of Persianate writing in the late modern period, see Robert Micallef and Sunil Sharma, eds, *On the Wonders of Land and Sea: Persianate Travel Writing* (Cambridge, Mass.: Ilex Foundation, 2013).

70 For Abu Talib Khan's biographical details here and below, see Gulfishan Khan, *Indian Muslim Perceptions of the West During the Eighteenth Century* (Karachi: Oxford University Press, 1998), 95ff. and also, Mushirul Hasan, ed. *Westerward Bound: Travels of Mirza Abu Taleb,* trans. Charles Stewart, ed. M. Hasan (New Delhi: Oxford University Press, 2005), Editor's introduction, citation xvii.

71 Abu Talib Khan, *The Travels of Mirza Abu Taleb Khan in Asia, Africa, and Europe,* trans. Charles Stewart, 3 vols (London: Longman, Hurst, Rees, Orme, and Brown, 1814), vol. 1, 2nd edn, 20–22.

72 Alam and Subrahmanyam, *Indo-Persian Travels,* 245.

73 M. Hasan, Editor's Introduction, xiv.

74 Khan, *The Travels of Mirza Abu Taleb Khan,* vol. 1, 53–4.

75 Ibid., 55.

76 Ibid., 48.

77 Ibid., 87, 96.

78 Ibid., 31.

79 Ibid., 109.

80 Ibid., 80, 83–4.

81 Ibid., 99.

82 Ibid., 40–2. For a recent account of Persian travel writing with respect to Burma, by another author who was an acquaintance of Abu Talib, see, Arash Khazeni, 'Indo-Persian Travel Writing at the Ends of the Mughal World', in *Past and Present,* 243 (2019), 141–74.

83 See for instance Aaron Jaffer, *Lascars and Indian Ocean Seafaring,*

1760-1860: Shipboard Life, Unrest and Mutiny (Martlesham: Boydell Press, 2015).

84 Mirza Abu Taleb Khan, 'Vindication of the Liberties of the Asiatic Women', in *Asiatic Annual Register*, 1801, 101–7.

85 Khan, 'Vindication', 101; all citations below, 101–7.

86 For more on Abu Talib's views of Britain, see Partha Chatterjee, *The Black Hole of Empire: History of a Global Practice of Power* (Princeton: Princeton University Press, 2012), 120–3.

87 Khan, *The Travels of Mirza Abu Taleb Khan*, vol. 1, 74.

88 Khan, *The Travels of Mirza Abu Taleb Khan*, vol. 2, chapter XVII; citation 104 and 129, 178.

89 Khan, *The Travels of Mirza Abu Taleb Khan*, vol. 2, 81.

90 Ibid., vol. 1, 23–6

91 Ibid., vol., 51, 69–70.

92 Khan, *The Travels of Mirza Abu Taleb Khan*, vol. 3, 172. Citation above from 166 and 176.

93 Kumkum Chatterjee, 'History as Self-Presentation: The Recasting of a Political Tradition in Late-Eighteenth Century Eastern India', in *Modern Asian Studies* 32, no. 4 (October 1998), 913–48, at 924. For context on these writers see: Jamal Malik, ed., *Perspectives of Mutual Encounters in South Asian History, 1760-1860* (Leiden: Brill, 2000) and also the forthcoming work of Robert Travers.

94 For Ghulam Husain's biography, see Iqbal Ghani Khan, 'A Book with Two Views: Ghulam Husain Khan's "An Overview of the Modern Times"' in Jamal Malik, ed., *Perspectives of Mutual Encounters in South Asian History, 1760-1860* (Leiden: Brill, 2000), 278–97; see also Gulfishan Khan, *Indian Muslim Perceptions of the West During the Eighteenth Century* (Karachi: Oxford University Press, 1998), 84ff. and Robert Travers, 'The connected worlds of Haji Mustapha (c.1730-91): A European Cosmopolitan in eighteenth-century Bengal', *Indian Economic and Social History Review* 52, no. 3 (2015), 297–333.

95 Ghulam Husain Khan Tabatabai, *A translation of the Seir mutaqharin or, View of modern times, being an history of India, from the year 1118 to year 1194*, trans. Haji Mustafa, 3 vols (Calcutta, 1789), vol. 3, 335.

96 For I'tisam al-Din's biography, see Khan, *Indian Muslim Perceptions*, 72ff.

97 Tabatabai, *A translation*, vol. 3, 337.

98 Ibid., 333.

99 Mirza Sheikh I'tesamuddin, *The Wonders of Vilayet: Being the Memoir, originally in Persian, of a Visit to France and Britain in 1765*, trans. Kaiser Haq (Leeds: Peepal Tree Press, 2002), 22.

100 I'tesamuddin, *The Wonders of Vilayet*, 27.

101 Ibid., 28.

102 Ibid., 28, 31–2.

103 Ibid., 34.

104 Ibid., chapter 3 for commentary on Mauritius and for citations in next paragraph too.

105 Ibid., 41–2.

106 Ibid., 47–9.

107 For more on this, see David Armitage, *The Declaration of Independence: A Global History* (Cambridge, Mass., 2007).

108 Cited in Armitage, *The Declaration*, 121.

109 For the history of science in the global age of revolutions, see P. Manning and D. Roods, eds., *Global Scientific Practice in an Age of Revolutions, 1750-1850* (Pittsburgh: University of Pittsburgh Press, 2016).

110 This follows the aim of my previous work, *Islanded: Britain, Sri Lanka and the Bounds of an Indian Ocean Colony* (Chicago: University of Chicago Press, 2013).

111 For the conceptual history of revolution, see Tim Harris, 'Did the English Have a Script for Revolution in the Seventeenth Century?', in Keith Baker and Dan Edelstein, eds, *Scripting Revolution: A Historical Approach to the Study of Revolutions* (Stanford: Stanford University Press, 2015), 25–40; David R. Como, 'God's Revolutions: England, Europe, and the Concept of Revolution in the Mid-Seventeenth Century', in Baker and Edelstein, eds, *Scripting Revolution*, 41–56. And for a more classic account, see Hannah Arendt, *On Revolution* (Harmondsworth, 1963).

112 On empire within the age of revolutions, see Jeremy Adelman, 'An Age of Imperial Revolutions', *American Historical Review* 113, no. 2 (April 2008), 319–40.

2 IN THE SOUTH PACIFIC:
TRAVELLERS, MONARCHS AND EMPIRES

1 For details of the stand-off outside Surabaya, see John Dunmore, *French Explorers in the Pacific*, 2 vols (Oxford: Clarendon Press, 1959–65), vol. 1, 328–31; Frank Horner, *Looking for La Pérouse: D'Entrecasteaux in Australia and the South Pacific, 1792-1793* (Carlton, Vic.: Melbourne University Press, 1995), chapter 14; Bruny d'Entrecasteaux, *Voyage to Australia and the Pacific 1791* (Carlton, Vic.,: Melbourne University Press, 2001), trans. Edward Duyker and Maryse Duyker, introduction, xxx–xxxix; Roger Williams, *French Botany in the Enlightenment: The Ill-fated Voyages of La Pérouse and his Rescuers* (Dordrecht: Kluwer Academic Publishers, 2003), chapter XIII; and Seymour L. Chapin, 'The French Revolution in the South Seas: The Republican Spirit and the d'Entrecasteaux Expedition', *Proceedings of the Western Society for French History* 17 (1990), 178–186. Citation from E. P. De Rossel, ed., *Voyage de Dentrecasteaux: Envoyé à la*

Recherche de La Pérouse, 2 vols (Paris: De l'Imprimerie Impériale, 1823), vol. 1, 471, cited in Dunmore, *French Explorers*, 327 and also Dianne Johnson, *Bruny d'Entrecasteaux and His Encounter with Tasmanian Aborigines: From Provence to Recherche Bay* (Lawson, NSW: Blue Mountain, 2012), chapter 14. Since this chapter was written, the following work has also appeared and was consulted at a late stage: Bronwen Douglas et al., eds, *Collecting in the South Seas: The Voyage of Bruni d'Entrecasteaux, 1791-1794* (Sidestone Press: Leiden, 2018).

2 See Horner, *Looking for La Pérouse*, 213; Dunmore, *French Explorers*, vol. 1, 330–31.

3 Horner, *Looking for La Pérouse*, 219.

4 Johnson, *Bruny D'Entrecasteaux*, 72.

5 D'Entrecasteaux, *Voyage*, xxxvi.

6 See M. La Billardière, *An Account of a Voyage in search of La Pérouse, undertaken by order of the Constituent Assembly of France and Performed in the Years 1791, 1792 and 1793 translated from the French*, 2 vols (London: J. Debrett, 1800), vol. 1, xix. For the intriguing and diverse paths taken by the collections of this expedition, see Douglas et al, eds., *Collecting in the South Seas*.

7 For analysis of the relationship between these three voyages, see Nicole Starbuck, *Baudin, Napoleon and the Exploration of Australia* (London: Pickering and Chatto, 2013), introduction.

8 As far as is possible, Aotearoa/New Zealand is used as a compound to denote the conjoinasns of modern-day New Zealand. Where Māori traditions, intellectual concepts and cosmology are in view below Aotearoa is used without New Zealand and New Zealand is used below as a name employed by colonists.

9 Cited in Williams, *French Botany*, 107. It is interesting that the bid to launch an expedition to search for d'Entrecasteaux still had to appeal to the name of the king: see Frank Horner, *Looking for La Pérouse*, 7.

10 For discussion of La Pérouse's agenda see Dunmore, *French Explorers*, 261–2. For the explorer's biography and further details of the mission see also, John Dunmore, *Pacific Explorer: The Life of Jean-François de La Pérouse, 1741-1788* (Palmerston North: Dunmore Press, 1985), esp. chapter 13.

11 Later however he wrote of how he would not call at Tahiti because it was so well known: 'possibly it is to the credit of the expedition's leader, and certainly to the benefit of the crews, if one can go round the world without calling at O-Taity', La Pérouse to Fleurieu, dated Avatska Bay, 10 September 1787, translated and republished in John Dunmore, ed., *The Journal of Jean-François de Galaup de La Pérouse* (London: Hakluyt Society, 1995), 512–520, at 517.

12 Dunmore, *Pacific Explorer*, 203.

13 La Pérouse to the Minister, dated Avatska 10 September 1787, in Dunmore, ed., *The Journal*, 510–2, at 510.

14 La Pérouse to the Minister, dated Avatska 10 September 1787, in Dunmore, ed., *The Journal*, 510–2, at 510, 511 and La Pérouse to Fleurieu dated Manila 8 April 1787 in Dunmore, ed., *The Journal*, 509–10, at 509.

15 La Pérouse to the Minister, dated Manila 7 April 1787, in Dunmore, ed., *The Journal*, 505–6, at 506.

16 La Pérouse to the Minister, dated Avatska 29 September 1787, in Dunmore, ed., *The Journal*, 533–4, at 533.

17 Jean-François de Galaup, Comte de La Pérouse, *The Voyage of La Pérouse Round the World, in the Years 1785, 1786, 1787 and 1788 translated from the French*, ed. M. L. A. Milet Mureau (London: John Stockdale, 1798), ii.

18 James Burney, *A Memoir on the Voyage of d'Entrecasteaux in search of La Pérouse* (London: Luke Hansard, 1820), 4–8, at 8.

19 Leslie R. Marchant, 'La Pérouse, Jean-François de Galaup (1741–1788)', *Australian Dictionary of Biography*, National Centre of Biography, Australian National University, http://adb.anu.edu.au/biography/la-perouse-jean-francois-de-galaup-2329/text3029, accessed 4 October 2013.

20 La Pérouse to the Minister, dated, 7 February 1788, in Dunmore, ed., *The Journal*, 541–2.

21 See Dunmore, *The Pacific Explorer*, for a detailed account of the family's reaction to this, esp. chapter 12.

22 John Hunter, *An Historical Journal of the Transactions at Port Jackson and Norfolk Island, with the Discoveries which have been made in New South Wales and in the Southern Ocean, since the publication of Philip's Voyage* (London: John Stockdale, 1793), 240.

23 D'Entrecasteaux, *Voyage to Australia*, 16.

24 Ibid., 81–2.

25 See the reproduction of the image in Bronwen Douglas, 'In the Event: Indigenous Countersigns and the Ethnohistory of Voyaging', in Margaret Jolly et al., eds, *Oceanic Encounters: Exchange, Desire, Violence* (Canberra: ANU Press, 2009), 175–198.

26 La Billardière, *An Account*, vol. 1, 279–280.

27 Jocelyn Linnekin, 'Ignoble savages and other European visions: The La Pérouse affair in Samoan history', *The Journal of Pacific History* 26, no. 1 (1991), 3–26.

28 Dillon, *Narrative and Successful Result*, vol. 2, 159–69.

29 'Rapport sur le voyage', in Muséum d'Histoire Naturelle, cited in Starbuck, *Baudin*, 2.

30 See Starbuck, *Baudin*, 21 and also Bernard Smith, *Imagining the Pacific* (Hong Kong, 1992), 48.

31 See Ralph Kingston, 'A not so Pacific voyage: The "floating laboratory"

of Nicolas Baudin', *Endeavour* 31, no. 4 (December 2007), 145–51, at 146.

32 Cited in Starbuck, *Baudin*, 137.

33 Anthony Brown, *Ill-starred Captains: Flinders and Baudin* (London: Chatham, 2001), 390 and 401.

34 Brown, *Ill-starred Captains,* 389 and 395.

35 For a commemorative souvenir of the two captains' engagement with Mauritius, see *Encounter Mauritius 2003: Commemoration of the Bicentenary of the Presence of Nicolas Baudin and Matthew Flinders in Mauritius* (Port Louis: Mauritius Govt Press, 2003).

36 See, for instance, Carol E. Harrison, 'Projections of the Revolutionary Nation: French Expedition in the Pacific, 1791-1803', *Osiris* 24 (2009), 33–52.

37 Letter dated 4 November 1804 from Matthew Flinders to Ann, cited in Brown, *Ill-starred Captains*, 394.

38 Details and citations connected to observations in New Zealand, from d'Entrecasteaux, *Voyage to Australia*, 159–60. For further observations on these plants see also La Billardière, *An Account*, vol. 2, 76–7.

39 D'Entrecasteaux, *Voyage to Australia*, 181–2.

40 See Robert Langdon, 'The Maritime Explorers', in Noel Rutherford, ed., *The Friendly Islands: A History of Tonga* (Melbourne: Oxford University Press, 1977), 40–62, 54–5 and also Peter Suren, ed., *Essays on the History of Tonga*, 3 vols (Nuku'alofa, Tonga: Friendly Islands Bookshop, 2001–6), vol. 2, 41–3.

41 D'Entrecasteaux, *Voyage to Australia*, 173.

42 Ibid., 190.

43 D'Entrecasteaux, *Voyage to Australia*, 186.

44 Ibid., 187.

45 For Cook's interest in the royal line of Tonga see, Langdon, 'The Maritime Explorers', 50–1.

46 D'Entrecasteaux, *Voyage to Australia*, 184.

47 La Billardière, *An Account*, vol. 2, 116.

48 Ibid. vol. 2, 128.

49 This paragraph relies on Christine Ward Gailey, *Kinship to Kingship: Gender, Hierarchy and State Formation in the Tongan Islands* (Austin, Texas: University of Texas Press, 1987).

50 The image, as well as the insight, arises out of a new book on d'Entrecasteaux's voyage: see Billie Lyt-berg and Melenaite Taumoefolau, 'Sisi Fale – Tongan Coconut Fibre Waist Garment', in *Collecting in the South Sea*, 85–87.

51 La Billardière, *An Account*, vol. 2, 129.

52 Patty O'Brien, *The Pacific Muse: Exotic Femininity and the Colonial Pacific* (Seattle: University of Washington Press, 2006), 198.

53 Gailey, *Kinship to Kingship*, 178ff. For the history of this period of Tonga, and for further discussion of material in this paragraph and the next, see I. C. Campbell, *Island Kingdom: Tonga, Ancient and Modern* (Christchurch: Canterbury University Press, 1992), 60.

54 See Suren, ed., *Essays*, vol. 3, 187ff.

55 Gailey, *Kinship to Kingship*, 179.

56 Cited in Harry Liebersohn, *The Travelers' World: Europe to the Pacific* (Cambridge, Mass.: Harvard University Press, 2006), 168.

57 Nicholas Thomas, *Islanders*, 22.

58 William Mariner, *An Account of the Natives of the Tongan Islands in the South Pacific Ocean*, 2 vols (London: J. Murray, 1817), vol. 1, xx, footnote. For some details of Mariner's time in Tonga see also, I. C. Campbell, *Gone Native in Polynesia: Captivity Narratives and Experiences from the South Pacific* (Westport, Conn.: Greenwood Press, 1998), 52–9.

59 Mariner, *An Account*, vol. 1, 46 and see also, Suren, ed. *Essays*, vol. 3, 67.

60 Mariner, *An Account*, vol. 1, 61.

61 Campbell, *Gone Native in Polynesia*, 54 and Suren, ed. *Essays*, vol. 3, 69–70.

62 See J. Orlebar, *A Midshipman's Journal on Board H.M.S. Seringapatam During the Year 1830*, ed. Melvin J. Voigt (California: Tofua Press, 1976), 72. Gunson estimates that there were 'eighty aliens' from Europe and 'the more distant Pacific islands' who resided in Tonga from 1796 to 1826: 'The Coming of Foreigners', in N. Rutherford, ed., *Friendly Islands: A History of Tonga* (Melbourne: Oxford University Press, 1978), 90–113, at 90.

63 For an account of the other survivors from the *Port au Prince* see Suren, ed., *Essays*, vol. 3, 74. There were 26 survivors, excluding the Hawai'ians.

64 Mariner, *An Account*, vol. 1, 101.

65 Ibid., 100.

66 Ibid., 420.

67 For a further discussion of the spread of money and a Tongan critique of it see Suren, ed., *Essays*, vol. 3, 192.

68 Jonathan Lamb, Vanessa Smith and Nicholas Thomas eds, *Exploration and exchange: A South Sea Anthology* (Chicago: Chicago University Press, 2000), 191–3.

69 For discussion of this, see: Nigel Statham, 'Manuscript XIX: Mafihape's Letter to William Mariner (1832)', *Journal of Pacific History* 43, no. 3 (December 2008), 341–66.

70 From the translation in Statham, 'Mafihape's Letter', 353.

71 Dillon, *Narrative and Successful Result*, vol. 1, 285–6.

72 In a letter dated London 8 May 1837 to J. H. Cook who brought him the letter he writes: 'I regret that I have been able to translate very little of my kind Mother's Epistle – partly from having forgotten the language, but principally from the orthography differing materially from that used

by me.' This letter is pasted at the front of Mariner, *An Account*, vol. 1; a copy is at the Mitchell Library, State Library of New South Wales, Sydney (hereafter MLS): C 797, vol. 1.

73 Campbell, *Gone Native in Polynesia*, 59.

74 Suren, ed., *Essays*, vol. 3, 144.

75 Suren, ed., *Essays*, vol. 3, 85.

76 See '"Port-au-Prince" Pirate Ship Discovery in Tonga', in *New Zealand Herald*, 9 August 2012: http://www.nzherald.co.nz/world/news/video. cfm?c_id=1503076&gal_cid=2&gallery_id=127358, accessed 22 June 2017.

77 Cited in Rod Edmond, *Representing the South Pacific from Cook to Gauguin* (Cambridge: Cambridge University Press, 1997), 73.

78 *The Poetical Works of Lord Byron: Complete in One Volume*, arranged by Thomas Moore et al. (New York: D. Appleton and Co., 1850), 174.

79 Suren, ed., *Essays*, vol. 3, 71. See also Nelson Eustis, *The King of Tonga* (Adelaide: Hyde Park Press, 1997), 20–1.

80 Thomas, *Islanders*, 24

81 From Suren, ed., *Essays*, vol. 3, 84. The reference here is to the voyage of HMS Seringapatam, under Captain Waldegrave.

82 For 'beachrangers' and escaped convicts see Augustus Earle, *A Narrative of a Nine Months' Residence in New Zealand* (London: Longman, 1832), 52–3. See also Earle's depictions of the Bay of Islands, at the National Library of Australia (hereafter NLA), Canberra.

83 See, for instance, 'Bay of Islands, New Zealand', watercolour, 1827–8, NLA: PIC Solander Box A36 T113 NK 12/75; and 'Entrance to the Bay of Islands', watercolour, 1827, NLA: PIC Solander Box B5 T104 NK 12/66.

84 'Tepoanah Bay of Islands New Zealand a Church Missionary Establishment', watercolour, 1827, NLA: PIC Solander Box C18 T176 NK 12/139.

85 On this see the excellent and recently published work, Tony Ballantyne, *Entanglements of Empire: Missionaries, Māori, and the Question of the Body* (Durham, NC: Duke University Press, 2014).

86 The broad outline of the history of New Zealand which follows draws on Keith Sinclair, *Oxford Illustrated History of New Zealand* (Auckland: Oxford University Press, 1990) and also M. N. Smith, *New Zealand: A Concise History* (Cambridge, 2005). It has also been heavily influenced by the revisionist reading of this period and the 'musket wars' in Angela Ballara, *Taua: 'Musket Wars', 'Land Wars' or Tikanga?: Warfare in Māori Society in the Early Nineteenth Century* (Auckland: New Zealand, Penguin Press, 2003) and also the work of Judith Binney, for instance in *The Legacy of Guilt: A Life of Thomas Kendall* (Wellington: Oxford University Press, 2005) and Judith Binney, *Stories Without End: Essays, 1795-2010* (Wellington: Bridget Williams Books, 2010), and more recently and since this chapter was first drafted, Ballantyne, *Entanglements*, and Frances Steel, ed., *New*

Zealand and the Sea: New Historical Perspectives (Wellington: Bridget Williams Book, 2018).

87 See Ballara, *Taua*, 67–69.

88 See ibid., 114–5; for the missionaries' reference to a 'council of war'. For reference to the 'rude parliament', see Earle, *A Narrative of Nine Months' Residence*, 180.

89 Augustus Earle, *Sketches Illustrative of the Native Inhabitants and Islands of New Zealand* (London: New Zealand Assoc., 1838); see also NLA: PIC vol. 532, U 2650 NK 668/9.

90 On the latter see Ballantyne, *Entanglements*.

91 For Marsden's biography, his agriculture and the origin of the mission, see, John Rawson Elder, ed., *The Letters and Journals of Samuel Marsden, 1765-1838* (Dunedin: Otago University Council, 1932), 18, 35 and 44. For the first voyage see, 'Marsden's First New Zealand Journal.'

92 See, for instance, 'Marsden's First New Zealand Journal', in Elder, ed., *The Letters and Journals*, 57–131, 85–6.

93 Samuel Marsden to Rev. J. Pratt of the Church Missionary Society, dated 22 September 1814, in Elder, ed., *The Letters and Journals*, 132–3, at 133.

94 See for instance Earle, *Narrative of Nine Months' Residence*, 45

95 For the explanation given to Marsden, see 'Marsden's first New Zealand Journal, 1814', in Elder, ed., *The Letters and Journals*, 87–8. For Marsden's account in the *Sydney Gazette*, see Patricia Bawden, *The Years Before Waitangi: A Story of Early Māori/European Contact in New Zealand* (Auckland: Institute Press, 1987), 46. See also Tony Simpson, *Art and Massacre: Documentary Racism in the Burning of the Boyd* (Wellington: New Zealand, Cultural Construction Company, 1993).

96 For this view and Berry's and Marsden's larger place in the politics of Sydney, see Tony Simpson, *Art and Massacre*.

97 Earle, *Narrative of Nine Months' Residence*, 152.

98 J. S. Polack, *New Zealand: being a narrative of travels and adventures during a residence in that country between the years 1831 and 1837* (London: Richard Bentley, 1838), 165–66.

99 Christina Thompson, 'A Dangerous People whose Only Occupation is War: Māori and Pakeha in 19th-century New Zealand', *Journal of Pacific History* 32, no. 1 (June 1997), 109–19, 112; see also Judith Binney, *The Legacy of Guilt*, 36. For Marsden's account of the shooting of his friend, see 'Marsden's First New Zealand Journal', in Elder, ed., *The Letters and Journals*, 61–2.

100 This follows the argument in Ballara, *Taua*.

101 Ballara, *Taua*, 454.

102 See James Belich, *The New Zealand Wars and the Victorian Interpretation of Racial Conflict* (Auckland, 1986).

103 James Busby, British Resident at New Zealand to the Secretary of State, dated the Bay of Islands, 16 June 1837, MLS: MLMSS 1668 (typescript copy), 206.

104 Ballara, *Taua*, 400ff.

105 See Earle, *A Narrative of a Nine Months' Residence*, 53–4. For Earle's images of 'King George', see 'King George, N Zealand costume', watercolour, 1828, NLA: PIC Solander Box A37 T122 NK 12/84 and 'The residence of Shulitea, chief of Kororadika, Bay of Islands', watercolour, 1827, NLA: PIC Solander Box A36 T109 NK 12/71.

106 Details of Hongi's biography draw upon Angela Ballara, 'Hongi Hika', in *Dictionary of New Zealand Biography, Te Era: The Encylopaedia of New Zealand*, http://www.teara.govt.nz/en/biographies/1h32/hongi-hika, accessed 10 September 2014.

107 For this criticism presented to Marsden, see 'Marsden's Second New Zealand Journal', in Elder, ed., *The Letters and Journals*, 143–221, 204. For more information on this, see also Ballantyne, *Entanglements*, 73–4.

108 Cited in Ballara, *Taua*, 191, from White, *The Ancient History of the Māori: His Mythology and Traditions: Ko nga tatai korero whakapapa a te Mori me nga karakia o nehe*, 6 vols, vol. X (Wellington: George Didsbury, 1887–90), vol. 10.

109 For commentary on the novelty of these plantations, see Ballara, *Taua*, 56.

110 Ballara, *Taua*, 190.

111 J. B. Marsden, ed., *Memoirs of the Life and Labours of the Rev. Samuel Marsden* (Cambridge: Cambridge University Press, 2011), 142.

112 For Hongi in Cambridge, see Binney, *Legacy of Guilt*, 73; also Dorothy Ulrich Cloher, *Hongi Hika: Warrior Chief* (Auckland, New Zealand: Penguin, 2003), chapter 5.

113 Cloher, *Hongi Hika*, 137.

114 Binney, *The Legacy of Guilt*, 14, 74.

115 Cited in Binney, *The Legacy of Guilt*, 74, from Creevey to Miss Ord, October 1820.

116 From Ballara, 'Hongi Hika'; also Smith, *New Zealand*, 33–4.

117 Ballara, 'Hongi Hika.'

118 For a critique of the iconic status of Te Rauparaha, see Ballara, *Taua*, 34.

119 Peter Butler, ed. *Life and Times of Te Rauparaha By His Son Tamihana Te Rauparaha* (Waiura: Martinborough: Alister Taylor, 1980), p. 41.

120 Ibid., 70.

121 Ibid., 74–5.

122 See the biography of Te Rauparaha, Steven Oliver, 'Te Rauparaha', in the *Dictionary of New Zealand Biography, Te Ara – the Encyclopedia of New Zealand*, http://www.teara.govt.nz/en/biographies/1t74/te-rauparaha, accessed 15 September 2014.

123 Claudia Orange, *The Treaty of Waitangi* (Wellington: Bridget Williams Books, 1987), 6–8; also Elder, ed., *Letters and Journals*, 81.

124 For a reference to the king's ships and king's warriors, see Earle, *Narrative of a Nine Months' Residence,* 164–5. For another reference to the king's ships, see Richard A. Cruise, *Journal of a Ten Months' Residence in New Zealand, 1820,* ed. A. G. Bagnall (Christchurch: Pegasus Press, 1957), 27.

125 Richard Bourke to James Busby, Government House, 13th April 1833, MLS: Governor's Despatches and Enclosures, A1267/13 (typescript copy), 1200–10. For Busby's address on his arrival to the Māori chiefs, see James Busby, *Letter of the Right Honorable Lord Viscount Goderich and Address of James Busby Esq. British Resident to the Chiefs of New Zealand* (Sydney: Gazette Office, n.d.). For Busby's account of the *Elizabeth* affair, see 'A Brief Memoir Relative to the Islands of New Zealand', in James Busby, *Authentic Information Relative to New South Wales* (London: Joseph Cross, 1832), 57–62, 64–6.

126 For Busby as the king's man and also the signing of the 1835 declaration, see Orange, *Treaty of Waitangi,* 13, 21. For the 1835 treaty, see 'A Declaration of Independence of New Zealand', in Orange, *Treaty of Waitangi,* appendix 1, 256. For the process of choosing the, flag see: 'Extract of a Letter from the British Resident of New Zealand to the Colonial Secretary, 22 March 1834, MLS: Governors' Despatches and Correspondence', A1267/13 (typescript copy), 1417–8. For commentary on the flag and on a possible constitution, see James Busby, British Resident at New Zealand, dated 16 June 1837, Bay of Islands to Secretary of State, MLS: MLMSS 1668 (typescript copy), p. 207. For the dockyard of New Zealand, see Earle, *Narrative of a Nine Months' Residence,* 25–6.

127 James Busby to Alexander Busby dated 10 December 1835, Waitangi, MLS: MLMSS 1349 (typescript copy), 97.

128 James Busby to Alexander Busby dated 22 June 1833, Bay of Islands, MLS: MLMSS 1349 (typescript copy), 29; see Ballantyne, *Entanglements,* 233.

129 'A brief Memoir relative to the Islands of New Zealand, submitted to the Right Hon. the Secretary of State for the Colonies, July 1832', in James Busby, *Authentic Information Relative to New South Wales* (London: Joseph Cross, 1832), 57–62, 60.

130 James Busby, British Resident at New Zealand to the Secretary of State, dated 16 June 1837, Bay of Islands, MLS: MLMSS 1668 (typescript copy), 207–9.

131 See for instance James Busby to Alexander Busby dated 5 May 1837, Bay of Islands, MLS: MLMSS 1349 (typescript copy), 131. Later in life Busby developed his views of the relation between the British monarchy, the House of Commons and colonial governors and assemblies in James Busby, *The Constitutional Relations of British Colonies to the Mother Country* (London: National Association for the Promotion of Social Science, 1865).

132 Richard Bourke to Rt. Honble Viscount Glenelg, dated 10 March 1836, MLS: Governors' Despatches and Enclosures, A1267/5 (typescript copy), 752.

133 *Correspondence with the Secretary of State Relative to New Zealand* (London: W. Clowes, 1840), 7, enclosure in letter from James Stephen to John Backhouse dated Downing Street, 12 December 1838.

134 This account of Thierry's quest draws from Binney, *The Legacy of Guilt*, appendix 3, titled 'Conquering Kings their Titles Take'. See also J. D. Raeside, 'Thierry, Charles Philippe Hippolyte de', in *Dictionary of New Zealand Biography, Te Ara – the Encyclopedia of New Zealand,* http://www.teara.govt.nz/en/biographies/1t93/thierry-charles-philippe-hippolyte-de. Also see correspondence in MLS: Governors' Despatches and Correspondence, A1267/19 (typescript copy), 2387ff. For growing French and American interest, see Orange, *Treaty of Waitangi*, 9. For Busby on how Thierry's activities may lead to further French involvement in New Zealand, see James Busby to Alexander Busby, 13 June 1839, Bay of Islands, MLS: MLMMS 1349 (typescript copy), 209.

135 James Busby to Alexander Busby, 9 April 1839, Bay of Islands, MLS: MLMMS 1349 (typescript copy), 187.

136 James Busby to the Colonial Secretary of New South Wales, 24 September 1838, MLS: Governors' Despatches and Enclosures, A1267/17 (typescript copy) 2172–5, at 2174.

137 James Busby to Alexander Busby, 5 September 1839, Bay of Islands, MLS: MLMMS 1349 (typescript copy), 245.

138 James Busby to Alexander Busby, 9 August 1836, Bay of Islands, MLS: MLMMS 1349 (typescript copy), 107. For another episode connected to violence between American mariners and settlers in New Zealand, see Statement of James Busby, British Resident at New Zealand and James R. Clendon, US Consul, 17 August 1839, Bay of Islands, MLS: Governors' Despatches and Enclosures, A1267/19, (typescript copy), 2362–5. For the rights of Americans with regard to fishing and land, see memorandum entitled 'How far American or other Foreign Interests may be affected by the occupation of New Zealand' and other correspondence, MLS: Governors' Despatches and Enclosures, A1267/19 (typescript copy), 2501ff.

139 'The Treaty of Waitangi' in Orange, *Treaty of Waitangi*, appendix 2, 258; see also Smith, *New Zealand*, 51.

140 Letter from R. Davis to James Busby, 29 June 1839, Waimate, MLS: MLMSS 1668 (typescript copy), 213.

141 Letter from James Busby to R. Davis, 11 July 1839, Waitangi, MLS: MLMSS 1668 (typescript copy), 213.

142 Letter from James Busby to Alexander Busby, 29 July 1839, Bay of Islands, MLS: MLMSS 1349 (typescript copy), 221.

143 'A Declaration of Independence of New Zealand', in Orange, *Treaty of Waitangi*, appendix 1, 256.

144 James Busby, British Resident at New Zealand to Secretary of State, 16 June 1837, Bay of Islands, MLS: MLMSS 1668 (typescript copy), 212: 'They prayed His Majesty "would continue to be their parent, and that he would become their protector" – The sentiment and the Language were their own.'

145 Lachy Paterson, 'Kiri Mā Kiri Mangu: The Terminology of Race and Civilisation in the Mid-Nineteenth-Century Māori-Language Newspapers', in Jenifer Curnow, Ngapare Hopa and Jane McRae, eds, *Rere Atu, Taku Manu!: Discovering History Language, and Politics in the Māori Language Newspapers* (Auckland: Auckland University Press, 2002), 78–97, at 91.

3 IN THE SOUTHWEST INDIAN OCEAN: WORLDS OF REVOLT AND THE RISE OF BRITAIN

1 The material on Onkruijdt's encounter with Paerl draws substantially upon Russel Viljoen, *Jan Paerl, A Khoikhoi in Cape Colonial Society, 1761-1851* (Leiden: Brill, 2006).

2 Ibid., 44–5.

3 Ibid., 47.

4 Ibid., 64, citing Onkruijdt to Van der Graaff, 26 October 1788, Western Cape Archives, Cape Town (hereafter WCA): CA C570, 51.

5 Ibid., 53, citing Onkruijdt to van der Graaff, 15 October 1788, WCA: CA C570, 19–20.

6 Details from Ibid., 19.

7 Ibid., 28.

8 Material in this paragraph draws upon Leonard Guelke, 'Freehold farmers and frontier settlers, 1657–1780', in Richard Elphick and Hermann Giliomee, *The Shaping of South African Society, 1652–1840* (Cape Town: Maskew Miller Longman, 1989), 2nd edn, 66–101 and P. J. van der Merwe, *The Migrant Farmer in the History of the Cape Colony, 1657-1842*, trans. Roger B. Beck (Athens, Ohio: Ohio University Press, 1995). See also O. F. Mentzel, *A Geographical and Topographical Description of the Cape of Good Hope*, trans. G. V. Marais and J. Hodge, 3 vols (Cape Town, 1944), vol. 3, 80: '[Swellendam] also ranks as a parish, but has so far neither church nor clergyman, nor is it likely to get one easily, because its inhabitants are scattered over such a vast area.'

9 Van der Merwe, *The Migrant Farmer*, 121, citing *landdrost, heemraden* and Military Officers from Swellendam to Governor, 17 March 1775, WCA: Petition, Reports etc., C1265.

10 William Patterson, *A Narrative of Four Journeys into the Country of the Hottentots and Cafaria in the Years 1777, 1778 and 1779* (London: Johnson, 1789), 84.

11 Anders Sparrman, *A Voyage to the Cape of Good Hope, Towards the Antarctic Polar Circle, and Round the World: But Chiefly into the Country of the Hottentots and the Caffres, from the year 1772 to 1776,* 2 vols. (London: Printed for G.G.J. and J. Robinson, 1785), vol. 1, 262–4.

12 Van der Merwe, *The Migrant Farmer,* 113, citing François Valentijn, *Oud en Nieuw Oost-Indiën: Vervattende een Naaukeurige en Uitvoerige Verhandelinge van Nederalnds Mogentheyd in die Gewesten,* 2 vols (Dordrecht: J. van Braam, 1724), vol. 2, 51.

13 See Hermann Giliomee, *The Afrikaners: Biography of a People* (Cape Town: Tafelberg, 2003), 61 for the introduction of a pass system.

14 Mentzel, *Geographical and Topographical Description,* vol. 3, 263.

15 Giliomee, *The Afrikaners,* 64 and quotation from 66.

16 This paragraph relies on Clifton C. Crais, *White Supremacy and Black Resistance in Pre-Industrial South Africa* (Cambridge: Cambridge University Press, 1992), for the point about 'Xhosa', see 18

17 See Crais, *White Supremacy and Black Resistance,* 51

18 For more on this see Susan Newton-King, *Masters and Servants on the Cape Eastern Frontier, 1760-1803* (Cambridge: Cambridge University Press, 1999), chapter 4. For the contested question of the relationship between Khoikhoi and San and whether they were interchangeable, see Penn, *The Forgotten Frontier,* 'Introduction'.

19 This paragraph is based on Simon Schama, *Patriots and Liberators: Revolution in the Netherlands, 1780-1813* (London: Fontana Press, 1992) and also Pepijn Brandon and Karwan Fatah-Black, '"The Supreme Power of the People": Local Autonomy and Radical Democracy in the Batavian Revolution (1795-1798)', *Atlantic Studies* 13 (2016), 370–388.

20 See the discussion of patriot sources in André Du Toit and Hermann Giliomee, *Afrikaner Political Thought: Analysis and Documents* (Berkeley, Calif.: University of California Press, 1983), chapter 2. The particular source from 1779 is 'The Burgher Petition to the Dutch Chamber of Seventeen, 9 Oct. 1779' on 39–41, citation 40.

21 For more on Cape patriotism, see Robert Ross, 'The Rise of the Cape Gentry', *Journal of Southern African Studies* 9, no. 2 (April 1983), 193–217, at 210. It is also worth noting here a book which was published just as this work went to press: Teun Baartman, *Cape Conflict: Protest and Political Alliance in a Dutch Settlement* (Leiden: Leiden University Press, 2019).

22 See Du Toit and Giliomee, *Afrikaner Political Thought,* 'Petition from some inhabitants to the governor and Political Council of the Cape, 17 Feb. 1784', 41–44, citation 43. For the origin of the document in Holland, see 29.

23 This paragraph draws upon H. Giliomee, 'Democracy and the Frontier: A comparative study of Bacon's Rebellion (1676) and the Graaff-Reinet Rebellion (1795-1796)', *South African Historical Journal* 6, no. 1 (1974): 30–51, esp. 35–7.

24 Giliomee, *The Afrikaners*, 73

25 Cited in Giliomee, 'Democracy and the Frontier', 40, Letter of Van Jaarsveld and A. P. Burger, 7 May 1795, WCA: VC 68.

26 All quotations that follow from Andrew Barnard to Robert Brooke, dated Cape of Good Hope 23 August 1797, WCA: Acc 1415 (74).

27 'Letter from the Earl Macartney to the Right Honourable Henry Dundas, dated Castle of Good Hope August 14 1797', in G. M. Theal, *Records of the Cape Colony*, 36 vols (London: William Clowes, 1897-1905), vol. 2, 148–9; quotation from 148.

28 'Declaration of Alexander Dixon, mate of the brig *Hope*, an English whaler, who arrived at False Bay on the 11th of August 1797', in Theal, *Records of the Cape Colony*, vol. 2, 149–151, quotation from 150.

29 'The Deposition of Frans Nicholas Petersen, third Mate of the *Hare*, Dutch Prize, which arrived in Simon's Bay on the Evening of the 10th August 1797', in Theal, *Records of the Cape Colony*, vol. 2, 153–4.

30 Barnard to Dundas, 19 October 1799, WCA: Acc 1715 (74).

31 The term 'second Gibraltar' was meant to indicate the futility of building a fort at Algoa Bay and was used by Barnard in a letter to Dundas, 7 December 1799, WCA: Acc 1715 (74).

32 Barnard to Dundas, 7 December 1799, WCA: Acc 1415 (74); and Barnard to Dundas, 9 March 1800, WCA: Acc 1415 (74).

33 This description relies on Newton-King, *Masters and Servants*, 213–5. All quotations however are from Andrew Barnard to Lord Macartney, dated 25 February 1799 and Barnard to Henry Dundas dated 21 September 1799, WCA: Acc 1415 (74).

34 Barnard to Henry Dundas, 17 August 1799, WCA: Acc 1415 (74). For how government adopted the tactic of cutting the supply of ammunition to frontier *boers*, see Giliomee, *The Afrikaners*, 58–59.

35 For more on this, see Newton-King, *Masters and Servants*, chapter 9, citation from 229.

36 John Barrow, *An Account of Travels into the Interior of Southern Africa*, 2 vols. (London, 1801), vol. 1, 96.

37 Barnard to Henry Dundas, 17 August 1799, WCA: Acc 1415 (74). For the need for 'some severe examples' to make peace, see Barnard to the Earl Macartney, 14 October 1801.

38 Nigel Worden, *Slavery in Dutch South Africa* (Cambridge: Cambridge University Press, 1985), 132–3.

39 From Worden, *Slavery*, 135.

40 See ibid., 127.

41 The framework of this paragraph relies substantially on Nigel Worden, 'Armed with Swords and Ostrich Feathers: Militarism and Cultural Revolution in the Cape Slave Uprising of 1808', in Richard Bessel, Nicholas Guyatt and Jane Rendall, eds, *War, Empire and Slavery 1770-1830*

(Basingstoke: Palgrave Macmillan, 2010), figures taken from 133. For comparison with another Dutch context of slave revolt, see W. Klooster and Gert Oostindie, eds, *Curaçao in the Age of Revolutions, 1795-1800* (Leiden: KITLV Press, 2011).

42 'Examination of Louis', WCA: CJ 516. For the description of Louis as a keeper of a wine-house, see 'Examination of the Prisoner James Hooper', WCA: CJ 516. For reference to England, Scotland and America, see 'Examination of the Prisoner Michael Kelly', WCA: CJ 516.

43 'Examination of the Prisoner Michael Kelly', WCA: CJ 516.

44 'Sentence in a Criminal Case, His Majesty's Fiscal, William Stephanus van Ryneveld Esq. Prosecutor for the Crown', WCA: CJ 802.

45 Quotations from 'Deposition of Jacomina Hendrina Laubscher', WCA: CJ 515.

46 'Examination of Louis', WCA: CJ 516; see also 'Examination of Abraham, Slave of John Wagenane', WCA: CJ 516.

47 'Sentence in a Criminal Case, His Majesty's Fiscal, William Stephanus van Ryneveld Esq. Prosecutor for the Crown', WCA: CJ 802.

48 'Examination of Louis', WCA: CJ 516.

49 'Sentence in a Criminal Case, His Majesty's Fiscal, William Stephanus van Ryneveld Esq. Prosecutor for the Crown', WCA: CJ 802.

50 Worden, 'Armed with Swords and Ostrich Feathers', 129. See 'Examination of Louis', WCA: CJ 516, for how Louis had his jacket tailored and bought swords and epaulets in 'the English shops'.

51 'Examination of the Prisoner Michael Kelly', WCA: CJ 516; for more on the feathers and how they were acquired, see 'Third Examination of the Prisoner James Hooper', WCA: CJ 516.

52 Nicole Ulrich, 'International Radicalism, Local Solidarities: The 1797 British Naval Mutinies in Southern African Waters', *International Review of Social History* 58, no. S21 (December 2013), 61–85, at 84.

53 See for instance, documents in WCA: CO/9, especially, Letters from Charles Felck to the Governor of this Cape of Good Hope, 8 December 1807, 4 January 1808 and 11 February 1808. This was also apparent in the proceedings of the court, where slave-owners were cast as Christians while slaves were not. See for instance the formulation in 'Sentence in a Criminal Case, His Majesty's Fiscal, William Stephanus van Ryneveld Esq. Prosecutor for the Crown', WCA: CJ 802. For example, the rebel leaders made sure that 'neither Slaves nor Christians should make their escape', from farms under siege.

54 I thank Prof. Nigel Worden for making this comment in addition to other observations on this chapter. For material connected to Islam in slave resistance, see Nigel Worden and Gerald Groenewald, eds, *Trials of Slavery: Selected Documents Concerning Slaves from the Criminal Records of the Council of Justice at the Cape of Good Hope, 1705-1794* (Cape Town: Van Riebeeck Society, 2005).

55 'Examination of Louis', WCA: CJ 516.

56 This paragraph relies on Abdulkader Tayob, *Islam in South Africa: Mosques, Imams, and Sermons* (Gainesville: University of Florida Press, 1999), chapter 2.

57 This paragraph and what follows draw upon Charles Grant, *The History of Mauritius or the Isle of France and Neighbouring Islands, composed primarily from the papers and memoirs of Baron Grant* (London: W. Bulmer and Co, 1801), 525–6; Albert Pitot, *L'Île de France: Esquisses Historiques (1715-1810)* (Port Louis, Mauritius: E. Pezzani, 1899), 137ff.; Sydney Selvon, *A New Comprehensive History of Mauritius*, 2 vols (Mauritius: Bahemia Printing, 2012), vol. 1, chapter 22; Raymond d'Unienville, *Histoire Politique de l'Île de France (1791-1794)* (Port Louis: L. Carl Achille, 1982), 12ff. and archival documents cited below from the National Archives of Mauritius.

58 Selvon, *A New Comprehensive History*, 203, 206.

59 [Citoyen Gouverneur, vous étiez le représentant d'un roi que l'amour du peuple avait conservé au faîte de la véritable grandeur mais que la souveraineté du peuple a renversé parce qu'il n'a pas su être le Roi des Français . . . La royauté est éteinte à jamais en France; mais l'autorité dont elle était dépositaire est maintenue. Le pouvoir exécutif subsiste dans toute sa force. Vous êtes toujours dans une colonie le représentant de ce pouvoir qui ne saurait exister en des mains plus sûres. Vous le prouvez bien par l'empressement avec lequel cédant au vœu de l'Assemblée vous venez prêter dans son sein le serment de fidélité à la République française. Jurez d'être fidèle à la République française et de la maintenir de tout votre pouvoir]. From d'Unienville, *Histoire Politique*, 15–16.

60 '*État vers dépenses de Monsieur le Comte Mac-némara pendant son séjour au camp de Tippo Sultan devant les lignes de Travancor*', in A75, National Archives of Mauritius (hereafter NAM), Port Louis.

61 Pitot, *L'Île de France*, 144.

62 ['du désir d'une indépendance qu'ils savent bien ne pouvoir jamais avoir lieu dans un état monarchique' and 'des assemblées tumultueuses & composées de matelots (. . .) facile à égarer par la vaine espérance d'une égalité chimérique'], Ordinance dated 2 June 1790, Dossier concernant Macnémara 1790, A75, NAM, Port Louis.

63 Pitot, *L'Île de France*, 146–7.

64 Charles Pridham, *An Historical, Political and Statistical Account of Mauritius and its Dependencies* (London: T and W Boone, 1849), 57.

65 W. Draper Bolton, *Bolton's Mauritius Almanac and Official Directory* (Mauritius: A. J. Tennant, 1851), xxxi.

66 For a discussion of the beheading of Maroons see Megan Vaughan, *Creating the Creole Island: Slavery in Eighteenth-Century Mauritius* (London: Duke University Press, 2005), 186–8.

67 Grant, *History of Mauritius*, xv, for comment about how the Revolution of France, attacked 'the class of its people to which I belong'.

68 Selvon, *A New Comprehensive History*, 209.

69 See Mohibbul Hasan, *History of Tipu Sultan* (Calcutta: World Press, 1971), 183–4.

70 James Gunnee [de Montille], 'The Agency of (Free) Coloured Elites in Mauritius, 1790-1865' (BA dissertation, University of Cambridge, 2012), 11.

71 For the growth of the free coloured community and their politics see, Vijaya Teelock, *Mauritian history: From its beginnings to modern times* (Port Louis, Mahatma Gandhi Institute, 2001), 154–6. For the politics of membership of the Colonial Assembly as it affected the free coloured peoples and women, see d'Unienville, *Histoire Politique*, 48, 57–8, 60–3.

72 Selvon, *A New Comprehensive History*, 209.

73 Auguste Toussaint, *History of Mauritius*, trans. W. E. F. Ward (Basingstoke: Macmillan, 1977), 49; see also Grant, *The History of Mauritius*, 531.

74 [[Le décret abolissant l'esclavage] servit le malheur des hommes libres et des esclaves, et allumeroit entr'eux une guerre civil, qui ne s'éteindroit que par la destruction entière des uns ou des autres, et peut-être même des deux partis]. From Samuel de Missy and Pierre-Michel Broutin to the deputies of the Colonial Assembly, 24 June 1793, NAM: 'Lettres reçues des députés de l'Île de France à Paris, 1793 – 1801', A 10B.

75 D'Unienville, *Histoire Politique*, 96–100.

76 Ibid., 132.

77 [Nous nous empressons de nous faire connaître à vous; et désirons, frères et amis, entretenir une correspondance fraternelle dont le but est et sera de déjouer les complots des ennemis de la République française. . . de reformer les abus; faire renaître la paix, l'unité et tranquillité publique]. From 'Popular society of Sans-culottes' of the canton of St. Benoît in Reunion Island to the Sans-culottes of Port Louis', 1 June 1794, NAM: 'Assemblée Coloniale; Lettres émanant de la Société des Sans-culottes, 1793-1795', D 64.

78 Selvon, *A New Comprehensive History*, 212.

79 Pridham, *An Historical*, 58–60, for both the idea of the talismanic effect of the announcement of the abolition of slavery and the fear of Haiti.

80 Megan Vaughan, 'Slavery, Smallpox, and Revolution: 1792 in Île de France (Mauritius)', in *The Society for the Social History of Medicine* 13, no. 3 (December 2000): 411–428. For the famine that impacted the third Colonial Assembly see: d'Unienville, *Histoire Politique*, 10–11.

81 Bolton, *Bolton's Mauritius Almanac*, xx–xxi.

82 John Jeremie, *Recent Events in Mauritius* (London: Hatchard and Son, 1835), 3.

83 Selvon, *A New Comprehensive History*, 212–4.

84 Ibid., 217

85 This paragraph draws on Vaughan, *Creating the Creole Island*, 257; see also Nigel Worden, 'Diverging Histories: Slavery and its Aftermath in the Cape Colony and Mauritius', *South African Historical Journal* 27, no. 1 (1992) 3–25, 8 and Teelock, *Mauritian History*, 88.

86 Selvon, *A New Comprehensive History*, 215.

87 Vaughan, *Creating the Creole Island*, 232.

88 For details of the delegations: Pridham, *An Historical*, 64. For an account of the arrival of an embassy from Île de France in Rangoon in Burma, with news of the age of revolutions, see Michael Symes, *An Account of an Embassy to the Kingdom of Ava* (London: W. Bulmer and Co., 1800), 397.

89 The discussion of the link between Mauritius and Mysore combines archival material cited below, with critical reading of J. Salmond, *A review of the origin, progress and result of the late decisive war in Mysore; in a letter from an officer in India: with notes; and an appendix comprising the whole secret state papers found at Seringapatam* (London: Luke Hansard, 1800); Grant, *The History of Mauritius; Official Documents Relative to the Negotiations Carried on by Tippoo Sultaun with the French nation and other Foreign States for Purposes Hostile to the British Nation to which is added proceedings of a Jacobin Club Formed at Seringapatam by the French Soldiers in the Corps Commanded by M. Dompart* (Calcutta: Printed at the Honourable Company's Press, 1799); and M. Hasan, *History of Tipu Sultan* (Calcutta: The World Press, 1971), 287–91 and S. P. Sen, *The French in India 1763-1816* (New Delhi: Munshiram Mahoharal, 1971), 547–55. This citation from *Official Documents*, 79.

90 See M. Shama Rao, *Modern Mysore: From the Beginning to 1868* (Bangalore: The Author, 1936), 178.

91 Kate Brittlebank, *Tipu Sultan's search for legitimacy: Islam and kingship in a Hindu domain* (Delhi: Oxford University Press, 1997).

92 Hasan, *History of Tipu Sultan*, 117. For a recent account of Tipu's diplomacy and its aims, see Kaveh Yazdani, *India, Modernity and the Great Divergence, Mysore and Gujarat* (Leiden: Brill, 2017), 289–99.

93 All the material connected to this paragraph and the next two derives from 'Narrative of the Proceedings of Tippoo Sultaun's Ambassadors', in Grant, *A History of Mauritius*, 535ff.

94 'Bazard fait le 1er Pluviôse an 6e pour les ambassadeurs de Typoo Sultan', 20 January 1798, *Documents concernant les relations avec Tippou Sultan, 1787 – 1799*, A101, NAM, Port Louis.

95 Hasan, *History of Tipu Sultan* (Calcutta: World Press, 1971), 287–8; see also letter written aboard the frigate *La Penrose*, dated 18 April 1798, NAM, A101.

96 See Salmond, *A review*, appendix B, no. 7, 'The Representatives of the Colony of the Isle of France to Tippoo Sultaun' and also appendix B,

no. 10, 'Dated Isle of France, Port North West, the 18th Ventose, 6th year of the French Republic'; A port master and shipbuilder did return to Mysore, see Salmond, *A review*, appendix B, no. 18, Letter from the Captain of the ships of War of the French Republic to Tipu Sultan, 28 April 1798; see also Grant, *The History of Mauritius*, 543.

97 Grant, *A History of Mauritius*, 536

98 Petition by Malartic, Done at Port North-West, 30 January 1798, cited in Rao, *Mysore*, 179.

99 'Volontaires français au service du pacha Tipoo Sultan', 21 April 1798, A101, NAM.

100 Teelock, *Mauritian History*, 19.

101 See for instance Barnard to Lord Macartney, 25 February 1799, and Barnard to Henry Dundas, 6 April 1799, WCA: Acc 1415 (74).

102 Aniruddha Ray, 'France and Mysore', in Irfan Habib, ed., *State and Diplomacy under Tipu Sultan: Documents and Essays* (New Deli: Tulika, 2001), 120–39, 134. For the proclamation in Cape Town, see 'Translation of a proclamation' in Theal, *Records of the Cape Colony*, vol. 2, 246–7.

103 Sen, *The French in India*, 553, citing Minute of Governor General Wellesley, 12 August 1798.

104 Kate Brittlebank, *Tipu Sultan's Search for Legitimacy: Islam and Kingship in a Hindu Domain* (Delhi: Oxford University Press, 1997), 28.

105 The controversial papers of the club appear in *Official Documents*.

106 See, for instance, Jean Boutier, 'Les lettres de créances du corsaire Ripaud', working paper available at: https://halshs.archives-ouvertes.fr/halshs-00007971/document, accessed 19 July 2018.

107 Kate Brittlebank, 'Curiosities, Conspicuous Piety and the Maker of Time: Some Aspects of Kingship in Eighteenth-Century South India', *South Asia: Journal of South Asian Studies* 16, no. 2 (1993): 41–56, 44.

108 Grant, *The History of Mauritius*, 192.

109 Ibid., 188.

110 See Sen, *The French in India*, 549.

111 *Official Documents*, 180.

112 For the reform of the army, see Nigel Chancellor, 'Tipu Sultan, Mysore State, and the Early Modern World' (Conference paper presented in Mysore, 2010).

113 *Official Documents*, 183.

114 Salmond, *A review*, appendix B, 'Letter dated 2nd April 1797, Tippoo Sultan the Victorious to the Representatives of the People residing in the Isles of France and La Réunion'. For kingship in relation to Tipu, see Brittlebank, *Tipu's Search for Legitimacy*.

115 See Partha Chatterjee, *The Black Hole of Empire: History of a Global Practice of Power* (Princeton: Princeton University Press, 2012), 85–93.

116 Adrian Carton, 'Shades of Fraternity: Creolization and the Making of Citizenship in French India, 1790-1792', *French Historical Studies* 31, no. 4 (2008), 582–607, 597.

117 M. Gobalakichenane, 'The French Revolution and the Tamils of Pondicherry (1790-1793)', *East and West* 50, no. 1/4, (December 2000), 295–308, 299.

118 Sen, *French in India*, 427–429.

119 This relies on Carton, 'Shades of Fraternity.'

120 Gobalakichenane, 'The French Revolution', 305.

121 Carton, 'Shades of Fraternity', 601.

122 Translated copy, order from the Prince of Orange to the Governor of Cape of Good Hope, Kew, February 27, 1795 in Theal, *Records of the Cape Colony*, vol. 1, 28

123 For information related to De Suffren, see Sen, *The French in India*, chapter IX.

124 For the attack: L. C. F. Turner, 'The Cape of Good Hope and Anglo-French rivalry, 1778-1796', *Historical Studies: Australia and New Zealand* 12, no. 46 (1966) 166–185, at 182ff.

125 See, for instance, letter from Mr William Eliot, Secretary of the Embassy and Acting Minister Plenipotentiary at The Hague to Lord Grenville, dated The Hague, 16 April 1794 in Theal, *Records of the Cape Colony*, vol. 1, 16–17.

126 Letter from Admiral Elphinstone and General Craig to Commissioner Sluysken and the Council of Policy, 29 June 1795, in Theal, *Records of the Cape Colony*, vol. 1, 92–6, quotation 93.

127 These quotations from ibid. 95–6.

128 Turner, 'The Cape of Good Hope'.

129 See for instance letter from G. M. Malet, Bombay, to Earl Macartney, 1 August 1797, WCA: BO 228; and letter from Roebuck Abbott &co, Fort St. George, to the Governor in Council, Fort St. George, 15 July 1798, WCA: BO 228. For gunpowder, see letter from John Stratchey to Barnard Esq, Secretary of the Government at the Cape Colony, 9 October 1797, WCA: BO 228.

130 See Peter Marshall, 'British Assessments of the Dutch in Asia in the Age of Raffles', in *Itinerario* 12, no. 1 (March 1988), 1–16.

131 Letter from Francis Baring to Henry Dundas, 12 January 1795, in Theal, *Records of the Cape Colony*, vol. 1, 19–23, quotation from 22.

132 Cited in Turner, 'The Cape of Good Hope', 181.

133 For the increasing Francophone culture of the Cape in this period, see Nigel Worden, Elizabeth van Heyningen and Vivian Bickford-Smith, eds., *Cape Town: The Making of a City: An Illustrated Social History* (Claremont, South Africa: David Philip Publishers, 1998), 81–3, citation from 81.

134 For the seized letters from the Cape of this period, see Danelle van Zyl-Hermann, '"Gij kent genoegt mijn gevoelig hart": Emotional life at the Occupied Cape of Good Hope, 1798-1803', *Itinerario* 35, no. 2 (August 2011), 63–80; cited letter: 70 fn. 47. For more biographical history of this period see, James Wilson, 'The Anglo-Dutch Imperial Meridian in the Indian Ocean World, 1795-1820', (PhD thesis, University of Cambridge, 2018).

135 See, for instance, letters of Andrew Barnard dated Castle of Good Hope, 11 July 1798 and 4 December 1798, WCA: Acc 1415 (74). In the latter: 'A Dutch Gentleman of the name of Prediger arrived here on board an American ship from Batavia . . . his behaviour and conversation since he came here have been perfectly correct, nor are his friends here amongst those who profess Jacobin principles.' Also, 'Applications to reside in the colony, October 1795-July 1798', WCA: BO 93; 'Reports on strangers, 1797', WCA: BO 195. For a Dutch man who is reluctant to return to Europe, see the petition of Jan Gerritt Myesart, 21 June 1798, WCA: BO 93: 'as being arrived in his mother country / Amsterdam / he found every thing in such a disorder that he was obliged to leave it and ship on board of the above named ship. . .' For the need to watch the 'improper concourse of Foreigners, and particularly of French and Dutch, to the Cape', see Letter from War Office to the Earl Macartney, dated Parliament Street, 14 January 1797, in Theal, *Records of the Cape Colony*, vol. 2, 36–7. For passports, see Proclamation of Major General Francis Dundas, 22 September 1801, in Theal, *Records of the Cape Colony*, vol. 4, 74–5.

136 Letter from the Burgher Senate to Earl Macartney, dated 16 June 1797, WCA: BO 3.

137 Letter dated 25 January 1799, WCA: Acc 1415 (74). For discussion of the 'Great Fire of Cape Town' of 23 November 1798, see Worden, van Heyningen, and Bickford-Smith, eds, *Cape Town*, 112.

138 See, for instance, Wilson, 'Anglo-Dutch Imperial Meridian', chapter 1 and also chapter 3 for material on registration of travellers.

139 Sen, *The French in India*, 442–4.

140 The following material and quotations arise from 'Précis historique de ce qui s'est passé au siège de Pondicherry en 1793', Bibliothéque National de France: 'Correspondance de Fresne', NAF 9373, 418–34.

141 For other accounts of the fall of Pondichéry see Sen, *The French in India*, 445–9; see also A. Iramacami, *History of Pondicherry* (New Delhi: Sterling Publishers, 1987), 142; see long detailed memoir, 1 footnote 4, 1, Mss 2200.

142 'Précis historique'.

143 Between 1793 and 1803 it is estimated that 'corsair activity' brought some £2,500,000 to Mauritius. See Teelock, *Mauritian History*, 95–6. For an early proposal to take Mauritius, justified because of privateering

undertaken out of the island, see Barnard to Dundas, 19 October 1799, WCA: Acc 1415 (74). See Private and Confidential Letter from Sir George Yonge to the Right Honourable Henry Dundas, dated Cape Town, 29 March 1800, in Theal, *Records of the Cape Colony*, vol. 3, 94ff.: 'The only annoyance at present to the Cape and indeed to India, Is the Mauritius . . . Whether it is adviseable to attempt the Reduction of this nest of Pirates, Is more than I can pretend to judge.'

144 A. Barry, Chief Secretary of Government, 28 July 1810, St. Denis, NAM: Secret Proceedings of the Diary, HA23. For terms of proclamation and how it was drafted, see letter from R. Farquhar to Lieut Keating, dated St. Denis, 30 July 1810, NAM: HA 23.

145 Letter from Charles Telfair to Captain A. Barry, dated Headquarters [Bourbon], 10 August 1801, NAM: HA 23.

146 Letter from Henry Keating to Robert Farquhar, dated Headquarters [Bourbon], 3 August 1810, NAM: HA 23.

147 See letter from R. Farquhar to Lieut Keating, dated St. Denis, 30 July 1810, NAM: HA 23. Farquhar writes that he had furnished a British officer with a 'rough sketch of Grand Port which lays down the Shoal directly on the mouth of the passage by the Isle de la Passe on which Marengo & other smaller vessels have struck together with the soundings into the very heart of that harbour'. Also, letter from Henry Keating to Robert Farquhar, dated St. Denis, 31 July 1810, NAM: HA 23.

148 Letter from Capt. Pym to Commander Rowley, dated 24 August 1810, Isle de la Passe, NAM: HA 23.

149 These images are in the collection of the National Maritime Museum, Greenwich, London (hereafter NMM), see PAF4779-PAF4786.

150 'Isle of France, No.1: View from the Deck of the Upper Castle Transport, of the British Army Landing', April 1813, NMM: PAF4779.

151 'Isle of France, No.5: The Town, Harbour, and Country, Eastward of Port Louis', April 1813, NMM: PAF4783.

152 Marc Serge Rivière, *'No Man is an Island': The Irish Presence in Isle de France/Mauritius, (1715-2007)*, (Rose-Hill, Mauritius: Edition de l'Océan Indien, 2008), 59.

153 Carmichael, *Account*, 57–8.

154 'Return of Captured Musquets, Ammunition, Flints, Barrels of Power, on the Isle of France', dated 17 January 1811, NAM: HA 14.

155 This paragraph relies on Selvon, *A New Comprehensive History*, 249–52.

156 [Les Anglais sont venus pour établir une ferme et perpétuelle amitié avec les habitans de l'Île de France, qui trouveront à vendre leurs denrées d'excellentes conditions, et qui jouiront de tous les avantages du Commerce comme tous les autres sujets de Sa Majesté Britannique]. From, Proclamations du Gouverneur Farquhar, December 1810, NAM: HA 51.

4 IN THE PERSIAN GULF:
TANGLED EMPIRES, STATES AND MARINERS

1 There aren't many histories of the Persian Gulf. For some exceptions, see Lawrence G. Potter, ed., *The Persian Gulf in History* (Basingstoke: Palgrave Macmillan, 2009) and Lawrence G. Potter, ed., *The Persian Gulf in Modern Times* (Basingstoke: Palgrave Macmillan, 2014). Also William Floor, *Persian Gulf: A Political and Economic History of Five Port Cities, 1500–1730* (Washington, D.C.: Mage Publishers, 2006). These are recently joined by J. E. Peterson, ed., *The Emergence of the Gulf States* (Bloomsbury: London, 2016). For an account of India's connections to the Gulf, see J. Onley, *The Arabian Frontier of the British Raj: Merchants, Rulers, and the British in the Nineteenth-century Gulf* (Oxford: Oxford University Press, 2007).

2 For this route, see Anne Bulley, *The Bombay Country Ships 1790–1833* (Richmond: Curzon, 2000), 135, and also J. B. Kelly, *Britain and the Persian Gulf, 1795–1880* (Oxford: Clarendon Press, 1968), 53.

3 Denis Piat, *Pirates & Privateers of Mauritius* (Singapore: Editions Didier Millet, 2014), 89–90. The account below of the taking of the packet draws upon Charles Belgrave, *The Pirate Coast* (London: G. Bell and Sons, 1966), 29–31; Anne Bulley, *The Bombay Country Ships 1790–1833* (Richmond: Curzon, 2000), 132–3; Charles Davies, *The Blood-red Arab Flag: An Investigation into Qasimi Piracy* (Exeter: University of Exeter Press, 1997), 258–62, and 'Sufferings of Captain Youl, &c. of the Fly Cruiser', in *Mariner's Chronicle or Interesting Narratives of Shipwrecks* (London, 1826), 149–50 and R. W. Loane, *Authentic Narrative of the Late Fortunate Escape of Mr. R. W. Loane* (Bombay: Ferris & Co, 1805). Other sources from the India Office Archives are cited below.

4 'Report from Mr. Loane of his proceeding and suffering', dated Bombay 5 February 1805, BL: IOR, Bombay Public Proceedings, P/343/20.

5 Letter from the Resident of Bushire to the Secretary of Government, Bombay, dated 2 July 1805, BL: IOR, Bombay Public Proceedings, P/343/25.

6 Quotations in this paragraph and the next, unless noted, from Loane, *Authentic Narrative*, 3, 6–8 and 29, 33.

7 There is a debate about whether these political units were made into states by Europeans and by the needs of imperial diplomacy. See, for instance, Shohei Sato, *Britain and the Formation of the Gulf States: Embers of Empire* (Manchester: Manchester University Press, 2016). See also n. 47 below for reference to this in the primary sources.

8 James Silk Buckingham, *Travels in Assyria, Media and Persia*, 2 vols (London: Henry Colburn and Richard Bentley, 1830), 2nd edn, vol. 2, 218.

9 This paragraph and the next draw upon Loane, *Authentic Narrative*, 16–17, 20, 22–7 and 33; quotation from 17.

10 This paragraph draws upon Loane, *Authentic Narrative*, 50 and 56.

11 *Mariner's Chronicle*, 150.

12 This paragraph draws upon Loane, *Authentic Narrative*, 68, 71–2.

13 Loane, *Authentic Narrative*, 27 and 38.

14 See Loane, *Authentic Narrative*, 40. See also: *Mariner's Chronicle*, 150.

15 Loane, *Authentic Narrative*, 98.

16 Buckingham, *Travels in Assyria*, vol. 2, 221–2 and 224.

17 'Report from Mr. Loane of his proceeding and suffering' dated Bombay 5 February 1805, BL: P/343/20.

18 These details of Shaikh Rahma's plunder of the *Hector* arise from Davies, *The Blood-Red Arab Flag*, 75. For further details of the fate of the *Alert* and the close attention paid by the British to tracking plundered goods, see J. A. Saldanha, ed., *The Persian Gulf Précis: Selections from State Papers, Bombay, Regarding the East India Company's Connections with the Persian Gulf, with a Summary of Events, 1600–1800*, 8 vols (Simla, 1906; and Gerrards Cross, Bucks: Archive Edition, 1986), vol. 3, 65–8.

19 On this see D. T. Potts, 'Trends and Patterns in the Archaeology and Pre-modern History of the Gulf Region', in J. E. Peterson, ed., *The Emergence of the Gulf States* (Bloomsbury: London, 2016), 19–42, 33.

20 Loane, *Authentic Narrative*, 109–111.

21 Secret and Political Dept. No. 159 of 1804 in Saldanha, ed., *The Persian Gulf Précis*, vol. 3, 67.

22 For more on the rise of the Wahhabi movement in Arabia and the Gulf, see Michael Crawford, 'Religion and Religious Movements in the Gulf, 1700–1971', in Peterson, ed., *The Emergence of the Gulf States*, 43–84; J. B. Kelly, *Britain and the Persian Gulf, 1795–1880* (Clarendon Press, 1968); Davies, *Blood-Red Arab Flag* and Madawi Al-Rasheed, *A History of Saudi Arabia* (Cambridge: Cambridge University Press, 2010). See also the work of Francis Robinson for an overview of colonial engagements with Islam. For instance, Francis Robinson, *Islam, South Asia, and the West* (New Delhi: Oxford University Press, 2007).

23 See Davies, *The Blood-Red Arab Flag*, 248. According to Risso, the Qawasim took about a one-fifth share of the booty arising from maritime violence at Ras al-Khaimah. See: Patricia Risso, 'Cross-Cultural Perceptions of Piracy: Maritime Violence in the Western Indian Ocean and Persian Gulf Region During a Long Eighteenth Century', *Journal of World History* 12, no. 2 (Fall 2001), 293–319, at 312.

24 For the execution see Tuson, *Records of the Emirates*, 35; also Kelly, *Britain and the Persian Gulf*, 45–7. And more recently for more on this campaign, Virginia Aksan, *Ottoman Wars, 1700–1870: An Empire Besieged* (Harlow: Pearson, 2007), 308–10.

25 C. A. Bayly, 'The 'Revolutionary Age in the Wider World, c.1790–1830', in Richard Bessel, Nicholas Guyatt and Jane Rendall, eds, *War, Empire*

and Slavery, 1770–1830 (Basingstoke: Palgrave Macmillan, 2010), 21–43, at 31.

26 Crawford, 'Religion', 56.

27 For more on this, see Giovanni Bonacina, *The Wahhabis seen through European Eyes (1772–1830)* (Leiden: Brill, 2011), citation, 7.

28 Letter from Harford Jones, Baghdad to Jacob Bosanquet, Chairman of the Court of Directors of the East India Company, 1 December 1798, enclosing an essay on the Wahhabis, reproduced in A. L. Burdett, ed., *The Expansion of Wahhabi Power in Arabia: British Documentary Records,* 8 vols. (Cambridge: Cambridge University Press, 2013), vol. 1, 125–35, citations here from 125 and 130, italics mine.

29 Ibid., 130.

30 See, Risso, 'Cross-cultural perceptions of piracy', 299–300.

31 For detailed dissection of these expeditions and their motivations see, Davies, *Blood-red Arab Flag,* 'Afterword', 277–95 and the more recent Potts, 'Trends and Patterns in the Archaeology and Pre-Modern History of the Gulf Region', esp. 31ff.

32 Davies, *Blood-red Arab Flag,* 190.

33 Extract from Bombay Political Consultations, 26 December 1809, quoting a letter from the Imaum [Imam] of Muscat to the Hon J Duncan, Governor of Bombay, received 25 December in Burdett, ed., *The Expansion,* 260–3, this quotation 261.

34 R. Temple, I. Clark and W. William Haines, 'Sixteen views of places in the Persian Gulph', NMM: PAF4793ff.

35 Report of Captain J Wainwright, commanding HMS *La Chiffonne,* off Ras ul Khyma to Rear Admiral Drury, 14 November 1809, in Burdett, ed., *The Expansion,* 255–9.

36 Political Dept. Diary No. 339 of 1809, instructions issued to the Commanders of the expedition in Saldanha, ed., *The Persian Gulf Précis,* vol. 3, 46.

37 For the idea of the Ras al-Khaimah and associated ports as 'headless', see Davies, *Blood-red Arab Flag,* 190.

38 Letter from Jonathan Duncan, Governor of Bombay, Fort St. George to the Rt. Hon. Lord Minto, Governor General, 6 April 1810, in Burdett, ed., *The Expansion,* 267–8, this quotation from 268.

39 See Davies, *Blood-red Arab Flag,* 197.

40 See ibid., 208; for an earlier truce between Ras al-Khaimah and the East India Company, including the clause 'they [Qawaism] will respect the flag and property of the Honourable East India Company' see: 'Agreement between Shaikh Sultan b. Saqr and the East India Company, 6 February 1806' in Penelope Tuson, ed., *Records of the Emirates: Primary Documents: 1820–1960,* 12 vols (Cambridge: Cambridge University Press, 1990), vol. 1, 3ff.

41 The words of Mrs. Thompson, wife of Captain T. Perronet Thompson, cited in H. Moyse-Bartlett, *The Pirates of Trucial Oman* (London: Macdonald & Co.), 130.

42 On this, see Nelida Fuccaro, 'Rethinking the History of Port Cities in the Gulf', in Potter, ed., *The Persian Gulf in Modern Times*, 23–46.

43 All quotations and discussion based on 'General Treaty with the Arab Tribes of the Persian Gulf, 1820', in Tuson, ed., *Records of the Emirates*, 13–15.

44 'Sir William Grant Keir's reports on the conclusion of the treaties and operations in the Arabian Gulf, January – February 1820', in Tuson, ed., *Records of the Emirates*, 47–117, information on 49–50.

45 Yet there is evidence that the directions to use flags and signals were not fully followed even in the immediate aftermath of the Keir agreement. See 'Letter dated 26 November 1821 from Mr. Meriton', in Saldanha, ed., *The Persian Gulf Précis*, vol. 3, 129.

46 For the history of slavery in the Gulf, see Thomas M. Ricks, 'Slaves and Slavers in the Persian Gulf, 18th and 19th Centuries: An Assessment', *Slavery & Abolition: A Journal of Slave and Post-Slave Studies* 9, no. 3 (1988), 60–70. See also Patricia Risso, *Oman & Muscat: An Early Modern History* (London & Sydney: Croom Helm, 1986), 101 for historic trade in slaves from Africa.

47 For debate in the sources about whether the Qawasim were a state, see Political Dept. Diary No. 339 of 1809, instructions issued to the Commanders of the expedition, in Saldanha, ed., *The Persian Gulf Précis*, vol. 3, 47.

48 See, for instance, 'The Coast from Bushire to Basadore in the Persian Gulf', surveyed by Lieuts. G. B. Bucks and S. B. Haines, 1828', NMM: G354:4/19.

49 In between these two truces were others: the 1835 Maritime Truce and the 1843 Maritime Truce. See, for instance, M. Reda Bhacker, *Trade and Empire in Muscat and Zanzibar: Roots of British Domination* (London and New York: Routledge, 1992).

50 These comments and quotations from 'Government of Bombay's instructions to Major-General Sir William Grant Keir on the expedition to the "Pirate ports", 27 October and 27 November 1819', in Tuson, ed., *Records of the Emirates*, 35–43.

51 For an introduction to the period of the history of Oman below what follows has drawn upon J. Jones and N. Ridout, *A History of Modern Oman* (Cambridge: Cambridge University Press, 2015), Risso, *Oman & Muscat*, and Reda Bhacker, *Trade and Empire*.

52 See, for instance, Jones and Ridout, *A History of Modern*, 12.

53 See Reda Bhaker, *Trade and Empire*, 20; Risso, *Oman & Muscat*, 171.

54 See, for instance, Calvin H. Allen, 'The State of Masqa in the Gulf and

East Africa, 1785–1829', *International Journal of Middle East Studies* 14, no. 2 (May 1982): 117–27.

55 Reda Bhaker, *Trade and Empire*, 27, 34.

56 Material on the history of Oman here and in following paragraphs draws upon Risso, *Oman & Muscat*; quotation from appendix II. For the original, see C. U. Aitchison, *A Collection of Treaties, Engagements and Sanads relating to India and Neighbouring Countries*, 14 vols (Calcutta: Superintendent Govt. Printing, India, 1929–33), 5th edn, vol. 11, 287–8.

57 This language may be compared for instance with the letter from Sa'id bin Sultan to the British: 'my friends were those of the English; that the foes of the English were my foes; that their allies were my allies; that our State, and property, and cities and territories were identified and that there existed no separate interest.' Translation of a letter from Political Department Diary No. 411 of 1814, His Highness Syyud Saeed the Imam of Muscat to Mahomed Aleekhan in Saldanha, ed., *The Persian Gulf Précis*, vol. 3, 53.

58 Simon Layton, 'Commerce, Authority and Piracy in the Indian ocean world, c.1780–1850' (PhD thesis, University of Cambridge, 2013), 87. Layton pays particular attention to the role of Bahrain in British policy in the Persian Gulf and also as a topic that inflects the relationship between Oman and the British.

59 Kelly, *Britain and the Persian Gulf*, 11.

60 Jones and Ridout, *A History of Modern Oman*, 44.

61 See Kelly, *Britain and the Persian Gulf*, 101ff.; Risso, *Oman and Muscat*, 175ff.

62 Risso, *Oman and Muscat*, 179–80.

63 Ibid., 99.

64 See, for instance, Lawrence Potter, 'Arabia and Iran', in Peterson, ed., *The Emergence of the Gulf States*, 100–25, at 104.

65 For British observations on Muscat, see Davies, *The Blood-red Arab Flag*, 47.

66 Details of the fall of the Safavid empire are drawn from John Foran, 'The Long Fall of the Safavid Dynasty: Moving Beyond the Standard Views', *International Journal of Middle East Studies* 24, no. 2 (May 1992), 281–304 and also William Floor and Edmund Herzig, eds., *Iran and the World in the Safavid Age* (London: I.B. Tauris, 2012). For a comparative history of Eurasian empire, see Stephen Dale, *The Muslim Empires of the Ottomans, Safavids and Mughals* (Cambridge: Cambridge University Press, 2010).

67 Foran, 'The Long Fall', 284.

68 For Zand Persia, see John R. Perry, *Karim Khan Zand: A History of Iran, 1747–1779* (Chicago: University of Chicago Press, 1979).

69 Perry, *Karim Khan Zand*, 159–61.

70 Translation of a Letter from the Imam Ahmad Been Sayeed, received without date the 6 November 1774, BL: IOR, Bombay Public Proceedings, P/341/40.

71 For the age of revolutions context to Qajar Persia, see Joanna de Groot, 'War, Empire and the "Other": Iranian-European Contacts in the Napoleonic Era', in Richard Bessel, Nicholas Guyatt and Jane Rendall, eds, *War, Empire and Slavery, 1770–1830* (Basingstoke: Palgrave Macmillan, 2010), 235–55.

72 This is the argument in C. A. Bayly, *Imperial Meridian: The British Empire and the World, 1780–1830* (Cambridge: Cambridge University Press, 1989), chapter 2. But for a recent persuasive critique of the thesis of 'tribal breakout', see Jagjeet Lally, 'Beyond "Tribal Breakout": Afghans in the History of Empire' *Journal of World History*, 29, 2018, 369–97.

73 'Correspondence of Henry Willock, British Legation at Tehran to the Marquis of Hastings concerning the alleged endeavours of the Imam of Muscat to induce the Persian Shah to attempt the capture of the island of Bahrain, April 1819', in Richard Schofield, ed., *Islands and Maritime Boundaries of the Gulf*, 20 vols (Oxford: Redwood Press, 1990), vol. 1, 291–4, quote 294. See this correspondence also for Oman's links with Persia in this period, as also the British, in order to exercise a counter-weight against Egypt.

74 For the idea of 'fear', see Frederick F. Anscombe, *The Ottoman Gulf: The Creation of Kuwait, Saudi Arabia and Qatar* (New York: Columbia University Press, 1997), 16.

75 For slavery in the Gulf, see Ricks, 'Slaves and Slave Traders'. But enslaved people were not the only trade between East Africa and Oman: see Reda Bhacker, *Trade and Empire in Muscat and Zanzibar*, 75.

76 See Robert Carter, 'The History and Prehistory of Pearling in the Persian Gulf', *Journal of the Economic and Social History of the Orient* 48, no. 2 (2005) 139–209, at 151.

77 See Patricia Risso, 'Muslim Identity in Maritime Trade: General Observations and Some Evidence from the 18th Century Persian Gulf/ Indian Ocean Region', *International Journal of Middle East Studies* 21, no. 3 (August 1989), 381–92, at 387.

78 Risso, *Oman and Muscat*, 142; for the wider context of French–British competition in Muscat, see chapter 8.

79 Political Dept. Diary No. 339 of 1809, instructions issued to the Commanders of the expedition, in Saldanha, ed., *The Persian Gulf Précis*, vol. 3, 45.

80 For the contemporary British explanation, see Robert Taylor, 'Extract from Brief Notes containing historical and other information connected with the Province of Oman, Muskat and the Adjoining Country. . .

prepared in the year 1818', in Schofield, ed., *Islands and Maritime Boundaries*, vol. 1, 247–76, esp. 274–76.

81 See Potter, 'Patterns', 106.

82 'Report of Henry Willock, British Charge d'Affaires at Tehran on efforts made to enlist the cooperation and assistance of the Persian and Muscati Governments in Captain Sadlier's forthcoming expedition to suppress the piratical activities of the Qawasim in the southern Gulf, 26 December 1819, in Schofield, ed., *Islands and Maritime Boundaries*, vol. 1, 305–6.

83 'Report of Henry Willock', 312.

84 'Minutes of a Conference between their Excellencies the Persian Ministers and His Britannick Majesty's Charge D'Affaires on the 22nd December 1819' in Schofield, ed., *Islands and Maritime Boundaries*, vol. 1, 329–36, citation 331.

85 See, for instance, Report dated 14 August 1821 by Dr. Jukes, Political Agent at Kishm, in Saldanha, ed., *The Persian Gulf Précis*, vol. 3, 127. In particular: 'The whole of the Persian shore of the Gulf is in possession of different Arab tribes, and though they may have little differences and quarrels among themselves, they would cordially unite to repel any attack the Persians might make to accept or subdue any of them.'

86 'Imam's letter to the Governor of Bombay, 1821', in Saldanha, ed., *The Persian Gulf Précis*, vol. 3, 122.

87 Letter from Tehran dated 10 March 1820, from Willock to Keir, in Schofield, ed., *Islands and Maritime Boundaries*, vol. 1, 435–8, citation 447.

88 Letter from Tehran dated 10 March 1820 from Willock to Keir, in Schofield, ed., *Islands and Maritime Boundaries*, vol. 1, 446–7.

89 Translation of a note addressed by His Excellency Mirza Abdul Wahab [Persian Minister of Foreign Affairs] to His Britannick Majesty's Charge d'Affaires' in Schofield, ed., *Islands and Maritime Boundaries*, vol. 1, 639–42, citation 641.

90 See Saldanha, ed., *The Persian Gulf Précis*, vol. 3, 139–42.

91 This account of the launch of the *Shah Alum* arises from *Asiatic Journal and Monthly Miscellany* 8 (1819), 394, and Ruttonjee Ardeshir Wadia, *The Bombay Dockyard and the Wadia Master Builders* (Bombay: Godrej, 1957), 237.

92 See Wadia, *Bombay Dockyard*, chapter 6; also W. T. Money, *Observations on the Expediency of Shipbuilding at Bombay* (London: Longman, 1811). Note the Money family were involved in the country trade themselves, while William who drafted this text worked in the Bombay Marine.

93 Amalendu Guha, 'Parsi Seths as Entrepreneurs, 1750–1850', *Economic and Political Weekly* 5, no. 35 (August 1970), M107–M115, and also Michael Mann, 'Timber Trade on the Malabar Coast, c.1780–1840', *Environment and History* 7, no. 4 (November 2001), 403–25, 404.

94 Money, 'Observations', 50, 56.

95 See Bulley, *The Bombay Country Ships*, 2–3.
96 See Wadia, *The Bombay Dockyard*, appendix B, 355.
97 Amalendu Guha, 'The Comprador Role of Parsi Seths, 1750–1850', *Economic and Political Weekly* 5, no. 48 (November 1970), 1933–6.
98 For details on the Wadia family, see Dosabhai Framji Karaka, 'Distinguished Parsis of Bombay', in J. B. Sharma and S. Sharma, eds, *Parsis in India* (Jaipur: Sublime Publications, 1999), 86–146, 93ff.
99 Details from Bulley, *The Bombay Country Ships*, 12ff.; also Wadia, *The Bombay Dockyard*, 172.
100 See the rules in Wadia, *The Bombay Dockyard*, facing 202.
101 From Wadia, *The Bombay Dockyard*, 208, cited from *Bombay Courier*, 23 June 1810.
102 Citation from Wadia, *The Bombay Dockyard*, 208.
103 See image in Bulley, *The Bombay Country Ships*, facing 14.
104 Money, 'Observations on the Expediency of Shipbuilding at Bombay', 60–1.
105 Jamsetjee Bomanjee's representation, dated 21 January 1805, BL: IOR, Bombay Public Proceedings, P/343/20.
106 John R. Hinnells and Alan Williams, Introduction in Hinnells and Williams, eds., *Parsis in India and the Diaspora* (Routledge: London, 2007), 1.
107 Guha, 'Parsi Seths as Entrepreneurs', also Hinnells and Williams, Introduction, 2.
108 F. A. Bishara and Risso, 'The Gulf, the Indian Ocean and the Arab World', in Peterson, ed., *The Emergence of the Gulf States*, 160–6, 162.
109 See Bulley, *The Bombay Country Ships*, 33 and appendix B in Wadia, *The Bombay Dockyard*. For more on the trade in timber from India to Oman in this period, see Risso, *Oman and Muscat*, 4, 81.
110 See Money, 'Observations', 65.
111 Kelly, *Britain and the Persian Gulf*, 116, 124, 129. For the ban, see also F. Warden, 'Historical sketch of the Joasmee tribe of Arabs from the year 1714 to the year 1819' in Tuson, ed,. *Records of the Emirates*, 247.
112 Kelly, *Britain and the Persian Gulf*, 157–8.
113 Mann, 'Timber Trade'. There was also the worry that control over shipbuilding in India by Arabs would restrict trade, see, Bully, *The Bombay Country Ships*, 32–3.
114 Letter from the Madras Government dated 23 January 1805, expressing their agreement 'regarding the appointment of our Agent for the purpose of ascertaining the extent to which the forests of that province [Malabar] and Canara may be available towards the objects of ship-building', BL: IOR, Bombay Public Proceedings, P/343/20. See also other letters in this volume connected to inquiries directed to forests and wood.
115 Vincenzo Maurizi, *History of Seyd Said, Sultan of Muscat, with a new introduction by Robin Bidwell* (Cambridge: Oleander Press, 1984), 95.

116 Francis Warden, 'Historical Sketch of the Joasmee tribe of Arabs from the year 1714 . . .', in Tuson, ed., *Records of the Emirates*, 251.

117 For the decline of the Bombay shipyard, see David Arnold, *Science, Technology and Medicine in Colonial India* (Cambridge: Cambridge University Press, 2000), 102ff.; and for the wider context of building ships in India, see also Frank Broeze, 'Underdevelopment and Dependency: Maritime India during the Raj', *Modern Asian Studies* 18, no. 3 (July 1984), 429–57.

118 See, for instance, T. M. Luhrmann, *The Good Parsi: The Fate of a Colonial Elite in a Postcolonial Society* (Cambridge, Mass.: Harvard University Press, 1996), 17: 'Because they tried to assimilate, and did not turn to revolution, they reveal the postcolonial consequences of their assimilation more powerfully than do most other colonial elites.'

119 Christine Dobbin, 'The Parsi Panchayat in Bombay City in the Nineteenth Century', *Modern Asian Studies* 4, no. 2 (March 1970), 149–64.

120 This section relies on C. A. Bayly, *Recovering Liberties: Indian Thought in the Age of Liberalism and Empire* (Cambridge: Cambridge University Press, 2012), 118ff.

121 For an account of the journal, see Marwa Elshakry and Sujit Sivasundaram, eds., *Science, Race and Imperialism*, in *Victorian Science and Literature*, eds, Gowan Dawson and Bernard Lightman, 8 vols (London: Chatto and Pickering, 2011–12), vol. 6, 1–6, citation from 4.

122 From 'Houses of Parliament' in Jehangir Naoroji and Hirjibhoy Meherwanji, *Journal of a Residence of Two Years and a Half in Great Britain* (London: William Allen & Co., 1841), 164ff.

123 This paragraph draws heavily upon N. Benjamin, 'Arab Merchants of Bombay and Surat (c.1800–1840)', *Indian Economic and Social History Review* 13, no. 1 (1976): 85–95. See also Bulley, *The Bombay Country Ships*, 32–3.

124 Benjamin, 'Arab Merchants', 85.

125 Buckingham, *Travels in Assyria*, vol. 2, 430.

126 Ibid.

127 William Heude, *A Voyage up the Persian Gulf* (London: Strahan and Spottiswoode, 1819), 19.

128 Bulley, *The Bombay Country Ships*, 230–1.

129 Heude, *A Voyage*, 24.

130 Heude, *A Voyage*, Ibid.

131 'Heude's Voyages and Travels', *Edinburgh Review* 32 (July–October 1819), 111–18, at 113–14.

132 Heude, *A Voyage*, 34–5.

133 Ibid., 36.

134 Heude, Ibid., 36.

135 See Maurizi, *History of Seyd Said*, x.

136 Ibid., 164.

137 Ibid., 167.

138 Bulley, *The Bombay Country Ships*, 231.

139 Aaron Jaffer, "'Lord of the Forecastle": Serangs, Tindals and Lascar Mutiny, c.1780–1860', *International Review of Social History* 58, no. S21 (December 2013), 153–75, at 170. This work has now also been published in full as: Aaron Jaffer, *Lascars and Indian Ocean Seafaring, 1780–1860: Shipboard Life, Unrest and Mutiny* (Martlesham: Boydell and Brewer, 2015).

140 For the wider framework of *lascar* labour and the navigation laws etc, see Michael H. Fisher, 'Working across the Seas: Indian Maritime Labourers in India, Britain, and in Between, 1600–1857', *International Review of Social History* 58, no. S21 (December 2013), 21–45.

141 Bayly, *Recovering Liberties*, 28ff.

142 Broeze, 'Underdevelopment and Dependency'.

143 Michael H. Fisher, 'Finding Lascar "Wilful Incendiarism": British Ship-Burning Panic and Indian Maritime Labour in the Indian Ocean', *South Asia: Journal of South Asian Studies* 35, no. 3 (2012), 596–623.

144 George Annesley Earl of Mountnorris [George Viscount Valentia], *Voyages and Travels to India, Ceylon, the Red Sea, Abyssinia and Egypt* (London: W. Bulmer and Co., 1809), 380. 'Correspondence', *The Naval Chronicle* 15 (1806), 476.

145 Letter of the Superintendent of the Marine, Robert Anderson, dated Bombay 2 February 1805, BL: IOR, Bombay Public Proceedings, P/343/20. The term 'pirate' was also applied to the *lascar* rebels in the letter dated Bombay 7 February 1805, from Forbes &c, BL: IOR, Bombay Public Proceedings, P/343/20.

146 Jaffer, "Lord of the Forecastle", 166; quotation from 'Asiatic Intelligence – Bombay', *Asiatic Journal and Monthly Miscellany* 14 (1822), 98.

147 'The Memorial of Henry William Hyland late Master of the Grab Brig Bombay Merchant' dated 26 September 1821, BL: IOR, Bombay Public Proceedings, P/345/65.

148 Bulley, *The Bombay Country Ships*, 80.

149 F. Warden, 'Extracts from brief notes relative to the rise and progress of the Arab tribes of the Persian Gulf', in Tuson, ed., *Records of the Emirates*, vol. 1, 24–5.

150 On this, see Potter, ed., *The Persian Gulf in History*, 14–16.

151 See 'Statement shewing the Expence incurred in the Dockyards for the Honble Company's, Her Majesty's, French Government and Merchant Vessels from 1838 to 1842', NMM: Papers of Captain Sir Robert Oliver (1783–1848), MS94/006.

5 IN THE TASMAN SEA:
THE INTIMATE MARKERS OF A COUNTER-REVOLUTION

1 For Cora Gooseberry's biography, see Vincent Smith, 'Gooseberry, Cora (1777–1852)', *Australian Dictionary of Biography*, http://adb.anu.edu.au/biography/gooseberry-cora-12942, accessed 17 August 2017. Cora's Aboriginal names were: Kaaroo, Carra, Caroo, Car-roo or Barangan.

2 Two breastplates of Gooseberry are extant. One in the Mitchell Library, Sydney, under classmark, R 251B, and the other in the Australian Museum, Sydney, under classmark, B008454.

3 Throughout this chapter Sydney is used for the region around Sydney Cove, though in the early period the port was called Port Jackson, with Botany Bay to the south and Broken Bay to the north.

4 F. Wymark, 'David Scott Mitchell', MLS: Am 121/1/1-3, 21.

5 *Morning Chronicle* (Sydney), 19 June 1844, 2 for comparison of Cora with Pomare. For Pomare of Tahiti and gender, see Patricia O'Brien, '"Think of me as a Woman": Queen Pomare of Tahiti and Anglo-French Imperial Contest in the 1840s Pacific', *Gender & History* 18, no. 1 (April 2006), 108–29.

6 For Cora's name as goatfish see Vincent Smith, 'Moorooboora's Daughter', in *National Library of Australia News* 16, no. 9 (June 2006), 19–21.

7 This paragraph relies on Grace Karskens, *The Colony: A History of Early Sydney* (Crow's Nest, N.S.W.: Allen & Unwin, 2010), 401ff. For wider views of Aboriginal engagement with water, see Heather Goodhall and Allison Cadzow, *Rivers and Resilience: Aboriginal People on Sydney's Georges River* (Sydney: University of New South Wales Press, 2009).

8 See, for instance, George B. Worgan, *Sydney Cove Journal, 20 January–11 July 1788*, ed. John Currey (Malvern, Vic.: Banks Society, 2010), 53 or Tench, *1788*, ed. Flannery, 258.

9 These comments relate to 'Natives of New South Wales pre-1806' (unsigned, undated), MLS: DGB 10. See also the other linked album, 'Natives of New South Wales drawn from life in Botany Bay, ca. 1805', MLS: PXB 513 and R. Browne, 'Natives Returned from Fishing, 1820', MLS: SV/150.

10 See Inga Clendinnen, *Dancing with Strangers: The True History of the Meeting of the British First Fleet and Aboriginal Australians* (Edinburgh: Canongate, 2003), 223–4.

11 See Karskens, *The Colony*, 408.

12 Worgan, *Sydney Cove Journal*, 107.

13 Augustus Earle, 'Portrait of Bungaree, a native of New South Wales, with Fort Macquarie, Sydney Harbour, in background', NLA: Rex Nan Kivell Collection, NK118. For an interpretation, see David Hansen, 'Death Dance', *Australian Book Review* 290 (April 2007), 27–32. See also Vincent

Smith, *King Bungaree: A Sydney Aborigine Meets the great South Pacific Explorers, 1799–1830* (Kenthurst, New South Wales [N.S.W.]: Kangaroo Press, 1992), and Vincent Smith, *Mari Nawi: Aboriginal Odysseys* (Dural, N.S.W.: Rosenberg, 2010), chapter 10.

14 Entry for 11 February 1822, Diary of Lachland Macquarie, MLS: A774. See Smith, *King Bungaree*, 77ff.

15 Cited Smith, *King Bungaree*, 134–5, from Richard Sadlier, *The Aborigines of Australia* (Sydney: T. Richards, Government Printer, 1883), 56, commenting retrospectively on his first visit to Sydney as a naval lieutenant, and from Peter Miller Cunningham, *Two Years in New South Wales* (London: Henry Colburn, 1827).

16 For the role of attire in the Cape rebellion led by Louis van Mauritius, see Nigel Worden, 'Armed with Swords and Ostrich Feathers: Militarism and Cultural Revolution in the Cape Slave Uprising, 1808', in Richard Bessel, Nicholas Guyatt and Jane Rendall, eds, *War, Empire and Slavery, 1770–1830* (Basingstoke: Palgrave Macmillan, 2010), 121–38.

17 Jocelyn Hackforth-Jones, *Augustus Earle, Travel Artist* (Canberra: National Library of Australia, 1980), 74.

18 Smith, *King Bungaree*, 139.

19 *Views in New South Wales and Van Diemen's Land* (London: J. Cross, 1830), Description in National Library of Australia copy, PIC S48/A-J LOC 171.

20 See Jakelin Troy, *King Plates: A History of Aboriginal Gorgets* (Canberra: Aboriginal Studies Press, 1993), 5–6.

21 'DEATH OF KING BONGAREE', broadside dated 27 November 1830, reproduced in Geoffrey C. Ingleton, *True Patriots All, or News from Early Australia as told in a Collection of Broadsides* (Sydney: Angus and Robertson, 1988), 122.

22 R. H. W. Reece, 'Feasts and Blankets: The History of Some Early Attempts to Establish Relations with the Aborigines of New South Wales, 1814–1846', *Archaeology and Physical Anthropology in Oceania* 2, no. 3 (October 1967), 190–206, at 197.

23 Smith, *King Bungaree*, 145–6. Also Smith, 'Gooseberry, Cora' (1777–1852)'.

24 *Bell's Life in Sydney*, 31 July 1852.

25 Augustus Earle, 'The annual meeting of the native tribes of Paramatta', watercolour, NLA: PIC Solander A35 T95 NK12/57.

26 *Sydney Gazette and New South Wales Advertiser*, 19 January 1826.

27 Watkin Tench, *1788: Comprising a Narrative of the Expedition to Botany Bay and a Complete Account of the Settlement at Port Jackson*, ed. Tim F. Flannery (Melbourne: Text Publishing Co., 1996), 258. See the comment of Alan Atkinson, *The Europeans in Australia*, 2 vols (Melbourne: Oxford University Press, 1997), vol. 1, 153. For the comparison of Aboriginal Australians with French peasants, see: Nicole Starbuck, 'Neither Civilized

nor Savage: The Aborigines of Colonial Port Jackson through French eyes',
in Alexander Cook, Ned Curthoys and Shino Konishi, eds, *Representing
Humanity in the Age of Enlightenment* (London: Pickering & Chatto, 2013),
109–22.

28 Despatch No. 15 of 1814, dated 8 October 1814 from Macquarie to Earl
Bathurst, in *Historical Records of Australia* (hereafter *HRA*), 37 vols
(Canberra, 1914–23, 1997–2006), series 3, vol. 8, 368.

29 Mr. William Shelley to Governor Macquarie, dated Paramatta, 8th April
1814, in *HRA*, series 3, vol. 8, 370–1.

30 David Collins, *An Account of the English Colony of New South Wales*, 2
vols (London: Printed for T. Cadell and W. Davies, 1798–1802), vol. 2,
225.

31 Grace Karskens, 'Red Coat, Blue Jacket, Black Skin: Aboriginal Men and
Clothing in Early New South Wales', *Aboriginal History* 35 (2011), 1–36.
On dress, see for instance, Worgan, *Sydney Cove Journal*, 25–29, and also
Tench, *1788*, ed. Flannery, 42.

32 Now named Pumicestone Passage.

33 Smith, *Mari Nawi*, 106–7, and 113–16. As has been expertly argued by
Bronwen Douglas, Bungaree was a point of comparison in Flinders' project
of a comparative ethnology of Aboriginal peoples along the coast of
Australia. Bronwen Douglas, 'The Lure of Texts and the Discipline of
Praxis: Cross-Cultural History in a Post-Empirical World', *Humanities
Research Journal* 14, no. 1 (2007): 11–30, and Bronwen Douglas, *Science,
Voyages and Encounters in Oceania, 1511–1850* (Basingstoke: Palgrave
Macmillan, 2014), chapter 3.

34 For this citation and the commentary on nets and spears, see Collins, *An
Account*, vol. 2, 254.

35 *Sydney Gazette and New South Wales Advertiser*, 23 December 1804.

36 Elisabeth Finlay, 'Peddling Prejudice: A Series of Twelve Profile Portraits
of Aborigines of New South Wales', *Postcolonial Studies* 16, no. 1 (2013),
2–27.

37 See for instance the black-and-white and coloured versions of this lithograph of Matora: W. H. Fernyhough, 'A Series of Twelve Profile Portraits
of Aborigines of New South Wales' (Sydney, 1836), NLA: 8Ref 994.40049915
F366 Ncopy and PIC U2181-U2193 NK590 LOC.

38 For the domain and Aboriginal peoples, see Karskens, *The Colony*, 216–17.

39 Karskens, *The Colony*, 12.

40 *Sydney Morning Herald*, 16 July 1877, article probably written by Angas,
initialled, G.F.A. The same report is also made by W. A. Miles, see Smith,
King Bungaree, 146 and W. A. Miles, 'How did the natives of Australia
become acquainted with the Demigods . . .', *Journal of the Ethnological
Society of London (1848–1856)* 3 (1854), 4–50.

41 Karskens, *The Colony*, 410–11.

42 'Matthew Flinders' biographical tribute to his cat Trim, 1809, NMM: FLI 11, http://flinders.rmg.co.uk/DisplayDocument2410.html?ID=92, accessed 13 May 2015.

43 I will use Tasmania for clarity in what follows instead of the period term Van Diemen's Land. Critically, it is worth noting that Trouwunna and Lutruwita are Aboriginal names for the island.

44 Letter from Governor King to Lord Hobart, dated Sydney, New South Wales, 9 May 1803, in *Historical Records of New South Wales* (hereafter *HRNSW*), ed. F.M. Bladen, 7 vols (Mona Vale, N.S.W.: Lansdown Slattery, 1978–9), vol. 5, 132.

45 Proclamation by Philip Gidley King, Captain-General and Governor, dated 26 May 1804 in *HRNSW*, vol. 5, 379.

46 See Letter to the Minister of Marine, dated 11 November 1802 in François Péron, *French Designs on Colonial New South Wales: François Péron's Memoir on the English Settlements in New Holland: Van Diemen's Land and the Archipelagos of the Great Pacific Ocean*, ed. and trans. Jean Fornasiero and John West-Sooby (Adelaide, South Australia: The Friends of the State Library of South Australia, 2014), appendix B, 326–29.

47 Letter from Governor King to Lord Hobart, dated Sydney New South Wales, 14 August 1804, in *HRNSW*, vol. 5, 423. For an alleged collaboration between French and American interests in the southern fishery, see Jorgen Jorgenson, 'Observations', in *Jorgen Jorgenson's 'Observations'*, ed. Rhys Richards (Wellington: Paremata Press, 1996), 20–1.

48 Governor King to Sir Joseph Banks, dated Sydney 9 May 1803, in *HRNSW*, vol. 5, 132–8, citation from 134.

49 Lyndall Ryan, *Tasmanian Aborigines: A History Since 1803* (Crow's Nest, N.S.W.: Allen and Unwin, 2012), 43.

50 Governor King to Sir Joseph Banks, dated Sydney 9 May 1803, in *HRNSW*, vol. 5, 132–8, citation from 134.

51 Commodore Baudin to Governor King, dated Port Jackson, 16 November 1802, in *HRNSW*, vol. 4, 1006.

52 Péron, *French Designs*, ed. Fornasiero and West-Sooby, Introduction, 28.

53 On the use of the idea of invasion, see ibid., 102.

54 François Péron, 'Memoir on the English Settlements in New Holland, Van Diemen's Land and the Archipelagos of the Great Pacific Ocean', in Péron, *French Designs*, ed. Fornasiero and West-Sooby, 248.

55 Peron, 'Memoir on the English Settlements', 248–9.

56 Péron, *French Designs*, ed. Fornasiero and West-Sooby, Introduction, 108, 119.

57 See 'François Péron, Report to General Decaen, 1803', in ibid., appendix A, 312.

58 Peron, 'Memoir on the English Settlements in New Holland, Van Diemen's Land and the Archipelagos of the Great Pacific Ocean', 261.

59 Ibid., 264.

60 Ibid., 260.

61 Ibid., 280.

62 Tench, *1788*, ed. Flannery, 208. On the Irish maritime imagination of escape see, Grace Karskens, '"This spirit of emigration": The nature and meanings of escape in early New South Wales', *Journal of Australian Colonial History* 7 (2005), 1–34.

63 Tench, *1788*, ed. Flannery, 211.

64 'Report on Port Jackson', journal entry dated 28–29 Floréal, Year 10 [18–19 May 1802] by Jacques-Félix-Emmanuel Hamelin in Péron, *French Designs*, ed. Fornasiero and West-Sooby, 337–8.

65 Grace Karskens, 'The early colonial presence', in Bashford and McIntyre, *The Cambridge History of Australia*, vol. 1, 91–120, 113.

66 Péron, 'Memoir on the English Settlements in New Holland, Van Diemen's Land and the Archipelagos of the Great Pacific Ocean', 193.

67 Ibid., 191.

68 Matthew Flinders, *Narrative of a Voyage in the Schooner Francis 1798: Preceded and Followed by Notes on Flinders, Bass, the Wreck of the Sidney Cove, etc.*, ed. Geoffrey Rawson (London: Golden Cockerel Press, 1946), 12.

69 François Péron, *King Island and the Sealing Trade: A Translation of Chapters XXII and XXIII of the Narrative by François Péron published in the Official Account of the Voyage of Discovery to the Southern Lands undertaken in the Corvettes Le Géographe, Le Naturaliste and the Schooner Casuarina, During the Years 1800 to 1804, under the Command of Captain Nicolas Baudin*, ed. and trans. Helen Mary Micco (Canberra: Roebuck Society, 1971), 38.

70 For Péron's interest in Flinders' movements and also an indication of his errors, see, Péron, *King Island and the Sealing Trade*, ed. Micco, 17.

71 Ibid., 23.

72 Ibid., 23.

73 Ibid., 24.

74 Ibid., 25.

75 Ibid., 20.

76 For more on the ideology of natural improvement as part and parcel of this period, see Richard Drayton, *Nature's Government: Science, Imperial Britain and the 'Improvement' of the World* (New Haven and London: Yale University Press, 2000). For science and empiricism in the age of revolutions, see Patrick Manning and Daniel Rood, eds *Global Scientific Practice in the Age of Revolutions* (Pittsburgh, PA.: University of Pittsburgh Press, 2016).

77 Flinders, *Narrative of a Voyage*, 21.

78 See for instance Tench, *1788*, ed. Flannery, 65. For Péron's anthropology, see Shino Konishi, 'François Péron's Meditation on Death, Humanity and

Savage Society', in Cook, Curthoys and Konishi, eds *Representing Humanity*, 109–22.

79 For the environmental contrast between Tasmania and NSW, see James Boyce, *Van Diemen's Land* (Melbourne Vic.: Black Inc., 2008), 1–11.

80 For 'piracy' in the age of revolutions, see Simon Layton, 'Discourses of Piracy in an Age of Revolutions', *Itinerario* 35, no. 2 (August 2011), 81–97.

81 For the first colonial sealers' arrival, see Patsy Cameron, *Grease and Ochre: The Blending of Two Cultures at the Colonial Sea Frontier* (Launceston, Tasmania: Fullers Bookshop, 2011), 51, 61–2; 70 for 'seawolves'. See also: Brian Plomley and Kirsten Anne Henley, *The Sealers of Bass Strait and the Cape Barren Island Community* (Hobart: Blubber Head Press, 1990).

82 Rev. J. McGarvie, 'Manuscript on convict escapees', NLA: MS 400482; for Munro's assistance to escaped convicts, see Plomley and Henley, *The Sealers of Bass Strait*, 6; for a list of Eastern Straitsmen, see Cameron, *Grease and Ochre*, appendix 2.

83 Ryan, *Tasmanian Aborigines*, 74; and the paragraph also draws upon, 132–3.

84 On Van Diemen's Land as one of the most policed countries in the world at this point, see discussion in Boyce, *Van Diemen's Land*, 174.

85 For recent transnational readings of Robinson, see Anna Johnston and Mitchell Rolls, eds, *Reading Robinson: Companion Essays to Augustus Robinson's 'Friendly Mission'* (Clayton, Vic.: Monash University Press, 2012).

86 Papers of George Augustus Robinson, vol. 8, part 3, Van Diemen's Land, 31 Oct. 1830 – 28 February 1831, MLS: A 7029. For more on the status of abolitionist discourse in the Bass Strait, see Penny Edmonds, 'Collecting Looerryminer's "Testimony": Aboriginal Women, Sealers, and Quaker Humanitarian Anti-Slavery Thought and Action in the Bass Strait Islands', *Australian Historical Studies* 45, no. 1 (2014), 13–33.

87 Letter from W. Balfour, Naval Officer, to Lieutenant Governor Arthur, dated 30 May 1826: Tasmania Archives and Heritage Office, Hobart, (hereafter TAHO) CSO 1/36.

88 See for instance the tissue map of James Allen, the Medical Officer on Flinders Island from 1834 to 1837 and son-in law to Robinson, TAHO: NG 1419.

89 'An Act for the better preservation of the Ports, Harbours, Havens, Roadsteads, Channels, navigable Creeks and Rivers in Van Diemen's Land, and the better regulation of the Shipping in the same', TAHO: CRO29/1/14.

90 See Charles Bateson, *Dire Strait: A History of Bass Strait* (Sydney: Reed, 1973), 68–87.

91 'Register of Names and Descriptions of Native Women forcibly taken away by the sealers and retained by them on the Straits', MLS: DLADD219, Item 9.

92 From 'Register of Names and Descriptions of Native Women'; note that this murder is not the only one recorded in these papers.

93 Bateson, *Dire Strait*, 63.

94 Henry Reynolds, 'George Augustus Robinson in Van Diemen's Land', in Johnston and Rolls, eds., *Reading Robinson*, 161–70, 167.
95 'Register of Names and Descriptions of Native Women'.
96 Cameron, *Grease and Ochre*, 18–19, 42–3.
97 James Kelly, 'Discovery of Port Davey and Macquarie Harbour, 12 December 1815 – 30 January 1816', TAHO: MM 134, 49. See also the description of the Kelly voyage in Bateson, *Dire Strait*, 41; for some other discussion of Briggs see Plomley and Henley, *The Sealers of Bass Strait*, 18 and Cameron, *Grease and Ochre*, 74–5.
98 For dancing as marking the culmination of 'reciprocal exchange', see Cameron, *Grease and Ochre*, 96.
99 Kelly, 'Discovery', 72.
100 'Papers of George Augustus Robinson', vol. 8, part 2, Van Diemen's Land, 30 September – 30 October 1830, MLS: A7029, part 2.
101 Cameron, *Grease and Ochre*, 137.
102 George Augustus Robinson's journal, Van Diemen's Land, 25 January – 24 July 1830, A7027, MLS: A7027, 240 for this sketch.
103 Cameron, *Grease and Ochre*, 95.
104 George Augustus Robinson's journal, Van Diemen's Land, 25 January – 24 July 1830, MLS: A7027, 251–2.
105 Ibid., 254.
106 Cameron, *Grease and Ochre*, 32.
107 George Augustus Robinson's journal, Van Diemen's Land, 25 January – 24 July 1830, MLS: A7027, 245, for the biography see Russell, *Roving Mariners*, 104.
108 George Augustus Robinson's journal, Van Diemen's Land, 25 January – 24 July 1830, MLS: A7027, 250–1.
109 For discussion of whether to describe these events as a genocide, see Ann Curthoys, 'Genocide in Tasmania: The History of an Idea', in A. Dirk Moses, ed., *Empire, Colony, Genocide: Conquest, Occupation, and Subaltern Resistance in World History* (New York: Berghahn Books, 2008), 229–52.
110 See Cameron, *Grease and Ochre*, 83–6, and Cameron makes the argument about the survival of Tasmanian aborigines from this community.
111 Ryan, *Tasmanian Aborigines*, 63; Plomley and Henley, *The Sealers of Bass Strait*, 56.
112 Russell, *Roving Mariners*, 14, 100.
113 Ibid., 15.
114 Ibid., and Nigel Prickett, 'Trans-Tasman stories: Australian Aborigines in New Zealand sealing and shore whaling', in G. R. Clarke, F. Leach and S. O'Connor, eds, *Islands of Inquiry: Colonization, Seafaring and the Archaeology of Maritime Landscapes*, (Canberra: Australian National University Press, 2008), 351–66.

115 Dutton's story draws considerably upon Russell, *Roving Mariners,* 111ff. For Dutton as pioneer, see J. G. Wiltshire, *Captain William Pelham Dutton: First Settler at Portland Bay, Victoria: A History of the Whaling and Sealing Industries in Bass Strait, 1828–1868* (Portland, Vic.: Wiltshire Publications, 1994).

116 'Log Book of the Barque Africaine, commanded by William Dutton from Launceston, Van Dieman's Land on a Whaling Voyage', NLA: MS 6824.

117 Lynette Peel, ed., *The Henty Journals: A Record of Farming, Whaling and Shipping at Portland Bay* (Carlton South, Melbourne: Melbourne University Press: 1996), 46.

118 This draws upon: Nigel Prickett, 'Trans-Tasman stories: Australian Aborigines in New Zealand sealing and shore whaling', in Clarke, Leach and O'Connor, eds, *Islands of Inquiry,* 351–66 and also Russell, *Roving Mariners,* chapter 3.

119 For his Māori name, see Russell, *Roving Mariners,* 48.

120 Russell, *Roving Mariners,* 58.

121 Prickett, 'Trans-Tasman stories', 353,

122 Ibid.

123 Citations in Russell, *Roving Mariners,* 56–7.

124 Smith, *Mari Nawi,* 179.

125 Lynette Russell, '"The Singular Transcultural Space": Networks of Ships, Mariners, Voyagers and "Native" Men at Sea, 1790–1870', in Jane Carey and Jane Lydon, eds, *Indigenous Networks: Mobility, Connections and Exchange* (New York and London: Routledge, 2014), 97–113, 101.

126 Smith, *Mari Nawi,* 177.

127 Ibid., 169.

128 Russell, *Roving Mariners,* 55; Smith, *Mari Nawi,* 169.

129 Tony Ballantyne, *Webs of Empire: Locating New Zealand's Colonial Past* (Vancouver: University of British Columbia Press, 2012), 126. For the story of the North Island and whaling see, for instance, Rhys Richards, 'Jorgen Jorgenson in New Zealand in 1804 and 1805', in *Jorgen Jorgenson's 'Observations',* edited and introduced by Rhys Richards.

130 Angela Wanhalla, *In/visible Sight: The Mixed-Descent Families of Southern New Zealand* (Wellington: Bridget Williams Books, 2009).

131 Richards, 'Jorgen Jorgenson in New Zealand', 73–4.

132 For the officers and their trades, see D. R. Hainsworth, *The Sydney Traders: Simeon Lord and his Contemporaries, 1788–1821* (Melbourne: Cassell Australia, 1972), chapter 1.

133 For the glut of sealskins in New Zealand, see Richard, 'Jorgen Jorgenson in New Zealand', 56. See also Hainsworth, *The Sydney Traders,* chapter 5.

134 Jorgen Jorgenson, *History of the Origin, Rise and Progress of the Van Diemen's Land Company* (reprinted, Hobart: Melanie Publications, 1979; original, 1829), 3.

135 'Van Diemen's Land Company Annual Reports, 1826–1831', NLA: MS 3273.
136 For an analysis of the violence between Aboriginal peoples and the company, see Ryan, *Tasmanian Aborigines*, 166ff.
137 Colonel William Wakefield Diary, 1839–1842', Alexander Turnbull Library, Wellington (hereafter TLW): qMS 2103, 26.
138 Raymond Bunker, 'Systematic colonization and town planning in Australia and New Zealand', *Planning Perspectives* 3, no. 1 (1988), 59–80, at 68.
139 For Edward on whalers see Prickett, 'Trans-Tasman stories'.
140 Colonel William Wakefield Diary', 24. For further biographical information about Richard Barrett, see Julie Bremner, 'Richard Barrett', http://www.teara.govt.nz/en/biographies/1b10/barrett-richard, accessed 14 May 2015.
141 'Colonel William Wakefield Diary', 49.
142 Ibid.
143 Ibid., 155.
144 Ibid., 156.
145 One might compare the status of Barrett with James Munro, the sealer of the Bass Strait, who was appointed as government agent in 1825 and later settled in Launceston. See Plomley and Henley, *The Sealers of Bass Strait*, 20 and 38.
146 For further discussion of the rising and changing status of a whaler in New Zealand, see the discussion of Johnny Jones in Ballantyne, *Webs of Empire*, 135–6.
147 See West, *History of Tasmania*, 90–3 and 108. For Jorgenson's biography, and details of his sealing and whaling, see James Dally, 'Jorgen Jorgenson (1780–1841)' at http://adb.anu.edu.au/biography/jorgenson-jorgen-2282, accessed 14 May 2017.
148 Richards, 'Jorgen Jorgenson in New Zealand', 82–3.
149 Ibid., 84.
150 Hainsworth, *The Sydney Traders*, 88.
151 Margaret Steven, *Merchant Campbell, 1769–1846* (Melbourne: Oxford University Press, 1965), 60–1.
152 Bateson, *Dire Strait*, 17
153 Steven, *Merchant Campbell*, cited 293.
154 Ibid., 299.
155 'Articles of indenture', TAHO: CRO29/1/15.
156 Agreement, dated 31 March 1834, made by James Kelly, MLS: James Kelly Papers, A2588. See also papers in Hobart, for example 'Whaling articles of agreement for the Brig Amity', TAHO: CRO29/1/5.
157 For more on Kelly, see Susan Lawrence, *Whalers and Free Men: Life on Tasmania's Colonial Whaling Stations* (North Melbourne, Vic.: Australian Scholarly Publishing, 2006).
158 For 'whitening' in Sydney, see Karskens, *The Colony*, 533ff.
159 'Colonel William Wakefield Diary', 457.

160 Lisa Ford and David Andrew Roberts, 'Expansion, 1820–50', in Bashford and McIntyre, *The Cambridge History of Australia*, 2 vols (Cambridge University Press, 2013), vol. 1, 121–48. For tensions in the emergence of bourgeois culture, see Penny Russell, *Savage or Civilised?: Manners in Colonial Australia* (Sydney: New South Wales Press, 2010). For tensions in the status of philanthropy and differing orders of gender, see Alan Lester and Fae Dussart, 'Masculinity, "Race", and Family in the Colonies: Protecting Aborigines in the Early Nineteenth Century', *Gender, Place & Culture: A Journal of Feminist Geography* 16, no. 1 (2009), 63–75.

161 Letter from Robert Campbell, dated Sydney, 18 July 1821, in 'Letter book, 1821', MLS: Robert Campbell Papers, ML 1348.

162 Letter from Robert Campbell, dated George Street, 26 October 1821, in 'Letter book, 1821', MLS: Robert Campbell Papers, ML 1348.

163 Lawrence, *Whalers*, 21–2.

164 Ibid., 22.

165 Ibid., 19.

166 For the maritime swing in histories of Australia and New Zealand see Frances Steele, 'Uncharted Waters? Cultures of Sea Transport and Mobility in New Zealand Colonial History', *Journal of New Zealand Studies* 12 (2011), 137–54 and also, Cindy McCreery and Kirsten McKenzie, 'The Australian Colonies in a Maritime World', in Alison Bashford and Stuart Macintyre, eds *The Cambridge History of Australia*, vol. 1, 560–84. Also important is Tracey Banivanua Mar, 'Shadowing Imperial Networks: Indigenous Mobility and Australia's Pacific Past', *Australian Historical Studies* 46, no. 3 (2015) 340–55; The twinning of Australia and New Zealand follows, for instance, Tony Ballantyne, *Entanglements of Empire*, but it is unusual for the period. Frances Steele, ed., *New Zealand and The Sea*, appeared in the final stages of editing this book and is a welcome addition to the literature on the maritime Tasman world.

167 See, for instance, Rachel Stanfield, *Race and Identity in the Tasman World, 1769–1840* (London: Pickering & Chatto, 2012).

168 Māori had names for the waters around their islands; the Tasman Sea was Te Tai-o-Rēua.

6 AT INDIA'S MARITIME FRONTIER: WATERBORNE LINEAGES OF WAR

1 I use Burma and Burmese as terms current in the period for the nation now called Myanmar.

2 *Epistles Written on the Eve of the Anglo-Burmese War*, trans. and ed. Maung Htin Aung (The Hague: Martinus Nijhoff, 1968).

3 'Epistle from the courtier Son' in *Epistles*, 31–3, citations from 32.

4 See, for instance, Maung Htin Aung, *The Stricken Peacock: Anglo-Burmese*

Relations, 1752–1948 (The Hague: Martinus Nijhoff, 1965), vii. For the earlier view that the Burmese were certain of victory see, for instance, G. E. Harvey, *History of Burma: From the Earliest Times to 10 March 1824* (London: Frank Cass, 1967, reprint Yangon, n.d.), 303–4.

5 'Epistle from an anxious Father to his Son', in *Epistles*, 45.

6 Thant Myint-U, *The Making of Modern Burma* (Cambridge: Cambridge University Press, 2001), 18.

7 See for instance, T. Abercromby Trant, *Two Years in Ava* (London: J. Murray, 1827), 9–10.

8 For details of the war see, for instance, Maung Htin Aung, *A History of Burma* (Columbia University Press: New York and London, 1967, reprint Yangon, n.d.), 210–32 and Thant Myint-U, *The Making of Modern Burma*, 17–20.

9 See, for instance, Henry Gouger, *Personal Narrative of Two Years' Imprisonment in Burmah* (London: John Murray, 1860), 103–4, for the bid to take Calcutta.

10 For Burmese understandings of geography in flux in this period, see Michael Charney, *Powerful Learning: Buddhist Literati and the Throne in Burma's Last Dynasty* (Ann Arbor, Mich.: Centres for South and Southeast Asian Studies, University of Michigan, 2006), 169–80. For the ideal, see Michael Aung Thwin, 'Jambudīpa: Classical Burma's Camelot', *Contributions to Asian Studies* 16 (1981), 38–61.

11 Victor B. Lieberman, *Strange Parallels: Southeast Asia in Global Context, c.800–1830*, 2 vols (Cambridge: Cambridge University Press, 2003), vol. 1, 198.

12 These appear to have been built by Messrs Snowball and Turner, see 'French and Shipbuilding', in Harvey, *History of Burma*, 353; also Trant, *Two Years in Burma*, 29 and Henry Havelock, *Memoir of Three Campaigns of Major-General Sir Archibald Campbell's Army in Ava* (Serampore, 1828), 49.

13 He is named as 'Sarkies', and was probably Manook Sarkies, see Allott, *The End of the First Anglo-Burmese War*, 4, 82.

14 See Bayly, *Empire and Information: Intelligence Gathering and Social Communication in India, 1780–1870* (Cambridge: Cambridge University Press, 1996), 122.

15 Trant, *Two Years*, 218–220.

16 Henry Bell, *Narrative of the Late Military and Political Operations in the Birmese Empire* (Edinburgh: Constable and Co., 1827), 64.

17 'One of the Birman Gilt War Boats Captured by Capt. Chads, R.N. in his successful expedition against Tanthabeen Stockade', painted by T. Stothard, R.A. from an original Sketch by Captn. Marryat, R.N. in Joseph Moore, *Rangoon Views and Combined Operations in the Birman Empire*, 2 vols (London: Thomas Clay, 1825–6), vol. 2, no. 4, BL: X 728; and *Notes*

to Accompany the Rangoon Views, 2 vols (London: Thomas Clay, 1825–6), vol. 2, no. 4, BL: X 728.

18 See the version of this image at the National Maritime Museum, 'One of the Birman Gilt War Boats Captured by Capt. Chads, R.N. in his successful expedition against Tanthabeen Stockade', NMM: PAG9121.

19 Trant, *Two Years in Ava*, 51–3, citation 53.

20 See Gouger, *Personal Narrative*, 19. For guns, see Than Tun, ed., *Royal Orders of Burma 1598–1885*, 10 vols (Kyoto: Centre for Southeast Asian Studies, 1983–90), vol. 5. There are recurrent orders in this volume connected to passage of guns; for instance, order dated 20 June 1806, 251 and orders 251ff.

21 Michael Charney, 'Shallow-draft Boats, Guns, and the Aye-ra-wa-ti: Continuity and Change in Ship Structure and River Warfare in Precolonial Myanma', *Oriens Extremus* 40, no. 1 (1997), 16–63.

22 See for instance Moore, *Birman Empire*, for this sequence.

23 See for instance 'The Combined Forces under Brigadier Cotton, C.B. and Capt. Alexander C.B. & Chads R.N. passing the Fortress of Donabue to effect a junction with Sir Archibald Campbell on the 27th March 1825', drawn by T. Stothard, R.A. from a sketch by Capt. Thornton, RN in Moore, *Birman Empire*, vol. 2, no. 6.

24 Anna Allott, *The End of the First Anglo-Burmese War: The Burmese Chronicle Account of how the 1826 Treaty of Yandabo was Negotiated* (Chulalongkorn University Press: Bangkok, 1994), a translation of a portion of the Burmese court chronicle the 'Kòn-baung-zet Maha Ya-zawin-daw-gyí', from the year 1826, 32.

25 For petroleum, see Trant, *Two Years in Ava*, 40, also John Crawfurd, *Journal of an Embassy from the Governor General of India to the Court of Ava*, 2 vols (London: Published for Henry Colburn and R. Bentley, 1834), 2nd edn, vol. 1, 97. For further discussion of this, see Sujit Sivasundaram, 'The oils of empire', in Helen Anne Curry, Nicholas Jardine, James Secord, and Emma C. Spary, eds, *Worlds of Natural History* (Cambridge: Cambridge University Press, 2018), 379–400.

26 Havelock, *Memoir of Three Campaigns*, 169.

27 'Marryat's private logbook and record of services, 23 September 1806 to 21 April 1815', NMM: MRY/6. For Burmese use and British responses to 'fire rafts', see also Havelock, *Memoir of Three Campaigns*, 130, 168.

28 Introduction, in Tun, ed., *Royal Orders*, vol. 5, xiii–xiv.

29 John Crawfurd, *Journal of an Embassy from the Governor General of India to the Court of Ava* (London: Henry Colburn, 1829), 1st edn, 112.

30 For a starting point with the *parabaik* in London, see *Catalogue of the Burney Parabaiks in the India Office Library* (London: British Library, 1985).

31 Allott, *The End of the First Anglo-Burmese War*, 73.

32 Ibid., 12.

33 For the indemnity see: Aung, *The Stricken Peacock*, 31.

34 Allott, *The End of the First Anglo-Burmese War*, 26.

35 Crawfurd, *Journal of an Embassy*, 1st edn, 116.

36 'Journal of a visit to Windsor, London, Richmond etc with a description and sketches of Indian idols etc. brought by Capt. Marryat from Burmah by Rev. John Skinner', transcribed by Russell Skinner, BL: Add MS 33697, 163.

37 Crawfurd, *Journal of an Embassy*, 2nd edn, vol. 1, 295, where the *Diana* was shown to the king. The *Diana* was assembled in Kidderpore in India in 1823, under the superintendence of a Scottish engineer, and was sold to Government for use in the Anglo-Burmese war. It remained on the Tenasserim coast after the end of the war, and with some intervals, until 1835, when she was broken up. See C. A. Gibson-Hill, 'The Steamers in Asian Waters, 1819-1839', *Journal of the Malayan Branch of the Royal Asiatic Society* 27, no. 1 (May 1954), 120-62.

38 'The Conflagration of Dalla, on the Rangoon River', drawn by Moore in *Birman Empire*, vol. 1, no. 17, BL: X 728.

39 Havelock, *Memoir of Three Campaigns*, 210 and 212.

40 Gouger, *Personal Narrative*, 293.

41 Ibid., 294.

42 Trant, *Two Years in Ava*, 178. For discussion of the relative strengths of steamboats and warboats, see Charney, 'Shallow-draft Boats'.

43 Crawfurd, *Journal of an Embassy*, 1st edn, 40, 45, 98.

44 Ibid., 445.

45 Havelock, *Memoir of Three Campaigns*, 241.

46 Crawfurd, *Journal of an Embassy*, 1st edn, 89.

47 Ibid., 321, 328.

48 Charney, 'Shallow-draft Boats', 60; Charney, 157.

49 Havelock, *Memoir of Three Campaigns*, 34.

50 Trant, *Two Years in Ava*, 33-4.

51 Ibid., 34. For a recent story about the quest to find a bell, see: http://www.bbc.co.uk/news/world-asia-28832296, accessed 20 July 2015.

52 For 'rifling', see John Butler, *A Sketch of the Services of the Madras Regiment* (London: Smith & Elder, 1839), 23.

53 Ibid, 22, 17.

54 See F. B. Doveton, *Reminiscences of the Burmese War* (London: Allen, 1852), 196-7.

55 Ralph Isaacs, 'Captain Marryat's Burmese Collection and the Rath, or Burmese Imperial State Carriage', *Journal of the History of Collections* 17, no. 1 (January 2005) 45-71, at 51.

56 Ibid., 46.

57 Catalogue description of 'Seated, dry lacquer Buddha', donated by Frederick Marryat, British Museum: 1826, 0211.1.

58 Ibid., 52.

59 Ibid., 51–56.

60 For the moveable seat, see *The Rath; Or, Burmese Imperial State Carriage, and Throne, Studded with 20,000 Precious Stones Captured in the Present Indian War which is now Exhibiting as Drawn by Elephants at the Egyptian Hall, Piccadilly* (London: Printed for the Proprietors, 1826), 8.

61 The same comparison of the carriage, the Shwedagon and the royal war-boat was made in *The Rath*.

62 'The Rath, Or Burmese Imperial State Carriage', *The Times*, 19 November 1825, 2.

63 For an account of the ethnic homogenisation undertaken by Ava, and the attempt to incorporate the Mons of Pegu and elsewhere within such a composite eighteenth-century polity, see Charney, *Powerful Learning*, chapter 6.

64 Lieberman, *Strange Parallels*, 183.

65 Aung, *The Stricken Peacock*, 14–16 see also Harvey, *History of Burma*, 353, 155–6, and Michael Symes, *Journal of his Second Embassy to the Court of Ava*, ed. with an introduction by G. E. Hall (London: Allen and Unwin, 1955), xxi.

66 Symes, *Journal*, xxx.

67 Aung, *The Stricken Peacock*, 22; see also 'Symes Instructions, dated 30 March 1802', reproduced in Symes, *Journal*, 106–8. For his biography see ibid., lxii.

68 Michael Symes, *An Account of an Embassy to the Kingdom of Ava, in the Year 1795*, 2 vols (Ediburgh: Constable & Co., 1827, first edn 1800), vol. 2, 147.

69 'Symes Journal', dated 3 October 1804, in Symes, *Journal*, 146.

70 Symes Journal', dated 15 November 1804, in ibid., 181.

71 'Appendix 1, Letter from the Rev. Padre Don Luigi De Grondona To Lieut. Canning' dated Amarapura, 2nd October 1802, in ibid., 237.

72 Symes to Lumsden, dated Rangoon 9 August 1802, reproduced in ibid., 134.

73 Tun, ed., *Royal Orders*, vol. 6, orders dated 24 March 1807 and 1 November 1807.

74 Symes, *Journal*, lxxxix.

75 See *A Description of the Burmese Empire, compiled chiefly from Native Documents by the Rev. Father Sangermano*, trans. William Tandy (Rome: Oriental Translation Fund, 1833), 177.

76 Aung, *The Stricken Peacock*, 21.

77 Letter from the Commissioner of Pegu to the Secretary of the Government of India, dated 27 September 1859, 'Protection of French Subjects at Ava', National Archives of Myanmar, Yangon: AG 1/1 Acc No.7975.

78 Aung, *A History of Burma*, 257–9.

79 'Scrap album of official documents, press cuttings etc. relating to Capt. Marryat', NMM: MRY/11-12.
80 See Isaacs, 'Captain Marryat's', 48.
81 'Frederick Marryat's Signal book' (n.d.), NMM: MRY/5.
82 Isaacs, 'Captain Marryat's', 48.
83 'Captain Marryat's Framed and Original Sketch of Napoleon Bonaparte', NMM: MRY/8. Compare this to 'Sketch of Bonaparte, as laid out on his Austerlitz campbed', NMM: PAF5963. The first (MRY/8) is in pen and ink; the second (PAF5963) is in pencil. See also NMM: MRY/7, for another image, titled, 'Original sketch taken by Capt. Marryat at St Helena, a few hours after the Emperor's death'.
84 Trant, *Two Years in Ava*, 15.
85 For a comparison with Napoleon in Egypt, see Havelock, *Memoir of Three Campaigns*, 43.
86 Gouger, *Personal Narrative*, 7.
87 Ibid., 33.
88 This follows the work of Michael Charney, *Southeast Asian Warfare, 1300–1900* (Brill: Leiden, 2004), who argues for the need to think of the regional contours of warfare in Southeast Asia, due to the similarities of demography, geography and climate.
89 I use the term Sri Lanka for the present nation and Lankan for people coming from the island. Ceylon is used as the colonial name for this island.
90 Tun, ed., *Royal Orders*, vol. 5, order passed on 18 March 1806, 212–3.
91 Ibid., order passed on 1 May 1806, 229–230.
92 Ibid., order passed on 29 May 1806, 240.
93 Ibid., vol. 6, orders passed on 4, 6 and 8 July 1807, 56–7.
94 Ibid., order passed on 21 January 1810, 166–7 and order passed on 26 December 1810, 306.
95 Ibid., vol.6, order passed on 31 January 1810, 172.
96 Kitsiri Malalgoda, *Buddhism in Sinhalese Society: A Study of Religious Revival and Change* (Berkeley: University of California Press, 1976), 87ff.
97 Malalgoda, *Buddhism*, 97–9.
98 See, for instance, Sujit Sivasundaram, *Islanded: Britain, Sri Lanka, and the Bounds of an Indian Ocean Colony*, chapters 1 and 3 for points made in this paragraph.
99 See, for instance, Sujit Sivasundaram, 'Appropriation to Supremacy: Ideas of the "native" in the rise of British imperial heritage', in Astrid Swenson and Peter Mandler, eds., *From Plunder to Preservation: Britain and the Heritage of Empire. c.1800-1940* (Oxford: Oxford University Press, 2013), 149–70. Also for more detail and for a fascinating example of the role of the literati and monks in orchestrating the reformulation

of religion and kingship in this period in Burma, Charney, *Powerful Learning*.

100 Sivasundaram, *Islanded*, for an extended account of the war, see, for instance, 212–14, 255–7.

101 Citations from the *Ingrisi Hatana* are from a full translation undertaken from Sinhala to English in collaboration with Prof. Udaya Meddegama of the University of Peradeniya, Sri Lanka. Copies are available to view at the Museum Library, Colombo National Museum (CNM), see, for instance, K11.

102 Ibid.

103 Ibid.

104 On this see the important revisionist work of Gananath Obeyeskere which has come out since this chapter was first drafted: *Doomed King: A Requiem for Sri Vickrama Rajasinha* (Colombo: Perera-Hussein, 2017).

105 Channa Wickremesekera, *Kandy at War: Indigenous Military Resistance to European Expansion in Sri Lanka, 1594–1818* (Colombo: Vijitha Yapa, 2004), 60–3.

106 Ibid., chapter 3.

107 *Sivasundaram, Islanded*, 71–2, 91.

108 Ibid., chapter 2.

109 Obeyesekere, *The Doomed King*, 138

110 *Ingrisi Hatana.*

111 *Vadiga Hatana* from translation undertaken by Prof. Udaya Meddegama from Kusuma Jayasuriya, *Waduga Hatana* (Colombo: Department of Cultural Affairs, 1966).

112 Extracts of Letters from Major Hardy to His Excellency the Governor, National Archives, Kew (hereafter TNA): CO 54/56.

113 *Ahalepola Hatana* from translation undertaken with Prof. Udaya Meddegama from K. F. Perera, *Ehalepola Hatanaya* (Colombo: Subhadraloka Press: Colombo, 1911).

114 'Narrative of Eknellegode Nilame', dated Ratnapura 20 July 1816, TNA: CO 54/61.

115 This quote and the one below arise from Ibid.; Kumari Jayawardena, *Perpetual Ferment: Popular Revolts in Sri Lanka in the 18th and 19th Centuries* (Colombo: Social Scientists' Association, 2010), 75.

116 Sivasundaram, *Islanded*, chapter 1.

117 'Narrative of Eknellegode Nilame'.

118 Jayawardena, *Perpetual Ferment*, 73–4.

119 Despatch from Brownrigg to Bathurst, dated Colombo 5 November 1816, TNA: CO 54/61.

120 P. E. Pieris, *Sinhale and the Patriots, 1815–1818* (reprinted Delhi: Navrang, 1995), 134, 136–7.

121 Captain L. De Bussche, *Letters on Ceylon, Particularly Relative to the Kingdom of Kandy* (London: J. J. Stockdale, 1817), 130–1.

122 Despatch from Brownrigg to Bathurst, dated Colombo 5 November 1816, TNA: CO 54/61.

123 Pieris, *Sinhale and the Patriots*, 328.

124 Jayawardena, *Perpetual Ferment*, 73.

125 William Thorn, *Memoir of the Conquest of Java* (London: T. Egerton, 1815), x–xi. For the use of the descriptor 'French' see for instance the fall of Batavia commentary by Thorn, 31–33. See also commentary on the plasticity of the term 'Dutch' in imperial contexts in Jos Gommans, 'Conclusion', in Catia Antunes and Jos Gommans, eds, *Exploring the Dutch Empire: Agents, Networks and Institutions, 1600–2000* (London: Bloomsbury Academic, 2015), 267–78.

126 See, for instance, letter to the Secret Committee of the Hon'ble Court of Directors, dated 26 October 1810, BL: Raffles-Minto Collection, Mss Eur F148/1. For how the French flag had replaced the Dutch flag, see 'Mr. Raffles' Reports on Java and the Eastern Isles', addressed to Lord Minto, dated Batavia, 20 September 1811, BL: Raffles-Minto Collection, Mss Eur F148/7, point 17. For the arrival of the news in 1810 in the Yogya court of the annexation of Holland by the French, see, Peter Carey, *The Power of Prophecy: Prince Dipanagara and the End of an Old Order in Java, 1788–1855* (Leiden: KITLV Press, 2007), 275–6.

127 Letter from Minto, dated Batavia, 2 September 1811, in Thorn, *Memoir*, 89.

128 'Mr. Raffles' Reports on Java and the Eastern Isles', addressed to Lord Minto, dated Batavia, 20 September 1811, BL: Raffles-Minto Collection, F148/7, point 64.

129 See for instance, Peter Carey, 'The Destruction of Java's Old Order', 171.

130 Gommans, 'Conclusion', 276. For the social history of Batavia in this period, see Ulbe Bosma and Remco Raben, *Being 'Dutch' in the Indies: A History of Creolisation and Empire, 1500–1920* (Singapore: National University of Singapore Press, 2008), and also Jean Gelman Taylor, *The Social World of Batavia: European and Eurasian in Dutch Asia* (Madison, Wisc.: University of Wisconsin Press, 1983).

131 Letter from Minto to Major General Abercromby, dated Fort William, 3 September 1810, BL: Raffles-Minto Collection, Mss Eur F148/1.

132 H. Vetch, 'Thorn, William (1780–1843)', rev. Francis Herbert, *Oxford Dictionary of National Biography*, Oxford University Press, 2004; online edn, Oct 2005 [http://www.oxforddnb.com/view/article/27338, accessed 21 July 2015].

133 Some vessels joined the Java expedition from Bengal too.

134 John Crawfurd, *History of the Indian Archipelago*, 3 vols (Edinburgh: Constable & Co, 1820), vol. 1, 308.

135 Ibid., 13.

136 Ibid., 193, 240.

137 'Mr. Raffles' Reports on Java and the Eastern Isles', addressed to Lord Minto, dated Batavia, 20 September 1811, BL: Raffles Minto Collection, Mss Eur F148/7, point 39.

138 Ibid., point 74.

139 'The Maritime Code of the Malays translated from the Malayu Language', in Mr. Raffles' Memoir on the Malayu Nation and a Translation, BL: Raffles-Minto Collection, Mss Eur F 148/9.

140 Letter from J. Hewett to Governor Robert Farquhar, dated Fort William, 20 May 1811, NAM: HA 5.

141 Thorn, *Memoir*, 5.

142 Ibid., 7.

143 Ibid., 11.

144 Later, this route generated some controversy and was seen to be a risky choice, given the conditions of the seas and winds at this time of the year. See, for instance, Commodore Hay, 'Draft of a letter with a Report of the Malabar's Passage': 'the route taken was utterly unwarranted by Reason or Experience', BL: Raffles-Minto Collection, Mss Eur F 148/10.

145 D. C. Boulger, *Life of Sir Stamford Raffles* (London: Horace, Marshall &Son, 1897), 57. For Raffles taking the credit for pushing Lord Minto to pursue the expedition, see Sophia Raffles, *Memoir of the Life and Public Services of Sir Thomas Stamford Raffles* (London: J. Murray, 1830), 116. For Raffles organising the survey in order to clarify the route of the Java expedition, see, 'Mr. Raffles' Reports on Java and the Eastern Isles', addressed to Lord Minto, dated Batavia, 20 September 1811, BL: Raffles-Minto Collection, Mss Eur F148/7, point 25.

146 'Mr. Raffles' Reports on Java and the Eastern Isles', addressed to Lord Minto, dated Batavia, 20 September 1811, BL: Raffles-Minto Collection, Mss Eur F148/7, point 25.

147 Thorn, *Memoir*, 12–13.

148 Ibid., 27. For the drama surrounding Mackenzie's landing in Java, see W. C. Mackenzie, *Colonel Colin Mackenzie, First-Surveyor-General of India* (Edinburgh: W. & R. Chambers, 1952), 110–14.

149 For the numbers of the forces see, Boulger, *Life*, 70.

150 Thorn, *Memoir*, 18.

151 Minute, dated Fort William, 29th November 1811, BL: Lord Minto's Minutes, Raffles-Minto Collection, Mss Eur F/148/15.

152 Thorn, *Memoir*, 21, 24.

153 Colonel Gillespie's report, dated Weltevreden, 11 August 1811, BL: Raffles-Minto Collection, Mss Eur F 148/10.

154 'Plan of the Route of the British Army, Under the Command of Lieut.

General Sir Samuel Auchmuty, from the day of their landing at Chillingching in Java on the 4th August 1811 to the assault on the enemy's lines at Cornellis on the 26th August 1811', BL: Raffles-Minto Collection, Mss Eur F148/10; 'Plans, Charts, Memorandum and details connected with the expedition against the Dutch Islands', BL: Raffles-Minto Collection, F148/10.

155 Crawfurd, *History*, vol. 1, 4.

156 Thorn, *Memoir*, 45; quotation from Minute, dated Fort William, 6 December 1811, BL: Lord Minto's Minutes, Minto-Raffles Collection, Mss Eur F148/15.

157 Ibid., 26.

158 Ibid., 33.

159 For the Dutch view once again that the climate would create 'intemperance' and 'fatigue' in the run-up to the battle of Cornelis, see Minute dated Fort William, 6 December 1811, BL: Minto-Raffles Collection, Lord Minto's Minutes, Mss Eur F148/15.

160 Boulger, *Life*, 74–5.

161 Thorn, *Memoir*, 95.

162 Ibid., 107.

163 Ibid., 'Native Powers.'

164 Ibid., 156.

165 Ibid., 134 and 138.

166 Crawfurd, *History*, vol. 1, 14.

167 'Mr. Raffles' Reports on Java and the Eastern Isles', addressed to Lord Minto, dated Batavia, 20 September 1811, BL: Raffles-Minto Collection, Mss Eur F148/7, point 33.

168 Carey, *The Power of Prophecy*, 205–6. Carey notes that the Yogya treasury was estimated at one million Spanish dollars in gold and silver coins in 1808, excluding diamonds. This entire treasury was lost between 1808 and 1812.

169 Citation from Carey, *The Power of Prophecy*, 261.

170 Treaty with the Sultan of Mataram, BL: Raffles-Minto Collection, Mss Eur F148/23. For Minto's proclamation on the liberal and enlightened principles of the new British government, see Carey, *The Power of Prophecy*, 283–4.

171 Carey, *The Power of Prophecy*, 348–65.

172 Carey, *The British in Java: 1811–1816: A Javanese Account* (Oxford: Oxford University Press, 1992), 118.

173 Ibid., 87.

174 Ibid., 103, 107. For the Yogya view of the sepoy as offensive, see Carey, *The Power of Prophecy*, 303.

175 Seda Kouznetsova, 'Colin Mackenzie as a Collector of Javanese Manuscripts', in *Indonesia and the Malay World* 36 (2008): 375–94. For his survey of the Solo river, see Mackenzie, *Colonel*, 135–9. 'As President

of the Commission on Java, Lieutenant-Colonel Mackenzie has visited almost every part of that island, the considerable and important collections which have been made by the Commission, added to the interesting documents which have been procured by his personal diligence and research, will form a body of most useful and interesting information . . .', cited in Mackenzie, *Colonel*, 161, from 'General orders on the farewell of Mackenzie', who left Java on 18 July 1813.

176 Jurrien van Goor, *Prelude to Colonialism: The Dutch in Asia* (Hilversum: Uitgeverij Verloren, , 2004), 93.

177 See for instance for Sri Lanka, Alicia Schrikker, *Dutch and British Colonial Intervention in Sri Lanka, 1780–1815: Expansion and Reform* (Leiden: Brill, 2007).

178 This view of the unhealthy airs of Batavia was widely held at this time, see J. J. Stockdale, *Sketches, Civil and Military, of the Island of Java and its Immediate Dependencies* (London: J. J. Stockdale, 1812), 2nd edn, 128–9, who writes here that Batavia is 'one of the most unwholesome spots upon the face of the globe', 'along this shore the sea throws up all manner of filth, slime, mollusca, dead fish, mud, and weeds, which putrefying with the utmost rapidity by the extreme degree of heat, load and infect the air with their offensive miasmata.' This book is a translation of earlier accounts by Dutch and French writers collected by Samuel Auchmuty; this quote is from a French account by C. F. Tombé.

179 For Mackenzie on the *kraton*, see Mackenzie, *Colonel*, 153.

180 For his role in the military events on Java, see Mackenzie, *Colonel*, chapter 15.

181 The discussion of the Opium War that follows draws upon: Julia Lovell, *The Opium War: Drugs, Dreams and the Making of China* (London: Picador, 2011), and Robert Bickers, *The Scramble for China: Foreign Devils in the Qing Empire, 1832–1914* (Penguin: Allen Lane, 2011).

182 Cited in Tonio Andrade, *The Gunpowder Age: China, Military Innovation, and the Rise of the West in World History* (Princeton: Princeton University Press, 2016), 249.

183 Cited in ibid., 256 and chapter 16 for a broader discussion about military divergence which feeds into this paragraph.

184 See Glenn Melancon, 'Honour in Opium? The British Declaration of War on China, 1839–1840', *The International History Review* 21, no. 4 (1999), 855–74, at 863.

185 For more on this, see Melancon, 'Honour in Opium?'

186 *The Chinese Repository* 5 (1836), 172–3.

187 John L. Rawlinson, *China's Struggle for Naval Development, 1839–1895* (Cambridge, Mass.: Harvard University Press, 1967), 11.

188 Ibid., 13.

189 Ibid., 16.
190 Andrade, *The Gunpowder Age*, 262.
191 Ibid., 258.
192 Ibid., 263.
193 Ibid., 264.
194 Benjamin Elman, *On Their Own Terms: Science in China, 1550–1900* (Cambridge, Mass.: Harvard University Press, 2005), 360. This paragraph draws upon Elman's survey of shipbuilding in China.

7 IN THE BAY OF BENGAL:
MODELLING EMPIRE, GLOBE AND SELF

1 'Scientific Expedition to the Equator, Instructions', dated 2 July 1822, Fort St. George, BL: IOR, P/245/33, this quote and that at the start of next paragraph.
2 For the origins of the observatory, see 'Description of an Astronomical Observatory Erected at Madras', dated Madras, 24 December 1792, Royal Astronomical Society, London (hereafter RAS): MSS Madras/2.
3 Goldingham writing to Colonel Mackenzie, cited from S. M. Razaullah Ansari, 'Early Modern Observatories in India, 1792–1900', in Uma Das Gupta, ed., *Science and Modern India: An Institutional History, c.1784–1947* (Delhi: Pearson, 2011), 349–80, at 353. For more on the history of Madras Observatory, see the writings of Rajesh Kochar available online, http://rajeshkochhar.com/tag/madras-observatory, accessed 12 January 2018. At a late stage, this chapter benefited from discussion with Prashant Kumar who is completing a PhD at the University of Pennsylvania which includes an account of the social history of the Madras Observatory.
4 See Matthew Edney, *Mapping an Empire: The Geographical Construction of British India, 1765–1843* (Chicago: University of Chicago Press, 2009), 172–3.
5 See W. H. Sykes, 'On the Atmospheric Tides and Meteorology of Dukkun (Deccan), East Indies', *Philosophical Transactions of the Royal Society of London* 125 (1835), 161–220, at 175.
6 Joydeep Sen, *Astronomy in India, 1784–1876* (London: Pickering and Chatto, 2014), 43–4. See John Goldingham, 'Corresponding Observations of Eclipses of Satellites of Jupiter, 1796', RAS: MSS Madras/5.
7 John Goldingham, 'Of the Geographical Situation of the Three Presidencies, Calcutta, Madras, and Bombay, in the East Indies', *Philosophical Transactions of the Royal Society of London* 112 (1822), 408–30, at 408.
8 John Goldingham, 'Experiments for ascertaining the Velocity of Sound, at Madras in the East Indies', *Philosophical Transactions of the Royal Society of London* 113 (1823): 96–139, 186.

9 See for instance, John Goldingham, 'Some Account of the Sculptures at Mahabalipooram: usually called the Seven Pagodas', *Asiatic Researches* 5 (1799): 69–80; see also, Markham, *A Memoir*, 239.

10 For one excellent account in line with this interpretation of the collection of data in this period, see Jan Golinski, *British Weather and the Climate of the Enlightenment* (Chicago: University of Chicago Press, 2011).

11 Fort St. George, 27 January 1809, BL: Madras Public Consultations, IOR, E/4/930.

12 J. Warren, 'An Account of the Comet which Appeared in the Months of September, October and November, 1807', dated Madras Observatory, 1 January 1808, RAS: MSS Madras/6, and R. C. Kapoor, 'Madras Observatory and the Discovery of C/1831 A1 (The Great Comet of 1831)', *Journal of Astronomical History and Heritage* 14 (2011), 93–102, at 97, 100.

13 Fort St. George, 27 January 1809, BL: Madras Public Consultations, IOR, E/4/930.

14 For ships as the 'hardware', see D. Miller, 'Longitude Networks on Land and Sea: The East India Company and Longitude Measurement "in the Wild", 1770–1840', in Richard Dunn and Rebekah Higgitt, eds, *Navigational Enterprises in Europe and its Seas, 1730–1850* (Basingstoke: Palgrave Macmillan, 2016), 223–47, at 227.

15 'Description of an Astronomical Observatory.'

16 See 'Copy of Report of Company's Astronomer on the Length of the Pendulum at the Equator, Transmitted and Presented to the Netherlands Government', 1824–30, BL: IOR, Z/E/4/42/E475.

17 'Scientific Expedition to the Equator, Instructions.'

18 J. Warren, 'Paper on the Length of the Simple Pendulum at the Madras Observatory', RAS, MSS Madras/8.

19 For more details see Sophie Waring, 'Thomas Young, the Board of Longitude and the Age of Reform' (PhD thesis, University of Cambridge, 2014), 96–7. For Kater's researches, see also 'Henry Kater, 'An account of experiments for determining the variation in the length of the pendulum vibrating seconds, at the principal stations of the Trigonometrical Survey of Great Britain', *Philosophical Transactions of the Royal Society of London* 109 (1819), 337–508.

20 Clements Robert Markham, *A Memoir on the Indian Surveys* (London: W. H. Allen & Co., 1871), 48.

21 J. Ivory, 'Short Abstract of M. de Freycinet's Experiments for Determining the Length of the Pendulum', *Philosophical Magazine* 68 (1826), 350–3, citation from 352.

22 Waring, 'Thomas Young', 146–7.

23 F. Mountford, Assistant Surveyor General, to the Chief Secretary of Government, dated 2 January 1822, BL: IOR, F/4/760.

24 John Goldingham, 'Report on the Length of the Pendulum at the

Equator', in Goldingham, ed., *Madras Observatory Papers* (Madras, 1826), 105–6.

25 Ibid., 'Report', 109. Further information below is drawn from this report.

26 Letter from John Goldingham to the Secretary of Government, dated 22 January 1824, Madras Observatory, BL: IOR, F/4/760.

27 Goldingham, 'Report', 113.

28 I thank Rachel Leow for suggestions on how to decipher the name 'Gaunsah Lout'.

29 Goldingham, 'Report', 114.

30 Elizabeth Graves, *The Minangkabau Response to Dutch Colonial Rule in the Nineteenth Century* (Singapore: Equinox, 2010), 49ff.; see also Azyumardi Azra, *The Origins of Islamic Reformism in Southeast Asia* (Honolulu: University of Hawaii Press, 2004).

31 Azra, *The Origins of Islamic Reformism*, 145.

32 Goldingham, 'Report', 114–15.

33 See Ivory, 'Short Abstract', 353.

34 This relies on but disagrees with Sen, *Astronomy in India*, 89 and for Warren's assistants, below, see 90.

35 Warren, 'Paper on the Length of the Simple Pendulum at the Madras Observatory'.

36 Warren, 'An Account of the Comet'.

37 For instance, note the depersonalized reporting in 'Transit Observations, 1840–51', RAS: MSS Madras/9, 3 vols.

38 John Warren, *Kala Sankalita: A Collection of Memoirs* (Madras: College Press, 1825), p. v.

39 Letter from John Warren to the Senior Member and Members of the Board of Superintendence for the College, dated 28 December 1826, Madras, BL: IOR, P/245/76.

40 Fort St. George, 25 January 1828, BL: Madras Public Consultations, IOR, E/4/935.

41 Letter from John Warren to the Senior Member and Members of the Board, dated 28 December 1826, BL: IOR, P/245/76.

42 Fort St. George, 25 January 1828, BL: Madras Public Consultations, IOR, E/4/935.

43 Warren, *Kala Sankalita*, xiii.

44 Fort St. George, 25 January 1828, BL: Madras Public Diaries and Consultations, India Office Records, E/4/935.

45 See the claim in E. Danson, *Weighing the World: The Quest to Measure the Earth* (Oxford: Oxford University Press, 2006), 204.

46 Material on Warren relies on R. K. Kochhar, 'French Astronomers in India', *Journal of the British Astronomical Association* 101, no. 2 (April 1991), 95–100. For milestones see 97.

47 See Dunn and Higgitt, eds, *Navigational Enterprises*.

48 This relies on A. C. Sanderson, 'The British Community in Madras, 1780–1830' (MPhil thesis, University of Cambridge, 2010). See also, Søren Mentz, 'Cultural Interaction between the British Diaspora in Madras and the Host Community, 1650–1790', in Haneda Masashi, ed., *Asian Port Cities, 1600–1800: Local and Foreign Cultural Interactions* (Singapore: National University of Singapore Press, 2009), 162–74.

49 James Capper, *Observations on the Winds and Monsoons* (London: C. Whittingham, 1801), 171.

50 For more on the writing of weather diaries, see Jan Golinski, *British Weather and the Climate of Enlightenment* (Chicago: University of Chicago Press, 2007).

51 Capper, *Meteorological and Miscellaneous Tracts* (Cardiff: J. D. Bird), 130.

52 Ibid., 128.

53 Ibid., 128–9.

54 Ibid., 198–9

55 Capper, *Observations*, xxii.

56 Ibid., 124.

57 Ibid., 125.

58 Ibid., 116. For more on Capper's commitment to the influence of 'electric fluid', see Peter Rogers, 'The Weather Theories and Records of Colonel Capper', *Weather* 11 (October 1956) 326–9.

59 Capper, *Observations*, xxvi–xxvii.

60 Thomas Forrest, *Treatise on the Monsoons in East-India* (London: J. Robson, 1783), 7. For Forrest's biography, see, D. K. Bassett, 'Thomas Forrest: An Eighteenth Century Mariner', *Journal of the Malaysian Branch of the Royal Asiatic Society* 34, no. 2 (1961), 106–22.

61 Thomas Forrest, *Voyage from Calcutta to the Mergui Archipelago* (London: J. Robson, 1792), i.

62 Forrest, 'Idea of Making a Map of the World', in *Voyage*, 139ff.

63 See for instance the transliterated annotations made by Forrest alongside the Jawi Malay script, on a map of Maguindanao, 'Map of the southern portion of 'Magindano', *c.*1775, BL: Add Mss 4924. See also Thomas Suarez, *Early Mapping of Southeast Asia* (Singapore: Periplus Editions, 1999), 251.

64 Quotations from Marcus Langdon, *Penang: The Fourth Presidency of India, 1805–1930* (Penang: Areca Books, 2013), 6–7, dated 25 January 1786 and 27 July 1787.

65 Ibid., 18, letter dated 29 April 1780.

66 Ibid., 20–1.

67 See D. K. Bassett, 'Thomas Forrest.'

68 Langdon, *Penang*, 11.

69 Letter from John Crawfurd, Resident, Singapore, to the Secretary to the Government of Fort William, dated 3 August 1824, National Archives of Singapore (hereafter NAS), Foreign Secret Department Files, copied from

the National Archives of India, NAB 1673 (microfilm). Such a view of Singapore as extending out to sea was also part of how J. T. Thomson saw his terrain as surveyor of Singapore. See letter from J. T. Thomson to Lieut. H. L. Thuillier, Deputy Surveyor General of Bengal, dated Singapore, 22 June 1847, in NAS: 'Letters: J. T. Thomson', 526.9092 THO, 2 vols, vol. 1, 1–9.

70 Trocki, *Prince of Pirates,* 61 and 67.

71 Letter from Lord Aberdeen, dated the Foreign Office, 10th December 1845, NAS: NAB 1673.

72 James Horsburgh, *Bay of Bengal* (London: J. Horsburgh, 1825). For the density of sailing information in the period, see John Lindsay, *Directions to Accompany J. Lindsay's Charts of the Straits of Malacca* (London, 1795). Also see Robert Laurie and James Whittle, *The Oriental Navigator: or New Directions for Sailing to and from the East Indies* (Edinburgh: Printed by R. Morison, 1794).

73 George Romaine, 'A Sketch of the Bay of Bengal shewing the tracks of three Cruizers', BL: Add Mss 13910.

74 Langdon, *Penang,* 59–62.

75 Peter Borschberg, Makeswary Periasamy and Mok Ly Yng, *Visualising Space: Maps of Singapore and the Region, Collections from the National Library and National Archives of Singapore* (Singapore: National Library Board, 2015), 88, and Daniel Ross, *Plan of Singapore Harbour, 1819* (London: J. Horsburgh, 1820). The commentary on early maps of Singapore benefits from, 'Geo-Graphics', exhibition, 2015.

76 For the pre-nineteenth-century history of Singapore straits, see other work by Peter Borscheberg, *The Singapore and Melaka Straits: Violence, Security and Diplomacy in the 17th Century* (Singapore: National University of Singapore Press, 2010).

77 Sketch of the land round Singapore Harbour, 7 February 1819, TNA: ADM 344/1307, item 1.

78 Anon., 'Plan of the Island of Singapore' (1822), BL: IOR, X/3347.

79 Letter from John Crawfurd, Resident, Singapore to the Secretary to the Government of Fort William, dated 3 August 1824, NAS: NAB 1673.

80 Ian Proudfoot, 'Abdullah vs Siami: Early Malay Verdicts on British Justice', *Journal of the Malaysian Branch of the Royal Asiatic Society* 80, no. 1 (June 2007), 1–16, from 'Retrenchments', a poem by Siami, translated by Proudfoot, at 13. The following section on Abdullah and Siami draws upon: John Bastin, 'Abdulla and Siami' in *Journal of the Malaysian Branch of the Royal Asiatic Society* 81, no. 1 (June 2008), 1–6; Diana Carroll, 'The "Hikayat Abdullah": Discourse of Dissent', *Journal of the Malaysian Branch of the Royal Asiatic Society* 72, no. 2 (1999), 91–129; Amin Sweeney, 'Abdullah Bin Abdul Kadir Munsyi: A Man of Bananas and Thorns', *Indonesia and the Malay World* 34 (2006), 223–45; Raimy

Ché-Ross, 'A Malay Poem on New Year's Day (1848): Munshi Abdullah's Lyric Carnival', *Journal of the Malaysian Branch of the Royal Asiatic Society* 81, no. 1 (June 2008), 49–82 and Raimy Ché-Ross, 'Munshi Abdullah's Voyage to Mecca: A Preliminary Introduction and Annotated Translation', *Indonesia and the Malay World* 28 (2000), 173–213.

81 Bastin, 'Abdulla and Siami', 4.

82 Abdullah Bin Abdul Kadir, *The Hikayat Abdullah,* ed. and trans. A. H. Hill (Malaysian Branch of the Royal Asiatic Society, Kuala Lumpur: Academe Art, 2009), 102, for this reference. For an argument about how Abdullah retrospectively constructed his relationship with Raffles and the dangers of reading this text as fact and an eye-witness account, see Sweeney, 'Abdullah Bin Abdul Kadir Munsyi'.

83 For Abdullah on the *hajj* see Raimy Ché-Ross, 'Munshi Abdullah's Voyage to Mecca'.

84 *The Hikayat Abdullah*, 234 and 297, for citations in this paragraph.

85 For the arrival of steam vessels in the waters around the Malay Peninsula, see C. A. Gibson-Hill, 'The Steamers in Asian Waters, 1819–1839', *Journal of the Malayan Branch of the Royal Asiatic Society* 27, no. 1 (May 1954), 120–62.

86 'Teks Ceretera Kapal Asap', in Amin Sweeney, ed., *Karya Lengkap Abdullah bin Abdul Kadir* (Jakarta: KPG, 2006), jilid 2, 271–304, citations and information from 275 and 278.

87 For another discussion of the importance of sight to belief, see J. T. Thomson, *Some Glimpses into Life in the Far East* (London: Richardson & Company, 1865), 330–1.

88 *The Hikayat Abdullah*, 290. For Abdullah's engagement with the missionary press, see Jan Van der Putten, 'Abdullah Munsyi and the missionaries', *Bijdragen tot de Taal-, Land-en Volkenkunde* 162, no. 4 (2006), 407–40. For the take-off of printed works, and in particular the missionary attention to science and technology, see Ian Proudfoot, *Early Malay Printed Books* (Academy of Malay Studies: University of Malaya, 1993), introduction, 11–19.

89 *The Hikayat Abdullah*, 290. For the point that these were among the fastest vessels in Singapore, see C. Skinner, 'Abdullah's Voyage to the East Coast, Seen Through Contemporary Eyes', *Journal of the Malaysian Branch of the Royal Asiatic Society* 39, no. 2 (1966), 23–33, 25.

90 *The Hikayat Abdullah*, 291.

91 For Abdullah's enjoyment of *pantuns* on his visits to Melaka, see Sweeney, 'Abdullah Bin Abdul Kadir Munsyi', 224.

92 Amin Sweeney, ed., *Karya Lengkap Abdullah bin Abdul Kadir Munsyi* (Jakarta: KPG, 2005), jilid 1, 162, verse 42. I thank Siti Nur'Ain for working alongside me and translating and answering questions on Malay. See also *The Story of the Voyage of Abdullah Bin Abdul Kadir Munshi,* trans. A. E.

Cooper (Singapore: Malaya Pub. House, 1949), 64, 'The time has come! The anchor's weighed! / Flash oars! Blaze guns! We must depart. / Deep in the breech the bullet lies; / Love lies still deeper in my heart.'

93 Raimy Ché-Ross, 'Munshi Abdullah's Voyage to Mecca', translation, 'The story of Abdullah bin Abdul Kadir Munshi's Voyage from Singapore to Mecca', 186.

94 *The Hikayat Abdullah*, 40.

95 Sujit Sivasundaram, *Islanded,* 271ff.

96 For the account of his encounter with the doctor, see *The Hikayat Abdullah*, 199–203, citation from 200.

97 *The Hikayat Abdullah*, 203.

98 Ibid., 204.

99 Diana Carroll, 'The 'Hikayat Abdullah', 92–3.

100 See the persuasive case mounted by Tim Harper, 'Afterword: The Malay World: Besides Empire and Nation', *Indonesia and the Malay World* 41, no. 120 (2013), 273–90, as also the other essays in this special issue.

101 Cited in J. J. Sheehan, 'A Translation of the Hikayat Abdullah', *Journal of the Malaysian Branch of the Royal Asiatic Society* 14 (1936), 227–8. This follows the view of Mark Frost and Yu-Meil Balasingamchow, *Singapore: A Biography* (Singapore: Éditions Didier Millet, 2009), 76: 'Strictly speaking he was Jawi Peranakan – a local-born Muslim of mixed Arab, Indian and Malay ancestry.'

102 See Frost and Balasingamchow, *Singapore: A Biography,* 76.

103 This was probably Captain Robert Smith of the Bengal Engineers, who had previously been superintending engineer and executive officer at Penang. See, Robert Smith, *Views of Prince of Wales' Island Engraved and Coloured by William Daniell From the Original Paintings of Robert Smith* (London: s.n., 1821).

104 *The Hikayat Abdullah*, 237–8 for Abdullah and Smith.

105 For his biography, see John Hall-Jones, *The Thomson Paintings: Mid-Nineteenth Century Paintings of the Straits Settlements and Malaya* (Singapore: Oxford University Press, 1983), ix–xi, and John Hall-Jones and Christopher Hooi, *An Early Surveyor in Singapore: John Turnbull Thomson in Singapore, 1841–1853* (Singapore: National Museum, 1979).

106 Thomson, *Some Glimpses*, chapter 58.

107 For Horsburgh's biography from the *Oxford Dictionary of National Biography* see: http://www.oxforddnb.com/view/article/13810.

108 Letter from J. T. Thomson to Colonel Butterworth, Governor of Singapore, Malaccca and P.W. Island, dated 25 August 1846, Singapore, NAS: Files of the Military Department, Marine Branch, copied from the National Archives of India, NAB 1672 (microfilm). For the idea of it towering above the seas, see the report of its erection from Governor of P.W. Island, Singapore and Malacca to Fort William, dated 9 March

1850, NAS: NAB 1672. See also J. A. L. Pavitt, *First Pharos of the Eastern Seas: Horsburgh Lighthouse* (Singapore Light Dues Board: Donald Moore Press, 1966).

109 J. T. Thomson, 'Account of the Horsburgh Lighthouse', *Journal of the Indian Archipelago and Eastern Asia* 6, no. 1 (1852), 376–498, 377. For further details on the building of the Horsburgh Lighthouse, see also NAS: Files of the Home Department, Marine Branch, copied from the National Archives of India, NAB 1671 (microfilm) and files in NAB 1672.

110 Minutes of the Marine Department of India, dated 5 September 1849, NAS: NAB 1671. See also letter dated 5 September 1849, BL: Marine Department, IOR, E/4/801, consulted on microfilm at National Archives of Singapore.

111 Thomson, 'Account', 430.

112 Letter from J. T. Thomson to T. Church, Resident Councillor, dated January 1852, NAS: NAB 1671. For another account of the conditions on the rocks see letter from J. T. Thomson to T. Church, Resident Councillor of Singapore, dated Singapore 8 March 1848, NAS: 'Letters: J. T. Thomson', 526.9092 THO, vol. 1, 42–4.

113 For the variety of labourers used on the rocks and how they spoke eleven different languages, see Letter from J. T. Thomson to Allan Stevenson, Engineer to the Northern Lighthouse Board, dated Singapore 28 September 1851, NAS: 'Letters: J. T. Thomson', vol. 2, 177–82.

114 Thomson, 'Account of the Horsburgh Lighthouse', 378.

115 For Thomson giving the number as eighty, see letter from J. T. Thomson to T. Church, Resident Councillor, dated Singapore, 10 August 1850, NAS: 'Letters: J. T. Thomson', vol. 1, 122–3. Other information from Hall Jones and Hooi, *An Early Surveyor in Singapore*.

116 For the two-part sketch, see plate 38 and plate 39, Hall Jones and Hooi, *An Early Surveyor in Singapore*. For Thomson's investment in these images and his desire to get engravings from London, see letter from T. Church, Resident Councillor to the Governor of Prince of Wales Island, Singapore and Malacca dated Singapore, 17 January 1852, NAS: NAB 1671. Also, 'Horsburgh Lighthouse Engravings Account', dated Singapore August 1852, NAS: 'Letters: J. T. Thomson', 526.9092 THO, vol. 2, 216.

117 Thomson, 'Account of the Horsburgh Lighthouse', 396.

118 Ibid., 397.

119 Ibid., 395.

120 Ibid., 437.

121 Wilbert Wong Wei Wen, 'John Thomson and the Malay Peninsula: The Far East in the Development of His Thoughts' (Undergraduate thesis, University of Otago, 2014).

122 Plate 31, Hall Jones and Hooi, *An Early Surveyor in Singapore*. For details

of the events surrounding this image, see Thomson, 'Account of the Horsburgh Lighthouse', 422.

123 Thomson, 'Account of the Horsburgh Lighthouse', 424. For Thomson's account of these events in the period itself see, letter from J. T. Thomson to T. Church, Resident Councillor, dated Singapore 29 May 1850, NAS: 'Letters: J. T. Thomson', 526.9092 THO, vol. 1, 114–16.

124 For his need to leave for Britain, see letter from J. T. Thomson to T. Church, Resident Councillor, dated Singapore 3 August 1853, NAS: 'Letters: J. T. Thomson', 526.9092 THO, vol. 2, 223–4. For his final removal, see letter from J. T. Thomson to T. Church, Resident Councillor, dated 28 December 1854, NAS: 'Letters: J. T. Thomson', 526.9092 THO, vol. 2, 228–9. See also Thomson, 'Account', 424, 431.

125 Thomson, 'Account of the Horsburgh Lighthouse', p. 416.

126 Ibid., 459–64.

127 Letter from T. Church, Resident Councillor to the Governor of Prince of Wales Island, Singapore and Malacca, dated Singapore, 17 January 1852, NAS: NAB 1671. For the revolving light, see letter from Colonel Butterworth, Governor, to the Undersecretary of Government, Fort William, dated 12 June 1848, NAS: NAB 1672.

128 For one such dispute, see letter from J. T. Thomson to T. Church, Resident Councillor, dated Singapore 20 October 1847, NAS: 'Letters: J. T. Thomson', 526.9092 THO, vol. 1, 27.

129 This comment picks up the exhibition entitled, 'Geo-Graphics: Celebrating Maps and their Stories', which was open in early 2015.

130 See. C. M. Turnbull, *The Straits Settlements: Indian Presidency to Crown Colony* (London: University of London Press, 1972).

131 'Number of Square Rigged Vessels and Native Craft touching at Singapore in the year 1836/7', NAS: Military Department, Marine Branch Papers, copied from the National Archives of India, NAB 1672 (microfilm).

132 See J. T. Thomson, *Plan of Singapore Town and Adjoining Districts* (1846), which shows plantations and the division of the land into plots.

133 J. T. Thomson and S. Congalton, *The Survey of the Straits of Singapore* (1846), and J. T. Thomson and S. Congalton, *The Survey of the Straits of Singapore* (1855). See also Charles Morgan Elliot, *Chart of the Magnetic Survey of the Indian Archipelago* (1851).

134 Letter from J. T. Thomson to Lieut. H. L. Thuillier, Dept. Surveyor General, Bengal, dated Singapore 27 December 1847 NAS: 'Letters: J. T. Thomson', 526.9092 THO, vol. 2, 240.

135 Letter from J. T. Thomson to T. Church, Resident Councillor, dated Singapore 6 April 1848, NAS: 'Letters: J. T. Thomson', 526.9092 THO, vol. 1, 48–55, quotations from 53. For the view that they were moving on to Johor, see letter from J. T. Thomson to Lieut. H. L. Thuillier, n.d., 1849, NAS: 'Letters: J. T. Thomson', 526.9092 THO, vol. 2, 250–1.

136 Trocki, *Prince of the Pirates*, 19.

137 Letter from J. T. Thomson to T. Church, Resident Councillor, dated Singapore 27 May 1851, NAS: 'Letters: J. T. Thomson', 526.9092 THO, vol. 2, 159–64, quotation from 161. For discussion of the rise of municipal government and also its relation to concerns to do with sanitation in early Singapore, see Brenda S. A. Yeoh, *Contesting Space: Power Relations and the Urban Built Environment in Colonial Singapore* (Kuala Lumpur: Oxford University Press, 1996), 31–2.

138 Turnbull, *The Straits Settlements*, 3.

139 Ibid., 242 ff. For two examples of attempts to use steam power to suppress piracy, see Letter from the Governor of Prince of Wales Island, Singapore and Malacca to the H. Torrens, Secretary to Government, Fort William, dated 27 September 1840, NAS: NAB 1673, and two decades later, letter from Colonel Cavenagh to the Secretary of the Government of India, dated Singapore, 1st October 1860, NAS: NAB 1671.

140 For port rules connected to the man-of-war at Singapore harbour see: despatch from the Governor of Prince of Wales Island, Singapore and Malacca to the Secretary to the Government of India, Fort William, dated 15 December 1857, NAS: NAB 1671.

141 Letter from Colonel Butterworth, Governor, 'Remarks upon the proposal of erecting a lighthouse at Singapore to the Memory of James Horsburgh', dated 31 January 1830, NAS: NAP 1672; see also letter from J. T. Thomson to J. Church, Resident Councillor, dated Singapore, 2 November 1830, NAS: NAP 1672, and letter from J. T. Thomson to T. Church, Resident Councillor, dated Singapore, 20 November 1850, NAS: 'Letters: J. T. Thomson', 526.9092 THO, vol. 1, 129–38.

142 Citation from Frost and Balasingamchow, *Singapore: A Biography*, 105.

143 Citation here and below from Raimy Ché-Ross, 'A Malay Poem on New Year's Day', 67–73.

144 Harper, 'Afterword'.

8 ACROSS THE INDIAN OCEAN: COMPARATIVE GLANCES IN THE SOUTH

1 Peter Burroughs, 'The Mauritius rebellion of 1832 and the abolition of British colonial slavery', *Journal of Imperial and Commonwealth History* 4, no. 3 (1976), 243–65, at 249, and Richard Allen, *Slaves, Freedmen and Indentured Laborers in Colonial Mauritius* (Cambridge: Cambridge University Press, 1999), 15.

2 Allen, *Slaves, Freedmen and Indentured Laborers*, 17.

3 Antony Barker, 'Distorting the record of slavery and abolition: The British anti-slavery movement and Mauritius, 1826–37', *Slavery and Abolition* 14, no. 3 (1993), 185–207, 141.

4   See for instance the now outdated Hugh Tinker, *A New System of Slavery: The Export of Indian Labour Overseas, 1830–1920* (London: Oxford University Press, 1974); and also Sujit Sivasundaram, 'The Indian Ocean', in David Armitage, Alison Bashford and Sujit Sivasundaram, eds, *Oceanic Histories* (Cambridge: Cambridge University Press, 2017), 31–60 for a discussion of how this debate has now given rise to a more complex picture of the relations of different types of labourers.

5   Satyendra Peerthum, '"Fit for Freedom": Manumission and Freedom in Early British Mauritius, 1811–1839', in A. Sheriff et al., eds, *Transition from Slavery in Zanzibar and Mauritius: A Comparative History* (Dakar, Senegal: Codesria, 2016), 69–88.

6   Peerthum, '"Fit for Freedom"', 89.

7   See Burroughs, 'The Mauritius Rebellion', and also Daniel North-Coombes, 'Slavery, Emancipation and the Labour "Crisis" in the Sugar Industry of Mauritius, 1790–1842', *Tanzania Zamani* 3, no. 1 (January 1997), 16–49, at 27.

8   This is the argument of Megan Vaughan, *Creating the Creole Island: Slavery in Eighteenth-Century Mauritius* (Durham, N. C. and London: Duke University Press, 2005), chapter 10.

9   Burroughs, 'The Mauritius Rebellion', 247–8.

10 Sateyndra Peerthum, '"Making a Life of their Own": Ex-Apprentices in Early Post-Emancipation Period, 1839–1872', in A. Sheriff et al., eds, *Transition from Slavery*, 109–40.

11 Allen, *Slaves, Freedmen and Indentured Laborers*, chapter 2.

12 Cited in James de Montille, 'The Coloured Elite of the District of Grand Port, Mauritius' (MPhil Dissertation: University of Cambridge, 2016), 63.

13 Burroughs, 'The Mauritius Rebellion', 243.

14 Edward Blackburn, 'Memorandum of some of the observations made by the Chief Justice in Council on the present state of the Colony with reference to the departure of Mr. Jeremie', dated 9 July 1832, TNA: CO 167/162. See also letter from Edward Blackburn to Governor Charles Colville, dated 14 August 1832, Port Louis, NAM: HA 20/2.

15 John Jeremie, *Recent Events at Mauritius* (London: S. Bagster, 1835), 6.

16 Barker, 'Distorting the Record', 6.

17 Burroughs, 'The Mauritius Rebellion', 253.

18 Jeremie, *Recent Events at Mauritius*, 28, and also *The Mauritius, an Exemplification of Colonial Policy* (Birmingham: B. Hudson, 1837), 8.

19 'Address by Mr. Jeremie to some of the Inhabitants of Mauritius convened by the Governor on the 7th July 1832', NAM: HA 20/2.

20 This paragraph draws on Burroughs, 'The Mauritius Rebellion', 256.

21 For an account of what happened when the *Ganges* arrived, see Letters from W. Staveley to Charles Colville, Governor, dated 14 August 1832, NAM: HA 20/2; for earlier incident, see above Chapter 3.

22 *Le Cernéen*, 7 July 1832. 'Cet évènement fut le dernier signal pour l'explo-sion du sentiment public. Toutes les affaires furent dèslors suspendues. Toutes les boutiques, tous les magasins furent spontanément fermés. La milice s'arma, et s'augmenta de tous les citoyens.'

23 Letter from John Jeremie to Governor Colville, dated 25 June 1832, NAM: H/20.

24 Jeremie, *Recent Events*, 43.

25 Sydney Selvon, *A New Comprehensive History of Mauritius*, 2 vols (Mauritius: Bahemia, 2012), vol. 1, 289.

26 John Jeremie, Report dated 18 March 1835, TNA: CO 167/187.

27 Letter from James Simpson to John Finniss, Police Office, dated Mahebourg, 29 March 1833, TNA: CO 167/178. And also for another reference to the events of the French Revolution as the 'real counterpart of this', see letter from John Jeremie to Governor Colville, dated Port Louis, 22 July 1832, TNA: CO 167/162.

28 Charles Pridham, *England's Colonial Empire: An Historical, Political and Statistical Account of Mauritius* (London: T. & W. Boone, 1849), 138.

29 Anthony Barker, *Slavery and Antislavery in Mauritius, 1810–33* (Basingstoke: Macmillan, 1996), chapter 2.

30 *Le Cernéen*, 13 July 1832. 'nous avons fait retentir de toute la force de nos faibles poumons la grande voix de la presse.'

31 'Observations relative to the actual state of the colony by a member of the meeting assembled at Govt House on Saturday 7TH inst.', dated 12 July 1832, signed J. Laing, TNA: CO 167/162.

32 Burroughs, 'The Mauritius Rebellion', 246.

33 'Observations relative to the actual state.'

34 Cited in Burroughs, 'The Mauritius Rebellion', 261.

35 Letter dated 30 April 1834 from John Jeremie to E. G. Stanley, Secretary of State for the Colonies, TNA: CO 167/178, 625.

36 Letter from John Jeremie to E. G. Stanley dated 30 April 1834.

37 *Le Cernéen*, 24 July 1832.

38 Jeremie, *Recent Events*.

39 Report from John Jeremie to E. G. Stanley, dated Port Louis, 21 June 1834, TNA: CO 167/178; and 'Address by Mr. Jeremie to some of the Inhabitants', NAM.

40 Report from John Jeremie to E. G. Stanley dated Port Louis, 21 June 1834, TNA: CO 167/178.

41 Ibid.

42 Ibid.

43 Ibid.

44 Ibid.

45 Ibid.

46 Jeremie, *Recent Events*, 37.

47	Report from John Jeremie to E. G. Stanley dated Port Louis, 21 June 1834, TNA: CO 167/178.

48	*La Balance*, 7 April 1834.

49	De Montille, 'The Coloured Elite', 71.

50	Report from John Jeremie to E. G. Stanley dated Port Louis, 21 June 1834, TNA: CO 167/178.

51	*La Balance*, 21 April 1834.

52	Hugh Strickland and A. G. Melville, *The Dodo and its Kindred* (London: Reeve and Benham, 1848), iv.

53	See, for instance, letter from Charles Telfair, Civil Assistant, to Captain Barry, Chief Secretary to Government, dated 8 August 1810; and also, letter from A. Barry, Chief Secretary to Charles Telfair, dated St. Denis, 8 August 1810; NAM: HA 23.

54	R. Farquhar, 'Notes on the first Establishment of Madagascar, and explanatory of its relations with & dependency on the Isle of France, taken from the Records in the Isle of France', TNA: CO 167/960.

55	Ibid.

56	Selvon, *A New Comprehensive History*, vol. 1, 266.

57	The relations between the government of Mauritius and polities on the East African coast continued into a later period too as witnessed by the extensive correspondence between Mauritius and Johanna, Zanzibar and Muscat. See NAM: HB 2.

58	Paper titled 'By Radama, King of Madagascar', NAM: HB/4. See further letters in HB/4 for how Radama brought in duties and restrictions on trade in 1827.

59	See letters in NAM: HB/4. For the names of the Indian convicts who were released from Mauritius to assist with Radama's cultivation plans, see letter from G. Barry to Mr. Hastie, Government Agent at Madagascar, dated Port Louis, 30 June 1825, NAM: HB/4, further documents in this folder show that more Indian convicts were sent to Madagascar.

60	Letter from J. Hastie, dated Tamatave, 25 February 1826, NAM: HB/4, and also letter from Commodore Nourse to Mr. Hastie, dated Bambatooka Bay, 8 December 1823, NAM: HB/5.

61	Gwyn Campbell, 'Madagascar and the Slave Trade, 1810–1895', *Journal of African History* 22, no. 2 (April 1981) 203–27.

62	Letter from Rainimaharo, Chief Secretary of Madagascar to the Governor of Mauritius, dated Antananarivo, 21 July 1840, NAM: HB 2/2

63	Letter from Mr. Campbell to the Hon Colonial Secretary, dated Port Louis, 19 October 1840, NAM: HB 2/2.

64	Campbell, 'Madagascar and the Slave Trade', 212.

65	Marina Carter and Hubert Gerbeau, 'Covert Slaves and Coveted Coolies in the Early 19TH Century Mascareignes', *Slavery and Abolition* 9, no. 3 (1988), 194–208, at 194.

66 'Proclamation in the Name of His Majesty George 3rd', signed at Port
     Louis, 27 April 1815 by R. T. Farquhar, TNA: CO 167/960.

67 Auguste Billiard, *Voyage aux Colonies Orientales, ou Lettres Écrites des Îles
     de France et de Bourbon* (Paris: Ladvocat, 1822), 64.

68 Richard B. Allen, 'The Mascarene Slave-Trade and Labour Migration in
     the Indian Ocean during the Eighteenth and Nineteenth Centuries',
     Slavery and Abolition 24, no. 2 (2003), 33–50.

69 Cited in Carter and Gerbeau, 'Covert Slaves', 203. 'exposés sans pitié sur
     le rivage de la mer, n'attendant plus que la mort pour terme de leurs
     cruelles soufrances'.

70 Pridham, *England's Colonial Empire*, 251.

71 Hubert Gerbeau, 'Engagees and coolies on Réunion Island: Slavery's Masks
     and Freedom's Constraints', in C. Emmer, ed., *Colonialism and Migration:
     Indentured Labour Before and After Slavery* (Dodrecht: Kluwer, 1986),
     209–36.

72 Letter from R. Farquhar to Earl Bathurst, dated Port Louis, 20 April 1815,
     TNA: CO 167/960.

73 Letter from R. Farquhar to Earl Bathurst, dated Port Louis, 18th September
     1815, TNA: CO 167/960.

74 For the citation here see Charles Darwin, *Journal of Researches into the
     Natural History and Geology of the Countries Visited During the Voyage of
     H.M.S. Beagle Round the World* (London: John Murray, 1845), 2nd edn, 484.

75 Governor Farquhar wrote: 'Mauritius has been considered as the Malta of
     this hemisphere – it is a Rock which deserves its importance, wealth &
     prosperity from the fortunate union of its geographical position, as a citadel
     or Military post, and as the emporium of Mercantile resort, between both
     hemispheres with the incomparable superiority of its Harbour', from R.
     Farquhar to Earl Bathurst dated Port Louis, 1 June 1816, TNA: CO 167/190.

76 This follows Pridham, *England's Colonial Empire*, 256; see also statistics
     to do with ship arrivals, 382–3.

77 'Documents concerning the establishment of a dockyard', NAM: HA 74/7.

78 Late Official Resident, *An Account of the Island of the Mauritius and its
     Dependencies* (London, 1842), 28–9. For another account of the trades in
     Port Louis, see Pridham, *England's Colonial Empire*, 251.

79 This follows the description provided by Bradshaw for his view of 'Port
     Louis, from the Offing', in T. Bradshaw, *Views in the Mauritius, or Isle
     de France* (London: James Carpenter, 1832).

80 Bradshaw, *Views in the Mauritius*, 4–5.

81 Plate 3 in M. J. Milbert, *Voyage Pittoresque à l'Ile de France* (Paris: A. Nepveu,
     1812). For a later surveyors map of Port Louis showing its municipal limits,
     see, J. L. F. Target, *Plan of Port Louis and its Environs* (1858), TNA.

82 For population figures, see James Backhouse, *A Narrative of a Visit to the
     Mauritius and South Africa* (London: Hamilton, Adams, 1844), 4; Pridham,

England's Colonial Empire, 393; and Auguste Toussaint, *Port Louis: A Tropical City* (London: George Allen, 1973), trans. W. E. F. Ward, 67; see also *Mauritius Blue Book*, 1835, Cambridge University Library (hereafter CUL) RCS.L.BB.483.1835.

83 A. J. Christopher, 'Ethnicity, Community and the Census in Mauritius, 1830–1990', *Geographical Journal* 158, no. 1 (March 1992), 57–64.

84 'Reports of a Medical Commission Assembled Under the Presidency of W. A. Burke', NAM: HA 68/2.

85 'Mauritius', *Oriental Herald and Colonial Intelligencer* 3 (London: Madden & Co., 1839), 648–50, at 649.

86 Letter from R. Farquhar to Earl Bathurst, Port Louis, 11 October 1816, TNA: CO 167/960.

87 Letter from Farquhar to Bathurst, 11 October 1816.

88 Pridham, *England's Colonial Empire*, 263.

89 Billiard, *Voyage aux Colonies*, 39: 'le féu détruisit en un instant les travaux et les fortunes d'un siècle.'

90 See 'Papers relative to the fire of 1816', and also 'Organisation of a Fire Brigade, 1823' in NAM: HA 16/8–9.

91 Letter from Police Office to G. A. Barry Esq. Chief Secretary, dated 4 July 1823, NAM: HA 16/9.

92 'Scheme proposed for a better organization of the Police Force in Mauritius', NAM: HA 19/2.

93 Pridham, *England's Colonial Empire*, 353; Toussaint, *Port Louis*, 68.

94 Pridham, *England's Colonial Empire*, 354.

95 Bradshaw, *Views in the Mauritius*, 5.

96 'Correspondence Relative to the Enclosing of the New Bazaar in Stone Walls, 1828', NAM: HA 7/4.

97 Toussaint, *Port Louis*, 76–7.

98 Pridham, *England's Colonial Empire*, 263.

99 Toussaint, *Port Louis*, 70.

100 'Papers relative to the *Conseil de Commune Générale*, 1818–1820', NAM: HA 14/6.

101 'Papers relative to the disturbance which took place in the Theatre of Port Louis on the night of 16 August 1823', NAM: HA 19/5.

102 Backhouse, *A Narrative of a Visit*, 4.

103 Bradshaw, *Views in the Mauritius*, 5.

104 See above, Chapter 3, XX.

105 J. Barnwell and A. Toussaint, *A Short History of Mauritius* (London: Government of Mauritius, 1949), 61; for the consumption of burgundy see Pridham, *England's Colonial Empire*, 264.

106 Barnwell and Toussaint, *Short History*, 173.

107 Backhouse, *A Narrative of a Visit*, 27–8. For another Protestant account bemoaning the moral neglect of Mauritius, see *A Modern Missionary:*

Being the Brief Memoir of the Rev. John Sarjant, late of Mauritius (London: John Mason, 1834).

108 Petition to Governor Gomm from shopkeepers in Port Louis, dated Port Louis, Mauritius 27 October 1843, NAM: RA 747.

109 Billiard, *Voyage aux Colonies*, 39. 'La parcourent toutes les nuances de couleur, depuis le rose pâle jusqu'au rouge cuivré, et jusqu'au noir le plus foncé.'

110 Billiard, *Voyage aux Colonies*, 40. 'les productions et les physionomies des quatre parties du monde'.

111 Backhouse, *A Narrative of a Visit*, 12.

112 A. J. Christopher, 'Ethnicity, Community and the Cènsus'.

113 Bradshaw, *Views in the Mauritius*, 4.

114 Pridham, *England's Colonial Empire*, 262.

115 For Ollier's biography, see de Montille, 'The Coloured Elite', from which I take these details in the para. below, see especially 72–3.

116 Charles Wesley, 'Remy Ollier, Mauritian Journalist and Patriot', in *Journal of Negro History* 6, no. 1 (January 1921), 54–65, at 64.

117 Toussaint, *Port Louis*, 88–9.

118 Letter from Committee of Election to the Municipal Corporation to the Colonial Secretary and attached 'List of Voters', dated 22 January 1850, Port Louis, NAM: RA 1082.

119 Letter from L. Lechelle, Mayor to the Governor, dated Port Louis, 30 March 1850 and letter from L. Lechelle, Mayor to the Governor, dated Port Louis, 30 March 1850, NAM: RA 1082.

120 'The Municipal Council', *Commercial Gazette*, 12 June 1850; see also, letter from L. Lechelle to the Colonial Secretary, dated Port Louis, 7 January 1851, NAM: RA 1130 and other documents in RA1130 for the cutting of stones.

121 Letter from L. Lechelle, Mayor to the Governor, dated Port Louis, 27 April 1850, NAM: RA 1130.

122 Letter from the Procureur Advocate Général, dated 9 March 1850, NAM: RA 1082, and letter dated 30 March 1850, above. For more elaborate rules connected to fires, see 'Municipal Regulations for the Town of Port Louis in Conformity with the Ordinance in Council no.16 of 1849', NAM: RA 1082.

123 Letters from L. Lechelle to the Governor, dated Port Louis, 9 April 1850, and dated Port Louis 21 April 1850, NAM: RA 1082.

124 *Le Cernéen*, 4 and 22 June 1850, 10 October 1850. I thank James de Montille for these two references.

125 Letter from L. Lechelle, Mayor to James Macaulay Higginson, Governor, dated Port Louis, 8 September 1851, NAM: RA 1130.

126 The discussion of Cape Town below has benefited from using the following as a starting point: Nigel Worden, Elizabeth Van Heyningen and Vivian Bickford-Smith, *Cape Town: The Making of a City: An Illustrated Social History* (Cape Town: David Philip, 1998).

127 Shirley Judges, 'Poverty, Living Conditions and Social Relations: Aspects of Life in Cape Town in the 1830s' (Master's thesis, University of Cape Town, 1977).

128 Ibid.

129 James Sturgis, 'Anglicisation at the Cape of Good Hope in the early nineteenth century', *Journal of Imperial and Commonwealth History* 11, no. 1 (1982), 5–32, at 10; see also Hermann Giliomee, *The Afrikaners* (Tafelberg: Cape Town, 2003), 197ff.

130 Giliomee, *The Afrikaners*, 198

131 Worden, van Heyningen and Bickford-Smith, *Cape Town*, 117.

132 Kirsten McKenzie, *Scandal in the Colonies: Sydney and Cape Town, 1820–1850* (Carlton, Vic.: Melbourne University Press, 2004), 56.

133 Judges, 'Poverty', 83.

134 Robert Ross, *Status and Respectability in the Cape Colony, 1750–1870* (Cambridge: Cambridge University Press, 1999), 81.

135 Timothy Keegan, *Colonial South Africa and the Origins of the Racial Order* (Cape Town and Johannesburg: David Philip, 1996), 166.

136 Sturgis, 'Anglicisation at the Cape'.

137 Kirsten McKenzie, "My Own Mind Dying with Me': Eliza Fairbairn and the Reinvention of Colonial Middle-Class Domesticity in Cape Town', *South African Historical Journal* 36, no. 1 (1997), 3–23.

138 A. Bank, 'Liberals and Their Enemies: Racial Ideology at the Cape of Good Hope 1820 to 1850' (PhD thesis, University of Cambridge, 1995), 17.

139 This follows my argument in Sujit Sivasundaram, 'Race, Empire and Biology before Darwinism', in Denis Alexander and Ron Numbers, eds, *Biology and Ideology* (Chicago: University of Chicago Press, 2010), 114–28.

140 Ross, *Status and Respectability*, 43.

141 K. McKenzie, 'The *South African Commercial Advertiser* and the Making of Middle-Class Identity in Early Nineteenth-Century Cape Town' (Master's thesis, University of Cape Town, 1993), 222.

142 Keegan, *Colonial South Africa*, 110.

143 Worden, Van Heyningen and Bickford-Smith, *Cape Town*, 88.

144 D. Warren, 'Merchants, Commissioners and Wardmasters: Municipal Politics in Cape Town, 1840–54' (Master's thesis, University of Cape Town, 1986).

145 Ibid., 94.

146 See for instance Ross, *Status and Respectability*, chapter 3.

147 K. McKenzie, 'Dogs and the Public Sphere: The Ordering of Social Space in Early Nineteenth-century Cape Town', *South African Historical Journal* 48, no. 1 (2003), 235–51, at 224.

148 This is in keeping with the argument of McKenzie, *Scandal in the Colonies*.

149 McKenzie, 'The *South African Commercial Advertiser*', 146.
150 For Cape colonists looking to the Caribbean, see McKenzie, *Scandal in the Colonies*, 140.
151 *Cape of Good Hope Observer*, 17 July 1849.
152 McKenzie, *Scandal in the Colonies*, 174; Ross, *Status and Respectability*, 161; Eric A. Walker, ed., *The Cambridge History of the British Empire*, 8 vols (Cambridge, 1929–63), vol. 8, 2nd edn, 379.
153 *South African Commercial Advertiser*, 6 June 1849; and 11 August 1849; italics in original.
154 *South African Commercial Advertiser*, 10 November 1849.
155 *Cape of Good Hope Observer*, 17 July 1849.
156 Cited in Walker, ed., *The Cambridge History of the British Empire*, vol. 8, 377.
157 *South African Commercial Advertiser*, 14 April 1849.
158 *South African Commercial Advertiser*, 5 May 1849.
159 *Cape Town Mail*, 20 May 1849.
160 Keegan, *Colonial South Africa*, 227.
161 *South African Commercial Advertiser*, 8 August 1849.
162 *South African Commercial Advertiser*, 20 June 1849.
163 *Cape Town Mail*, 14 July 1849.
164 Miles Taylor, 'The 1848 Revolutions and the British Empire', in *Past and Present* 166, no. 1 (February 2000), 146–80.
165 *Cape of Good Hope Observer*, 17 July 1849.
166 *Cape of Good Hope Observer*, 24 July 1849
167 *Cape of Good Hope Observer*, 9 October 1849.
168 *Cape of Good Hope Observer*, 9 October 1849
169 *South African Commercial Advertiser*, 4 August 1849; the term 'pest ship' also appeared in the *Cape Town Mail*, 12 May 1849.
170 Cited in Walker, ed., *The Cambridge History of the British Empire*, vol. 8, 379.
171 *South African Commercial Advertiser*, 30 December 1848.
172 Cited in Warren, *Merchants*, 208.
173 Stanley Trapido, 'The Origins of the Cape Franchise Qualification of 1835', *Journal of African History* 5, no. 1 (1964): 37–54.
174 *South African Commercial Advertiser*, 16 May 1849.
175 Taylor, 'The 1848 Revolutions'.
176 Christopher Holdridge, 'Circulating the African Journal: The Colonial Press and Trans-Imperial Britishness in the Mid Nineteenth-Century Cape', *South African Historical Journal* 62, no. 3 (2010), 487–513, 508–9.
177 *South African Commercial Advertiser*, 28 October 1848; *Cape Town Mail*, 4 November 1848.
178 *South African Commercial Advertiser*, 2 December 1848.
179 See McKenzie, *Scandal*, 177; for 'moral dung heap': *South African*

Commercial Advertiser, 18 September 1849. For another comparison with New South Wales, Norfolk Island and Van Diemen's Land see, *Cape Town Mail*, 23 June 1849.

180 *Cape Town Mail*, 8 September 1849.

181 This relies on McKenzie, *Scandal in the Colonies*, 176.

182 This material arises from, Holdridge, 'Circulating the African Journal', 506.

183 *Cape Town Mail*, 8 December 1849; 29 December 1849.

184 *South African Commercial Advertiser*, 21 March 1849.

185 *South African Commercial Advertiser*, 21 July 1849; 22 August 1849; and 15 September 1849.

186 On this see the inaugural editorial in the *Mauritius Times*, 15 July 1848.

187 *Le Cernéen*, 23 June 1848; and, *Le Cernéen*, 11 July 1848.

188 *Le Cernéen*, 4 July 1848. For further sentiments along these lines see: *Le Cernéen*, 6 July 1848.

189 *Le Cernéen*, 6 October 1848. 'Il est intutile de dire qu' à l'égard du gouverne-ment métropolitain, nos efforts seront toujours ceux de sujets dévoués et fidèles, et qu'un des premiers devoirs que nous impose cette qualité est de l'éclairer sur les conséquences de sa politique commerciale à l'égard de cette belle Dépendance de la Couroune britannique, afin d'en appeler de l'Angleterre abusée à l'Angleterre mieux informée.'

190 *Mauritius Times*, 10 October 1848 and 12 October 1848.

191 Report from Central Police Office, dated 6 October 1848 written by A. D'Courcy Potterton, Police Officer, TNA: CO 167/302.

192 *Mauritius Times*, 18 October 1848.

193 Letter dated Port Louis, from James Egbert Simmons to Mrs Simmons, 25 February 1848, CUL: Add 9549/9; see also *Le Cernéen*, 11 October 1848, and the despatch from William Gomm to Earl Grey, dated 9 October 1848, TNA: CO 167/302; also despatch from William Gomm to Earl Grey, dated 14 October 1848, TNA: CO 167/302.

194 Despatch from William Gomm to Earl Grey, dated 14 Oct 1848, TNA: CO 167/302.

195 *Mauritius Times*, 13 October 1848.

196 *Le Mauricien*, 13 October 1848.

197 *Le Cernéen*, 14 October 1848.

198 Letter from d'Épinay to William Gomm, dated 6 October 1848, TNA: CO 167/302.

199 *Mauritius Times*, 7 November 1848.

200 *Mauritius Times*, 10 November 1848.

201 *Mauritius Times*, 7 November 1848.

202 *Mauritius Times*, 9 December 1848.

203 *Mauritius Times*, 24 July 1849.

204 *Mauritius Times*, 24 July 1849.

205 Letter from James Egbert Simmons to Mrs. Simmons, dated Port Louis,

8 December 1849, CUL: Add 9549/39. There is also one letter written by Caroline Simmons to Mrs. Simmons, CUL: Add 9549/79.

206 Letter to Mrs. Simmons from James Simmons, dated Port Louis, 21 August 1848, CUL: Add 9549/16.

207 Letter to Mrs. Simmons from James Simmons, dated Port Louis, 16 December 1849, CUL: Add 9549/40.

208 Letter from James Simmons to Mrs Simmons, dated Port Louis, 17 December 1851, CUL: Add 9549/70.

209 Letter from James Simmons to Mrs Simmons, dated Port Louis, 18 June 1852, CUL: Add 9549/77.

210 Letter from James Simmons to Mrs. Simmons, dated Port Louis, 21 August 1849, CUL: Add 9549/34.

211 Letter from James Simmons to Mrs. Simmons, dated Port Louis, 14 October 1848, CUL: Add 9549/18.

212 Letter from James Simmons to Mrs. Simmons, dated Port Louis, 6 October 1852, CUL: Add 9549/83.

213 Letter from James Simmons to Mrs. Simmons, dated Port Louis, 24 June 1848, CUL: Add 9549/14.

214 A series of early articles were about steam, see for instance 'Steam Communication', *Commercial Gazette*, 20 July 1850. For a contract on the conveyance of mails on steamships between Mauritius and Aden made in 1852, see NAM: HA 74/10.

215 'Representative Governments for the Colonies – Mauritius', *Commercial Gazette*, 3 June 1850. For a comparative glance to Mauritius in order to advance a local issue in Cape Town, see comments on a grant to Mauritius by Parliament, *Cape Town Mail*, 31 March 1849.

216 'The new Constitution of the Cape – Mauritius', *Commercial Gazette*, 9 October 1850.

217 Barnwell and Toussaint, *A Short History*, 192.

218 Letter dated Port Louis, 30 October 1850, *Commercial Gazette*, 31 October 1850. Two years earlier *Le Cernéen* had already pointed out the greater political freedoms enjoyed by Bourbon.

219 *Commercial Gazette*, 31 October 1850. 'si, à chaque fois que les questions qui nous touchent de près et qui sont résolues par d'honorables gentlemen qui n'ont jamais rien vu de Maurice, qui ne savent peut-être pas où elle est située, et qui, à coup sûr, ne se doutent pas des mœurs, des coutumes et de l'esprit de la population, si ces questions étaient discutées par des hommes capables par leur expérience et, en quelque sorte, obligés par devoir de réfuter les fausses allégations et les lourds sophismes entassés si souvent contre nous et contre les colonies en général; si nous avions, au sein même du Gouvernement métropolitain, des avocats désintéressés, il y a long-temps que les abus dout nous nous plaignons encore auraient cessé, et que des institutions conformes à notre esprit et à nos vœux, dont la Municipalité est la première pierre, nous auraient été accordées.'

220 *Cape Town Mail*, 2 December 1848.

221 *Le Cernéen*, 25 and 28 September 1848; or for instance 11 November 1848. Also, *Le Mauricien*, 23 August 1848.

222 Taylor, 'The 1848 Revolutions.'

223 Sujit Sivasundaram, *Islanded*, 313.

224 For instance after the 1848 rebellion, *Le Mauricien*, 27 November 1848, noted the similarity between the two colonies: 'That Colony resembles in most respects Mauritius.

225 *Le Cernéen*, 21 October 1848. 'Les Ceylonais ne sont pas plus heureux que nous; les biens ruraux sont surchargés de dettes et se vendent a vil prix, lorsqu'on trouve à les vendre.' For another comparative analysis of Mauritius and Ceylon, see *Le Mauricien*, 9 November 1849.

226 *Le Mauricien*, 28 August 1848.

227 *Mauritius Times*, 18 November 1848. 'Inutile de dire que nous ne croyons pas aux professions libérales de foi des Hollandais et des Créoles francais: ils veulent de la liberté – comme le Ceylon Times et son partie, – pour les Blancs afin d'exterminer les Noirs ou des les reduire en esclavage.'

228 *South African Commercial Advertiser*, 28 October 1848.

229 *Cape Town Mail*, 18 November 1848.

230 *Cape Town Mail*, 25 November 1848.

CONCLUSION

1 For an excellent recent history of imperial history in Britain, see Joanna de Groot, *Empire and History Writing in Britain, 1750-2012* (Manchester: Manchester University Press, 2013).

2 The biographical details are taken from Anthony A. D. Seymour, 'Robert Montgomery Martin: An Introduction', in Seymour, ed., *History of the British Colonies: Possessions in Europe, Gibraltar* (Grendon: Gibraltar Books, 1998), i–xiv, and also from F. H. H. King, 'Robert Montgomery Martin', in *Oxford Dictionary of National Biography*.

3 Laidlaw, *Colonial Connections*, 172–3

4 Seymour, 'Robert Montgomery Martin', x–xii.

5 Robert Montgomery Martin, 'Report', in *Statistics of the Colonies of the British Empire* (London: W. H. Allen & Co., 1839), v.

6 Robert Montgomery Martin, *History of the British Colonies*, 5 vols (London: James Cochrane, 1835), vol. 1, 492.

7 Ibid., 405, 410.

8 Laidlaw, *Colonial Connections*, 188.

9 Robert Montgomery Martin, *History of Austral-Asia* (London: John Mortimer, 1836), 35.

10 Ibid., 120.

11 Ibid., 123.

12 Ibid.
13 Ibid., 127.
14 Ibid., 133.
15 Ibid.
16 Ibid., 205.
17 Ibid., 295.
18 Martin, *History of the British Colonies*, vol. 4, 377
19 Robert Montgomery Martin, *History of Southern Africa* (London, 1836), 286.
20 Ibid., 305.
21 Ibid., 306.
22 For a current debate on how to write the history of Britain in a global moment, see the roundtable discussion, 'Britain and the World: A New Field?', *Journal of British Studies*, 57, no. 4 (October 2018), 677–708.
23 In a vast literature, two important recent histories of the British empire are John Darwin, *The Rise and Fall of the British World System, 1830-1970* (Cambridge: Cambridge University Press, 2009); and Philippa Levine, *The British Empire: Sunrise to Sunset* (Harlow: Pearson, 2007). For a biographical approach, see Miles Ogborn, *Global Lives: Britain and the World, 1550-1800* (Cambridge: Cambridge University Press, 2008).
24 This follows a view I advanced and called 'recyling' in: *Islanded*.
25 On the importance of acknowledging the violence of empire, see for instance the roundtable, 'Imperial History by the Book', *Journal of British Studies* 54, no. 4 (October 2015), 971–97 and also Richard Drayton, 'Where Does the World Historian Write From?: Objectivity, Moral Conscience and the Past and Present of Imperialism', *Journal of Contemporary History* 46, no. 3 (July 2011) 671–85.
26 See for instance Bernard Porter, *The Absent-Minded Imperialists: Empire, Society and Culture in Britain* (Oxford: Oxford University Press, 2006).
27 Zoe Laidlaw, *Colonial Connections, 1815-1845: Patronage, the Information Revolution and Colonial Government* (Manchester: Manchester University Press, 2005).
28 This account of Marryat draws upon, Tim Fulford, 'Romanticizing the Empire: The Naval Heroes of Southey, Coleridge, Austen, and Marryat', *Modern Language Quarterly* 60, no. 2 (June 1999), 161–96.
29 Frederick Marryat, *Masterman Ready: or, The Wreck of the Pacific*, 3 vols (London: Longman, 1841-2), vol. 1, 269.
30 Ibid., vol. 2, 49.
31 Ibid., vol.2, 161.
32 Ibid., vol. 2, 163.
33 Ibid., vol. 3, 175.
34 This account of Martineau follows, Deborah Logan, General Introduction in Logan, ed., *Harriet Martineau's Writing on the British Empire*, 5 vols (London: Pickering & Chatto, 2004), vol. 1, xv–xliii, xvi.

35 Catherine Hall, 'Epilogue: Imperial Careering at Home', in David Lambert and Alan Lester, eds, *Colonial Lives Across the British Empire: Imperial Careering in the Long Nineteenth Century* (Cambridge, Cambridge University Press, 2006), 353.

36 Logan, ed., *Harriet Martineau*, vol. 1, 156.

37 Ibid., 190.

38 Ibid., 195.

39 The last work to approach this period across a broad span was C. A. Bayly, *Imperial Meridian*.

40 For further information on the translation of the *Mahavamsa* and its printing under British patronage, see Sivasundaram, *Islanded*, chapter 3.

41 This follows Sivasundaram, 'Materialities in the Making of World Histories', in Ivan Gaskell and Sarah Carter, eds, *Oxford Handbook of History and Material Culture: World Perspectives* (forthcoming).

42 For Grey as collector, see Donald Jackson Kerr, *Amassing Treasure for All Times: Sir George Grey, Colonial Bookman and Collector* (Otago: Otago University Press, 2006). For Grey's publication of Māori materials, see 88–9.

43 George Grey, *Polynesian Mythology and Ancient Traditional History of the New Zealand Race* (London: J Murray, 1855), 1.

44 There were debates surrounding 'the new imperial history', exemplified for instance in Kathleen Wilson, ed., *A New Imperial History: Identity and Modernity in Britain and the Empire, 1660-1840* (Cambridge: Cambridge University Press, 2003). For these debates see Dane Kennedy, *The Imperial History Wars: Debating the British Empire* (London: Bloomsbury, 2018). See also A. L. Stoler and Frederick Cooper, eds, *Tensions of Empire: Colonial Cultures in a Bourgeois World* (Berkeley: University of California Press, 1997); Catherine Hall, *Civilising Subjects: Metropole and Colony in the English Imagination, 1830-1867* (Cambridge: Polity, 2002); and Antoinette Burton, *After the Imperial Turn? Thinking with and Through the Nation* (Durham, N.C.: Duke University Press, 2003). For capital and empire, see P. J. Cain and A. G. Hopkins, *British Imperialism: Innovation and Expansion, 1688-1914* (London: Longman, 1993). For the environmental turn which this book represents, see for instance David Armitage, Alison Bashford and Sujit Sivasundaram, eds, *Oceanic Histories* (Cambridge: Cambridge University Press, 2018).

AFTERWORD

1 'Nicholas Pike: Naturalist, Author, Soldier and Consul' opened on 18 September 2018, when I was in Mauritius.

Index

Abdullah, Shaikh, of Ajman, 126, 127
Abdullah bin Abdul Kadir, 268–71, 272,
  280–1, 283, 284
Abercrombie, General, 150
Aboriginal Australians: agency of, 165, 169,
  178, 179, 282; Bennelong in London,
  169; breastplates given to, 166–7, 172;
  Bungaree's voyages with Europeans,
  169, 175–6, 179, 202; colonial gift-giving,
  169–70, 172; colonial trope of alcohol
  addiction, 167; displacement of from
  historical memory, 178–9; Earle's
  images of, 169, 170–2, *173*, 174; Eora
  (clans in coastal Sydney region), 166–8;
  execution of *Black Tommy*, 336–7; and
  fishing, 167–8, 169, 172, 176, 179; as
  greeters to Sydney, 169, *170*, 170–2, *171*,
  179; imperial programmes of schooling,
  172, 175; as maritime travellers, 193;
  Martin's writings on, 336–8; policy of
  'whitening' unleashed, 200; possessions
  at Mitchell Library, 166–7; racial characterisations of, 172, 174–5, 282, 342;
  racist colonial characterisations, 172,
  174–5, 342; and republicanism, 174;
  status of indigenous histories, 188–91;
  women as cultural go-betweens in
  Sydney, 178; women fishing with hook
  and line, 167–8, 169, 172, 179
Aboriginal Tasmanians: agency of women,
  189–90, 191–3, 201, 202; brutal depopulation of, 186, 187, 189, 192–3, 196, 197,
  203; continuing heritage of, 192–3;
  'extermination of the native' narrative,
  196; Martin's writings on, 338; perspectives and traditions, 192–3; resistance to

colonialism, 186–7, 282; Robinson's
  reserve for, 187–8; transportation/
  confinement to Bass Strait, 187, 189;
  travelling of the oceans by, 193;
  women's interaction with sealers, 186,
  188, 189–90, 191–3, 201, 202
Aborigines Protection Society, 17, 336
Abu Talib Khan Isfahani, Mirza, 27–33, 36,
  37
Admiralty Islands, 46, 47
Afghanistan, 242
Africaine (Dutton's ship), 194
age of revolutions: and Dillon's voyage
  (1825-6), 16, 17–20, 21–4, 26; empire
  adopts language of, 26, 39, 77–8, 97,
  131–3, 221, 243; empire alters course of,
  39; exclusion due to race, 100, 110–11,
  122, 311; Gulf as space on mental globe
  of, 163; language of nations and citizenship, 42, 97–103, 107, 108–11, 116, 122, 136;
  liberty as key concept, 31, 37–8; as long-
  lasting label of history writing, 1–2;
  'motives of humanity' phrase, 20, 26;
  multiple senses of word 'revolution,'
  38–9; news from Europe, 40–2, 43, 50,
  97–103, 116, 287, 315–17, 321; notions of
  natural territory, 148; Parsis as agents
  in, 154–6; revolts in Sydney, 181–2;
  revolts of enslaved peoples, 80, 82,
  92–5; 'revolution' as unstable term of
  reference, 130–1; revolutionary status of
  Wahhabi movement, 130–3; and South
  Asian elites, 27–37, 104–9, 154–6; Tipu's
  alleged republican sympathies, 107–9;
  traditional focus on Atlantic, 1, 37–8,
  122; *trekboer* patriotic revolt, 87–92;

Image Credits

INTRODUCTION

0.1 © Victoria and Albert Museum, London

0.2 © National Maritime Museum, Greenwich, London

0.3 © State Library of New South Wales

0.4 © Augustus Earle, National Library of Australia, NK12/126.

0.5 © The National Archives, ref. MPG1/532 (5)

0.6 © Bugis nautical map on cowhide, AH 1231, c.1816, Kaart: VIII.C.a.2, Special Collections, Utrecht University Library.

CHAPTER 2

2.1 © Pictures from History / Bridgeman Images

2.2 © Collection Nationaal Museum van Wereldculturen. Coll.no. RV-34-6

2.3 © Musée du quai Branly - Jacques Chirac, Dist. RMN-Grand Palais

2.4 © The Trustees of the British Museum

2.5 © The History Collection / Alamy Stock Photo

2.6a © Sujit Sivasundaram

2.6b © Sujit Sivasundaram

2.7 © Augustus Earle, National Library of Australia, NK12/139

2.8 © Augustus Earle, National Library of Australia, NK 668

2.9 © Augustus Earle, National Library of Australia, NK12/84

2.10 © Icas94 / De Agostini / Bridgeman Images

2.11 © Barry, James, active 1818-1846. Barry, James: [The Rev Thomas Kendall and the Maori chiefs Hongi and Waikato]. Ref: G-618.

Alexander Turnbull Library, Wellington, New Zealand. / records/23241174

CHAPTER 3

3.1 © National Gallery of Victoria, Melbourne, Joe White Bequest, 2010
3.2 © National Maritime Museum, Greenwich, London
3.3 © British Library Board. All Rights Reserved / Bridgeman Images
3.4 © Sujit Sivasundaram
3.5 © Sujit Sivasundaram
3.6 © British Library Board. All Rights Reserved / Bridgeman Images
3.7 © The Stapleton Collection / Bridgeman Images
3.8 © National Maritime Museum, Greenwich, London

CHAPTER 4

4.1 © National Maritime Museum, Greenwich, London
4.2 © National Maritime Museum, Greenwich, London
4.3 © National Maritime Museum, Greenwich, London
4.4 © National Maritime Museum, Greenwich, London
4.5 © Bridgeman Images

CHAPTER 5

5.1 © State Library of New South Wales
5.2a © State Library of New South Wales
5.2b © State Library of New South Wales
5.3 ©The Art Archive/Shutterstock
5.4 © Bridgeman Images
5.5 © Augustus Earle, The National Library of Australia NK12/57.
5.6 © Fernyhough, W. H. (William Henry), Series of Twelve Profile Portraits of Aborginies of New South Wales; The National Library of Australia
5.7 © The Picture Art Collection / Alamy Stock Photo
5.8 © Sujit Sivasundaram; Mitchell Library, State Library of New South Wales

CHAPTER 6

6.1 © National Maritime Museum, Greenwich, London
6.2 © British Library Board. All Rights Reserved / Bridgeman Images
6.3 © The Stapleton Collection / Bridgeman Images
6.4 © Sujit Sivasundaram
6.5 © National Maritime Museum, Greenwich, London
6.6 © Sujit Sivasundaram

CHAPTER 7

7.1 © University of Cambridge, Institute of Astronomy Library
7.2 © University of Cambridge, Institute of Astronomy Library
7.3 © University of Cambridge, Institute of Astronomy Library
7.4 © JMM Photography/Shutterstock
7.5 © The Picture Art Collection / Alamy Stock Photo
7.6 © Hocken Collections, Uare Taoka o Hākena, University of Otago, 92/1217 a12197

CHAPTER 8

8.1 © BLM Collection / Alamy Stock Photo
8.2 © Archives Charmet / Bridgeman Images